Handbook of Dialogical Self

In a boundary-crossing and globalizing world, the personal and social positions in self and identity become increasingly dense, heterogeneous and even conflicting. In this handbook scholars of different disciplines, nations and cultures (East and West) bring together their views and applications of dialogical self theory in such a way that deeper commonalities are brought to the surface. As a 'bridging theory', dialogical self theory reveals unexpected links between a broad variety of phenomena, such as self and identity problems in education and psychotherapy, multicultural identities, child-rearing practices, adult development, consumer behaviour, the use of the internet and the value of silence. Researchers and practitioners present different methods of investigation, both qualitative and quantitative, and also highlight applications of dialogical self theory.

HUBERT J. M. HERMANS studied psychology at the Catholic University of Nijmegen. In 1973 he became associate professor of psychology at the University of Nijmegen and in 1980 full professor at the same university. Since 2002 he has been president of the International Society for Dialogical Science (ISDS) and since 2006 editor-in-chief of the *International Journal for Dialogical Science* (IJDS). For his scientific contributions to society, he was honoured with a Knighthood in the Order of The Netherlands Lion in 2002.

THORSTEN GIESER received his MA in social anthropology and religious studies from the University of Heidelberg, Germany, and attained his Ph.D. in social anthropology at the University of Aberdeen, UK. He is a Fellow of the Royal Anthropological Institute, with a particular interest in the cultural phenomenology of intersubjective experience, perception, embodiment and empathy, and is now a lecturer in social anthropology at the University of Koblenz-Landau, Germany.

Handbook of Dialogical Self Theory

Edited by

Hubert J. M. Hermans and Thorsten Gieser

CAMBRIDGE UNIVERSITY PRESS

CAMBRIDGE
UNIVERSITY PRESS

The Edinburgh Building, Cambridge CB2 8RU, UK

Published in the United States of America by Cambridge University Press, New York

Cambridge University Press is part of the University of Cambridge.

It furthers the University's mission by disseminating knowledge in the pursuit of
education, learning and research at the highest international levels of excellence.

www.cambridge.org
Information on this title: www.cambridge.org/9781107681064

© Cambridge University Press 2012

First published 2012
First paperback edition 2013

A catalogue record for this publication is available from the British Library

Library of Congress Cataloguing in Publication data

Handbook of dialogical self theory / edited by Hubert J. M. Hermans,
Thorsten Gieser.
    p. cm.
  ISBN 978-1-107-00651-5 (Hardback)
    1. Self.   2. Identity (Psychology)   I. Hermans, H. J. M.
II. Gieser, Thorsten.   III. Title.
  BF697.H335 2011
  155.2–dc22

                                                       2011015042

ISBN 978-1-107-00651-5 Hardback
ISBN 978-1-107-68106-4 Paperback

Contents

Figures

Tables

Contributors

EMILY ABBEY is an assistant professor at Ramapo College of New Jersey, USA, where she studies adult development.

CHARL ALBERTS is a senior lecturer at the Department of Psychology at the University of Fort Hare, Alice, South Africa. His main research interest revolves around identity formation among Afrikaners in a post-apartheid South African context.

HERMAN BAERT is a full professor in the Center for Human Resources Development and Training and Lifelong Learning of the Katholieke Universiteit Leuven, Belgium.

SHALINI BAHL, Ph.D., is the founder of iAM Business Consulting, Amherst, USA.

JOHN BARRESI is retired and currently a research professor of psychology and philosophy at Dalhousie University, Canada.

MARIE-CÉCILE BERTAU is a lecturer in psycholinguistics at the University of Munich, Germany, working on language in the traditions of cultural-historical psychology (Vygotsky) and dialogical linguistics (Jakubinskij, Bakhtin).

SUNIL BHATIA is an associate professor of human development at Connecticut College, USA. He studies identity formation in various cultural contexts, and he also directs the Holleran Center for Community Action and Public Policy at his college.

KENNETH R. CABELL is a Ph.D. candidate in cultural and social psychology at Clark University, USA.

NANDITA CHAUDHARY is a reader at the Department of Human Development and Childhood Studies, Lady Irwin College, University of Delhi, India.

ELŻBIETA CHMIELNICKA-KUTER, Ph.D., is an assistant professor in the Department of Personality at the John Paul II Catholic University of Lublin, Poland.

GIANCARLO DIMAGGIO is a psychotherapist at the Third Center of Cognitive Psychotherapy in Rome. He is professor of the psychotherapy of personality disorders at Scuola di Specializzazione in Psicologia Clinica II – University 'La Sapienza' – Rome, Italy.

SHAUN GALLAGHER holds the Moss Chair of Excellence in Philosophy at the University of Memphis, USA, and is research professor of philosophy at the School of Humanities, University of Hertfordshire, UK.

THORSTEN GIESER, Ph.D., is a lecturer in social anthropology at the University of Koblenz-Landau, Germany.

ALEX GILLESPIE is a senior lecturer in social psychology at the University of Stirling, UK, working on identity, communication, thought and language.

MIGUEL M. GONÇALVES is professor of psychology at the School of Psychology, University of Minho, Portugal.

HUBERT J. M. HERMANS is an emeritus professor at the Radboud University of Nijmegen, The Netherlands, and is the creator of dialogical self theory. He is scientific director of the International Institute for the Dialogical Self.

AGNIESZKA HERMANS-KONOPKA, Ph.D., specializes in work with emotions, art and awareness in the dialogical self approach. She is program director of the International Institute for the Dialogical Self, The Netherlands.

VINCENT W. HEVERN is a professor of psychology at Le Moyne College, USA, and edits several online scholarly initiatives, including *NarrativePsychology.com*.

DAVID Y. F. HO is Distinguished Professor in the Department of Psychology at Renmin University of China, Beijing, China.

CAROL A. JASPER is a Ph.D. student researching the impact of success and failure upon adolescent identity development at the University of Stirling, UK.

DOROTA KOBYLIŃSKA is an assistant professor in experimental social psychology at the University of Warsaw, Poland.

REINEKKE LENGELLE is a visiting professor in the Masters of Arts Integrated Studies Program at Athabasca University, Canada.

M. BEATRICE LIGORIO is professor of educational psychology and E-learning at the University of Bari, Italy.

GRAHAM LINDEGGER is a professor in the School of Psychology, University of KwaZulu-Natal, South Africa.

JOHN T. LYSAKER is a professor of philosophy in the Department of Philosophy at Emory University, USA.

PAUL H. LYSAKER is a clinical psychologist at the Roudebush Veterans Affairs Medical Center and a professor of clinical psychology in the Department of Psychiatry at the Indiana University School of Medicine, USA.

FRANS MEIJERS leads the Research Group of Professional Development in Vocational and Organisational Learning at The Hague University, The Netherlands.

TOON VAN MEIJL is associate professor in the Department of Anthropology and Development Studies and Academic Secretary of the Centre for Pacific and Asian Studies, University of Nijmegen, The Netherlands.

HELEN R. MOORE is a Ph.D. student studying relational adaptation following acquired brain injury at the University of Stirling, UK.

MASAYOSHI MORIOKA is a professor of psychology at the Graduate School of Human Development and Environment, Kobe University, Japan.

ROBERT A. NEIMEYER is a professor of psychology at the University of Memphis, USA, where he studies loss and grief from the standpoint of constructivist psychology.

DINA NIR is the head of the Negotiation Program in the Department of Business at Ono Academic College, Israel, and is a guest lecturer in the Department of Psychology at the Herzliya Interdisciplinary Centre, Israel.

PIOTR K. OLEŚ is a professor of psychology and head of the Department of Personality at the John Paul II Catholic University of Lublin, Poland.

MAŁGORZATA PUCHALSKA-WASYL, Ph.D., is an assistant professor in the Department of Personality at the John Paul II Catholic University of Lublin, Poland.

PETER T. F. RAGGATT is a senior lecturer in psychology at James Cook University, Queensland, Australia.

ANTÓNIO P. RIBEIRO is a Ph.D. student in clinical psychology at the School of Psychology, University of Minho, Portugal.

JOHN ROWAN is a Fellow of the British Psychological Society and works in London, UK, as an independent consultant. He is also a poet and mystic.

KATARZYNA STEMPLEWSKA-ŻAKOWICZ is a professor of psychology at the Helena Chodkowska University of Management and Law, Warsaw, Poland.

SETH SURGAN is an assistant professor of psychology at Worcester State University, USA.

HUBERT SUSZEK is an assistant professor in the Department of Psychology at the University of Warsaw. He also works as a psychotherapist at the Psychotherapy Center of the Nowowiejski Hospital in Warsaw, Poland.

JAAN VALSINER is a cultural-developmental psychologist working at Clark University, USA.

LENI M. F. VERHOFSTADT-DENÈVE, Ph.D., is emeritus professor of clinical developmental psychology at Ghent University, Belgium, and founder of the School of Experiential-Dialectical Psychodrama. She is a member of the Royal Flemish Academy of Belgium for Science and the Arts.

LISA S. WHITTAKER is finishing her Ph.D. at the University of Stirling, UK, studying recognition and identity, and she is also a programme executive with the Prince's Trust, Scotland.

ANNEMIE WINTERS is a Ph.D. student at the Center for Human Resources Development and Training and Lifelong Learning of the Katholieke Universiteit Leuven, Belgium.

BARTOSZ ZALEWSKI is an assistant in the Department of Psychological Assessment at the Warsaw School of Social Psychology, Poland.

RENATA ŻURAWSKA-ŻYŁA, Ph.D., works at the Psychological-Pedagogical Counseling Center in Tomaszów Lubelski, Poland.

Epigraph

The self is an oral society in which the present is constantly running a
dialogue with the past and the future inside of one skin.
David Antin, USA

We must have our say, not through violence, aggression or fear. We must
speak out calmly and forcefully. We shall only be able to enter the new
world era if we agree to engage in dialogue with the other side.
Tahar Ben Jelloun, Morocco

Introductory chapter
History, main tenets and core concepts of dialogical self theory[1]

Hubert J. M. Hermans and Thorsten Gieser

Dialogical self theory (DST) is built neither as a *grand theory*, pretending to offer a comprehensive explanation of much of human behaviour, nor as a *mini-theory* that is focused on a fairly narrow segment of human functioning. It is also not a system of thought that aims to combine or integrate two or more existing mini-theories in a synthesizing way. It is rather a *bridging theory* in which a larger diversity of theories, research traditions and practices meet, or will meet, in order to create new and unexpected linkages.

The notion of bridging theory might not suggest that there are bridges only, linking existing insights or practices without offering them an original and new perspective. Instead, it is a theory *itself* with its own identity and specific conceptual framework. However, this framework is formulated in such an open way that different, separated or even contradictory conceptual systems or approaches can find a platform which enables them to meet other theories, research traditions and practices, in the service of their further development and scrutiny.

As this handbook shows, the openness and specific conceptual identity of DST as a bridging theory create an interface for 'unexpected meetings'. As the reader will see, contributions presenting social-psychological experimental research or personality correlates find their place in the same framework as explorations into transcendental awareness. Or, psychotherapeutic traditions in the West are presented, and theoretically linked, with psychotherapeutic practices emerging in the East. Or, contributions about acculturation problems are placed side by side with an analysis of consumer behaviour, as phenomena with conceptual linkages at a deeper theoretical level.

A bridging theory as a 'meeting place for strangers' does not mean that this theory is not affected by its visitors. Like many other theories, its tenets can be confirmed, refuted, revised, enriched or further developed. It even can disappear from the scene when it would lose its credibility, fertility or truth pretensions, or when it would lose its network function. What is the core of DST as a bridging theory?

Summary of dialogical self theory

Before sketching the theory's historical roots, we summarize it here. It brings together two basic concepts, self and dialogue, that are usually seen as stemming from different psychological or philosophical traditions. The self has strong historical roots in American pragmatism, in theorists like William James, George H. Mead and Charles Sanders Peirce, while dialogue is a central concept in the writings of main figures in European traditions, like Martin Buber and Mikhail Bakhtin. Moreover, in many discussions self and dialogue are seen as different on the internal-external axis. While the self is considered, at least in Western traditions, as a reflexive concept that deals with the question of which processes take place 'internally', that is, *within* the person, dialogue is taking place 'externally', that is, *between* person and other. By bringing the two concepts together in the combined notion of 'dialogical self', the between is interiorized into the within and reversibly, the within is exteriorized into the between. As a consequence, the self does not have an existence separate from society but is part of the society; that is, the self becomes a 'mini-society' or, to borrow a term from Minsky (1985), a 'society of mind'. Society, from its side, is not 'surrounding' the self, influencing it as an external 'determinant', but there is a society-of-selves; that is, the self is in society and functions as an intrinsic part of it. The consequence is that changes and developments in the self automatically imply changes and developments in society at large and reversed. In other words, self and society are not mutually exclusive but inclusive (Hermans 2001). (For the process of negotiations between people *and* within the self, see Nir's chapter.)

In a most succinct way the dialogical self can be conceived of as a *dynamic multiplicity of I-positions*. In this view, the *I* emerges from its intrinsic contact with the (social) environment and is bound to particular positions in time and space. As such, the embodied *I* is able to move from one position to the other in accordance with changes in situation and time. In this process of positioning, repositioning and counter-positioning, the *I* fluctuates among different and even opposed positions (both within the self and between self and perceived or imagined others), and these positions are involved in relationships of relative dominance and social power. As part of sign-mediated social relations, positions can be voiced so that dialogical exchanges among positions can develop. The voices behave like interacting characters in a story or movie, involved in processes of question and answer, agreement and disagreement, conflicts and struggles, negotiations and integrations. Each of them has a story to tell about their own experiences from their own perspective.

As different voices, these characters exchange knowledge and information about their respective *me*'s, creating a complex, narratively structured self. (For the processes of positioning, repositioning and counter-positioning in educational contexts, see Ligorio's chapter; see also Hermans and Hermans-Konopka 2010.)

Before we deal with DST in more detail, we will outline its historical background. Focusing on some of its inspirers, we will show how the theory is emerging from the thoughts of historical forerunners.

James' transcendence of Cartesian dualism between self and other

For an understanding of the dialogical self, it makes sense to start with a basic distinction introduced by William James (1890), between the *I* and the *me*, seen by Rosenberg (1979) as classic in the psychology of the self. In James' view, the *I* is equated with the self-as-knower or the self-as-subject, while the *me* is equated with the self-as-known or the self-as-object. In order to understand the relation between self and other, it should be noted that James was well aware of the gradual transition between *me* and *mine*. He noted that the self-as-known is composed of all that the person can call his or her own, 'not only his body and his psychic powers, but his clothes and his house, his wife and children, his ancestors and friends, his reputation and works, his lands and horses, and yacht and bank-account' (1890: 291). As this frequently cited quotation suggests, people and things in the environment belong to the self, as far as they are felt as 'mine'. This means that not only 'my body' but also 'my mother' and even 'my opponent' are part of the self as 'extended' to the environment. The extended self contrasts with the Cartesian self, which is based on a dualistic conception, not only between self and body but also between self and other. In the extended self, the other belongs to the self and is not simply 'outside the skin'. With his gradual transition between self and non-self, later confirmed by a series of experiments by Rosenberg (1979), James paved the way for later theoretical developments in which oppositions to and negotiations with the other-in-the-self, in close connection with the actual other, are part of an extended, multivoiced process. (For the extension of the self in a psychodramatic context, see Verhofstadt-Denève's chapter.)

From Mead's 'generalized other' to 'collective voices'

In DST it is assumed that dialogue is innovative. This goes back to one of the great insights of Mead (1934) that selves are not only representatives of society and are deemed to conform to existing institutional structures, but are also able to *create and innovate* them. He was well aware of the problems that emerge when social processes are limited to the internalization of the attitude of the other within the self. In such a case, the self would be just a copy of external social roles and the members of society no more than 'slaves of customs'. There would be no innovations that bring social changes in society and no renewal of existing institutions. Being aware of this problem, Mead introduced a distinction between *I* and *Me*:

I have been undertaking to distinguish between the 'I' and the 'me' as different phases of the self, the 'me' answering to the organized attitudes of the others which we definitely assume and which determine consequently our own conduct so far as it is of a self-conscious character. Now the 'me' may be regarded as giving the form of the 'I.' The novelty comes in the action of the 'I,' but the structure, the form of the self is one which is conventional. (1934: 209)

In Mead's view, innovation is part of the capacity of the *I*, while the social rules and conventions of the generalized other are placed in the *Me*. One of his favourite examples is the artist, who is usually seen as unconventional. However, artists are not complete 'outsiders', because they accept certain rules of expression. In this context, Mead refers to the Classical Greek artists, who were, at the same time, innovators and supreme artisans in their society, introducing an originality that made their contribution unconventional.

Mead's distinction between the *I* and the *me* is somewhat different from that of James, but at the same time it goes an important step further. In his thorough analysis of the self, James (1890) emphasized three aspects of the *I*: identity, that is, sameness over time; distinctness from others; and 'volition', which referred to the 'appropriation' and 'rejection' of thoughts (see also Damon and Hart 1982). James and Mead agree on the 'agentic' qualities of the *I*. The latter did this by referring to its innovative potentials, whereas the former made a strong case for its capacity to appropriate and to reject. In James' own terms, 'There must be an agent of the appropriating and disowning; but that agent we have already named. It is the Thought to whom the various constituents are known. That Thought is a vehicle of choice as well as of cognition; and among the choices it makes are these appropriations, or repudiations, of its "own"' (1890: 340).

Mead and James agree on the agentic capacity of the *I*, and, moreover, both emphasize the social qualities of the self (see James' discussion of the 'social self' and Mead's treatment of 'society'). However, Mead elaborated, even more than James, on the immediate and pervasive significance of the other for, and even *in*, the self, and he did so by introducing such influential concepts as the 'generalized other' and 'taking the role of the other'.

As Mead has convincingly demonstrated, the generalized other is necessary for a society that is in need of social rules which are shared and understood by all the participants of a (societal) game. However, as Ritzer (1992) observes, Mead's interest in the *unity* of society and the 'objective' attitude of the generalized other had the disadvantage that he did not elaborate a systematic theory of macro-social conflicts, social differences, and ethnic- and gender-based inequality. As a consequence, Mead's theory is based on a 'homogeneous society' metaphor, with a heavy emphasis on micro-social, game-like processes. Moreover, the 'generalized other', like social and emotional rule in general, has become a more complex phenomenon in a world society that, as the result of the process of globalization and localization, has led to the emergence of a variety of interfaces between cultures (see Surgan and Abbey's chapter and van Meijl's chapter). At these interfaces, different and even conflicting social and emotional rules, which 'worked' within the boundaries of relatively isolated groups or cultures, have lost their meaning as general principles on a world scale.

When, in a globalizing society with an increasing intensity of intercultural contacts, there are different 'generalized others', they can be in touch with each other, oppose or inspire each other, or even suppress or silence each other. As such, they can be conceived of as 'collective voices' that speak through the mouth of individual speakers and, in the case of people with different social or cultural backgrounds, can even meet each in one and the same self, as exemplified by such multiple identities as those of an Algerian woman participating in an international football competition but afterward praying in a mosque, English-speaking employees living in India but giving technical training courses via the internet to adolescents in the USA, or a Muslim working in The Netherlands who feels under pressure to hide his religious beliefs because he is afraid that his Dutch colleagues would reject him if he were to express them openly. The focus here is on intercultural processes that lead to the formation of a multiplicity of cultural positions or voices coming together in the self of a single individual (Pieterse 1995). These examples have in common that different cultural voices are involved in various kinds of social relationships and produce positive or negative meanings in fields of uncertainty. In other words, the processes of globalization and localization are not just realities outside the individual but are rather incorporated as a constituent of a dialogical self in action.

The notion of voice brings us to another source of inspiration: the Russian dialogical school. We will make a move from the self as a central concept in American pragmatism to the other basic component of DST, the notion of dialogue.

From Bakhtin's polyphonic novel to the relevance of dominance and social power

In James' quotation above, we see a foreshadowing of several 'characters' whom he sees as belonging to the *mine*: my wife and children, my ancestors and my friends. Such characters are more explicitly elaborated in Bakhtin's metaphor of the 'polyphonic novel', which brings together the notions of dialogue and multiplicity of voices. This metaphor was presented in his book *Problems of Dostoevsky's Poetics* (1973), which emerged after extensive reading of Dostoevsky's literary productions. The metaphor derives from the idea that in these works there is not a single author at work – Dostoevsky himself – but *several* authors or thinkers, represented by characters such as Myshkin, Raskolnikov, Stavrogin, Ivan Karamazov and the Grand Inquisitor.

In these novels each character figures as the author of his or her own ideology, and not as the product of Dostoevsky's finalizing artistic vision. That is, the characters are not treated as obedient slaves in the service of an omniscient author-thinker who is standing *above* his characters, but they come forward as independent thinkers, each with his or her own ideology and view of the world. Rather than a number of different characters in a *unified* objective world, there is a *plurality* of consciousnesses. As in a polyphonic musical work, like a canon or fugue, a multiplicity of voices accompany and oppose one another in dialogical ways. In this way, Dostoevsky creates a diversity of perspectives, portraying characters conversing with the Devil (Ivan Karamazov and the Devil), with their alter egos (Ivan Karamazov and Smerdyakov), with the superior part of themselves (the double), and even with caricatures of themselves (Raskolnikov and Svidrigailov). As part of this novelistic construction, the notion of dialogue allows the author to differentiate the inner world of one and the same individual in the form of an interpersonal relationship. By transforming an 'inner' thought of a particular character into an utterance, dialogical relations emerge between this utterance and the utterance of imagined others. This dialogical construction makes it possible to contract temporally dispersed events into spatial oppositions that are simultaneously present (in this way creating a 'landscape of the mind'). In Bakhtin's terms, 'This persistent urge to see all things as being coexistent and to perceive and depict all things side by side and simultaneously, *as if in space rather than time*, leads him [Dostoevsky] to dramatize in space even the inner contradictions and stages of development of a single person' (Bakhtin 1973: 23; emphasis added). By considering temporally distributed thoughts and experiences as a polyphony of spatial oppositions, Bakhtin is able to treat a particular idea in the context of both internal and external dialogues, exposing and developing the idea from a multiplicity of perspectives. (For an empirical investigation of the polyphonic novel in a group of novelistic authors, see the chapter by Żurawska-Żyła, Chmielnicka-Kuter and Oleś in this book.)

Towards the other on the subject level

The polyphonic novel as multivoiced and dialogical allows for the further development of the extended self in the sense of James. Let's revisit for a moment the passage from James in which he considers as 'mine', not only his yacht and bank account, but also, to the annoyance of some feminist commentators, also his wife, children and friends. The reference to such divergent extensions derives from the implicit assumption that what one considers as 'mine' refers to something possessed, in full agreement with the 'appropriative' (volitional) nature of the Jamesian *I*. As James' statement suggests, the other is considered as 'mine', which can be appropriated or possessed, but not as a 'you' that can be addressed. The other is approached on the object level but not the subject level.

In his influential study of dialogue, Martin Buber (1970) was well aware of the fundamental difference between the other as subject and the other as object. In his view, the *I* is a member of a pair that manifests itself in two fundamentally different ways: as *part* of an *I–you* relationship (subject–subject relationship) and as *part* of an *I–it* relationship (subject–object relationship). The term *I* is not a single word having a meaning in itself but, rather, is part of the word pair *I–you* or *I–*it, representing two completely different attitudes to the world. Only in the *I–you* relation is there an encounter, where the *you* as the other is addressed as an independent other, yet is embedded in a relation. In contrast to James' appropriating *I*, the encounter between *I* and *you* in Buber's case is unthinkable without a receptive attitude, which is the cradle for emergence of deeper meanings.

In contrast, the *I* as part of the *I–it* relation is an objectifying, rather than a dialogical *I*. The term '*it*' signifies an act of observation, classification, thinking or using, but it is never an actual being-in-relationship.

The *it* is the result of an act of observation. However, as an objectified reality, the *it* is only an abstraction from the living experience of the human being living *with* others and with nature.

Buber's *I–thou* relationship that allows one to address the other on the subject level is in agreement with a statement by Bakhtin (1973: 51): 'For the author the hero is not "he", and not "I" but a full-valued "thou", that is another full-fledged "I".' For DST it is of crucial importance to consider the other, as an extended self, on the subject level. Put briefly, the other, as real, imagined or remembered, can be addressed as an *I*-position as part of an extended self. Along these lines it is possible to go beyond what Sampson (1985) depicted as the 'self-contained identity' as an ideological construction in Western culture. In his view, this identity is characterized by three features: (1) a sharp distinction between self and non-self; (2) the other as outside the self; and (3) an attitude of having the environment under control. (For a contrasting view, see Chaudhary's chapter on Indian culture, in which self and other are intensely intertwined.)

Otherness and alterity *in* the self

It is a central feature of DST that every party involved in the process of dialogue receives a voice to speak from his or her specific point of view and is given the space to express his or her concern in its particularity and uniqueness. Therefore, dialogical relationships require the responsibility of all parties involved to contribute to a democratic society in such a way that voices are not silenced, denied or suppressed on the basis of race, gender, age or any other social or personal characteristic. This consideration led Cooper and Hermans (2007) to analyse the literature on 'alterity' that refers to the acceptance and respect of the 'otherness' of the other. In the tradition of the founding philosopher of alterity, Emmanuel Levinas (1969), otherness is often equated with the face of another human being, while the internal sphere of the self is characterized by sameness and identity. However, such an association between self and sameness does not sufficiently take into account the differentiation, diversity and even oppositions of a multivoiced, dialogical self with its relatively autonomous parts characterized by alterity. Cooper and Hermans (2007) argued that, in the context of DST, the notions of 'difference', 'otherness' and 'alterity' can be usefully extended from the *inter*personal realm to the *intra*personal one. In this way, alterity can be found and experienced not only between the self and the actual other, but also between different *I*-positions within the self. The introduction of the notion of self-otherness is not to suggest that alterity exists within a self-contained, isolated monad. Rather, it is to emphasize that otherness enters the self from the most explicitly 'external' realms to the most seemingly 'internal' ones, whether expressed by the voices of actual others, imagined others or the different voices of 'oneself' (Cooper and Hermans 2007). (For the development of a methodology in which the *actual* other is included in dialogical relationships, see Jasper *et al.*'s chapter.)

Social dominance and power

The constitutive function of alterity in dialogical relationships requires an exploration of the question of to what extent dominance and social power enable or restrict such relationships. As far as dialogues are taking place in a society of people, with its traditions, established positions and social rules, they do not take place in a social vacuum, free from any element of dominance and power. As Linell (1990) has emphasized, meanings are not entirely constructed *ab novo* in monadic interactions but rather belong to a cultural capital inherited and invested in by new actors throughout history. This heritage implies that the micro-context of dialogical relationships cannot be understood without some concept of macro-frames as organizational, institutional and ethnographic contexts. Every utterance has a history in preceding dialogues and an embeddedness in situation and culture, as Gadamer (1989) has extensively argued.

Asymmetry exists even in *each* individual act–response sequence, by the simple fact that one participant knows more about a particular topic, has more information available or has more expertise in a particular field than the interaction partner. Moreover, speakers have a certain privilege in being able to take initiatives and display their view. There are various ways in which a party can dominate or control the 'territory' to be shared by the partners involved in social exchange.

As part of the reciprocal process that is usually described as turn-taking, actors continually alternate the roles of 'power holder' and 'power subject', as Linell (1990) has extensively demonstrated. For example, by making the most initiatory moves in a conversation, one party strongly determines the unfolding local context. As a consequence, the subordinate party allows, or must allow, his or her contributions to be directed, controlled or inhibited by the interlocutor's moves (interactional dominance). Or, the person who talks a lot in a conversation prevents the other party from taking a turn (amount of talk). Or, one party predominantly introduces and maintains topics and perspectives on topics (topic dominance). In this case, the party who determines the topic of the conversation may achieve a high degree of dominance that may be expressed not only in the content of the talk, but also in the direction that the conversation takes as a whole. Or, one of the interacting partners is dominant not so much by talking much but by introducing a few but really important things that strongly influence the further direction of the talk (strategic dominance). In other words, the process of turn-taking is only possible by allowing parties to be temporarily dominant in the course of exchange. Its necessity as an element of organized turn-taking demonstrates that relative dominance and organized verbal dialogue are not mutually exclusive but rather inclusive.

Social power plays a more structural role when societal institutions are taken into account. This can be illustrated by placing the play of question and answer and relationships of agreement and disagreement, the basic forms of dialogue in the sense of Bakhtin (1973), in a macro-context. When differences in social power between parties are minimal or do not interfere, as in a talk between two good friends, the dialogical process is reciprocal; that is, the interacting parties feel relatively free to ask questions of each other at any time in the exchange. Contrastingly, in a legal interrogation, in which power differences are more pronounced, questions and answers are highly asymmetrical, one party posing the questions and the other forced to answer. There is a succession of questions and answers but the free interchange is seriously constrained by the rules and expectations determined by the institutional context. In a similar way, relationships of agreement and disagreement are constrained by institutional positions. In schools that aim to stimulate personal responsibility and creativity as part of the learning process, pupils are permitted to disagree not only with their classmates but even with their teachers, if such disagreements are allowed as signs of a creative or independent thinking. However, even in such open educational climates, power differences play a subtle role and structure dialogical relationships even where they seem to be absent. Suppose, a student, who does not understand a mathematical problem, asks the teacher for help. The teacher then explains how the solution can be found and finally asks, 'Do you understand now?' When the student answers, 'Yes', there is no certainty that he has really understood the explanation, because the answer is a 'claimed answer'; that is, the student may feel the expectation of the teacher that he is a good student and may give the expected answer in line with the authority of the teacher. Or, if the boss asks to borrow the car of one of his employees, this request and the employee's response may entail an embarrassment that is absent if the same request is made by one employee of another. Or, when two people disagree on a particular subject and one or both parties become defensive, repeating their own point of view again and again, the disagreement may escalate and transform into a power game. In other words, question and answer, like agreement and disagreement, are not automatically forms of dialogue in which both parties can express and further develop their positions. When participating in social contexts, individual voices and their dialogical relationships are to a great extent expressions of institutional and historically bound collective voices and, at the same time, limited by them. As a consequence, power differences structure and constrain, overtly or covertly, both the process and the content of dialogical relationships. (For dominance and power in acculturation processes, see Bhatia's chapter; for the same phenomena in educational institutions, see Winters *et al.*'s chapter.)

To what extent is our brain dialogical?

The dialogical self is structured and constrained not only by societal processes but also by the functioning of the brain. Lewis (2002), for example, observed that children and adults, in situations of stress, feel the urge to return to 'ordinary' self-positions that offer sufficient safety, security and relaxation. This observation raises the question of to what extent dialogue is possible if the person constantly and automatically wants to return to security-providing positions. In order to address this question, Lewis analyses short phrases such as 'That was stupid' or 'You are dumb' that a person (or an imagined other) is saying to himself when involved in a task. In such situations, Lewis observes, there is neither a clear-cut other voice nor much turn-taking, and no explicit sequence of question and answer. He assumes that these utterances come from voices of significant others in the remote past whose positions are incorporated as stabilized parts into the extended domain of the self. Internal 'dialogues' of this kind are usually inchoate and sublingual, and there is not much development of a dialogue with another voice. These observations suggest that, on this sublingual level, we are more conservative and monological than innovative and dialogical.

Elaborating on his study of short, self-directed statements, Lewis (2002) presents a neuroscientific model that is consistent with Schore's (1994) analysis of the dialogical functioning of the brain. According to this analysis, the (higher) orbitofrontal cortex produces, in its linkage to the (lower) conservative, subcortical limbic system, an affectively charged sense of an interpersonal respondent, which is based on stabilized expectancies from many past interactions. This model shows how relatively stable, sublingual or prelingual voices put constraints on the higher linguistic, dialogical processes. Such quick and sublingual reactions are not necessarily a disadvantage, as they may add, in specific situations, to our action readiness and behavioural efficiency. Although these reactions are adaptive in some situations, they put constraints on the flexibility of dialogical relationships with others and reduce the openness to the alterity of the different voices in and outside the self.

Dialogue is not always there

The fact that dialogue between and within people is constrained, both by societal power differences and by the connection of the higher with the lower parts of the brain, is reason to give attention to the difference between dialogue and monologue and to their mutual relation. In the literature there are different and partly contrasting views on the relationship between dialogue and monologue. Bakhtin (1984: 293), for example, has a very broad view on dialogue as he assumes that dialogue is always there: 'Life by its very nature is dialogic. To live means to participate in dialogue...' In contrast, for Buber (1970), life is not always dialogical, because, as we have already seen, in some situations people are involved in *I–thou* relationships, and in other situations in *I–it* relationships. Bohm (1996), a quantum physicist interested in philosophy, also argues that dialogue is there only under specific circumstances, particularly when people are involved in a common creative process and generate new meanings that were not present in the starting point:

A dialogue can be among any number of people, not just two. Even one person can have a sense of dialogue within himself, if the spirit of the dialogue is present. The picture or image that this derivation suggests is of a stream of meaning flowing among and through us and between us. This will make possible a flow of meaning in the whole group, out of which may emerge some new understanding. It's something new, which may not have been in the starting point at all. It's something creative. And this shared meaning is the 'glue' or 'cement' that holds people and societies together. (1996: 6–7)

On the issue of the question of 'whether dialogue is there always or sometimes', DST is on the side of Buber and Bohm. For this theoretical choice, we propose two basic reasons. First of all, it is our opinion that in order to know the nature of dialogue it is important to know its constraints, just as it is, by analogy, important to understand human freedom in direct relation to the question of determinism. We can learn much about dialogue when we focus also on its constraints. Therefore, it makes sense to consider dialogue and monologue as two sides of the same coin. This conception prevents the conception of dialogue to become so broad that it is identical to 'communication', with the risk that all possible kinds of communication, including commands and even misleading rhetoric, would be considered as 'dialogical'. (For extreme forms of monologicality in the internet, see Hevern's chapter.)

The second reason is that, from the perspective of DST, dialogue is something 'precious'. It is the social expression of a human capacity that not only is valuable in itself but also must be fostered and developed in the service of self and in a society in which people are willing and able to create new and innovative meanings, solve problems in productive cooperation, and take the alterity of other people and their own selves into account for the welfare of themselves and society. (For the crucial role of innovative moments in psychotherapy, see Gonçalves and Ribeiro's chapter.)

The continuum between dialogue and monologue

Although dialogue and monologue can be considered – at the conceptual level – as qualitatively different, they can be described, from an analytical point of view, as representing different degrees on a continuum. Take, for example, two participants involved in an interchange who try to dominate or 'win' the discussion, do not listen carefully to each other, are not aware of possible misunderstandings that are slipping through and make no effort to unveil them, and do not allow themselves to learn from their preceding interchange. In this case, the 'exchange' moves to the monological end of the continuum. On the contrary, it moves to the dialogical end of the continuum when the participants listen to the other's point of view, allow each other the space to give expression to their own experiences and specific points of view, are motivated to uncover possible misunderstandings and are able and willing to correct them, and *learn* from each other on the basis of their preceding interchange. Between these polar opposites, there are many situations in which the interchange shows a *mixture* of both dialogical and monological elements. For example, person A listens to the other party in an emphatic way and corrects or develops parts of his initial point of view on the basis of the preceding interchange and even shares this with person B. In the same discussion, however, person A neglects or even ignores other elements which are brought in by person B, who then feels understood at some points but misunderstood at others.

Analysing dialogue and monologue in terms of variations on a continuum not only has the advantage of taking into account constraining circumstances, but is also in agreement with the positional nature of dialogical relationships. That is, some positions have the tendency to move the interchange to the monological end of the continuum, while others bring it to the dialogical end. For example, the official positions of judge and suspect limit their interchange in accordance with their societal definition; or, the teacher who has the task of evaluating the performance of his pupil at an examination does so on the basis of educational criteria and not on the basis of the preferences of the student; or, a general, confronted with an emergency, has to take a decision without consulting his subordinates. Not only social but also personal positionings influence the movements on the continuum. When husband and wife are in a defensive or angry position, their interchange will be very different from the situation in which they position and express themselves as loving each other. Depending on the nature of their relationship, the angry and closed position may create a need in the partners to 'move' in the direction of a loving and open position. As this example suggests, social and personal positions (e.g. loving wife, critical colleague, punishing father, informal politician) make combinations that have immediate implications for their place on the continuum and for their movements on it. (For empirical support of the relationship between dialogue and openness, see Oleś and Puchalska-Wasyl's chapter; for experimental evidence of the effect of 'tolerant' and 'intolerant' postions on the monological stereotyping of minority groups, see Stemplewska-Żakowicz *et al.*'s chapter.)

Some basic concepts of dialogical self theory

In this section we summarize some of the main concepts that are central to DST: *I*-position, third position, meta-position, promoter position and the process of depositioning (for extensive discussion of the process of positioning, see Raggatt's chapter).

I-position

The notion of *I*-position acknowledges the multiplicity of the self, while preserving, at the same time, its coherence and unity. The *I*, subjected to changes in time and space, is intrinsically involved in a process of positioning and is distributed by a wide variety of existing, new and possible positions (decentring movements). *I*-positions have their relative autonomy in the self, have their own specific history, and show different developmental pathways (see Barresi's chapter). At the same time, the *I* appropriates or owns some of them and rejects or disowns others (centring movements). Those that are appropriated are experienced as 'mine' and as 'belonging to myself' and, as a consequence, they add to the coherence and continuity in the self. By embedding *I*-positions in dialogical relationships and processing them in 'dialogical spaces', both within and between selves, they are 'lifted up' to the level of mutual enrichment and alterity. At the same time, *I*-positions structure and constrain such relationships.

The seemingly static notion of '*I*-position' refers, in fact, to a highly dynamic process of positioning, repositioning and counter-positioning, in which persons place themselves or are placed vis-à-vis other positions in personal or social spaces, in this way giving expression to their sense of agency (see Gallagher's epilogue). People can position themselves as congruent or discongruent with basic human experiences and emotions like anguish, ecstasy, anxiety, desire or safety. (For the role of emotions in the self, see Dimaggio's chapter, Morioka's chapter and Neimeyer's chapter.)

Third position

When two positions are involved in a conflict, they can, under specific conditions, be *reconciled* in a third position in which the conflict between the original positions is lessened and mitigated. At the same time, the third position profits from the energy originating from the two positions in the service of its further development. For example, Branco *et al.* (2008) describe the story of Rosanne, a Catholic woman in Brazil, who defined herself as lesbian. Her internal conflict focused on the 'Catholic daughter' versus the 'lesbian woman'. The purpose of the investigators was to show the creative strategies Rosanne used to weave a relative self-integration out of strongly contradictory beliefs and values. She discovered that her inner conflict led her to develop a (third) position of a *missionary*. As a Christian woman, she decided to help forsaken and lost people, including many gays and lesbians, and this gave her a way to reconcile her lesbian nature with traditional Christian values, practices and beliefs. (For the development of a hybrid third position in a conflicting intercultural context, see Surgan and Abbey's chapter; for ambivalent third positions, see Raggatt's chapter.)

Meta-position

Self-reflection is generally seen as a basic human capacity. In terms of the present theory, it refers to 'extra-positionality', the self moving above itself and taking a 'helicopter view'. Consider the example of a tennis player. As long as he is in the game, the best he can do is to be fully in the flow of the action. Any moment of self-criticism or self-doubt would interfere with the effectiveness of the performance. As long as he is fully engaged in the moment of action, he is just *in* the position of the player and 'in the act'. However, after the game, there is time for critical self-reflection. At this level he evaluates his performance and may decide to improve his skills or to follow a different strategy next time. On this (first) level of self-reflection, he thinks of himself in the position of a tennis player only. However, he has the possibility to move to a second and higher level of self-reflection, where he considers his position as tennis player in the context of a broader variety of positions. On this level, he may start to reflect on his future. Does he want to make tennis a career? What will happen when his physical condition declines? At this level he examines the connection between his position as a tennis player in the context of other significant positions, such as father, husband or student gifted in languages. Finally, he reaches a point where he has the feeling of taking a well-balanced decision which he considers as relevant to his future.

A meta-position, sometimes also described as an 'observing ego' or 'meta-cognition', permits a certain distance from one or more other positions, although it can be attracted, both cognitively and emotionally, towards some positions more than others (see Bahl's chapter on consumer behaviour). It provides an overarching view so that several positions can be seen simultaneously and relevant linkages between positions become visible. Depending on the nature of the contact with others, and the positions evoked, a person can take different meta-positions. They allow, in Damasio's term (2010), 'off-line thinking' that enables the person to delay immediate reactions or gratification and facilitates the *organization* of the self beyond the moment. They take a broader array of specific *I*-positions into account and have an executive function. As mediated by higher cortical brain activity, they have the potential to influence the lower emotional circuits of the brain so that long-term planning becomes possible. (For the functioning of a meta-position in psychotherapy, see Dimaggio's chapter and Ho's chapter; for its place in educational processes, see Winters and colleagues' chapter; and for its function in a case of multiple personality, see Barresi's chapter.)

Promoter positions

When the self functions as a successive multiplicity of unrelated *I*-positionings such that each follows its own course and specific development over time, a confusing cacophony of voices lacking any insightful organization emerges (for the notion of cacophony in schizophrenia, see Lysaker and Lysaker's chapter). In order to understand the *organization* of the self from a developmental perspective, a special concept, a promoter position, is required to create order and direction in what James would depict as the 'blooming, buzzing confusion' of *I*-positions. While meta-positions facilitate coherence and organization in the self from a spatial point of view, promoter positions do so from a temporal perspective.

Promoter positions (Valsiner 2004; see also Valsiner and Cabell's chapter) imply a considerable openness towards the future of the self and have the potential to produce and organize a diverse range of more specialized but qualitatively different positions in the service of the development of the self as a whole. Due to their openness and broad bandwidth, they have the potential to synthesize a variety of new and already existing positions in the self and reorganize the self towards a higher level of development. Promoter positions function as innovators of the self, *par excellence*.

Typically, significant others – real, remembered, anticipated or imaginary – who play a role in one's self temporarily or for a longer period, serve as promoter positions. Significant others, like one's father, mother, other family members or teachers, may exert their long-lasting influence as promoters of one's development (or as anti-promoters, in case they function as an impediment to one's development). But also inspiring figures in the arts, science, politics, literature, film or music may serve as promoter sources that have the potential of facilitating the development of existing *I*-positions and generating new ones. As a result of their openness to the future, promoters are given a stabilized and influential place as others-in-the-self that populate the extended (external) domain of the self.

Imagined figures as well as actual figures may function as promoter positions. Some people return, particularly in a period of stress or pain, to an image or picture of a deceased family member from which they receive support and strength (see Neimeyer's chapter). People with a religious or spiritual background often consult the image or statue of Buddha, Christ or other holy person, and many people have daily dialogical contact with an image of divinity that figures as the 'ultimate promoter position'. (For transpersonal personifications, see Rowan's chapter; for the influential role of ancestors in South African culture, see Lindegger and Alberts' chapter.) Depending on the influence of such positions, the consultation of imagined significant others can create a 'position shift' similar to the imagined role reversals in early childhood (for the role of imagination in pretend play, see Bertau's chapter).

Also in the internal domain of the self, promoter positions may emerge. For example, some people derive a developmental impetus of *I*-positions, as in 'I as always going on, never giving up', or 'I as artistic', or 'my call in life'. Such positions may be particularly influential because they help people to find their way in a great diversity of situations, and they open vistas for future developments in the self. Sometimes external and internal positions are closely linked together, as when somebody says, 'I'm a high achiever in order to prove that I'm not subject to the limitations imposed on my father', or 'I'm taking revenge for the injustice done to my loved ones.' The close and highly dynamic interconnections between external and internal positions may account for the way the self *responds* to the variegated societal influences to which the self is subjected.

In summary, the main argument that we want to develop in this section is that self and society are closely interconnected, leading to the conception of the self as a 'society of mind'. This society is populated by internal positions and external positions (perceived, remembered or imagined others), which in their mutual dynamic relationships construct and reconstruct each other in reciprocal ways. External positions influence internal ones and vice versa. In fact, external positions as constructions of the other in the self mediate between internal positions and the actual others as 'objective realities' outside. Dialogue between the self and the actual other is needed in order to confirm, correct or further develop the way others are reconstructed as external positions in the self. External positions find themselves always in a field of tension between the urge of the self to keep contact with 'outside reality' and the need to structure the images of the other in the self on the basis of the needs of internal positions. It is at the heart of the present theory that internal dialogues within the self and external dialogues with actual others are both needed in order to reach a cross-fertilization of the mini-society of the self and the macro-society at large.

Transcendental awareness as a process of depositioning

Do the processes of positioning, dialogue and monologue have the last word? Is the person doomed to be constantly involved in these processes? Is the person always located in specific locations in the landscape of the mind destined to live within the limiting horizons of specific *I*-positions? Such questions stimulate an exploration of the farther reaches of the human self in terms of the process of depositioning. Let's start with an experience reported by the spiritual scholar Jiddu Krishnamurti in 1922:

On the first day while I was in that state and more conscious of the things around me, I had the first more extraordinary experience. There was a man mending the road; that man was myself; the pickax he held was myself; the very stone which he was breaking up was a part of me; the tender blade of grass was my very being, and the tree beside the man was myself. I also could feel and think like the roadmender and I could feel the wind passing through the tree, and the little ant on the blade of grass I could feel. The birds, the dust and the very noise were a part of me. Just then there was a car passing by at some distance; I was the driver, the engine, and the tires; as the car went further away from me, *I was going away from myself. I was in everything*, or rather *everything was in me*, inanimate and animate, the mountain, the worm and all breathing things. All the day I remained in this happy condition. (quoted by Forman 1999: 375; emphasis added)

The distinctive nature of this experience is that the person is *beyond* any position and, at the same time, he is *in* everything and everywhere. The boundaries of the self become highly permeable and the self is extended to an unusual degree. The person feels united with people, animals and even objects that are normally perceived as 'outside', 'external' or 'not me'. Instead of successive turn-taking and explicit dialogue, there is an immediate and direct identification with the environment as a whole, including all of its manifestations and details. The person feels unified with an unlimited environment without any sign of pathological disintegration.

This form of depositioning (for other types, see Foreman 1999) deviates significantly from the Jamesian *I*, which is considered to be involved in a continuous process of 'appropriation' and 'repudiating' (James 1890: 340). Rather, this special state of mind can be described, with the title of a chapter of Deikman (1999): 'I = awareness.' The *I* is more receptive than appropriative, and it is open to a high degree, as reflected by Krishnamurti's words, 'rather everything was in me'.

The experience of space is not lost (e.g. 'the car went further away') but is felt as strongly expanded beyond the individual, who is far from self-contained. Therefore, transcendental awareness can be seen as the most far-reaching answer to Sampson's discription of the self as a 'self-contained identity', the preferred Western model of the self with its sharp boundaries between self and non-self, with the other as purely outside the self and the typical attitude of control of the environment.

It should be emphasized that awareness as a route of depositioning is of a different nature than the process of meta-positioning as described earlier. While a meta-position requires a self-reflexive distance towards more specific positions in the form of thoughts, considerations and comparisons, awareness is direct, non-conceptual, non-categorizing and unmediated by explicit signs or symbols. While meta-positioning requires some conceptual 'work' on the self, awareness can only take place by pure attention. In addition, meta-positions can be influenced and coloured by specific positions (e.g. 'I as critical of myself' or 'I as self-ridiculing myself'), in contrast to awareness, which is non-judgemental and non-evaluative (for the process of depositioning, awareness and silence, see Hermans-Konopka's chapter).

It would be a misunderstanding to assume that states of expanded awareness are the exclusive domain of people who are 'gifted mystics', or the result of long-lasting meditative practices. In various forms they can be part of the experiences of everyday life. It may happen when you reach, after a long walk, a mountain top with a view of a fabulous landscape; when you enjoy great music or become deeply impressed by a work of art; when you have an extraordinary experience of love or have accomplished something, alone or together, that gives the feeling of rising 'above' or 'beyond' yourself; or when feeling part of a group that unites people from different religions, ethnic groups or cultures. At such moments, we feel *expanded* beyond ordinary boundaries while feeling most *close* to ourselves. Such moments of immediate and deep encounter with something beyond our usual self-definition are not possible by any form of mediated and explicit turn-taking. It is more like Buber's *I–thou* connection. As far as the word 'turn' is applicable, the turns are falling together in an immediate encounter with an expanded reality. (For the role of non-verbal aspects in dialogical relationships, see Morioka's chapter; see also Gieser's 2006 analysis of 'shape-shifting' in cultural anthropology.)

Conclusion

In the course of this chapter, we have referred several times to two basic movements to which the self is subjected: centring (organizing and stabilizing) movements and decentring (disorganizing and destabilizing) movements. Both movements are, in their equivalence, seen as necessary for the development of a dialogical self (Hermans and Hermans-Konopka 2010). In line with a modern model of the self, dialogue can be centring and unifying; for example, when participants arrive at common meanings via productive agreement and cooperation. In line with a postmodern model, dialogue can also be decentring, in situations where participants succeed in realizing a productive exchange via disagreement or social conflict from which they learn to their mutual benefit.

We started this chapter with the statement that DST is a bridging theory. In our view, centring and decentring movements are not only typical of the self as the subject matter of the theory, but also characteristic of the theory itself, as materialized by the different chapters of this handbook. The topics addressed, the (sub)disciplines, and the cultures and countries of the authors are diverse enough to move the whole enterprise into very different directions. At the same time they find their common ground in the formulation of an open theory that aims to provide some conceptual foundations that are coherent enough to face the challenge of different applications and interpretations. In the field of tension between the two movements, this book may serve as an invitation to contribute to a new field of theory, research and practice that finds its context in a globalizing society.

NOTE

1 This introduction provides a summary of the theory and a context of the chapters of the handbook. A more extended exposure of the theory is given by Hermans and Hermans-Konopka (2010).

REFERENCES

Bakhtin, M. (1973) *Problems of Dostoevsky's Poetics* (Ann Arbor, MI: Ardis)

Barge, J. K. and Little, M. (2002) Dialogical wisdom, communicative practice, and organizational life, *Communication Theory*, **12**, 375–397

Bohm, D. (1996) *On Dialogue* (New York: Routledge)

Branco, A. U., Branco, A. L. and Madureira, A. F. (2008) Self-development and the emergence of new *I*-positions: emotions and self-dynamics, *Studia Psychologica*, **6**, 23–39

Buber, M. (1970) *I and Thou: A New Translation with a Prologue 'I and You' and notes by Walter Kaufmann* (Edinburgh: T. & T. Clark)

Cooper, M. and Hermans, H. J. M. (2007) Honoring self-otherness: alterity and the intrapersonal, in L. Simão and J. Valsiner (eds.), *Otherness in Question: Labyrinths of the Self* (Greenwich, CT: Information Age), 305–315

Damasio, A. (2010) *Self Comes to Mind: Constructing the Conscious Brain* (New York: Pantheon)

Damon, W. and Hart, D. (1982) The development of self-understanding from infancy through adolescence, *Child Development*, **4**, 841–864

Deikman, A. J. (1999) 'I' = awareness, in S. Gallagher and J. Shear (eds.), *Models of the Self* (Thorverton, UK: Imprint Academic), 421–427

Forman, R. K. C. (1999) What does mysticism have to teach us about consciousness?, in S. Gallagher and J. Shear (eds.), *Models of the self* (Thorverton, UK: Imprint Academic), 361–377

Gadamer, H.-G. (1989) *Truth and method*, 2nd rev. edn. Trans. and rev. J. Weinsheimer and D. G. Marshall (New York: Continuum)

Gieser, T. (2006) How to transform into goddesses and elephants: exploring the potentiality of the dialogical self, *Culture & Psychology*, **12**, 443–459

Hermans, H. J. M. (2001) The dialogical self: toward a theory of personal and cultural positioning, *Culture & Psychology*, **7**, 243–281

Hermans, H. J. M. and Hermans-Konopka, A. (2010) *Dialogical Self Theory: Positioning and Counter-Positioning in a Globalizing Society* (Cambridge University Press)

James, W. (1890) *The Principles of Psychology* (London: Macmillan), vol. I

Levinas, E. (1969) *Totality and Infinity: An Essay on Exteriority.* Trans. A. Lingis (Pittsburgh, PA: Duquesne University Press)

Lewis, M. D. (2002) The dialogical brain: contributions of emotional neurobiology to understanding the dialogical self, *Theory & Psychology*, **12**, 175–190

Linell, P. (1990) The power of dialogue dynamics, in I. Marková and K. Foppa (eds.), *The Dynamics of Dialogue* (New York: Harvester Wheatsheaf), 147–177

Mead, G. H. (1934) *Mind, Self, and Society* (University of Chicago Press)

Minsky, M. (1985) *The Society of Mind* (New York: Simon & Schuster)

Pieterse, J. N. (1995) Globalization as hybridization, in M. Featherstone, S. Lash and R. Robertson (eds.), *Global Modernities* (London: Sage), 45–68

Ritzer, G. (1992) *Sociological Theory*, 3rd edn (New York: McGraw-Hill)

Rosenberg, M. (1979) *Conceiving the Self* (New York: Basic Books)

Sampson, E. (1989) The decentralization of identity: toward a revised concept of personal and social order, *American Psychologist*, **11**, 1203–1211

Schore, A. N. (1994) *Affect Regulation and the Origin of the Self: The Neurobiology of Emotional Development* (Hillsdale, NJ: Lawrence Erlbaum)

Straus, E. W. (1958) Aesthesiology and hallucinations, in R. May, E. Angel and H. F. Ellenberger (eds.), *Existence: A New Dimension in Psychiatry and Psychology* (New York: Basic Books), 139–169

Valsiner, J. (2004) The promoter sign: developmental transformation within the structure of the dialogical self, paper presented at XVIII Biennial Meeting of the International Society for the Study of Behavioral Development, Ghent

Part I

Theoretical contributions

Introduction

Hubert J. M. Hermans and Thorsten Gieser

The chapters in this section will deal with theoretical issues around dialogical self theory (DST). They have in common that they elaborate on particular aspects that have a central place in the theory or develop them further.

A detailed overview of the main concepts of DST is presented in Raggatt's chapter. This overview enables the author to elaborate on both the simultaneity (synchronic extension) and the succession (temporal extension) of the position repertoire. Inspired by the work of Charles Sanders Peirce, he then focuses on the concepts of 'ambiguous third position' and 'dialogical triad', arguing that they provide important tools for conceptualizing both differentiation and integration in the formation of a dialogical self.

In his chapter Barresi too describes the spatial and temporal aspects of DST. He does so by proposing a three-dimensional model of the dialogical self, which adds a reflective dimension to the spatial and temporal dimensions of *I*-positions, with special attention to the function of meta-positions in the organization of the self. Taking recent advances in DST into account, he presents a case study of multiple personality in order to illustrate in a radical way some theoretical issues associated with temporality that are not generally acknowledged.

In her chapter on the developmental origins of the dialogical self, Bertau presents an extensive review of literature that shows how in the early years of life intersubjective processes take place *before* language develops. She does so by discussing a wide variety of phenomena that can be considered as precursors of the later, full-grown dialogicality. Among them are the preference for melodies to which the child was exposed prenatally and the prosodic features of the mother's language (melody, intensity and rhythm), imitation and provocation in tongue protrusion as signs of inborn intersubjectivity, the experienced distinction between self-touches and other touches, the joint attention of parent and child to objects in the environment, pretend play, and imaginary companions.

In their contribution Valsiner and Cabell offer two mutually relatable ideas to the discourse of DST in order to make sense of the dialogical self's complexities: self-making and synthesis. Elaborating on the concept of *self-making*, they argue that the ever-developing, ever-transitioning and ever-dynamic dialogue requires attention to the mediating (semiotic) devices people use – within their own mind and within the immediate environment – to cultivate their life space. In their discussion of the concept of *synthesis*, the authors maintain that tension, created by the hyper-production of self-made meanings in the self, requires synthesis. Inspired by the philosopher Johann Gottlieb Fichte, they make a case for a hierarchical structure of the dialogical self, without losing its focus on its dynamic nature.

In a cultural-anthropological analysis, van Meijl poses the fundamental question of how individuals connect various cultural identifications within the self in the context of migration that is characterized by rapid social and cultural change. The author shows how an increasing number of cultural positions in multicultural societies may destabilize the dialogue between various identifications that is required in order to strike a balance in the self. He exemplifies this process by describing the multicultural dilemmas of Samoan youngsters in New Zealand. On the basis of these observations, he then introduces Marilyn Strathern's notion of the 'partible person', consisting of a composite of social relations; therefore, it is not an individual but rather a 'dividual'. Finally, he compares this notion with the dialogical self and demonstrates how the two concepts complement and enrich each other.

In his chapter on acculturation strategies, Bhatia argues that acculturation for many transnational immigrants is essentially a contested, dynamic and dialogical process. In this light, he refers to a fourfold classification of acculturation strategies: 'assimilation', 'integration', 'separation' and 'marginalization'. He critically discusses these strategies in mainstream cross-cultural psychology where they are typically considered as universal, mutually exclusive and exempt of social power. In order to redress these tendencies, he presents examples from his own research on Indian diasporas in order to demonstrate how the concept of voice in DST allows us to make the claim that race, ethnicity and culture do not entail a movement towards assimilation, marginalization, separation *or* integration in a new culture. Rather, there is an ongoing, *simultaneous* dialogical movement between voices that are at once assimilated, integrated, privileged and marginalized.

In her contribution, Verhofstadt-Denève compares DST and her 'phenomenological-dialectical personality model', inspired as it is by psychodramatic approaches. She shows that there are considerable similarities on the theoretical level, but marked differences in the methods applied for exploring and stimulating intra- and interpersonal dialogues. She compares the psychodramatic approach with Hermans' self-confrontation method (SCM) and personal position repertoire (PPR) method, which can be used to assess *I*-positions and stimulate dialogical processes. She shows how in psychodrama the protagonist has the opportunity to really meet the antagonist, an encounter that intensifies and surpasses the self-reflexive dimension as typical of the SCM and PPR method. She argues that, in a psychodramatic approach, the dialogical relationship between protagonist and antagonist is sustained on the level of *action* that vividly actualizes the here-and-now nature of dialogical exchange between significant *I*-positions.

In an intercultural context, Surgan and Abbey propose to investigate the processes of positioning and repositioning on three levels of analysis: *personal, social* and *societal*. Specifically, they examine the creation of novel 'third positions' by transnational migrants to the USA and treat these positions as expressions of the process of *hybridization*. They discuss the case study of a person who constructed a hybrid identity after moving back and forth between Latin American and North American social environments. In this case the process of hybridization results neither in a position of independence nor in one of interdependence, but in a form of 'interdependent independence', expressing not so much 'helping myself' or 'receiving help from others', but rather 'asking for help comfortably'.

In her chapter on the functioning of the dialogical self in India, Chaudhary discusses the social setting of Indians as it has evolved from ancient times. She shows that the application of DST to Indian selves is effective because it allows for the explication of 'otherness in the self', for the context-dependence of behaviour, and for the combination of personal and social functioning. She discusses a range of phenomena that are central in the Indian self as a 'society of the mind', such as *strategic silence* (as an effective strategy in awkward social situations), *social ventriloquism* (talking on behalf of another person), *indirect address* (speaking to A what is intended for B), and *position shift* (a significant other takes the position of 'I', as when a person may say not 'I want you to ...' but 'father wants you to ...'). With these and other features, the author demonstrates how a diversity of phenomena typical of the Indian self can be explained in DST terms.

In his chapter on 'human digital ecology', Hevern articulates three propositions: (1) the internet alters the personal and social experience of Cartesian space and time; (2) it may foster *or* undermine dialogical exchange depending upon the degree of anonymity and isolation of their users; and (3) it facilitates extreme forms of monologicality, including what might be termed 'voices of darkness and the irrational'. Hevern demonstrates that the advent of cyberspace, as a completely new spatial form in human experience, undermines both traditional and modernist ways of understanding how people function intra- and interpersonally. He observes, within the uncertainty engendered by its complex and ever-more diversifying ecology, that the internet allows increasing opportunities for the dynamics of positioning and repositioning and voices and counter-voices.

In their chapter on schizophrenia, Lysaker and Lysaker describe models of self-disturbance from psychoanalytic, phenomenological and existential vantage points in order to compare them with DST. From the latter perspective, they discuss three different forms of self-experience: a *barren* self, in which persons experience themselves as flat or even empty of self-positions; a *monological* self, in which one or a few positions (e.g. *I* as persecuted or *I* as possessing a special status) are silencing other positions; and a *cacophonous* self, where the person feels overwhelmed or lost in a storm of positions that may never again cohere. The authors make clear that, whereas the other perspectives (psychoanalytic, phenomenological and existential) all seem to speak more generally of sense of self in schizophrenia, DST enables them to distinguish among three kinds of self-experience (barren, monological and cacophonous) and to recommend distinct psychotherapeutic approaches for each.

In their analysis of the social situation in the new South Africa, Lindegger and Alberts are interested in a comparison of Western psychotherapies which historically have been embraced by the white sector of the population and traditional African healing favoured mainly by black people. They notice that under the influence of urbanization, globalization and transformation, hybrids of these two forms of therapeutic healing are produced. They find in DST a conceptual framework that enables them to articulate not only the differences but also the deeper commonalities and possible reconcilability of the two therapeutic approaches. In the second part of their contribution, they report the results of interviews with white South African families, which reveal a great deal of 'threat narratives' (e.g. referring to the 'black danger'). They end their chapter by discussing the necessity of innovative dialogues that take into account the alterity of the racial other in the new South Africa.

1 Positioning in the dialogical self: recent advances in theory construction

Peter T. F. Raggatt

The literature on the dialogical self has grown significantly over the past two decades. The two guiding metaphors of a dialogical approach, namely that the self takes the form of both a 'conversation' and a 'mini-society', have been inspirational for researchers working across many topics in social, cultural and clinical psychology, and in neighbouring social sciences (e.g. Barresi 2002; Bhatia and Ram 2001; Chandler 2004; Fogel *et al.* 2002; Gieser 2006; Hermans 2001; Hermans and Dimaggio 2004; Hermans and Hermans-Konopka 2010; Hermans and Kempen 1993; Hevern 2004; Josephs 2002; Lewis 2002; Lysaker 2006; Raggatt 2000, 2006; Sampson 1993; Stiles 1999; Tappan 2005). Fundamental to dialogical self theory (DST) is the proposition that the self has extension in both *space* and *time* through processes of *positioning*. Inspired particularly by William James (1890), Mikhail Bakhtin (1981, 1984) and George Herbert Mead (1934), Hermans (2001) has conceptualized the dialogical self as an extended 'position repertoire'. The repertoire contains a variety of interacting 'internal positions' (e.g. *I* as adventurer, *I* as pessimist), 'external positions' (e.g. the imagined voice of my father), and 'outside' positions (e.g. interlocutors, significant others, groups). In this dynamic arrangement, positioning processes are at play on multiple levels: in our 'self-talk', in our relationships, in the social orders we inhabit, and in our cultural activities. As the engine of DST, therefore, the concept of positioning has a broad range of convenience with applications at different levels of engagement. Because of this breadth, an integrated, nuanced and comprehensive theory of positioning is needed.

If the dialogical self is an extended position repertoire in time and space, then it must have features of both *simultaneity* (synchronic extension) and *succession* (temporal extension). This conceptualization presents significant challenges for theory building, a problem I aim to address in this chapter. As mentioned, we are positioned in our internal dialogues, in our intimate exchanges and everyday dealings, in our cultural pursuits, and indeed in our historical embedding in culture.

Until recently, however, the literature on the dialogical self has lacked a systematic account of these complex processes (Raggatt 2007). In the first part of this chapter, then, I consider recent developments in positioning theory. The aim is to give a broad overview and synthesis of positioning processes. In this I will draw particularly on the recent work of Hermans (Hermans and Hermans-Konopka 2010), as well as other scholars.[1] In the second part of the chapter, I consider some promising avenues for future work on understanding positioning mechanisms. In particular, I will focus on the concepts of 'ambiguous third position' and 'dialogical triad', arguing that they provide important tools for conceptualizing both integration and differentiation in the formation of a dialogical self.

A synthesis of positioning terms and processes

Hermans and Hermans-Konopka (2010) have recently presented a wide-ranging discussion of positioning processes. Here I will take the liberty of summarizing their ideas along with other recent contributions to positioning theory (e.g. Raggatt 2007; Valsiner 2004). For brevity, Table 1.1 presents a synthesis and glossary of key positioning terms (only brief definitions are given). The terms are organized thematically under 'basic elements', 'dynamic elements', 'developmental processes' and 'cultural/historical processes'. Table 1.1 is intended to point towards a more comprehensive model of positioning processes. In what follows, I will give a brief commentary on each thematic component of the table. The basic elements in positioning theory (Table 1.1) have already been mentioned here. Most fundamental are the concepts of '*I*-position' and 'counter-position', which set up the grounds for extension, multiplicity and decentralization in the self. When the *I* takes up a position in relation to the world, or one is positioned by others, movement is immediately implied by a range of potential counter-positions, whether these positions are internal to the self or have origins outside. In either case, some degree of dynamic, developmental or cultural tension is implied by the process of positioning and counter-positioning. It is precisely these processes that require more rigorous specification in theory and research (Raggatt 2007). At the cultural level, for example, the process of globalization has created opportunities for innovation of the self across borders and cultural divides that are new (Hermans and Dimaggio 2007). At the same time, countervailing processes of localization emerge (or re-emerge), and these can lead, in their defensive forms, to race tensions and conflicts, to a closing-off

Table 1.1 *A glossary of terms in positioning theory*

	Brief definition
Basic elements	
I-position[1]	A location appropriated by the *I* within an extended field or 'position repertoire'
Counter-position[1]	An alternate (often conflicting) location appropriated by the *I*
Internal position[1]	An *I*-position with a distinctive inner voice and personal history
External position[1]	An 'other-in-the-self'; the voice of a teacher, a parent, a partner
Outside position[1]	Persons, groups, institutions in the outside world
Dynamic elements	
Core position[1]	A position on which the functioning of other positions depends
Meta-position[1]	A superordinate position – the product of two or more positions
Promoter position[1,2]	A position which gives order and direction in the development of the position repertoire
Shadow position[1]	A disowned or less conscious position that produces negative affect
Third position[1]	A mediator between two conflicting positions
Ambiguous third position[3]	Part of self, other, object or event with 'multi-stable' meaning value
Dialogical triad[3]	Two opposing *I*-positions mediated by an ambiguous position with multi-stable or structurally ambiguous meaning value
Developmental processes	
Social positioning[4]	Positioning from 'outside'; e.g. by virtue of gender, status, ethnicity
Reflexive positioning[4]	Positioning from 'inside'; e.g. through conflicts over self-esteem
Decentring processes[1,5]	Centrifugal movements that differentiate or disorganize the existing position repertoire so that it becomes open to innovation
Centring processes[1,5]	Centripetal movements that contribute to the organization and integration of the position repertoire
Cultural/historical processes	
Globalization[1]	Cultural processes of boundary crossing, hybridization and innovation
Localization[1]	Cultural processes of development based on local values, traditions and practices
Premodern model of self[1,6]	Self subordinate to soul, community and religious authority
Modern model of self[1,6,7]	Separation of self from other, subject from object, public from private
Postmodern model of self[1,8]	Plurality, decentring of subject, multiple sites for self-engagement

[1] Hermans and Hermans-Konopka 2010.
[2] Valsiner 2004.
[3] Raggatt 2010.
[4] Raggatt 2007.
[5] Bakhtin 1981.
[6] Danzinger 1997; Taylor 1989.
[7] Richardson *et al.* 1998.
[8] Gergen 1991.

of new positions, and even to a resurgence of fundamentalisms characteristic of the pre-modern era (Hermans and Hermans-Konopka 2010; Kinnvall 2004).

Under what I have called 'dynamic elements' in Table 1.1, Hermans and his co-author have made a number of contributions to the problem of specifying the organization and developmental trajectory of the dialogical self. Of central concern for organization are questions about the relative differentiation versus integration of the self. In terms of development, the question to be addressed concerns the dynamics of decentralizing and centralizing movements as the dialogical self emerges or 'grows'. In the dialogical tradition (e.g. Bakhtin 1981, 1984, 1990) decentralizing movements are fundamental – multiplicity trumps unity, and any experience of unity is viewed as an achievement and as having a temporary or proscribed status. Consequently, integration is not defined as an end state, as in humanistic and modernist conceptions (e.g. Erikson 1963; Maslow 1954; McAdams 1993). To capture integrating and centralizing movements in the self, Hermans proposes the concepts of 'meta-position' and 'core position'. A meta-position (Table 1.1) acts a little like an overseer, observing the functioning of a limited set of interacting internal and external positions that are simultaneously available to awareness. Note that this implies a hierarchical structure in the self. But Hermans and his co-author argue that meta-positions can themselves be subject to domination by other positions that will mask 'insight' or an 'overview'. In fact there may be a *multiplicity* of meta-positions available to the dialogical self, each with its own purview. Hermans and Hermans-Konopka write:

A meta-position is not to be considered a 'control centre' of the self or an agency that guarantees the unity and coherence of the self in advance ... a meta-position is typically [the product of] ... one or more internal and external positions ... [D]epending on time and situation, different meta-positions emerge. (2010: 148)

On this view there is really no dominant centralizing tendency that can be equated with a fully integrated self. The concept of core position (Table 1.1), similarly, does not denote a central headquarters for the self but rather a dominant position with a wide range of convenience. A position is a core position when a large number of other positions are affected by its functioning. Presumably, core positions assemble a large domain of other positions linked by important events, persons, objects and life narratives (Raggatt 2006).

Developmental trajectories, both centralizing and decentralizing, must also be theorized in positioning terms, and, here, key innovations in positioning theory have emerged in recent years (Hermans and Hermans-Konopka 2010; Raggatt 2010; Valsiner 2004). The concept of 'promoter sign', first proposed by Valsiner (2004), can be used to model both centralizing and decentralizing movements. A promoter sign, or 'promoter position' (the term used by Hermans), can be internal or external to the self. Its primary purpose is to facilitate development, and this may take place either by centralizing movements (e.g. by facilitating a coalition of older positions) or by decentralizing movements (e.g. by allowing or facilitating the innovation of the self by new positions). Hermans and Hermans-Konopka (2010) identify a range of promoter positions, including internal positions that emerge in therapy to provide the grounds for positive change, and external positions that act as guides and inspirations, and are typically constituted by significant others, places or contexts. Hermans and Hermans-Konopka write:

Promoter positions ... stimulate the development of the self. Typically, significant others – real, remembered, anticipated or imaginary ... serve as promoter positions. Inspiring figures in the areas of art, science, politics, novels, film or music or art may serve as promoter sources that open the self by their appeal to already existing I-positions and their potential to engender new ones. (2010: 234)

Hermans and Hermans-Konopka also identify 'third' positions (Table 1.1), which they define as fulfilling a primarily integrating role, mediating between two other conflicting positions; for example, a valued other helps me to express both my artistic and practical selves. The result is centralizing movements. In my view, however, this definition rather limits the scope and potential of third positions. I have recently proposed, for example, that *ambiguous* third positions can be used to understand decentralizing movements that are important in the formation of new positions (Raggatt 2010). In this formulation, 'dialogical triads' are comprised of two opposing *I*-positions that are *simultaneously* polarized and attracted by a mediating third position that has dynamic *ambiguous* properties. The third term may take the form of another person, an event or an object that, in semiotic terms, is structurally ambiguous; for example, a partner may promote conflict by being both accepting and rejecting of you; or a boss may be alternately supportive and hostile, producing decentralizing movements. In the second part of this chapter, I will argue that ambiguous third positions of this type *provide the very grounds for the emergence of multiplicity in the self*. (For another case of ambiguous third position, see also Surgan and Abbey's chapter.)

Under 'Developmental processes' in Table 1.1, an important distinction is made between 'social positioning' – positioning with origins in the external domain, and 'reflexive' positioning – arising from conflicts between internal positions. Several authors have discussed this distinction (Hermans 2001; Raggatt 2007; Tan and Moghaddam 1995). Within the framework of DST, this means we must distinguish between the influence of '*others*-in-the-self' (external positions) and '*otherness*-in-the-self' (internal positions). The mechanisms of positioning would appear to differ in the two cases. In developmental terms, social positioning must be considered *primary*, consistent with Vygotsky's (1978) views on the social formation of mind and the importance of the other in development. Bertau (2008) has observed, in Vygotsky's (1929) account of 'interiorization', a process that begins with social positioning – the child is initially oriented towards the other, is shaped by the other's speech and actions. But soon the child starts to disregard the other for the sake of an 'interior' world in which the other may be reconstructed or imagined. Hence, what begins as a social positioning process can be transformed into the potential for reflexive positioning. The child moves towards and away from the other in the construction of internal and external positions. Eventually different internal positions can have exchanges. Translating these early processes to questions of later development, I have argued that social positioning reflects the impact of others, and of cultural and institutional prescriptions that define the contours of the self (e.g. one's status, gender, class or ethnic group). Reflexive positioning, on the other hand, *recognizes that people construct and narrate their own lives in ongoing 'micro-dialogues' that have moral and ethical underpinnings.* Elsewhere, for example, I have argued that such reflexive dynamics can be summarized along a few core existential needs – to maintain esteem, to express agency and autonomy, to seek communion with others, and to maximize pleasure (Raggatt 2007). Reflexive positioning involves dialogical tension between opposing positions around these themes. Social positioning may also take on many forms. I have focused in my own research on the effects of power in social settings involving hierarchies. At least three forms meet this criterion: occupational/status conflicts, gender conflicts and social-class conflicts (there are presumably many others). Their inclusion recognizes that social positioning is sanctioned by power differences which give rise to uncertainties and to tensions in different social settings. In studies in which life history material was coded for social and reflexive positioning, I have shown how these categories interact in interesting ways (Raggatt 2008, 2011). For example, esteem concerns (reflexive positioning) interact with cross-gender conflicts (social positioning), but only for women, while for men agency concerns (reflexive positioning) and occupational status conflicts (social positioning) interact.

Under cultural/historical processes in Table 1.1, I have included two sets of countervailing forces, also discussed by Hermans and Hermans-Konopka (2010). All these processes are *simultaneously* at play in positioning theory. Processes of globalization are closely linked to the postmodern model of the self. As noted earlier, globalization exerts decentralizing pressures by creating opportunities for innovation of the self across cultures and national boundaries. The emergence of the World Wide Web, for example, has created global virtual communities and networks. Mass migrations have created widespread diasporas that were not anticipated half a century ago (Hermans and Dimaggio 2007). These cultural level processes promote hybridizing and decentralizing movements in the self. At the same time, countervailing processes of centralization and localization are important. Under the influence of Enlightenment individualism and consumerist capitalism, for example, the modern model of the self reproduces centralizing movements (Danzinger 1997; Taylor 1989). Localization manifests in cultural enclaves and diaspora communities that can preserve and extend long traditions while also closing off the potential for new positions (Hermans and Hermans-Konopka 2010; Kinnvall 2004).

As we look at the historical processes captured in the premodern, modern and postmodern models of the self (Table 1.1), it is tempting to link DST explicitly to the postmodern model – DST, after all, emphasizes plurality. But Hermans and Hermans-Konopka emphasize that this view is misleading because the dialogical self, in historical terms, is a product and amalgam of the traditional, the modern and the postmodern views of the self. These cultural models are defined as simultaneously present, active and themselves in dialogue.

Positioning in dialogical triads: the role of 'third' positions as mediators

In the second part of this chapter, I want to focus more closely on 'third' positions as crucial mediators for the formation of a dialogical self. We have seen that 'promoter' positions can mediate both innovation and integration of the position repertoire by *intervening* between positions that are in tension or conflict. Mediation requires at least a *triad* of two positions plus a third as mediator. I propose that *triadic formulations have a wide range of application to positioning theory.* In the field of linguistics, Charles Sanders Peirce (1931) long ago introduced the concept of 'thirdness' as a means to conceptualize semiotic mediation. When this principle is applied to language, Peirce argued, meaning becomes dependent on the triadic relationship between an object, its signifier and a third term, which Peirce called the 'interpretant' (defined broadly as the interpretative tradition of a culture). The power of triadic formulations involving thirdness is that they can be arranged in multiple complex structures. Indeed, triad models in various forms have emerged since the time of Peirce, including 'communication' triads (sender–recipient–object of reference; Buhler 1990), 'epistemic' triads (ego–alter–object; Marková 2003), and 'developmental' triads (child–parent–object; Zittoun *et al.* 2007). In the context of developmental triads, for example, Hermans and Hermans-Konopka (2010) observe that infants may be positioned by their mothers (the third term in this illustration) as 'good' or 'bad', depending on their behaviour. If repeated sufficiently by the caregiver, 'good' and 'bad' may become *affective-charged and polarized internal positions* in childhood that are elaborated in later experience through reflexive positioning. Here, positioning is a mediated process. From the beginning it takes place in indirect ways (in this case, through the mother), rather than directly from the child to the world.

Ambiguous third positions

In thinking about the importance of mediation in positioning theory, it will be helpful to identify a special class of 'ambiguous third' positions that play an important role in the formation of position repertoires. Hermans and Hermans-Konopka (2010) make reference to ambiguous thirds, but without elaborating on their implications. For example, they observe that *I*-positions may be 'owned' or 'disowned', appropriated or rejected, or seen as either 'part of me' or 'not part of me'. They write:

> Some *I*-positions are located in the vague and ambiguous border-zone between self and non-self which can be characterized as 'identity-in-difference' (Gregg, 1991), that is, they belong to me and do not belong to me *at the same time*. (2010: 142)

I think these ambiguous 'border-zone' positions provide one of the keys to understanding our multiplicity. When some aspect of our experience in the form of an *ambiguous object* – another person, an event or some other symbolic reference – is simultaneously appropriated as part of the self and rejected as 'not part of me', then we have the kernel around which the formation of *I*-positions and counter-positions can emerge. Although not writing explicitly about the dialogical self, the American personality psychologist Gary Gregg (1991, 1995) has pinpointed a similar process. In his detailed case histories of 'self representation', Gregg identified certain core positions that are 'multi-stable or structurally ambiguous' (1995: 617). For example, 'Faith' is a working-class girl from a traditional Italian immigrant family who rises to the position of company chief executive. During interview, she describes herself as a 'diamond in the rough'. Through a detailed description of the case material, Gregg shows how this structurally ambiguous symbol can be read from two different *I*-positions. In one reading, she is 'pure', 'precious', 'refined' and 'sophisticated'. In another, she is 'crude', 'dirty', 'street-wise' and 'tough'. Here, the symbol of the 'rough diamond' is an ambiguous mediator. It is multi-stable and structurally ambiguous. Commenting on the juxtaposition of Faith's 'refined', middle-class and 'tough', working-class positions, Gregg writes:

Most theorists assume that the operative roles [for self-representation] are those actually enacted by the individual [and that these] ... are therefore primarily micro-social (daughter, sister, student, tennis player, and so on). But the self-representations that continually reappear [in the case material] tend to derive from macro-social relations... Hence, Faith's continual switching of refined ... middle-class style and tough ... working-class style to manage her face-to-face personal relationships at work and at home. Most important, Faith does not simply 'clean up' her act in middle-class roles and 'talk dirty' in working class roles, but deploys *both styles in both settings*, deliberately monitoring and managing the aesthetic tension between the two to her strategic advantage. (italics added; 1991: 188)

Gregg's analysis shows how Faith's use of the 'rough diamond' metaphor captures the *simultaneity* of the 'refined' and 'crude' positions in her life.

Thirdness and looking into a mirror

The importance of symbolic mediation for the dialogical self is nicely illustrated in the experience of looking into a mirror, an experience which highlights the need for triadic formulations. What we see in the mirror is a *double* – it is, in embodied terms, the Jamesian *me* in counter-position to the *I* (James 1890). (Hence, there are two positions.) But the image in the mirror is incomplete. It is only a *partial* image of the *Me* that might be seen by a third-person other. In his essay 'Author and Hero in Aesthetic Activity', Bakhtin observes that looking into a mirror is a disquieting experience because it is characterized by 'a peculiar emptiness, ghostliness [and] vaguely oppressive loneliness' (1990: 28–29). While mirroring 'simulates' the relationship between a position and a counter-position, there remains an *absence*. The mirror's reflection 're-presents' the self but *devoid of context*. For this, the view from a third position is needed. At this point, then, Peirce's concept of thirdness meshes with the dialogical approach. We can conceptualize this form of symbolic mediation by using 'dialogical triads'.

A dialogical triad is comprised of an *I*-position, a counter-position and an *ambiguous third* – typically another person, event or some object of signification that has structurally ambiguous properties. Because of these properties, ambiguous thirds can *initiate* decentralizing movements in the self. In the remainder of this chapter, I will try to illustrate how this triadic conception can provide an analytic framework for understanding the *formation* of *I*-positions and counter-positions.

Case illustration: dialogical triads in the case of Sean

In my work I have endeavoured to illustrate the mechanisms discussed here using dialogical triads that pinpoint multi-stable or structurally ambiguous third-term positions in the repertoires of research participants. I will illustrate the arguments developed here by a case example. First, I summarize the methodological approach. Then a synopsis of the life of Sean (a pseudonym) is briefly sketched. With this background in place, the text focuses on a sequence of three interrelated dialogical triads taken from the case material. The triads reveal the 'doubled' symbolic features of ambiguous thirds.

Method in outline

I use a narrative approach to the assessment of the dialogical self, examining positioning in terms of conflicting storied accounts elicited through in-depth interviews (e.g. Raggatt 2000, 2006). Like Hermans, this work makes the assumption that dominant positions and counter-positions have their own internally coherent stories to tell. Research participants are interviewed over two sessions, and must complete a series of questionnaires and rating scales. Initially, participants are asked to list 24 life history constituents, including six significant people, six life events, eight objects and places and four aspects of body image (liked and disliked body parts). Participants are then required to sort these constituents into associated groups or clusters (typically, between two and six clusters are produced) and to provide a self-relevant identifier for each cluster (e.g. creative self, spiritual self, victim). In this way, important positions and counter-positions are revealed, under the assumption that these positions comprise life history details. Participants are sometimes also asked to rate their constituents pair-wise, for similarities and differences. These ratings can then be cluster analysed to reveal associated constituents, and this output can be analysed and interpolated with the participants' qualitative sorting of material, and with their commentary on the life history material given in audiotaped interviews.

Synopsis: the life of Sean

Sean was 43 years old at the time of data collection. He was born in Northern Ireland and emigrated to Australia with his working-class family as a 10-year-old. His father was a foundry worker who played soccer for Northern Ireland as a young man, but who subsequently became, in Sean's words, 'a violent alcoholic'. His mother suffered from prolonged bouts of depression and was repeatedly hospitalized throughout Sean's childhood. Crucially for the argument here, Sean remembers being 'mothered' by his sister who was 11 years older than he. After he emigrated to Australia, Sean's teenage years were marked by success on the sports field, but also by family trauma. After his mother died of cancer when he was 18, Sean developed problems with the use of heroin and alcohol that eventually led to chronic addictions. Sean spent the first decade of his adult years battling to stay alive. In his thirties, Sean joined Alcoholics Anonymous and formed a lasting relationship with a counsellor. These decisions helped bring about positive changes in his life.

I-positions in Sean

In sorting his life history constituents, Sean identified *I*-positions that he called, in order of emergence, the 'Good Guy', the 'Lost Boy', the 'Addict' and the 'Magician'. Here, we will only be concerned with the opposing positions of Good Guy and Lost Boy.

Sean tells me that the Good Guy and the Lost Boy are both positions that he recognizes from childhood, and that they have remained important throughout his life. Early in childhood, the Good Guy was linked to his older sister as primary caregiver and, later, to his achievements in the sporting arena. Like his father, Sean was a champion at sports. He recalls: 'I dominated everything in sporting achievement . . . it was the way I built up my self-esteem.' Sean was a champion footballer and later he became an elite-level cricketer, playing in Australia's national competition. But while Sean's sister and his life as a cricketer are important for the Good Guy, *at the same time* these symbols of esteem are implicated in the emergence of the Lost Boy. When Sean was seven years old, his sister *secretly* emigrated to Australia. This was an event that was never explained to Sean. The family kept the sister's emigration plans a closely guarded secret until after she had left Northern Ireland. Sean emphasizes the importance of this event in his life. He says, 'My sister *was* my

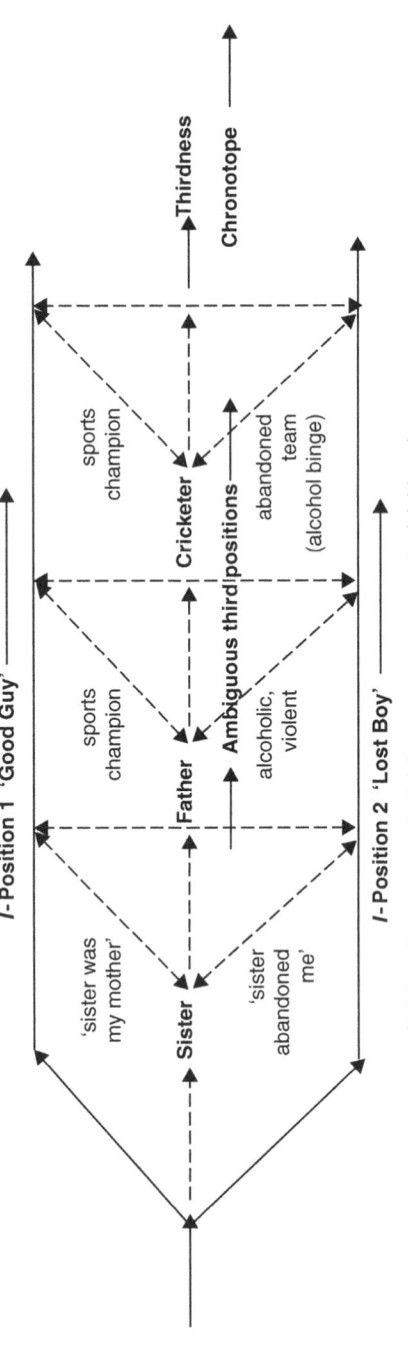

Figure 1.1 Hypothetical tracking of *I*-positions and ambiguous thirds in the case of Sean.

mother. It was the first great absence in my life.' In Sean's account, then, this traumatic event is the kernel for the emergence of the Lost Boy as counter-position to the Good Guy. And here, the sister is a key *ambiguous third* in this splitting movement. She is a 'Janus head' that can be used to explain some of the positioning dynamics at play in Sean's world.

Three dialogical triads

Figure 1.1 shows a hypothetical segment of Sean's extended position repertoire for the domain <Good Guy – Lost Boy>, configured in a chain of three dialogical triads. In childhood, Sean's sister, his surrogate mother, abandons him. This is the kernel event that produces decentralizing and counter-positioning movements in Sean's early position repertoire. Sean's father is also a key ambiguous third, notably later in Sean's teenage years. The father constitutes the second 'ambiguous third' depicted in Figure 1.1. The father had been a sports champion in Sean's early childhood, but by the time Sean reached his teens his father had descended into alcoholism. This is precisely the script that is recapitulated in Sean's adult life, and so the father stands for both the Good Guy sportsman in Sean, and the Lost Boy who later succumbs to addiction. A significant event from adulthood helps constitute the last triad shown in Figure 1.1. In this event, Sean, as a young man, abandons his cricket team comrades at an airport while in transit to an important interstate match. He goes on an alcoholic 'bender', blacks out and resurfaces 'confused and disoriented' in a strange city three days later. Here, the Good Guy and the Lost Boy are intensely polarized in the symbol of the 'lost cricketer', drunk, abject and derelict.

In Bakhtinian terms, Figure 1.1 portrays a form of 'personal chronotope' (Bakhtin 1981) – in this case a pattern of time–space relations for two of Sean's dominant *I*-positions (see also Raggatt in press). The ambiguous thirds that form triads in this example are the Janus heads or fulcrums around which these (counter-)positions emerge. For Sean, his sister and father are profoundly Janusian, simultaneously occupying the space of both his most pleasant and unpleasant memories. In this way such mediators also invoke centralizing and decentralizing movements in the self; for example, 'I want to be like my father, but at the same time I don't want to be like him.' In summary, the tension between centralizing and decentralizing movements of the self is represented here in a sequence of dialogical triads defined by ambiguous thirds that are *doubled* – the sister as *both* mother and betrayer; the father as *both* champion and drunkard; the cricketer as *both* elite and abject.

Conclusion: the future of positioning theory

In the first half of the chapter, I suggested that positioning theory can be conceptualized in terms of a set of basic and dynamic elements that are subject to developmental processes, and that these processes have, first, social and, later, also (self-)reflexive origins. Basic elements include internal and external *I*-positions and counter-positions. Dynamic elements include the concepts of core position, meta-position, promoter position and third position. The combination of basic and dynamic elements can lead to both centralizing (integrating) and decentralizing (differentiating) movements in the position repertoire (Table 1.1). Outside forces, both historical and cultural, also drive positioning movements, and these can lead variously to innovation, disorganization, integration or restriction of the position repertoire.

In the second half of the chapter, I suggested that the principle of mediation is particularly important for understanding the mechanics of positioning processes, and that here, the concept of 'thirdness' provides an important tool for understanding these mechanisms (see also Raggatt 2010). Ambiguous third positions show how the self has a fundamentally semiotic, as well as narrative, foundation. The application of a semiotic approach inspired by Peirce (1931) to questions of positioning dynamics and structure yields a potentially important tool for advancing DST. Using a case example, I showed how the approach successfully allows us to plot the *formation* of *I*-positions and counter-positions through an analysis of life history data. The evidence provided in the case of Sean was of a special class of third positions that are 'doubled', 'multi-stable' or 'structurally ambiguous' with respect to their symbolic significance. These objects are in a form akin to the classical double-faced figure of Janus from Roman mythology. They are symbols with twin faces looking simultaneously to opposing *I*-positions. While they divide the self, at the same time their multi-stability provides the grounds for integration. Sean's sister and his father are elements that link as well as differentiate the Good Guy and the Lost Boy.

In closing, I believe that triadic models and templates offer considerable promise as a conceptual tool for further theoretical and empirical work on the dialogical self. For the future, an integrated and more comprehensive understanding of positioning processes offers the possibility to further consolidate DST as a significant innovation in both theoretical and applied psychology. If we are to advance understanding of the dialogical self, we need to specify conceptual frameworks that can account for the various forms of positioning discussed here. This chapter has tried to make a move in that direction by presenting a provisional classification system for positioning elements and processes and by showing how that system can be applied to empirical and discursive studies of the dialogical self. I hope that the conceptual framework used here may prove useful for future theoretical and empirical work.

ACKNOWLEDGEMENTS

I would like to thank Marie-Cécile Bertau and John Barresi for helpful comments on earlier drafts of this chapter. The research was supported by Merit Research Grants to the author from James Cook University.

NOTE

1 Harré and Van Langenhove (1991, 1999) and their colleagues also use the term 'positioning theory' in the context of discourse analytic work.

REFERENCES

Bakhtin, M. (1981) *The Dialogic Imagination*. Ed. M. Holquist and trans. M. Holquist and C. Emerson (Austin, TX: University of Texas Press)
(1984) *Problems of Dostoevsky's Poetics*. Ed. and trans. Caryl Emerson (Minneapolis, MN: University of Minnesota Press)
(1990) *Art and Answerability*. Trans. Vadim Liapunov (Austin, TX: University of Texas Press)
Barresi, J. (2002) From 'the thought is the thinker' to 'the voice is the speaker': William James and the dialogical self, *Theory & Psychology*, **12**, 237–250
Bertau, M.-C. (2008) Voice: a pathway to consciousness as 'social contact to oneself', *Integrative Psychological and Behavioral Sciences*, **42**, 92–113
Bhatia, S. and Ram, A. (2001) Locating the dialogical self in the age of transnational migrations, border crossings and diasporas, *Culture & Psychology*, **7**, 297–309
Buhler, K. (1990) *Theory of Language: The Representational Function of Language* (Amsterdam: John Benjamins)
Chandler, M. J. (2004) Bridging the antinomy between personal and cultural identities, paper presented at the Third International Conference on the Dialogical Self, Warsaw, Poland
Danzinger, K. (1997) The historical formation of selves, in R. D. Ashmore and L. Jussim (eds.), *Self and Identity: Fundamental Issues* (New York: Oxford University Press), 137–159
Erikson, E. (1963) *Childhood and Society*, 2nd edn (New York: W. W. Norton)
Fogel, A., de Koeyer, I., Bellagamba, F. and Bell, H. (2002) The dialogical self in the first two years of life: embarking on a journey of discovery, *Theory & Psychology*, **12**, 191–206
Gergen, K. J. (1991) *The Saturated Self* (Oxford: Basil Blackwell)
Gieser, T. (2006) How to transform into goddesses and elephants: exploring the potentiality of the dialogical self, *Culture & Psychology*, **12**, 443–459

Gregg, G. S. (1991) *Self-Representation: Life Narrative Studies in Identity and Ideology* (New York: Greenwood Press)
(1995) Multiple identities and the integration of personality, *Journal of Personality*, **63**, 617–641
Harré, R. and Van Langenhove, L. (1991) Varieties of positioning, *Journal for the Theory of Social Behaviour*, **21**, 393–407
(eds.) (1999) *Positioning Theory* (Oxford: Blackwell)
Hermans, H. J. M. (2001) The dialogical self: toward a theory of personal and cultural positioning, *Culture & Psychology*, 7, 243–281
Hermans, H. J. M. and Dimaggio, G. (eds.) (2004) *The Dialogical Self in Psychotherapy* (New York: Brunner and Routledge)
(2007) Self, identity and globalization in times of uncertainty: a dialogical analysis, *Review of General Psychology*, **11**, 31–61
Hermans, H. J. M. and Hermans-Konopka, A. (2010) *Dialogical Self Theory: Positioning and Counter-Positioning in a Globalizing Society* (Cambridge University Press)
Hermans, H. J. M. and Kempen, H. J. G. (1993) *The Dialogical Self: Meaning as Movement* (San Diego, CA: Academic Press)
Hevern, V. W. (2004) Threaded identity in cyberspace: weblogs and positioning in the dialogical self, *Identity: An International Journal of Theory and Research*, **4**, 321–335
James, W. (1890) *The Principles of Psychology* (London: Macmillan), vol. I
Josephs, I. E. (2002) 'The Hopi in me': the construction of a voice in the dialogical self from a cultural psychological perspective, *Theory & Psychology*, **12**, 161–174
Kinnvall, C. (2004) Globalization and religious nationalism: self, identity, and the search for ontological security, *Political Psychology*, **25**, 741–767
Lewis, M. D. (2002) The dialogical brain: contribution of emotional neurobiology to understanding the dialogical self, *Theory & Psychology*, **12**, 175–190
Lysaker, J. (2006) 'I am not what I seem to be' (commentary on Wiley), *International Journal for Dialogical Science*, **1**, 41–46
Marková, I. (2003) *Dialogicality and Social Representations* (Cambridge University Press)
Maslow, A. (1954) *Motivation and Personality* (New York: Harper and Row)
McAdams, D. P. (1993) *The Stories We Live By: Personal Myths and the Making of Identity* (New York: William Morrow)
Mead, G. H. (1934) *Mind, Self and Society* (University of Chicago Press)
Moore, C. and Lemmon, K. (eds.) (2001) *The Self in Time: Developmental Perspectives* (Hillsdale, NJ: Lawrence Erlbaum)
Peirce, C. S. (1931) Thirdness, in C. Hartshorne, P. Weiss, and A. W. Burks, (eds.), *Collected Papers of Charles Sanders Peirce* (Cambridge University Press), vol. V
Raggatt, P. T. F. (2000) Mapping the dialogical self: towards a rationale and method of Assessment, *European Journal of Personality*, **14**, 65–90
(2006) Multiplicity and conflict in the dialogical self: a life-narrative approach, in D. P. McAdams, R. Josselson and A. Lieblich (eds.), *Identity*

and Story: The Narrative Construction of the Self (Washington, DC: American Psychological Association Press), 15–35

(2007) Forms of positioning in the dialogical self: a system of classification and the strange case of Dame Edna Everage, *Theory & Psychology*, **17**, 355–383

(2008) Interaction of personal and social positioning in the formation of the dialogical self: a study of Australian adults, *Studia Psychologica*, **6**, 149–172

(2010) The dialogical self and thirdness: a semiotic approach to positioning using dialogical triads, *Theory & Psychology*, **20**, 400–419

(2011) Gender, embodiment, and positioning in the dialogical self: do men and women see eye to eye?, in E. Aveling, I. Kadianaki, M. Märtsin, B. Tyler, B. Wagoner and L. Whittaker (eds.), *Dialogical Science: The Self in Communication, Culture and Society* (Greenwich, CT: Nova Science Publishers), 213–227

(in press) Personal chronotopes in the dialogical self: a developmental case study, in M.-C. Bertau, M. Gonçalves and P. Raggatt (eds.), *Dialogic Formations: Investigations into the Origins and Development of the Dialogical Self* (Charlotte, NC: Information Age Publishing)

Richardson, F. C., Rogers, A. and McCarroll, J. (1998) Toward a dialogical self, *American Behavioral Scientist*, **41**, 496–515

Sampson, E. (1993) *Celebrating the Other: A Dialogic Account of Human Nature* (San Francisco, CA: Westview Press)

Stiles, W. B. (1999) Signs and voices in psychotherapy, *Psychotherapy Research*, **9**, 1–21

Tan, S.-L. and Moghaddam, F. M. (1995) Reflexive positioning and culture, *Journal for the Theory of Social Behaviour*, **25**, 387–400

Tappan, M. B. (2005) Domination, subordination and the dialogical self: identity development and the politics of 'ideological becoming', *Culture & Psychology*, **11**, 47–75

Taylor, C. (1989) *Sources of the Self: The Making of the Modern Identity* (Cambridge, MA: Harvard University Press)

Valsiner, J. (2004) The promoter sign: developmental transformation within the structure of the dialogical self, paper presented at the XVIII Biennial Meeting of the ISSBD, Ghent, Belgium

Vygotsky, L. S. (1929) The problem of the cultural development of the child, *Journal of Genetic Psychology*, **36**, 415–434

(1978) *Mind in Society: The Development of Higher Psychological Processes* (Cambridge, MA: Harvard University Press)

Zittoun, T., Gillespie, A., Cornish, F. and Psaltis, C. (2007) The metaphor of the triangle in theories of human development, *Human Development*, **50**, 208–229

2 Time and the dialogical self

John Barresi

Introduction

Although time is recognized as an important factor relating dialogical selves, space is the primary metaphor used when discussing alternative *I*-positions in dialogical relations (e.g. Hermans 2001, 2002; Hermans and Kempen 1993; Raggatt 2000). However, more recently, there has been a growing theoretical interest in the temporal dimension of dialogicality (e.g. Bertau and Gonçalves 2007; Bhatia and Ram 2001; Gillespie 2005, 2007; Hermans and Dimaggio 2004; Hermans and Hermans-Konopka 2010; McAdams 2006; Märtsin 2010; Raggatt 2010; Valsiner 2001). This interest has taken several forms. For instance, Hermans and Hermans-Konopka (2010) devote a chapter of their review of dialogical self theory (DST) on the historical development in the West in conceptions of self, from traditional, to modern, to postmodern, all of which they see as embedded in our current understanding of the self. Taking a more ontogenetic approach to the temporal dimension, Bertau and Gonçalves (2007) recently edited a volume of papers devoted to the early development of the dialogical self and the forms it takes from preverbal to early verbal development. A longer, life-historical perspective on temporal transformations in the representation of the dialogical self is found both in clinical (e.g. Hermans and Dimaggio 2004) and in non-clinical case studies (e.g. Gillespie 2005; McAdams 2006; Raggatt 2010, in press). Finally, although short-term change through time in dialogical relations has often been described, the micro-dynamics of change through time in dialogical relations and structural variations of *I*-positions has increasingly become theorized in a variety of models of change (e.g. Hermans and Hermans-Konopka 2010; Märtsin 2010; Valsiner 2001).

In a previous paper, I presented a three-dimensional model of the dialogical self (Barresi 2002a), which added a reflective dimension and a temporal dimension to a spatial dimension of *I*-positions. The vertical dimension of the model represents the individual's degree of self-reflection, where hierarchically subordinate selves are sometimes organized under higher-order integrative selves. The horizontal dimension focuses on how the individual conceives of the temporal extension of selves, which can be temporally narrow or extend throughout a lifetime. Finally, the lateral dimension represents the individual's understanding of how personal selves connect with the selves of others. Sometimes these selves are conceived as distinct from each other, but at other times the boundary between self and other is indistinct or integrated in a shared 'self' or '*we*-position' of a group or culture. The main focus of my discussion was on how this three-dimensional model of selves emerges in early development and transforms throughout the lifetime of the individual.

In the present chapter, I will first provide an updated version of this model, which takes into account more recent discussions of the *temporal* dimension and how it relates to the *reflective* and *social* dimensions of self. I am particularly interested here in the theoretical distinction between what is called a meta-position and what I will call a primary *I*-position. A meta-position is an *I*-position which refers to other *I*-positions, typically primary *I*-positions, though it can also refer to other meta-positions (cf. Barresi 2002b, 2007a; Hermans and Hermans-Konopka 2010; Lysaker and Lysaker 2005). Whereas primary *I*-positions tend to focus on action with respect to an immediate sense of self (a self that may itself be a product of lower-level primary *I*-positions integrated through a meta-position), meta-positions often take a reflective and temporally extended view of self in determining one's course of action. As a consequence of taking this extended view, it is from meta-positions that we typically engage in imaginative reflection on other *I*-positions and sometimes provide them with voices of their own. It is often assumed that at any particular point in time, the person can be disposed to reflect over a range of *I*-positions and facilitate dialogue among them. However, because of issues involving dominance in *I*-positions and lack of empathy with the point-of-view of other *I*-positions that sometimes occurs, we cannot generally assume that the person, when occupying a particular *I*-position, even a quite general meta-position, can freely imagine and give voice to other *I*-positions, both in self and in others (Barresi 2002b; Cooper and Hermans 2007). Also, typically, life moves on from one to another *I*-position, without any or much reflection. As a result, 'dialogue' between *I*-positions is more often implicit in their transitions and reorganization than explicit as inner voices of one *I*-position to another, or empathic representation of alter-positions through a meta-position (e.g. Barresi 2002b; Hermans and Hermans-Konopka 2010; Lysaker and Lysaker 2005; Märtsin 2010; Valsiner 2001). After providing an updated version of the three-dimensional model in light of these advances in theory, I will go on to consider a case study of multiple personality previously considered in another context (Barresi 1994) in order to illustrate in a radical and concrete way certain temporal aspects of the model and important theoretical issues associated with temporality that are not generally acknowledged.

The development and transformation
of a three-dimensional model of the dialogical self

According to the present revised version of the three-dimensional model (Barresi 2002a), the infant in early development neither unifies the many primary *I*-positions of self into a unified meta-position representing the *embodied self*, nor distinguishes between the embodied *I*-positions of self and other. Different body parts are involved in a variety of situational object-directed activities (what Barresi and Moore 1996, call 'intentional relations'), but only rarely are several body parts integrated with each other into a single coordinated *I*-position and directed at a common object. Sometimes activity involves the infant alone, but at other times it involves the infant with an adult. In these latter circumstances the infant participates in the socially interactive situation without any reflective consciousness of its distinction from the other person. Gradually, the infant becomes more fully acquainted with the powers of its own body, and also becomes aware of variations in its coordinated and joint activity with another individual. At this point, from the middle to the end of the first year, the infant is becoming pre-reflectively aware of its self both as an integrated being with a common orientation or *I*-position towards the world immediately presented to the infant and sometimes as part of a larger, goal-oriented unit or *we*-position involving another person. But the infant still does not have reflective awareness of itself as a distinct individual with its own particular *I*-positions that differ from the *I*-positions of another person (Barresi 2007a, b; Barresi and Moore 1996; Moore and Barresi 2009).

It is around the middle of the second year that the toddler begins to distinguish itself as an individual with its own distinct first-person *I*-positions from those of other individuals (Barresi and Moore 1996; Moore and Barresi 2009). This is an important achievement, because the toddler is now able to adopt a reflective meta-position that can localize concurrent primary *I*-positions that are different between self and another person, and can represent them as occurring in different individuals. In order to do this, the toddler needs a concept of 'self' and 'person' that can be applied not only to self, but also to another person

(Barresi in press). This concept of person and self attributes to each individual a first-person perspective as well as a third-person appearance to other persons. Yet, even with this distinction in hand, the difference between self and other, as *embodied selves*, each with its own distinct first-person *I*-positions, is often nested within a distinction between 'we' and 'they' at a non-reflective level. As a result, there are many shared *we*-positions with close others that are not yet identified as such and distinguished from *we*-positions of strangers. This embedding of partially reflective *I*-positions within non-reflective *we*-positions occurs at even higher group and cultural levels as well, and it becomes a lifetime task to be able to reflect on our collective *we*-positions as they appear from positions outside our immediate group or cultural context (see Barresi 2008 for an example involving racism; Hermans and Hermans-Konopka 2010 for a general overview view of intercultural and global positioning).

Early in the development of the dialogical self, the focus is on spatial relations of *I*-positions, where each primary *I*-position represents a particular sense of self, with its own action orientation and voice. This occurs both for parts of a single embodied self that become connected to each other by meta-positions in an individual's deliberated actions, and for self and others as distinct embodied locations of *I*-positions acting separately or in unison at a point in time. Dialogicality occurs when these different object-oriented positions interact and are joined together or distinguished at one time. There is little dialogical activity that stretches across time. Because of linguistic development during this period, these various positions of self and other become articulated in interaction, and as a result dialogical relations become more complex than preverbal relations. However, they are still mainly spatial, with memory for past positions and anticipations of future positions developing slowly from the second to the fourth year.

However, a major change occurs during the fourth and fifth years of development. It is at this time that self-reflection enters more fully into the temporal domain and the child becomes capable of moving imaginatively among *I*-positions not only across space but also across time (Barresi 2001; Moore and Lemmon 2001). The child of this age becomes able to represent self and others and their points of view at a particular time and their changes across time. The child is able to conceive of its own past and future representations of reality as distinct from its present representations, and it begins to appreciate itself as well as others as beings extended in time. It is at this time that a temporally extended *mental self* is formed. Before this time, experiences unfold but are not connected together into an autobiographical stream. Now, retrospective memory and anticipation of the future has this structure.

Free-floating imagination, which develops at this time, becomes the key tool for representing diverse points of view and *I*-positions that vary not only across space but also across time (Barresi 2001; Martin and Barresi 1995; Moore *et al.* 1998; Thompson *et al.* 1997). As William Hazlitt pointed out long ago, '[Imagination] must carry me out of myself into the feelings of others by one and the same process by which I am thrown forward as it were into my future being, and interested in it' (1805/1969: 3; quoted by Martin and Barresi 1995: 466). Indeed, it is imagination that makes possible reflection upon distinct, relatively stable *I*-positions from different times and forms new, temporally extended meta-positions and eventually narrative meta-positions out of them. Once the child conceives of self as extended in time, he or she can conceive of situational or dispositional selves or *I*-positions that also extend through time or reappear from time to time. As the child becomes older, these extended dispositional and situational self-positions from different times become dialogically related to each other as conflict arises between them in choice situations, or inconsistency is perceived in reflection. However, until adolescence, no serious attempt can be made to resolve inconsistency, or to structure a coherent narrative representation of self, due to the lack of ability to represent self abstractly.

A process of self-conscious formation of integrative meta-positions that constitute our identities as *narrative selves* typically begins in adolescence (McAdams 2006). Narrative is used as a reflective strategy to integrate various primary *I*-positions and meta-positions, whose origins range from the distant past through to the present, into coherent meta-positions for the future. It becomes a lifelong struggle to acquire and maintain unified, and fairly continuous reflective meta-positions that can make sense of, and to some extent control, our actions across the diverse situations that we face as adults, who continue to transform as biological, psychological and social beings until death terminates the process. While there may be no single narrative meta-position that provides unity to our lives, often we work at a variety of stories of self with significant temporal extension. These stories bind together primary *I*-positions, which are continually changing, into coherent wholes that persist as narrative meta-positions that contribute significantly to future actions. The younger adult tends to live mainly in the present and, through intense reflection on possible interpretations of past and future positions, tries to form an integrated narrative identity; but, inevitably, that adult generates inadequate and inconsistent stories that displace each other or enter into dialogical relations with each other and lead to new stories. By contrast, mature adults are centred in their lives and, from a variety of relatively stable narrative meta-positions that have minimal conflict with each other, can look backward and forward with almost equal vision. In old age, the look backward from reflective narrative meta-positions takes on special importance, and narrative reconstructions of the past that extend through the life of the individual and hold it together in a meaningful way are stressed. With respect to the future, the emphasis in old age turns on living well in the present, rather than in orienting to a distant future – at least with respect to one's own lifetime.

In sum, from a temporal point of view, the dialogical self that is seen at a particular point in time is composed of *I*-positions whose origin, transformation and significance are distributed across time, both from the past and into the future. As we develop, and in particular in adulthood, various primary *I*-positions are integrated into reflective meta-positions of varying temporal extent, with positions of both sorts displacing each other across time in a variety of new syntheses that are ever transforming through time (Barresi 2002b). Some meta-positions that emerge early in development become primary positions for further development by meta-positions with wider scope. Of particular importance is the development of meta-positions that are inherently temporal in structure. The temporally extended mental self that develops in the fourth year is such a compounded meta-position, as are versions of narrative self that emerge during adolescence. In order more fully to understand the dialogical self, we need to uncover this temporally organized transformational structure. In the next few sections of this chapter, we will consider a case study in which the temporal organization of the dialogical self becomes especially apparent through dissociation of phenomenal mental selves, each with their own temporally integrated narrative meta-structure and with changing dialogical relations to other mental selves.

B.C.A.: a case study in multiplicity and temporality of phenomenal mental selves

At the beginning of the twentieth century, the Boston neurologist, Morton Prince, treated two cases of multiple personality or dissociative identity disorder. B.C.A. was the name given to the patient in Prince's second case. Her case is less famous than the Beauchamp case (Prince 1906), but from an empirical and theoretical point of view, she is the more interesting. Prince published a number of studies of her case (e.g. Prince 1910, 1914/1921, 1919, 1923) and Nellie Parsons Bean, the patient, published two autobiographies in the first person from reflective narrative meta-positions of two of the three main personalities in the case (B.C.A. 1908, 1908–9). Nellie also corresponded with Prince from all three main personality or reflective meta-positions, A, B and C, during the course of her therapy, and continued to do research on dreams with Prince and his associate Dr Waterman after she completed therapy. At one point she hoped to write a book of her own on her dreams, but that never came about. Much of the material on her case is currently at the Francis A. Countway Library of Medicine at Harvard University, and I have previously used this material to provide a more exhaustive psychogenesis of her case (Barresi 1994) than that provided by Prince (1919). Here, I will draw on this previous analysis, as well as on other materials in the collection.

In the case of B.C.A., the event that caused the dissociation of personality was a kiss that Nellie received from a man in a sanatorium while recovering from mental illness after her husband died. The man was also a patient there. The kiss apparently burst her apart through the complex of emotions it elicited. What remained were two relatively stable personalities or phenomenal mental selves that were later called A and B by Prince. The original person was recovered two years later, when these two personalities and their various partial syntheses, called C, finally fused sufficiently that the original Nellie before the kiss was revived and the memories associated with A, B and C as dominant alternating personalities were restored to her (Barresi 1994).

A and B emerged out of relatively stable I-positions that had a long history well before forming separate personalities with their own stable reflective meta-positions. Before the split, Nellie experienced these two conflicting sides of her personality from a single, self-conscious meta-position as part of her phenomenal stream of consciousness and temporally extended mental self. It was only after the split that Nellie, in her two distinct, self-conscious meta-positions A and B, would reflect back on her past and see their pre-existence as opposing I-positions in Nellie. In this reflection backward, Nellie as A saw herself as the dutiful wife, while Nellie as B saw herself as the happy young girl who never committed herself to marriage, so was always pulling Nellie apart, wishing to escape this responsibility. After her husband's death this pulling apart ceased during a period of mourning, while the committed wife position dominated, but she also became ill from overwork and depression. Meanwhile, the other side was building subconscious strength. So when she was finally sent by her doctor to the sanatorium, this latter side, the young, happy and healthy B side, who did not take on the responsibilities that so dragged the wife down, began to appear suddenly for short periods of time when Nellie would forget about her duties to her son Robert and her sisters, and instead would tramp through the woods as she had done before marriage, but would never do as the mature, dutiful wife, or her extension as *A*.

Immediately following the kiss and break-up of the personality, Nellie, in these two distinct *I*-positions, *A* and *B*, took turns being the dominant consciousness, while the other side was subconscious, but also often co-conscious. So, at least some of the time, each of these *I*-positions was aware of what the other self as a dominant, conscious *I*-position was doing, and would critique it from her own co-conscious position. At these times, there was one continuous stream of conscious activity in Nellie but one inhabited by two stable and continuous *I*-positions existing concurrently but in fierce opposition, one being dominant for a period of time and overriding the motivations of the other. In a sense it was the way Nellie had been before her husband died, only more extreme with more distinct and incompatible *I*-positions that, apparently, were now two distinct, temporally extended, mental selves. Before his death, there was some sort of compromise between the two sides, each having a voice that would be listened to by the other and integrated into a common, temporally extended, reflective meta-position that was Nellie's mental self. Now there were no more compromises; the inner voice was probably not even heard by the dominant *I*-position, and the two sides had become distinct mental selves.

Eventually, these two sides became reflectively aware of their distinct *I*-positions and became distinguishable to themselves as mental selves. This occurred after Prince began treating Nellie, when the two *I*-positions reorganized as two clearly independent streams of consciousness, with separable memory systems and alternating states of dominant consciousness. After one particular session of hypnosis, Nellie as *A* no longer had memory for any of subsequent activities that she did when *B* was dominant, though Nellie as *B* remained co-conscious of *A*'s activities. But both sides were now able more clearly to distinguish events following the kiss, where one or the other *I*-position dominated behaviour to the exclusion of the other, while the other as a co-conscious *I*-position criticized it, but had no apparent influence on the dominant *I*-position's behaviour. Nellie as *A*, in particular, viewed activities that she could remember from her *B* state as 'insane' and not her, and she was terribly embarrassed by what she, as *B*, did in that state, while Nellie as *B* thought that A was suicidally depressed and dangerous both to herself and to *B*.

Some professionals would claim that Prince 'created' the two personalities through hypnosis, but I have argued previously (Barresi 1994) that hypnosis only facilitated the formation of a memory barrier between the two pre-existing personalities, and I have agreed with Prince (1919) that dissociation of these personalities and mental selves occurred with the kiss. Because of its focus on *I*-positions, not consciousness, DST cuts through this issue. In contrast to those professionals who emphasize memory and apparent unity of consciousness, DST focuses on intrinsic differences between core *I*-positions. It seems less important to identify the source of the dissociation in this case, than to understand the history of that dissociation with respect to *I*-positions that developed in Nellie and the role that various reflective meta-positions played in Nellie's transformations in phenomenal self-consciousness.

This is a distinct advantage of DST. Whatever their source, *B* and *A* (who is later replaced by the partially synthesized *C* from elements of *A* and *B*) represent *I*-positions that individually develop through time and stand initially opposed to each other. Their first appearance as opposing *I*-positions began with Nellie's marriage and her difficulty dealing with her sexual responsibilities. But at this time a single, continuous, phenomenal, self-conscious meta-position and mental self, aware of the opposing motivational positions, held together the two *I*-positions. Much later the kiss led to a more permanent separation of the two *I*-positions, with one subconscious and the other conscious, and a loss of the meta-position that held these two sides of Nellie's personality together. Once the memory barrier was formed, these *I*-positions became clearer in their self-understanding and in their conscious opposition to each other. But they also at that time attempted individually through narrative reconstruction, as well as collectively, through automatic writing in a question-and-answer mode and commenting on each other's writings, to make sense of their emergence out of Nellie's life history, and to resolve their conflicts. Indeed, the final re-emergence of Nellie two years after the dissociation occurred in the context of *B* writing her autobiography and thinking about the kiss and its aftermath. She was also feeling more empathic than previously with the partially synthesized *C* personality that currently coexisted with her. Both were working on autobiographies, and because Nellie in both of these *I*-positions was devoted to Prince and helping him, these *I*-positions were no longer so far apart. Indeed, as B.C.A.'s later dreams show, this devotion to Prince was beginning to turn into love, a love that may have played a significant role in the process of putting Nellie back together.

Self-recollection, appropriation and the development of *I*-positions in B.C.A.

There are a number of theoretically illuminating aspects for DST in the development and expression of the multiple *I*-positions of B.C.A. One that we have already encountered, and worth further discussion, is the activity of reconstructive self-analysis. Morton Prince, as therapist, was, of course, interested in the prehistory of the emergent personalities of *B* and *A*, and this may have been part of the stimulus for Nellie in her *B* and *A* I-positions to reconstruct their origins in the life history of Nellie before the dissociation. But Nellie in each of these *I*-positions became quite involved in this reconstruction, and it is mainly through these self-analyses that Prince was eventually able to write his own psychogenesis of the case (Prince 1919). Of particular importance were the letters and autobiography of *B*, as she was both the most unusual part of B.C.A. and the part of Nellie that more or less had continuous consciousness throughout the period of dissociation, and even beyond. Even after re-synthesis *B* continued to appear as an accessible hypnotic state of Nellie that provided information about Nellie's dreams.

In one of *B*'s important letters that contributed to her autobiography, Nellie as *B* describes her origin in the 'shock' of marriage and Nellie's 'shrinking' from the sexual relations with her husband:

After marriage we began to pull different ways. I can't make it very clear – the division was nebulous but I think I am now made up of all the impulses which began to come then. I was not an I then you know but to understand what I write you will have to call me so. I remember them now as my thoughts but at that time had never thought of myself as a 'self' … [S]omeway that shrinking became part of the system of thought we are calling 'me' (B). (letter, undated, Bean, 1907–1913; cited by Barresi 1994: 18)

Nellie as *B* then describes how this shrinking may have reduced for a while in her marriage until her husband became ill:

[W]ith that all this undercurrent seemed to become synthesized and a true division took place: not that I was an I even then but there was a double train of thought – she, X or A, is conscious of that, you know. All that shrinking became intensified – she suffered very much – and this internal rebellion increased more and more, and also the intensity of her self-reproach…

I think the rebellion was myself Dr. P. but A knew.

Then after his death she thought she had killed him you know.

I think all this division springs from that one cause [i.e. sexual desire] – first because she had no feeling of that kind and now because she has. So you see, it seems to me that I was there, as a separate train of thought, from the time of her marriage – pulling a different way all the time from the way she had to go and not wanting to live the life she had to live, but I really came as a self at Nashua [the sanatorium]. I ruled A for weeks before I came – she can't understand about that time, she was so well and strong and happy – but it was I. She has told you about that, and these thoughts and impulses and acts were mine not hers. (letter, undated, Bean, 1907–1913; cited by Barresi 1994: 18–19)

One of the interesting aspects of this narrative is how Nellie as *B* appropriates to her self, some but not all of the motivations of Nellie, whom she calls *X* in her original form. But she knows that *A* remembers these rebellious motives, as well as she does. *B* also describes how these motivations and the *I*-position associated with them became her as a separate self or '*I*', but one that did not originally think of her self as an '*I*'. In more typical individuals, where we do not have dissociations like this and we can remember past experiences more or less continuously without gaps, there is an experience of having a single stream of consciousness and one temporally extended, phenomenal, mental and embodied self. Regardless of whether we presently wish to take ownership of past motivations or not, we accept them as past states of our embodied and temporally extended mental self, as *I*-positions that we have been in, not as positions of an 'alter' who is not self (cf. Cooper and Hermans 2007). But *B* here claims that things she remembers as happening to Nellie can be divided into her 'own' thoughts and those of *A* or *C*. A typical person adopting a meta-position of reflecting on the past and constructing a self-narrative that links past memories to the present self might select some motivations and actions as more truly her self or as an emergent part of her current *I*-position; but she would also acknowledge other actions as what she was like in the past, though not part of her current narrative sense of self. But Nellie as *B* here is quite specific in setting boundaries between memories that were her own and those that were not. Moreover, she views this history from the point of view of the ontogenesis or psychogenesis of her 'self' as a distinct continuous '*I*', or reflective meta-position (her mental self). Early on, these motivations are seen as an *I*-position of the pre-dissociation Nellie, one of her opposing *I*-positions, but later they are seen as her own 'self' or reflective *I*-position, an *I*-position that had grown in strength and eventually became a dominant and independent personality and mental self, which became dissociated from the rest of Nellie with the kiss.

In the letter we have been considering, Nellie as *B* traces her history to the beginning of Nellie's marriage, with a gradual development from that time. A month later she has different idea:

My theory is this. I think that long ago – twenty years, you know, at the time of that shock [i.e. the sexual act with her husband] – I became 'split off' from the main personality (is that right?) and that I dropped into the subconscious region – wherever that is – I disappeared; and I was nineteen years old. Then a shock of something the same nature brought me back and, as I had had no independent life – now don't laugh – I was still nineteen. That is why that affair with Mr. H. [the man who kissed her] seemed all right and why I was so well and gay and happy – as a girl of nineteen would be. Do you see how I reason it?

Now I am quite different from what I was a year ago. You see that, do you not? My point of view is different – I am much older. (letter, 28 November 1907, Bean 1907–1913; cited by Barresi 1994: 20)

What is different and intriguing about this idea, compared to her previous letter, is that, developmentally, she feels that she did not mature beyond 19 after marriage, until she reappeared as a separate, independent, *I*-position at Nashua. However, after her reappearance, she continued to mature. It is as if this happy girl side of Nellie's personality that had no knowledge of and no interest in sexuality did not get a chance to develop once she got married, and the responsible wife became the dominant *I*-position. However, this side could reappear and could continue to mature after her husband died. In the end the depressed wife *I*-position of *A* disappears, and various *C*s appear that at least partially integrate the happier, and younger, side of Nellie's personality with the mature *A* side of her personality. However, this new integration still differs from *B* in that sexuality is included and also matures.

After Nellie, as she was at the time she was kissed, reappears two years later, and recovers continuous memories of *A*, *B* and *C*, she continues to develop and looks back on her life in a way that seems to have integrated some of the happy young girl, but now one that also has a different attitude to sexuality. In a letter written five years after her dissociation, she writes:

One fact, which I am sure is true and which may have some bearing on the case of B.C.A., is that I matured very slowly . . . I enjoy things which women who are past forty do not usually care for – dancing, riding, tramping, gymnastics, etc. As far as pleasures are concerned I stopped living when I was little more than thirty [probably when her husband's illness began], and it seems sometimes as if all the pleasure I should have felt, but did not, was pent up within me unused. If the conditions of my life were different I should be very active and gay.

Then as to love, I loved my husband truly and deeply, and I love him just the same now; he was one of the finest men I have ever known; but nevertheless, if love should come to me again, if I should meet the 'right man' I could love him with a depth and passion impossible to me at any time before in my life. It is a little as if I had not been really awake before. (letter, 29 July 1911, Bean (1907–1913); cited by Barresi 1994: 37)

What is important to note here with respect to the issue of time and the dialogical self is that each relatively stable *I*-position has its origin in time and can have its own unique developmental history. Some *I*-positions that might be formed in childhood never outgrow their childish perspective, while other positions mature because they have become dominant *I*-positions, or an integrated part of dominant meta-positions. In therapy, or due to life events, some undeveloped

I-positions can become part of later integrated meta-positions, thus being allowed to develop once again. This seems to have happened in Nellie's case. After Nellie's period of mourning for her husband, and the period of dissociation of personality, when *B* had a life of her own for a while, the happy girl that *B* thinks of as herself finally got a chance to mature. When pre-dissociation Nellie who disappeared at Nashua re-emerged, it was a new Nellie, one who, after incorporating her experiences as *A*, *B* and *C* during the intervening period, could develop a different orientation to sexuality and to happiness from the unhappy and guilt-ridden widow.

Dissociation and early development in B.C.A.: the history of love

Nellie had a long-standing phobia of cats and many of Nellie's dreams involve cats. They appear whenever anxiety or fear is a major emotional response in her dream state. In many of the earlier dreams, cats often surround her. In one described in Prince's (1910) article on her dreams, she is being chased by wild men with clubs and is told by one of them that she must walk through a sea of cats in front of her without speaking a word. When faced with cats in her dreams, she always shudders and 'shrinks' from them. Consistently in her dreams, there is a strong analogy between her feelings about cats and her feelings about sexual relations with men.

A revealing picture of the relationship between cats and men in Nellie's mental structure is depicted in a dream published by George Waterman (1910). In this dream, love is depicted as a 'monstrosity':

He had a long striped body like a tiger. His legs were short, like an alligator's legs, so that his body lay close to the ground; the feet had long claws; he had a long neck like a giraffe; the head was that of a man and yet seemed different, more as if it belonged to a statue of marble, a sort of Apollo. It was horrible and terrible . . . She said, 'Who are you?' and the animal replied, 'I am Love.' She was frightened and ran away. (Waterman 1910: 204)

Symbolically, the giraffe-like neck above a low body appears as a graphic representation of the erect male organ. But the figure also combines the aggressive feline properties of tiger-like stripes as well as long claws. In discussing the dream she said 'that she would not portray Love as a gentle and protecting angel [as in a picture she recalled], but as a figure made up of the body of a lion, the claws of a tiger, and the head of an angel; because, while love attracts and lures one on, it always rends and tears one' (Waterman 1910: 206).

How did cats and sex come to have this meaning for Nellie? And does it have anything to do with her dissociation of personality? When she was about five years old she was left in a room alone with a white kitten that had an epileptic fit. Although she apparently screamed for help, no one came immediately to rescue her. The result of this experience was a permanent phobia of cats – in particular of white cats. Young Nellie was apparently overwhelmed by this emotional experience and developed amnesia for the event. As an adult, she could no longer recall the event even under hypnosis. Prince (1914/1921: 16–19) discovered the event which caused her phobia through the use of automatic writing.

It might be wondered how such an event could have the causal power to produce Nellie's dissociative identity disorder. Certainly, many frightening events occur to children and even produce phobias without ever producing personality dissociations. It is not my claim that this event alone produced Nellie's adult personality dissociation. We have already discussed other causal factors that entered into her final dissociation with the kissing incident, and I discuss other factors in my previous paper (Barresi 1994). What I am claiming is that the cat seizure provided a traumatic shock that shattered Nellie's phenomenal sense of self when it was still too fragile to defend itself against the emotional consequences of the cat's fit. She was at the age when a mental self, extended in time, is first formed. The result of the event was dissociation of the experience, and, as a result, dissociation of other experiences became available to her as a means of defence for later emotional traumata of a similar sort. Eventually, she used it in her conflict over sexuality as described above.

However, because of the close relation of love for a kitten and love for a man, there is a closer connection between the earlier and subsequent dissociation. In the dream that depicts love as a phallic cat, love is not just a metaphor of love between men and women for Nellie, but also seems grounded in her earliest experience of love – her love for the epileptic cat that 'lured' her on, but 'rent and tore' her. Still, as we saw earlier in Nellie's letter to Prince about B.C.A., her attitude towards love and sex changed over the years. She was more ready for sexual love than she had ever been in her marriage, and if the opportunity arose she felt that she could love 'with a depth and passion impossible to [her] at any time before in [her] life'. Unfortunately, she never did remarry, and may not have been able to satisfy this passion.

Theoretically, I think that the main lesson to be learned from this example is that the I-positions that we see in adult personalities can have long histories that go back to early childhood. Conflicts that arise at that time between alternative motives and affective relations to particular objects can later generalize to similar objects, but at new levels. What was once a child's ambivalent love and fear of a kitten turned into ambivalence over sexual relations with Nellie's husband, and eventually into a dissociation of Nellie's personality. But as time passes and situations bring forth particular *I*-positions in conflict, there is also an opportunity to resolve this conflict. In the present case, the kiss that caused the later dissociation led to a new reintegrated Nellie, who was now open to sexual desire, and a change in her attitude toward love.

Conclusion

In the present chapter, I have tried to introduce some theorizing about the temporal dimension of the dialogical self that is often ignored because of the usual focus on space rather than time. I have provided a sketch of a developmental and life historical account of how time enters into the psychology of a person with respect to different aspects of self. In the example given, I have tried to focus on a more limited set of issues. The first issue is how reflective meta-positions appropriate and incorporate primary self-positions for which they have empathy, as part of their *I*-position, while *I*-positions, for which they do not have empathy, do not. B.C.A. presents an extreme version of this appropriative activity. Nellie in her several personalities recognized different actions from the past as their own actions, while others were viewed as evidence either of temporary insanity or of some other self. Secondly, dissociation here provides a window on how reflective meta-positions grow through time as phenomenal selves. James (1890) described how the stream of consciousness of a single personality grows through the process of appropriation between neighbouring thoughts (cf. Barresi 2002b). Usually, in the typical case, we have only one such continuous stream of consciousness and with it one continuously developing mental self. But in the case of dissociation, several such mental selves occur. In the present case, we have traced the development of such mental selves. The third issue that I have focused on in the case of B.C.A. is how development occurs with respect to changing orientations to ambivalent objects that elicit opposing primary *I*-positions and sometimes meta-positions. To illustrate this, I have traced the history of love for another living being, starting with a kitten, in the life history of Nellie Bean. While there is much more to say about the temporal properties of the dialogical self that is not pursued here, I hope that this chapter will facilitate further work on time and the dialogical self.

ACKNOWLEDGEMENTS

This chapter is based in part on manuscript material in the Morton Prince papers at the Francis A. Countway Library of Medicine, which reserves rights to the use of material not previously released for publication. I wish to thank the staff at the library for their generous assistance in obtaining access to and in using the Prince papers. I also wish to thank the Dalhousie Research Development Committee for a grant to support travel to see these papers, and to the Social Science Research Council for support in writing this chapter. Ray Martin and Peter T. F. Raggatt provided very helpful comments on previous versions of the present chapter, and I thank them for their assistance.

REFERENCES

Barresi, J. (1994) Morton Prince and B.C.A.: a historical footnote on the confrontation between dissociation theory and Freudian psychology in a case of multiple personality, in R. Klein and B. Doane (eds.), *Psychological Concepts and Dissociative Disorders: Reverberation and Implications* (Hillsdale, NJ: Erlbaum), 85–129

(2001) Extending self-consciousness into the future, in C. Moore and K. Lemmon (eds.), *The Self in Time: Developmental Perspectives* (Hillsdale, NJ: Lawrence Erlbaum), 141–161

(2002a) A three dimensional model of the dialogical self, paper presented at the Second International Conference on the Dialogical Self, Ghent

(2002b) From 'the thought is the thinker' to 'the voice is the speaker': William James and the dialogical self, *Theory & Psychology*, **12**, 237–250

(2007a) Consciousness and intentionality, *Journal of Consciousness Studies*, **14**, 77–93

(2007b) The origins of autism: commentary on 'Autism as a downstream effect of primary difficulties in intersubjectivity going with abnormal development of brain connectivity' by Filippo Muratori and Sandra Maestro, *International Journal for Dialogical Science*, **2**, 119–124

(2008) Black and white like me, *Studia Psychologica*, **8**, 11–21

(in press) On seeing our selves and others as persons, *New Ideas in Psychology*. doi:10.1016/j.newideapsych.2009.11.003

Barresi, J. and Moore, C. (1996) Intentional relations and social understanding, *Behavioral and Brain Sciences*, **19**, 107–122

B.C.A. (a.k.a. Nellie Parsons Bean) (1908) My life as a dissociated personality, *Journal of Abnormal Psychology*, **3**, 240–260

(1908–1909) An introspective analysis of a co-conscious life (my life as a dissociated personality) by a personality (B) claiming to be co-conscious, *Journal of Abnormal Psychology*, **3**, 311–334

Bean, N. P. (a.k.a. B.C.A.) (1907–1913) Unpublished letters and notes to M. Prince, 1907–1913, in Papers of Morton Prince, 1890–1916 (inclusive), B ms c83, Francis A. Countway Library, Harvard University

Bertau, M.-C. and Gonçalves, M. (2007) Special issue on the developmental origins of the dialogical self, *International Journal for Dialogical Science*, 2, 1–324

Bhatia, S. and Ram, A. (2001) Locating the dialogical self in the age of transnational migrations, border crossings and diasporas, *Culture & Psychology*, 7, 297–309

Cooper, M. and Hermans, H. J. M. (2007) Honoring self-otherness: alterity and the intrapersonal, in L. Simão and J. Valsiner (eds.), *Otherness in Question: Labyrinths of the Self* (Greenwich, CT: Information Age Publishing), 305–315

Gillespie, A. (2005) Malcolm X and his autobiography: identity development and self-narration, *Culture & Psychology*, 11, 77–88

(2007) Time, self and the other: the striving tourist in Ladakh, north India, in L. Simão and J. Valsiner (eds.), *Otherness in Question: Development of the Self* (Greenwich, CT: Information Age Publishing), 163–186

Hazlitt, W. (1969) *Essay on the Principles of Human Action and Some Remarks of the Systems of Hartley and Helvetius*, new edn (Gainesville, FL: Scholars' Facsimiles and Reprints)

Hermans, H. J. M. (2001) The dialogical self: toward a theory of personal and cultural positioning, *Culture & Psychology*, 7, 243–281

(2002) The dialogical self as a society of mind: introduction, *Theory & Psychology*, 12, 147–160

Hermans, H. J. M. and Dimaggio, G. (2004) *The Dialogical Self in Psychotherapy* (New York: Brunner and Routledge)

Hermans, H. J. M. and Hermans-Konopka, A. (2010) *Dialogical Self Theory: Positioning and Counter-Positioning in a Globalizing Society* (Cambridge University Press)

Hermans, H. J. M. and Kempen, H. J. G. (1993) *The Dialogical Self: Meaning as Movement* (San Diego, CA: Academic Press)

James, W. (1890) *The Principles of Psychology* (London: Macmillan), vol. I

Lysaker, J. and Lysaker, P. (2005) Being interrupted: the self and schizophrenia, *Journal of Speculative Philosophy*, 19, 1–21

Martin, R. and Barresi, J. (1995) Hazlitt on the future of self, *Journal of the History of Ideas*, 56, 463–481

Märtsin, M. (2010) Identity in dialogue: identity as hyper-generalized personal sense, *Theory & Psychology*, 20, 436–450

McAdams, D. (2006) The problem of narrative coherence, *Journal of Constructivist Psychology*, 19, 109–126

Moore, C. and Barresi, J. (2009) The construction of common-sense psychology in infancy, in P. D. Zelazo, M. Chandler and E. Crone (eds.), *Developmental Social Cognitive Neuroscience* (New York: Psychological Press), 43–62

Moore, C., Barresi, J. and Thompson, C. (1998) The cognitive basis of prosocial behaviour, *Social Development*, 7, 198–218

Lemmon, K. and Moore, C. (2001) Binding the self in time, in C. Moore and K. Lemmon (eds.), *The Self in Time: Developmental Issues* (Mahwah, NJ: Lawrence Erlbaum Associates), 163–179

Prince, M. (1906) *The Dissociation of a Personality: A Biographical Study in Abnormal Psychology* (New York: Longmans)

(1910) The mechanism and interpretation of dreams, *Journal of Abnormal Psychology*, **5**, 139–195

(1914/1921) *The Unconscious: The Fundamentals of Human Personality, Normal and Abnormal* (New York: Macmillan)

(1919) The psychogenesis of multiple personality, *Journal of Abnormal Psychology*, **12**, 225–280

(1923) Complete loss of all sensory functions except hearing but including coenesthesis and visual images of body, *Journal of Abnormal Psychology*, **18**, 238–243

Raggatt, P. (2000) Mapping the dialogical self: towards a rationale and method of assessment, *European Journal of Personality*, **14**, 65–90

(2010) The dialogical self and 'thirdness': a semiotic approach to positioning using dialogical triads, *Theory & Psychology*, **20**, 400–419

Thompson, C., Barresi, J. and Moore, C. (1997) The development of future-oriented prudence and altruism in preschool children, *Cognitive Development*, **12**, 199–212

Valsiner, J. (2001) Process structure of semiotic mediation in human development, *Human Development*, **44**, 84–97

Waterman, G. (1910) Dreams as a cause of symptoms, *Journal of Abnormal Psychology*, **5**, 196–210

3 Developmental origins of the dialogical self: early childhood years

Marie-Cécile Bertau

Introduction

Because dialogical self theory (DST) is initially grounded in a therapeutic approach (Hermans, Kempen and van Loon 1992), development was first conceived in terms of the dynamics of a mature self. The theory's growing importance and increasing multidisciplinarity have resulted in elaborating several developmental issues: in infancy, in young adults, and regarding significant processes such as cultural transition and motherhood (Bertau and Gonçalves 2007; Bertau *et al.* in press; Hermans and Hermans-Konopka 2010; Josephs 2003).

In this vein the chapter looks for the incipient dialogues of a self at its beginning. The hope is to contribute to the developmental question in regard to processes already in place *before* language, as performed by the child, enhances its dialogical power. As will be seen, human beings develop modes of exchanges from pregnancy on: from their start in life they are positioned within alterity. Hence, the perspective offered here contributes to a further decentring from the Cartesian ego.

The frame for an ontogenetic perspective will be set first, followed by considerations on time and form. A chronological view of the significant moments in development is then given. The last section addresses developmental changes bound to the so-called displaced practices particularly related to language.

Setting the frame

As Rochat (2006) put it, the infant's world is defined by self, other and objects as related 'ontological categories'. A closer look at these categories reveals their complex relational and internal richness.

Firstly, each self is in relation to another self; 'ego' and 'alter' are thus paired dialogical positions resulting in individuals not merely existing next to each other, but always in alter–ego relations.[1] This defining alter–ego relationship is displayed and explored in different positions, in specific forms of activities, and in specific views on the three basic categories: self, others, objects. Thus, the infant is differently positioned by a peer than by her mother or her older sister. She positions herself differently with that person, and performs in these relations activities in a specific way (e.g. negotiating an object); this will result in the self's different views of her world. According to the framework of DST, this interactional multiplicity forms and manifests the self's external and internal multiplicity, its dynamics in space and time.

Secondly, objects play a positional and positioning role in alter–ego relations; they are embedded in culturally specific activities and are not neutral. Objects are given, forbidden, labelled and talked about. They circulate within the community with specific values and meanings, and are 'semiotically chargeable'. A significant other introduces the object to the infant, or accompanies its discovery, leaving his or her traces in it as attributed values and meanings. In this positioning activity, the infant gains access to the object's culturally and individually determined 'life form', entailing 'crystallized otherness' (Bertau 2007). This can be assumed to have an impact on the important step of joint attention reached by 9 months of age.

Hence, the challenge to an ontogenetic perspective is that two of the three related categories (self, other, object) show external *and* internal relational complexity because of their dialogical, tensional co-being. Indeed, any dialogical relation is a tensional one, a feature accounting for the dynamic nature of the relation and leading it beyond mere additivity. Tensional relations open the duality to further transformations and lead to qualitatively new outcomes (Josephs and Valsiner 1998), and this is clearly a condition for development. Openness is counterbalanced by conservative routines on both external social and internal dialogical relationships, preserving the self from too much innovation (Hermans and Josephs 2003). The dialogical self is thus open *and* closed, in unfolding and developing dynamics. As a result, the three categories are not just juxtaposed entities, but exhibit their dialogical complexity as relational-tensional movements, and these performances change and develop through time, as the infant grows.

Time and form

Time is surprisingly not a self-evident topic in developmental studies; it seems that the focus on individual cognition eliminates the *performative* aspect of *activities with others and self*. Shared and experienced time is grounded in a possibly innate *sense of time* crucial for communication.

Trevarthen (1999: 157) thus underscores the 'infants' acute sensitivity to timing of expressions' narrowly related to intersubjectivity, and addresses the palpable experience of time and duration of acts and moves, stressing the central role of the sense of time in movements and moving (stepping, jumping, caressing, talking).

Hence, movements in time are experienced by the baby bodily, in so far as her time experience is related to perceptual experiences concerning her own body. These experiences entail the unique combination of proprioception and double-touch stimulation, specify the baby's own body as a differentiated entity in the environment (Rochat 2001), and represent an early form of embodied dialogical activity (Fogel 1993). As soon as the baby begins to move through space (from rolling over to walking eventually), she experiences bodily repositionings leading to different views of the world (Hermans and Hermans-Konopka 2010), and new possibilities of acting on the world, other and self.

Others participate in these experiences from the start with evaluations ranging from bodily to verbal comments: acts of positioning. The infant's view of the world becomes simultaneously a world view, and a conceptual horizon is built. Adults' attitudes towards the infant's body are already found in the ways they hold, put down or feed the baby and are responded to by her in body tonus (Gratier 2008) and rhythmic structures (Jaffe *et al.* 2001). Both parties construct together through their mutually oriented body dynamics a common space-time, where dialogical exchanges such as vocalizations (Gratier 1999) or object negotiation (Lyra 2007) gain specific forms. As a result, the infant performs self-dialogues and other-dialogues very early in complementary ways to each other; moreover, both dialogue types are based in bodily experiences in space and time.

The qualitative microgenetic research undertaken, for instance, by Fogel and de Koeyer-Laros (2007) traces developmental change in shared time. When we follow the exchange activities of a mother–infant communicative system across time, the relational-historical process through which the infant develops its dialogical self becomes visible. This process entails repeated encounters between individuals with specifically performed positions. New forms of communication emerge because of the performance of 'the same' on a historical basis, allowing for references, abbreviated forms and innovations (Lyra and Bertau 2008): 'what occurred earlier' conditions each new developmental period (Fogel and de Koeyer-Laros 2007). Thus, highlighting the time aspect leads to acknowledging the *historicity* of relations; that is, the history of the inherently relational form of perception and action in the infant's self (Fogel 1993) and the history of caregiver–infant exchanges, constructing patterns convertible into a new formation.

Acknowledging experienced and shared time results in a conceptual shift from related *entities* to relational *acts*: the in-between is a duration, specifically formed by the entities, and this very act defines them *as* related, and related in *this* way. Thus, the engaged entities are shown as specifically related, positioned ones. In regard to the infant, focusing on relational performance means that there is no need for a concept of self to be able to fulfil the movement. Rather, self will be developed by relational acts as a position, understood as a 'dynamically changing process' (Fogel 1993); repeated relational performances refine the position dynamics. This radical relational view can be said to be specific to a developmental theory in the frame of DST, where a 'core self' does not one day develop into a narrative and multiple one, but where self is dialogical from the beginning (Fogel 1993).[2] The *movements in time and space* are defining for selves as dialogical.

Each performance will adopt a specific formation so as to be recognizable and sharable by the interactants; forms are hence the necessary corollary to time. They exist as performed, in duration, and they are commonly perceptible by the interacting partners, such as a way of vocalizing, of giving, of attentiveness. Further, they crystallize into ad hoc and conventional patterns. This can entail a symbolic dimension, as with verbal forms, which can eventually be detached from the common space-time and serve individual imaginative purposes.

Significant moments in development

Up to now, there is no fully formulated model regarding the ontogenesis of the *dialogical* self. Developing *dialogicality* can be followed through a host of communication acquisition studies, showing evidence for an early and sensitive adjustment to the needs of interpersonal verbal dialogues; the development of *self* is also addressed in a rich literature. But the issue is to trace the developing dialogicality of the developing self. The chronology given is thus an approach with hints to significant moments within the first two years of life and a glimpse into further development.

Pregnancy and birth

A general tendency can be seen in developmental psychology over the last decades, reaching increasingly into young age: the view that child and infant actively participate in their own development. This tendency has now reached foetal psychology. Following DiPietro (2010), an early mutual adjustment of foetus and mother can be assumed, where the foetus comes to play an active role in both its own ontogeny and pregnancy outcomes, preparing a successful transition to its postnatal environment. Investigating especially foetal motor activity as related to stimulation of the maternal sympathetic nervous system, DiPietro (2010) could establish a significant stability of time patterns within individual maternal–foetal pairs. Thus, a very early synchrony on a neurophysical level with individual characteristics can be assumed, a *dyad-specific timing*.

As pregnancy cannot be studied outside societal influences, the mental representations future mothers are constructing of their mother-hood in relation to their sociocultural situation complement the mutual bodily adjustment. Thus, the transition to motherhood is determined by the woman's understanding of her new position in relation to a societal construction shaping early mothering techniques and attitudes as the 'Right Way to mother' (van den Bergh 2010).[3] From a dialogical stance, the future mother experiences specific transformations of her dialogical self within a tensional field involving societal and own expectations (Duarte and Gonçalves 2007). Hence, the synchrony with the foetus establishes, within this net of diverse influences, voices of individual and cultural kinds (Hermans 2001).

We must add to the neurophysical synchrony the important fact that the foetus develops hearing around the sixth month of gestation, coupled with auditory learning. This leaves traces in the newborn's preferences for melodies to which she was exposed prenatally, for the prosodic features of her mother's language (melody, intensity and rhythm), and for her voice (Mampe *et al.* 2009; Trevarthen 1999), which is *actively* sought by 3-day-old newborns (DeCasper and Fifer 1980).

This attunement to melody and rhythm can be seen as the continu-ation of prenatal synchronization. Speech, music and voice are shapes unfolding in time, building an auditory gestalt, discernible on the basis of sounds and noises. These non-arbitrary and recurrent forms function like a point of entry for the foetus, and the infant will be able to join the previsible sequence of events, which are perceptible actions of the other. Sharing and co-acting are possible because of these forms-in-time, inde-pendently of intentionality or of a cognitive representation of self and other on the infant's side.

Thus, auditory preferences show the infant as actively expecting the other, in position to start exchange. Recent investigations reveal the earliness and the degree to which the newborn is already attuned to its specific environment. Comparing 2–5-day-old newborns from

monolingual French and German families, Mampe *et al.* (2009) analysed their crying sound patterns and established that the surrounding
speech prosody influences the newborn's first productions. From a
Bakhtinian perspective, these specific cry forms can be seen as replies
after the listening period in the womb. Newborns relate themselves to
the other by using a recognizable form of expression, a reply and an
address driving the intersubjective system construction. This form is
appealing to the mother, as it elicits her child-directed speech and
vocalizations, and thus her position as mother.

Right after birth, newborns show capacities which support and further
develop the intersubjective system between themselves and the mother
and other caregivers. According to the investigation by Rochat and
Hespos (1997) with 24-hour-old babies, newborns appear to discrimin-
ate between self- and non-self-stimulation (a touch of the cheek);
notably, this finding points to an early *directedness to the other*: compared
with the stimulation of their own hand on their cheek, the newborns
turned significantly more to the stimulation of the experimenter's finger.
Self- and other touches are not confused, a condition for early precursors of self-dialogues and other-dialogues to take place.

Precursors of self-dialogues can be seen as occurring in the self-
exploration infants are engaged in from birth. They bring their legs or
their hands into the field of view for long periods of visual-haptic exploration, and in touching themselves, they experience proprioception and
double-touch stimulation. In this, they explore an early, embodied form
of dialogicality: body experiences are taken with respect to their different
aspects, such as the touching hand and the touched one, along with the
time it takes to do the touching, re-experienced in repeated movement
cycles. The different perspectives infants have towards their activity can
be viewed as emerging *I*-positions: the tactile perspective of the touching
hand, the proprioceptive perspective of the touched one, and the visual
perspective of eyes and head following the event (Fogel *et al.* 2002).

The infant experiences multiple sensory modalities interacting with
each other. According to Fogel *et al.* (2002), the infant utilizes this vivid
integration to interpret her experiences – an integration understood
by Fogel and colleagues as 'dialogue between multiple *I*-positions' that
is 'fundamental for the development of the infant's embodied self, in
relation to her environment' (Fogel *et al.* 2002: 195–196). Hence, the
dialogical self builds first as a bodily experienced self. As previously
mentioned, the dialogues of the infant's significant others accompany
and embed the infant's emerging dialogicality of self.

Concerning other-dialogues, a characteristic form of dialogue with
newborns is grounded in their imitational skills. These are enabled by

selective orientation and preferences; they are particularly alert to the eyes of a person speaking, and can see well enough to imitate facial expressions and gestures of a friendly attentive person (Trevarthen 1999). But imitation is not only responsive, as Nagy and Molnar (2004) show, in investigating the baby's *initiatives* within an imitation sequence.

In their study, a cycle of imitative turns between an adult and a newborn (3–54 hours old) is constructed that permits the baby to take not only a responsive but also an initiative turn. This in turn provokes the missing response by the adult, a response anticipated by the regular timing introduced. The dialogical quality of the infant's activities is correlated with heart rate: provocative imitations are shown to be anticipated by heart deceleration indicating preparation for an expected stimulus. This study illustrates well the aspect of a shared timing, building up a small relational history made of exchanged similarities: a co-regulative action, requiring self-action to be performed in relation to the other's action. Timing and taking up the other's bodily performance show time and form as supports of earliest proto-conversations between partners on the body level.

First months and years

A significant turning point emerges at 6–8 weeks of age, building markedly on the infant's sense of timing and earlier developed mother–infant synchrony. It is a turning point for both parties, described as a change in stance to each other: a conversational stance (Rochat 2001), related to primary intersubjectivity in the infant (Trevarthen 1979). At this age, the infant's wakeful time increases dramatically, and periods when the infant is alert and actively exploring the environment increase also in duration and frequency (Rochat 2001). The infant's attention is more sustained, and motor coordination is stronger and more efficient (Trevarthen 1999). Hence, the infant is now more present, more accessible by others; this is sustained by emerging social and contingent behaviour.

Thus, around 6 weeks, infants produce socially elicited smiling in face-to-face interactions with social partners, showing a first clear sign of positive social affective attunement (Rochat 2001), which has, in turn, a significant impact on the adult's interactional and emotional engagement (Rochat *et al.* 1999). Discovering their infant as a person, parents frame their interactions in terms of fine-tuning, especially regarding the time and form of games (Rochat *et al.* 1999). Highly scaffolded and ritualized face-to-face exchanges and proto-conversations emerge, and others 'become a sounding board to the infants, a sort of running commentary' (Rochat 2001: 353). Correspondingly, infants show growing social expectation (Rochat *et al.* 1999) as well as emerging triadic competencies (Rochat 2001).

This new social stance is a response to social others, at the same time highly provocative for these others: they turn to the baby in a specific way so that jointly built time structures (games, proto-conversations) can emerge, in which both partners are highly active. This not only permits the infant to engage in joint communicative activities but also gives her access to the attention *of the other to herself*.

Reddy (2003) values the infant's diverse emotional reactions at 2 months of age as reactions to the other's attention to *self as a whole*; for example, they smile more when adults make eye contact with them. This responsivity is complemented by about 4 months by active 'calling vocalizations' as attempts to direct the other's attention to self. Following this are experiences of other's attention *to acts* by the self, understood as a specific aspect of the self (her gaze). Again, there is responsivity: the infant follows the other's gaze, as to a frontal target. This step is followed by the attention of the other to an *external object in hand* (0;9–0;11[4]), a step related to the beginning of showing/giving play; the last steps involve the other's attention to a *distant object*, as when the child moves across the room to fetch it, and by the other's attention to an *object distant in time* and to *absent targets*.

As a result, one can observe a development of the other's attention that the infant reacts and responds to and that goes from self to a gradually more distant object as focus. These steps are seen by Reddy as preparatory to conceptual representation of self and other emerging at 1;6. Joint attention of both partners to an external object at the end of the first year is thus informed by these precursors due to an *affective* engagement. Awareness of the other's attention permits dialogical, or positioning, relationships before a conceptual representation of self is established.

It is remarkable how the caregiver adjusts to the infant's development in differentiating her focus of attention, thereby creating a system of relevance. I assume that its function is to continue the infant's first perceptual-bodily orientations in terms of *I*-positions, refining and enriching these in the sense of other-and-object-related positions. Hence, the forms of another's attention make different self aspects of the active infant salient: her self, her gaze and her activities with objects in proximity, then in spatial and finally in temporal distance. Every form of relevance marking is rooted in the relationship of the partners that functions as the anchor for a first relation to external reality. Hence, intersubjectivity serves, firstly, mutuality and dialogicality, and not external reference; intersubjectivity in terms of external reference will develop in subsequent joint attention.

The affective quality of the other's awareness to self can be assumed to link to the infant's embodied dialogical self with *I*-positions as sensory experiences, connecting these with the felt awareness of the other. This link results in external dialogue, which has creative potential for the self, enriching the infant's *I*-positions and contributing to the interpersonal dialogue, as the following segment shows.

Fogel and colleagues present the case study of the interactions of a mother and her infant, Susan. At 2 months of age, Susan shows coordination between several *I*-positions based on sensory experiences. As she integrates these positions, 'she becomes aware of herself in her body'. Her mother serves 'as an amplifier, facilitating integration of the infant's sensory dialogue through social dialogue' (Fogel *et al.* 2002: 196). Susan lies on the floor and looks at her mother, who speaks melodically to her while slowly shaking a rattle above her. The mother says, 'Your sister Jane is here watching you today. She wanted to see what we do when we come here.' Susan then touches the rattle with one hand and touches her face with the other.

The authors comment on this episode:

Here, Susan is processing multiple embodied positions within herself. She experiences different forms of proprioceptive feedback through the sensation of one hand touching her face and the other touching the rattle. The rattle and face are different locations in space in relation to the infant's body (i.e. left vs right, face vs hand). In addition, the experience of each position is coloured by Susan's attention to mother visually, audibly, and tactually as she makes contact with the rattle. Susan's experience of her mother acts as an additional I-position for the infant through social dialogue. (Fogel *et al.* 2002: 196)

The *I*-positions the dialogical self experiences are constructed through the real experiences of the baby's own body in relation to a location and an environment, in relation to a significant person's way of attention and address, and, lastly, in relation to the object called into the interaction and handled in an addressive way to the infant. So, *I*-positions are anchored in perceptual and social reality, and are highly dynamic. The mother's way of being attentive to the infant generates a relational position including Susan's experience of her mother as acting with an object, and of the experience of her mother's attention to her.

Bateson (1975) coined the term 'proto-conversation'. Since then, proto-conversations have been studied with increasingly sophisticated technical means in regard to the timing and the structures of the partner's vocal-verbal contributions, revealing the subtle attunement of temporally organized gesture and vocal expression (e.g. Gratier 1999, 2003; Rochat *et al.* 1999). Bateson's term addresses joint performances and focuses on the importance of vocal exchange as affirmation and maintenance of social contact; it thus underscores the new social stance of the partners. Further, as each actual practice with its specific self–other experiences becomes part of the next practice, proto-conversations are shown to be genuine dialogues where partners construct through interdependent acts mutuality and historicity with the potential of innovation.

Voice is here to be given special attention in different respects. First, it is well known that the mother's vocalizations and her child-directed speech lead the infant into the acquisition of language (e.g. Papoušek *et al.* 1992). Besides, it has been established that the communicative function of maternal vocalizations, in terms of expressing emotions and giving melodic forms to different speech acts (comfort, prohibition, approval), is well understood by the infant by the fourth month (Fernald 1992). Lastly and most importantly, the mother's voice adds a psycho-cultural dimension to her utterances in addition to a teaching one. As stated previously, the mother–infant communication system is shaped by the individual and cultural voices of the mother's dialogical self. Thus, any maternal utterance positions the mother as belonging to a certain culture along with specific values and concepts, especially of mothering, but also with various familial and social norms. The maternal voice nevertheless has its 'prosodic signature', precisely known and sought by the newborn, a vocal style ranging from canonical to idiosyncratic (Gratier 2008), together with the maternal psychophysiological characteristics (depressed, happy, healthy); this complex internal polyphony positions the infant, and functions like a running subtext. Disturbances in the mother's psychological health (depression) and identity position (migration) have effects on her voicing and on the mother–infant proto-conversations (Gratier 1999; Muratori and Maestro 2007; Robb 1999).

In the second half of the first year, the infant is said to discover that she has a unique perspective on the world (Fogel *et al.* 2002). This moment in development is also addressed under the terms of joint attention (Tomasello 1993) and secondary intersubjectivity (Trevarthen and Hubley 1978), and by the emergence of a subjective sense of self (Stern 1985). Rochat (2001) speaks of the intentional stance of the infant, with social referencing, pointing, gaze following and joint attention establishing the triangle self–other–object; further, infants begin actively to involve others in their explorations of the surrounding world, entailing the other as resource of help and knowledge.

In the framework of DST, the focus on the infant's self, as it appears especially in Fogel's and Stern's accounts, is to be questioned. Rather, and following the relational view advocated here, co-being and dialogical practices are to be highlighted. These shared experiences lead to shared perspectives and a pragmatic knowledge of subjectivity. This knowledge entails common actions and the other's subjectivity within these actions, such as how the infant can get the other's attention; it does not require an awareness of the infant's own, separate subjectivity, or a *concept* of a subjective self. Hence, sensitive experiences of dialogicality precede the awareness of one's own perspective, and the concept of a separate subjectivity is formed later, at around 1;6 (Barresi in this volume; Reddy 2003).

The following episode allows us to understand how practical subjectivity develops within shared experience. Fogel and de Koeyer-Laros (2007) give a microanalytic account of the 9-month developmental transition within mother–infant exchanges, when the infant is pounding on a table while her mother is participating and commenting. Although Susan's *I*-positions are still embodied, she takes for the first time a clear distance from her direct bodily experience by comparing it with that of the mother. What develops through repeated dialogical play across more than 30 weeks (26–40 weeks) is the infant's awareness of her unique role in the play, together with the ability to choose, initiate and refuse. The difference between self and other is *performed* through differences in ways of acting, making the infant's own embodied *I*-positions clearly her own ones, while also relating them to the other's interactive and communicative activities.

Towards displaced practices

Within the second year a significant shift in the self–other–world relationships occurs, especially enhanced with the child's entry into performed verbal language. 'Decoupled practices' can take place, performed by the individual on the basis of social ones and by their means, but now for the infant's own purposes and turned away from an actual other. These deviations from the common reality are strategies of the self to come to an understanding of this very reality, a process which contributes to the construction of the self's dialogicality, also in terms of self reflection.

It is around the first birthday that the infant begins to actively produce verbal language, with a significant jump in lexical acquisition around 1;6 leading to combinations and thus to productive grammar (Grimm and Weinert 2002). Children become increasingly able to confer a verbal and conventional form on their intentions and acts, they gain access to symbolic meanings and to different speech genres, and they enhance their narrative capacities. It can be assumed that these new forms will have a formative effect on the self's dialogue, on its articulation in both senses of the term. This is indexed by infants' and children's monologues (Nelson 2006; Pickert 1981), as well as by self dialogues with imaginary companions (Klausen and Passman 2007). These forms of self-directed speech produce the ability to retrace various experiences of self in different positions and to construct an observing, organizing and eventually a reflective position. Characteristic of these forms is a displacement leading from actual to imaginary others, and the forms of self activities have a replay or play character permitting further distancing.

The most important gain of verbal language is its symbolic character, offering and demanding imagination, leading beyond the here-and-now into past, future and fictitious activity fields. Language development and symbolic or pretend play are closely intertwined (Vygotsky 1967); both are a means of activity displacement. Role-pretend play with peers allows us to trace the development of the metacognitive and metalinguistic skills needed for this play's organization, especially in terms of attribution and change of roles (Andresen 2002). Pretend play is further related to a developing theory of mind and allows heightened levels of reasoning (Lillard 2001). In this, pretend play can be assumed to support the development of a reflective stance in the dialogical self, explicitly involving self–other positioning.

Role-pretend play is first performed with others in the social space, and then by the self alone. Explicit multivoicedness is performed, whereby partners can play and experiment with *I*-positions that do not even exist. This is the case with 'Susan and the lion', an episode reminding us that the world of infants and children is a 'zoo-full of beings' (Goffman 1981), with voices and positions that the self can use as resources.

In the following episode (Fogel *et al.* 2002), the function of voice becomes clear, matching Susan's development towards language as performed symbolic activity. The mother's voice works as a supporting structure for the child's 'voicing in' the common dialogue as an individual voice. It also demonstrates the possibility of performing not only the two actual roles embodied by the partners, but also multiple and embedded voices.

Mother and child (1;5) have played the lion game with a lion puppet many times with clear roles, the mother always being the lion. Then a change occurs as the child puts the puppet on her own hand and acts with the voice of the lion, as she previously experienced the mother doing it. The child aligns with the voice of the mother *as lion* that nevertheless belongs to the mother and hence reflects her perspective (on lions, on her child, on their mother–daughter relationship). Hence, the mother's voice leads the child into a new position and at the same time conveys the perspective, meaning and form of that position. As the authors point out,

[d]uring this episode, Susan is experimenting and playing with new *I*-positions and their corresponding emotions: being frightened if you are followed by a lion, being frightening if you are playing the lion. She explores them as she physically embodies the lion with her hand... In this way, she traverses from the role of the child to the role of the lion-adult, and vice versa. Susan is now able to imagine and act in both roles... A new voice exchanges information with the old one, resulting in a more complex and narratively structured self. (Fogel *et al.* 2002: 201)

It is important to add that Susan is exploring the new role not only via her hand but also via *her voice*; that is, via the actual performance of a differently sounding vocal event ('Roar!'). This sensible experience is accompanied by the role's emotions (frightening vs. being frightened) and actions (moving the puppet in a specific way). The new voice is thus a psychological phenomenon, derived from the actual experience. The connection formed here between experience and psychological phenomenon can be seen as the moment when the infant moves from a pragmatic to a conceptual knowledge of subjectivity. The voice as psycho-physical phenomenon represents well this passage, belonging to the domain of social activities as well as to the individual psychic domain.

Interiorization is grounded in such practices because it continues and deepens the positional manifoldness of social language activity in the individual domain (Bertau 2008). It takes the voice of the other as its means for individual psychological purposes such as remembering, problem solving and self-regulation. Language is interiorized as semiotic means and as the speech of significant others, entailing experienced multivoicedness.

Inner speech along with imagery is seen by Morin (2005) as one of three sources of self-awareness, defined as a sophisticated form of consciousness. Inner speech is for Morin the most powerful cognitive process of self-awareness, postulating that not using inner speech for introspective purpose will impede self-awareness development. On the contrary, extensively talking to oneself will probably generate a rich and well-articulated self-concept.[5] These effects are due to language: through naming and categorizing states, and engaging in language-based modes of representation, an individual can acquire the capacity to reflect upon them; these reflections can be communicated and discussed in internal dialogues. The notion of inner voice is to be added (Steels 2003), permitting the simulation of the other's speaking and thus the exploration of that perspective, together with the simulated performance of complete dialogues with others.

As a result, I assume that inner speech is an important means for the internal formation, organization and regulation of the dialogical self's dialogicality. This means is incipient in the self-talk of children, and this, in turn, is grounded in multivoiced plays. Time as mutual synchronization is the central aspect to all these types of speech, reaching into preverbal proto-conversations and into exchanges and adjustments of two bodies. Self comes to be within the rhythm of intersubjectivity, first in a fully concrete sense. It then detaches itself gradually from the actual presence of the other, and becomes able to perform self-talk and internal dialogues.

Nevertheless, the self remains within the pulse of self–other time that confers on it structure and organization, allowing it to be a whole, progressing and transforming in time. DST is different from other self theories in the respect that it opens up to the rhythmicity of selfness–otherness, forming a dynamic unity (Valsiner 2005). Thus, developing a dialogical self means for the self to be in rhythm with an other. Performing this interactional rhythm is performing self, an unfinished construction over time.

ACKNOWLEDGEMENT

I am grateful to John Barresi for his excellent comments on previous drafts of this chapter.

NOTES

1 The first term of this duality is 'alter' for developmental reasons, ego-centrism being rejected on this basis. Thus, the starting point in life is 'alter'; this does not, however, result in a dominating role for this position (Bertau in press).

2 Fogel formulates an explicit criticism of the objective view of self (1993: 144–146); Reddy (2003) argues in a similar vein against the contention that the cognitive skills of a 12–18-month-old infant are needed to be aware of being attended by the other.

3 Roland (2011) addresses the Indian conception of multiple motherhood; this carries its own normative construction of the 'Right Way'.

4 0;9 is to be read as 9 months old (0 years, 9 months). This style (general format: year;month;week;day) was introduced by the developmentalists Clara and William Stern at the beginning of the twentieth century and is now widespread.

5 Morin (2005) is aware of the fact that one can engage in dysfunctional self-talk, as in the case of an anorexic women saying to herself, 'I am too fat'; thus, it is not the mere possibility of inner speech which matters, but its quality.

REFERENCES

Andresen, H. (2002) *Interaktion, Sprache und Spiel. Zur Funktion des Rollenspiels für die Sprachentwicklung im Vorschulalter* (Tübingen: Narr)

Bateson, M. C. (1975) Mother–infant exchanges: the epigenesis of conversational interaction, in D. Aaronson and R. W. Rieber (eds.), *Developmental Psycholinguistics and Communication Disorders* (New York: New York Academy of Sciences), 101–113

Bertau, M.-C. (2007) Encountering objects and others as a means of passage, *Culture & Psychology*, **13**, 335–352

  (2008) Voice: a pathway to consciousness as 'social contact to oneself', *Integrative Psychological and Behavioral Science*, **42**, 92–113

  (in press) Voices of others for self, voices of others in self: polyphony as means and resource for constructing and reconstructing social reality, in M. Riemslagh, A. Liégois, J. Corveleyn and R. Burggraeve (eds.), *'After You': The Ethics of the Pastoral Counselling Process* (Leuven: Peeters)

Bertau, M.-C. and Gonçalves, M. (2007) Looking at 'meaning in movement' in development: introductory reflections on the developmental origins of the dialogical self, *International Journal for Dialogical Science*, **2**, 1–13

Bertau, M.-C., Gonçalves, M. and Raggatt, P. (eds.) (in press) *Dialogic Formations: Investigations into the Origins and Development of the Dialogical Self* (Charlotte, NC: Information Age Publishing)

Bruner, J. (1975) The ontogenesis of speech acts, *Journal of Child Language*, **2**, 1–19

DeCasper, A. and Fifer, W. (1980) Of human bonding: newborns prefer their mother's voice, *Science*, **208**, 1174–1176

DiPietro, A. (2010) Psychological and psychophysiological considerations regarding the maternal-fetal relationship, *Infant and Child Development*, **19**, 27–38

Duarte, F. and Gonçalves, M. (2007) Negotiating motherhood: a dialogical approach, *International Journal for Dialogical Science*, **2**, 249–275

Fernald, A. (1992) Meaningful melodies in mother's speech to infant, in H. Papoušek, U. Jürgens and M. Papoušek (eds.), *Nonverbal Vocal Communication: Comparative and Developmental Approaches* (Cambridge and Paris: Cambridge University Press; Éditions de la Maison des Sciences de l'Homme), 262–282

Fogel, A. (1993) *Developing Through Relationships: Origins of Communication, Self, and Culture* (University of Chicago Press)

Fogel, A., de Koeyer, I., Bellagamba, F. and Bell, H. (2002) The dialogical self in the first two years of life: embarking on a journey of discovery, *Theory & Psychology*, **12**, 191–205

Fogel, A. and de Koeyer-Laros, I. (2007) The developmental transition to secondary intersubjectivity in the second half year: a microgenetic case study, *Journal of Developmental Processes*, **2**, 63–90

Goffman, E. (1981) *Forms of Talk* (Philadelphia: University of Pennsylvania Press)

Gratier, M. (1999) Expressions of belonging: the effect of acculturation on the rhythm and harmony of mother–infant vocal interaction, *Musicae Scientiae*, Special Issue, 93–122

(2003) Expressive timing and interactional synchrony between mothers and infants: cultural similarities, cultural differences, and the immigration experience, *Cognitive Development*, **18**, 533–554

(2008) Liminal spaces and narratives of voice and body in infant vocal interchange (commentary on Morioka), *International Journal of Dialogical Science*, **3**, 143–154

Grimm, H. and Weinert, S. (2002) Sprachentwicklung, in R. Oerter and L. Montada (eds.), *Entwicklungspsychologie* (Weinheim/Basel: Beltz), 517–550

Hermans, H. J. M. (2001) The dialogical self: toward a theory of personal and cultural positioning, *Culture & Psychology*, **3**, 243–281

Hermans, H. J. M. and Hermans-Konopka, A. (2010) *Dialogical Self Theory: Positioning and Counter-Positioning in a Globalizing Society* (Cambridge University Press)

Hermans, H. J. M. and Josephs, I. E. (2003) The dialogical self between mechanism and innovation, in I. E. Josephs (ed.), *Dialogicality in Development* (Westport, CT, and London: Praeger), 111–126

Hermans, H. J. M., Kempen, H. J. G. and van Loon, R. J. P. (1992) The dialogical self: beyond individualism and rationalism, *American Psychologist*, **47**, 23–33

Jaffe, J., Beebe, B., Feldstein, S., Crown, C. L. and Jasnow, M. D. (2001) *Rhythms of Dialogue in Infancy* (Boston, MA, and Oxford: Blackwell)

Josephs, I. E. (ed.) (2003) *Dialogicality in Development* (Westport, CT, and London: Praeger)

Josephs, I. E. and Valsiner, J. (1998) How does autodialogue work?, *Social Psychology Quarterly*, **61**, 68–83

Klausen, E. and Passman, R. H. (2007) Pretend companions (imaginary playmates): the emergence of a new field, *Journal of Genetic Psychology*, **167**, 349–364

Lillard, A. P. (2001) Pretend play as twin earth: a social-cognitive analysis, *Developmental Review*, **21**, 495–531

Lyra, M. C. D. P. (2007) On abbreviation: dialogue in early life, *International Journal for Dialogical Science*, **2**, 15–44

Lyra, M. C. D. P. and Bertau, M.-C. (2008) Dialogical practices as basis for self, *Studia Psychologica*, **6**, 173–193

Mampe, B., Friederici, A. D., Christophe, A. and Wermke, K. (2009) Newborns' cry melody is shaped by their native language, *Current Biology*, **19**, 1994–1997

Morin, A. (2005) Possible links between self-awareness and inner speech, *Journal of Consciousness Studies*, **12**, 115–134

Muratori, F. and Maestro, S. (2007) Autism as a downstream effect of primary difficulties in intersubjectivity going with abnormal development of brain connectivity, *International Journal for Dialogical Science*, **2**, 93–118

Nagy, E. and Molnar, P. (2004) Homo imitans or homo provocans? Human imprinting model of neonatal imitation, *Infant Behavior and Development*, 27, 54–63

Nelson, K. (ed.) (2006) *Narratives from the Crib* (Cambridge, MA, and London: Harvard University Press)

Papoušek, H., Jürgens, U. and Papoušek, M. (eds.) (1992) *Nonverbal Vocal Communication: Comparative Developmental Approaches* (Cambridge and Paris: Cambridge University Press; Éditions de la Maison des Sciences de l'Homme)

Pickert, S. (1981) Imaginative dialogues in children's private speech, *First Language*, 2, 5–20

Reddy, V. (2003) On being the object of attention: implications for self–other consciousness, *Trends in Cognitive Sciences*, 7, 397–402

Robb, L. (1999) Emotional musicality in mother–infant vocal affect, and an acoustic study of postnatal depression, *Musicae Scientiae*, Special Issue, 123–154

Rochat, P. (2001) Social contingency detection in infant development, *Bulletin of the Menninger Clinic*, 65, 347–360

(2006) *Le Monde des bébés* (Paris: Odile Jacob)

Rochat, P. and Hespos, S. J. (1997) Differential rooting response by neonates: evidence for an early sense of self, *Early Development and Parenting*, 6, 105–112

Rochat, P., Querido, J. G. and Striano, T. (1999) Emerging sensitivity to the timing and structure of protoconversation in early infancy, *Developmental Psychology*, 35, 950–957

Roland, A. (2011) *Journeys to Foreign Selves: Asians and Asian Americans in a Global Era* (New Delhi: Oxford University Press)

Steels, L. (2003) Language re-entrance and the 'inner voice', *Journal of Consciousness Studies*, 10, 173–185

Stern, D. (1985) *The Interpersonal World of the Infant: A View from Psychoanalysis and Developmental Psychology* (New York: Basic Books)

Tomasello, M. (1993) On the interpersonal origins of self-concept, in U. Neisser (ed.), *The Perceived Self: Ecological and Interpersonal Sources of Self-Knowledge* (Cambridge University Press), 174–184

Trevarthen, C. (1979) Communication and cooperation in early infancy: a description of primary intersubjectivity, in M. Bullowa (ed.), *Before Speech: The Beginning of Human Communication* (London: Cambridge University Press), 321–347

(1999) Musicality and the intrinsic motive pulse: evidence from human psychobiology and infant communication, *Musicae Scientiae*, Special Issue, 155–215

Trevarthen, C. and Hubley, P. (1978) Secondary intersubjectivity: confidence, confiding and acts of meaning in the first year, in A. Lick (ed.), *Action, Gesture and Symbol: The Emergence of Language* (London: Academic Press), 183–229

Valsiner, J. (2005) General synthesis. Recurring agendas: integration of developmental science, in J. Valsiner (ed.), *Heinz Werner and*

Developmental Science (New York: Kluwer Academic/Plenum Publishers), 391–424

Van den Bergh, B. R. H. (2010) Some social and historical scientific considerations regarding the mother–fetus relationship and parenthood, *Infant and Child Development*, **19**, 39–44

Vygotsky, L. S. (1967) Play and its role in the development of the child, *Soviet Psychology*, **5**, 6–18

4 Self-making through synthesis: extending dialogical self theory

Jaan Valsiner and Kenneth R. Cabell

> He – Why do you want to leave him?
> She – To give a sense of heroism to my life.
> He – I don't understand. Don't you love him anymore?
> She – I'm incapable of separating desire and love. For me they are the same thing.
> He – You no longer desire him?
> She – I still desire him.
> He – And so?
> She – But I told you: I want to give a sense of heroism to my life.
> To suffer by imposing suffering upon myself.   (Petrignani 2000: 115)

The dialogical nature of human paradoxical feelings can be found everywhere. The feelings of ambivalence set the stage for an opposition – a tension between the feeling of 'love' for the other and the feeling of 'still wanting to leave him' that 'feed-in' and 'work through' each other. The oppositions in the ambivalent feelings become synthesized into a higher semiotic field – a hyper-generalized life philosophy of *heroism* that is marked by *suffering*. The self is complex in its dynamics of self-construction and self-organizing – but how can psychology make sense of it?

In this chapter we offer two mutually relatable ideas into the discourse of dialogical self theory (DST) to make better sense of the complex self in structural dynamics and development:

1. Self-making: An increased focus on the ever-developing, ever-transitioning and ever-dynamic dialogical self (DS) alludes to the fluid phenomena of *self-culture*. The individual uses mediating devices – within one's own mind and within the immediate environment – to cultivate the life space. Therefore, just like farmers who cultivate their land, individuals cultivate themselves and their surroundings. It is through a process of 'cultivation' that the self's relationship to the environment – including the self's relationship to its selves – acquires a semiotic (that is, cultural) meaning. Consequently, as various *I*-positions within the self engage in dialogue, they constantly cultivate themselves – reconstructing, renegotiating and reorganizing meanings

of selves, in relationship to each other and the environment. As long as there is self-dialogue, there will remain self-making (Valsiner 1999).

2. Synthesis: An increased focus on the ever-developing, ever-transitioning and ever-dynamic DS alludes to the hyper-production of self-made meanings. Often, these meanings – either momentarily fleeting or ontologically stable – can coexist but provide tension (such as in the case of ambivalence). The overcoming of such tension requires the notion of synthesis. The focus on synthesis has been central in chemistry – but has failed to find its way into psychology since it was first suggested in the 1820s. A specific solution to the problem of causality in chemistry – through the notion of catalysis – has likewise remained beyond the borders of psychology. The development of DST through adoption of the focus on catalytic processes within the DS is likely to bring the focus of psychologists back to the emergence of novel forms through synthesis. The dynamics of the dialogical processes – a general term for interacting positions – within a particular field of catalytic conditions are best viewed as *dialectical* in their nature – with a focus on different forms of *tensions* between the opposite positions and their overcoming (synthesis) (see also Verhofstadt-Denève's chapter, in this handbook). This direction extends the previous effort to chart a typology of possible relations between *I*-positions (Valsiner 2002).

The general ethos of these two directions for theoretical innovation of the DS field is that of abstract conceptualization of the dynamic processes of constant self-organization and self-creation of the DS. While the topographic view of the DS has been well articulated over the past two decades (Hermans 2001, 2002), it is the capturing of the dynamics of the self-making that has posed major theoretical problems. These problems haunt all of psychology (Valsiner 1998); hence, our coverage of the DS here is only a microcosm of a slow but persistent innovation that a number of areas in psychology – cultural and developmental – are currently undergoing (Valsiner 2009). If we look at the efforts to make sense of the dialogical nature of the self from a historical angle, we can find how over two centuries the efforts to conceptualize that facet of human nature have periodically appeared (Fichte 1794; Külpe 1892; Maimon 1794, 1797, 2010; Rosenkranz 1843) and disappeared in the ambivalent self-negotiation of psychology as a science.

A dialogical self: dynamic multiplicity

The notion of 'the self' is an abstraction. Psychology is filled with abstractions that turn dynamic processes into static depictions of their outcomes – and then spend much effort to turn such depictions back into ones that capture the dynamic processes. Thus, the idea that something seemingly as fixed as 'the self' could be multiple in itself is an example of such a return to the complex reality of the phenomena. William James' coverage of the structure of the self as multiple back in 1890 has been one of the starting points of DST. That focus on multiplicity remained non-dynamic in James' presentation – the structure of the many facets of the self did not include the view of the self as a dynamic system. Mikhail Bakhtin's literary philosophy in the 1920s–1970s (e.g. Bakhtin 1981, 1986) provided the DST with an opportunity to return to a dynamic look at the multiplied structure of the self. Yet the conceptual problem – the static nature of the categories that are used to depict phenomena of dynamic kinds – remains. Different perspectives that have emphasized the multiplicity-in-unity of the self have made it clear that the use of fixed, unitary, point-like descriptors of the self (e.g. traits) constitutes a theoretical impasse for psychology (Märtsin 2010).

However, recognizing the dialogical nature of the self is a way of capturing a multiplicity-in-unity that substantively transcends the static nature of traditional accounts of personality in psychology (Hermans 1995, 2001; Hermans and Hermans-Konopka 2010; Hermans and Kempen 1993). The conceptual structure of DST overcomes the entified notion of the self. The self is a process of relating between its components (Ferreira *et al.* 2006; Gillespie 2006, 2007; Leiman 2002, 2004; Linell 2009; Salgado and Gonçalves 2007; Salgado and Hermans 2005) as well as arriving at new states of itself (e.g. abbreviation – Lyra 1999; dialectical synthesis – Marková 2003). Within the DS, the interacting *I*-positions are embedded within a self-structure, supportive of a particular hierarchical organization. It is the dynamics of a systemic relating within a particular self-structure that is essential for a developmental model of DST. Therefore, the loci of focus in DST should be on the topography of *I*-positions in conjunction with the relationships between *I*-positions as they undergo dynamic transformation within a particular self-structure. The hierarchical structure of a system provides the vertical relationship between *I*-positions. These relationships take different forms (Valsiner 2002), among which the dominant–dominated relationship plays a key role.

A hierarchical structure of dynamic kind is important to understand not only the role of asymmetry in power dynamics of the DS system but also of the role of regulation. *I*-positions can regulate downwards in the hierarchy, inhibiting the voice of those *I*-positions it dominates, sometimes silencing them completely. Such *I*-positions become *T*-positions ('taboo positions') – *I*-positions that are no longer discernible – yet play a role in the whole. They are analogous to 'black holes' in astronomy. The hierarchical organization of the DS entails two modes of regulation. *I*-positions that are *regulating upwards* can promote the voice of those *I*-positions at the top of the hierarchy, sometimes powerful enough to allow for monologization. Such upward regulation allows for rapid construction of semiotic hierarchies (Valsiner 2001). It is paralleled by *downward regulation* that constrains the relationships of the *I*-positions at the lowest level of the topographical map of the DS. This form of regulation is crucial for maintaining the vertical 'depth' of the hierarchical organization within manageable limits. The organization of the system provides also for the horizontal relationships of *I*-positions – these are usually seen in topological models of DST. The regulation of *I*-positions in dialogue also occurs on the horizontal plane. These structural dynamics introduce an important reconception in DST: dialogue does not only occur horizontally between two juxtaposed positions, but also vertically within the hierarchical structure of the self. In addition to *I*-positions, that structure includes *T*-positions that are functional – yet not explicit – in the DS.

The dynamics of dialogue: communicative zones in the self-system

The structural and organizational components of DST can be developed even further through the theoretical understanding of the mind as a psychological field in which three communicative zones are constantly being negotiated and renegotiated – the zone of promoted talk, the zone of inhibited talk and the zone of possible talk. The mind as a semiotic demand setting (Valsiner 2000: Chapter 7 and Epilogue) is a complementary innovation that foregrounds the dynamics of dialogue within the self-system.

Dialogue can occur regarding anything – this is the zone of possible talk. But this zone becomes constrained given the 'atmosphere' in the society of the mind – that is to say, that particular semiotic catalysers 'set the stage' for the direct regulations of what is (and what is not) allowed in the dialogical discourse (discussed further below). Various positions with various ideological perspectives and value-laden voices engage in a self-preservation game to guarantee their survival within the DS system. *I*-positions act as semiotic regulators, regulating (via inhibiting or promoting) what is dialogued about. Therefore, out of the whole field of possible talk emerge two smaller zones – the zone of promoted dialogue and the zone of taboo dialogue – the inhibited sub-part of the field (Figure 4.1).

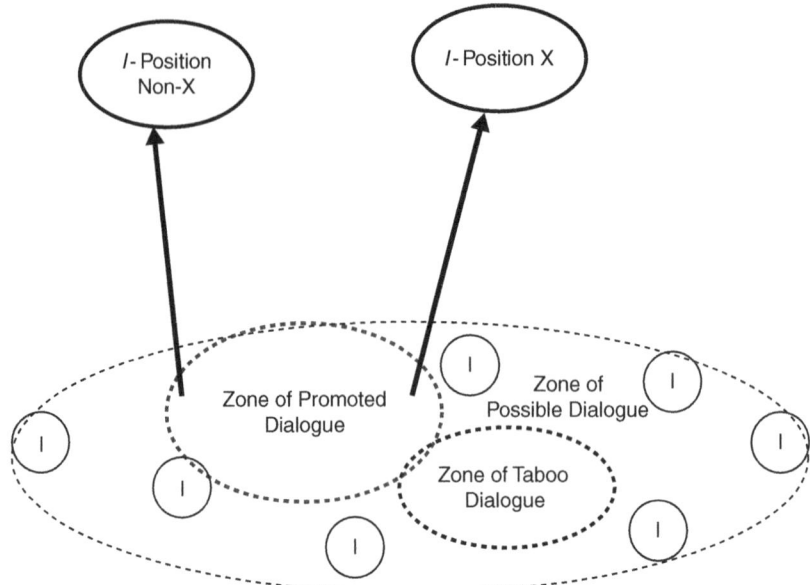

Figure 4.1 Vertical construction of *I*-positions on the basis of a
structured field of dialogicality.

Such developments are seen in dialogical interactions between the
individual and society. Thus, it is no surprise to see such a model within
the society of the mind. Consider a political system that provides the
general atmosphere to promote dialogue in line with a certain life philosophy or moral/ethical code while inhibiting dialogue regarding other
contradictory value systems. A contextually supported political system
may result in some voices being heard more often (or at least, more
dominantly) than others. This can be mapped on to the DS, in which
hierarchical systems of *I*-positions and their corresponding voices interact. But how these *I*-positions systemically relate (i.e. what positions are
more dominant than other; what positions are more influential than
others; what positions are heard more than others; etc.) depends on
the contextual support of the system. Such contextual support can be
conceptualized as the catalytic conditions of the system.

Catalytic processes within the dialogical self: supporting development

The concept of catalysis was introduced into chemistry by Jöns Jakob
Berzelius in 1836 (see overview by Steininger 2008: 57). It became

recognized as an indispensable notion in chemistry over the rest of the nineteenth century, leading to Wilhelm Ostwald getting a Nobel Prize for it in 1909 (Ostwald 1900: 109, 1909). It has proliferated well into the biological sciences and has been a major alternative to the traditional view of causal processes. Alwin Mittasch in his *Catalysis and Determinism* (1938) extended the notion of catalysis outwards from science to general philosophy of living matter, and to introduce the notion of catalytic causality (Heinemann 1938).

In general, 'catalysis' is a broad term that refers to a process that provides the conditions necessary – but not by themselves sufficient – to produce a particular qualitative change in a system. Thus, the catalyst does not cause a particular reaction to happen, nor does it cause a particular result. Instead, catalysis supports the reaction and enables the production of the outcome. The abstract qualities of catalysis include:

(1) a type of contextual support
(2) enabled regulation within the system
(3) the production of novel qualities.

It is the presence of the catalytic agent (and only its presence) that provides the conditions necessary – a type of contextual support – for the enablement (or disablement) of regulation that produces a novel qualitative outcome.

Imported into the social sciences – specifically, psychology – the notion of the catalyst remains similar in respect to the abstract qualities of its role within a system but diverges in the delegation of each quality. In its application to the semiotic version of DST, we can think of the role of some signs – semiotic catalysts – enabling (or disabling) the regulatory roles of other signs. The regulatory roles of signs enabled by the catalyst actively and directly promote or inhibit various processes within the psychological system, ultimately leading to the qualitative change in the system and the production of novelty.

Semiotic catalysers exist in the background of the system, providing a directional flavouring that guides psychological processes. They 'set the stage' in a way that provides contextual support for the immediate future-oriented semiotic regulation of the self. Therefore, the main quality of the semiotic catalyser is to provide the conditions necessary – the contextual support – that guide and direct the employment of semiotic regulators (Cabell 2010, in press). Yet they are not equal to promoter signs (Valsiner 2004), generalized and abstracted signs directly regulating the future direction of the self. The semiotic catalysers orient and support – yet they do not specifically act upon psychological processes. They create the 'general atmosphere' – so to speak – for the future-directed actions of the DS. They are – in terms of our contemporary psychology – 'the context' that makes a particular phenomenon possible.

Depending on the contextual support of the semiotic catalyser, various semiotic regulators can be enabled (or disabled) to act directly on the *I*-positions and their dialogues. Regulators can, for example, promote the abstraction and generalization of an *I*-position (construction of a meta-position), or a synthesis of *I*-positions can occur (construction of fused *I*-positions or the development of a coalition of positions). Other contextual support can lead to particular dominant-submissive hierarchies, resulting in various system organizations and corresponding to a multiplicity of psychological outcomes.

Conformity and independence: the contextual support of social guidance

Solomon Asch's classic study on independence and conformity can be viewed in light of catalytic conditions. Asch had a group of confederates and one test subject compare the length of a line to three other lines and indicate which of the three lines was the same length as the original line. The confederates were instructed to indicate the obviously wrong answer and the study tested to see if the test subject would conform or remain independent. The results showed significant results towards conformity on the critical trials. Asch remarked that the study grew out of the

circumstances that invested the situation of the minority person with significance, from his doubts and sufferings, his strengths and weaknesses. (Asch 1956: 24; emphasis added)

It is interesting to see Asch's reference to the circumstances – the contextual support – for the semiotic regulation of conformity and/or independence of the minority person. More specifically, Asch refers to parts of the study in which the circumstances provided the conditions necessary for the regulated emergence of doubts and sufferings. The fluctuating self dialogue of the participants is seen as Asch (1956) quotes his participants:

'First I thought something was the matter with me or most of them' [o]. 'I was sure they were wrong, but not sure if I was right' [3] – a statement that nicely illustrates the hold that group opinion can have. Going in the same direction was the following statement of a subject who, after exclaiming, 'Everybody here's crazy but me,' added: 'seeing they had the power of numbers, I thought they must be right somehow, but it wasn't what I saw, and I think I was right' [o]. 'Either these guys were crazy or I was – I hadn't made up my mind which... I was wondering if my judgments really were as poor as they seemed to be, but at the same time I had the feeling that I was seeing them right. *It was a conflicting situation*' [8]. (1956: 28; emphasis added)

The self-report of a conflicting situation is important here. The catalytic conditions provided contextual support that guided the construction of ambivalent feelings. Therefore, one *I*-position regulated the flow of experience that voiced a dissent from the group and a consent to independence. The other *I*-position promoted the flow of experience that voiced consent with the group and dissent with independence. The tension caused by the dialogue between conflicting *I*-positions can be seen as a catalytic condition in itself, guiding psychological functioning towards transcending the tension and conflict and allowing the self to move forward and think/act accordingly. The ability of human psychological processes to arrive at new synthetic meanings (Salvatore in press) – based on tensions – and make use of those as contextual features of the situation – shows how catalytic processes work in DS. The arrival at the description 'this was a conflicting situation' sets up conditions for understanding the context – and eliminating the previous tension.

Dialectic processes in the dialogical self: a new focus on synthesis

The theoretical move of DST into the developmental domain makes it necessary to return to ideas long abandoned in psychological science – that developmental thought cannot operate without clear conceptualization of *emergence*, as the whole developmental paradigm is predicated upon the construction of novel forms (Baldwin 1906, 2010; Valsiner 1998). Yet it is precisely the process of emergence that has been difficult to capture by our formal conceptual systems – in all areas of science. The conceptual difficulty is predicated upon development being a relationship between what already is and what does not exist at the given time. Furthermore, the presence of various catalytic conditions that enable – but do not cause – new developments further complicates the picture.

Dialectics reconsidered: Johann Gottlieb Fichte, Salomon Maimon and Georg Wilhelm Hegel

The idea of the unity of opposites and their role in the process of emergence of novelty was obvious to German philosophers. Johann Gottlieb Fichte (1762–1814) – considered to belong to the 'idealist' group – and his contemporary Salomon Maimon (1753–1800) are the originators of the dialectical philosophy in European philosophical traditions. They antedated the better known – and widely disputed – legacy of Georg Wilhelm Hegel (1770–1831). Much of the potentially positive thought of the German dialectical thinkers in the nineteenth century has been ignored in psychology (see Leary 1980). Yet for the needs of DST, we need to go further back in history to the pre-Hegel period. Importantly, it is Fichte – rather than Hegel (Mueller 1958) – who initiated the analytical frame widely known in dialectical philosophy – the thesis–antithesis–synthesis triad – in his 1794 book *Grundlage der gesamten Wissenschaftlehre* (Fichte 1794; in English, Fichte 1868). The starting point of his focus was the question of how a human being can know what is conceptually necessary for any knowledge to come into being. It was a philosophical effort that was explicit in its transcendental effort in relation to Kantian antinomies. Fichte borrowed the focus on synthesis from Salomon Maimon (1794, 1797; in English, 2010), who was, like Fichte, creating a subjective, idealist world view.

Absence of the predicate and its implications

It is not a surprise that efforts to understand how the DS functions share the starting point with subjective-idealist philosophical traditions. The simple – yet perplexing – question about the self is – *how can we discover that something we call 'self' exists at all*? There is no self without the self-maker – and the self-maker needs the ability to enter into a dialogue with oneself even to ask that question. Discovering one's own self creates ever new dialogicality within the self. Once released, dialogicality will be wandering endlessly through the soul fields of the self.

Yet, in the beginning is a word – and an indeterminate one! Fichte's starting point was the most basic statement the self makes – *I am* (*Ich bin*) (Figure 4.2). This is a *maximally indefinite* statement about a *very definite* being – the utterer oneself. Its indefinite nature is achieved by way of loss of the predicate. The discussion of the indefinite quality of the 'I' is elaborated by Yair Neuman:

unlike other linguistic signs, the sign 'I' has no clear reference. The sign 'tree' indicates the concept of a tree, the sign 'number' corresponds to the object well defined by mathematicians, but what object does the sign 'I' indicate? The answer is that the sign 'I' fulfills the mysterious function of associating the lived experience of the individual with a communicable and social form of expression. (Neuman 2009: 17)

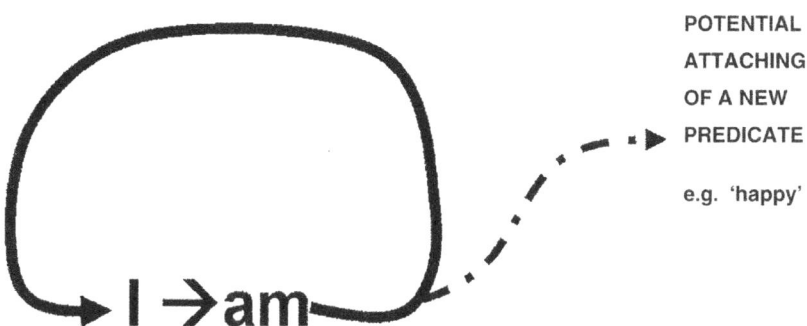

Figure 4.2 The binding of new predicates in the process of self-recursivity.

The experience – immediate and social – is the negotiation ground on which the indefiniteness of the concept 'I' becomes specified – by attaching predicates to itself. In some sense – considering every statement about *I* in the infiniteness of irreversible time – the 'I' has a hyper-generalized predicate – itself. Emergence of other predicates begins from that – seemingly nebulous – state. All derivations – 'I am a man', 'I am happy', etc. – set the focus on the stated quality (man, happy), rather than upon the experiencing self. The semiotic nature of the 'I' is an abstraction that moves the utterer away from the very act of uttering – *Tathandlung* (rather than *Tatsache* – i.e. fact).[1] In the subjective-idealist perspective such *fact-handling* is central – the world outside is being posited by it.

How would such a maximally indefinite statement be limited by specifiable constraints? In classical logic this is achieved by identity statements (e.g. 'A is A'). Similarly, Fichte creates the limiting predicate within the positioning agent itself.

This self-recursivity of the self can be viewed as the starting point of the DS – in fact it is a dynamically recursive focus on the duality of the self ('I am' and 'I am' are not repetition of the same, but a dialogue of the self-in-being). This trick of establishing a predicate-in-oneself[2] fortifies the indeterminacy of the *Ich* who makes a claim of being oneself – that is determinate. Yet, such determined indeterminacy – a repetitive cycle of assertions about the *I* – closes the door to any conceptualization of development, and similarly to all applications of classical logic that require the identity statement ('A is A') rather than accept variability in A over time. This developmental quality of binding new predicates to the *I* is the basis upon which any DS perspective is developed. The binding of new predicates (constructions of selves) allows for a qualitatively different *I* (construction of the self).

Creating the predicate through *oppositing*

From the point of view of DST, it is very interesting to note how Fichte's argumentation about the general principles of dialectics was formulated by turning the notion of self (*I*, the *Ich*) into a relationship with non-*I* (*nicht-Ich*). The key move that makes creating such a relationship possible is the treatment of the opposites as separate-but-connected (*inclusive separation* – Valsiner 1987), rather than apply to them the either/or assumptions of classical logic (*exclusive* separation). The *Ich* and *Nicht-Ich* are *opposed* (German: *Satz des Gegensetzens* – Fichte 1794: 25) – they constitute parts within the same whole. The opposites exist *through* each other – leading to the relationship.[3] Yet being in the relationship is only a starting point of becoming the new opposition. Both of the opposing parts of the whole (A and non-A) relate with themselves in their new version – synthesis – through the other. This synthetic relationship leads to the overcoming of the previous tension. Here Fichte situates the notion of overcoming (*aufheben*) in the case of double negation. That latter notion – relevant to later development of dialectical philosophy – is built upon the idea of *reciprocal determination* (or *relation* in Kant – Fichte 1868: 108 – in German, *Wechselbestimmung*[4] – Fichte 1794: 60). The fact that Fichte invents a new term is relevant to making sense of this beginning point of dialectical thought – the reciprocal determination takes the form of determining a change of each part of the oppositions in the system by the processes that work through their counterpart. That work takes the form of limiting (*Einschränkung*) of the other. Such mutual limiting sets the stage for synthesis of the new.[5] This is Fichte's point of opposites relating with one another by 'moving through' so that the relating leads to synthesis. The action of A through non-A ('thesis') limits the non-A, resulting in an 'antithesis' that – acting through A – leads to both limited A and non-A in a new state ('synthesis').

Conclusion: the study of the process structure of relations

DST has constructed and maintained itself as complex. However, it is exactly the complexity of the dynamics within a self-organized and self-structured system that is crucial to develop further. DST introduces the centrality of *relationships between components* of the differentiated self – positing their nature as one or another form of mutuality – such as mutual coordination, mutual contradiction, dialectical overcoming of oppositions by synthesis of new ones, and so on – *between I*-positions. Our focus on the DS leads to the unresolved problem of how to construct the hierarchical structure of the DST without losing its focus on the dynamic nature of self-organization. There is a constructive tension between the 'map-making' of *I*-positions and the 'position-making' functions of the map. The distribution of *I*-positions becomes open for further development by the success of constructing the hierarchy of positions.

The construction of any hierarchy of positions starts with a particular contextual support. Embedded within a particular 'atmosphere', the enablement (or disablement) of regulation can begin to structure various positions and their relations to one another. Often, positions become opposed in which their dialectical synthesis provides qualitative breakthrough within the DS system.

Qualitative breakthrough is the core of any development. The dynamics of the DS allow for a constantly fluctuating picture of the self-culture and self-construction processes. Such a semiotic version of DST requires the use of various sign functions and sign productions to provide the framework for a dynamic developmental self. The use of semiotic mediators, such as semiotic catalysers and semiotic regulators, is crucial for understanding the self system. Regulators in the self-system – such as promoter signs and inhibitory signs – can result in the semiotic demand setting of the self. This hierarchical regulation of the DS is captured in the need to consider some of the *I*-positions as dominant guidance tools that organize other positions ('promoter positions' – Hermans and Hermans-Konopka 2010) and other *I*-positions as dominant guidance tools that organize other positions ('taboo positions'). The DS can grow through innovative moments in the flow of meaning construction ('*I*-moments' – see Bento *et al.* in press; Cunha *et al.* in press; Gonçalves and Ribeiro in this volume). What emerges from this making of the self-reflexive (dialogical) self is the focus on dynamic hierarchical regulation of one's action through constant positioning and repositioning towards others and the world (Dimaggio *et al.* 2010; Hermans 2001, 2002; Leiman 2002, 2004). The structure of DS needs to allow flexible self-construction (and self-demolishing) of the hierarchical functional order.

NOTES

1 Fichte 1794: 10; discussion in Ryue 1997: 144–150. Contrast with another predicate-less expression: 'it is'.
2 The appropriate contrast here – thinking of Fichte's dialogue with Kant – is the latter's 'thing-in-itself' (*Ding-an-sich*). By moving from the thing-in-itself

to the thing-as-predicate-for-itself, Fichte opens the possibility of a dynamic view – that could become dialogical, and dialectical.

3 The non-A in this case is not *absence* of A, but presence of something else that is non-A. Non-A can be seen as being 'empty of A' – but this emptiness is a form of fullness (with something else, or with A to come, or to be remembered from the past). For example, in the meaning system of the Sa'dan Toraja (Sulewesi, Indonesia), the 'empty earth' – the time between the rice harvest and the planting of new crop – is described as full of fertility. The apperception of the expected future makes a non-A an example of *being posited in the A* (even if absent at the time). The notion of 'empty fullness' (kenosis) of the body of the Christ in discourses in Christianity is an occidental example (Tsintjilonis 2006: 565 and 563).

4 In analogy with *Wechselwirkung* – reciprocal action, mutual effect. *Bestimmung* here fits in the sense of allocation, appropriation and modification (reference to process), while *Wirkung* refers to outcome (result, effect, consequence).

5 The idea of mutual constraining sets the stage for contradictions – non-A limiting A in contrast to A limiting non-A – leading to tension.

REFERENCES

Asch, S. E. (1956) Studies of independence and conformity: a minority of one against a unanimous majority, *Psychological Monographs*, **70**, 9, 1–70

Bakhtin, M. M. (1981) *The Dialogic Imagination* (Austin, TX: University of Texas Press)

(1986) *Speech Genres and Other Late Essays* (Austin, TX: University of Texas Press)

Baldwin, J. M. (1906) *Thought and Things: A Study of the Development and Meaning of Thought, or Genetic Logic.* Vol. I: *Functional Logic, or Genetic Theory of Knowledge* (London: Swan Sonnenschein & Co.)

(2010) *Genetic Theory of Reality* (New Brunswick, NJ: Transaction)

Bento, T., Cunha, C. and Salgado, J. (in press) Dialogical theory of selfhood, in J. Valsiner (ed.), *The Oxford Handbook of Culture and Psychology* (New York: Oxford University Press)

Cabell, K. R. (in press) Catalysis: cultural constructions and the conditions for change, *Journal of Integrated Social Sciences*, **2**

(2010) Mediators, regulators, and catalysers: a context-inclusive model of trajectory development, *Psychology & Society*, **3**, 26–41

Cunha, C., Gonçalves, M. and Valsiner, J. (in press) Rehearsing renewal of identity: re-conceptualization on the move, in M.-C. Bertau, M. Gonçalves and P. Raggatt (eds.), *Investigations into the Origin and Development of the Dialogical Self* (Charlotte, NC: Information Age Publishing)

Dimaggio, G., Hermans, H. J. M. and Lysaker, P. (2010) Health and adaptation in a multiple self, *Theory & Psychology*, **20**, 379–399

Ferreira, T., Salgado, J. and Cunha, C. (2006) Ambiguity and the dialogical self: in search for a dialogical psychology, *Estudios de Psicologia*, **27**, 19–32

Fichte, J. G. (1794) *Grundlage der gesamten Wissenschaftslehre* (Leipzig: Christian Ernst Gabler)
(1868) *The Science of Knowledge* (Philadelphia, PA: Lippincott)

Gillespie, A. (2006) *Becoming Other: From Social Interaction to Self-Reflection* (Greenwich, CT: Information Age)
(2007) The social basis of self-reflection, in A. Rosa and J. Valsiner (eds.), *The Cambridge Handbook of Sociocultural Psychology* (Cambridge University Press), 678–691

Heinemann, F. H. (1938) Philosophy in German: philosophy of nature, *Philosophy*, **13**(51), 338–344

Hermans, H. J. M. (1995) The limitations of logic in defining the self, *Theory & Psychology*, **5**, 375–382
(2001) The dialogical self: toward a theory of personal and cultural positioning, *Culture & Psychology*, **7**, 243–281
(2002) The dialogical self as the society of mind, *Theory & Psychology*, **12**, 147–160

Hermans, H. J. M. and Hermans-Konopka, A. (2010) *Dialogical Self Theory: Positioning and Counter-Positioning in a Globalizing Society* (Cambridge University Press)

Hermans, H. J. M. and Kempen, H. J. G. (1993) *The Dialogical Self: Meaning as Movement* (San Diego, CA: Academic Press)

Külpe, O. (1892) Das Ich und die Aussenwelt, *Philosophische Studien*, **7**, 394–413

Leary, D. E. (1980) German Idealism and the development of psychology in the nineteenth century, *Journal of the History of Philosophy*, **18**, 299–317

Leiman, M. (2002) Toward semiotic dialogism: the role of sign mediation in the dialogical self, *Theory & Psychology*, **12**, 221–235
(2004) Dialogical sequence analysis, in H. J. M. Hermans and G. Dimaggio (eds.), *The Dialogical Self in Psychotherapy* (Hove: Brunner-Routledge), 255–269

Linell, P. (2009) *Essentials of Dialogism: Aspects and Elements of Dialogical Approaches to Language, Communication and Cognition* (Charlotte, NC: Information Age Publishing)

Lyra, M. C. D. P. (1999) An excursion into the dynamics of dialogue, *Culture & Psychology*, **5**, 477–489

Maimon, S. (1794) *Versuch einer neuen Logik oder Theorie des Denkens* (Berlin: Erns Felisch)
(1797) *Kritische Untersuchungen über das höhere Erkenntnis- und Willensvermögen* (Leipzig: Gerhard Fleischer und Jüngern)
(2010) *Essay on Transcendental Philosophy* (London: Continuum)

Marková, I. (2003) *Dialogicality and Social Representations* (Cambridge University Press)

Märtsin, M. (2010) Identity in dialogue: identity as hyper-generalized personal sense, *Theory & Psychology*, **20**, 436–450

Mead, G. H. (1912) The mechanism of social consciousness, *Journal of Philosophy*, **9**, 401–406
(1913) The social self, *Journal of Philosophy*, **10**, 374–380

Mittach, A. (1938) *Katalyse und Determinismus* (Berlin: Springer)

Mogk, A. and Bukau, B. (2010) When the beginning marks the end, *Science*, 327, 966–967

Mueller, G. E. (1958) The Hegel legend of 'thesis-antithesis-synthesis', *Journal of the History of Ideas*, 19, 411–414

Neuman, Y. (2009) Peter Pan's shadow and the relational matrix of the 'I', *Semiotica*, 176, 15–27

Ostwald, W. (1900) *Grundlinien der anorganischen Chemie* (Leipzig: Wilhelm Engelmann)

(1909) On catalysis. Nobel Lecture, 12 December. Retrieved from http://nobelprize.org/nobel_prizes/chemistry/laureates/1909/ostwald-lecture.html

Petrignani, S. (2000) Body, in M. F. Cutrufelli (ed.), *In the Forbidden City* (University of Chicago Press), 115–127

Rosenkranz, K. (1843) *Psychologie oder die Wissenschaft vom subjective Geist* (Königsberg: Bornträger)

Ryue, H. (1997) Die Differenz zwischen 'Ich bin' und 'Ich bin Ich', in W. H. Schrader (ed.), *Die Grundlage der gesamten Wissenschaftslehre von 1794/95 und der transcendentale Standpunkt* (Amsterdam: Rodopi), 143–156

Salgado, J. (2007) The feeling of a dialogical self: affectivity, agency and otherness, in Simão and Valsiner (eds.), *Otherness in Question*, 53–72

Salgado, J. and Gonçalves, M. (2006) The dialogical self: social, personal, and (un)conscious, in A. Rosa and J. Valsiner (eds.), *The Cambridge Handbook of Sociocultural Psychology* (Cambridge University Press), 608–624

Salgado, J. and Hermans, H. J. M. (2005) The return of subjectivity: from a multiplicity of selves to the dialogical self, *Electronic Journal of Applied Psychology*, 1, 3–13

Salgado, J. and Valsiner, J. (2010) Dialogism and the eternal movement within communication, in C. Grant (ed.), *Beyond Universal Pragmatics: Studies in the Philosophy of Communication* (Bern: Peter Lang), 101–121

Salvatore, S. (in press) Social life of the sign: sense-making in society, in J. Valsiner (ed.), *The Oxford Handbook of Culture and Psychology* (New York: Oxford University Press)

Schwennesen, N. and Koch, L. (2009) Visualizing and calculating life: matters of fact in the context of prenatal risk assessment, in S. Bauer and A. Wahlberg (eds.), *Contested Categories: Life Sciences in Society* (Farnham: Ashgate), 69–87

Simão, L. M. and Valsiner, J. (eds.) (2007) *Otherness in Question: Labyrinths of the Self* (Charlotte, NC: Information Age Publishing)

Steininger, B. (2008) Katalysator – Annäherung an einen Schlüsselbegriff das 20. Jahrhunderts, in E. Müller and F. Schmieder (eds.), *Begriffsgeschichte der Naturwissenschaften* (Berlin: Walter de Gruyter), 53–71

Tsintjilonis, D. (2006) Monsters and caricatures: spirit possession in Tana Toraja, *Journal of the Royal Anthropological Institute*, 12, 3, 551–567

Valsiner, J. (1987) *Culture and the Development of Children's Action* (Chichester: Wiley)

(1998) The development of the concept of development: historical and epistemological perspectives, in W. Damon and R. Lerner (eds.),

Handbook of Child Psychology, 5th edn. Vol. I: *Theoretical Models of Human Development* (New York: Wiley), 189–232

(1999) I create you to control me: a glimpse into basic processes of semiotic mediation, *Human Development*, **42**, 26–30

(2000) *Culture and Human Development* (London: Sage)

(2001) Process structure of semiotic mediation in human development, *Human Development*, **44**, 84–97

(2002) Forms of dialogical relations and semiotic autoregulation within the self, *Theory & Psychology*, **12**, 251–265

(2004) The promoter sign: developmental transformation within the structure of dialogical self, paper presented at the Biennial Meeting of the International Society for the Study of Behavioural Development (ISSBD), Ghent

(2007a) *Culture in Minds and Societies* (New Delhi: Sage)

(2007b) Looking across cultural gender boundaries, *Integrative Psychological and Behavioral Science*, **41**, 3–4

(2009) Integrating psychology within the globalizing world: a requiem to the post-modernist experiment with Wissenschaft, *Integrative Psychological and Behavioral Science*, **43**, 1–21

5 Multiculturalism, multiple identifications and the dialogical self: shifting paradigms of personhood in sociocultural anthropology

Toon van Meijl

The beginning of the new millennium is characterized by massive movements of people in search of work, money, pleasure and prestige. People have always been on the move to a lesser or larger extent, but contemporary movements of migrants are qualitatively different from those in the past. In recent decades, revolutionary innovations have taken place in communication and information technology, and these enable migrants to maintain contact with relatives at home much easier than before. As a consequence, the world has become virtually a smaller place, in which transnational connections among people transcend the everyday lives of migrants.

The emergence of transnational networks has far-reaching implications for the transformation and differentiation of culture, cultural identities, and the self of individuals. After all, migration societies are rapidly diversifying and changing into multicultural orders. The putative cohesion of societies that formerly were, at least ethnically, more uniform than today is also swiftly challenged by a rise of ethnic groupings, with different languages and different cultural customs. Not only does the growing mix of peoples with different cultural backgrounds in many societies around the globe entail a growing multiplicity of culture at social levels, but it is also reflected in the self of individuals, who are more and more involved in a multitude of social networks in different culture areas.

A growing number of cosmopolitan citizens are engaged in a variety of cultural milieus, with due consequences for their cultural identities. Indeed, their cultural identities are no longer similar to the cultural identity of the majority of the people around them, but they are first and foremost characterized by cultural differences. They are also becoming more flexible since it has gradually become more essential to be able to relate to different circumstances. As a corollary, the variability of contemporary identities demands the replacement of the relatively static concept of identity with the more dynamic concept of identification. Furthermore, it is important to make explicit that identifications are no longer singular as they invariably involve multiplicity (van Meijl 2010).

The multiple identifications of individuals living in multicultural circumstances, however, raise new questions regarding the relationship between the various cultural dimensions of their self. This chapter examines the fundamental question of how individuals connect various cultural identifications and different representations thereof within the self. The focus will be on the mediation of multiple identifications within individual constructions of self in the context of migration that is characterized by rapid social and cultural change. Especially migrant youngsters face enormous difficulties in expressing their cultural identities in terms of traditional aspects of culture, such as language, religion and ritual, yet they cannot discard their ethnicity. The question is therefore how they deal with these dilemmas and how they constitute their self in and through cultural differences? More specifically, how do 'traditional' and post-migrant expressions of culture intersect within the self of young individuals growing up in multicultural circumstances? And how may we conceive of individual selves who are not unified but torn between a number of different, possibly conflicting cultural positions and identifications? In other words, how can cultural differences within individuals be acknowledged without representing their identifications as negative, fragmented, damaged or in crisis?

In this chapter, I examine these questions from the perspective of dialogical self theory (DST), which offers a powerful tool for the analysis of multiple identifications of migrants in multicultural societies. Furthermore, this chapter will discuss the implications of a dialogical perspective on the multiple identifications of multicultural persons for the concept of the individual. The main question behind this thread is whether an increasing number of cultural positions in multicultural societies may destabilize the dialogue between various identifications that is required for a successful balance between different dimensions of the self. This question will be addressed in light of recent shifts in notions of personhood in cultural anthropology that are the result of innovations in the interpretation of Melanesian ethnography. The notion of the partible person, who is a composite of social relations and therefore not individual, but dividual, has emerged from this debate. In the final section, this term will be compared and contrasted with the dialogical self, all with an eye on the tenability of the concept of the individual. I begin, however, with an ethnographic excursion into the dilemmas of multicultural youngsters in the Pacific.

Multicultural dilemmas

The impact of migration is nowhere near as pervasive as it is in the Asia-Pacific region, which accounts for almost 40 per cent of the millions of people who cross national borders each year (Goss and Lindquist 2000). Limited prospects for economic growth and climate change cause people to try their luck elsewhere. The largest migration streams are from Polynesia, with half a million Polynesians living abroad today, which is about 25 per cent of the total population. Approximately 250,000 of those are living in New Zealand, where they make up 7 per cent of the total population. Furthermore, it is interesting that for some groups, such as Cook Islanders, Niueans and Tokelauans, the numbers resident in New Zealand exceed, often considerably, those resident in the origin societies (Macpherson, Spoonley and Anae 2001).

The transnational connections between Pacific people in New Zealand and their places of origin indicate that an increasing number of diasporic youngsters are growing up between two or more shores, developing multiple identifications with more than one place in and beyond New Zealand. Since migrants from Samoa and Tonga make up the largest Polynesian groups in New Zealand, their situation has been investigated in some detail (Anae 1997, 2001; Lee 2003, 2004; Small 1997). Some 60 per cent of Samoans and Tongans resident in New Zealand were born there, but continue to be raised in Pacific style by parents who were born overseas. In New Zealand, these migrant children are generically identified as Samoans or Tongans, although within Samoan and Tongan communities a distinction is gradually being made between those who were born in the Pacific and those who were born in New Zealand. In both cases, however, the main label of identification continues to refer to a territory that is far removed from the country in which they are growing up, a phenomenon that has been described as deterritorialization by the cultural anthropologist Appadurai (1996). It goes without saying that this paradoxal relationship between the customary label of someone's identity and the circumstances in which a person is raised generates confusion. The Samoan anthropologist Melani Anae (2001: 106) has encapsulated the perplexity following this mix-up in the following verse:

> I am a Samoan – but not a Samoan
> To my aiga in Samoa, I am a Palagi
> I am a New Zealander – but not a New Zealander
> To New Zealanders, I am a bloody coconut, at worst,
> A Pacific Islander, at best,
> To my Samoan parents, I am their child.

The confusion begins when someone's Samoan identity is challenged by island-born members of one's extended family (*aiga*) or church community, which are rather influential in Pacific Islander communities, while at the same time one's identity as a New Zealander is challenged by *Papalagi*, New Zealanders of European descent. For many youngsters, these emotional challenges to their identity as both Samoan and New Zealander entail insecurity and lack of control. It reinforces their awareness that some social and cultural attitudes and behaviour derived from their new world are opposed to prior behavioural and sociocultural norms proceeding from the Pacific. As a consequence, their sense of self is divided between two cultural positions that are generally considered contradictory.

The prime source of identity confusion among Pacific youngsters growing up in New Zealand, Australia and the USA is the inability to speak the first language of their parents and grandparents. Although many might be able to understand their 'mother tongue', at least to some extent, their lack of proficiency prevents them from participating in activities organized by the extended family or other institutions that are founded on a Pacific Island basis, such as churches. For that reason, too, many young people no longer think of themselves as 'real Pacific Islanders', nor are they viewed as such by their parents and other family members whose first language is not English. Thus, the level of fluency in a Pacific language becomes a sign for which dimension of an adolescent's upbringing is more dominant: those more fluent in a Pacific Island language than in English are still regarded as real Pacific Islanders, whereas those who prefer to communicate in English are frequently considered as more New Zealander, Australian or American.

The question whether Pacific youngsters are torn between two cultures or whether some sometimes manage to constitute a balanced identity 'between two shores' has been examined most extensively for Tongan youngsters living in Australia by Helen Lee (2003). She demonstrates in great detail that young people are increasingly able to shift between identities in different contexts. These shifts may involve significant transformations in appearance (clothing, hairstyle, etc.) and behaviour according to whether they are at home, church or school, or socializing with peers. She hastens to add, however, that more youngsters are struggling to combine different roles that are expected of them in different domains of society: 'One minute you're a Tongan and the other, you are stepping out of that circle to join the rest of society' (Lee 2003: 137).

Indeed, the cultural dilemmas faced by these Pacific youngsters are increasingly common around the world since more and more people are constantly moving across cultural landscapes (Castells 1996). People for whom multiculturalism is the order of the day have no option but to mediate their multiple identifications by engaging in a dialogue between different cultural positions (see also van Meijl 2006). The notion of the dialogical self provides a deep understanding of strategies that may be deployed to cope with cultural dilemmas.

Multicultural societies and the dialogical self

The theory of the dialogical self offers a sophisticated analytical framework for the study of multicultural identifications since it suggests the relation of plural, competing cultural positions of multicultural youngsters to the notion of a person as a composite of multiple, often contradictory self-understandings. DST is also useful for the appreciation of the multiple identifications of people living in multicultural societies since it relates the increasing cultural complexity that is associated with the distribution of cultural meanings, practices and forms across populations with multivoicedness and dialogue among various cultural positions of the self.

In this context, it suffices to summarize that DST is inspired, on the one hand, by William James' (1890) classic distinction between *I* and *me*, and, on the other hand, by Bakhtin's (1984 [1929]) metaphor of the polyphonic novel, which allows for a multiplicity of positions among which dialogical relationships may be established. On the interface between these traditions, Hermans and Kempen (1993) have argued that the *I* has the ability to move from one spatial position to another in accordance with changes in situation and time. The *I* fluctuates among different and even opposed positions, and has the capacity to endow each position with a voice so that dialogical relationships between positions can be established. Bakhtin (1981: 360) especially proves very useful for the purpose of acknowledging the dialogue in which multicultural youngsters find themselves. He describes so-called 'hybrids' as having two voices, two languages, two consciousnesses, two epochs, being situated at 'the collision between differing points of view on the world' but also 'profoundly productive historically' and 'pregnant with potential for new world views'. Thus, Bakhtin creates the possibility for the self to be conceived of as a dynamic multiplicity of different and even contrasting positions or voices that allow mutual dialogical relationships.

Hermans (2002) has also drawn attention to the similarities between self and society, both functioning as a polyphony of consonant and dissonant voices since there is no essential difference between the positions a person takes as part of the self and the positions people take as members of a heterogeneous society (see also Hermans and Hermans-Konopka 2010). As a consequence, the dialogical self may be considered a 'society of the mind' (Hermans 2002) to the extent that different and contrasting cultures are represented in the diverse repertoire of collective voices playing a part in a multivoiced self. This insight, in turn, raises questions regarding the mixing of cultural positions or voices. Should we conceptualize of different cultural identifications of people living in multicultural societies as two separate cultural positions that are available and between which a person shifts from time to time, or, alternatively, is a third position emerging that may be a mixture of two original positions? And if a 'third space' emerges for the construction of a new, hybrid self (Bhabha 1990: 211), do the original positions retreat or even vanish, or do they continue to be accessible in their original form depending on changes taking place in spatial positions?

For several reasons, the conception of the self as multivoiced and dialogical has proved a valuable device for the analysis of the dynamic connections between the global and the local at the level of personal identifications (Hermans and Dimaggio 2007). First, in a globalizing world people are no longer living in bounded and relatively isolated societies that are radically different from other societies. Instead, an increasing number of people are living on the interfaces between societies, implying intimate contact with different cultural customs. And the increasing interconnectedness of societies and peoples leads not only to an increasing contact between different cultural groups but also to an increasing contact between different cultural conceptions within individual persons. Intercultural contact leads to the emergence of a multiplicity of cultural positions or voices coming together in the self of single individuals. And such positions may become engaged in mutual negotiations, agreements, disagreements, tensions and conflicts. The global–local nexus is, in other words, not just a reality outside the individual, but it is has also penetrated the self of multicultural individuals who have no option but to engage in a dialogue between their various cultural positions.

In contrast to societies in the past that tended to be more isolated, bounded and perhaps also homogeneous at least to some extent, contemporary societies are increasingly characterized by strong cultural differences, contrasts and oppositions. These require dialogical relationships in order to maintain some sort of equilibrium within society. When the world becomes more heterogeneous and multiple, however, the self of individuals making up that world also becomes more heterogeneous and multiple. For that reason, too, the self of individuals can only cope with its own differences, contrasts, tensions and uncertainties by developing dialogical relationships between the various dimensions of their lives. This requires a conception of the self in which processes of question and answer, agreement and disagreement, and negotiations between different parts of the self are recognized as intrinsic features of dealing with diversity.

A third reason why a dialogical conception of the multicultural self is required to orchestrate the dynamic relationship between global and local institutions is intertwined with the need to interact with people from a different cultural background by recognizing and accepting their alterity. This is necessary in a world in which divisions between different cultures can only be bridged by means of dialogical exchange. After all, only dialogue may contribute to making cultural differences meaningful and comprehensible (Hermans and Kempen 1998). Since other persons and groups with different cultural customs are increasingly part of an extended self in terms of a multiplicity of contradictory voices or positions, a dialogical conception of the self seems therefore also indispensable.

Here, it is important to highlight that a multiplicity of *I* positions is to be distinguished from a number of possible selves, the concept which still featured in the groundbreaking work of William James. The difference is that a number of possible selves are generally assumed to constitute part of a multifaceted self with one centralized *I* position, whereas the dialogical self 'has the character of a decentralized, polyphonic narrative with a multiplicity of *I* positions' (Hermans, Kempen and van Loon 1992: 30). This aspect of the dialogical self, too, is essential to make sense of the self of multicultural youngsters, who are torn between different cultural positions. Their cultural self is divided between home and more public spaces beyond home, and the shift from one position to another is even literally represented by a different voice, speaking either a Pacific language or English, or a mixture of the two in the form of a new patois that is emerging among youngsters meeting in multicultural spaces.

Another important feature of dialogical relationships between self and other is dominance, which Hermans and Kempen (1993: 73) exemplify with reference to the relationship between self and community. If the self is defined as a multiplicity of different *I*-positions, it may be argued that the community is not only able to address the self in a variety of positions, but also to let the self know how these positions, and the way the self functions in them, are approved. Exactly this occurs also in multicultural societies when young people are unable to express their cultural identity in terms of their parents' cultural background and likewise fail to subscribe to ideological notions of authenticity. In those situations, the self of adolescents growing up in multiple settings is usually monitored by the community approving or disapproving their behaviour and concomitant construction of a cultural position. Thus, communities also have the capacity to make some positions more dominant than others. And the dominance of cultural communities in the positioning process not only organizes but also restricts the multiplicity of possible positions in the public arena of multicultural societies.

An important implication of this form of cultural dominance is that some identifications are strongly developed, whereas others are suppressed or even disunited from self. Indeed, the prevalence of one identification implies the occasional neglect or suppression of another identification. Specific experiences, particularly negative experiences, may lead to the active suppression or even splitting of unwanted positions, slowing down the dialogical movements between different identifications. Dominance of one position over another may even reduce dialogical interchange to such an extent that monologue might seem a more appropriate term to describe the impact of cultural domination on the self. Monologue and dialogue, however, must not be considered as diametrically opposed to each other, but they characterize the theoretical boundaries of a graded continuum (Hermans and Hermans-Konopka 2010: 53–54). Thus, suppressed positions may be silenced by the strength of a dominant position, but they will rarely vanish completely from the repertoire of cultural positions and voices. For that reason, too, it may be argued that dialogical exchange between multiple identifications, albeit sometimes low key, will continue to characterize adolescents' constructions of multicultural realities as well as the position of their own self within it.

The dialogical self, then, is not a substance or an essence in its own right, as it exists only in a tensile relationship with all that is other and, most importantly, with other selves (see also Gardiner 1992: 73). For the same reason, the dialogical self is not a whole or a unified composition; instead, it is based on the assumption that there are many *I*-positions that can be occupied by the same person. At the same time, the dialogical self is intensely social, not in the sense that a self-contained individual enters into social interactions with other outside people, but in the sense that other people occupy positions within a multivoiced self (Hermans *et al.* 1992: 29).

The implications of this view of the – dialogical – self for the conception of the person as an individual in the West are, of course, revolutionary. DST transcends the separation between the individual and society by demonstrating that modern persons are not autonomous since the self is populated by others, including persons to whom the self feels close and persons to whom the self feels opposed. Contrary to the individualistic conception of the self, then, the most important implication of the dialogical perspective on the self is that it is not an intrapsychic but a relational phenomenon that transcends the boundaries between the inside and the outside, between self and other. Methodologically, this view has been elaborated in the form of an analogy between, on the one hand, the spatialization of the dialogical relations between the different *I*-positions, and, on the other hand, the simultaneity of voices within a self's discourse. This compelling perspective on the self has been extraordinarily influential over the past two decades since it makes a decisive contribution to the process of transcending the Cartesian *cogito* by tackling the pitfalls of individualism and rationalism (Hermans *et al.* 1992).

The Cartesian conception of the self is traditionally phrased in terms of the expression '*I* think', assuming that one centralized *I* is responsible for all steps in reasoning and thinking. William James made a first step towards escaping from what is known as the objection of solipsism against this assumption of Descartes, who in fact defined the existence of individual consciousness as separated from the existence of other people. In the conception of self as dialogical, this philosophical issue of individuality is finally resolved to the extent that the self is intricately interwoven with the other: the *I* is distinct from other people, but the *me* includes the perspective of the other in the self. In addition, the dialogical notion of the self constitutes a step beyond the Cartesian assumption that mental processes are essentially different from the body and other material extensions, since the body is included as part of the – material – self. The intrinsic relation between *I* and *me* precludes not only the supposition of a completely distinct *I*, but also a disembodied relationship between the *I* and the body. Thus, the dialogical conception of the self as multiple and extended exceeds the Cartesian *cogito* and opens up the avenue for a radical revision of the deeply entrenched notion of the person as individual.

In recent years, the transgression of the individual in the dialogical self has acquired new meaning in online communication. This is popular among migrants who are engaged in maintaining transnational connections with their kin in their home countries (see also Bhatia's chapter), but the internet makes it also possible for multicultural youngsters to diffuse their multiple identifications across various networks, online and off-line (Landzelius 2006) (see also Hevern's chapter). Since virtual networks enable them to escape from the pressure to abide by cultural traditions, their increasing participation in online communities often reflects a decreasing commitment to local activities. Thus, communication over the internet is not only a crucial resource to maintain a sense of community across boundaries (Howard 1999), but it also provides a platform to transgress boundaries and criticize cultural traditions, which some consider as suffocating (Morton 1999). The implications of this relatively new form of social interaction is that the self has become partible since it may be divided into online and off-line identifications. DST offers the tools to examine the interaction between various parts of the divided self. As such, it also concurs with comparative discussions about notions of personhood in cultural anthropology.

The partible person and the (in)dividual

Melani Anae (see above) sighed that she is a Samoan and not a Samoan, a Palagi, a New Zealander and not a New Zealander, a 'coconut', a Pacific Islander, a child, a person and what not. Indeed, she has difficulty to conceive of herself as one, undividable person. Her self is made up of a variety of different personas as she holds different cultural positions. And she did not seem to feel unified as one person, although she is perfectly capable of switching between different positions in different cultural contexts and also of (re)combining existing positions into new ones. DST makes it possible to analyse her dynamic self comprising a variety of cultural positions without diagnosing her as a person suffering from a dissociative identity disorder. For that reason, too, DST has far-reaching implications for the concept of the individual. It contributes to the further destabilization of the dichotomy between Western individualism and non-Western dividualism, which is deeply embedded in Western traditions of thinking.

The essentialist construction of an autonomous individual with a unitary and stable self in the West has always been grounded in a contrasting assumption that people in non-Western societies do not possess an individuated self that is differentiated from the other. As a corollary, a sociocentric model has long dominated Western perceptions of the non-Western self, presupposing that in non-Western societies a self is inseparable from the surrounding community. Although this dichotomy has been contested in recent years (e.g. Kusserow 1999; Murray 1993), the advancement and refinement of the dialogical self demonstrates that in the end the differences between the self of people in the West and the self of people in other parts of the world should not be exaggerated. In the long run, this may also help to bring about the inevitable dialogue between people with different cultural identities (see also Hermans and Kempen 1998).

The notion of the dialogical self makes it possible to bridge the divide in thinking about personhood in different societies since its implications for the concept of the individual are very similar to the implications of anthropological thinking about personhood in non-Western societies. In recent history, the debate about the person in anthropology has been enriched especially by ethnographic contributions from Melanesia, in particular the work by Marilyn Strathern. In her book *The Gender of the Gift* (1988), Strathern reflects on Melanesian notions of personhood, but her work is highly relevant to the dialogical self and social psychology at large since her analysis of Melanesian sociality is embedded in pioneering reflections about Western orthodoxies regarding the relationship between individual and society. Her insightful descriptions of the extent to which Melanesian persons are deeply embedded in social networks raise an issue that is very similar to the questions raised by the dialogical self, namely whether persons may still be represented as non-partible or as *in*-dividual?

Indeed, the innovation of Strathern's perspective lies mainly in the novelty of her image of the person as, just like the dialogical self, relationally constituted. For her the Melanesian person is not a unitary 'individual' but a 'dividual', multiply or plurally constituted of earlier contributions by other persons (Strathern 1988: 13). In Melanesia, according to Strathern, persons are constructed as the composite site of the relationships that produced them. Singular persons may be seen as a social microcosm, as the composite of collective relationships, as composite persons so to speak. The multiple and partible nature of composite persons is only revealed in social practice, when singular persons externalize their internal components in kinship or exchange relationships. Agency in this context consists therefore mainly in a process of personal decomposition.

Let me unpack this succinct description of what has become known in anthropology as the notion of the 'partible person', to begin with a quotation:

> Far from being regarded as unique entities, Melanesian persons are as dividually as they are individually conceived. They contain a generalized sociality within. Indeed, persons are frequently constructed as the plural and composite site of the relationships that produced them. (Strathern 1988: 13)

As Hermans (2002) argues that the self is a 'society of the mind', Strathern (1988: 13) argues that '(t)he singular person can be imagined as a social microcosm'. Both draw attention to the substantial links between people as constitutive of their web of social relationships. In Melanesia, however, these are predetermined by kinship relationships.

Furthermore, in Melanesia it is widely assumed that children are formed by the mixing of substances from both the mother and the father, menstrual blood and semen, which, in turn, are believed to be responsible for the constitution of female and male parts of the body. This understanding of procreation, positing different male and female parts in the reproduction of the person, appears to be quite common throughout Melanesia (Busby 1997: 270).

The implication of this belief for the gender of a person is, of course, that to some extent men and women are equivalent. The assumption that a body contains both male and female parts permits a conceptualization of the person as non-gendered, or rather, in Strathern's (1988: 183) terms, as cross-sex. A person's gender is imagined as dually or sometimes even multiply composed, as a result of which persons are effectively non-gendered or androgynous. Strathern does make clear that anatomical classifications of persons as either male or female are usually unproblematic, but that a gendered, single sex identity of Papuans is not self-evident. Only in ritual practices is the corporeal body represented as exclusively male or exclusively female. Since gender is principally displayed or revealed in ritual, while it fades away again after ritual performances, it may be described as performative. As such, gender is also inherently unstable.

The fluctuation of the gendered state of a person has also far-reaching implications for the concept of the body, which is regarded as 'a register, a site of . . . interaction' between male and female features of the person (Strathern 1988: 131). Since these reflect the genealogical connections with the mother and the father, the body may also be considered as 'a microcosm of relations'. As a consequence, it has no inherent properties or capacities either:

(I)f the body is composed of relations, if it shows the imprint of past encounters, then the relations are not in a state of stasis. . . These internal relations must either be further built upon or must be taken apart and fresh relationships instigated. (Strathern 1988: 131)

Since in Melanesian imagery a series of genealogical relationships is revealed in the body, it can be argued that first and foremost it is composed of specific actions of other persons. The Melanesian person, however, cannot be thought of as a mere locus of historic roles or a constellation of prior statuses. Instead, the social person in Melanesia appropriates its own history through the genealogical connections that are embedded in the body (Strathern 1988: 132). As the dialogical self shifts the focus from external roles to internal positions, the Melanesian person is likewise a nodal point in a web of historic relationships. This perception of the person as a bundle of relationships must also be understood against the background of Melanesian procreation theories, on the basis of which different body parts are identified as of either gender. Thus, a unitary identity encompasses within itself other identities, which in gender terms may belong to the opposite sex (Strathern 1988: 122).

'In being multiple', Strathern (1988: 185) argues, the Melanesian person 'is also partible, an entity that can dispose of parts in relation to others'. Strathern illustrates her view of the partibility of the so-called composite person, or the dividual, with a complex ethnographic analysis of the exchange relationships that are so highly characteristic of Melanesia (Gell 1999). It is beyond the scope of this chapter to expand on Melanesian exchange, but it is relevant to make explicit the implications of Strathern's analysis for the relation between individual and society (cf. Strathern 1991). In this context, Strathern draws on indigenous narratives in order to compare and contrast Melanesian with non-Melanesian perspectives on relationships.

In a comparative analysis of indigenous and Western world views, the nature of Melanesian perspectivism is crucial. In a Melanesian view, perspectives generally take on the form of analogies, which are based on similarities between signs that in the Western view do not structurally correspond. In Western perspectives, on the contrary, the focus is usually on homologies, on structural correspondence between signs that are considered as related (see also Wagner 1977). Consequently, in the Melanesian view, different perspectives are mutually interchangeable when they are based on analogical relationships. In the Melanesian view a particular perspective may be exchanged for an analogical perspective that is considered as completely different from the Western viewpoint. Since there is no structural difference between the forms in which persons and relations appear, for example, Melanesians may regard a member of a lineage as both like and unlike the lineage itself. Rather than being considered as part of a whole lineage, there is no structural difference between members and lineages. By the same token, lineages are generally not viewed as wholes made up of distinct members. Indeed, one may instantly turn into another: in my body the genealogical connections of the entire lineage are represented. The point is that in Melanesia there are no principles of organization that are not also found in the constitution of the person. No switch of perspective between person and relations is required in order to observe social relations. A person is social relations, and social relations is a person, but also a whole network of relationships. Exchanging perspectives only differentiates one set of relations from another, as it does one kind of person from another.

Projecting this insight onto the mirror imagery of Western societies makes it apparent that we do not normally see relations when observing a person, since we do switch perspectives in the representation of the relation between person and group, or individual and society. From a Western perspective the relation between person and group is, rather than an analogy, a homology of part and whole. This image of the person as a part cut from a whole, however, is, according to Strathern, in need of revision in light of the insights in the creativity of other, notably Melanesian recombinations of parts and wholes, of persons and groups, of groups and society. Strathern (1994: 216) cogently argues that Melanesians generally do not experience fundamental problems with the question of how to fit together parts of a whole, nor with bits and pieces that have to be reconfigured for the sake of an authentic community or a real society. In light of this insight, I would argue, it has become inevitable to revise the Western perspective on the relation of person to group, which departs from the proposition that persons are foremost members of cultural groupings or a society, and that they should therefore be regarded as having a pre-existing identity (Strathern 1994: 206–207). Thus, the pioneering contribution to the anthropology of the person by Marilyn Strathern may also be used to develop a critique of Western discourses regarding the person, and, more specifically, regarding the assumed boundedness and individuality of the person in Western societies. As such, it arrives at conclusions regarding the individual that are remarkably similar to the conclusions that can be drawn from DST.

Concluding remarks

The ethnography of some non-Western societies demonstrates that persons are not universally considered as unitary 'individuals'. Instead, persons are frequently regarded as 'dividuals', multiply or plurally constituted of earlier contributions by other persons (e.g. Marriott 1976; Piot 1999). In Melanesia, for example, persons are constructed as the composite site of the relationships that produced them. Singular persons are seen as a social microcosm, as the composite of collective relationships, as composite persons so to speak.

This view of the composite person parallels the discourse of DST to the extent that it is also centred on the view of a person as a composite of many, often contradictory, *I*-positions, self-understandings and identities, the loci of which are not confined to the body but extend into the surrounding environment. This notion of the person implies that it is no longer equalized to the individual, but, instead, it is regarded as dividual, as partible. The person is, in other words, a composition of relationships through which the self is deeply intertwined with others. Thus, the person also extends outside its own self, and this conception simultaneously destabilizes the boundedness of the person within the body. The destabilization of the individual and the disembodiment of the self from the body constitute the two main similarities between the partible person and the dialogical self. Ultimately, the dialogical self may therefore also imply the end of the concept of the individual.

Apart from the striking similarities between the partible person and the dialogical self, there are, of course, also differences. The notion of the partible person has been developed in an anthropological discourse grounded in Melanesian ethnography, while the concept of the dialogical self emerged primarily in Western psychology. This raises the question of to what extent the partible person may be involved in dialogue and, by the same token, the extent to which the dialogical self is partible. Although the precise relationship between partibility and dialogue may be established only in empirical research, the principle of rapport is based on complementarity, as may be inferred from the analysis of the highly dynamic identifications of people living in multicultural circum-stances. Although the cultural dilemmas faced by many youngsters growing up in multicultural societies may lead to the increasing partibility of their identifications, as in online and off-line spaces, the possibility that a new hybrid self made up of two or more different cultural positions may emerge cannot be excluded. Hermans and Hermans-Konopka (2010: 325) have recently also demonstrated that the increasing partibility of positions does not necessarily contradict the reintegration of positions at other times or in other spaces. Decentring movements of the self may well parallel centring movements of the self.

Since decentralization is generally complemented by the centralization of the self, the relationship between partibility and dialogue can be considered as a continuum. Interestingly, both ends of this continuum shift the attention away from the connotations of the concept of indi-viduality, and this resonates with the problems identified in the analysis of the multiple identifications of multicultural youngsters. Only divi-duality makes it possible to do justice to the full range of cultural positions held by multicultural youngsters who cannot abandon their ethnic genealogies yet simultaneously interrelate with cosmopolitian culture as a matter of course. Rather than attempting to squeeze the variety of cultural positions held by multicultural youngsters into a conception of them as indivisible individuals, it is instead more realistic, even more human, to depart from their partibility into a series of inter-connected yet distinct cultural identifications which are in continuous dialogue. As the partibility of self is rapidly becoming more and more standard among people living in multicultural circumstances, a dialogical perspective is necessary to take into account all aspects of people's lives without suppressing part or whole at any moment.

REFERENCES

Anae, M. (1997) Towards a NZ-born Samoan identity: some reflections on 'labels', *Pacific Health Dialog*, **4**, 128–137

(2001) The new 'Vikings of the Sunrise': New Zealand-borns in the Information Age, in C. Macpherson, P. Spoonley and M. Anae (eds.), *Tangata O Te Moana Nui: The Evolving Identities of Pacific Peoples in Aotearoa/ New Zealand* (Palmerston North: Dunmore Press), 101–121

Appadurai, A. (1996) *Modernity at Large: Cultural Dimensions of Globalization* (Minneapolis, MN: University of Minnesota Press, Public Worlds), vol. I

Bakhtin, M. (1981) *The Dialogical Imagination: Four Essays* (Austin, TX: University of Texas Press)

(1984) *Problems of Dostoevsky's Poetics* (Minneapolis, MN, and London: University of Minnesota Press)

Bhabha, H. K. (1990) *Nation and Narration* (London: Routledge)

Busby, C. (1997) Permeable and partible persons: a comparative analysis of gender and body in South India and Melanesia, *Journal of the Royal Anthropological Institute*, **3**, 261–278

Castells, M. (1996) *The Information Age: Economy, Society and Culture*. Vol. I: *The Rise of the Network Society* (Oxford: Blackwell)

Gardiner, M. (1992) *The Dialogics of Critique: M. M. Bakhtin and the Theory of Ideology* (London and New York: Routledge)

Gell, A. (1999) Strathernograms, or the semiotics of mixed metaphors, in A. Gell (ed.), *The Art of Anthropology: Essays and Diagrams*. London School of Economics Monographs on Social Anthropology, vol. 67 (London: Athlone), 29–75 (edited posthumously by E. Hirsch)

Goss, J. and Lindquist, B. (2000) Placing movers: an overview of the Asian-Pacific migration system, *The Contemporary Pacific*, **12**, 385–414

Hermans, H. J. M. (1998) Moving cultures: the perilous problems of cultural dichotomies in a globalizing society, *American Psychologist*, **53**, 1111–1120

(2002) The dialogical self as a society of mind, *Theory & Psychology*, **12**, 147–160

Hermans, H. J. M. and Dimaggio, G. (2007) Self, identity, and globalization in times of uncertainty: a dialogical analysis, *Review of General Psychology*, **11**, 31–61

Hermans, H. J. M. and Hermans-Konopka, A. (2010) *Dialogical Self Theory: Positioning and Counter-Positioning in a Globalizing Society* (Cambridge University Press)

Hermans, H. J. M. and Kempen, H. J. G. (1993) *The Dialogical Self: Meaning as Movement* (San Diego, CA: Academic Press)

Hermans, H. J. M., Kempen, H. J. G. and van Loon, R. J. P. (1992) The dialogical self: beyond individualism and rationalism, *American Psychologist*, **47**, 23–33

Howard, A. (1999) Pacific-based virtual communities: Rotuma on the World Wide Web, *The Contemporary Pacific*, **11**, 160–175

James, W. (1890) *The Principles of Psychology* (London: Macmillan), vol. I

Kusserow, A. S. (1999) Crossing the great divide: anthropological theories of the Western self, *Journal of Anthropological Research*, **55**, 541–562

Landzelius, K. (ed.) (2006) *Native on the Net: Indigenous and Diasporic Peoples in the Virtual Age* (London and New York: Routledge)

Lee, H. M. (2003) *Tongans Overseas: Between Two Shores* (Honolulu: University of Hawai'i Press)

     (2004) All Tongans are connected: Tongan transnationalism, in V. S. Lockwood (ed.), *Globalization and Culture Change in the Pacific Islands* (Upper Saddle River, NJ: Pearson Prentice-Hall), 133–148

Macpherson, C., Spoonley, P. and Anae, M. (eds.) (2001) *Tangata O Te Moana Nui: The Evolving Identities of Pacific Peoples in Aotearoa/New Zealand* (Palmerston North: Dunmore Press)

Marriott, M. (1976) Hindu transactions: diversity without dualism, in B. Kapferer (ed.), *Transactions and Meaning: Directions in the Anthropology of Exchange and Symbolic Behavior* (Philadelphia: Institute for the Study of Human Issues), 109–142

van Meijl, T. (2006) Multiple identifications and the dialogical self: Maori youngsters and the cultural renaissance, *Journal of the Royal Anthropological Institute*, **12**, 917–933

     (2010) Anthropological perspectives on identity: from sameness to difference, in M. Wetherell and C. T. Mohanty (eds.), *The Sage Handbook of Identities* (London: Sage), 63–81

Morton, H. (1999) Islanders in space: Tongans online, in R. King and J. Connell (eds.), *Small Worlds, Global Lives: Islands and Migration* (London and New York: Pinter), 235–253

Murray, D. W. (1993) What is the Western concept of self? On forgetting David Hume, *Ethos*, **21**, 3–23

Piot, C. (1999) *Remotely Global: Village Modernity in West Africa* (University of Chicago Press)

Small, C. (1997) *Voyages: From Tongan villages to American Suburbs* (Ithaca, NY, and London: Cornell University Press)

Strathern, M. (1998) *The Gender of the Gift: Problems with Women and Problems with Society in Melanesia* (Berkeley, CA: University of California Press)

     (1991) *Partial Connections* (Savage, MD: Rowman and Littlefield, ASAO Special Publications no. 3)

     (1994) Parts and wholes: refiguring relationships, in R. Borofsky (ed.), *Assessing Cultural Anthropology* (New York: McGraw-Hill), 204–217

Wagner, R. (1977) Analogic kinship: a Daribi example, *American Ethnologist*, **4**, 623–642

6 Acculturation and the dialogical formation of immigrant identity: race and culture in diaspora spaces

Sunil Bhatia

The race-related riots in the towns of Bradford, Oldham and Burnley in the UK in the summer of 2001; the rise in post-9/11 hate acts against South Asian immigrants – especially Muslim immigrants in the UK and the USA; the violent uprising and nightly torching of cars in Paris suburbs in 2006; the murder of Theo van Gogh in The Netherlands in 2004; the 'honour killings' in Germany in 2008; the recent increase in racially motivated 'curry-bashing' attacks in 2009 on Indian students in Australia; and the French parliament's decision in June 2010 to ban the wearing of full-face veils, such as the burka, hijab and niqab, in public places have brought to the forefront issues related to ethnic identity and acculturation. As I was finishing this chapter, other events have also taken centre stage in the US media. Terry Jones, the pastor of a small church in Florida in the USA, has decided to mark 11 September by burning copies of the holy Koran. On 5 September, *The New York Times* published an article titled 'American Muslims Ask, Will We Ever Belong'. In that article, Eboo Patel, the leader of an interfaith youth project in Chicago, said, 'I am more scared than I have ever been—more scared than I was after Sept. 11.'

These acculturative events and the heated rhetoric dramatizing them have forced psychologists to rethink how we define acculturation in a world where international borders are becoming porous, and journeys, travel and migration between geographical spaces are common. What does it mean to 'belong' as a transnational immigrant with ties to multiple societies, homes, religion and identities? What does it mean for transnational immigrants to integrate and assimilate in their new world? Rethinking acculturation research so that it includes the varied, sometimes contradictory, and often racialized and politicized experiences of new immigrants provides a very valuable site from which psychology has an opportunity to remake itself as a field that continues to be relevant in a world that is rapidly becoming transnational, diverse and global.

In this chapter, I argue that acculturation for many transnational immigrants is essentially a contested, dynamic and dialogical process. In particular, I use examples from the Indian diaspora to demonstrate that such a dialogical process involves a constant moving back and forth between various cultural voices that are connected to various sociocultural contexts and are shaped by issues of power and constructions of otherness (Bhatia 2007, 2008, 2010; Bhatia and Ram 2004, 2009). In contrast to cross-cultural psychology's conception of acculturation, I use selective examples from an extensive ethnography done on the Indian diaspora (see Bhatia 2007) to highlight the larger sociocultural and political contexts that are implicated in both the dynamics of acculturation and the dialogical formation of immigrant identity.

Acculturation, immigration and psychology

The displacement of millions of migrant labourers, refugees and professionals from the postcolonial 'Third World' to the 'First World', and the formation of numerous migrant 'ethnic enclaves', is now one of the most important defining features of the twenty-first century. Furthermore, questions about migration and the construction of identity are paramount today as the rate of immigration to the USA rapidly increased in the 1990s to 'nearly a million new immigrants per year' (Suárez-Orozco and Suárez-Orozco 2001: 55). This kind of identity negotiation is commonplace in European migrant communities that consist of Mexican-Americans, Chinese-Canadians, Turkish-Germans, French-Algerians, Moroccan-Dutch and British-Indians. These non-European/non-white diasporic communities bring into sharp relief the sense of constantly negotiating between here and there, past and present, homeland and hostland, self and other. Such negotiations have not been adequately recognized or understood in many of the existing acculturation models in psychology (Bhatia and Ram 2001; Chirkov 2009; Rudmin 2009).

Traditionally, much of mainstream psychology has been occupied with developing universal, linear models and theories of immigrant identity, acculturation and adaptation. For instance, cross-cultural psychologists have studied topics such as acculturation and acculturative stress (Berry 1998), socialization and enculturation (Camilleri and Malewska-Peyre 1997), and bicultural identity (LaFromboise, Coleman and Gerton 1998). Prominent in acculturation research is the model of acculturation strategies proposed by Berry and his colleagues (e.g. Berry 1980, 1990, 1997). For the last three decades, this acculturation model has been the most widely used in the social sciences in North America and Europe, and it continues to provide the conceptual foundations for numerous empirical and experimental studies on acculturation and immigrant identity (Bhatia and Ram 2009). These authors' prolific output, and the fact that several major introductory books on psychology (e.g. Halonen and Santrock 1996; Travis and Wade 1997; Westen 1997) cite them extensively, indicate that their model of acculturation strategies is one of the most influential on the subject as developed in cross-cultural psychology.

Acculturation strategies refer to the plan or the method that individuals use in responding to stress-inducing new cultural contexts. A fourfold classification is proposed which includes 'assimilation', 'integration', 'separation' and 'marginalization'. Berry and his colleagues suggest that an *assimilation* strategy occurs when individuals decide not to maintain their cultural identity by seeking contact in their daily interaction with the dominant group. When the individuals from the non-dominant group 'place a value on holding on to their original culture' (Berry and Sam 1997: 297), and seek no contact with the dominant group, they are pursuing a *separation* strategy. When individuals express an interest in maintaining strong ties in their everyday life both with their ethnic group and with the dominant group, the *integration* strategy is defined. The fourth strategy is *marginalization*, in which individuals 'lose cultural and psychological contact with both their traditional culture and the larger society' (Berry 1998: 119). The optimal acculturation strategy for immigrants is integration, which 'appears to be a consistent predictor of more positive outcomes than the three alternatives' (Berry and Sam 1997: 318). Integration implies both the preservation of home culture and an active involvement with the host culture.

Central to the theory of integration strategy is the assumption of universality. Berry and his colleagues take the position that although there are 'substantial variations in the life circumstances of the cultural groups that experience acculturation, the psychological processes that operate during acculturation are essentially the same for all the groups; that is, they adopt a *universalist perspective* on acculturation' (emphasis in original; Berry and Sam 1997: 296). Drawing and developing upon previous research, Berry and his colleagues maintain that other psychological processes, such as 'behavioural shifts', 'culture shedding', 'culture shock' and 'acculturative stress', are also experienced in varying degrees by an individual undergoing acculturation (Berry 1998; Berry and Sam 1997). So what are these universal psychological processes? What does it mean to say that all groups manifest the same kind of 'psychological' thinking during the acculturation process? What is the basis for analytically separating the psychological from the cultural?

Are the 'psychological processes' similar for individuals who migrate to the USA from Western European countries such as the UK and Germany, as opposed to, say, individuals who migrate from previously colonized countries such as India and Kenya?

In contrast to these psychological models of acculturation discussed above, the notion of 'diasporas' has become increasingly utilized to understand immigrant experiences, and in the last decade there has emerged a distinct area referred to as 'diaspora studies' (for a review, see Tölöyan 1996). The term 'diaspora' emphasizes the ongoing negotiations that many immigrants undertake at multiple levels with their host culture and their native homeland (Hall 1991). Race has always played a key role in US state-sponsored immigration, naturalization and citizenship laws (López 1996; Mohanty 1991). Moreover, given the existence of racial prejudice in American and European society, non-European/non-white immigrants have been more likely to face exclusion and discrimination than their European counterparts. Subsequently, through personal and collective remembering, tales of discrimination, hardships and sheer exploitation are kept alive in most non-European, non-white immigrant communities. Such narratives have played a large part in constructing and maintaining what are known as diasporas.

Diasporas distinctly attempt to maintain (real and/or imagined) connections and commitments to their homeland *and* to recognize themselves and act as a collective community. In other words, people who simply live outside their ancestral homeland cannot automatically be considered diasporas (Tölöyan 1996). Tölöyan attributes the expanding usage of this term in part to the acceleration of immigration to the industrialized worlds; to the lack of assimilation of many immigrant groups; to institutional links with the homeland; to sustained work by many immigrant groups to create and maintain their own religious institutions, language schools, community centres, newspapers, radio stations; and to the American university itself, where many diasporan elites have converged to forge theoretical sites to address immigrant identity and transnational locations. Diasporas are usually formed when the immigrant community in question does not find its culture represented in the mainstream host culture and when immigrants experience the absence, erasure (e.g. through intentional efforts to promote assimilation into the host's mainstream culture) and silencing of their culture by members of and practices within the host culture. For non-European/non-white transnational diasporic communities in particular, there is a constant and politicized negotiation of the meaning of 'here' versus 'there', 'then' versus 'now', homeland and hostland, and self and other (Glick-Schiller, Basch and Szanton-Blanc 1995).

The Indian diaspora in Yankee land

There are approximately 1.7 million Indians who live in various diasporic communities across the USA. According to the 2000 US census, the Indian-American community is one of the fastest growing immigrant communities in the USA. From 1990 to 2000, there was a 106% increase in the growth rate of Indian-Americans, compared to the average 7% growth rate in the general population. This shift marks the largest growth in the Asian-American community (Bhatia 2007). By all accounts, the immigration reform of 1965 is considered as being most significant and profoundly influential for the history of Indian immigration. The 1965 Immigrant Act fundamentally changed the background of the Indian migrants in the USA. Within a very short span of time, Indian migrants in the USA made the transition from being 'pariahs to elite' (Rangaswamy 2000: 40). Unlike the first wave of the Punjabi Sikh diaspora, the second wave of Indian migrants are highly skilled professionals. They are medical doctors, engineers, scientists, university professors, and doctoral and postdoctoral students in mostly science-related disciplines, such as chemistry, biochemistry, mathematics, physics, biology and medicine. Prashad (2000: 75) writes that between 1966 and 1977, 83 per cent of Indians who emmigrated to the USA were highly skilled professionals, comprising about '20,000 scientists with Ph.Ds, 40,000 engineers, and 25,000 doctors'. These professional Indians have made their 'home' in suburban diasporas in towns and cities all across America.

Despite achieving tremendous economic success in the USA, the professionals in the Indian diaspora experience varying levels of racism and discrimination in their workplace and their suburban communities. The skin colour, bindi, sari, food, gods and goddesses, and 'thick accents' of the professional Indians become the main vehicles through which much of the racism is directed towards various members of the Indian diaspora by their suburban neighbours and co-workers. For example, Deepali, a biochemist, struggles to find play dates for her daughter, Karishma, because her daughter is seen as different by her suburban neighbours. Venkat, a top-level executive at the local computer company, talks about many painful occasions when both his children asked him why they were brown and different from white children. Neelam, a university professor, talks about how her daughter's bindi was ripped off by a 6-year-old boy on the first day of school. How do these professional, elite, transnational migrants understand their racial designation as non-white people or 'people of colour'?

Dialogical self, voice and identity

I employ DST to understand how professional Indians, living in a Connecticut suburb in the eastern USA, negotiate their multiple ethnic and racial identities. Prior work on the dialogical self and migration has shown that acculturation is essentially a dialogical process (Bhatia 2002; Cresswell 2009; Hermans and Dimaggio 2007; Hermans and Hermans-Konopka 2010; Tardif-Williams and Fisher 2009). Such a process involves a constant moving back and forth between *I*-positions that are both constructed and constrained by issues of race, sexuality and gender. More specifically, the dialogical model of self allows us to analyse how the 'voices' of the larger majority play an important role in shaping the identity of migrants living in diaspora spaces.

In the last decade, a number of psychologists have adopted DST to understand the multiple and shifting contours of individual identity (Hermans and Kempen 1993; Hermans and Hermans-Konopka 2010; Josephs 1998; Ragatt 2000; Sampson 1993; Valsiner 2000; Wertsch 1991, 1998). Drawing on Bakhtin's concept of polyphony and multi-voicedness, Hermans constructs a dialogical conception of self. One important dimension of the polyphonic novel is the distinction between 'logical' and 'dialogical' relationships. Hermans, Kempen and van Loon (1992) outline this difference by using Bakhtin's examples: 'life is good' and 'life is good'. They suggest that from an Aristotelian perspective, these two phrases are connected by a relationship of identity and are exactly the same. However, from a dialogical point of view, they may be described as a sequence in a conversation that involves two separate persons in agreement with each other. These two phrases can be seen as different utterances or speech acts. Thus, the first phrase, 'life is good', is a statement, and the second phrase, 'life is good', is a confirmation (Hermans *et al.* 1992: 27).

The polyphonic novel – with its multitude of characters, each with his or her own voice and ideological positions that are independent but yet linked to the voices of the *other*, through internal or external dialogue – plays a crucial role in the formulation of the dialogical self (Bakhtin 1984). As with Dostoevsky's characters, Hermans and his colleagues conceive of the self in terms of a number of dynamic but relatively autonomous *I*-positions that are in dialogue with both real, actual and imagined others. The '*I*' is not static but can move from one position to another with changes in time and circumstances:

The 'I' fluctuates among different and even opposed 'I' positions. The 'I' has the capacity to imaginatively endow each position with a voice so that dialogical relations between positions can be established. The voices function like interacting characters in a story, involved in the process of question and answer, agreement and disagreement. The dialogical self is conceived as social; not in the sense that a self-contained individual enters into social interactions with other outside people, but in the sense that other people occupy positions in the multivoiced self. (Hermans *et al.* 1992: 28–29)

From the point of view of the DST, individual *I*-positions can be in disagreement, contradiction, opposition and agreement. The concept of voice and positions in the dialogical self can be analysed by the metaphor of space. Hermans (1996: 44) argues that 'voice assumes an embodied actor located in space' acting and coordinating with other actors. Similarly, a position is always located in either relation or opposition to other positions. The concept of 'voice and position' can be metaphorically employed to define the dialogical self as an 'imaginal space' between different positions.

The concept of voice allows us to focus on the idea that an immigrant's racial and cultural identity emerges through a dialogical process that constantly moves back and forth between incompatible cultural positions (Bhatia 2002). Rather than posit migrant identity as an allocation of different cultural components in a fortuitous, congenial amalgam, the concept of dialogue and voice allows us to emphasize the constant contradiction, struggle and negotiation that immigrants experience between different cultural selves. It is this process of negotiation and contestation between different voices that adds varying levels of complexity to the study of identity in the diaspora (Bhatia 2002; Bhatia and Ram 2001, 2004).

Contradictions of cultural positions: an example

The majority of Indian participants documented in my book *American Karma: Race, Culture and Identity in the Indian Diaspora* (Bhatia 2007) faced varying levels of racism and discrimination, but were largely unwilling to frame their selves in terms of having a racial identity. On the surface, it would appear that these professional Indians have 'made it' in America and ultimately are integrated within the larger society. Their stories of racism and prejudice, however, force them to reposition their identities as the cultural other, as they carve out an isolated space for themselves in the suburban diaspora. These different voices represent the multiple, shifting and often conflicting cultural positions in the diaspora. Venkat, a 42-year-old Indian immigrant, began his interview by telling me that he had achieved a lot of his goals during his life. He has a doctoral degree in management and is director of the eastern region for sales and marketing in the PC division at the local multinational computer company. Venkat felt it was important to underscore the point that his 'Indianness' did not play any role in his accomplishments. He emphasized that it was his talent, hard work and persistence that put him on a successful trajectory in corporate America. Venkat remarked, 'I did my Ph.D., and in everything I did, I was successful. Every career or otherwise endeavours I have taken, I've done them well, and it has nothing to do with whether I am Indian or not.' Venkat said that his nationality did not put him at a disadvantage with his white co-workers because everyone experiences some form of discrimination and prejudice. He said:

If I was a white American male, you know, maybe there would be prejudice because I'm too short. So, it doesn't really matter. It doesn't really matter. Everybody has their own, you know, pet peeve, I guess. So being an Indian, I don't think it put me at a different spot. Or at least, that's how I feel.

In an earlier part of the interview, Venkat had mentioned that he was seen as 'Indian' and therefore 'different' by many of his co-workers, that his being a foreigner and having an accent would never allow him to achieve his full potential in corporate America. During our conversations, I recalled his earlier statements from the interview and asked Venkat whether or not he thought being Indian had ever specifically prevented him from getting promoted to the upper-level management. Venkat said that his Indian values, cultural habits and educational background had prepared him well to meet the challenges of his workplace, but that his being 'different' never affected his work life. According to Venkat, every person is subjected to some form of prejudice, including white Americans:

Yeah, there is discrimination, because you are Indian, but, okay, suppose you are a white American, okay. No difference whether your name ... or if you have a Jewish name. I know for sure a friend of mine, Schwiekert, it's a German name. He did not get a job in a company because the guy who was interviewing him thought he was Jewish. He's a white blond, blue eyes, can't get more white.

Venkat had mentioned to me that, 'had it not been for his Indianness', he would have risen much higher in his career. He was also disturbed about his son's and daughter's experiences with racism at their school. His daughter had once asked him, 'Why am I brown?' So I was surprised when Venkat told me that his Indianness had no adverse effects on his work life. What were the reasons behind the contradictions and inconsistencies in Venkat's interview?

Venkat and many other upper-class Indians describe themselves as privileged 'model minorities', but they are also positioned as outsiders, foreigners with 'thick accents', brown skin, and different customs and traditions. In order to counter these positions, many Indians actively place themselves as 'the same as' or 'similar to' the majority of Americans by invoking the *I*-positions of universal human nature ('racism is universal, everyone is prejudiced') and American benevolence ('America has given me success', 'America is a great country so why talk about racism?'), and by shoring up their professional identity ('I am a scientist so race or racism does not matter in performing one's role as a doctor, software engineer or biochemist').

Many of the Indians I interviewed made strategic attempts to convert their difference into positions of sameness. That is, some of the participants wanted to establish their identity as being very similar to the dominant majority. This kind of assertion is based on a dialogical relationship in which there is also a strategic identification with the voice that represents the dominant majority. Venkat's interview also illustrates the theoretical significance of the concept of positioning. Hermans and Hermans-Konopka explain: 'As a verb [*position*] it shows the dynamic aspect of the process of receiving, finding and taking one's place in the field of social relationships. There is an active *placing* of oneself in particular relationships. A significant theoretical advantage of the concept is that it can also be used in the passive form: being *positioned* by others, *being placed* by others and with oneself' (2010: 150). When Venkat is placed and positioned by others as a minority, he counter-positions his difference by invoking the 'voice of sameness'. Venkat establishes sameness or equivalence in identity by equating his experience of discrimination or prejudice with the experiences of the dominant majority. Venkat is placed in the field of contradictory and incompatible positions in which there is an acceptance of racial positions assigned to him by powerful others and a simultaneous rejection of these positions. In other words, by equating his experience of racial difference with other forms of prejudice that some white people experience, Venkat finds a way to form a strategic positioning with the dominant majority. Such an identification also involves seeing his voice and subject positioning as being equal to each other. Thus, Venkat's negotiations with self result in a 'higher density of cultural positions' that in turn create 'larger differences and even contradictions' in his self-repertoire (Hermans and Hermans-Konopka 2010: 150).

Venkat's narrative from the Indian diaspora is not an exception. On the one hand, many Indian professionals have clearly articulated that they did not reach the highest position in their company because they were Indian, but, on the other hand, they were not willing to be considered as having racialized identities. This simultaneous acceptance and rejection of their difference can be described as a 'double-voiced' discourse. This double-voiced discourse is carried out between both the individual's speaking voice and the dominant voice of the majority. Hermans and Kempen (1993: 77) note that 'each word that is spoken by an individual speaker is "double voiced": a word has always two directions, both towards the object of speech and towards a word originating from another person's speech.' The Indian migrants' attempt to establish sameness with the dominant majority represents a move towards demonstrating equivalence of power. The voice of the other originates from a group, a society or an institute and tends to occupy a strong presence in the mind of those individuals who are from the minority groups.

The role of power and race in the dialogical self

Drawing on Linell's concept of power in dialogical relations, Hermans and Kempen (1993) note that interactional dominance deals with a 'pattern of asymmetry in terms of initiative-response' structure. Concepts of social power and dominance play an important role in the theory of the dialogical self (see Hermans and Salgado 2010). The dominant party is the one who makes the most invitatory moves: the contributions that strongly determine the unfolding local context. The Indian immigrants' move towards establishing equality with the dominant majority then represents an attempt to reposition the interactional dominance between their many interior voices. These immigrants were identifying with their white colleagues and were representing themselves as no longer being the subordinate party whose voices are controlled and regulated by the hegemonic majority. This repositioning of self in relation to the dominant other implies that the participants are reasserting their power as agents capable of reshaping their assignations. Such back-and-forth play between voices of difference and voices of sameness also implies that the participants were foregrounding or backgrounding their Indianness strategically as situations unfolded at work (Bhatia 2007).

These identifications are strategic because they reveal how professional participants use their multiple voices and shifting *I*-positions to reconstruct meanings about their difference. These dialogical strategies, choices and tactics are used by many Indian professionals to understand their racial identities and cope with their sense of difference in the work world. Seeing themselves primarily as scientists or engineers allows them to create sameness with their American co-workers and also provides these Indian professionals with a conceptual framework to describe their identities that transcends culture, race and gender issues. These dialogical strategies also demonstrate that many Indians, despite experiencing racism and discrimination in their life, are ambivalent about their racial identity and are often very reluctant to see themselves as raced, 'brown people'.

What role does race play in the Indian immigrants' subjective understanding of their identity as a group? The responses of the Indian migrants from the diaspora show that, in some cases, there is direct resistance on the part of the participants to cast their identities in racial terms. In other cases, they have an ambiguous view about their racial identities. Prashad (2000) writes that Indians in the USA are aware that they are not part of mainstream, American, 'white' culture, but they also realize that they are not 'black' either. On one hand, he writes, *desis* (Indians living abroad) have denied their 'blackness' in America, 'partly out of a desire for class mobility'. On the other hand, he says, 'Indians have formed political connections with other minority groups to express solidarity, but mostly the alliances with minority groups have been formed to gain some of the resources for advancement guaranteed to historically oppressed minorities by the states' (Prashad 2000: 94–99). Indian-Americans are comfortable with the idea that they differ from mainstream America in terms of culture and ethnicity, but not in terms of their racial identity. George (1997) explains:

What is refused by nearly all upper and middle class South Asians is not so much a specific racial identity but the very idea of being raced. The only identity that is acknowledged is the cultural and ethnic one of being no more and no less than 'Indian-American'. (1997: 29)

The Indian diaspora's reluctance to be cast as persons of colour – as having a racial identity – can be explained in several ways. George states that many South Asians living in the USA want to make themselves racially invisible. The move towards invisibility is made by constructing their personhood in terms of class and cultural formations. For example, there is a tendency among many Indian-Americans to represent themselves to Americans as being from the glorious ancient Indian civilization, the spiritual and cultural East, or the pure Aryan race.

Such a stance, notes George (1997), is intended to reposition their negative portrayal as 'immigrants of colour' to a positive ascription of belonging to a superior culture. This stance is intended to distance Indian-Americans from other people and communities of colour residing in the USA. She explains: 'Recognizing this commonality across ethnicity supplied by brownness of one's skin requires that one surrender the comfort offered by a seemingly race-free but culturally value-loaded Indianness' (George 1997: 43).

Many participants form the Indian diaspora – who describe themselves as model minorities – are from upper-caste/class positions in India, and they also bring with them racial attitudes about caste and class-based hierarchies from their homeland to their new world. These strategies, according to George, should be read as 'symptomatic of the upper-caste South Asian determination to occupy a position that is simultaneously privileged and unmarked: the place of invisibility' (1997: 45). This desire to occupy the place of invisibility and to be seen as 'Aryan' is demonstrated repeatedly in the history of Indian migration to the USA. It is important to keep in mind that the idea of denying, erasing or muting one's racial identity is not tantamount to a 'straightforward desire for whiteness' (George 1997: 42). Furthermore, George tells us that the confusion about racial identity in the South Asian diaspora can be best described by using the term 'ambiguous non-whites'. This term, she notes, 'allows for an identity as non-white and as white (because it is ambiguous): in either case the racial marker around which identity revolves is white' (1997: 43). The acculturation processes of these migrant groups involve a dynamic repositioning of the dimensions of race, ethnicity, nationality, language and class. Some of these migrant communities actively changed the identities that were given to them, and some other migrant groups found it difficult to change the identities that were assigned by others.

Acculturation as a dialogical and multivoiced process

In contrast to the model of acculturation research discussed above, the responses of the Indian participants of this chapter suggest that there is an ongoing and simultaneous dialogical negotiation with the voices of assignations and assertions. Arguing against the universal models espoused by cross-cultural psychologists, Tardif-Williams and Fisher (2009) write that Bakhtin's dialogical theory

> may help to shift thinking away from conceiving acculturation change as a fixed process that occurs solely within an individual, and disrupts ideas that some fixed, pre-set meaning exists beyond the interaction and active engagement of people with each other, with cultural texts, or with cultural discourses... From a Bakhtinian perspective, cultural (and acculturative) meaning is negotiated, created, reproduced, experimented with, discarded and embraced by people in their daily interactions; culture and acculturative processes reflect a set of discourses or representations... In this way, acculturation is an *unfinalizable* dialogue, always a work in progress. (2009: 155)

This dialogical view of acculturation where cultural meanings are negotiated and strategically positioned can be applied to understand the

narratives produced in the Indian diaspora. In conclusion, the acculturation experiences of the professional Indians – and their strategic deploy-
ment of their voices – are shaped by their class positions back home and
the history of multicultural discourse about race and otherness in America. Thus, a dialogical perspective on acculturation processes challenges
three assumptions made by the dominant theories of acculturation in
cross-cultural psychology.

The first assumption relates to theories about immigrants' integration
struggles. One of the assumptions inherent in the integration strategy
proposed by traditional acculturation theorists is that immigrants can
somehow 'positively' assimilate the values and ideologies of both the
dominant, mainstream group and their own ethnic group. Recall that the
concept of 'acculturation strategies' and 'bicultural competence'
assumes that all immigrants can possibly achieve a happy, balanced
blend that entails 'becoming effective in the new culture and remaining
competent in his or her culture of origin' (LaFromboise et al. 1998:
148). Those immigrants who do not achieve this goal are considered to
be experiencing higher acculturative stress (Berry 1998) and are not as
physically or psychologically healthy (LaFromboise et al. 1998). To
suggest that the acculturation process merely involves 'culture shedding', 'some behavioural shift' or the 'unlearning of one's previous
repertoire', as much scholarship on acculturation in psychology demonstrates, implies that one can float in and out of cultures, shedding one's
history and politics, and replacing them with a new set of cultural and
political 'behaviours' whenever needed. Advocating the strategy of 'integration' as an end point or examining acculturation in terms of universal
categories overlooks the multiple, contested and sometimes painful
voices that are associated with 'living in-between' cultures (Bhatia
2008).

Second, DST shows that the power of the dominant majority to place
and position minorities as others, foreigners or outcasts plays an important role in the acculturation process of immigrants. Assimilation or
integration is not an option for many first-generation Indian immigrants,
like Venkat or Rohan, because they were described as the racial and
cultural other when they arrived in America. The identity negotiations
that they undertook in the diaspora began the moment they were marked
as the other. We see how this otherness is constructed through assigning
exotic or negative cultural meanings to the bindi, sari and 'thick accents'.
In many cases, the construction of otherness was downright racist and
extremely disruptive to the children and families of the Indian diaspora.
Furthermore, it is not clear what the term 'integration' means exactly.
How does one know when one is 'integrated', or not, within the host

culture? Who decides whether an immigrant is pursuing a strategy of marginalization, integration or separation? The identity of middle-class Indians in the local diaspora is made up of different voices, but these voices share an asymmetrical relationship with each other. Although most professional Indians try to counter the racist assignations that are made by many Americans, by asserting that they are equal to the dominant majority, there is an inherently unequal relationship of power between the voices of assignation and voices of assertion.

Third, the acculturation process illustrates that the diasporic immigrant identity is not fixed by some core, singular, essential, universal 'trait' and 'attitude' or a personality 'attribute'. Thus, the concept of voice in the DST allows us to make the claim that the Indian immigrants rework the different voices related to their racial and cultural otherness. Their heritage or ethnicity does not entail a movement towards assimilation, marginalization, or separation and integration in a new culture. Rather, there is an ongoing, simultaneous dialogical movement between the voices that are at once assimilated, integrated, privileged and marginalized (Hermans and Hermans-Konopka 2010).

Thus, when one considers how many diasporic immigrants are 'coming to terms' with their identity and negotiating and renegotiating their selfhood in the 'First World', we realize the usefulness of the model of DST that is proposed by Hermans and his colleagues. The dialogical model of acculturation not only highlights the tensions and contradictions of living with hyphenated identities in the 'First World', but also poses a challenge to cross-cultural psychology's notion of acculturation strategies in general and the concept of integration strategy in particular.

REFERENCES

Bakhtin, M. (1984) *Problems of Dostoevsky's Poetics* (Minneapolis, MN: University of Minnesota Press)

Berry, J. W. (1980) Acculturation as varieties of adaptation, in A. Padilla (ed.), *Acculturation: Theory, Models and Some New Findings* (Boulder, CO: Westview Press), 9–25

(1990) Cultural variations in cognitive style, in S. Wapner (ed.), *Bio-psycho-social Factors in Cognitive Style* (Hillsdale, NJ: Erlbaum), 289–308

(1997) Immigration, acculturation and adaptation, *Applied Psychology: An International Review*, **46**, 5–68

(1998) Acculturative stress, in P. B. Organista, K. M. Cren and G. Marin (eds.), *Readings in Ethnic Psychology* (New York: Routledge), 117–122

Berry, J. W. and Sam, D. (1997) Acculturation and adaptation, in J. W. Berry, M. H. Seagull and C. Kagitçibasi (eds.), *Handbook of Cross-Cultural Psychology: Social Behavior and Applications* (Needham Heights, MA: Allyn and Bacon), vol. III, 291–326

Bhatia, S. (2002) Acculturation, dialogical voices and the construction of the diasporic self, *Theory & Psychology*, **12**, 55–77

(2007) *American Karma: Race, Culture, and Identity and the Indian Diaspora* (New York University Press)

(2008) 9/11 and the Indian diaspora: narratives of race, place, and immigrant identity, *Journal of Intercultural Studies*, **29**, 21–29

(2010) Theorizing cultural psychology in transnational contexts, in S. R. Kirschner and J. Martin (eds.), *The Sociocultural Turn in Psychology: The Contextual Emergence of Mind and Self* (New York: Columbia University Press), 205–227

Bhatia, S. and Ram, A. (2001) Rethinking 'acculturation' in relation to diasporic cultures and postcolonial identities, *Human Development*, **44**, 1–17

(2004) Culture, hybridity and the dialogical self: cases from the South-Asian diaspora, *Mind, Culture, and Activity*, **11**, 224–241

(2009) Theorizing identity in transnational and diaspora cultures: a critical approach to acculturation, *International Journal of Intercultural Relations*, **33**, 140–149

Camilleri, C. and Malewska-Peyre, H. (1997) Socialization and identity strategies, in J. W. Berry, P. R. Dasen and T. S. Saraswathi (eds.), *Handbook of Cross-Cultural Psychology. Vol. II: 2 Basic Processes and Human Development* (Needham Heights, MA: Allyn and Bacon), 41–67

Chirkov, V. (2009) Critical psychology of acculturation: what do we study and how do we study it, when we investigate acculturation?, *International Journal of Intercultural Relations*, **33**, 94–105

Cresswell, J. (2009) Towards a post-critical praxis: intentional states and recommendations for change in acculturation psychology, *International Journal of Intercultural Relations*, **33**, 162–172

George, R. M. (1997) 'From expatriate aristocrat to immigrant nobody': South Asian racial strategies in the southern Californian context, *Diaspora*, **6**, 27–59

Gilroy, P. (1993) *The Black Atlantic: Modernity and Double Consciousness* (Cambridge, MA: Harvard University Press)

Glick-Schiller, N., Basch, L. and Szanton-Blanc, C. (1995) From immigrant to transmigrant: theorizing transnational migration, *Anthropological Quarterly*, **68**, 48–63

Hall, S. (1991) Old and new identities, old and new ethnicities, in A. D. King (ed.), *Culture, Globalization, and the World-System: Contemporary Conditions for the Representation of Identity* (Binghamton, NY: State University of New York), 41–68

Halonen, J. S. and Santrock, J. W. (1996) *Psychology: Contexts of Behavior* (Dubuque, IA: Brown and Benchmark)

Hermans, H. J. M. (1996) Voicing the self: from information processing to dialogical interchange, *Psychological Bulletin*, **119**, 31–50

Hermans, H. J. M. and Dimaggio, G. (2007) Self, identity, and globalization in times of uncertainty: a dialogical analysis, *Review of General Psychology*, **11**, 31–61

Hermans, H. J. M. and Hermans-Konopka, A. (2010) *Dialogical Self Theory: Positioning and Counter-Positioning in a Globalizing Society* (Cambridge University Press)

Hermans, H. J. M. and Kempen, H. J. G. (1993) *The Dialogical Self: Meaning as Movement* (San Diego, CA: Academic Press)

   (1998) Moving cultures: the perilous problems of cultural dichotomies in a globalizing society, *American Psychologist*, **53**, 1111–1120

Hermans, H. J. M., Kempen, H. J. G. and van Loon, R. J. P. (1992) The dialogical self: beyond individualism and rationalism, *American Psychologist*, **47**, 23–33

Hermans, H. J. M. and Salgado, J. (2010) The dialogical self as a mini-society, in S. R. Kirschner and J. Martin (eds.), *The Sociocultural Turn in Psychology: The Contextual Emergence of Mind and Self* (New York: Columbia University Press), 183–204

Hernandez, D. J. (1999) Children of immigrants, one-fifth of America's children and growing: their circumstances, prospects, and welfare reform, master lecture presented at the biennial meeting of the Society for Research in Child Development, Albuquerque, New Mexico

Josephs, I. (1998) Constructing one's self in the city of the silent: dialogue, symbols and the role of 'as-if' in self-development, *Human Development*, **41**, 180–195

   (2002) 'The Hopi in me': the construction of a voice in the dialogical self from a cultural psychological perspective, *Theory & Psychology*, **12**, 161–173

Khan, S. (1998) Sexual exiles, in S. D. Dasgupta (ed.), *A Patchwork Shawl: Chronicles of South Asian Women in America* (New Brunswick, NJ: Rutgers University Press), 62–71

Kibria, N. (2002) *Becoming Asian American* (Baltimore, MD: Johns Hopkins University Press)

LaFromboise, T., Coleman, L. K. and Gerton, J. (1998) Psychological impact of biculturalism: evidence and theory, in P. B. Organista, K. M. Cren and G. Marin (eds.), *Readings in Ethnic Psychology* (New York: Routledge), 123–155

López, H. I. F. (1996) *White by Law: The Legal Construction of Race* (New York University Press)

Mazumdar, S. (1989) Racist responses to racism: the Aryan myth and South Asians in the United States, *South Asia Bulletin*, **9**, 47–55

Mohanty, C. T. (1991) Cartographies of struggle: Third World women and the politics of feminism, in C. T. Mohanty, A. Russo and L. Torres (eds.), *Third World Women and the Politics of Feminism* (Bloomington, IN: Indiana University Press), 2–47

Prashad, V. (2000) *The Karma of Brown Folk* (Minneapolis, MN: University of Minnesota Press)

Raggatt, P. (2000) Mapping the dialogical self: towards a rationale and method of assessment, *European Journal of Personality*, **14**, 65–90

Rangaswamy, P. (2000) *Namaste America: Indian immigrants in an American Metropolis* (University Park, PA: Pennsylvania State University Press)

Rong, X. L. and Prissele, J. (1998) *Educating Immigrant Students: What We Need to Know to Meet the Challenge* (Thousand Oaks, CA: Corwin Press)

Rudmin, F. (2009) Constructs, measurements, and models of acculturation and acculturative stress, *International Journal of Intercultural Research*, **33**, 106–123

Sampson, E. (1993) *Celebrating the Other: A Dialogic Account of Human Nature* (Boulder, CO: Westview Press)

Segall, M. H., Lonner, W. J. and Berry, J. W. (1998) Cross-cultural psychology as a scholarly discipline: on the flowering of culture in behavioral research, *American Psychologist*, **53**, 1101–1110

Suárez-Orozco, M. M. and Suárez-Orozco, C. (2001) *Children of Immigration* (Cambridge, MA: Harvard University Press)

Tardif-Williams, C. Y. and Fisher, L. (2009) Clarifying the link between acculturation experiences and parent–child relationships among families in cultural transition: the promise of contemporary critiques of acculturation psychology, *International Journal of Intercultural Relations*, **33**, 150–161

Tölöyan, K. (1996) Rethinking diaspora(s): stateless power in the transnational moment, *Diaspora*, **5**, 3–35

Travis, C. and Wade, C. (1997) *Psychology in Perspective*, 2nd edn (New York: Addison Wesley)

Valsiner, J. (2002) Forms of dialogical relations and semiotic auto-regulation within the self, *Theory & Psychology*, **2**, 251–265

Wertsch, J. V. (1991) *Voices of the Mind: A Sociocultural Approach to Mediated Action* (Cambridge, MA: Harvard University Press)

(1998) *Mind as Action* (New York: Oxford University Press)

Westen, D. (1997) *Psychology: Mind, Brain and Culture* (New York: Wiley)

7 Psychodrama: from dialogical self theory to a self in dialogical action

Leni M. F. Verhofstadt-Denève

Introduction

In a comparison of the theoretical and practical aspects of dialogical self theory (DST) (Hermans and Hermans-Konopka 2010; Hermans and Kempen 1993) and *phenomenological-dialectical* theory and practice (Verhofstadt-Denève 1988, 2000, 2007), we will focus on a confrontation of two crucial key elements from both theories, namely the model of the 'multivoiced self characterized by moving *I*-positions', and the central 'phenomenological-dialectical personality model' (Phe-Di P model). This analysis aims to demonstrate that while the theories underlying both models show great similarities, there appear to be marked differences in the methods applied for exploring and stimulating intra- and interpersonal dialogues. Therefore, the theoretical analysis will be complemented by a comparative methodological-practical issue.

In various publications, Hermans has convincingly emphasized the connection between DST and the self-confrontation method (SCM) (Hermans and Kempen 1993), and later also with the construction of a personal position repertoire (PPR) (Hermans 2001b). Similarly, Verhofstadt-Denève described the strong relationship between the phenonomenological personality model and experiential-dialectical psychodrama (Dillen *et al.* 2009; Verhofstadt-Denève 1988, 2000, 2001, 2003; Verhofstadt-Denève *et al.* 2004). A brief analysis of (1) SCM and PPR, and of (2) various types of dialogues activated in psychodrama aims to demonstrate that the application of action and drama techniques in addition to SCM and PPR would constitute an effective complement to the constructive stimulation of 'internal and external imaginal dialogues' and thus offer an added value to the service of DST. Moreover, psychodrama could also be enriched if used in conjunction with SCM and PPR. A deliberate combination of the SCM, PPR and psychodrama techniques therefore holds a real challenge for the future.

Theory

Hermans' model of moving I-positions

The self can be represented as a space composed of a multiplicity of positions, represented by dots in two concentric circles (Figure 7.1).

Internal positions, depicted by dots within the inner circle, are felt as part of myself (e.g. *I* as a mother, *I* as an ambitious worker, *I* as an enjoyer of life), whereas *external positions*, depicted by dots within the outer circle, are felt as part of the environment (e.g. my children, my colleagues, my friend John) (Hermans 2001a). Within the realm of internal positions, a distinction has been made between 'social positions' and 'personal positions'. Social positions can be equated with the traditional term 'role' (e.g. father, husband). Personal positions, on the other hand, receive their form from the particular ways in which individual people organize their own lives (e.g. *I* as a perfectionist, *I* as a dreamer) (Hermans 2001b). Many positions, however, are simply *outside* the subjective horizon of the self, and the person is simply not aware of their existence. As possible positions, however, they may enter the self-space at some moment in time depending on changes in the situation (Hermans 2001a).

In order to facilitate dialogical processes, positions were approached as voiced positions, able to tell their stories and implied meaning units. Three kinds of (imaginal) interchange can be distinguished: internal–external, internal–internal and external–external (Hermans 2001b).

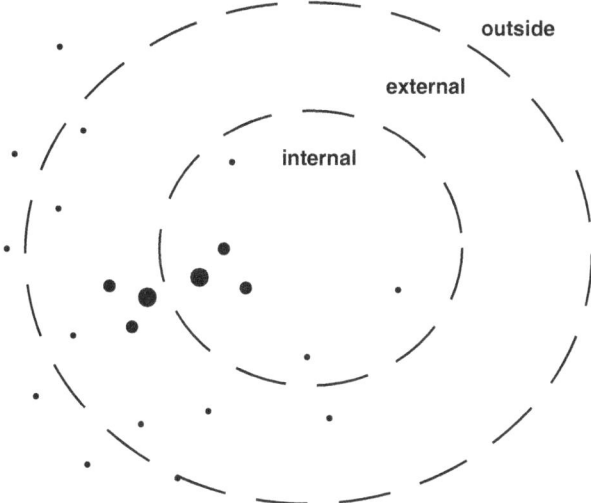

Figure 7.1 Positions in a multivoiced self.

Although intra- and interpersonal dialogues are strongly interwoven, it is necessary to make a distinction between imagination and reality as defined by a particular community. An imagined intrapersonal dialogue (*within the self-space*) may take an entirely different direction in from an interpersonal actual dialogue (*between different persons*). The actual words of the actual other may even force me to reconstruct my opinion as the interaction develops. In fact, the actual other questions, challenges and changes existing positions in the self, and is able to introduce new ones (Hermans 2001a). In the next part we will present a succinct analysis of the Phe-Di P model with systematic references to Hermans' model of moving *I*-positions.

The phenomenological-dialectical personality involved in 'intrapersonal' and 'interpersonal' dialogues

Earlier publications give a detailed description of the basic principles of developmental psychotherapy and the underlying phenomenological-dialectical personality theory (Verhofstadt-Denève 1988, 2000, 2001). We shall confine ourselves to the main ideas here (see Figure 7.2).

In this model, *phenomenological* refers to the unique subjective content and meaning which all human beings attach to themselves and sur-rounding world. *Dialectical* refers to the underlying process which causes these contents to be created and to develop.

The phenomenological content: intrapersonal dialogues

The basic content of the model harks back to William James' *I–me* self-model, as does the view of the self proposed by Hermans. The Phe-Di P model views the person as a dynamic *I–me* relationship, in which the *I* (as subject) is capable of reflection on the *me* (as object). For example, a people can reflect on their capacities and weaknesses. The ability to reflect belongs to the *I*; the result of reflection (capacities and weaknesses) belongs to the *me*.

In the model, the *I* is the person's thinking, feeling, willing, acting, observing and evaluating component. It experiences, reflects, organizes, selects and integrates in terms of self-esteem and recognition by (signifi-cant) others (see below). The *I* is therefore more process than content. The *me* can be observed. It is a semantic system resulting from the reflection by the *I*. What is the result of the reflection process of the *I* on the *me*? The *I–me* relation creates several phenomenological self-constructions. The interpretations of the social and material world are also part of the *I–me* since they all involve personal constructions and (re)creations. The properties I attribute to my friend become part of myself. In the sometimes chaotic multiplicity of person and world

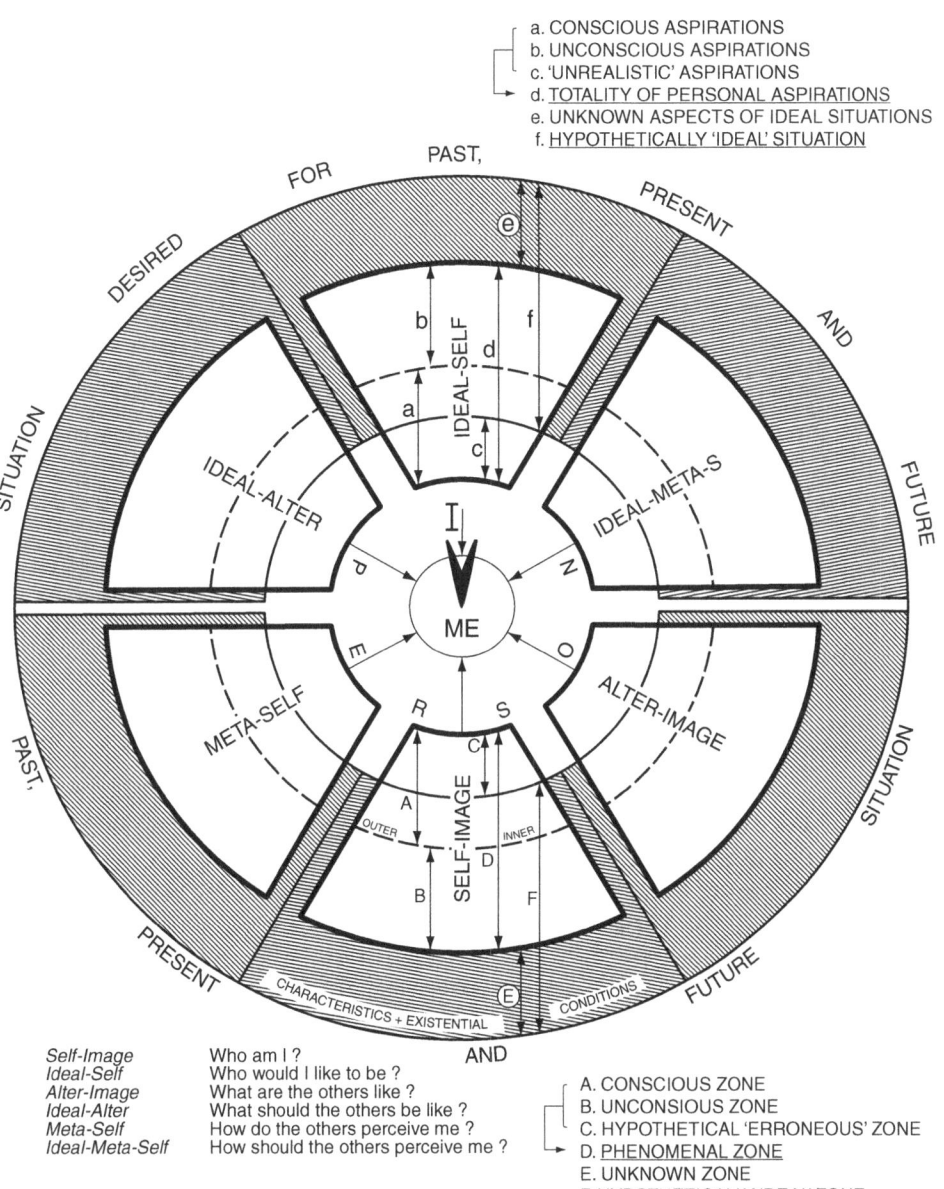

Figure 7.2 The phenomenological-dialectical personality model.

interpretations, we distinguish six *me*-constructions (or *me*-dimensions), each corresponding to a central question (see Figure 7.2):

Central I-questions	**me-constructions**
1. *Who am I?*	*self-image*
2. Who would I like to be?	ideal self
3. *What are others like?*	*alter image*
4. What should others be like?	ideal alter
5. *How do others perceive me?*	*meta-self*
6. How should others perceive me?	ideal meta-self

These six questions constitute the basis of a therapeutically practicable and 'living' personality model consisting of six *me*-constructions. For every human being, the starting point is a unique, subjective (phenomenological) interpretation of oneself and one's surrounding social and material reality at different levels of consciousness, knowing, time and action.

The content of the personality constructions, as a result of the *I–me* reflection, will be briefly illustrated by self-descriptions from one of my clients. Kevin, a 17-year-old boy, had a fight with his drunk father in order to protect his mother; the father as a result was permanently paralysed, and Kevin suffers from extreme guilt feelings.

The first two constructions relate to the self:

1. *As I am in the world in which I am living (self-image)*: 'I am Kevin. I'm 17. I have no friends. I no longer trust anyone. Everything used to be nicer in the past; we were a real family then and my parents loved me. I'm a bad son to them. Life has become meaningless and I don't think this is going to change.'
2. *As I would like to be in a world in which I would want to live (ideal self)*: 'I'm Kevin as I would like to be. I have friends I can trust, and a girlfriend who truly loves me. I get along well with my parents. Weather permitting, I occasionally take my dad out for a walk in his wheelchair. I often give my mum a hand in the household and sometimes look after my brothers. We love each other.'

The third and fourth constructions concern my creation of the other(s):

3. *As they exist as persons in their world (alter image)*. Kevin speaks as his mother: 'I'm Kevin's mother. I am 39 years old. I have a large family and my husband's in a wheelchair. He has fortunately stopped drinking. I sometimes feel very tense, but I keep fighting for my husband and my children.'
4. *As I believe they should be in an ideal world (ideal alter)*. Kevin as his mother: 'I'm Kevin's mother and I feel quite happy. My husband has become

friendlier, gentler, also towards the children. We're again forming the warm family we used to be. I can better cope with the situation now.'

Both alter images relate to the construction of our meaningful material and social world. They are the 'others inside us', so to speak. These others are of course very closely related to our self-image. They contribute towards positive or negative self-esteem.

When thinking about the others in greater depth, I am inevitably confronted with the question of how the others view me and what I mean to them (meta-self). Basically, the meta-self is part of the alter image, but given its considerable therapeutic importance, this dimension is treated as a separate *me*-construction:

5. *My construction of the image others have formed of me and my world (meta-self)*. Kevin as his mother: 'You can't trust Kevin. He's much too quick-tempered, he doesn't control himself at all, and this caused this nasty accident. The police came. He ran away. How on earth can he do something like this to his parents! He's depressive now. I can't stand it any longer.'
6. *My construction of the way others should perceive myself and my world (ideal meta-self)*. Kevin as his mother: 'I think Kevin's a good lad – he loves me a lot and he protected me from my bullying husband, who used to beat me. He saved my life. If only my husband hadn't been so aggressive, Kevin wouldn't have had to stop him and he wouldn't have fallen! Kevin's certainly not to blame for the accident. Kevin has a girlfriend and he recently got a job at the post office. I know he's happy and this makes me happy too.'

In summary: the construction of the self-image and ideal self not only implies an active conversation with *oneself* about one's own qualities, weaknesses and strengths, but also includes social self-related questions (cf. 'social roles'): 'Who am *I* in relation to others? What is my task to them as a son, a brother?' Both contents are highly comparable to Hermans' 'internal personal *I*-positions' and 'internal social *I*-positions', respectively (see Figures 7.1, 7.2 and 7.3). In contrast, the four other dimensions, alter self and ideal alter; meta-self and ideal meta-self, are the result of our personal construction of these significant others – 'What are they like?, What do they think and feel?' and 'What image do they have of me?' – comparable to Hermans' 'external *I*-positions' (see Figures 7.1, 7.2 and 7.3).

It is important that the content of the six dimensions can be analysed by the same basic features such as time, location, consciousness, possibilities of alternative interpretations, and (un)known concepts (see Figure 7.2).

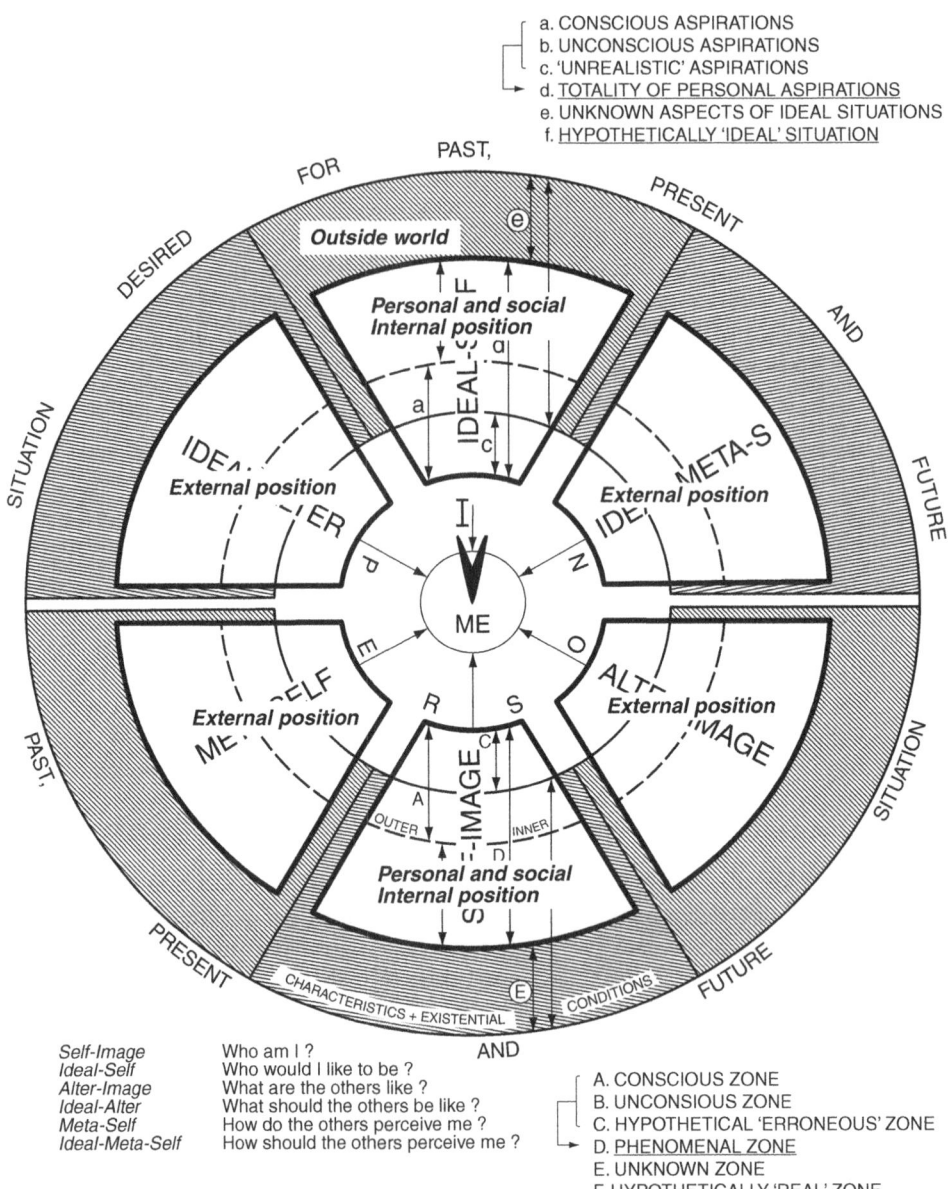

a. CONSCIOUS ASPIRATIONS
b. UNCONSCIOUS ASPIRATIONS
c. 'UNREALISTIC' ASPIRATIONS
d. TOTALITY OF PERSONAL ASPIRATIONS
e. UNKNOWN ASPECTS OF IDEAL SITUATIONS
f. HYPOTHETICALLY 'IDEAL' SITUATION

Self-Image	Who am I ?	A. CONSCIOUS ZONE
Ideal-Self	Who would I like to be ?	B. UNCONSIOUS ZONE
Alter-Image	What are the others like ?	C. HYPOTHETICAL 'ERRONEOUS' ZONE
Ideal-Alter	What should the others be like ?	D. PHENOMENAL ZONE
Meta-Self	How do the others perceive me ?	E. UNKNOWN ZONE
Ideal-Meta-Self	How should the others perceive me ?	F. HYPOTHETICALLY 'REAL' ZONE

Figure 7.3 The multivoiced self-positions (see Figure 7.1) in relation to the phenomenological-dialectical personality model (see Figure 7.2).

Each of the six dimensions can be reflected upon from the three different *time perspectives*; for example, Kevin has an image of himself and of his father in the past, the present and the future. Moreover, in each dimension we can make a distinction between the *external(outer) aspect* (the things one says, and one's concrete actions) and the *internal (inner) aspect* (what one thinks and feels).[1]

For example, during a psychodrama session, Kevin said, shouting at his father:

K: *Oh shut up! Look at yourself! What did you do with your life? Misfit!* (external expression of alter image).

DIRECTOR   *What are you thinking of now? What do you feel? Go one step*
(TO K):   *to the left and try to say what is going on in your mind –*
                    your father can't hear you now.

K can now express his internal part, 'acting from a new *I*-position as if another person was speaking from a different space':

K (THINKING   *I feel bad … guilty. Why am I saying all this? I know he feels*
ALOUD):   *miserable, and strangely enough I pity him. Sometimes*
                   I think I still love him? (internal content of self-image).
                   K becomes emotional and softly weeps.

Therapeutic sessions should offer the possibility to work with external and internal hidden contents.

It is obvious that the *I–me* reflection is not confined to the *conscious* level (Figure 7.2, zones A and a). One need not be a convinced Freudian to acknowledge the huge impact of the *unconscious* on the development of the *me*-constructions (Figure 7.2, zones B and b).

As subjectively involved interpreters, '*errors*' *and* '*gaps*' can occur in the way we perceive and construe our own and other people's qualities and performances (Figure 7.2, zones C and c). It goes without saying that there are no strict criteria for assessing whether an interpretation is correct or erroneous. '*Erroneous*' has a relative (situational) meaning largely determined by historical, cultural and social traditions. From a clinical-therapeutic point of view, it is essential that the therapist should unconditionally start from taking the client's subjective phenomenological constructions of himself and the others, no matter how bizarre and unrealistic these constructions may appear to be. Starting from here, and supported by a safe therapeutic climate, the client can himself discover more adequate, or at least alternative, interpretations of himself and the world.

In addition to the 'erroneous' interpretations of myself and my material and social world, there are the hypothetical characteristics and conditions upon which I cannot reflect because I do not know them (yet).

These so-called *unknown contents* are in keeping with Hermans' concept of the *outside world* (Figures 7.1, 7.2 and 7.3, zones E and e). Unknown elements are fundamentally different from unconscious ones. Unknown contents are literally those *I do not know*, those I have not yet been confronted with at whatever level of consciousness. Unconscious contents are those *I may prefer not to know*. Unconscious contents are dynamic forces which intrinsically determine our behaviour considerably. The influence of unknown contents may also be decisive, but essentially they do not belong to my person, such as social forces I am (not yet) aware of, but which I will possibly have to address later, and unknown elements inside or outside this world which we will probably never know, such as the infinitesimally large and the infinitesimally small in a cosmic reality.

Interpersonal dialogues between 'real' persons

So far, we have discussed intrapsychic phenomenological constructions and dynamics within one single person. Such subjective internal actions typically occur when we are alone, as when we are (day)dreaming, writing a text or driving a car. However, interpersonal contacts with other persons are highly frequent as well. Like Hermans, we distinguish imagined dialogues (within the self space) and actual dialogues (between different persons). We meet other people in the train, in the streets and so on. We sometimes learn from them and they at times make us correct our phenomenological contents. This is even more true for real-life contacts in discussions after a lecture, at work or with a friend, or in chat or email conversations. These interpersonal dialogues involve an intensely complex combination of intra- and interpsychic dynamics in both persons and offer scope for mutual corrections of intra- and interpsychic phenomenological constructions. These insights are essential for resolving conflicts between persons, groups and cultures.

Dialectical processes

As stated above, the six *me*-constructions of the person refer to the content or the result of the *I–me* reflection. The dialectical refers to the dynamic relationship between the constructions. The assumption is that the six personality dimensions need to relate to each other as dialectical oppositions moving through three stages (thesis, antithesis, synthesis) following a double negation (see also Verhofstadt-Denève 2000, 2007). For instance, there is an inevitable opposition between the self-image and the ideal self. If both were to coincide completely, the development process between these two poles would stagnate (for elaborations, see Riegel 1979; Verhofstadt-Denève 2000, 2007; Verhofstadt-Denève *et al.* 2003).

How is the dialectical component materialized? During a psychodrama action, the protagonist (Kevin) can begin by presenting himself in the *I*-form (i.e. self image or thesis stage; cf. Hermans' 'internal personal *I*-position'). In a second stage, he moves into his ideal self and formulates in the *I*-form whom he would like to be or become (i.e. antithesis stage; cf. Hermans' 'moving to opposite internal *I*-position'). According to Fichte (1810, drawing on Hegel), this transition from the first to the second state implies the *first negation* – here the negation of the self-image in favour of the ideal self; or, formulated differently, the self-image remains historically present but is shifted towards the background in favour of the ideal self. In this stage, the opposition between the two images (or *I*-positions) is therefore felt most strongly.

However, after taking the role of the ideal self, this ideal self is negated as well by the return to the initial position: his self-image (this is the *second negation*) (i.e. synthesis stage, or as could be formulated as Hermans' 'a move to the initial *I*-position'). According to Hegel, the result of this triadic process is that the two poles concerned (self-image and ideal self) will be changed, 'aufgehoben', or raised to a qualitatively higher level of development, mainly through the experienced opposition between self-image and ideal self during the discordant antithesis stage (Verhofstadt-Denève 2000, 2007).

To conclude: in the phenomenological personality model (as in Hermans' way of thinking), the *me* is clearly a 'multivoiced self' with six main dimensions which can interact and be in conflict. Interestingly, the content of the six self-constructions shows a high congruence with the *I*-positions in Hermans' multivoiced self. As demonstrated above, both models have clear correspondences. Moreover, we think that differences do not so much relate to the basic theoretical assumptions as to the methodological-clinical field of application.

Practice

The self-confrontation method (SCM), the personal position repertoire (PPR) and dialogues with 'imaginal figures'

Hermans' SCM involves a thorough self-investigation, which is of great diagnostic importance as a useful starting point for clinical practice. However, the self-critical Hermans discovered a number of limitations in the SCM which made this method inadequate to meet the versatility of DST. For extensive information about this rich procedure and the development of practical examples, we refer to Hermans and Hermans-Jansen (1995). In his view, the SMC is too exclusively focused on 'self'-investigation, with clients telling their story as 'passionate storytellers' to a therapist, but from which two fundamental aspects are missing in relation to the DST.

First of all, the social aspect is under-represented in this investigation. The stories generally remain confined to pure self-descriptions *without focus on the external* I-*positions*. A second limitation resides in the fact that in the traditional use of the SCM, clients are not urged to *express and explore themselves in an actively dialogical way* in relation to the basic acceptance of a multivoiced, dialogical self-concept. Therefore, the PPR method was developed as a complement to the SCM. The PPR is a research tool in which both internal and external I-positions can be made explicit and be charted in a clear matrix (for a full overview of the procedure together with the development of a case, see Hermans 2001b).

The PPR definitely fulfils the social dimension of DST in its explicit focus on the external I-positions. The possibility which the PPR offers for determining an organized structure of the internal and external I-positions at different moments meets the basic DST principle of the self as a complex, narratively organized structure, *extended* to the *social* environment (Hermans 2001a). The PPR method was devised in order to assess the organization of I-positions, but in itself it does not explore dialogical relationships between the different positions. However, by inviting some of the positions to formulate valuations from their own perspective, and exchanging them with other I-positions, the method was further adapted in dialogical ways. As such, the PPR method can be used in better accordance with the dialogical aspect of DST: 'The voices function like interacting characters in a story, involved in a process of question and answer, agreement and disagreement' (Hermans 2001b). The combination of SCM and PPR seemed a good step towards real dialogues.

Like the SCM, the PPR can be administered repeatedly, thus revealing shifts in the hierarchy of I-positions. These shifts are discussed with the therapist, and from these discussions the main oppositions in the I-positions can be distilled. Some good examples can be found in the PPR study of Mary, who defined herself as a *witch* in certain circumstances, besides her ordinary position as *Mary* (see Hermans and Hermans-Jansen 1995). The innovative nature of this approach resides in the fact that the valuations which Mary formulated via the SCM were also evaluated by the witch. In other words, the SCM helps the client to formulate valuations from a specific *I*-position and to subsequently answer them from another *I*-position. 'As the different affective profiles suggest, Mary and the witch were adversaries in some situations ... but could cooperate quite well in other situations... As part of this strategy, the incompatible position is not "cured" or treated as an undesirable symptom, but taken seriously as a partner with whom it is possible to get "on speaking terms". Instead of removing a "maladaptive" part of the self, the position repertoire is enriched and broadened in such way that a health-promoting reorganisation of the self can take place' (Hermans 2006). What is essential here is that for the first time a real dialogue arises between the two internal *I*-positions. For instance, Mary moves into the position of the witch, who 'becomes a part of herself', and from this position she formulates a statement directed towards herself. As will appear below, it is this very dialogue which is systematically, and even more directly and actively, applied in psychodrama.

Psychodrama

Almost all therapies stimulate self-reflection (cf. the *I–me* dynamic) in order to help the client to find a more adequate redefinition of self and significant others. We also suggest a stimulation of intense self-reflection, but with lively dialogues directly in the personal context of the phenomenological self space, through the deliberate application of action and drama techniques. This method differs substantially from other therapies (and from the SCM and PPR practice) in which the client – in a dialogue with a therapist – mainly tells a story *about* himself in relation to significant others, comparable to the position of an interested external observer. In a training group in which both a client-oriented experiential therapy and a psychodrama therapy were taught, participants formulated the essence of psychodrama as follows.

In experiential therapy, you are standing on *the bank of your self-river* and you reflect on the flow, which you watch and contemplate intensely, in dialogue with an empathic therapist. And of course this is highly valuable. Moreover, in psychodrama the therapist (director) helps you to *take the plunge into your flow of life* and to start 'real', direct intra- and interpsychic dialogues within a specific time frame and space, which is inevitably accompanied by a sudden, more intense, consciousness and emotionality. It is a dialogue rather with yourself and with the others in you, than with the therapist, who is constantly watching you from the river bank. The therapist does not take the plunge into the process together with you, so he can always save you from the current, and once in a while, when you risk becoming flooded by the strong experiences, this is indeed what he does, after which you can watch and contemplate the process you are going through from the river bank, together with the therapist, from a meta-position, and you can decide whether you are ready to jump back into the river. It is an ongoing, challenging alternation of a *contemplation* from a meta-position and a *stepping into* your own flow of life, with an accepting director offering no content himself but constantly monitoring your strength.

The expert application of psychodrama techniques can enable the 'protagonist' to *really step into his/her own personal universe* (Moreno and Moreno 1969; Verhofstadt-Denève 2000). As a result, in a specific space and time frame, he can actually look round, feel, think, talk, dialogue, fight, reorganize power structures and integrate. The idea is that a direct, in-depth *I–me* action should enable participants to find alternative constructions and organizations in relation to themselves and their material and social world. The main task of the psychodrama director is to create an atmosphere providing the greatest possible feeling of security, unconditional respect and mutual acceptance from all group members. The director is a 'facilitator' who, through the creation of a safe and structured methodological framework, gives the protagonist the confidence to step into his or her universe.

We will try to illustrate this procedure through the elaboration of a number of dialogue types corresponding to Hermans' theory of moving *I*-positions, namely (1) internal–external, (2) internal–internal and (3) external–external interchanges.

Some examples of possible dialogues between personality constructions

Dialogue between self-image and alter image or 'imaginal internal–external dialogue'

Here Kevin (K) is the protagonist (as mentioned above) in a group of eight adolescents who work under the supervision of a director (Dir). Kevin starts to tell in the *I*-form who he is (self-image or an internal *I*-position) and creates a concrete familiar situation.

DIR.: *Kevin, you're going to see your father now. Where do you want to meet him? What time is it? What are you going to do?*

K: *He's in the kitchen in his wheelchair, it's 7 pm.*

DIR.: *OK, tell us what the kitchen looks like. Where's the door, where's the worktop?*
     K describes the kitchen, and a few chairs and a table are brought in. (These simple objects considerably enhance Kevin's affective involvement in this specific situation.)

DIR.:   *I know it's difficult for you to meet your father, but here you can safely give it a try. If you like, you can choose somebody from the group to represent your father* ('antagonist').

K: *OK, I'll take Bob.* Bob enters the inner group space.

DIR.:   *OK, Kevin, come here and stand behind Bob. You will now try to become your father and tell us who you are, using the I-form* (i.e. role-taking). *Take your time, Kevin. Bob, you will listen very carefully so that you know how to represent Kevin's father.*

K: *I am Kevin's father. I am 42. I am paralysed, tired. I've lost all my strength and vitality. I watch TV all day long, I feel angry and sad. The only reason I go on living is my youngest son, Jerry. He's the only one left who loves me* (this is a part of Kevin's alter image, his father and brother – cf. the move to an external *I*-position – we now proceed to Kevin's meta-self, another external *I*-position).

DIR.   (addressing Kevin in the role of his father): *Well, father of Kevin, what do you think about your eldest son?*

K   (still playing the role of his own father): *He is the cause of all this misery. I might have been dead. I wish I was. As a child he was such a lovely kid. But how much he has changed!* (Kevin's meta-self). Kevin is finding it hard to cope and starts crying softly.

DIR.:   *OK, Kevin, take your time. Come here, you can now be yourself again, you are no longer your father. Who are you now?*

K: *I'm Kevin, I had a difficult moment just now. I don't know why, I don't usually cry, but it came so suddenly!* (again Kevin's self-image; cf. the switch to the internal *I*-position and an example of a dialectical process: from the self-image to the alter image and meta-self returning to the self-image).

The above example describes the experiencing of oppositions between dimensions (or *I*-positions) of the person. The following example illustrates oppositions within one dimension.

Dialogue within the self-image or 'imaginal internal–internal dialogue'
The following example comes from a psychodrama session with students in clinical psychology. They wish to learn psychodrama through personal experiences. Here is how Jane (the protagonist) formulated this experience.

The director asks who would like to be the protagonist. I feel like stepping forward but I hesitate. I wait a little, and suddenly I can hear myself say, 'Yes, I would like to!' My 'critical self' urges me to accept the challenge. The director asks me to take a chair which represents *myself as a totality*. During role-taking in the *I*-form, I discover various – even opposed – aspects in myself. First I choose a red chair for the enthusiastic, naive and somewhat foolish part in me. With the help of the group members who double[2] me, I call this part my *wild exuberance*. In a dialogue between myself, as my wild exuberant part and my father, I feel a strong disapproval, strong emotions come up.[3] Returning to myself as a totality gives me a relaxed feeling. Then I choose a chair for my second component, the *critical and evaluating spirit*. I then step out of this system, looking at things from a distance, considering and arranging things (cf. mirroring technique).[4] Back into the system, I discover my third component, which I call my *emotional self*. I position myself, my totality and my three components in a specific meaningful place in the room. I consecutively become each component, and the director constantly asks: *Who are you? What would you want to be like? How do important others perceive you? How should the others perceive you? How does Jane perceive you? How do the other components perceive you? What do you think of them?* The fact that I give answers in the *I*-form, from each of the respective positions, has a highly clarifying effect, structuring the whole. The end of the action is now near, and by way of conclusion I can say something to my three components and to the whole self. I feel moved and I stammer something like 'I'm glad to have all of you!'

This result is completely in agreement with Hermans. Instead of removing a 'maladaptive' part of the self, the position repertoire is enriched and broadened in such way that a health-promoting reorganization of the self can take place (Hermans 2006).

Dialogue between alter images or 'imaginal external–external dialogue'
For instance, in one of the sessions, Kevin enacts an animated dialogue between his parents. He alternately becomes his father and his mother, always speaking in the *I*-form when filling in their respective alter and meta-images (i.e. role-taking), and in the *you*-form for the dialogue, while moving in space from one role to the other.

Dialogue with deceased persons or 'imaginal dialogue with imaginal others'
In principle, this is a special form of a dialogue of the first type, namely self-image vs. alter image/meta-self or 'imaginal internal–external dialogue', in which the significant other is a deceased person who in an imaginary way is constantly present for the person in an active dialogue and plays a supportive role. The training group consists of 15 therapists. Pierre (P), a 36-year-old clinical psychologist, suddenly said that he wanted to confide a closely guarded secret to the group. This was his story:

P:	*As you know, I lost my twin brother Serge in a car crash when I was 14. He was killed instantly, but I survived the crash. However, what you don't know is that Serge has always been with me. He's here now too. We often talk to each other, but he sometimes frightens me and makes me feel guilty, and that's what I would like to work on now, here in this group.*
DIR.:	*Pierre, would you like to choose someone from the group as a symbol for your brother Serge?*
P:	*Yes, Jean-Marc.* Jean-Marc steps forward.
P (standing behind Jean-Marc):	*I am Serge, I'm 14 years old, I was killed in a car crash, but I will always be there for Pierre.*
DIR.:	*Pierre, become yourself again, and if you wish you can say something to Serge.*
P:	*Serge, I'm glad you're here, it means I'm never alone, but sometimes I also feel fear and guilt towards you.*
DIR.:	*Pierre, become your brother Serge again.*
DIR. (to Pierre as Serge):	*Serge, you've heard what Pierre has said.*
P (as Serge):	*Yes, but I don't understand this; there's no reason why he should be afraid of me or feel guilty. He could have been killed instead of me. There's nothing he could have done about this, was there?*
DIR.:	*Pierre, become yourself again and listen to your brother Serge.*
JEAN-MARC (group member playing Serge):	*Yes, but I don't understand this; there's no reason why you should be afraid of me or feel guilty. You could have been killed instead of me. There's nothing you could have done about this, was there?* Pierre hears his brother's words and becomes highly emotional.
P:	*He's never said this to me before. This is completely new, and it's quite a relief* (Pierre then moves over to his brother and embraces him).

The answer of Pierre is remarkable, since these are the very words which Pierre himself used in the position of his brother Serge, and now he is surprised to hear these words via his brother as if they were totally new. This role-taking and dialogue process initiates a lively, exteriorized self-dialogue or dialectical movement between the self-image and an imaginary significant other (or alter image). There are clear correspondences between this dialogue and the dialogue that emerged between Hermans' (2006) client and the portrait, *Mercedes de Barcelona*, but with Pierre the internal action is supported vigorously by his personally becoming the other in a concrete spatial and temporal context.

Psychodrama and dialogical self theory

It is clear that the DST supports a much broader and richer inter- and intrapersonal activity than what a client expresses through the SCM method, even in combination with a PPR investigation. The technique of the dialogue with imaginal figures was indeed a major step in a dialogical direction. However, psychodrama can probably play an even more important role here. Practice does show that the combination of speaking, thinking, feeling and acting provides a very strong stimulus within the complex process of self-actualization and self-reorganization.

Both the SCM and psychodrama can generate a picture of an individual's personality structure, while both can also engender personality development. But the two methods appear to have different accents. The SCM emphasizes a more systematic survey of the structure and process of the self at different developmental moments, whereas psychodrama, thanks to its strong affective-relational, emotional and cognitive involvement, probably has a more direct therapeutic impact. From this perspective, both methods are mutually complementary.

It would therefore appear useful to initiate a psychodrama series by means of an SCM and PPR investigation (by way of a diagnostically convenient pre-test) and to investigate the changes within the person on the basis of a second test after the final psychodrama session. Similarly, we would suggest that, after a SCM and PPR investigation, short action sequences could be inserted following the reflective conversations with the therapist in which the 'passionate storyteller' is encouraged by the therapist 'to really make the step into his/her story' and – based on the choice of the theme after an SCM/PPR investigation – to engage in real multivoiced self-dialogues in psychodrama.

In psychodrama the protagonist can really meet the antagonist. This encounter intensifies and surpasses the imaginary self-reflective dimension. The intense physical and mental action enables the protagonist to experience the self and significant others as part of a multivoiced self, not only in the mind but also by meeting and being those significant others in concrete situations in specific times and spaces. This experience makes the protagonist intensively feel not only the differences, disharmonies, power struggles and tensions, but also the similarities and harmony between self and other. Action gives personal identity a vivid relational component.

In this way, the quite diagnostic-organizational accent of SCM and PPR could be complemented by a more explicit social and therapeutic stance through the generation of powerful affective-emotional processes in the psychodramatical action. Therapeutically oriented learning processes also appear to be more lasting after emotional releases. Many researchers have proposed that a focus on client emotion is essential for any therapy to produce long-term client change (Lyddon *et al.* 2006). In this context I can also refer to Greenberg's action-oriented, emotion-focused therapy (Ellioth *et al.* 2004).

To conclude, the SCM could, on the one hand, give a more objective diagnostic added value to psychodrama in keeping with the phenomenological personality model, while psychodrama, on the other hand, could be a useful complement to the SCM, when there could be effectively a move from one *I*-position to the other, in order to really meet *and become* the antagonists in a concrete time and self space as an exteriorization – a coming alive – of imagined *I*-positions. In other words, action and drama techniques give the client the opportunity to really enter into the personal '*society of mind*' (Hermans and Hermans-Konopka 2010) and be directly involved in internal social processes such as the fight for dominance, dialogue and integration. These actions are completely in congruence with the richness of DST. A combination of the SCM, the PPR, *and* action and drama techniques thus appears to be a genuine challenge to clarify the inherent relationship between DST and a self in vivid *dialogical action* (see also Ho's chapter).

NOTES

1 It should be noted that 'internal' and 'external' have another meaning here as in Hermans' model of moving *I*-positions.
2 Doubling is a typical psychodrama technique in which group members can help the protagonist by formulating statements in the *I*-form as if the protagonist herself was speaking. The protagonist can always deny or change the statements.
3 Refers to the part of herself that is most opposed to the father's view. Cf. Hermans: the narrow relationship between internal and external *I*-positions.
4 Cf. Hermans' meta-position (Hermans 2004: 23).

REFERENCES

Dillen, L., Siongers, M., Helskens, D. and Verhofstadt-Denève, L. (2009) When puppets speak: dialectical psychodrama within developmental child psychotherapy, *Journal of Constructivist Psychology*, **22**, 55–82

Ellioth, R., Watson, J. C., Goldman, R. N. and Greenberg, L. S. (2004) *Learning Emotion-Focused Therapy: The Process-Experiential Approach to Change* (Washington, DC: American Psychological Association)

Fichte, J. G. (1976) Die Wissenschaftslehre, in ihrem allgemeinen Umrisse dargestellt [1810] [The science of knowledge in its general outline]. Trans. Walter E. Wright. *Idealistic Studies*, **6**, 106–117

Hermans, H. J. M. (2001a) The dialogical self: toward a theory of personal and cultural positioning, *Culture and Psychology* (Special Issue: Culture and the Dialogical Self: Theory, Method and Practice), **7**, 243–281

(2001b) The construction of a personal position repertoire: method and practice, *Culture and Psychology* (Special Issue: Culture and the Dialogical Self: Theory, Method and Practice), **7**, 323–365

(2004) The dialogical self: between exchange and power, in H. J. M. Hermans and G. Dimaggio (eds.), *The Dialogical Self in Psychotherapy* (Hove and New York: Brunner-Routledge), 14–28

(2006) Moving through three paradigms, yet remaining the same thinker, *Counselling Psychology Quarterly*, **19**, 5–25

Hermans, H. J. M. and Hermans-Jansen, E. (1995) *Self-Narratives: The Construction of Meaning in Psychotherapy* (New York: Guilford Press)

Hermans, H. J. M. and Hermans-Konopka, A. (2010) *Dialogical Self Theory: Positioning and Counter-Positioning in a Globalizing Society* (Cambridge University Press)

Hermans, H. J. M. and Kempen, H. J. G. (1993) *The Dialogical Self: Meaning as Movement* (San Diego: Academic Press)

Lyddon, W. J., Yowell, D. R. and Hermans, H. J. M. (2006) The self-confrontation method: theory, research, and practical utility, *Counselling Psychology Quarterly*, **19**, 27–44

Moreno, J. L. and Moreno, Z. T. (1969) *Psychodrama: Action Therapy and Principles of Practice* (Beacon, NY: Beacon House), vol. III

Riegel, K. F. (1979) *Foundations of Dialectical Psychology* (New York: Academic Press)

Verhofstadt-Denève, L. (1988) The phenomenal-dialectic personality model: a frame of reference for the psychodramatist, *Journal of Group Psychotherapy Psychodrama and Sociometry*, **41**, 3–20

(2000) *Theory and Practice of Action and Drama Techniques: Developmental Psychotherapy from an Existential-Dialectical Viewpoint* (London: Jessica Kingsley Publishers)

(2001) Affective processes in a multivoiced self in Action, in H. Bosma and S. Kunnen (eds.), *Identity and Emotions: A Self-Organizational Perspective* (Cambridge University Press), 141–150

(2003) The psychodramatical 'social atom method': dialogical self in dialectical action, *Journal of Constructivist Psychology*, **16**, 183–212

(2007) Existential-dialectical psychodrama: the theory behind practice, in C. Baim, J. Burmeister and M. Maciel (eds.), *Psychodrama: Advances in Theory and Practice* (New York: Brunner-Routledge), 111–126

Verhofstadt-Denève, L., Dillen, L., Helskens, D. and Siongers, M. (2004) The psychodramatical 'social atom method' with children: a developing dialogical self in dialectic action, in H. J. M. Hermans and G. Dimaggio, *The Dialogical Self in Psychotherapy* (Hove and New York: Brunner-Routledge), 152–170

Verhofstadt-Denève, L., Schittekatte, M. and van Leeuwen, K. (2003) Gender differences in developmental pathways on self-evaluation from adolescence into adulthood: the Flanders Longitudinal Study, *International Journal of Adolescent Medicine and Health*, **15**, 139–152

8 Identity construction among transnational migrants: a dialogical analysis of the interplay between personal, social and societal levels

Seth Surgan and Emily Abbey

In this chapter, we illustrate how phenomena on the personal, social and societal levels work together in the production of novel *I*-positions within the dialogical self. Specifically, we examine the creation of novel 'third positions' (Hermans and Hermans-Konopka 2010) by transnational migrants to the USA. We begin with a discussion of identity processes under globalization, highlighting the process of *hybridization* and its dialogical nature. Next, we will articulate three levels of analysis (personal, social and societal) and discuss their importance and mutual necessity before introducing Eleonora, a participant in a recent study of identity construction among transnational migrants to the USA. Eleonora's example will be used to illustrate the process of hybridization, through which a novel 'third position' emerges and is voiced. Our analysis will focus on the construction of novel forms of symbolic action through which a (hybrid) 'third' position instantiates itself and seeks intelligibility. In the final section of this chapter, we will discuss the dynamics of hybridization and how processes on the personal and social levels of analysis are linked to societal-level formations.

Identity processes in transnational migrants: why hybridization?

Globalization is changing many aspects of our human experience, including the relationship between transnational migration and identity construction. According to Glick-Schiller *et al.* (1995), a distinction can be made between old and new modes of immigration. 'Old' immigration came with a heavy emphasis on assimilation. That is, the decision to leave home came along with an expectation that one would actively seek membership in the host culture and forsake connection with the home culture. This model rests upon the assumption of *disconnection* between 'home' and 'host' cultures within the person's life course. Globalization, in contrast, promotes an opposite world view: one of profound *connection*.

Globalization has opened the door to greater discretionary transnational migration and ushered in a 'new' immigration. For these 'new' immigrants (Glick-Schiller *et al.* 1995), the decision to leave home is often made in pursuit of education, love, adventure or simply a more pleasing life. Easy access to communication, information and transportation often means that 'home' may be decentred as cosmopolitanism is becoming more popular worldwide (Hermans and Dimaggio 2007). The new immigration brings with it *transnational* migrants and personal worlds that are full of tension, mixture and creation in ways that were rare – and not supported by dominant modes of thinking about immigration – at earlier points in human history. As an ethos of globalization has taken hold within the social sciences, the concepts of hybridization and hybridity (Bhabha 1994, 1996; Kraidy 2003; Pieterse 1995, 2001; Yao 2003) have become increasingly popular as ways of referring to instances of cultural mixture and creativity. The realities of globalization put the concept of hybridization at centre stage in our quest to understand the dynamics of identity construction among transnational migrants.

What is hybridization?

The term 'hybrid' comes from the Latin *hybrida*, which refers to the offspring of a tame sow and a wild boar (Young 1995: 6). As such, the idea of hybrid*ization* connotes: (1) a biological (or at least biologistic) process by which a new generation is produced through combination of existing forms, and (2) that the members of the 'parent' generation are of pure kinds that will be mixed. In the socio-historical context of colonization and slavery, it is easy to see how derogatory connotations of miscegenation and half-breeds – uncivilized transgressions of the natural (or even God-given) order of things – might have become attached. More recently, transformed by their place within a contemporary discourse of globalization and border-blurring, 'hybrid' and 'hybridization' have become celebrated terms that highlight the fertile and dynamic nature of human cultural life. As such, they have been incorporated into the lexicon of cultural analysis:

> What we are calling a hybrid construction is an utterance that belongs, by its grammatical and compositional markers, to a single speaker, but that actually contains mixed within it two utterances, two speech manners, two styles, two 'languages,' two semantic and axiological belief systems. (Bakhtin 1981: 304–305)

Bakhtin highlights the critical aspect of all hybrid creations: tension. A hybrid creation is not an easy or straightforward synthesis. There is an 'internal' tension between form and function. Although the utterance, on its surface, appears to belong to a single speaker (by virtue of its surface features), the single utterance somehow expresses, combines or transforms multiple meaningful and value-laden perspectives. This 'internal' tension produces an 'external' tension between the utterance and its audience. As a hybrid construction, the utterance itself is not intelligible within the confines of dominant discourses. Hybrid constructions have the potential not only to combine features of categories that are held as different within the existing sociocultural order, but also to problematize, transgress and shed light upon the status quo.

Hybridization as a dialogical process and the emergence of 'third' positions

If we transpose this notion of hybridity to the domain of identity construction, we can see that hybrid identities exist under constant threat. By virtue of the mismatch with more widely accessible modes of representation and interpretation – and despite their important political value – hybrid subjects are under constant threat of not being intelligible on the social scene. This perhaps motivated Rushdie (1992) to compare life as a hybrid subject to the effort involved in straddling two stools while inevitably slipping between them. Even in its best moments (i.e. the straddling moments, as opposed to the slipping ones), there is struggle. Bringing the stools together (and making a bench) is impossible, as is choosing one or the other stool on which to sit comfortably.

Rushdie's 'stools' can be equated with I-positions within dialogical self theory (DST). DST (Hermans 1996, 2000, 2001; Hermans and Kempen 1993) portrays the self as a set of interacting 'positions', each of which is grounded in the external world and 'voiced' by the I (self-as-knower). Positions may reflect relevant self-concepts (e.g. I as man/woman), important relationships and social others (e.g. I as husband/wife), professional affiliations (e.g. I as psychologist), and even affiliation with larger-scale social structures (e.g. I as American). A person's self not only emerges as an inventory of voiced positions, but also takes on its particular quality through the nature of the interactions between positions, which are regulated by the construction of signs of different kinds (Valsiner 2005). Voices within the dialogical self can agree or disagree, can establish dominance hierarchies, can maintain or destroy those hierarchies, and can work together to create novel syntheses.

Hybridization can occur in situations where multiple I-positions are simultaneously active and cannot simply coexist, either because of conflict or because of the creative urge towards synthesis. This situation

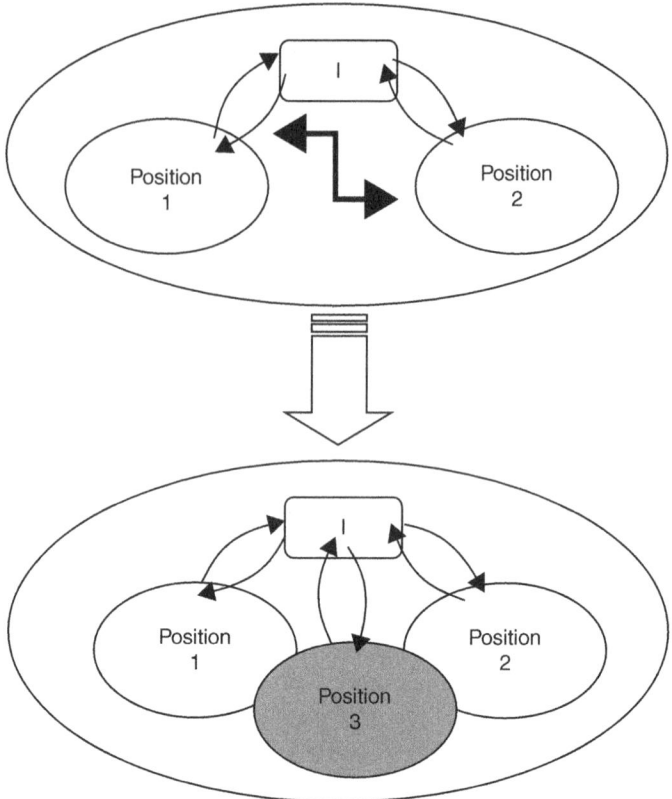

Figure 8.1 The emergence of a hybrid 'third' position (position 3, shaded) through tense action of the *I* within a hybrid space between position 1 and position 2.

leads to the production of a space of *tense action* that the *I* occupies between *I*-positions. In this metaphorical space, the *I* may produce a novel position – a 'third' position that emerges from the tense relationship between *I*-positions but does not deny or remove their differences (Hermans and Hermans-Konopka 2010: 191; see also Raggatt's chapter in this volume). This new position is not reducible to any previously existing position (see Figure 8.1). While the new position may include aspects of previously existing positions, the work of postcolonial and Chicana feminist thinkers (e.g. Anzaldua 1999; Bhabha 1996; Hasnat 1998; Lugones 1996; Radhakrishnan 1996) has demonstrated that hybridity also includes the creation of novel forms of cultural life that cannot be identified with previously existing forms.

Third positions may function to mitigate the conflict between existing *I*-positions and may exert a unifying or integrative influence on the self. To illustrate this idea, Hermans and Hermans-Konopka (2010) refer to Rosanne, a Brazilian woman interviewed by Branco *et al.* (2008), who struggles with her *I*-positions as lesbian and Catholic. Rosanne constructs a 'third position' as a missionary whose calling is to guide members of the gay community to the Catholic Church as a way of helping them deal with their often-conflicted family situations. According to Hermans and Hermans-Konopka (2010: 158), such 'third' positions are created through 'strategic processes' that bridge the gap and interconnect socially opposing *I*-positions. In what follows, we look more closely into the process by which 'third' positions emerge. We suggest that *third positions are created through the process of hybridization* and that hybridization itself can take on many forms. Before looking more closely at the process of hybridization, however, we must articulate the three-levelled framework within which our examination will take place.

Understanding hybridization: three levels of analysis

We approach hybridization through three co-necessary levels of analysis: the personal, social and societal. Briefly, the personal level of analysis includes processes by which the individual connects, compares, synthesizes and draws inferences from available ideas (Falmagne 2009: 806) as well as processes of affective construction and self-regulation (Valsiner 2007). Personal-level processes draw upon but cannot be reduced to collectively available cultural resources. The dynamics of the *I*'s tense action within the hybrid space are describable on the personal level of analysis. The social level of analysis includes local (discursive) interactions. For example, the social level of analysis includes the processes of negotiating relational identity positions (e.g. teacher vs. student). The societal level of analysis includes discursive and material processes that configure social positions and interactions (Falmagne 2004, 2009). For example, the educational/academic system as a whole structures the field within which 'teacher' and 'student' identity positions are assumed, but cannot be reduced to local interactions by which people take on (or negotiate, contest, shed or swap) those positions.

The three levels of analysis are dialectically engaged with one another (Falmagne 2009) and mutually implied in any moment of action. For example, in her work on reasoning, Falmagne (2004, 2009; Abbey and Falmagne 2008) demonstrates how the three levels of analysis are intertwined within an individual's struggle to deal with an algebra teacher who requires a method that the participant finds unnecessarily complicated. On the societal level of analysis, there are several relevant discourses on rationality and emotion (e.g. social knowledge, intuition, rationalism; Falmagne 2009: 808). On the personal level, the participant is agentive in her ways of managing, integrating and silencing multiple perspectives on epistemic authority. The dynamics of that sense-making process define the functioning of the personal level. In the process of making sense of this situation, however, the person simultaneously acts on the social level, establishing herself as a particular kind of person by insisting on trusting herself rather than automatically submitting to the authority emanating from the front of the classroom. As Abbey and Falmagne (2008) point out, that 'identity work' only 'works' because of the existence of a societal-level discourse/structure of authority (i.e. based on status or expertise). This societal-level formation provides the meaning of and configures the identity positions implicated by the participant's action on the social level. Without such societal-level discourse/structure, the participant's move would either be meaningless or have a different meaning (Abbey and Falmagne 2008). In this way, the personal, social and societal levels are always entwined and guarantee the polyvalence of action.

Voicing *I*-positions through symbolic action in everyday settings

Mundane as they may seem, everyday actions – like deciding how to do your algebra – can be seen as meaningful in light of the relations between the personal, social and societal levels of analysis. These activities can function as personal symbols, as described by Josephs (1997: 517): 'symbols that are related to individual motivation and make sense only in relation to the life history of the individual'. This approach to the pervasive symbolism of everyday life aligns with Boesch's symbolic action theory:

On one hand, we structure our experienced reality according to factual, instrumental, spatio-temporal – i.e., 'realistic' – qualities which allow social communication and coordination; but we also, and jointly, structure our experience in relation to situations and actions significant to our I-world relationship, thereby establishing a kind of biographical consistency. (Boesch 1997: 426)

Boesch's perspective on symbolic action encourages us to look at the rich personal and social connotations of everyday activities. Such connotations are what make everyday activities important media for the voicing of *I*-positions. *I*-positions are voiced through symbolic action, which implicates all three levels of analysis at every moment. That action has a particular form, involves particular cultural tools (meanings, objects), and symbolically expresses a meaningful and value-laden perspective on the world. According to Boesch (2001: 482), the 'ever-present goal of our actions is relating ourselves to our social, cultural and natural worlds, actual as well as past and anticipated'. In what follows, we will analyse the emergence of 'third' *I*-positions by examining how specific forms of symbolic action and their connotations develop within the hybrid space between established *I*-positions. We will then discuss that process in light of the interplay of the three levels of analysis.

Developing 'third positions' through symbolic action: an interview study

As part of a recent study on identity construction among transnational migrants to the USA, the first author (Surgan 2006) conducted a set of open-ended interviews with twelve participants from four continents. Participants varied by age (24–51) and length of time spent in the USA (2–32 years). Consistent with the notion of the 'new immigration', the participants were relatively homogeneous in terms of their reasons for coming to the USA (personal, professional and educational reasons). During the interviews, participants were asked about everyday life practices within the context of their transnational migration. Conversation focused on changes, resistance to change and the significance of those practices within the process of adjusting to life in the USA. Participants' talk about selected everyday practices was analysed with an eye towards the symbolic aspects of those actions. The role of meaning as a tool by which people establish feelings of being 'at home' is impossible to overestimate. Consider one of Boesch's examples:

the feeling of meaningfulness marks the difference between familiarity and strangeness. I walk along a shopping street – windows full of all kinds of goods, clothes hanging on outside stalls . . . all of it means something, although what exactly I may ignore, but it belongs to a society whose habits . . . are familiar. However, should I walk in an Arabian Suk, even the smell there would be strange . . . and soon, without a guide, I feel lost. All that, of course, means something to those living here, but to me, it is meaningless – or rather, it signifies a threat, loss of self-confidence, helplessness. (Boesch 2007: 310)

Although these may sound like the reflections of a person who simply does not enjoy travelling, this passage illustrates how even everyday activities like shopping, listening to music or enjoying an idle afternoon can be seen as arenas where established and emerging systems of meaning come into contact. Such arenas are where, in very concrete terms, personal-cultural activity and creativity can be seen in action.

Eleonora Lebednick: reconstructing 'independence'

Eleonora Lebednick was born in Cuba in 1955 to a Lithuanian father and a Costa Rican mother. On Eleonora's seventh birthday, her father was forced to escape Cuba and fled to Florida. Four days later, the rest of the family left for Costa Rica. After nine months apart, the family reunited in Florida for a month and moved together to Puerto Rico, where Eleonora's father ran an arm of his business. In 1972, Eleonora returned to the USA for college. During college, she was 'back and forth' between the USA and Puerto Rico. After graduation (1976), she returned to Puerto Rico, where she worked for two years and married before moving to Philadelphia and then to New Jersey, where she earned a Ph.D. She and her husband then moved back to Puerto Rico (1982–5) and had two daughters. After returning to the USA, the family visit Puerto Rico two or three times a year. Much of the Lebednick family remains in Puerto Rico, where they are well established and well respected. At the time of her interview, Eleonora was teaching high-school Spanish in the middle Atlantic USA and was planning to move back to Puerto Rico with her family. Soon after this interview, Eleonora and her family returned to Puerto Rico, where they still live.

Recalling her college days, Eleonora portrayed herself as having been securely Puerto Rican, not needing to display her heritage or pursue friendships with other Puerto Ricans. Her *I*-position as Puerto Rican was inherently compatible with her evolving *I*-position as American. This compatibility had at least two sources. Geographically, Puerto Rico 'sort of belongs to the whole area of North America'. Culturally, the Puerto Rican popular media of her time was already quite 'American'. Textbooks, TV shows and popular music were all directly imported from the USA. In this phase of her story, the two positions reinforce each other in a stability-bound form of dialogue that comes close to what Valsiner (2002) called mutual in-feeding (see also Gonçalves and Ribeiro's chapter in this volume).

The relation between her two *I*-positions changed as Eleonora grew older and had a family of her own. It became more important for her to maintain relationships with other Latin Americans and she claims that now 'most of my GOOD friends are Latin'. This change was motivated by her desire for her daughters to 'be aware of where their roots are'. As her adult life develops, we can see Eleonora more actively cultivating a Puerto Rican counter-position (in relation to *I*-as-American), which becomes a strong tool in the process of raising her daughters. Eleonora and her husband invest much time and money to ensure that their daughters will grow up to be 'authentic' Puerto Ricans, not 'tourists' or 'New Yoricans', with whom Eleonora strongly *dis*-identifies (calling them 'strange birds', 'radical', 'not me' and part of 'a different reality'). In this scene, the Puerto Rican *I*-position enters into its first explicit dialogue with *I*-as-American while dominating others completely, as Eleonora works discursively to pre-emptively short-circuit any possibility of construing her daughter's (and, by identification, her own) Puerto Ricanness as anything less than authentic.

Eleonora's efforts to cultivate certain basic values in her daughters reflects the notion that the process of positioning and counter-positioning opens a field in which the construction of a novel third position becomes possible (Hermans 2008). In this field, Eleonora sees a fundamental tension between the American and Latin approaches to 'independence'. It is here that Eleonora strays from her black-and-white thinking and stumbles into the murky waters of hybridization. The ability to rely on one another for help is a feature of Puerto Rican life that Eleonora would like her daughters to maintain. She, however, feels that this is 'very much missing' in American life – in contrast to Puerto Rico, where help is freely offered by the members of the community. Eleonora remarks, 'If there's a child around, there will always be twenty people around to help the child.' According to Eleonora, American-style independence includes too much emphasis on solitary self-sufficiency. In America, help is not freely offered, and asking for help comes with a certain amount of shame.

In discussing her hopes for her daughters, Eleonora describes what she considers an ideal mixture of American and Latin versions of independence. A person, according to Eleonora, should be able to take care *of oneself* but not necessarily *by oneself*. That is, people should be the primary agent in ensuring their own welfare and should not wait for others to help them. In this way, the basic axiological framework of American-style independence is in effect. However, Eleonora considers the ability to ask for help comfortably – and seeing others as cooperative instead of selfishly competitive – to be an important tool for taking care of oneself. This form of independence – a kind of interdependent independence – is a prototypically hybrid creation. Emerging from between familiar cultural forms, it is a form of symbolic action by which a novel 'third' position – a trans-Caribbean *I*-position – is enacted (see Figure 8.2). (For the notion of a 'third ambiguous position', see Raggatt's chapter.)

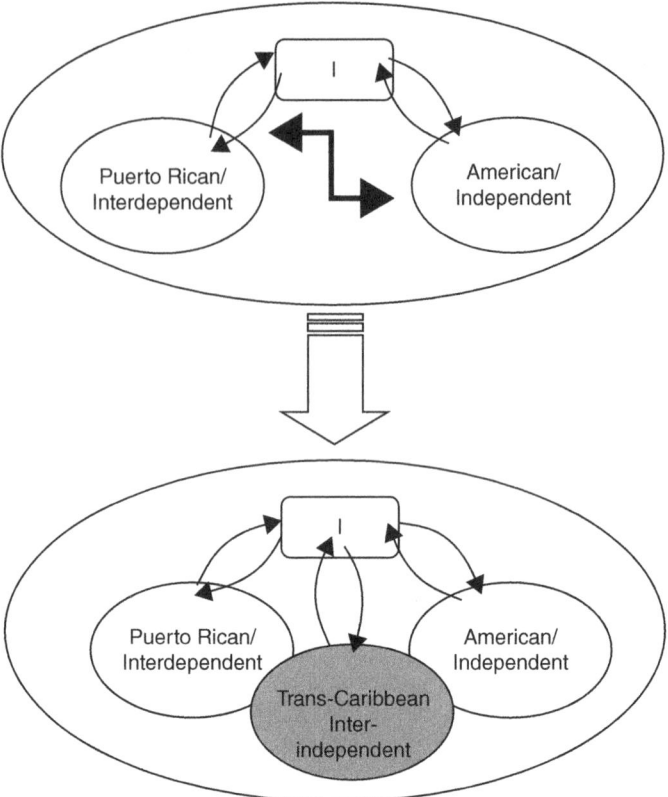

Figure 8.2 The emergence of Eleonora's hybrid trans-Caribbean *I*-position through symbolic action.

Analysing the emergence of third positions: forms of hybridization

Each *I*-position within the self system entails meaningful and value-laden (i.e. 'axiological') commitments to forms of action. In so far as a single position dominates the self system, the person's actions fit that perspective on the world and serve a particular set of meanings and values. In cases of hybridization, no existing position dominates completely. The *I* occupies a tense space between established positions, none of which are capable of adequately organizing action. In the process of voicing a new third position, the *I* draws upon and transforms aspects of existing *I*-positions, including the forms of action to which those positions are committed and the underlying semiotic/axiological framework that those positions entail.

Hybridization can take many forms, producing third positions that draw upon existing *I*-positions in different ways. For example, Eleonora's trans-Caribbean *I*-position emerges through a particular form of hybridization. In her construction, the act of getting help from others is transposed into the meaningful and axiological framework of American-style self-sufficiency. This form of hybridization might be described as *assimilatory transposition*. 'Assimilatory' here refers to the fact that the basic semiotic-axiological framework is that of the 'host' society. Specifically, Eleonora subscribes to the American-style notion that the individual should be the primary agent in one's own well-being. A behavioural element from her 'home' repertoire (i.e. comfortably expecting and pursuing help from others) is transposed into this existing axiological framework, yielding the hybrid form of action (and concomitant third *I*-position) that she hopes to cultivate in her daughters.

In contrast to Eleonora's mode of hybridization, a person may adopt a new set of behaviours that is more popular within the host community, but use those practices in service of meanings and values from home. This was the case for Elira Carconi, a young Albanian woman who struggled to maintain her existing values regarding time with friends while functioning within the dominant pattern of work/leisure of the USA. Since arriving in the USA, Elira has scaled back the amount of time that she spends with friends. On the social scene, this allows her to conform superficially to the prevailing norms of American social life and helps her avoid the label of being 'the needy friend'. Reduced time with friends also allows Elira to survive the institutional demands of post-graduate student life. However, the significance of time with friends was never subordinated to the perceived American focus on 'all work and no play'. We could call this form of hybridization *conservative transposition*. Here, 'conservative' indicates that something has been preserved from 'home'. In this case, the basic semiotic-axiological framework is that of the 'home' society. A behavioural element from 'American life' is transposed into the set of meanings and values that characterize Albanian social life as this participant experienced and understood it.

Rosanne's case (Branco *et al.* 2008), which Hermans and Hermans-Konopka (2010) present as a example of the construction of a third position, can also be seen as an example of hybridization, even though her story does not include transnational migration. In Surgan's (2006) study, participants discuss how they negotiate the tensions between existing *I*-positions (e.g. *I*-as-Albanian) and an emerging position of *I*-as-American. Similarly, Rosanne's case includes a tension between an existing *I*-position that has long been powerful within her life (i.e. *I*-as-Catholic) and a more recently emerging position (i.e. *I*-as-lesbian). In Rosanne's case, a breakthrough is made when she reconstructs some fundamental aspects of Catholicism and takes on the role of missionary. In this case, Rosanne takes a form of behaviour (i.e. being a missionary) that is well-established within the Catholic framework but uses that behaviour to serve a novel set of values. One might refer to this form of hybridization as *conservative resignification*. As in Elira Carconi's case, 'conservative' indicates maintenance of something from the 'home' (in this case, Catholic) way of life: becoming a missionary. 'Resignification' refers to the fact that Rosanne created a novel axiological framework within which the activity of being a missionary finds its personal-cultural significance. Specifically, Roseanne comes to her particular version of 'love' by wrestling with and, to a certain extent, distancing herself from the version of Catholicism with which she grew up. It is her 'personal theology' (Hermans and Hermans-Konopka 2010: 157) that gives personal sense to her work as a missionary.

Hybridization and inequality within the dialogical self: the centrality of expressive dominance

The stories told by Eleonora, Elira and Rosanne all demonstrate the notion that, in the process of hybridization, *I*-positions may not interact as equal partners. In Eleonora's case, the American position dictated the basic framework within which the act of seeking help was made meaningful. In other words, her American *I*-position held *expressive dominance* over her Puerto Rican *I*-position. Radhakrishnan nicely highlights this aspect of hybridization:

When someone speaks as an Asian-American, who is exactly speaking? If we dwell in the hyphen, who represents the hyphen: the Asian or the American, or can the hyphen speak for itself without creating an imbalance between the Asian and American components? ... True, *both components have status, but which has the power and the potential to read and interpret the other on its terms*? If the Asian is to be Americanised, will the American submit to Asianisation? (Radhakrishnan 1996: 211; emphasis added)

In Elira's case, the Albanian position held expressive dominance within the process of creating her novel third position. Rosanne created a novel 'personal theology', allowing her to occupy territory that might make her an outsider in both Catholic and gay communities.

Expressive dominance entails the ability of one position to provide the semiotic and axiological framework within which utterances and actions find their personal-cultural significance. This is a qualitative notion of dominance, compared to other, more quantitative notions that have been proposed (e.g. topic dominance, social dominance, amount of talk; Hermans and Dimaggio 2007; Hermans and Kempen 1995). Complete expressive dominance results in different forms of non-hybridization, including silencing of one position (accomplished discursively in many ways, as Eleonora illustrated in relation to 'New Yoricans'). In cases of hybridization, such dominance is *incomplete*. That is, both *I*-positions participate in the creation of the third position, but on unequal terms. As was illustrated in the previous section, different forms of hybridization are possible, and it is the form of hybridization that gives the new third position its particular character. A full typology of hybridization processes has been elaborated elsewhere (Surgan 2006, 2007), but is beyond the scope of this chapter. In order to understand why particular forms of hybridization are more likely to appear in particular cases, it is necessary to go beyond the personal level of analysis and connect the dynamics of *I*-positions with phenomena at the social and societal levels.

The dynamics of power on the psychological level and beyond: *I*-positions under societal guidance

Up to this point, we have focused on the creation of third positions through hybridization on a personal, private level (i.e. the self). We conceptualized *I*-positions as entailing meaningful and value-laden commitments to particular forms of action and examined the emergence of a novel hybrid *I*-position through the adoption or construction of specific forms of *symbolic* action. Action itself was analysed in terms of its surface features (observable form) and its symbolic capacity for semiotic and axiological expression. We elaborated the dynamics of hybridization in terms of *expressive dominance* and used that concept to describe a variety of ways in which the *I* can draw upon existing positions. Approaching the notion of hybridization through the lens of expressive dominance brings the issue of power to centre stage. It is here that DST can be extended across the personal, social and societal levels of analysis. Indeed, Hermans and Dimaggio (2007: 50) note that '[t]he notion of dominance points to the necessity of a linkage between the three levels'.

The work of producing novel forms of symbolic action, performed on the personal level of analysis, is, simultaneously, part of the 'identity work' of assuming a new position in the social sphere (as Falmagne's analysis of reasoning suggests). In other words, the symbolic forms of action by which novel *I*-positions are instantiated on the personal level also *externalize* the person's hybrid self, bringing it to the social scene. Such actions are part and parcel of making an identity claim, which may be heard, questioned, silenced, punished or even celebrated, by social others within their assumed roles in relation to the subject. A person's ability to accomplish a particular form of positioning depends upon the degree to which the identity being claimed is intelligible to relevant social others. As Abbey and Falmagne (2008) illustrate, positioning only works because the social interactions within which positioning occurs are configured by wider, societal-level discourses.

Consider an example from our first instance of 'immigration': our arrival on this planet through childbirth. Societal discourses surrounding childbirth range from 'Childbirth as natural' to 'childbirth as medical/ technological achievement'. When a newborn child must spend its earliest days in an incubator, these discourses clash in the life world of the mother. At this moment, the much-valued physiological, nurturing relationship between mother and child (which has been operating throughout pregnancy) is interrupted by the technical realities of childbirth as a medical procedure. The mother is forced into an outsider role as a machine assumes control over the life-sustaining aspects of motherhood. She must find another way of instantiating her *I*-position as mother. This rupture prompts personal-cultural dynamics that have been nicely brought to light by Landzelius (2001). By engaging in the symbolic action of decorating the incubator (with teddy bears, greeting cards, photos, etc.), the mother is able to enact a new version of motherhood. Thus, even an *I*-position that is as apparently natural as '*I*-as-mother' is configured by the norms and laws of childcare and family structure within a social group, as well as its technological inventions. It is important to note that, in this example, the symbolic action is *mediated*. It is accomplished through the use of particular cultural tools (e.g. teddy bears). These cultural tools are useful exactly because of their significance within societal-level discourses of childhood, home, family and caring. In this way, *I*-positions taken on by each person are configured by societal-level discourses and inhabited through the person's symbolic action, making *I*-positions real for the person himself or herself and intelligible to others.

Societal-level formations function as constraints on and promoters of forms of hybridization and, therefore, the emergence of third positions. Human history contains many examples of institutionalized suppression of particular forms of symbolic action. For example, when Jews were not allowed to study the Torah under ancient Hellenistic rule (but gambling was acceptable), the game of spinning the *dreidel* was invented. The dreidel is a spinning top inscribed with four Hebrew letters. Each letter is assigned a gambling-related function. The letters, however, also form the acronym of the sentence, 'A great miracle happened there.' Playing dreidel gave Jews a way of collectively remembering and covertly retelling the story of the Hanukkah miracle under conditions of harsh oppression. Similarly, when African slaves in Brazil were not allowed to practise fighting (but dancing was acceptable), *capoeira* was invented. Capoeira is an acrobatic art form that combines the actions and postures of a martial art with the music, singing and atmosphere of a dance. These are examples of *conservative synthesis*, where novel practices are synthesized in order to maintain something from 'home'. In these examples, oppressed groups found ways of expressing previously existing values in societal contexts where particular forms of symbolic action were outlawed (and others were promoted).

In a similar vein, societal-level formations may promote (but not determine) forms of dialogical relationships between *I*-positions. Indeed, Hermans and Hermans-Konopka (2010: 11) note that 'societal power differences are reflected in the relative dominance of positions in the self'. For example, consider the easy coexistence and mutual support between Eleonora's Puerto Rican and American *I*-positions during her college days. This configuration was supported by the context of formal education and the (somewhat peculiar) history of economic and political relations between Puerto Rico and the USA. On the one hand, conventionalized naming of world regions (propagated through societal valuing of formal education) legitimated Eleonora's claim about the geographical connection between Puerto Rico and the USA. The history of economic and political relations between the two countries is also relevant. As Eleonora pointed out, textbooks, music and television programmes were all directly imported from the USA. As a Commonwealth of the USA, many structural features of Puerto Rico's economic and political system are modelled after, borrowed from or even incorporated into corresponding systems in the USA. These societal and historical factors configure the social field within which identities are constructed and within which the personal dynamics of the self system operate.

General conclusions

One of the most exciting innovations in DST has been the introduction, by Hermans and Hermans-Konopka (2010), of the concept of third positions. This concept suggests that tensions between positions (whether full of conflict or creative energy) can be the starting point for the further development of the self system. With the emergence of a third position, relationships of tension are transformed into conciliation and creation. Throughout this chapter, we have tried to describe the process by which third positions can emerge. Thus, one of the contributions of this chapter to DST is the notion of *hybridization*. In this chapter, we have conceptualized hybridization as a dialogical process that involves selective combination and synthesis of *I*-positions. *I*-positions are meaningful and value-laden perspectives on the world that are voiced through the symbolic qualities of everyday action. Using several examples, we have illustrated the idea that hybridization occurs through the construction of novel forms of symbolic action, which cannot be reduced to previously existing forms. These novel forms of symbolic action instantiate and voice the emerging third position.

Another contribution of this chapter to DST is the claim that hybridization can take many forms and follow many trajectories. In other words, there are many ways in which third positions can emerge from the tension between *I*-positions. In this chapter, we have presented cases of *conservative* and *assimilatory transposition* as well as *conservative synthesis* and *conservative resignification*. These forms of hybridization (as well as others not discussed here) describe the many ways in which novelty may emerge either in terms of the semiotic/axiological framework expressed through symbolic action or in the observable form of the symbolic action itself. Different forms of hybridization can produce very different third positions, yet all have the same beginning: tension between *I*-positions. Therefore, the exact character of the third-position-in-the-making cannot be deduced by examining the *I*-positions that are currently in tension. We hope that our description of various hybridization processes helps us see the variety of ways in which the dialogical self can innovate itself, finding qualitatively novel patterns of form and function.

Finally, beyond describing several forms of hybridization by which third positions develop, we have explicated the emergence and interrelatedness of different forms of hybridization. To that end, we have argued that understanding the emergence of specific forms of hybridization in specific cases requires us to go beyond the personal level of analysis. Working through tensions between *I*-positions (on the personal level) entails identity-related positioning within the social field, which is configured by discursive and material formations on the societal level. As Hermans and Hermans-Konopka (2010: 158) suggest, the relative dominance of *I*-positions reflects societal power structures. In this chapter, we have conceptualized dominance within the process of hybridization in terms of *expressive dominance*, or the ability of one position to dictate the terms within which symbolic action gains its personal-cultural significance. This may be a more useful notion of dominance to carry forward. Further research into the relationship between specific societal-level formations and the dynamics of expressive dominance would strengthen the ability of DST to address the personal, social and societal levels of analysis while maintaining a focus on the dynamic and developmental potential of DST.

REFERENCES

Abbey, E. and Falmagne, R. J. (2008) Modes of tension work within the complex self, *Culture and Psychology*, **14**, 95–113
Anzaldua, G. (1999) *Borderlands/La Frontera* (San Francisco: Aunt Lute Books)
Bakhtin, M. (1981) *The Dialogic Imagination: Four Essays* (Austin, TX: University of Texas Press)
Bhabha, H. (1994) *The Location of Culture* (London: Routledge)
   (1996) Culture's in-between, in S. Hall and P. du Gay (eds.), *Questions of Cultural Identity* (Thousand Oaks, CA: Sage), 53–60
Boesch, E. E. (1997) Reasons for a symbolic concept of action, *Culture and Psychology*, **3**, 423–431
   (2001) Symbolic action theory in cultural psychology, *Culture and Psychology*, **7**, 479–483
   (2007) A meditation on message and meaning, in W. J. Lonner and S. A. Hayes (eds.), *Discovering Cultural Psychology: A Profile and Selected Readings of Ernest E. Boesch* (Charlotte, NC: Information Age), 309–330
Branco, A. U., Branco, A. L. and Madureira, A. F. A. (2008) Self-development and the emergence of new I-positions: emotions and self-dynamics, *Studia Psychologica*, **8**, 23–40
Falmagne, R. J. (2004) On the constitution of 'self' and 'mind': the dialectic of the system and the person, *Theory & Psychology*, **14**, 822–845
   (2009) Subverting theoretical dualisms: discourse and mentalism, *Theory & Psychology*, **19**, 795–815
Glick-Schiller, N., Basch, L. and Blanc, C. S. (1995) From immigrant to transmigrant: theorizing transnational migration, *Anthropological Quarterly*, **68**, 48–63
Hasnat, N. (1998) Being 'Amreekan': fried chicken versus chicken tikka, in S. D. Dasgupta (ed.), *A Patchwork Shawl: Chronicles of South Asian Women in America* (New Brunswick, NJ: Rutgers University Press), 33–45
Hermans, H. J. M. (1996) Voicing the self: from information processing to dialogical interchange, *Psychological Bulletin*, **119**, 31–50
   (2000) Valuation, innovation and critical personalism, *Theory & Psychology*, **10**, 801–814
   (2001) The dialogical self: toward a theory of personal and cultural positioning, *Culture & Psychology*, **7**, 243–281
   (2008) The dialogical self: state of the art, keynote address delivered to the 5th International Conference on the Dialogical Self, Cambridge, UK
Hermans, H. J. M. and Dimaggio, G. (2007) Self, identity, and globalization in times of uncertainty: a dialogical analysis, *Review of General Psychology*, **11**, 31–61

Hermans, H. J. M. and Hermans-Konopka, A. (2010) *Dialogical Self Theory: Positioning and Counter-Positioning in a Globalizing Society* (Cambridge University Press)

Hermans, H. J. M. and Kempen, H. J. G. (1993) *The Dialogical Self: Meaning as Movement* (San Diego, CA: Academic Press)

(1995) Body, mind, and culture: the dialogical nature of mediated action, *Culture & Psychology*, 1, 103–114

Josephs, I. E. (1997) Playful fighting vs fighting for dominance, *Culture and Psychology*, 3, 511–520

Kraidy, M. M. (2003) *Hybridity, or the Cultural Logic of Globalization* (Philadelphia: Temple University Press)

Landzelius, K. M. (2001) Charged artifacts and the detonation of liminality: teddy-bear diplomacy in the newborn incubator machine, *Journal of Material Culture*, 6, 332–344

Lugones, M. (1996) Purity, impurity and separation, in B. Laslett and R. E. B. Joeres (eds.), *The Second Signs Reader* (University of Chicago Press), 275–196

Obeyesekere, G. (1981) *Medusa's Hair: An Essay on Personal Symbols and Religious Experience* (University of Chicago Press)

Pieterse, J. N. (1995) Globalization as hybridization, in M. Featherstone, S. Lash and R. Robertson (eds.), *Global Modernities* (London: Sage), 45–68

(2001) Hybridity, so what? The anti-hybridity backlash and the riddles of recognition, *Theory, Culture & Society*, 18, 219–246

Radhakrishnan, R. (1996) *Diasporic Mediations: Between Home and Location* (Minneapolis, MN: University of Minnesota Press)

Rushdie, S. (1992) *Imaginary Homelands: Essays and Criticism 1981–1991* (London: Granta)

Surgan, S. (2006) Stories of home: otherness and identity in immigration narratives, unpublished Ph.D. thesis, Clark University, Worcester, MA

(2007) Conceptualizing hybridization, paper presented to the 12th Biennial Conference of the International Society for Theoretical Psychology, Toronto, Canada

Valsiner, J. (2002) Forms of dialogical relations and semiotic autoregulation within the self, *Theory & Psychology*, 12, 251–265

(2005) Scaffolding within the structure of the dialogical self: hierarchical dynamics of semiotic mediation, *New Ideas in Psychology*, 23, 197–206

(2007) Human development as migration, in L. M. Simão and J. Valsiner (eds.), *Otherness in Question: Labyrinths of the Self* (Charlotte, NC: Information Age), 349–378

Yao, S. G. (2003) Taxonomizing hybridity, *Textual Practice*, 17, 357–378

Young, R. J. C. (1996) *Colonial Desire: Hybridity in Theory, Culture, and Race* (London: Routledge)

9   Negotiating with autonomy and relatedness:
     dialogical processes in everyday lives
     of Indians

Nandita Chaudhary

> If people were not different, they would have nothing to say to each
> other. And if they were not the same, they would not understand each
> other.   (Arendt 1958: 155)

In this chapter, the specific nature of dialogical relationships in the
Indian self and society will be explored. Taking selected dimensions of
the social setting of Indians as it has evolved from its ancient history as
an instance, I will attempt to provide an explication of the principles of
dialogical self theory (DST) as effective and expressive in defining the
functioning of the self, precisely because it allows for the inclusion of
otherness in the self, context-dependence of behaviour, and the combination of personal and social functioning of the self in the Indian
situation. Within this proposal it becomes possible to address issues of
self-construction through dialogue and not domination, through discussion and not determination, thereby allowing the presence of complex
and even conflicting processes in the organization of the self and its
community. I attempt to explain such features of social interactions
and personal reconstructions in terms of what Hermans refers to as a
'society of the mind' (Hermans and Hermans-Konopka 2010: 1).

The (historical) social setting

The Indian subcontinent has had a textured history of external influence
and internal strife, whether it was ancient invaders, colonial occupation,
globalization or, more recently, terrorism. Conflict, diversity, adaptation
and survival have thus been the mainstay of its people. Like a giant
organism, it has expanded, divided and survived, leaving within and
outside its shifting borders fractured identities as well as enhanced
cohesion. Although the country only gained independence from the
British in 1947, also a time at which its territory was divided, the idea

of India is ancient in the sense that the subcontinent has changed borders and leaders, but each subsequent occupation has become incorporated into the collective identity. For example, colonial occupation led to the widespread use of the English language and when the British left, Indians adopted this language as their own. Somehow, with its textured history and constant occupation, the reality of adaptive survival has been sustained. It is often mind-boggling even to attempt to understand how such massive diversity and distance (literally and metaphorically) has allowed the nation to survive. With a thousand-odd languages and many, many more ethnic communities, with tremendous ecological variation heightened by economic, religious and social diversity, India remains an immense mystery. At present, alongside enduring traditions and unending poverty, increased mobility, occupational expansion, economic progress, technological advancement and global influence are exerting new pressures on the enduring character of its people. Many scholars admit that these contemporary challenges are yet another instance of invasion of persistent patterns of living, something that Indians are quite adept at handling. The proverbial adaptability developed over centuries is considered to be the strength of its people. Over its history, Indians have accepted other ways of living, and there is sufficient evidence to suggest the presence of a capacity for selecting dimensions of 'foreign' influence and making it their own. Evidence of this can be seen in culinary, sartorial, linguistic, religious and other cultural practices inside the home as well as on the street. And the magical quality of these developments has been that the changes have occurred in many cases without losing older ways of living. In this sense, the 'multilingual' capacity of Indian communities has in many ways allowed outside influence to be organically incorporated without eroding the identity of Indianness (Sen 2005). There are elements of tradition in everyday life that can be attributed to beliefs and practices that are thousands of years old, and it is extremely important to understand that, in India, there is a characteristic interweaving of the past and present.

When I speak of Indianness, I do not imply a homogeneous, monolithic structure of a consolidated, coherent way of living. If anything, Indian culture provides us with the exact opposite of that which is implied by these adjectives. The number of people and the diversity in languages, ethnic practices, legends and spirituality make such statements rather improbable. Even the past is textured with variety and multiplicity. India 'does not have one past, but many pasts' (Ramanujan 1999: 187). To add to the texture of multiplicity is the fact that the past always has a constant presence in the present (Anandalakshmy 2010). As Thapar (2000) observes, 'At certain levels there are aspects of cultural traditions in India that can be traced to roots as far back as a few thousand years, but such a continuity must not be confused with stagnation' (2000: xxv).

Thus, we find that there is an intricate interweaving and interlocking of the various pasts, such that 'every description of tradition can be as a negation or contradiction of another' (Anandalakshmy 2010: 19). As Rich (2010) writes of her days as an American student of Hindi in the city of Udaipur,

This town is in a time warp, though it is hard to say which time. When neighbours wave and ask 'Who was that who walked you home?' I think the '50s. When the *rikshaws* whiz by, looking like Model Ts from the back, it's the muted Indian '20s. But when I go to the doctor and find myself next to a tribal woman with an enormous gold nose ring, or when I talk to a Rajput, a member of the autocratic warrior caste – the men have knife-straight backs and villainous handlebar moustaches – I can see the links to the Middle Ages so clearly, its startling... In the centre of time's web ... is the sly tugging present. (2010: 49, 52)

This sense of parallel historicity underlying technological advancement in every sphere of life is enormously difficult to comprehend especially for people who live in the homogeneous-appearing environments of techno-logically advanced nations. There is thus a collective 'multivoicedness' that characterizes Indian cultural reality. It is like living in a time machine which simultaneously creates periods of history along its journey. Perhaps the metaphor of the 'time machine' bears important analogies with the DST, since the functional, dynamic temporality and spatial fluidity of the ideas are quite similar.

Multivoicedness and adaptability: derived and discursive identities

Relationships among members of any group are guided by cultural, social and historical orientations that develop over centuries. In Indian communities, there exists a deep sense of relatedness with other people. Individuals are defined by whom they are related to, whom they spend time with. Interpersonal linkages are believed to be con-structive of identity. As Marriott (1990) argued, Indians can better be characterized as 'dividuals' and not individuals, precisely because of the fundamental 'otherness' of community living that is organized around hierarchy (Dumont 1970) in interpersonal dynamics. In the fields of anthropology and sociology, much has been written about the peculiarities of the Indian social order, based keenly on categories and classification rather than on individual attributes (Marriott 1991). There have been many debates about the quality of the Indian mind, and whether this feature is peculiar, or something that is fundamentally human; but there is no denying the fact that for the Indian, social positioning remains a critical feature of the dynamic organization of people with each other and about themselves. As a matter of fact, it could easily be contended that 'social positioning' has more emphasis among Indians than 'personal positioning' (Hermans and Hermans-Konopka 2010). From a very young age, children are constantly oriented towards highlighting the presence and influence of 'others' in their lives with a correspondingly subordinated emphasis on the self. This pattern is maintained by direct intervention, narrating mythical stories, leading by example and discussing others' transgressions (Chaudhary 2004). In this sense, identities could be seen as 'derived', implying that every person is defined by the cluster of 'others' around him or her. It is not that 'personal' attributes are ignored, but rather that the constellation of people and circumstances are essential ingredients of personhood. For example, we find that children are often addressed as 'son or daughter of X'. This expression also extends to adults, who are often addressed as 'mother or father of Y' rather than by their names. First names are often avoided, and are likely to generate a sense of embarrassment when their articulation is demanded. Kin terms remain the most common deictic terms, often even for people who are not family. Although urban life has diminished some of these practices, as naming becomes more significant due to legal requirements and the need for identifying individuals, the elaborate kin terminology in Indian languages finds proportionate attention in everyday discourse (see Chaudhary 2004 for more details). Thus, if we accept that personal and social positioning are two dimensions of self-configuration, there is clear evidence of a prevailing focus on the latter in Indian culture.

Among Indians, reality itself is believed to be contingent upon context. To risk an over-generalization to other religious and ethnic groups, Hindu Indians are predisposed towards a world view that places central importance on society over and above the individual. There is a basic unfamiliarity with the preoccupation of Western society described as 'ontological individualism' (Bellah *et al.* 1985). In contrast, the Hindu view of society is 'organismic' (Menon 2003: 434), implying fundamental interconnections and interdependence between people. Social relationships and even morality are believed to be natural and enduring where it is the context, the role and relative social positioning that determine personhood. The idea of a consistent, core selfhood is reserved for spiritual discourse, where it is believed that every living being has at its centre an atman, the basic self that transcends a single life and believed to be a quality of the divine '*paramaatman*', ideas that are tacitly evident in discourse about personhood.

Communicative constellations: the structure of conversational interface

The words that people use are believed to provide invaluable insight into the constellation of thought of their users. Language, as Sapir (1949: 162) said, is a symbolic guide to a culture. Of particular significance is the fact that the users of any language(s) are quite unaware of the priorities that are shared in the use of a language (Wierzbicka 1997). However, it is when translations are attempted, especially for cultural characteristic experiences or items, that one becomes aware of several difficulties in meaning transfer. In a delightfully multilingual society like India, knowledge of a single language is rare. Most people grow up hearing several languages (Mohanty 1994). Language interactions are framed by the orientations to reality. In this manner, we are able to uncover some of the different layers of life that surround any given process of human interaction. Instances of language use are provided here to display some of the intriguing patterns that prevail in everyday conversations since they are believed to contain critical cultural information.

Going by the proposal that language is a symbolic guide for and a reflection of cultural processes, and that vocabulary is a sensitive index to the culture of a people, such proliferation suggests the social need to mark minute relational details in person talk. It is such differences between languages that provide the handle for analysis of differences. In actual fact, the study of cultural diversity and human universality can only proceed through dynamic, dialogical discussions (Wierzbicka 2006). Thus, if we see the universal task of forms of address in language, the variety displayed in different languages provides us with the variation that exists in this basic human endeavour.

Conversational interface among Indians is usually multiparty. Whether it is in childcare or social gatherings, there is a tendency to use strategies of multiparty discourse. The reasons could relate to the density of social life, and it remains a matter of common practice that lengthy dyadic interaction is not common (Chaudhary 2004). Several important strategies have been documented from research on language use. These strategies are actively taught to young children, sometimes directly, and sometimes through leading by example. Clearly, the messages that children receive for conversation is that what one says and what words are used are not to be driven so much by internal states and personal arguments, but by the context: who are the people within earshot, and what is the relative positioning of the different persons in conversation. A failure to recognize, acknowledge and act with regard for these factors leads to the breakdown of conversation and social inter-action (Chaudhary 2004). The list below is a compilation of tactics that characterize social dynamics with the purpose of providing evidence for 'positioning' in everyday discourse.

1. *Strategic silence.* In situations of doubt, silence is an effective strategy. Whenever a person is in an awkward social situation or a personal demand is made that she may find formidable, it is quite all right not to say anything, and to look to another person for a fitting response. This is a common experience for researchers in the field who find that respondents just turn away in silence during an interview when they are unable or unwilling to grasp the situation.

2. *Social ventriloquism.* In a hierarchical setting, due consideration has to be paid to the social arrangement. One of the strategies I encountered in families was talking on behalf of another person. In such situations, the pronoun 'we' may be used to hint at a personal involvement in the remark. For instance, if a woman does not wish to join the others for a visit, she might say to (and on behalf of) her child, 'Say that we have a headache. And would rather stay home.' In Hindi pronouns, there is an interesting possibility that the equivalent of the first-person plural 'we' can also be applied to the person herself. Person reference vocabulary in Indian languages provides the substance for several critical opportunities for saving face and not directly addressing the other, strategies that are perhaps essential for maintaining individual agency in a dense social setting. These intricacies are mostly hidden from the light of academic analysis primarily because they are so hard to grasp and investigate, and also because we have mostly been guided by the study of problems emerging from cultures with better developed industries of psychological research. Such a lan-guage exchange would be completely missed by a person who has not been socialized as a native, and would seem so commonplace to an insider that it is likely, in either instance, to receive little academic attention.

3. *Indirect address, speaking to* A *what is intended for* B. If something disagreeable or playful needs to be said, another person closer to one's own social status can be utilized to make a point, with the intention that the message is carried to the intended party, who may be within hearing distance. In this manner, the message is communicated without compromising the status of the other person.

An example of this would be that if someone whom you cannot address directly is talking loudly, a child in the vicinity (who may be talking) may be told to keep his voice down. Children are very popular targets for this sort of manipulation with relationships, since such a remark would be quite common to make anyway.

4. *Position shift.* This is a pervasive technique used by adults while addressing 'other' people in the environment in the presence of children. One of the most common instances of the strategy is to address others by using the kin term from the perspective of the child. So a mother may say to a child, when she wants the child to come in, 'Father is calling you.' In this case a significant other (father) takes the position of *I*, and this can be seen as a sign of the strong interconnectedness of the different positions.

5. *Speaking on behalf of others.* As a complement to the earlier mentioned phenomenon of strategic silence, it is very common for people to speak on behalf of each other, knowing well that it is a strategy to be used in case of doubt. For people from a culture in which it is unusual to do this, conversations with Indians can be quite deceptive, as indicated by the following example. A foreign researcher visiting our institute went along with us to visit a nearby village. He asked a daughter-in-law from one of the families: 'How many children do you have?' When the question was translated for her, she covered her face with a veil and looked away, and her mother-in-law answered for her. The visitor concluded that to Indian women it was not clear how many kids they had!

6. *Using kin terminology as a default person deixis system for other people.* Unknown people are usually taken into the fold of family terminology. Thus, there is a conscious application of kin terms to make people feel included in a person's life. For instance, close friends of the mother can be addressed as *Masi* ('mother's sister' in Hindi) to give them a special place in a child's life (also see Rich 2010).

7. *Lower frequency of first-person references in conversation.* Adults tend to make proportionately fewer references to themselves in conversations with children. The adult usually drops the subject in a sentence. For instance, a question like 'Can Mummy open this for you?' may be spoken as 'Can open this for you?' or even more simply, 'Open?' In my research, I have found a substantially low level of self-referencing among mothers in conversation with their children notwithstanding the fact that 'person talk' was the most dominant feature of conversations with children (Chaudhary 2004). Person talk here refers to those utterances in which people were the topic of conversation as opposed to events, objects or ideas. Of course, this could be construed

as negation of the self, or simply as giving priority to the child and to others in the environment.

8. *Encouragement of context-driven multivoicedness.* From a very young age, children are socialized to act with consideration for the circumstances, mostly the company in which they are. Socialization practices are eagerly focused on *how* children behave in front of whom. Thus, there will be playful indulgence in the company of the mother and other women, whereas the same adult (the mother) may make a harsh reproach for intimacy by the child in the presence of an outsider (Kakar 1981). Another example can be found in the encouragement of children by both the family and the school to differentiate ways of speaking at home and at school. The active separation of 'formal school talk' and 'informal speech at home' is a task the child has to master, although it is important to note that all talk at home is not the same. Children will gradually learn that they have to 'speak' differently in the presence of different people, even within the intimacy of the home. They will be reprimanded for too much familiarity or formality, depending upon the audience of any action.

Regarding differences between home and school, children are often given different 'names' for home and school so that a clear distinction is encouraged between the two domains. The presence of numerous dialects and languages in Indian communities has been a rather confounding matter for educational policy for language teaching, and one of the important features of school discourse is that children are expected to subordinate the use of the familiar dialect or language of the home to the formal medium of instruction, which may be a regional or national language, depending on the location. According to Mohanty (1994), this often leads to the development of different strategies at school, sometimes resulting in a serious 'gap' in children's language and cultural development.

9. *Conversations are more like 'multilogues' than dialogues.* The *Wiktionary*[1] defines 'multilogues' as many-to-many conversations typically using collaborative tools of social networking websites. I am using this term here to display one type of conversation in Indian homes that tends to take place when many people are together. In my study of adult discourse with children, while analysing who was speaking and who was being spoken to, I found the presence of several utterances which were being addressed to 'everyone in general and no one in particular' (Chaudhary 2004). Additionally, while such conversations were taking place, there was a sort of recursion to phrases that people tagged from each other, emphasizing and amplifying critical elements

in discussion. Similar descriptions are found in Rich's (2010) account of her stay with her host family, an extended unit of an undetermined number of members during her study of Hindi in Udaipur, India. She reports one such conversation (2010: 36) in which we find the multilogue, especially where Jain 1 addressed his statement to 'the kitchen at large':

Over dinner, they'd ask questions simultaneously or in round robin:

JAIN 1:	How much did you pay for the radio?
ME:	Five hundred rupees? No, I think it was six.
JAIN 1 (TO THE KITCHEN AT LARGE):	She is telling us she paid five hundred rupees for the radio.
JAIN 2 TO JAIN 1:	Five hundred?
JAIN 1:	Yes. She is telling us five hundred.
JAIN 3 TO JAIN 1:	Five hundred? I think she is telling us six.
JAIN 4:	Yes. Six.
JAIN 5:	She is saying six. No. Maybe she is saying five hundred and sixty rupees?
ME:	I think that's what I paid, six.
JAIN 5:	Yes. She is saying six.
JAIN 1:	SIX HUNDRED RUPEES? She paid too much!
JAIN 2, 3, 4, 5:	Yes, yes, yes! She paid too much.

As this example shows, multilogues result in a considerable amount of moments of what Hermans and Hermans-Konopka (2010) label as 'collective positioning'; that is, that speakers tend to shift positions in social interactions, making delicate modifications in their self presentation as they do. As suggested in DST, these multiple positions between people also emerge within the self.

10. *Open positioning of the self towards others*. Another feature of spoken language in Hindi, particularly, is the tendency in conversation to mark the end of a statement with a question. For instance, Indians commonly say something like: 'This ball is red, no?', 'Sit, no?' or 'Sit, yes?' (both of the preceding imply the same intention). In this instance, the negative (or positive) ending with a question is utilized to enhance the request and turn it into persuasion. As Desai (2010) remarks:

Isn't it a typical Indianism to end questions in a negative? 'Right, no?' *'Hai na'* (Isn't it)? In our everyday language, we use the negative ending to a question all the time in an unconscious way. As a mannerism of language that we employ routinely, it is useful in pointing towards an underlying cultural characteristic. The negative in the question prevents an opinion or a suggestion from being an assertion. It includes the person being spoken to, allowing for his or her input. In some ways, the person is unconsciously apologising for having an individual opinion and is appeasing the other person by attaching a note of self-doubt at the end. The doubt is dangled for the purposes of etiquette, and gives the speaker an escape route if the listener were to disagree. The dangling negative inquisitor ... is a sign of a culture uncomfortable with prickly individualism and helped turn individual inquiry into collective assent. (Desai 2010: 115)

Taking this instance of a prevalent discourse strategy, I propose here that there is a proclivity for intersubjectivity and for otherness in commonplace conversations in which a speaker is always sensitive (sometimes too sensitive) to the nuances of the other person's position, and, anticipating this, uses language to engage the listener into agreement. Inevitably, there are many quarrels that can potentially ensue over inappropriate usage of language or what is seen as rude behaviour on the part of the other person, especially when there is inadequate consideration for the other. In India as a hierarchically oriented society, there are rules within rules that are quite binding, but also numerous variations, depending on family orientation, language, ethnic group, social status and religion. For example, the above strategy for persuasion by ending with a question would not be considered a requirement for engaging a person in a lower social status, an employee, for instance. Thus, one always has to be mindful about what is being said to the other person for amicable social interaction. Using persuasion inappropriately could be taken as a weakness (but is also an element in discourse strategies of the erstwhile royalty, who were considered so far above the ordinary person, that they could overuse politeness as a style rather than a strategy!).

The ten illustrations given above indicate how deeply (and differently) 'other' people construct everyday conversations in the lives of Indians; and one prevalent format for discourse is what can clumsily be called 'to everyone in general and no one in particular'. In the rather delicate social dynamics of the Indian family, such strategies go a long way in maintaining social cohesion, saving face and evading responsibility when the need may arise. Here we find evidence for an emphasis on externality of self-positioning, where the 'other person' gains precedence over and above the individual self, whether it is to include, to ignore (as in strategic silences) or to be deliberately excluded. This feature of Indian cultural life has important implications for the study of the (extended) self. The consonance between traditional patterns and contemporary adaptations of externality points towards a clear cultural orientation towards others. It is important, however, not to see this preponderance as absolute and overarching, as has often been advanced in cross-cultural psychology, that Indians are a collectivistic people. This would result in an oversimplification since it needs the complementarity and the dialogicality with internal positions, which, although not necessarily encouraged beyond a point in social life, are an inevitable dimension of the self. In the next section, I will argue for the active engagement with internal positions of the self in social interactions.

The constructive coexistence of personal and social positioning

Being sensitive to circumstances is thus a critical dimension in the socialization of young children to the extent that context becomes a far more critical consideration than consistency in conduct. Thus, the expectation is for children to learn quite quickly that they have to behave differently in the presence of different people. This multivoicedness is one of the basic principles of successful social dynamics in Indian community living. Yet it must not be assumed that this is an overarching orientation that converts all members into automatons of social compliance, completely under the influence of 'otherness'. Nothing could be farther from the truth. There are several spaces and opportunities for asserting personal agency within the framework of external positioning. Potentially, there will be personal and collective strife as a result of pressures from different forces. For instance, when orientation to one group conflicts with that towards another, or when a personal desire has to be subordinated to the requirements of a group, it could create social fractures. How are some of these conflicts dealt with? In Hindu theory of morality, for instance, the notion of *dharma* (or righteous action as defined by social and personal obligations) provides an important traditional format for the hierarchy of moral obligations, again subordinating the personal to the collective (Menon 2003). *Dharma* is defined on the basis of the specific role of a person within a given context, and these features will demarcate what will constitute righteous action. For instance, the *dharma* of a householder will require him or her to subordinate personal needs for the good of the family; failing to do so would be considered 'immoral' within such an ideology, even if it were personal advancement that was juxtaposed as a competing choice.

In spite of this hierarchy, autonomy is clearly an opposing force when we consider social cohesion and order. Dynamic combinations of autonomy and interdependence usually help to maintain cultural coherence. If this were not the case, globalization would have broken the social architecture of Indian society. After all, India has remained the largest political democracy despite the long-standing tradition of compliance and conformity with collective forces. Despite great technological advances and global influence, traditions have allowed other ways of being to enter into community and family life. To illustrate this dynamic from a study of beliefs about parents of young children (3–6-year-olds), adults' orientations towards the development of autonomy in children with specific reference to the cultural importance placed on relational interactions were investigated (Tuli and Chaudhary 2010). How do Indian middle-class parents balance interactions with their children with these seemingly opposing forces of interdependence and closeness, on the one hand, and independence and autonomy on the other? The interview sessions revealed that adults selectively guided the child towards autonomy in certain tasks like relationships with other children, toilet habits, sleep routines and play. For areas that were considered critical for development, like eating, respectful conduct towards elders and relationships within the extended family, there was a high degree of determinism of the child's conduct in the sense that each action was supervised and controlled.

Adult care of the young child seemed to be highly inconsistent if all domains were taken together. However, if the domains were analysed separately by focusing on areas of cultural priority, it was found that there were common areas across the families where adults would exercise extreme concern for guiding children towards conformity. In the specific example of 'food'-related conduct, which remains a cultural priority, adults were found to be feeding children well beyond the age when they could handle food on their own. According to the respondents, there were many reasons for this; children tend to waste food if they eat on their own, they take much more time when they are left to themselves, their choices of food that they like to eat is often not 'good', and when food is being prepared by a family member, wasting it is just not an option. However, when children go out on their own, either to play at school or in another person's home, the questions facing the substitute caregiver or the child would concern precisely these areas, food and socially appropriate conduct (towards elders). We labelled this strategy 'elective interdependence' whereby adults guide their children towards variability in social distance and individual agency depending on the situation (Tuli and Chaudhary 2010). What happens here is that the children are encouraged to be autonomous in certain situations (like interactions with peers) and affectionate and interdependent with grandparents (for instance) for the benefit of all parties: the valuable place of older people in the lives of children, the value of the sustained contact with and presence of older members of the family, and the important assistance that grandparents can provide in the care of young children. Strategically, adults encourage their children to approach older people for care, affection, closeness and favours as they grow. Both the independence and the affiliation or approach is closely guided by the parents and significant adults in a child's life. 'Elective interdependence' was used to characterize this strategy that mothers were found to be using with their children when they actively guided them towards finding support and care from older people within the family. This was believed to strengthen the relationship between the grandparents (or other adults) and children, without displaying the role of the parents who were encouraging this. The expression 'elective' was used because this was done very carefully. The child was not expected to be equally close to everyone as is sometimes assumed about people from 'collectivistic' cultures. Closeness and distancing is something that a child learns by guidance from a very early age.

In another study of adolescents' interactions with parents, it was found that domain-specific expectations of adults in the family were frequently cited sources of stress for them. In particular, the 'calculated' distancing of peers and continued closeness to family was seen as one of the most difficult demands for adolescents who were moving towards greater affinity with peers. The assistance of and cooperation with peers was suspect since it was believed to lead to potential exploitation in the competitive classroom and street; but family members were mostly seen as benevolent and therefore always to be approached with supplication. There were also different orientations expected towards family members depending on current disputes within large families, another source of stress for the young adolescent. Interestingly, it was the 13–15-year-olds who were most vulnerable to these complexities; from the findings, it emerged that by the time they were around 18, these young people had accepted and adapted to adult expectations while retaining their autonomy in social conduct in most cases (Chaudhary and Kaura 2001).

This dialogical adaptability towards conflicting positioning is characteristic of Indian personal existence and community living. In many instances, social compliance is extended as lip service to an older (and valuable) way of living. The commitment to self-expression is subjugated to the social order, even if it implies a compromise with the self as a temporary adjustment. As in the instance of the older adolescents in the above-mentioned study, experiencing attraction towards peers and affiliation for the family, they develop a practiced distinction in their behaviour in the two external positions, that with peers and that with family. Thus, we find here that the degree of consistency between external positions may also be much lower in such a social climate than in cultures that encourage internal consistency of self-processes. I will stretch this argument further to say that a person who has the capacity for an elastic self that can acclimatize itself to the context is considered to have attained personal maturity, despite the putative inconsistency from an individualism-oriented perspective.

Contextual considerations: ambivalence, ambiguity or dialogicality?

The ways in which ambivalence is dealt with in everyday interactions displays imaginative dialogicality, allowing for the coexistence of different ways of positioning and divergent opinions. From these research studies and scholarly writings, evidence is available to develop new combinations of known ways of dealing with situations, along with the constant creation of novel solutions to emerging problems. DST is well placed to achieve a reasonable understanding of such phenomena that would otherwise be packed into boxes with inappropriate labels, or, worse, left unattended since they would be hard to classify. We can see how social interactions guide the developing person towards active engagement with cultural reality while retaining individual agency. Without a dialogical orientation, these creative human endeavours of self-development would be difficult, if not impossible, to explain.

Conclusions

DST provides us with an effective framework for exploring the flexibility and fluency of the self-processes that characterize human interactions. I have demonstrated how the notions of personal and social positioning provide us with a valuable framework for finding both the exceptions and the regularities in the cultural dynamics of Indians. Previous attempts to understand the self have moved from looking at rather limited dimensions of self-processes, often tightly bound into incomprehensible dualities within which reluctant individuals are categorized. Within the processes of dialogicality, the reality of personal encounters and social processes is considered without being dismissed as redundant or peripheral to the self. Each of us creates a psychological self as we go about our everyday lives. Psychology theory has often forced us to be placed within circumscribed boxes (e.g. individualist vs. collectivist). Cultures and people must not be categorized into one or another kind, since every time we do that, we will fall seriously short of reasonable explanation for any phenomena under study (Chaudhary 2009). As a consequence, therefore, we have often been unable to comprehend the coexistence of divergent orientations both in shared reality and personal predisposition. Dichotomies of self-structures, like individualism and collectivism, are based on the assumption of a high-internal consistency of self-processes founded on cultural oppositions (Hermans and Kempen 1998). I have attempted to show how, within a culture that prioritizes sociality, the collective and ideological demand for a consistency in positions in the self is not constructed as a developmental goal. As a matter of fact, it is the capacity to adapt and change the self that gains respect from others. However, within this frame, a reasonably strong sense of personal agency and individuality (both spiritual and personal) seems to express itself in specific domains. It is, perhaps, the capacity for mastery in both cohesion of positions in the self and flexibility of positioning that would make for the most mature combination for a person (see also Surgan and Abbey in this volume). While advancing this debate, we are compelled to consider that our evaluations of cultures and individuals (others as well as our own) must be advanced with the knowledge of prevailing realities that may themselves be dialogical arrangements of conflicting forces.

NOTE

1 http://en.wiktionary.org/wiki/multilogue

REFERENCES

Anandalakshmy, S. (2010) *Through the Lens of Culture: Centuries of Childhood and Education in India*. Monographs of Bala Mandir Research Foundation (Chennai: Bala Mandir Research Foundation)

Arendt, H. (1958) *The Human Condition* (University of Chicago Press)

Bellah, R. N., Madsen, R., Sullivan, W. M., Swidler, A. and Tipton, S. M. (1985) *Habits of the Heart: Individualism and Commitment in American Life* (Berkeley, CA: University of California Press)

Chaudhary, N. (2004) *Listening to Culture: Constructing Reality from Everyday Discourse* (New Delhi: Sage)

  (2009) Social dynamics in complex family contexts and its study, in J. Valsiner, P. C. M. Molenaar, M. C. D. P. Lyra and N. Chaudhary (eds.), *Dynamic Process Methodology in the Social and Developmental Sciences* (New York: Springer), 383–404

Chaudhary, N. and Kaura, I. (2001) Approaching privacy and selfhood through narratives, *Psychological Studies*, **46**, 67–78

Desai, S. (2010) *Mother Pious Lady: Making Sense of Everyday India* (New Delhi: HarperCollins)

Dumont, L. (1970) *Homo hierarchicus: The Caste System and Its Implications* (University of Chicago Press)

Hermans, H. J. M. (2001) The construction of a personal positioning repertoire: method and practice, *Culture and Psychology*, **7**, 323–366

Hermans, H. J. M. and Hermans-Konopka, A. (2010) *Dialogical Self Theory: Positioning and Counter-Positioning in a Globalizing Society* (Cambridge University Press)

Hermans, H. J. M. and Kempen, H. J. G. (1998) Moving cultures: the perilous problems of cultural dichotomies in a globalizing society, *American Psychologist*, **53**, 1111–1120

Kakar, S. (1981) *The Inner World* (New Delhi: Oxford University Press)

Marriott, M. (1990) *India Through Hindu Categories* (New Delhi: Sage)
    (1991) On constructing an Indian ethnosociology, *Contributions to Indian Sociology*, **25**, 295–308

Menon, U. (2003) Morality and context: a study of Hindu understandings, in J. Valsiner and J. Connolly (eds.), *Handbook of Developmental Psychology* (London: Sage), 431–449

Mohanty, A. K. (1994) *Bilingualism in a Multilingual Society: Psychosocial and Pedagogical Implications* (Mysore: Central Institute of Indian Languages)

Ramanujan, A. K. (1999) *The Collected Essays of A. K. Ramanujan.* Ed. V. Dharwadkar (New Delhi: Oxford University Press)

Rich, K. R. (2010) *Dreaming in Hindi: Coming Awake in Another Language* (New Delhi: Tranquebar)

Sapir, E. (1949) *Selected Writings in Language, Culture and Personality* (Berkeley, CA: University of California Press)

Sen, A. (2005) *The Argumentative Indian: Writings on Indian History, Culture and Identity* (London: Penguin)

Thapar, R. (2000) *The Penguin Early History of India* (New Delhi: Penguin)

Tuli, M. and Chaudhary, N. (2010) Elective interdependence: understanding individual agency and interpersonal relationships in Indian families, *Culture and Psychology*, **16**, 477–496

Wierzbicka, A. (1997) *Understanding Cultures Through Their Key Words* (London: Oxford University Press)
    (2006) *English: Meaning and Culture* (London: Oxford University Press)

10   Dialogicality and the internet

Vincent W. Hevern

Printing with moveable type first appeared in Europe in the mid-fifteenth century. This technological innovation created a new environment in which both books and newly created forms of written communication (journals, newspapers, pamphlets, etc.) could be more easily and broadly disseminated than was ever possible by the hand-copying of texts. Within less than a century, the print 'revolution' had undermined or challenged traditional aspects of European life including the role of monasteries and the power of the Roman Catholic Church (Dondi 2010). In recent decades a range of scholars under the disciplinary umbrella of media ecology have argued that the result of print technology included a fundamental shift in human cognitive functioning and values for those living in cultures awash in printed books and similar media (Lum 2006). The printed word fostered an individual's encounter with texts as a private experience, emphasized the importance of objectivity and critical distance, and undermined the priority of immediate oral communication.

The advent of the internet (Net) in the closing decades of the twentieth century appears to be a technological innovation with potentially as profound and influential an effect upon human beings, individually and communally, as the coming of the printing press (Feldman 2002; Shirky 2010). Adapting a biological metaphor first suggested by Nardi and O'Day (1999) in respect to information systems more generally, Hevern (2005) detailed how the internet may be described as the *human digital ecology*. As a vast and interconnected environment for communication and information storage (i.e. as an ecology broadly conceived), the internet functions on a worldwide basis; incorporates a myriad of protocols for the exchange of visual, auditory, and other types of information; and continually evolves new and competing technological forms to permit that exchange. Further, inherent in the digital nature of the internet lies its unique character as so-called *cyberspace* in which users explore the internet's varied locales via their computers. Thus, the contents of communication online (1) exist virtually independent of particular geographic location (albeit dependent upon physical network linkages), (2) are disseminated almost instantaneously, (3) are easily transformable and (4) are stored and accessed for increasingly lower costs.

Use of the internet across the globe stood at roughly 360 million persons (or 6% of the world's population) in late 2000 (Internet World Stats 2009) but will expand to more than 2 billion (29% of the world population) by 2010 (Shirky 2010). Profound geographic differences characterize present internet use: in 2009, about 74% of North Americans, 60% of Australians and 52% of Europeans used the Net while only 19.4% of Asians, 6.8% of Africans and 28.3% of those living in the Middle East did. Thus, the Net is still far from functioning as a universal technology across cultures. Nonetheless, the past decade has witnessed the proliferation of tools for direct social interaction and exchange between individuals and among groups via the rapid development of new online technologies. Pre-millennial internet media (email, instant messaging or texting, personal webpages and weblogs) have been joined by a host of post-2000 innovations: wikis, peer-to-peer file-transfer protocols (such as BitTorrent), social networking utilities (Facebook, MySpace, Twitter), VOIP or voice over the internet protocol (e.g. Skype), and both graphic image (Flickr) and video (YouTube, Vimeo) sharing utilities, among other developments (Thelwall 2009b). These online elements form an environment often labelled 'Web 2.0' (O'Reilly 2007) as individuals use the Net not merely to access information created by professional web developers ('Web 1.0') but also to create and share with others like themselves their own concerns, ideas, beliefs, artistic and other personal achievements, and so on. The affordances of these multifaceted technological tools have, as I detail below, powerful social and psychological implications (Wellman *et al.* 2003).

Hermans and Dimaggio (2007) analyse globalization in our current age of uncertainty and describe the widespread emergence of both global and local voices which function in continuous interaction and negotiation to shape both self and identity of those living in this age. Hermans and Hermans-Konopka (2010) argue that contemporary selves, inheriting millennia of human cultural achievements, live 'in a world society that is increasingly interconnected and intensely involved in historical changes [so that] dialogical relationships are required not only *between* individuals, groups and cultures, but also *within* the self of one and the same individual' (2010: 1). Building on these analyses, this chapter examines crucial aspects of the internet, which functions as a particularly rich instantiation of the forces of globalization and the emergence of the self as dialogical. Indeed, since the 1993 creation of the World Wide Web (WWW), the Net has become for many both a prime force for and singular example of the processes of globalization itself (Berners-Lee 2000). A particularly helpful stance for this analysis, I believe, comes from the *media ecological* perspective employed here: that is, how media 'affect human perception, understanding, feeling, and value' as those media form an environment of increasingly complex message transmission and exchange (Postman 1970: 161).

Key aspects of dialogicality and the internet

The complex of these digital media – the Net as a collective environment – both mirrors and challenges the contemporary self as a dialogical 'society of mind' (Hermans and Hermans-Konopka 2010). Persons using the internet at any length experience the principal forces highlighted by Hermans and Hermans-Konopka (2010) as markers of globalization; that is, *complexity, ambiguity, knowledge deficiency* and *unpredictability*. The almost unimaginable complexity of the Net is suggested by a single statistic: in 2008, the computers of Google stored more than 1 trillion unique WWW addresses, 1000 times as many sites as found just 8 years earlier (Alpert and Hajaj 2008). The sheer size and diversity of materials found online challenge web browsers to make sense of what they encounter. In following sequential, but often random pathways through hypertext documents, browsers often experience a sense of ambiguity in evaluating what they encounter online. Even the so-called 'digital native' generation – those born in the late twentieth century who came of age simultaneously with the Net – at times lack the knowledge either to evaluate their findings or to use digital technology in an informed fashion (Bennett *et al.* 2008; Robinson and Schlegl 2005). Finally, the level of online technological innovation has been so rapid and broad that forecasts about what the Net will look like in the future have been, at best, informed guesses. The Net of today was unpredicted even 10 years ago. Consider that the site we now know as Facebook first appeared in a dormitory room at Harvard University in early 2004. Six years later, more than 500 million people worldwide had accounts on this one social networking tool (Kirkpatrick 2010). What the Net will look like in another decade is unknown.

Within the framework detailed above, let me highlight three more specific points of intersection between dialogical self theory (DST) (Hermans and Hermans-Konopka 2010) and how the internet functions dynamically as a globalizing experience. I suggest that

- The internet alters the personal and social experience of Cartesian space and time.
- The internet may foster or undermine dialogical exchange depending upon the degree of anonymity and isolation users experience.
- The internet facilitates the expression of extreme forms of monologicality including what might be termed 'voices of darkness and the irrational'.

These are not the only aspects of the online environment that can be examined from a dialogical stance. But I believe that they demonstrate a range of the ways in which DST finds support from and can contribute to a more profound understanding of life in cyberspace.

Point 1: the internet alters the personal and social experience of Cartesian space and time

In the globalizing era of late modernity, individuals find themselves marked in varying degrees by three models of the self emerging from collective human history: the self (1) as *traditional* and split between body and mind, (2) as *modern* and centralized as a united entity, and (3) as *postmodern* and decentralized across diverse social and cultural localities (Hermans and Hermans-Konopka 2010). DST proposes that persons must negotiate with themselves to find ways of integrating these models across the multiple environments faced in daily life. The Net as a digital ecology raises additional challenges to these demands.

Consider how alterations in the personal and social experience of Cartesian space and time are a direct function of the internet as a digital medium. Modernist understandings of physical space (*here* vs. *there*) have become obliterated as digital technological innovations first carve arenas of life space into 'online' versus 'off-line' territories and, more recently, meld both of these into newly joined configurations (Taekke 2002). With the post-millennial advent of widespread broadband, Wi-Fi, and 3G cellular telephone access to the internet in many nations, the notion of needing dedicated places to function online is more and more disappearing. In many regions, portable electronic devices such as the iPhone and notebook computers can link users to the Net almost ubiquitously: bedrooms, living rooms, classrooms, city streets, bookstores, airport waiting rooms all become locales to go online. Further, the very notion of cyberspace obliterates the need to settle upon a single physical location for individuals to encounter one another (Hevern 2005). Distance disappears as a consideration online since the Net can connect individuals one-on-one or many-to-many without the need for physical nearness. Hevern and Annese (2005) demonstrate that isolated individuals such as those socially stigmatized or with physical disabilities can engage in social encounters with many others online because of the nature of cyberspace. Further, in the aftermath of disasters such as the 2010 Haitian earthquake or political unrest such as the 2009 Iranian 'Green' revolution, new forms of online social media (e.g. Twitter) facilitate the dissemination of information from the scene, link affected families and friends separated by great distances, and engage the attention of sympathetic citizens across the world (Gilmore 2010).

Similarly, modernist conceptions of personal time as strictly linear and sequential (*then* vs. *now*) more frequently are experienced online as both parallel (multiple *nows*) and recursive (past experiences, relationships and voices *re-presenting* themselves) on the Net. For example, consider Facebook, mentioned earlier. Subscribers to this social network regularly find themselves contacted by or are themselves contacting individuals from different stages of their lives (during childhood, college and university, etc.) whom they discover are also members of the network (Kirkpatrick 2010). In such online encounters years – even decades of time – may have passed since pairs were last in contact. Thus, within the contemporary time frame of an online meeting, correspondents must present themselves simultaneously as they are today and as they were in some fashion at an earlier point in life.

The implications of these changes in the experience of space and time are profound in other ways. They make possible a far broader engagement in constructing personal identity as a 'society' of mind. How? DST argues that, in contrast to more traditional role theory, the self engages in a constant process of active positioning; the self is agentic and an original source of meaning (Hermans and Hermans-Konopka 2010). Within the context of the internet, Hevern (2004) and Hevern and Annese (2005) detail how the authors of both personal home pages and weblogs construct their identities online, using a broad array of elements: autobiographical writing; photographs; links to valued topics, resources or personal concerns across multiple domains (political, religious, familial, sexual, etc.); and so on – all markers of self-identity. In doing so, these individuals make quite visible varying positions within the self and, frequently, solicit commentary or dialogue from those encountering their self-presentation online. In recent years, the rise of social networking tools such as Facebook or MySpace and their integration into other online presentation utilities continues to give selves the means of expressing valued and quite varied positions with ease (Kirkpatrick 2010). This development of very active presentation technologies ought not to be surprising. Over the last decade, evolutionary biologists have focused more intently on the ways in which organisms engage in active processes of transforming their environments – behaviour which is called 'niche construction' – and, in so doing, achieve organism-specific advantages for survival and development (Laland *et al.* 2000). Similarly, in the ecology of the internet, users are not merely passive consumers of media (as in buying a newspaper or magazine or turning on a specific television programme) but actively contribute to self-definition by posting messages, uploading visual or sound productions (to YouTube, Flickr, etc.), and engaging others in extended conversations in chat rooms or comment threads, and similarly active processes.

Point 2: the internet may foster or undermine dialogical exchange depending upon the degree of anonymity and isolation users experience

When individuals use the internet actively either by developing personal web pages and weblogs or by posting to social networking sites, they engage in acts of identity disclosure and construction. Many forms of online self-expression encourage an exploration of identity dialogically since they occur within the inherently social setting of others who view and respond to what individuals say about themselves. Examining personal home pages and weblogs, Hevern (2004) and Hevern and Annese (2005) noted broad and diverse forms of self-presentation online as authors reviewed their own political, social, philosophical and spiritual beliefs and activities. Further, online exchanges sometimes permit significant levels of disagreement to emerge as conversants explore each other's way of seeing and acting within the world. Thus, for some weblog authors such as the political writer Andrew Sullivan or the actor/gaming developer Wil Wheaton, it is not uncommon for them to enter into extended discussions with those with whom they disagree in some fashion.[1] Over the decade that Sullivan has published his weblog *The Daily Dish*, he has given even his fiercest critics a hearing and responded to their arguments about his positions on issues such as politics, religion and literature.

Yet, for many online users, a willingness to express and explore controversial or personally delicate issues rests upon the degree of anonymity offered by the particular internet tool through which the communication takes place. Interviewing weblog creators, Hevern (2004) found that the willingness to explore certain aspects of personal identity such as sexual orientation came much more easily if online writers had a sense of either anonymity (by the use of a pseudonym) or felt a relative isolation from their 'real-life' world within the online niche in which they published. In chat rooms and other discussion venues, teens often resort to the use of alternative nicknames or monikers which hide their identity; in such environments, adolescents frequently become more adventurous in the topics they are willing to discuss (Subrahmanyam *et al.* 2006). Further, researchers following the anonymous participants within virtual gaming environments, such as *World of Warfare*, find sophisticated forms of social experience that may differ profoundly from what happens in 'real life'. Players develop reputations for various gaming skills amidst loose networks of others who serve as an audience, provide a sense of 'social presence' and 'spectacle', and confer status and image on the gamers they are watching (Ducheneaut *et al.* 2006).

The post-2000 arrival of widespread social networking tools such as MySpace, Facebook and Twitter seems to have affected important aspects of what individuals choose to do online (Thelwall 2009b). The very rationale of these tools rejects online anonymity or isolation for the most part and seeks to link individuals who either know each other already or desire to build future relationships. Thus, persons usually distinguish themselves on these sites by posting at least a modicum of identifying data (particularly their names, location and gender; Livingstone 2008; Valkenburg and Peter 2009). Yet, as users begin to build larger and larger networks of relationships at such sites they confront a conundrum: Do I want everyone with whom I am linked to know 'X' about myself and what I am thinking, or, if not, how must I shape my self-expression so that I only disclose what I am comfortable disclosing?

Social network users answer this challenge in multiple ways, as by limiting links to specific online others or by altering the subject matter that they post. The social networks of college students tend to distinguish between those who are 'off-line' and 'online' friends (Subrahmanyam *et al.* 2008). Expressing themselves online to a relative paucity of 'real-life' observers, these emerging adult students often adopt a greater degree of experimental or exploratory self-presentation than they do off-line. Livingstone (2008) reports that older adolescents in the UK tend to be more discriminating in the ways in which they present themselves in online forums compared to younger adolescents. Older adolescents either change the degree of frankness in their online self-expression or create 'zones of privacy' by limiting access to their online postings to a more circumscribed network of friends. Finally, in a broad study of teenagers using the social networking site MySpace, Thelwall (2009a) found that users tended to show a high degree of *homophily*; that is, on many variables such as ethnicity, religion, age, country, marital status and sexual orientation they tend to be quite similar to their cyberfriends.

These findings suggest that individuals in cyberspace engage in quite active processes of positioning as they choose to express particular *I*-positions according to the degree of their public notoriety. Many who are either anonymous or sequestered online within secure locales that protect their 'real-world' identities seem ready to explore innovative aspects of themselves. But, public internet forums such as Facebook or MySpace elicit a more univocal or less revelatory online presence as a function of the diversity of those who serve as a social audience. Shirky summarizes these behaviours by noting that 'intimacy doesn't scale' (2010: 200). Further, Thelwall observes, 'The findings here echo in a new context (interpersonal relationships) the fears ... that despite the online availability of diversity (of information and opinions) people may choose to cocoon themselves away from the unfamiliar' (2009a: 229).

Point 3: the internet facilitates the expression of extreme forms of monologicality including voices of darkness and the irrational

Heightened levels of uncertainty in the contemporary world confront the self with the need to cope in new ways. Hermans and Hermans-Konopka (2010) outline five major strategies that the self might adopt in response to uncertainty. Among these options are three forms – *giving the lead to one powerful position, boundary sharpening* and *position multiplication* – that may help explain the online emergence of extreme forms of monologicality and what might be termed 'voices of darkness and the irrational'. The more extreme forms of monologicality grow from the unique spatial (and temporal) configurations of the internet and its affordances that allow the self to enter into networked relationships with others with varying degrees of *anonymity, isolation* and *exclusivity.*

Relatively early in the Net's existence, researchers began to note a phenomenon by which moderate voices online were often drowned out by one side or another in any hotly contested subject area (Shirky 1995; Wallace 1999). Social dynamics promoting group conformity tend to exert strong pressure upon participants in many online environments (Wallace 1999). Spears *et al.* (1990) found that individuals who already leaned in one direction or another on controversial political and social issues tended to move towards more extreme positions in online rather than face-to-face interactions. This process appears akin to what Hermans and Hermans-Konopka (2010) describe in dialogical theory as *giving lead to one powerful position* which tends to dominate other positions. Individuals defer to a dominant stance and either join in expressing solidarity with it or remain silent.

More recent work has highlighted the degree to which extreme forms of monologicality online involve political ideologies, international relations and religious beliefs. Such monologicality often takes the form of relatively isolated complexes of interconnected and mutually referencing internet-based media that resolutely shun links to or do not give positive expression of alternative voices. Jamieson and Capella (2008) labelled this phenomenon among strongly partisan political media as the 'echo chamber' effect. They highlight ways in which various communication media, particularly the internet and political talk radio, tend towards ideological 'Balkanization' and heightened polarization among consumers of these media. According to DST, this phenomenon corresponds functionally to the self as it *sharpens the boundary* between itself and those groups, ideas or other positions that fall outside the boundary.

The process of boundary sharpening is demonstrated online by a continuing tension between *alterity* and *abjectivity* (as Hermans and Dimaggio 2007 term it). The cyberworld simultaneously champions the other as valued (*alters* like gays, the disabled or trauma survivors who build communities online; Hevern and Annese 2005), while providing the means to construct the other as hated (the *'abject'* - *enemy* of the self such as the immigrant or the religiously different believer who must be reviled in order to secure one's own personal identity in an uncertain world). A particularly clear expression of this phenomenon can be seen among those organizations in the USA labelled as 'hate groups' by the Southern Poverty Law Center: 'Currently, there are 932 known hate groups operating across the country . . . [a]nd their numbers are growing' ('Hate and extremism', 2010: paragraph 2). Commonly targeted others who serve as the objects of this hatred most frequently include Jews and other non-Christians, non-Whites, government employees, gays and other sexual minorities. These extremist groups identify themselves with names like Stormfront (the oldest White Christian Nationalist group in the USA), White Revolution (a neo-Nazi group), California Coalition for Immigration Reform (an anti-immigrant group which labels Mexican immigrants as 'savages'), Knights of the Ku Klux Klan, and the Nation of Islam (an anti-Semitic Black separatist movement founded in 1930).

Schafer (2002) has analysed online hate groups and identified important common features across sites. Central to their operation are extensive chat rooms and discussion boards in which like-minded individuals can share their beliefs across a range of topics. In so doing, 'the internet allows extremist groups to offer social support, regardless of geographic proximity. . . Members can also share information that is outside of the control of either the government or conventional media ... making this mode of communication more secure and appealing in the eyes of group adherents' (Schafer 2002: 72). Such sites often reiterate a set of common themes relating to the unacceptability of different abject others while filtering out voices that may disagree or offer alternative viewpoints. In this fashion, a kind of relentless monologicality sabotages the potential for fruitful dialogical exchange by site visitors beyond the hate expressed by the website. Rather than offering a dialogical encounter with others who are different, such websites illustrate how coalitions of abject positions can be assembled in order to voice strong boundaries between the self and the hated other.

A more specialized expression of monological positioning which is divorced from broader dialogical exchange comes in confronting the online growth of what might be termed 'voices of darkness and the irrational', *which for practical purposes otherwise could not function without the internet.* Examples of such voices would include those who traffic in child pornography, advocates of adult–child sexual relations, and promoters of self-injury and apparently destructive lifestyles such as the 'pro-anorexia' (or 'pro-ana') community.

Consider that the dissemination of explicit child pornography was highly circumscribed throughout the twentieth century (Wortley and Smallbone 2006). But 'the advent of the internet in the 1980s dramatically changed the scale and nature of the child pornography problem' (2006: 1) on a worldwide basis. Organized pornography rings involving an estimated 50,000 to 100,000 paedophile members across the globe arose online. Among those seeking explicit materials on the Net, recent research data suggest that about 10 per cent are consumers of child pornography (Seigfried 2008). Critical aspects of those seeking child pornography online include (1) sophisticated use of multiple internet data exchange tools (bulletin boards, listservs, Internet Relay Chat, Usenet newsgroups and password-protected chat rooms); (2) gravitation towards cybercommunities of like-minded individuals, who receive 'social validation, a sense of belonging, and support' in such groups (Bourke and Hernandez 2009: 188); and (3) a general lack of observable characteristics which might signal a tendency towards child pornography use. Wortley and Smallbone (2006) point out that online child pornography users 'are more than likely to be in a relationship, to be employed, to have an above-average IQ, to be college educated, and to not have a criminal record' (2006: 14).

These findings present researchers with an enigma: since few specific subject variables seem associated with child pornography use *per se*, what may be the contributory factors involved in such behaviour? From the perspective of both DST and media ecology, the seeming anonymity of cyberspace and the construction of highly specialized digital niches may remove the self from exposure to other cautionary voices opposed to such behaviour (Wortley and Smallbone 2006). In a sense, the overall effect of anonymity, the relative isolation of online child pornography sites, and their dedication to an exclusive concern with the trade of images of children engaged in sexual acts seems to block out more conventional social and legal voices opposed to such behaviour. Further, as Granic and Lamey point out, 'Conventional hierarchies are disrupted by a distributed, decentralized network [such as those found on the internet] in which power is spread among various people and groups and one voice does not dominate or pre-empt others' (2000: 104). While not dominated by the voices of either a single person or block of individuals, such sites do display the monologicality of a shared but highly focused concern. The absence of counter-voices objecting to the trade of child pornographic images builds upon the diffusion of responsibility inherent in such sites. With repeated visits, child pornography users appear to become habituated and desensitized to the implications of their actions.

The behaviour highlighted here – of individuals enmeshed simultaneously in online communities voicing aspects of 'darkness and irrationality' and in 'real-life' settings of relative social conformity – challenges any theory of the self and offers distinctive possibilities for DST. These phenomena can be represented by a hybridized form of the strategies used by the postmodern self in confronting uncertainty; namely, a multiplication of positions functioning in relative autonomy *and* the simultaneous sharpening of position boundaries *within the self* rather than between the self and others. This formulation of DST seems akin to what Rowan and Cooper summarize as 'simultaneous pluralism – the way in which a person can maintain a dynamic portfolio of alternative self concepts as they move through the world' (1999: 5), a viewpoint championed by Rappoport *et al.* (1999).

Concluding remarks

Humanity has completed only two decades of intensive involvement in online activity. What have we come to know about people's behaviour online? As DST would suggest, those who employ the internet do so generally in quite active, adaptive, social and storied ways (Hevern 2005). Yet, the emergence of this worldwide communication medium itself contributes to the broad phenomenon of globalization with its attendant changes to traditional ways of social life and custom. The internet challenges us to understand how people cope with the resulting uncertainty of this globalized world. Adopting a media ecological perspective regarding the Net, this chapter has pointed to a variety of ways that DST can explicate how people function in this new communications environment.

The notion of positions within the dialogical self rests upon the developmental grounding of the self as spatialized both physically and psychologically (Hermans and Hermans-Konopka 2010). The advent of a completely new spatial form in human experience, cyberspace, undermines both traditional and modernist ways of conceiving how people function intra- and interpersonally. Internet users no longer confront the limits of Cartesian space and time and have flocked to dialogical exchange online eagerly. Yet, within the uncertainty engendered by its complex and ever-more diversifying ecology, the internet seems to evoke differential forms of online behaviour and expression. For many, the self engages in novel and distinctive forms of dialogical exchange only behind the social boundaries afforded by anonymity and the relative isolation of different communication tools. For others, the uncertainty of postmodern forms of life finds expression when selves adopt relatively extreme forms of monologicality online that cast the world into a struggle between valued selves and despised abject others. Finally, the internet seems to permit the emergence of what I have termed here 'voices of darkness and the irrational'. The emergence of such voices appears to be facilitated by dual factors: distinctive positioning strategies of the self as well as the unique affordances of barricaded and relatively anonymous internet communication tools.

NOTE

1 Hevern (2004) offered an explicit review of the weblogs of both these authors. More than six years after that analysis, both bloggers are still quite active in writing online.

REFERENCES

Alpert, J. and Hajaj, N. (2008, 25 July) *We Knew the Web Was Big . . . The Official Google Blog*. Retrieved 11 June 2010 from http://googleblog.blogspot.com/2008/07/we-knew-web-was-big.html

Anderson, J. Q. and Rainie, L. (2010, 19 February) *The Future of the Internet IV*. Pew Internet and American Life Project. Retrieved 8 June 2010 from http://pewinternet.org/topics/Future-of-the-internet.aspx

Bennett, S., Maton, K. and Kervin, L. (2008) The 'digital natives' debate: a critical review of the evidence, *British Journal of Educational Technology*, **39**, 775–786

Berners-Lee, T. (2000) *Weaving the Web: The Original Design and Ultimate Destiny of the World Wide Web by Its Inventor* (San Francisco, CA: HarperCollins)

Bourke, M. L. and Hernandez, A. E. (2009) The 'Butner study' redux: a report of the incidence of hands-on child victimization by child pornography offenders, *Journal of Family Violence*, **24**, 183–191

Dondi, C. (2010) The European printing revolution, in M. F. Suarez and H. R. Woudhuysen (eds.), *The Oxford Companion to the Book* (New York: Oxford University Press), vol. I, 53–61

Ducheneaut, N., Yee, N., Nickell, E. and Moore, R. J. (2006, April) Alone together? Exploring the social dynamics of massively multiplayer online games, paper presented at the 2006 Conference on Human Factors in Computing Systems, Association of Computing Machinery, Montreal, Canada. Retrieved 10 June 2010 from http://portal.acm.org/citation.cfm?id=1124772.1124834

Feldman, M. P. (2002) The Internet revolution and the geography of innovation, *International Social Science Journal*, **54**, 47–56

Gilmore, G. (2010, 24 May) 10 reasons social media is important in a real crisis. Glen Gilmore and Social Media [weblog]. Retrieved 12 June, 2010 from http://glengilmoreblog.blogspot.com/2010/05/10-reasons-why-social-media-is.html

Granic, I. and Lamey, A. V. (2000) The self-organization of the Internet and changing modes of thought, *New Ideas in Psychology*, **18**, 93–107

Harding-Rolls, P. (2009) There's life beyond World of Warcraft. *Screen Digest*, 24 March 2009. Retrieved 20 May 2011 from www.greenfieldscommunications.com/releases/09/Screen_Digest_Life_beyond_World_of_Warcraft_240309_F.pdf

Hate and extremism (2010) Southern Poverty Law Center. Retrieved 8 June 2010 from www.splcenter.org/what-we-do/hate-and-extremism

Hermans, H. J. M. and Dimaggio, G. (2007) Self, identity, and globalization in times of uncertainty: a dialogical analysis, *Review of General Psychology*, **11**, 31–61

Hermans, H. J. M. and Hermans-Konopka, A. (2010) *Dialogical Self Theory: Positioning and Counter-Positioning in a Globalizing Society* (New York: Cambridge University Press)

Hevern, V. W. (2004) Threaded identity in cyberspace: weblogs and positioning in the dialogical self, *Identity: An International Journal of Theory and Research*, **4**, 321–335

 (2005) Dialogical selves in the human digital ecology, in P. K. Oleś and H. J. M. Hermans (eds.), *The Dialogical Self: Theory and Research* (Lublin, Poland: Wydawnictwo Katolicki Uniwersytet Lubelski), 15–26

Hevern, V. W. and Annese, S. (2005) Le homepage personali in rete: il sé a dialogo con l'altro [Personal home pages on the Web: the self in dialogue with the other], in M. B. Ligorio and H. J. M. Hermans (eds.), *Identità dialogiche nell'era digitale* [*Dialogical Identity in the Digital Age*] (Gardolo-Trento, Italy: Editioni Erickson), 41–63

Internet World Stats (2009) World internet usage statistics news and world population stats. Retrieved 10 March 2010 from www.internetworldstats.com/stats.htm

Jamieson, K. H. and Cappella, J. N. (2008) *Echo Chamber: Rush Limbaugh and the Conservative Media Establishment* (New York: Oxford University Press)

Kirkpatrick, D. (2010) *The Facebook Effect: The Inside Story of the Company that is Connecting the World* (New York: Simon & Schuster)

Laland, K. N., Odling-Smee, J. and Feldman, M. W. (2000) Niche construction, biological evolution, and cultural change, *Behavioral and Brain Sciences*, **23**, 131–175

Livingstone, S. (2008) Taking risky opportunities in youthful content creation: teenagers' use of social networking sites for intimacy, privacy and self-expression, *New Media and Society*, **10**, 393–411

Lum, C. M. K. (ed.) (2006) *Perspectives on Culture, Technology and Communication: The Media Ecology Tradition* (Cresskill, NJ: Hampton Press)

Nardi, B. A. and O'Day, V. L. (1999) *Information Ecologies: Using Technology with Heart* (Cambridge, MA: MIT Press)

O'Reilly, T. (2007) What is Web 2.0? Design patterns and business models for the next generation of software, *Communications and Strategies*, **65**, 17–37

Postman, N. (1970) The reformed English curriculum, in A. C. Eurich (ed.), *High School 1980: The Shape of the Future in American Secondary Education* (New York: Pitman), 160–168

Rappoport, L., Baumgardner, S. and Boone, G. (1999) Postmodern culture and the plural self, in J. Rowan and M. Cooper (eds.), *The Plural Self: Multiplicity in Everyday Life* (London: Sage), 93–106

Robinson, A. M. and Schlegl, K. (2005) Student use of the Internet for research projects: a problem? our problem? what can we do about it?, *Political Science and Politics*, **38**, 311–315

Rowan, J. and Cooper, M. (eds.) (1999) *The Plural Self: Multiplicity in Everyday Life* (London: Sage)

Schafer, J. A. (2002) Spinning the web of hate: Web-based hate propagation by extremist organizations, *Journal of Criminal Justice and Popular Culture*, **9**, 69–88

Seigfried, K. C. (2008) Self-reported online child pornography behavior: a psychological analysis, *International Journal of Cyber Criminology*, **2**, 286–297

Shirky, C. (1995) *Voices of the net* (Emeryville, CA: ZD Press)
    (2010) *Cognitive Surplus: Creativity and Generosity in a Connected Age* (New York: Penguin)

Siapera, E. (2006) Multiculturalism online: the internet and the dilemmas of multicultural politics, *European Journal of Cultural Studies*, **9**, 5–24

Spears, M., Russell, L. and Lee, S. (1990) De-individuation and group polarization in computer-mediated communication, *British Journal of Social Psychology*, **29**, 121–134

Subrahmanyam, K., Reich, S. M., Waechter, N. and Espinosa, G. (2008) Online and offline social networks: use of social networking sits by emerging adults, *Journal of Applied Developmental Psychology*, **29**, 420–433

Subrahmanyam, K., Smahel, P. and Greenfield, P. (2006) Connecting developmental constructions to the internet: identity presentation and sexual exploration in online teen chat rooms, *Developmental Psychology*, **42**, 395–406

Taekke, J. (2002) Cyberspace as a space parallel to geographical space, in L. Qvortrup (ed.), *Virtual Space: Spatiality in Virtual Inhabited 3D Worlds* (London: Springer-Verlag), 25–45

The 1000 most visited sites on the Web (2010, April) Google. Retrieved 1 June 2010 from www.google.com/adplanner/static/top1000/

Thelwall, M. (2009a) Homophily in MySpace, *Journal of the American Society for Information Science and Technology*, **60**, 219–231

(2009b) Social network sites: users and uses, in M. V. Zelkowitz (ed.), *Advances in Computing*, vol. 76 (Amsterdam: Elsevier), 19–73

Valkenburg, P. M. and Peter, J. (2009) Social consequences of the internet for adolescents, *Current Directions in Psychological Science*, **18**, 1–5

Wallace, P. (1999) *The Psychology of the Internet* (New York: Cambridge University Press)

Wellman, B., Quan-Haase, A., Boases, J., Chen, W., Hampton, K., Isla de Diaz, I. and Miyata, K. (2003) The social affordances of the internet for networked individualism, *Journal of Computer-Mediated Communication*, **8**, 3

Wortley, R. and Smallbone, S. (2006) *Child Pornography on the Internet* (Problem-Specific Guides Series No. 41). Office of Community-Oriented Policing Services: US Department of Justice. Retrieved 3 June 2010 from www.cops.usdoj.gov/files/RIC/Publications/e04062000.pdf

11 Schizophrenia and alterations in first-person experience: advances offered from the vantage point of dialogical self theory

Paul H. Lysaker and John T. Lysaker

With diverse roots in the work of Kierkegaard (1849/1980), Nietzsche (1886/1966), Dewey (1922/1988) and Bakhtin's literary analyses of Dostoyevsky (1929/1985), dialogical self theory (DST) suggests that a human being's sense of self across the events of a day and lifetime is not the accomplishment of a singular and stable self. Identity is not the experience of a core self that underlies, or directs, the full range of human experience and action. Instead, the coherence of self-perception and action flow out of dynamic dialogues simultaneously occurring within a person and between persons in purposive contexts (Hermans 1996; Hermans and Hermans-Konopka 2010). The term 'dialogue' is employed because different and semi-independent self-facets or 'self-positions' interact with one another, giving rise to a sense of self. Importantly, these positions may be similar or quite dissimilar, even contradictory. For instance, while one is drinking coffee in a lounge during a work break, one's sense of self could emerge from the interactions among sense of self as 'tired', 'a successful adult', 'worried about a daughter's application to college', 'envious of a colleague', 'missing a lover', 'entering a new stage of one's career' and so on. And the interactions among these different facets might change depending upon whether an old friend arrives unexpectedly, the drink is changed from coffee to gin, or a rival is seen to be engaged in deep conversation with an office mate.

On this view, the self is thus regarded as an interanimating constellation of elements or, better still, moments (whose genesis is a combination of embodied biological and eco-social forces as well as personal experiences). Self-experience specifically gains its richness from the number and depth of different self-positions that arise in and enable one to respond coherently to ongoing life experiences as one pursues various goals. For example, as one eats breakfast in a cold diner with an old friend after a sleepless night, various self-facets might come into play: self-as-friend, self-as-hungry, self-as-cold, self-as-tired, self-as-anxious, etc. Again, the sense of self in this example and many others arises out of exchanges or 'dialogues' between these various facets in particular contexts. Thus, for dialogical psychology, the sense of self is not given in an intuitive grasp of some stable, core self, but in a disclosure of some facet of the temporal, polyphonic constellation that each of us is.

While DST has been linked to a wide range of clinical innovations (Hermans and Dimaggio 2004) as well as innovations in socio-political theory (Hermans and Hermans-Konopka 2010), it has implications for understanding a range of perplexing psychiatric issues. In this chapter we will in particular discuss an application of this theory which may advance our understanding of schizophrenia.

While some still claim that schizophrenia is a myth (Boyle 2002), most contemporary research presents the difficulties experienced by persons diagnosed with schizophrenia as the effect of biological processes and/or social injustice. For example, it has been hypothesized that abnormal brain development *in utero*, or in early childhood or adolescence (Fish and Kendler 2005; McGlashan and Hoffman 2000; O'Donnell 2007) leaves individuals suffering from schizophrenia with brain activity insufficiently coordinated to respond to the multiple demands of daily life. Others suggest that social stigma, which unjustly equates mental illness with incompetence or dangerousness, leaves persons with schizophrenia without adequate levels of self-esteem and self-confidence (Markowitz 1998). Taken together, these views portray persons with schizophrenia as either not suffering from anything tangible or as unable to engage life meaningfully as a result of a range of impersonal forces. Neurobiological insult, concurrent social conditions or scientific delusions are seen as precluding healthy function, perhaps metaphorically assaulting an individual subjectivity on all fronts.

While these lines of research have greatly advanced our contemporary understanding of disability, as we have suggested elsewhere (Lysaker and Lysaker 2008), the portrait of the person suffering from schizophrenia which emerges from this is deeply problematic. Schizophrenia, whatever its aetiology, is a disorder that interrupts the lives of people who must continue to struggle to find and create security and meaning in a world of contingency. As Stanghellini has noted, if we fail to consider the first-person aspects of the illness, we may separate 'madness from the man who embodies it' (2004: 46). Similarly, Barham has suggested that someone with schizophrenia must be understood 'as an active participant in social life' in order 'to identify more adequately where he fails as a social agent' (1993: 78). Beyond this, overlooking schizophrenia's first-person dimensions risks objectifying persons with this condition and obscuring capacities they have which might enable them to interpret productively and address the challenges that unfold as a result of their illness.

Support for the importance of exploring the first-person experience of schizophrenia can be found in studies of outcome and recovery. Andresen and colleagues have suggested that those suffering from schizophrenia must overcome a 'loss of a sense of identity' (2003: 589). Others have suggested that recovery may require not only symptom remission but also changes in deeply subjective aspects of human experience, including a deepened experience of self and world and the development of a richer and more coherent personal narrative (France and Uhlin 2006; Lysaker and Lysaker 2008). Consistent with this, first-person accounts by individuals with schizophrenia describe alterations and over-all diminishment in basic self-experience. Recently, for example, Kean (2009) has written: 'What lies behind the symptoms is a tormented self, a highly personal experience unchangeable and irreplaceable by any physical treatment... [D]espite the "usual" voices, alien thoughts and paranoia, what scared me the most was a sense that I had lost myself, a constant feeling that my self no longer belonged to me' (p. 1). She continues: 'This has nothing to do with the suspicious thoughts or voices; it is purely a distorted state of being. The clinical symptoms come and go, but this nothingness of the self is permanently there' (2009: 1).

Kean's report is telling for several reasons. First, it, too, presents an experience of self-diminishment in the course of schizophrenia. Second, it further specifies that experience: 'my self no longer belonged to me'. The claim is not that the self belongs to some alien force, but that her 'self' no longer appears as her own, singular project. She no longer encounters herself as a being of her own making. In fact, where an ongoing sense of effective agency lay, only nothingness remains. Third, congruent with other findings (e.g. Lysaker and Buck 2008), her experiences of self-diminishment may persist or remit independently of changes in symptoms or other outcomes.

Indeed, empirical research has demonstrated that many have experienced things very similar to what Kean and others have described (Roe 2001; Saavedra *et al.* 2009). It has been commonly found that many with schizophrenia experience a significant loss of metacognitive capacity or previously held capacities to think meaningfully about thoughts and feelings. These deficits persist at the trait level, and are not simple reflections of a single symptom or neurocognitive deficit (Brüne 2005; Dimaggio and Lysaker 2010; Lysaker, Carcione *et al.* 2005). They also present unique impediments to psychosocial function and the maintenance of an evolving personal narrative (Corcoran *et al.* 2005; Lysaker *et al.* 2010a, 2010b).

While there is reason to attend to the first-person dimensions of schizophrenia, a better understanding of what transpires when persons with schizophrenia experience their own diminishment is needed. In response, this chapter will utilize DST to construct an account of experiences of self-diminishment in schizophrenia. Specifically, we will suggest that many disparate accounts of self-diminishment may be understood as involving lost or weakened capacities for intrapersonal and interpersonal dialogue. We then will outline how losses of this kind appear to assume at least three different forms. Finally, we will return to the claims of DST within a larger discourse concerning self-experience in schizophrenia and show how our account squares with a range of three other descriptions of alterations in self-experience, including those from psychoanalytic, phenomenological and existential perspectives. This will not only highlight the kind of contributions DST can make to this area of schizophrenia research, but it also will help consolidate the theoretical landscape from which researchers and clinicians address the phenomenon of self-experience in schizophrenia.

Sense of self in schizophrenia and the loss of dialogue

The phenomenon we wish to consider involves persons, diagnosed with schizophrenia, who experience themselves as having lost key aspects of their former selves. They are not without a self but have experienced a diminished self. They are aware of their loss and can poignantly describe it. But how is this possible? A credible answer must address how persons gain and reflect upon a sense of self. DST offers a powerful account of this process.

Drawing on DST, we have proposed that experiences of self-diminishment may reflect difficulty in sustaining dialogues among self-positions in worldly interactions as a result of any of a number of social and biological processes (Lysaker and Lysaker 2002, 2005, 2008). Specifically, a person's sense of self may radically transform as dialogues involving its many positions fail. If the processes that allow different self-facets to engage and interanimate one another were imperilled in the onset of social and biological factors linked to the illness, then dialogue, at least in part, would diminish, and this, in turn, would give one the sense that the richness and depth of oneself had diminished. In order to understand how a self could be diminished in such a manner, we have proposed three processes of dialogical compromise and linked them with three corresponding kinds of self-experience: barren, monological and cacophonous. Since this view was initially proposed, support for these hypotheses has been provided by a number of authors (Bradfield and Knight 2008; Meehan and Maclachlan 2007; Saavedra et al. 2009).

First, if no self-positions are able to interact meaningfully with another, an empty or *barren* state might follow in which persons experience themselves as being more or less nondescript or even empty. Such persons might have the sense that nothing much happens to them or that they are not going anywhere; that is, they would not experience themselves as protagonists in the stories of their lives. Alternatively, if one self-position dominates and orders most experience (e.g. 'self-as-in-danger' or 'self-as-flawless'), then the second kind of disturbance, a *monological* self-organization, would result, leading to a self-experience locked within one or a few facets. In such a state, persons might be able to experience themselves as bound to a recurring scenario (e.g. as persecuted or possessing special status) whose persistence rendered a previously felt sense of self inaccessible, even to the point that one so fixated might regard past facets as destroyed. In the third model, one in which self-positions appear and recede without any significant order, it seems possible that the ensuing sense of self would prove *cacophonous*, contributing to a sense of oneself as overwhelmed, lost or highly anxious in the light of having no explanations (not even a monological explanation). Moreover, such persons might have the experience that previously held senses of self had evaporated in a storm of self-positions that may never again cohere. In all three cases, then, the suggestion is that diminishing intrapersonal dialogues transform the sense of self in the direction of diminishment relative to previous senses of self. For example, one used to have good relations with siblings and friends, be ambitious but shy, and be a postal worker and a musician, but now one is empty or persecuted, or at sea in thoughts and feelings that do not cohere, and so one is just overwhelmed.

This model of self-experience in schizophrenia has also led to a more detailed model of how self-experience might be especially taxed by direct, interpersonal contact (Lysaker and Lysaker 2008). In particular, it has been suggested that social contacts may be overwhelming for persons with limited dialogical capacity. For one, encountering others could quickly call forth a number of different self-positions which, given impaired dialogical capacities, would prove difficult to integrate in an organized conversation. Second, being known by another person could call forth the matter of having to deal with how one is seen by that other person. With one's sense of self now involving both how one finds oneself and how one finds oneself regarded by another, the dialogical demands placed upon the sense of self would intensify. But with limited dialogical capacities, persons with schizophrenia might not be able to sustain the ensuing interanimation. While such exchanges might result in different experiences if one lives through a monological, barren or cacophonous self-organization, in each case it seems likely that rich, interpersonal contact would be experienced as a threat and intimacy avoided. And this, in turn, could lead to its own lines of self-experience rife with feelings of abandonment and alienation, which might complement or intensify the self-experience associated with compromised intrapersonal dialogue.

Of note, our work using DST is far from the first effort to understand disturbances in self experience. In the following sections we will, therefore, explore three other prominent and earlier views of disruption in self-disturbance. Specially, we describe models of self-disturbance from psychoanalytic, phenomenological and existential vantage points in order to be able to compare them later with the dialogical approach and then to further articulate the advances offered by DST.

Psychoanalytic views

Psychoanalysis was one of the first perspectives to observe that persons with schizophrenia openly report experiencing an altered or diminished sense of self. Freud (1957) asserted that schizophrenia occurs when persons fully detach themselves from the world and refocus all of their psychic energies upon themselves, undermining vital action towards non-self objects and events. In this state, the self is essentially disengaged from the world and trapped in an exclusive self-relation, which erodes the possibility of socially comprehensible emotions and daily experiences.

One implication of Freud's account is that psychoanalytic treatment or any form of psychotherapy related to depth psychology should prove impossible for people with schizophrenia. Several psychoanalysts, however, have reported success in psychotherapy for persons with schizophrenia and evolved a view of schizophrenia in terms of a desire for and terror of connection with others (e.g. Fromm-Reichmann 1954; Searles 1965; Sullivan 1962). Others (e.g. Bak 1954; Bion 1967) have suggested that schizophrenia involves experiences of emptiness and an inability to make meaning. In fact, some asserted that persons with schizophrenia were terrified that if meaning coalesced, a catastrophe would ensue, destroying either the individual with schizophrenia or the person with whom they were engaged. Despite their needs for love and closeness, persons with schizophrenia, according to this model, experience a world they need to avoid and even shield from their potentially destructive presence. These psychoanalysts thus locate within schizophrenia a frail self at times overrun by overwhelming affects and desires and threatened by the demands of reality and a potentially brutal conscience.

Summarizing this and other work, Frosch (1983) suggests that persons with schizophrenia constantly sense that their basic capacity for self-experience is on the verge of destruction.

Phenomenological views

Other theorists, with strong links to German and French philosophy and psychiatry, have studied the structures of consciousness in schizophrenia. Minkowski has suggested that schizophrenia involves a loss of 'vital contact with reality' (1987: 188). Due to a persistent lack of temporal synthesis, such persons lack enough integrated experience to sustain a sense of self. Having lost touch with the 'moving stream which envelops us at all points and constitutes the milieu' that renders life intelligible, such persons do not 'know how to live' (1987: 191). In other words, 'although [the person with schizophrenia] knows where he is, he does not feel as if he is in that place ... [T]he term "I exist" has no real meaning for him' (1987: 196).

Since Minkowski, phenomenological approaches to schizophrenia have been influenced by Blankenburg (2001), who argued that schizophrenia fundamentally undermines what he terms 'common sense', or the capacity to gauge, without explicit, self-conscious reflection, what any given situation demands. He observes that what is 'striking for those around the patient is that there is a withering away of a sense of tact, a feeling for the proper thing to do in situations, a loss of awareness of the current fashions ... a general indifference towards what might be disturbing to others' (2001: 306). Extending this logic, Stanghellini (2004) suggests that a loss of pre-reflectively operative, common sense, would fundamentally disrupt self-experience in the context of relatedness. So afflicted, one experiences a loss of continuity in things and events and experiences the *stuff* of one's self diminishing. Without a living connection to the world, one that establishes a dialogue between desire and the world's feedback, psychosocial dysfunction is less a lack of social skills than 'a defective dialectic between the two poles of the self: the individual characteristics embodied by the "I" and the social demands embodied by the "me"' (2004: 78). Moreover, in the wake of these disconnects, persons with schizophrenia are forced to confront their impoverished grasp of things, leaving them, Stanghellini suggests, suspended in a 'nothingness', a state that seems analogous to the looming threat noted by Frosch (1983).

But what is it that undermines self–world interaction and sense of self in schizophrenia? A reply must explore what undermines a fundamental capacity like 'common sense'. Mishara (2004) has presented two different approaches. The first, labelled 'Apollonian' following Nietzsche's dichotomization of personality types, suggests that common sense withers under a radical inward gaze. Along these lines, Sass (2000) suggests that the sense of self in schizophrenia is a matter of 'hyper-reflexivity' or extreme self-awareness. In such a position, persons with schizophrenia attend to themselves with an intense and fixed gaze that fragments the sense of self and renders spontaneity and a grasp of basic life processes impossible. Like Freud, Sass thus finds extreme narcissism characteristic of schizophrenia. Unlike Freud, however, who claimed that narcissism in schizophrenia leads to grandiosity or somatic delusions, hyper-reflexivity paradoxically causes persons to cease experiencing themselves as a subject of awareness.

In the contrasting view, the Dionysian, common sense fails because perceptual and automatic meaning processing are disrupted 'from below'. The problem is not too much reflection, but breakdowns in the preconscious processes that sustain connections between embodied feelings, judgements and a world shared by others. One might incline towards this explanation because the account offered by Sass, and the Apollonian view more generally, do not explain how excessive self-awareness automatically persists over time. Consistent with the Dionysian view, Parnas and Handest (2003) find an elemental lack of attunement to the world in schizophrenia, one that makes basic engagement impossible. They describe, for instance, someone in the early stages of disorder, who 'tended to lose the sense of whose thoughts originated in whom and [who] felt as if his interlocutor somehow "invaded him," an experience that shattered his identity and was intensely anxiety provoking' (2003: 129).

Phenomenological analyses of schizophrenia are distinguished by a structural focus on the disorder's first-person dimensions. They observe anxiety, feelings of emptiness and disordered psyches, but also tie these phenomena to breakdowns in perceptual capacities, what many call 'common sense'. They refer less to the troublesome affects noted by psychoanalysis and more to a sense of growing confusion and emptiness. In this way they point to more barren self-structure, whereas psychoanalysis at times seems more interested in monological and cacophonous self-structures as ways to survive overpowering affects.

Existential views

While phenomenological views are concerned with interpretations and perceptions of the world, another view can be discerned. Labelled by us and others as existential, another view has focused more on the self as it exists meaningfully as an actor in the world. A central proponent of this view, one suspicious of traditional interpretations of schizophrenia, Laing (1978) has suggested that persons with schizophrenia experience a disruption in their relationship with themselves. To have schizophrenia, according to Laing, is to be unable to feel 'together with' others or 'at home' in the world. As such, to experience schizophrenia is no longer to experience oneself as 'a complete person' (1978: 17).

In such states, it is unclear from moment to moment who or what one is, and the boundaries of self and other seem tenuous and unreliable. Moreover, one's world is terrifying, as if it were 'liable at any moment to crash in and obliterate all identity' (1978: 45). Perhaps in contrast to the phenomenological view, Laing locates the disturbance, not so much in a lack of perceptual atonement, but in the actual participation in the world, a participation that seems to dissolve even the most tenuous sense of identity. It is not common sense that is missing but the ability to sustain self-relationships while being immersed in activity.

Focusing more intently on the experience of the person with schizophrenia, Boss (1979) suggested that schizophrenia involves experiences of 'encroachment' by unnamed, external sources upon one's 'ability to be responsive and open to what is encountered' (1979: 235). He claims that 'First they cannot open themselves fully to the meaningful address of what they encounter ... so that they cannot respond with all their faculties to the normally accepted significance ... of those things and events. Second they are unable to maintain a free stance vis-à-vis their perceptions of what they encounter' (1979: 235). In view of this degree of personal destabilization, Boss regarded schizophrenia as the 'radically incomplete manifestation of the free and self-reliant selfhood that normally characterizes human beings. Therefore, schizophrenia is an illness that can be characterized only negatively' (1979: 236). Perhaps in contrast here with the psychoanalytic views, the issue is not affect dysregulation or the experience of intersubjectivity as threat, but somehow a set of self-relations which are sufficiently viable to withstand the pressures of meaningful participation in the world. It is in the address of what is encountered and not necessarily in intimate social situations in which the peril lies. In contrast to phenomenology, there also is a disappearing or fragmented self and not the hyper-reflexive being that excessive awareness precludes from being in the world.

Comparisons with dialogical models

When drawing from the four perspectives considered (DST, psychoanalysis, phenomenological psychiatry and existential psychiatry), a remarkably consistent portrait of self-experience in schizophrenia emerges, at least at the descriptive level. Each view reports an overall sense of compromised agency and a felt lack of meaning among persons diagnosed with schizophrenia. Each view also presents those experiences in a twofold manner. On the one hand, the world itself seems confused, disordered, even threatening. On the other hand, the self is also disordered, a site of confusion, pain, even antagonism. In other words, Laing seems to present a common view when he states that a person with schizophrenia experiences a 'rent in his relation with his world ... and a disruption in relation with himself'. We find this significant. It evinces a set of observations common to four distinct lines of inquiry into schizophrenia and opens up possibilities for further dialogue and possible collaboration.

Digging deeper into these observations, one can see that, with regard to world dislocation, DST, as well as psychoanalytic and existential views, stresses social dislocations and pays less attention to perceptual confusion than do phenomenological views. Similarly, phenomenological views seem less focused on the affective dimensions of self-experience than the other perspectives. Thus, while all observe an overall lack of vital contact with the world, different perspectives describe that point of contact in different ways or, rather, stress different dimensions of that contact. At this point, it seems prudent to regard these as different emphases and not contradictory perspectives. As 'emphases', they remind each view of its likely partiality, and encourage exploration.

The most notable difference between these perspectives, at least at the level of description, can be found in the account we have developed out of DST. Whereas the other perspectives all seem to speak more generally of the sense of self in schizophrenia, we have elected to distinguish among three kinds of self-experience (barren, monological and cacophonous) and to recommend distinct psychotherapeutic approaches for each (Lysaker and Lysaker 2008). We consider this an advantage because it reminds us that schizophrenia is not a univocal phenomenon. Moreover, it renders more salient various ways in which self–world interactions are undermined in lives beset by schizophrenia. For example, tempestuous affects are not significant in barren forms of self-organization whereas they are in cacophonous forms, albeit in a manner distinct from the more singular affective dimensions of monological forms of self-organization. Now, to be clear, our claim is not that with the help of DST we have clearly identified the three essential forms of disturbed self-experience in schizophrenia. Rather, our claim is more modest. It seems beneficial to introduce distinctions like these in order to draw with a finer pen the various ways in which self-experience in schizophrenia is structured.

At the level of explanation, starker differences are predictably evident. Because we cannot do justice to all of these divergences, we will focus on what distinguishes DST from each of the perspectives explored above. Some psychoanalytic models suggest that these alterations in self-experience are linked to early experiences with caretakers and/or psychological conflicts. One clear tenet of the dialogical model is that the kinds of disturbances in self-experience we are describing could have a range of roots, including early experiences as well as alterations in brain functioning that accompany the progress of schizophrenia as a neuro-biologically based illness. Second, in their focus on affect and desire, psychoanalytic accounts retain the sense of a univocal self overwhelmed by affect, thus suggesting that recovery lies with the reassertion of ego control over such affects and desires. DST, while not ignoring the affects (Hermans and Hermans-Konopka 2010; Lysaker and Lysaker 2005), situates the challenges they pose within the interanimating play of self-positions. One is thus not simply overcome by emotion or desire, but beset within a set of salient self-positions, such as self-as-son, self-as-nurse, self-as-tired, etc. By this model, the goal of ego control is replaced by the effort to access and/or develop other positions, such as self-as-client, self-as-friend, self-as-worker, etc., from which complex desires and affects can be explored and reintegrated into an enabling flow of self-positions.

An analogous difference distinguishes our dialogical view from some phenomenological views that suggest that a diminished sense of self is the eventual manifestation of pre-existing alterations in self-experience already under way early in life. The claim is that, early in life, a basic constitutional deficit prevents one from building an identity within initial interactions with caretakers. As a result, these persons cannot manage anxiety or threats to self-integrity prior to illness. Minkowski, for example, suggests that the disharmony of person and world is present before the symptoms of schizophrenia arise. In other words, prior to onset, one should find a life that has 'evolved in fits and starts ... not [as] a continuous line, supple and elastic but [as] one broken in several places' (1987: 206). A view grounded in DST would not expect this. Experiences of diminishment are so shattering because they contrast so starkly previously rich self-experience. Moreover, these losses are so striking because they happen to persons who recognize what is missing as a result of previously having known it so well and automatically.

Due to their invocation of univocal terms like 'common sense', several phenomenological views address experiences of diminishment in schizophrenia with reference to pre-reflectively operative, egological activity. Because DST stresses the interanimating play of self-positions in all human conduct, a term like 'common sense' strikes us as an abstract term for what is really a polyphonic process – common sense for self-as-lover is not common sense for self-as-brother. Yet, rather than simply note the disagreement, we would like to articulate some of the research questions it raises. First, do the breakdowns in pre-reflectively operative processes observed by researchers like Mishira, or the reliance on rote responses observed by Stanghellini, vary among the forms of self-organization proposed by DST, or, more generally, when different self-positions are animated? It could be that 'common sense' and 'dialogical interanimation' are related. For example, the difficulties observed by phenomenological inquirers might contribute to dialogical breakdowns and/or vice versa. Or, both might occur independently of one another. Second, do the phenomena observed by phenomenological inquirers vary across contexts, perhaps intensifying in intersubjective exchanges? We have observed (Lysaker, Johannesen *et al.* 2005) that some deficits associated with schizophrenia intensify during certain exchanges with others. For instance, self-experience may be threatened when the interaction stimulates a range of different aspects of the person with schizophrenia which are difficult to organize. Self-experience may also be threatened when the interaction involves the other person forming too many ideas to organize within an internal or external dialogue about the person with schizophrenia and again offering too many things. Thus, a question for future research is whether, contradicting some phenomenologists, self-diminishment may vary from one situation or self-position to another.

When brought into conversation with so-called 'existential' accounts, our dialogical view does not share Boss' assessment that schizophrenia can only be accounted for negatively. Like Laing, DST stresses that persons with schizophrenia not only undergo but also interpret and struggle with their fate. The self functions as a dynamic agentic multiplicity (Hermans and Hermans-Konopka 2010) and as such is always making sense in some way of experience. Those struggles may be wrought with pain and significantly compromised, but positive evidence of a self at work remains in the cases we have observed and described. Moreover, this knowledge enables therapeutic approaches that rebuild weakened capacities rather than seek their total reconstruction.

The four views we have detailed observe the depth of pain and disorientation felt by those whose self-experience has been disrupted over the course of schizophrenia. What a view derived from DST stresses, perhaps either more uniquely or strenuously than others, is that a salient dimension of such disruptions is how sharply they contrast with previous senses of self. A dialogical perspective points to a somewhat more continuous, experiential dimension within the lives undergoing the illness. By locating the sense of self within the interanimating play of self-positions, a dialogically informed perspective has helped us to see how disruptions in self-experience could emerge suddenly, exist in some moments and not others, and be repaired. Put another way, earlier healthy positions that have been relegated to the background during the illness, can be foregrounded and revitalized by the process of psychotherapy. Though the point is up for debate, we continue to hold that a dialogical view of self-diminishment also offers a more nuanced view of the kinds of self-experience that arise in schizophrenia. The foregrounding and backgrounding of self-positions may even offer a working model of the coming and somewhat mysterious going of illness among persons with schizophrenia.

In summary, we see great potential for the insights derived from the dialogical view to be synthesized with psychoanalytic, phenomenological and existential views of diminished self-experience in schizophrenia and so to evolve an ever deeper account of that phenomenon. Finally, these opportunities afforded by DST point to possible projects which might in parallel with ours explore how other medical and psychiatric illnesses might affect self-experience.

REFERENCES

Andresen, R., Oades, L. and Caputi, P. (2003) The experience of recovery from schizophrenia: towards an empirically validated state model, *Australian and New Zealand Journal of Psychiatry*, **37**, 586–594

Bak, R. C. (1954) The schizophrenic defense against aggression, *International Journal of Psychoanalysis*, **35**, 129–134

Bakhtin, M. (1985) *Problems of Dostoyevsky's Poetics*. Trans. C. Emerson (Minneapolis, MN: University of Minnesota Press)

Barham, P. (1993) *Schizophrenia and Human Value* (London: Free Association Books)

Bion, W. R. (1967) *Second Thoughts* (New York: Jason Aronson)

Blankenburg, W. (2001) First steps toward a psychopathology of 'common sense', *Philosophical Psychiatry and Psychology*, **8**, 303–315

Boss, M. (1979) *Existential Foundations of Medicine and Psychology*. Trans. S. Conway and A. Cleaves (New York: Jason Aronson)

Boyle, M. (2002) *Schizophrenia: A Scientific Delusion* (New York: Routledge)

Bradfield, B. C. and Knight, Z. G. (2008) Intersubjectivity and the schizophrenic experience: a hermeneutic phenomenological exploration, *South African Journal of Psychology*, **38**, 33–53

Brüne, M. (2005) Theory of mind in schizophrenia: a review of the literature, *Schizophrenia Bulletin*, **31**, 21–42

Corcoran, R., Mercer, G. and Frith, C. (2005) Schizophrenia, symptomatology and social inference: investigating theory of mind in people with schizophrenia, *Schizophrenia Research*, **24**, 397–405

Dewey, J. (1988) *Human Nature and Conduct* (Carbondale, IL: Southern Illinois University Press)

Dimaggio, G. and Lysaker, P. H. (2010) *Metacognition and Severe Adult Mental Disorders: From Basic Research to Treatment* (New York: Brunner-Routledge)

Fish, B. and Kendler, K. S. (2005) Abnormal infant neurodevelopment predicts schizophrenia spectrum disorders, *Journal of Child and Adolescent Psychopharmacology*, **15**, 348–61

France, C. M. and Uhlin, B. D. (2006) Narrative as an outcome domain in psychosis, *Psychology and Psychotherapy*, **79**, 53–67

Freud, S. (1957) *Neurosis and Psychosis*. Trans. A. and J. Strachev. *Collected Papers* (London: Hogarth Press), vol. II

Fromm-Reichmann, F. (1954) Psychotherapy of schizophrenia, *American Journal of Psychiatry*, **111**, 410–419

Frosch, J. (1983) *The Psychotic Process* (New York: International Universities Press)

Hermans, H. J. M. (1996) Voicing the self: from information processing to dialogical interchange, *Psychological Bulletin*, **119**, 31–50

Hermans, H. J. M. and Dimaggio, G. (2004) *The Dialogical Self in Psychotherapy* (Brunner-Routledge: London)

Hermans, H. J. M. and Hermans-Konopka, A. (2010) *Dialogical Self Theory: Positioning and Counter-Positioning in a Globalizing Society* (Cambridge University Press)

Kean, C. S. (2009) Silencing the self: schizophrenia as a self-disturbance, *Schizophrenia Bulletin*, **35**, 1034–1036

Kierkegaard, S. (1980) *The Sickness unto Death* (Princeton University Press)

Laing, R. D. (1978) *The Divided Self* (New York: Penguin Books)

Lysaker, J. T. and Lysaker, P. H. (2005) Being interrupted: the self and schizophrenia, *Journal of Speculative Philosophy*, **19**, 1–22

Lysaker, P. H. and Buck, K. D. (2008) Is recovery from schizophrenia possible? An overview of concepts, evidence and clinical implications, *Primary Psychiatry*, **15**, 60–66

Lysaker, P. H., Carcione, A., Dimaggio, G., Johannesen, J. K., Nicolò, G., Procacci, M. and Semerari, A. (2005) Metacognition amidst narratives of self and illness in schizophrenia: associations with insight, neurocognition, symptom and function, *Acta Psychiatrica Scandinavica*, **112**, 64–71

Lysaker, P. H., Dimaggio, G., Carcione, A., Procacci, M., Buck, K. D., Davis, L. W. and Nicolo, G. (2010a) Metacognition and schizophrenia: the capacity for self-reflectivity as a predictor for prospective assessments of work performance over six months, *Schizophrenia Research*, **122**, 124–130

Lysaker, P. H., Johannesen, J. K. and Lysaker, J. T. (2005) Schizophrenia and the experience of intersubjectivity as threat, *Phenomenology and the Cognitive Sciences*, **4**, 335–352

Lysaker, P. H. and Lysaker, J. T. (2002) Narrative structure in psychosis: schizophrenia and disruptions in the dialogical self, *Theory & Psychology*, **12**, 207–220

(2008) *Schizophrenia and the Fate of the Self* (Oxford University Press)

Lysaker, P. H., Shea, A. M., Buck, K. D., Dimaggio, G., Nicolò, G., Procacci, M., Salvatore, G. and Rand, K. L. (2010b) Metacognition as a mediator of the effects of impairments in neurocognition on social function in schizophrenia spectrum disorders, *Acta Psychiatrica Scandinavica*, **122**, 405–413

Markowitz, F. E. (1998) The effects of stigma on the psychological well-being and life satisfaction of persons with mental illness, *Journal of Health and Social Behavior*, **39**, 335–347

McGlashan, T. H. and Hoffman, R. E. (2000) Schizophrenia as a disorder of developmentally reduced synaptic connectivity, *Archives of General Psychiatry*, **57**, 637–648

Meehan, T. and Maclachlan, M. (2007) Self construction in schizophrenia: a discourse analysis, *Psychology and Psychotherapy*, **81**, 131–142

Minkowski, E. (1987) The essential disorder underlying schizophrenia and schizophrenic thought, in J. Cutting (ed.), *The Clinical Roots of the Schizophrenic Concept* (Cambridge University Press), 188–212

Mishara, A. L. (2004) Disconnection of the external and internal in the conscious experience of schizophrenia: phenomenological, literary and neuroanatomical archaeologies of self, *Philosophica*, **73**, 87–126

Nietzsche, F. (1966) *Beyond Good and Evil* (New York: Random House)

O'Donnell, B. F. (2007) Cognitive impairment in schizophrenia: a life span perspective, *American Journal of Alzheimer's Disease and Other Dementias*, **22**, 398–405

Parnas, J. and Handest, P. (2003) Phenomenology of anomalous self-experience in early schizophrenia, *Comprehensive Psychiatry*, **44**, 121–134

Roe, D. (2001) Exploring the relationship between the person and the disorder among individuals hospitalized for psychosis, *Psychiatry*, **62**, 372–380

Saavedra, J., Cubero, M. and Crawford, P. (2009) Incomprehensibility in the narratives of individuals with a diagnosis of schizophrenia, *Qualitative Health Research*, **19**, 1548–1558

Sass, L. A. (2009) *Madness and Modernism: Insanity in the Light of Modern Art, Literature, and Thought* (Philadelphia: John Benjamins)

Searles, H. (1965) *Collected Papers of Schizophrenia and Related Subjects* (New York: International Universities Press)

Stanghellini, G. (2004) *Disembodied Spirits and Deanimated Bodies* (Oxford University Press)

Sullivan, H. S. (1962) *Schizophrenia as a Human Process* (New York: Norton)

12   The dialogical self in the new South Africa

Graham Lindegger and Charl Alberts

Following forty-six years of the oppressive apartheid regime, 1994 saw the birth of the new democratic South Africa. This was the birth of what Desmond Tutu, then head of the Anglican Church in South Africa, and a spokesperson for this new democracy, called 'the rainbow nation'. Since then, there have been repeated calls to recognize, foster and celebrate this rainbow nation. Following the initial euphoria and the honeymoon phase of the new dispensation, there has been the growing realization of the challenges involved in consolidating this new society. South Africa is a multicultural society with nine official languages, each embodying distinctive identities and cultural values. In this diversity of ethnic groups and languages are two broad world views, that is, a broadly Western world view, privileged in the old South Africa, and a broadly African world view, privileged in the new South Africa. The forging of a unique African identity, reflected in ideas such as the African Renaissance, is an important project of the emerging South African society. The concept of 'transformation' has become one of the most widely used in public discourse in South Africa. This has referred to changes in legislation, social policy, employment practices and access to resources, but also to the emergence of new, transformed, personal identities for South Africans. This process has not been without considerable conflict and frustration, both for groups sharing a particular identity (e.g. Afrikaners), and for individuals within the new South Africa.

The authors of this chapter work as academic and applied psychologists in South Africa. Like other social scientists, we have attempted to understand and theorize the challenges in the process of transformation in various sectors in South Africa. We have found the theoretical framework of the dialogical self especially helpful in understanding many of the contemporary issues in South Africa. In this chapter we select two very different, but equally important challenges, to illustrate the broad applicability of the dialogical self to issues in contemporary South Africa. The first, from the field of clinical psychology, focuses on mental health interventions, one of the many challenges for the health-care system in

South Africa. This part of the chapter compares Western psychotherapy and traditional African healing. It is argued that these modes of therapeutic intervention are very different in appearance. However, we argue that in comparing them there is an important commonality; that is, that they both explicitly operate through dialogical processes, well described by dialogical self theory (DST). We also argue that DST is a useful framework for conceptualizing their differences. The second, from the field of social psychology, focuses on changing Afrikaner identity in South Africa. The theory of the dialogical self is an extremely useful theory to use to make understandable the complexities and psychological struggles among 'white' Afrikaans-speakers in confronting a dramatically changing and, for many, a threatening social context. The theory also provides liberating perspectives for communities and individuals caught up in contexts of fundamental social change, uncertainty and threat.

Psychotherapy and traditional African healing: a dialogical self perspective

In the transformation of public health services in South Africa, including and especially mental health services, there is a constant challenge of how to offer services that are both health appropriate and culturally relevant. One particular aspect of the debate about culture and mental health has focused on the relevance of Western psychotherapy versus traditional African healing (Straker 1994; Swartz 1998). On the one hand, there is a well-developed interest in psychodynamic psychotherapy, informed by contemporary object relations theory (ORT) (Straker 1994; Swartz 1998). In parallel, there is also a long-standing practice of traditional African healing (Mosue 2000; Straker 1994; Swartz 1998). While there is an acknowledgement of many commonalities to African healing in general (Vontress 1991), this chapter will focus primarily on traditional African healing practices in southern Africa, most especially among isiZulu- and isiXhosa-speaking people. It has been argued (Parle 2003; Straker 1994; Vontress 1991) that the predominant use by Africans of traditional healing, rather than Westernized medicine and psychotherapy, is a product of factors such as predominantly living in rural areas, lower literacy rates, being unable to afford the costs of Western treatments, and the historical underfunding of health services to black people (Swartz 1998). Western psychotherapies have historically been more embraced by the white sector of the population, and the traditional African healing by black people (Straker 1994). However, urbanization, globalization and transformation have produced hybrids of these two forms of therapeutic healing. In examining the interface of these two systems of therapy, we may inquire about their similarities, differences and possible reconcilability. In making this comparison, we heed the warning of Hermans about assuming that different groups are 'internally homogeneous and externally distinctive' (2001: 267). Instead we conceptualize these as different patterns of mental health intervention. One of the frequent problems in making these comparisons is the lack of appropriate conceptual framework. The work of Buhrmann and Gqomfa (1982) is one of the few attempts to compare these two approaches theoretically, on the basis of Jungian theory. DST has provided us with an ideal framework for this purpose. This section of this chapter briefly describes Western psychodynamic therapy and traditional African healing, and then goes on to use DST as a framework for comparison of these two approaches.

Object relations therapy (ORT) and traditional African healing

Psychodynamic therapy, based primarily on ORT, involves an intense, interpersonal relationship between two people (psychotherapist and client), based on a carefully moulded rapport (Lemma 2003). This intervention will be largely verbal in modality, based on the free associations of the client and the interpretations of the therapist/analyst, together with the evolution and resolution of a complex transference and counter-transference relationship (Lemma 2003). The treatment will usually involve regular, intensely private meetings over reasonably long periods of time, usually involving only the client and therapist, focused on the client's private, emotional experience or internal world. Occasionally, significant others of the client may be brought into the therapeutic process. ORT, the theoretical frame to conceptualize the client's experience, is essentially interested in the interface between the person's relationships with significant others and his psychological representations of these people or 'internal objects' (Ogden 1983). These psychological representations of significant others, or 'internal objects' as they are termed in ORT, are seen as playing a major role in the emotional economy of the person. The relationship between client and therapist, especially as played out in the transference, becomes the therapeutic vehicle through which these internal objects are made accessible and brought to some therapeutic resolution, in the hope of improving the client's state of well-being and his or her interpersonal relationships ('refs'), through recognition of and dialogue with these objects/people. Specialized interventions, such as dream interpretation, will be an important part of the therapeutic process.

Traditional African healing is likely to be quite different, at least on the surface. African cosmology is rooted in relationships (Gyekye 1997; Hewson 1998; Kambon 1992; Parle 2003; Vontress 1991). The system of relationships of which the person is part is both natural and supernatural (Sogolo 1993; Straker 1994), and includes relationships with family, community, the Earth, God, spirits, and ancestors or the living dead. Ancestors, in particular, are seen as having a strong influence over the lives of people (Buhrmann and Gqomfa 1982; Mosue 2000; Straker 1994; Thorpe 1991; Vontress 1991), and play an important role in the healing of illness or overcoming difficulties (Buhrmann and Gqomfa 1982; Ela 1995; Straker 1994). Health and happiness, including mental health, will be seen as a function of the equilibrium of these various relationships, whereas ill health or unhappiness will be seen as a function of disharmony or the influence of evil spirits (Hewson 1998; Straker 1994; Thorpe 1993). One form of illness is that which is the result of spirit possession, and there are well-documented descriptions of epidemics of spirit possession, such as the 'indiki spirit possession' in Zululand, South Africa, between 1890 and 1914 (Parle 2003). While the exact form of diagnosis and intervention in traditional African healing will vary, a common frame of reference for diagnosis is these multifaceted relationships of the client.

While there are many forms of healing and healing practitioners in traditional African healing, such as herbalism and faith healing, we are especially interested in culturally sanctioned healers called 'iZangoma' in isiZulu and isiXhosa. The task of these iZangoma (plural of *iSangoma*) focuses largely on diagnosing any disharmony in these relationships (Ela 1995; Hewson 1998; Thorpe 1991; Vontress 1991), especially the relationship with ancestors. The iSangoma functions as an intermediary between the visible and invisible worlds to diagnose and harmonize these relationships, and especially to transmit messages from the ancestors/living dead to the living (Ela 1995; Vontress 1991). Various ceremonies and rituals may be performed by the iSangoma to diagnose disequilibrium in these various relationships, such as 'bone throwing' and 'divining the bones' (Hewson 1998: 1030). Dreams are frequently seen as communications from the ancestors (Straker 1994; Thorpe 1991), and the iSangoma plays an important role in interpreting these dreams sent by ancestors (Buhrmann and Gqomfa 1982; Hewson 1998; Straker 1994), or using the dreams to facilitate communication with ancestors (Straker 1994). The healer is likely to assume a far more active and directive role in the healing than the Western psychotherapist. Once the problem has been diagnosed, various healing rituals will be prescribed and enacted by the iSangoma together with the client, usually aimed at the restoration of harmony in relationships with the living and the living dead. These rituals may involve wearing particular clothes, ritual washing, herbal medicines, sacrificing of animals, dancing and singing (Hewson 1998; Straker 1994), and interpretation of dreams (Buhrmann and Gqomfa 1982; Straker 1994; Thorpe 1991). In the case of the indiki epidemic referred to earlier, 'relatives and homestead heads would be required to present the amandiki [plural of *indiki*] with gifts and to sacrifice an animal, usually a goat, to drive the spirit away' (Parle 2003: 114). These rituals and ceremonies are invariably performed in the presence and with the active participation of other members of family, extended family and community. Further, 'it is the promotion of cohesiveness in community and family life that is served by the rituals and observances' (Straker 1994: 460). The healing process is likely to be explicitly religious or spiritual.

While these two approaches to healing or therapy appear on the surface to be radically different, and even irreconcilable, the framework of DST makes it possible to identify some important underlying commonalities, as well as to understand and explain the differences.

Dialogical theory as conceptual framework for comparison

Given that this book is devoted to DST, the basic elements of Hermans and Kempen's DST (1992) theory do not need to be repeated here, but will be assumed. However, we will highlight some elements of DST which have been most useful in the comparison of Western psychotherapy and traditional African healing. *First*, DST draws on Bakhtin's idea of the polyphonic novel with multiple authors, each with its own voice in dialogue with potential others. This dialogical relationship of the various *I*-positions, or voices, is with a variety of potential others. The self is effectively a mind space for the dialogue of these different voices or *I*-positions. Hermans and Kempen warn of the danger of 'real' or objective others being given any kind of ontological superiority in this dialogical relationship. They warn that the tendency to recognize only objective or actual others arises from 'an ethnocentric projection of certain narrow assumptions in Western social science' (1992: 214). *Second*, the challenge for each person is the construction of an effective dialogue of these various voices or *I*-positions with each other and with the other people in each version of the story, as part of the construction and maintenance of the self. It is the dialogical quality which is the

ultimate defining quality of the self. This interaction of the multiple
voices, or *I*-positions, of self may find resolution in various forms, one
being the harmonious dialogue of the various voices, and another being
the privileging of some voices and the subordination of others. *Third,* like
all narrative forms, the dialogical self is inevitably constructed of temporal and spatial dimensions. Each voice, or *I*-position, in the dialogue is
located in a particular spatial and temporal plane, which is an essential
context within which the *I*-position operates. Any voice articulating a
version of a narrative is located in a particular space and time. 'The self,
then, is successively or even simultaneously located in different positions
in an imaginal landscape and is able to move between these positions. In
short, the self is a process of dialogical movements in an imaginal space'
(Hermans and Kempen 1993: 44).

Explaining and comparing Western psychotherapy and traditional African healing

So how does the DST of Hermans and Kempen assist in the explanation
and comparison of patterns of healing seen in Western psychotherapy
and traditional African healing?

First, ORT and African cosmology are both relational in nature. ORT
is founded on the notion of the person as essentially relational, and
consciousness and the unconscious as relational. As Ogden's classical
definition reveals, ORT is constantly concerned with the relationship
which takes place within and between persons. 'Object relations theory...
is in fact fundamentally a theory of unconscious internal object relations
in dynamic interplay with current interpersonal experiences' (1983:
227). It is the effectiveness of this dialogue of internal and external
'objects', seen in the process of integration, which determines the mental
health and psychological maturity of each person. Psychodynamic therapy is inherently dialogical. ORT sees internal representations of self and
others as being in constant interaction and dialogue, producing mental
life. Ogden's description of ORT mirrors Hermans' (2001) description
of the relationship between internal and external positions in DST. In
Hermans and Kempen's terms, one important emphasis in ORT is on
'imaginal others' (1992: 214), especially as they play their role in an
unconscious, mental landscape. The task of psychodynamic psychotherapy could be seen as one of assisting each of the *I*-positions in the
imaginal landscape to articulate its voice, or, as Roland puts it, to find
'different ways of listening to and hearing such voices' (2001: 318).
The interpretations of the therapist play a critical role in speaking for
the unheard, subjugated (but influential) voices, or *I*-positions, of the

unconscious. Equally, dreams and other unconscious manifestations may express important, but subjugated, *I*-positions or voices. The therapist may also be instrumental in identifying 'ventriloquations' in particular *I*-positions. The ultimate task of psychotherapy is one of identifying all the person's *I*-positions and facilitating a dialogue between the various voices or *I*-positions making up the landscape of the self.

Traditional African cosmology is also both relational and dialogical, and can be well explained by DST. As described earlier, persons are defined by their relationship with other persons. There is no such entity in African cosmology as a person isolated from relationship with others. Life is about relationship and dialogue. This dialogue operates in the various planes of relationship (Kambon 1992; Sow 1980; Straker 1994). In terms of DST, we may argue that the dialogue of various *I*-positions operates in various spaces, some natural and some supernatural. The horizontal plane involves the dialogue with immediate family, extended family and community in social and physical space. The vertical plane involves the relationship with the living dead or the ancestors and God (Ela 1995; Straker 1994; Vontress 1991), in what is essentially a transpersonal space. While Westerners might have great difficulty with the idea of ancestors (and God, for that matter), DST emphasizes the importance of recognizing not only actual or objective others. Ancestors and other spirits play a vital role in the psychic life of persons, family and community, and in the landscape of the self of individuals. Each of these people represents a potential external position in DST terms. An ongoing relationship and dialogue of individuals with their families and their ancestors is essential for health and well-being (Hewson 1998; Thorpe 1991; Vontress 1991). The voice of the ancestors is articulated in many forms, including physical symptoms, external events and dreams (Straker 1994). As explained above, dreams may function as very real dialogues between people and their ancestors. The criterion of health and well-being is the harmony of persons in relationship on the vertical and horizontal planes, or in natural and supernatural spaces. Disharmony, illness and distress may be seen to arise from a failure of dialogue with all the persons that make up this relational landscape. The task of the traditional healer is one of discerning the locus of dysfunctional relationships on each plane, and facilitating the dialogue with these significant others or unheard voices, especially those of the ancestors. According to Mosue (2000), this is especially apparent in situations where people have forgotten or failed to recognize or heed the voices of the living dead. Interestingly, Hewson describes some aspects of the diagnostic rituals performed for clients in specifically dialogical terms. One of the healers interviewed in her study used bone throwing and divining, and referred to an occasion when 'the bones did not want to talk to me at first' (1998: 1030). This particular healer also described specifically talking to the ancestors of her client, and that 'the ancestors are speaking through the bones' (1998: 1031), a typical example of ventriloquation. Straker in her detailed case study describes the dreams of the siblings in this case as 'a real conversation between themselves and their father' who had recently been murdered (1994: 460).

Traditional African cosmology and healing, on the one hand, and ORT and psychodynamic therapy, on the other hand, are extremely similar in their relational understanding of persons, health and dysfunction and in their use of dialogical process as therapy. In this sense, they are both very different from, and equally unacceptable to, Western science and medicine. Both could be seen as 'magico-religious' or narrative rather than scientific perspectives (Frank 1993).

In Western psychotherapy the manifest or explicit dialogue is between the therapist and client, but the therapeutic process involves an implicit recognition and dialogue with important 'objects' existing in intrapsychic or social domains of the person's life (Ogden 1983). Hermans' description of the self is also implicitly an excellent description of this therapeutic process: 'The I moves in an imaginal space (which is intimately intertwined with physical space) from the one to the other position, creating dynamic fields in which self-negotiations, self-contradictions and self-integrations result in a great variety of meanings' (2001: 252). The therapist plays an important role in facilitating this dialogue and movement. In some forms of Western psychotherapy, especially family therapy, significant others in the client's life may be explicitly incorporated into the therapeutic process, and the therapist's role is the facilitation of dialogue between them. Methods such as dream interpretation often play an important role in the therapeutic process, with clients often being explicitly invited into dialogues with characters in dreams (Straker 1994). In DST terms each of the dream characters may be seen as representing a different internal or external *I*-position.

In traditional African healing the dialogue will commence between iSangoma and client, but then progress to incorporate dialogue with various others, most especially ancestors (Buhrmann 1986; Straker 1994). The iSangoma functions as a medium of dialogue between clients and their ancestors. The dialogue may partly be by the individual with ancestors. For example, Buhrmann and Gqomfa (1982) provide a detailed case example of intervention with a woman, Mrs T, through the medium of dream interpretation. The healing ceremony commenced when 'Mrs T made impassioned pleas to all the clan ancestors, calling them one by one by name', but then 'this led to a discussion between her and her uncle about her initial illness' (1982: 46). The authors go on to say that 'Sharing her memories, anxieties and dreams with the sympathetic multitudes, the living and deceased, had a healing effect' (1982: 48). On the other hand, the dialogue may be by the ancestors to the person or persons. This was seen clearly in Straker's (1994) case where ancestors were seen as directly speaking through the dream. In DST terms, each of these others may represent potential *I*-positions. The healing process explicitly involves dialogue with these internal and external *I*-positions.

Thus far, we have suggested that, different as they appear, both psychotherapy and traditional African healing operate through dialogical processes which are well explained by DST. But there are also some critical differences between psychotherapy and traditional African healing, in the ways and spaces in which this dialogue takes place. Again DST provides an extremely useful framework for understanding and explaining the differences. It is especially the DST notion of the spatial dimension of *I*-positions (Hermans 2001), narratives and dialogue that is helpful in examining the difference. Western societies, with their valuing of autonomy and self-sufficiency, tend to operate in a predominantly private and 'internal' or mental space. The preferred therapies are those that deal with the 'imaginal others' emanating from and residing 'inside' people in the unconscious, such as psychodynamic approaches dealing with 'internal objects' or psychological representations, or the interface of these imaginal others with external others, as in family therapy. While significant others such as partners, parents or children may be involved in psychotherapy, the internal space or mental landscape is central in the understanding and practice of most Western psychotherapies.

Traditional African societies, on the other hand, with their valuing of relationships and communality, operate in a predominantly social, interpersonal and 'external' space. This may be on a horizontal/natural level of relationships with family and community or a vertical/supernatural level of relationships with ancestors, spirits and God (Straker 1994). But even the latter is understood and enacted in a shared social space, rather than in a private mental space. In both Straker's (1994) and Buhrmann and Gqomfa's (1982) cases of dream interpretations, this is done in the presence of and with the social participation of family and community. The preferred interventions are those that operate in this social space of family and community, including divining the messages of ancestors, dream interpretation or sacrifice of animals. Where a Western therapist may seek the cause and solution of a personal problem 'within' the client, traditional African healers are more likely to seek the cause and solution in relationships on the 'outside', whether on the horizontal or vertical plane. It is in the space of the consulting room, the shared space with the therapist and the client's own mind, that healing takes place for psychotherapists. However, it is in the social space of the family/ community/ancestors that healing takes place for Africans. These spatial differences are critical for enacting meaningful dialogical processes leading to healing.

With rapid urbanization and social change in South Africa, there are interesting changes occurring in the social construction of identity, as will be described in the second part of this chapter. More people are living in the space between traditional African culture and modern globalization, or occupy a bicultural identity. This is well described by Hermans and Dimaggio (2007:31) as 'global and local voices' in parallel and 'the increasing number of voices and counter-voices'. The mental health difficulties arising for people in South Africa may occur in any of the possible relational spaces within which they live (social, intrapsychic, transpersonal/spiritual), and may be related to any of the objects/voices in these spaces, or be a function of any one of the multiple identities people occupy. Rapid social change is also reflected in changes in patterns of mental health usage. Many black people in South Africa seek psychotherapy, and a growing number of white people have become interested in ancestors and traditional healing. There are also hybrid forms of therapeutic intervention emerging. One of these is the emergence of white iZangomas (Schumaker *et al.* 2007). Each of these hybrid identities and/or novel therapeutic interventions opens up potentially new *I*-positions and alternate spatial domains in which they are voiced. Novel forms of therapeutic intervention, such as the combination of Western psychotherapy and traditional African healing described by Straker (1994), may also provide a context within which *I*-positions emerging from various parallel cultural identities may be dialogued.

The task of the contemporary therapist/healer working in South Africa is to discern the relevant voices, *I*-positions and relational others which play a key role in the presenting problem, and to decide the best space, or combinations of space, for the therapeutic dialogue to be enacted. The DST as framework allows mental health practitioners better to conceptualize the rich array of possible therapeutic interventions, and to intervene accordingly, rather than crudely to polarize Western psychotherapy and traditional African healing as mutually exclusive.

Afrikaner identity construction in post-apartheid South Africa

The second part of this chapter focuses on a very different issue in the new South Africa; that is, the construction of Afrikaner identity. This issue has been selected to show the broad range of applicability of DST to social-psychological issues in contemporary South Africa.

Hermans and Kempen (1998: 1111) argue, 'In an increasingly interconnected world society the conception of independent, coherent, and stable cultures becomes increasingly irrelevant. Processes of globalization are drawing people from different cultural origins into close relationships. . .' With the dismantling of the apartheid state in 1994, South Africans from all cultural and racial backgrounds have begun to experience the disintegration of the walls of separation in many spheres of life, and their lives have become increasingly more socially integrated and entangled. 'White' Afrikaans-speakers (Afrikaners), the most powerful group during the apartheid era and the architects of apartheid or racial segregation, have seen their position change to a minority group that is politically relatively powerless, even while enjoying significant economic wealth and power. Afrikaans-speaking 'whites' are often viewed as a group that is experiencing social transformation towards democracy and equality as a difficult and painful process. Many Afrikaners, both old and young, are grappling to define or redefine their identities in a post-apartheid era. Public discourse by and around Afrikaners reveals that while this new identity is taking multiple forms, for many it involves an attempt to integrate the values of the new South Africa with valued aspects of Afrikaner identity rooted in the old South Africa.

The second author recently conducted a study to investigate how 'white' Afrikaans-speakers construct identities of being Afrikaans and 'white'. A qualitative design was used and a social constructionist metatheory underpinned the investigation. Nine Afrikaner families, consisting of both parents and at least one youth (17–18 years of age) in secondary school, were invited to take part in family conversations about their 'white' Afrikaner identity. The families were all from middle-class socio-economic backgrounds in the Eastern Cape and were relatively traditional in their outlook. The nine family conversations were managed as focus groups (Wilkinson 2004), and the purpose was to allow family members to talk freely and interact with each other around their experiences as 'white' Afrikaans-speakers in the post-apartheid society. The interview schedule that was developed included questions and probes relating to family members' experience of being Afrikaner and 'white' in the new democratic South Africa: for example, who and what is an Afrikaner?; what is your experience of the new South Africa where 'whites' are not dominating to the same extent as in the past?; and what do you think of apartheid? A discursive and rhetorical analysis, using Billig's (1996) rhetorical approach, was utilized to analyse the transcribed texts of the family conversations.

(Threat) narratives of Afrikaner identity

Analysis of these interviews revealed that a large number of topics in the family conversations dealt with threat, both explicitly and implicitly. The narratives of threat related to social, economic, cultural, political and interpersonal domains of life. Talking about threat was usually conducted in the form of an argument and certainly not with the intention of entertaining the listener. These threat narratives generally lead to the negative conclusion: 'they are the problem'. For example, the racial Other is out to get back at us as Afrikaners for what was done to them during the apartheid past, or 'they' want to undermine and destroy our cultural heritage and language. All in all, the narratives of 'white' Afrikaans-speakers in the investigation were saturated with a sense of threat, loss and protest in the process of grappling with being Afrikaner and 'white' in contemporary South African society.

Analysis of the interviews also revealed that these narratives of threat were also dominated by ambivalence and contradictions. For example, the husband and father, Alan, in one of the family conversations responded to a question on the future of Afrikaners in South Africa: he started by stating that he thought the Afrikaner's future looks bright in South Africa. However, his subsequent argument repeatedly contradicted this optimistic construction, revealing a deep sense of threat and uncertainty relating to the survival of the Afrikaners' language and culture in a society where the 'enemy' or racial Other is the dominant group in government.

The ambivalent structure of Afrikaner threat narratives can also be seen in the use of disclaimers, mitigations and other forms of racist denial in the construction of these threat narratives. For example, Annette, one of the speakers in a family conversation, used the disclaimer, 'I don't have a pain or something that they pulled them up' (i.e. 'I don't object to the improved status of black South Africans'), before voicing her concern: 'But the one should not oppress the other.' In another family conversation, Eloize used the rhetorical strategy of mitigation to manage her threat talk: 'We will have to put up *a little bit* of a fight for our language and our culture.' When 'white' speakers express a negative opinion about black South Africans, particularly in a racially sensitive society like South Africa, the possibility exists that an utterance may be interpreted as a racist statement. 'White' speakers are often concerned that negative talk about black South Africans may be heard as biased, prejudiced or racist. What happens is that such discourse needs to be mitigated or managed in such a way that it will not be held against the speaker. Researchers like van Dijk (1987, 1992), Billig (1988) and others, in studies conducted in Western Europe, Britain and the USA, have shown that these are routine moves used in social face-keeping when 'white' speakers are talking about ethnic and racial affairs. The use of these discursive and rhetorical manoeuvers serves a particular function: Afrikaans-speaking 'whites' seem to manage their discourses of 'race' and threat so that they can be seen to be in harmony with the ideologies and values of the new democratic society, even while holding on to aspects of their cultural identity rooted in the past. They want to make sure that they are not misunderstood and that an unwanted inference like 'racist' is not made from what they say.

It may be argued from analysing the discourse of the family conversations that many Afrikaners at the present historical juncture seem to be experiencing a profound sense of threat and anxiety. The following extract from one of the family conversations illustrates this well. In this extract, the speaker, who is a 'white', Afrikaans-speaking teacher, is telling about an experience that she had teaching adjectives to a grade seven class consisting of black students.

I teach black children virtually the entire day but I think ... I don't know when racism will disappear from our schools even among our children if it ever will be corrected... I write on the board 'the black cat' immediately I hear but I am standing with my back a few say something about 'black' I let it go by... it is grade sevens [.] The next sentence [smiling] is hmm 'the boy is wearing a white shirt' and just there they [said] something ... I immediately [.] Maybe I shouldn't have [.] I snapped and I turned around and said: '*The problem lies with you.*'

The 'white', Afrikaans-speaking teacher hears remarks about 'black' and 'white' as she was writing on the board with her back towards the class. In annoyance she turns to the class and lashes out emotionally: 'The problem lies with you.' She accuses the children of being preoccupied with 'race'. It is evident from what the speaker is telling that she did not hear precisely what the children were saying, nor the context within which it was said. Ironically, it was she that hears what the children were saying as racist. She brings a racist framework to bear on what she had heard the children saying.

It is evident from this extract that the speaker has utilized the rhetorical strategy of reversal in her talk. As Billig (1988), van Dijk (1992) and others have emphasized, this strategy is an extreme form of denial of racism. Van Dijk (1992) reiterates that reversals are no longer a form of social defence, but a strategy of (counter-)attack – 'the problem lies with you'. It has been established by analysing the talk and text of forms of elite discourse, as well as everyday talk, that the rhetorical strategy of reversal has been often used by right-wing groups in different parts of Western Europe and the USA. The strategy of reversal was widely used by 'white' Afrikaans-speakers in the family conversations of the reported study. The frequent use by Afrikaners in the present study of the discursive and rhetorical strategy of reversal is an indication of the extent to which they experience their position as threatened and stigmatized in the contemporary South African situation.

Recitation of discourses of the past in constructing Afrikaner threat narratives

Analysis of the interview transcripts also revealed that often discourses of the past were recited or repeated in the construction of threat narratives. The following typical ways of constructing threat narratives were identified:

1. We should stand together as a separate ethnic group against threats from outside ('We are a small little group').
2. The purity of the Afrikaans language is threatened: 'The Afrikaner is something of the past . . . if you cannot speak Afrikaans, your language.'
3. Our valued moral principles are disappearing: 'Where are those moral principles today?'
4. The 'Swart Gevaar' (Black Danger) is threatening us: 'He was just wiped out . . . *then* already they had said . . . we are not going to allocate the bursaries to the whites.'

Rhetorically, the threat narratives wherein discourses of the past are recycled, are utilized as a criticism and protest against the changing order in South Africa. Furthermore, it is clear that the sense of threat among Afrikaners is closely associated with the loss of traditional identities and ways of making sense in the post-apartheid society. The loss is often constructed as a catastrophic loss where Afrikaners 'are gone' and are 'lost human beings'.

Dialogical self perspective on emerging Afrikaner identity

Hermans *et al.*'s (1992) conceptualization of the self and identity as multivoiced and dialogical has provided a useful conceptual framework to understand the complexities in the construction of threatened identities in contexts of dramatic social transformation like post-apartheid South Africa. The family interviews conducted in this study reveal the multiplicity and contrasting voices that are at work in the psyches of 'white' Afrikaans-speakers in contemporary South Africa. They also provide evidence of the attempt to maintain a traditional/local identity in parallel with an emerging global identity which is part of the new democratic South Africa. There are similarities between the reported study and the study by van Meijl (2006), who also used DST to make intelligible the fragmentation of self and the psychological struggle among urban Maori youth between a prescribed traditional cultural identity and forms of identification emanating from their also being rooted in a society that is predominantly European in its outlook (see also his chapter in this book).

The collective voices of the past, as seen in the recitation of discourses of a bygone era, continue to play a significant role in the identity construction of Afrikaners in the present. Afrikaners find themselves in a position where many continue to believe in or partially adhere to the discourses and ideologies of the past, but at the same time they are confronted with a transforming society where racism has been outlawed and apartheid discredited, leaving many Afrikaners deeply uncertain and threatened. The privileging of the identities of being Afrikaner and 'white', rooted in the time and space of the old South Africa, even while negotiating a contemporary identity in the new South Africa, is likely to complicate the process of becoming full citizens in the new South African society. There is little doubt that the South African society in transformation is saturated with upheavals, stresses and challenges. However, constructing such a bleak picture of the opportunities, rights and expectations of 'white' Afrikaans-speakers would inevitably lead to large numbers deciding to leave the country or withdrawing their energies from productive involvement in activities and projects of the new democratic society. If the findings of the study are transferable to Afrikaner families in other contexts in South Africa, it is not unimaginable that forms of extreme behaviour could possibly erupt among Afrikaners, including young people.

The ambivalent structure of Afrikaner threat narratives also seems to show the struggles of Afrikaners in dealing with realities in the new South Africa. The abundant mobilization among 'white' Afrikaans-speakers of the rhetorical strategy of reversal of racism (or 'projection' in psychoanalytic language) becomes intelligible against the backdrop of a transforming social context that often becomes too threatening and unbearable to deal with in a rational way.

Hermans and Dimaggio (2007) maintain that fundamental differences in an intensely interconnected society, like South Africa, require not only dialogical relationships between people to build a liveable world where threat can be diminished or eliminated, but also a self that is developing the capacity to deal with its own tensions, contrasts, differences, uncertainties and threats. Innovative dialogue is needed that takes into account the different perspective of the other person or group in its alterity. Alterity is a basic feature of well-developed dialogue, according to Hermans and Dimaggio (2007). It is vital that people in transforming societies, like Afrikaners in present-day South Africa, learn to deal with difference in constructive ways. What is needed, among other things, is that Afrikaners should increasingly venture into taking part in projects in close cooperation with the racial Other, from where they can stand in new *I*-positions and produce new narratives that will be increasingly free of threat, uncertainty and apathy, and where they can play their role as participating, constructive and moral citizens of a democratic South Africa.

Conclusion

The emerging democracy of the new South Africa provides an ideal social laboratory within which to study issues of self and identity. In this chapter we have selected two topical issues in South Africa, one from the field of mental health/psychotherapy and one from the field of social identity in post-apartheid society, to examine some issues of self and identity. We have found the theoretical framework of the dialogical self to be especially helpful in investigating these contested issues. In conclusion we mention the three points from DST which have been most helpful in considering these two issues. *First,* DST describes the self as a dialogue of *I*-positions or voices in an imaginal landscape, with some of these *I*-positions as more privileged and others as more subjugated. We have suggested that mental health problems leading to the need for therapeutic intervention, and issues of forging a new social identity in South Africa, both involve a dialogue with and of multiple voices or *I*-positions. The challenge in both the arenas of mental health services and social transformation is to find a way to facilitate the dialogue, rather than polarization, of these *I*-positions in the renegotiation of self and identity. The conflicts inherent in the renegotiation of Afrikaner identity in South Africa provide a demonstration of the complex challenges in this process, and the realignment of these different *I*-positions. *Second,* DST explains the way in which each voice or *I*-position making up the (dialogical) self is located in a particular time and space. We have suggested that traditional African healing and Western psychotherapy represent patterns of healing employing very different spaces for the enactment of the imaginal landscape of voices, but that these are both inherently dialogical in nature. We have suggested that effective therapeutic intervention involves the ability to discern the most appropriate space within which to facilitate the therapeutic dialogue. Equally, we might argue that the renegotiation of Afrikaner identity also involves voices from different times and spaces, some from the 'old' and some from the 'new' South Africa. The interviews with Afrikaners referred to in this chapter were conducted in the familiar space of 'home', which seemed also to be the locus of traditional Afrikaner identity. But we could expect that a different *I*-position of Afrikaner identity may have been revealed if the space of these interviews were a more public one. *Finally*, issues around psychotherapy and culture, as well those around renegotiating social identity, provide very good evidence of Hermans and Dimaggio's (2007: 31) claim that 'global and local voices are involved in continuous interchanges and negotiations'. Their interest is primarily in the 'impact of globalization on self and identity and at the same time a growing uncertainty... [and the] increasing number of voices and countervoices' (2007: 31). While some of the phenomena described in South Africa are no doubt the result of globalization, they are also part of the process of democratization and transformation. Our work on changing Afrikaner identity clearly shows the emergence of two parallel identities, one more traditional or local, and the other more modern or global. One of the greatest challenges for Afrikaners in South Africa may be seen as the harmonious dialogue of the voices/countervoices of these two identities which are maintained in parallel. The field of mental health/psychotherapy can also be seen as faced with the challenge of responding to the needs of the growing number of people in South Africa who do not have an exclusively 'Western' or 'African' identity, but rather both in parallel, typically characterized by the uncertainty referred to by Hermans and Dimaggio (2007).

REFERENCES

Billig, M. (1988) The notion of 'prejudice': some rhetorical and ideological aspects, *Text*, **8**, 91–110
  (1996) *Arguing and Thinking: A Rhetorical Approach to Social Psychology* (Cambridge University Press)
Buhrmann, M. V. (1986) *Living in Two Worlds: Communications Between a White Healer and Her Black Counterparts* (Wilmette, IL: Chiron Publications)

Buhrmann, M. V. and Gqomfa, J. N. (1982) The Xhoas healers of Southern Africa. 3. A family therapy session with a dream as central component, *Journal of Analytic Psychology*, **27**, 41–57

Ela, J.-M. (1995) *My faith as an African* (Maryknoll, NY: Orbis Books)

Frank, J. *Persuasion and Healing: A Comparative Study of Psychotherapy*, 3rd edn (Baltimore, MD: Johns Hopkins University Press)

Gyekye, K. (1997) *Tradition and Modernity: Philosophical Reflections on the African Experience* (Oxford University Press)

Hermans, H. J. M. (2001) The dialogical self: towards a theory of personal and cultural positioning, *Culture & Psychology*, **7**, 243–282

Hermans, H. J. M. and Dimaggio, G. (2007) Self, identity and globalization in times of uncertainty: a dialogical analysis, *Review of General Psychology*, **11**, 31–61

Hermans, H. J. M. and Kempen, H. J. G. (1993) *The Dialogical Self: Meaning as Movement* (San Diego, CA: Academic Press)

(1998) Moving cultures: the perilous problems of cultural dichotomies in a globalizing world, *American Psychologist*, **53**, 1111–1120

Hermans, H. J. M., Kempen, H. J. G. and van Loon, R. J. P. (1992) The dialogical self: beyond individualism and rationalism, *American Psychologist*, **47**, 23–33

Hewson, M. G. (1998) Traditional healers in Southern Africa, *Annals of Internal Medicine*, **128**, 1029–1034

Kambon, K. K. (1992) *The African Personality in America: An African Centred Framework* (Tallahassee, FL: Nubian Nation Press)

Lemma, A. (2003) *Introduction to the Practice of Psychoanalytic Psychotherapy* (Chichester: Wiley)

Mosue, L. (2000) The role of the dead-living in the African family system, Unpublished master's thesis, Pietermaritzburg, University of Natal

Ogden, T. (1983) The concept of internal object relations, *International Journal of Psychoanalysis*, **64**, 227–241

Parle, J. (2003) Witchcraft or madness? The amandiki of Zululand, 1894–1914, *Journal of Southern African Studies*, **29**, 105–132

Roland, A. (2001) Another voice and position: psychoanalysis across civilizations, *Culture & Psychology*, **7**, 311–322

Schumaker, L., Jeater, D. and Luedeke, T. (2007) Introduction, histories of healing: past and present medical practices in Africa and the diaspora, *Journal of Southern African Studies*, **33**, 707–714

Sogolo, G. (1993) *Foundations of African Philosophy: A Definitive Analysis of Conceptual Issues in African Thought* (Ibadan: Ibadan University Press)

Sow, A. I. (1980) *Anthropological Structures of Madness in Black Africa* (New York: International Universities Press)

Straker, G. (1994) Integrating African and Western healing practices in South Africa, *American Journal of Psychotherapy*, **48**, 455–467

Swartz, L. (1998) *Culture and Mental Health: A Southern African View* (Cape Town: Oxford University Press)

Thorpe, S. A. (1991) *African Traditional Religions: An Introduction* (Pretoria: Sigma Press)

van Dijk, T. A. (1987) *Communicating Racism: Ethnic Prejudice in Thought and Talk* (Newbury Park, CA: Sage)

(1992) Discourse and the denial of racism, *Discourse and Society*, **3**, 87–118

van Meijl, T. (2006) Multiple identifications and the dialogical self: urban Maori youngsters and the cultural renaissance, *Journal of the Royal Anthropological Institute (N.S.)*, **12**, 917–933

Vontress, C. E. (1991) Traditional healing in Africa: implications for cross-cultural counseling, *Journal of Counselling and Development*, **70**, 242–249

Wilkinson, S. (2004). Focus group research, in D. Silverman (ed.), *Qualitative Research: Theory, Method and Practice* (London: Sage), 117–199

Part II

Methods for studying the dialogical self

Introduction

Hubert J. M. Hermans and Thorsten Gieser

As a bridging theory (see introductory chapter), dialogical self theory (DST) needs a certain variety of methods for studying the broad variety of phenomena falling within its scope. In the present section, the main methods – some quantitative, others qualitative – are described together with their theoretical background.

In their chapter, Oleś and Puchalska-Wasyl present a method, the Internal Dialogical Activity Scale (IDAS), for assessing different kinds of dialogues within the self (e.g. identity dialogue, supportive dialogues and dialogues with imagined others). One of their questions is to what extent internal dialogical activity has a basis in basic personality traits. In order to address this question, they calculated correlations between the IDAS and the NEO-PI-R, an instrument to assess the so-called Big Five personality traits. Particularly relevant to DST are the correlations between internal dialogical activity and the trait 'openness to experience'. Moreover, they collected data, relevant to the experience of uncertainty, another concept relevant to DST.

Żurawska-Żyła and colleagues present an investigation of the dialogical self of six Polish novelists, who were willing to tell about their personal relationship with the characters that are central in their work. For this purpose, the authors developed a research method for studying the organization of *I*-positions, 'the spatial self-representation procedure', allowing for a graphical description of the self in terms of a spatial organization of *I*-positions. As part of this project, the novelists were invited to focus on their own *I-position as author* and to mark the relationships – if there were any – between this position and each of the selected characters of their novels. Their findings led this chapter's authors to make a distinction between two kinds of novels within the broader category of the Bakhtinian polyphonic novel: the 'multivoiced' and the 'dialogical' novel.

Stemplewska-Żakowicz and colleagues start their chapter by noting that DST, despite its variety of applications, has not yet been experimentally verified. For their purposes, they investigate the positional basis of DST from the perspective of a 'discursive mind model'. This model is based on the assumption that the mind consists of a number of auto-nomic, holistic modules linked to a specific social context and dependent on one's socialization history. Guided by this model, they perform a series of experiments in which they show that different (conscious or non-conscious) *I*-positions have different ways of perceiving and inter-preting the world. Of specific relevance to DST is the finding that participants tell different self-narratives from different *I*-positions and that these self-narratives are different in both form and content. Based on such experiments, the authors investigate to what extent the pos-itional structure of DST can be verified.

The process of self-negotiation in situations of internal conflict is central in Nir's chapter. Drawing on DST's tenet that the self functions as a society of mind, she proposes that just as in negotiations between people, the internal negotiation within the self may lead to either coer-cive win–lose or collaborative win–win processes. In order to assist people to manage their inner conflicts and transform coercive negoti-ations and decisions into integrative win–win outcomes, she presents a *four-stage intervention method* that can be used in both research and practice. The author argues that the method promotes a democratic and equality-based process in the self and encourages an active and unconditional process of internal listening.

Gonçalves and Ribeiro emphasize in their contribution that in DST dialogical relations allow innovation and transformation of existing pat-terns of self-organization. They observe that in many psychotherapeutic processes, innovation is blocked by a cyclical movement between two opposing voices, one dominant that organizes the client's problematic self-narrative, and one innovative but non-dominant. In their search for ways of escaping this stabilizing cycle, they focus on 'innovative moments' that have the potential of defreezing and transforming the existing organization of the self. For this purpose they have developed an 'Innovative moments coding system', which comprises five categories of innovative moments (action, reflection, protest, re-conceptualization and performing change) that can be observed in the course of psycho-therapy. The authors show how different innovative moments can be observed in different phases of psychotherapy.

Jasper and colleagues start their chapter noting that in dialogical self research a wide variety of methods have been used, such as experiments, self-report questionnaires, self-confrontation method, anthropological data, interview data and close textual analysis of biographical material. In a critical review, they argue that the available methodologies enable us to examine the voices within the dialogical self, but not the voices of significant others outside the self. Therefore, they introduce the inter-personal perception method of Laing as a means to enhance the ability of the researcher to examine systematically the voices of the self in direct relation with those of actual people around us. As the authors show, one of the advantages of using this method is that misunderstandings (one's view of the other's intentions does not match the actual view of the other) can be uncovered.

13 Dialogicality and personality traits

Piotr K. Oleś and Małgorzata Puchalska-Wasyl

Introduction: the dialogical self and the trait theory of personality

Dialogical self theory (DST) is an original, influential and very inspiring theory of personality rooted in constructivism and a phenomenological approach (Hermans 1996, 2002; Hermans and Hermans-Konopka 2010; Hermans and Kempen 1993). The notion of the dialogical self not only expresses the basic complexity and multifaceted character of the human self, but – what is especially distinctive – also proposes that human cognitive and emotional, as well as social, functioning is based on inner dialogical relationships between different *I*-positions. And it is far more than a reference to James' theoretical approach; it is a clear extension of his theory and a creative proposition for modern psychology of the self. However, like every new and inspiring theory, it should be confronted with other approaches, and any possible connections to leading theoretical propositions should be clarified.

Taking as our starting point the integrative models of personality proposed by either McCrae and Costa (1999) or McAdams and Pals (2006), we pose the main question, how is the dialogical self related to the three main domains of personality: basic tendencies (mainly traits), characteristic adaptations and the self-system? In this chapter, using a correlation approach, we try to show and comment on selected personality correlates of the internal dialogical activity, which seem to challenge DST. Thus, what are the relationships between inner dialogical activity and the variables from the three levels of personality: traits, characteristic adaptations and the self-concept?

According to the five-factor theory of personality, the core components of the personality system are basic tendencies (five traits),

Correspondence concerning this chapter should be addressed to Piotr Oleś, Department of Personality Psychology, John Paul II Catholic University of Lublin, Al. Raclawickie 14, 20–950 Lublin, Poland; email: oles@kul.lublin.pl. The research presented in this chapter was supported by the Foundation for Polish Science.

characteristic adaptations and self-concept (McCrae and Costa 1999). McAdams and Pals (2006) propose a similar model – personality organization on a very general level may be introduced as three broad domains: dispositional traits, characteristic adaptations and integrative life stories (McAdams and Pals 2006). Regardless of some differences on the third level, both models are more similar than different. When we pose a question about the relationship between internal dialogical activity as an expression of the dialogical self, and the variables representing the three levels of personality, the answer seems to be obvious when it concerns the level of the self: the dialogical self is a highly dynamic notion offering a new perspective for theoretical interpretation and research on the self. Each *I*-position represents a unique valuation perspective, and each *I*-position has the potential to relate in a dialogical way to any other internal *I*-position or external imagined figure. And the creation of various *I*-positions is very relevant to a rich, flexible, integrated and healthy system of personal meanings, in which numerous internal tendencies have the opportunity for full expression or representation.

Furthermore, dialogical activity is so basic and crucial for human functioning that it can be related to traits or neurobiological processes (see Lewis 2002; Linell 2007), which – like traits – belong to basic tendencies (Larsen and Buss 2005). Moreover, dialogicality is a core feature of dialectical thinking typical for adulthood (Sternberg *et al.* 2001). As such, internal dialogues have some adaptive functions, for they may lead to the solution of personal dilemmas and contribute to a process of understanding other people or various culture-rooted points of view, as well as leading to an agreement between two or more standpoints. Therefore, we assume that internal dialogical activity as a function of the dialogical self is directly related to characteristic adaptations.

Thus, our purpose is to explore how dialogicality is related to each of the three levels of personality, namely traits, characteristic adaptations and self-concept. Provided that people differ in the intensity of dialogicality, and that these differences can be empirically assessed, we intend to construct a scale to measure the general intensity of inner dialogues according to the individual differences approach (Oleś *et al.* 2010). We define internal dialogical activity as engagement in dialogues with imagined figures, the simulation of social dialogical relationships in one's own thoughts, and the mutual confrontation of the points of view representing different *I*-positions relevant to personal and/or social identity (Oleś 2009; see also Hermans 1996, 2002; Hermans and Kempen 1993; Josephs 1998; Marková 2005).

How inner dialogical activity can be measured

Assuming that the people have an insight into their inner dialogical activity, and that they are aware of the dialogues conducted in their thoughts, we tried to assess the intensity of the dialogicality. The Internal Dialogical Activity Scale (IDAS) was constructed by a deductive-rational approach; that is, the content of the scale was based on theoretical knowledge about the phenomenon under investigation. The initial set of items was generated after an intensive study of several related sources (Chmielnicka-Kuter 2005; Hermans 1996, 2002; Hermans and Kempen 1993; Josephs 1998; Marková 2005; Puchalska-Wasyl 2005; Raggatt 2000). The final version of the IDAS contains 47 items measuring the intensity of general dialogical activity and of seven kinds of internal dialogues measured by subscales. Below, we mention the names of these subscales, giving one clarifying example of an item for each of the scales.

- Pure dialogical activity (DA) – *I converse with myself.*
- Identity dialogues (ID) – *Sometimes I debate with myself about who I really am.*
- Supportive dialogues (SD) – *In some stressful situations, I attempt to calm myself with my thoughts.*
- Ruminative dialogues (RD) – *After failures, I blame myself in my thoughts and discuss how the failures could have been avoided.*
- Confronting dialogues (CD) – *Sometimes I think that my 'good' side argues with my 'bad' side.*
- Simulation of social dialogues (SS) – *Sometimes I continue a conversation with other people in my mind.*
- Taking a point of view (PV) – *Often in my thoughts I use the perspective of someone else.*

The items are designed in a Likert-type format with five alternative answers (from 1 = *I strongly disagree*, to 5 = *I strongly agree*). The total score is the sum of all the scores. The reliability of the total result is very high: Cronbach $\alpha = 0.93$ and stability $r_{tt} = 0.84$, measured at a 2-month interval. The internal consistency for the subscales is from 0.64 to 0.82, and the correlations between them and the total score are from 0.30 (RD) to 0.78 (SD), which means that the subscales have a 10% to 60% variance in common with the total scale (Oleś 2009).

What are the correlates of internal dialogical activity? We carried out several studies and replicated the results in different samples in order to get proper and certain results (Oleś *et al.* 2010). With reference to the general model of personality (McCrae and Costa

1999; McAdams and Pals 2006), the correlates were investigated on the levels of traits, characteristic adaptations (e.g. styles of attachment and empathy) and self-concept (e.g. self-knowledge, self-esteem or self-clarity).

Inner dialogical activity and personality characteristics

On the level of traits we computed the correlations between IDAS and the NEO-PI-R (Revised NEO Personality Inventory) (Costa and McCrae 1992). The results show a moderate correspondence between the intensity of internal dialogical activity and Neuroticism (0.34, $p < 0.001$), as well as Openness (from 0.27, $p < 0.01$ in adolescents, to 0.54, $p < 0.001$ in middle-aged adults). The relationship with Neuroticism was also replicated by the Eysenck Personality Questionnaire – Revised (EPQ-R) (0.39, $p < 0.001$). Generally, the higher the level of Neuroticism and Openness, the higher was the level of internal dialogical activity (Puchalska-Wasyl *et al.* 2008). This is probably modified by developmental factors since, in adolescents, internal dialogicality corresponds higher with Neuroticism than with Openness (in students, higher with Openness or Neuroticism, depending on the sample), while in the middle-aged samples the internal dialogical activity corresponds higher with Openness than with Neuroticism (Oleś *et al.* 2010). This implies that in adolescents internal dialogues are stimulated mainly by anxiety and personal problems, whereas in adults mostly by openness and curiosity. Adolescents may use internal dialogues for coping with the unknown, which tends mainly to reduce anxiety, while middle-aged adults use internal dialogues mainly for exploring new worlds and for dialectical thinking, which broadens the scope of personal possibilities (see Sternberg *et al.* 2001). However, one should remember that – according to the correlations – both kinds of relationships are present in each group, so the aforementioned age difference is a matter of emphasis.

These findings are indirectly supported by Puchalska-Wasyl (2006, 2007), who investigated the relationship between traits and internal dialogues which were evoked in a quasi-experimental way. The students who preferred internal dialogues to monologues as a form of internal mental activity differed in some personality traits measured by means of the NEO-PI-R. The persons preferring inner dialogues scored significantly higher on Openness and its facets, such as Fantasy, Aesthetics and Feelings, as well as higher on Self-Consciousness as a component of Neuroticism, and lower on Assertiveness as a component of Extroversion, than the participants preferring internal monologues (Puchalska-Wasyl *et al.* 2008).

A level of characteristic adaptations was represented by the attachment style measured by the Experiences in Close Relationships–Revised Questionnaire (ECR–R) (Fraley *et al.* 2000), and empathy measured by the Interpersonal Reactivity Index (IRI) (Davis 1980). The most striking result is the negative correspondence between the internal dialogues and the avoidant attachment (-0.44, $p < 0.001$), while the correspondence between the internal dialogical activity and the anxious style is positive (0.39, $p < 0.001$). The persons who are attached in an anxious style are prone to conduct internal dialogues, whereas those attached in the avoidant style are inclined to avoid mutual relationships among the *I*-positions representing parts of themselves or other people. On the one hand, these findings imply an analogy between internal dialogical activity and the social relationships of the person. Although the correlations are not high, they suggest that internal dialogues to some degree mirror social relationships: the more avoidant social bonds people have, the more rarely do they engage themselves in inner dialogical activity. On the other hand, anxious social relationships positively correspond with inner dialogical activity, which can be connected to the neuroticism of anxious persons and their motivation to test possible social contacts in advance by means of internal dialogue. Such relationships between the inner and outer world express very well the notion of the dialogical self as a 'society of mind' (Hermans 2002). Additionally, the internal dialogicality seems to function as a bridge or medium between one's own mind and the minds of others, for it is related to empathy (0.33, $p < 0.001$).

The highest correspondence might have been expected between measures of the self and internal dialogical activity, since they both belong to the third, narrative level of the personality, according to McAdams and Pals (2006). The results do not confirm this expectation. In a few independent studies we have not found any replicable pattern of significant relationships between internal dialogicality and several indices of self-concept measured by the Adjective Check List (Gough and Heilbrun 1983). Simultaneously, internal dialogicality is negatively related to mindfulness (-0.36, $p < 0.001$) as measured by the Mindful Attention/Awareness Scale (MAAS) (Brown and Ryan 2003). Probably, internal dialogues engage the mind; thus, they imply a lower level of mindful attention. The results also show a slight negative relationship between internal dialogical activity and self-esteem (-0.32, $p < 0.05$) measured by the Self-Esteem Scale (SES) (Rosenberg 1965), as well as self-concept clarity (-0.37, $p < 0.01$) measured by the Self-Concept Clarity Scale (SCC) (Campbell *et al.* 1996). High self-esteem and clear self-concept do not predispose the person to internal dialogues. Perhaps unclear self-concept gives space for the internal confrontation of different points of view, which may tend to clarify self-knowledge.

What are the implications of correlation studies for DST?

First of all, according to DST, it is possible to measure internal dialogical activity, provided that the person is able to reflect on his/her dialogical activity taking a meta-position which gives a bird's-eye view of a whole system of *I*-positions, their voices and relationships. Such a function of a meta-position is consistent with the notion of the dialogical self as a 'society of the mind' (Hermans 2002). However, the correlation research provides results suggesting interpretations going beyond the framework of DST. While the positions are constructed according to the representations of important inner and outer relationships, the phenomenon of dialogicality is influenced by more stable and non-contextualized personality characteristics. As such findings suggest, it makes sense to consider the phenomenon of dialogicality in relation to the integrative model of personality, for this can benefit our knowledge of the dialogical self.

The findings presented reveal that internal dialogical activity has foundations in the personality structure, especially in the traits of Openness and Neuroticism. Low Openness, by definition, implies low motivation for the exchange of ideas, so it is conducive to monologues rather than dialogues. High Openness gives rise to the interchange of ideas with a real or imagined partner and a readiness to share his or her ideas, as well as creating new ideas in a dialogue. The fact that dialoguing people are innovative in thinking (Openness to Experience) fits Hermans' description of dialogicality in terms of a healthy and creative exploration of the self (Hermans 2002, 2003; Hermans and Dimaggio 2007). It was also found that a more vivid and creative imagination (Fantasy), is typical of persons entering into internal dialogues, in comparison with persons preferring monologues. At the same time, dialoguing persons can better differentiate emotional states and appreciate them as an important part of inner life (Feelings). Additionally, internal dialogical activity is easier for those who have some self-doubts or not very high self-esteem (lower self-clarity and higher self-consciousness) (Oleś et al. 2010; Puchalska-Wasyl et al. 2008), which is relevant to the further exploration of the connection between dialogical activity and the experience of uncertainty (Hermans and Hermans-Konopka 2010).

Our results in general are consistent with the results concerning relationships between narratives and traits (McAdams et al. 2004; McGregor, McAdams and Little 2006), indirectly supporting the links between dialogicality and narrative thinking (Bruner 1990). In these studies, the negative emotional tone of a life narrative was associated with Neuroticism, the narrative themes of communion were correlated with Agreeableness, and the structural complexity of life narratives was associated with Openness. However, a positive narrative tone was not related to Extroversion (McAdams et al. 2004). Moreover, the level of happiness was higher in persons whose social goals and life stories were consistent with, and supported by, sociable personality traits (Roberts et al. 2004). Both results suggest a consistency between the traits and the features of life stories. On a general level, we have obtained very similar results: a consistency between the type of internal dialogues and traits. For example, people high in Neuroticism tend to conduct ruminative dialogues (the correlation between Neuroticism and ruminative dialogues as a subscale of the IDAS is $r = 0.44$, $p < 0.001$), and people high in Openness are prone to use internal dialogues for identity clarification (the correlation between Openness and identity dialogues in IDAS is $r = 0.57$, $p < 0.001$) (Oleś et al. 2010).

Nevertheless, we think it is too early to conclude that traits influence the type of internal dialogical activity; traits rather seem to affect the intensity of the dialogicality, and perhaps in a very general way they can correspond to a particular type of internal dialogue. At the same time, the lack of correlations with Extroversion suggests that inner dialogical activity is not a simple function (or expression) of higher brain arousal or a mental activity typical of low Extroversion (Pickering and Gray 1999). However, it should be emphasized that traits definitely do not explain the intensity and different types of internal dialogical activity in a sufficient way (Puchalska-Wasyl et al. 2008).

Simultaneously, characteristic adaptations such as, for example, the aforementioned attachment styles seem to colour the type of internal dialogue. Let us mention some more examples from our data. Secure attachment correlated positively with identity dialogues ($0.64, p < 0.001$) and negatively with ruminative dialogues ($-0.75, p < 0.001$) as measured by the subscales of the IDAS. Anxious attachment correlated with the simulation of social relationships (0.79, $p < 0.001$) as well as with ruminative dialogues (0.53, $p < 0.001$), whereas avoidant attachment correlated negatively with supporting dialogues (-0.67, $p < 0.001$) as well as identity dialogues (-0.45, $p < 0.001$), and slightly positively with ruminative dialogues (0.34, $p < 0.001$) (Oleś et al. 2010). This means that general patterns of adaptations correspond as follows with types of internal dialogues: security in social relationships inspires individuals to use internal dialogues in forming their identity and to avoid rumination, while, for example, anxiety in social relationships stimulates individuals to simulate and check interpersonal relationships in their imagination. As these data prove, some types of internal dialogues correspond to selected variables from the second level of personality organization – characteristic adaptations.

Finding correlates between dialogicality and variables like self-esteem or self-clarity, we showed that dialogicality also corresponds with the variables from the third level of personality organization – the self. However, in our opinion, DST is much more inclined to idiographic studies of inner voices, their organization, expressions and integration, than to the nomothetic correlation research. Looking for a correspondence between DST and the integrated model of personality, one can assume that the traits constitute a susceptibility to a higher or lower internal dialogical activity, while the characteristic adaptations probably influence the types of this activity in the form of the most typical inner dialogues (e.g. identity, supporting or ruminative ones), and also according to current personal problems, challenges or situations. On the self-level of personality organization, the relationship under reflection looks quite different. Regardless of some correlations, the core of this problem is that the system of personal meanings provides unique topics for inner dialogues. Thus, on this third level – the self – one's personal meaning system is responsible for the identity features given to the *I*-positions and their interchange and/or creative power. While on the levels of traits and characteristic adaptations, research on dialogicality is easily subjected to correlational and nomothetic studies, on the level of the self, internal dialogues should be investigated by an idiographic approach and qualitative research methods. In conclusion, firstly, we postulate the existence of personality predispositions for inner dialogical activity. Secondly, we propose three levels of qualitatively different relationships between the dialogical self and the variables from the integrative model of personality.

Summary of results

We would like to juxtapose our results with the main ideas of DST in order to emphasize that the findings presented are consistent with Hermans' conception, and confirm it. As we have tried to show, there is an analogy between internal dialogical activity and the social relationships of a person. In particular, the correspondence between the types of inner dialogue and attachment styles suggests that internal dialogicality mirrors, to some degree, the social bonds which people have. An analogical conclusion was drawn by Cooper (2003), who claimed that our internal dialogues have the same characteristics as those which are typical of our real interpersonal relationships. Against that background, Hermans' (2002) metaphor of the dialogical self as a 'society of the mind' is understandable as well.

The idea of the innovative potential of dialogue seems to find expression in the connection between Openness to Experience and internal dialogical activity, especially identity dialogues. People high in Openness, who are curious about not only their outer, but also their inner, world (Costa and McCrae 1992), are probably prone to pose many questions pertaining to their identity. The fact that they have an inclination to identity dialogues suggests that this kind of internal activity can bring them some new answers (Hermans 1999). At the same time, dialogue, particularly when the person is open to the input of others and willing to revise his/her original point of view on the basis of the interchange with the dialogical participant, necessarily implies some degree of uncertainty (Hermans and Hermans-Konopka 2010). When we think about the four aspects of uncertainty, namely complexity, ambiguity, deficit knowledge and unpredictability, we can consider it as something opposite to self-concept clarity as discussed above. Nevertheless, the fact that internal dialogical activity correlates positively with Neuroticism and negatively with self-esteem and self-concept clarity seems to confirm the thesis about a relationship between dialogue and the experience of uncertainty – a problem especially typical of adolescents who cope with increasing level of uncertainty.

On the one hand, in the context of this thesis one can give the following interpretative hypothesis concerning the above-mentioned correlation between dialogicality and Neuroticism, low self-esteem and unclear self-concept: a higher level of feelings of inferiority and ambiguity of the self may be stimulated by dialogical thinking, mainly when the person confronts two or more identity-relevant *I*-positions. On the other hand, a contrary hypothesis can be advanced: internal dilemma and conflicts can be worked through and resolved by means of inner dialogues. Both these interpretative hypotheses are only seemingly contradictory, since both of them can explain two different phases of the same process. As Hermans and Hermans-Konopka (2010) claim, the experience of uncertainty, as a consequence of a dialogue as an unpredictable process, can lead to anxiety and insecurity, but, at the same time, it can be reduced by going *through* a dialogical process in order to find a post-dialogical form of certainty.

Finally, it is worth noting that our results show that the different types of dialogue (e.g. ruminative dialogues or identity dialogues) have very different correlations with external variables, such as different attachment styles. This suggest that in the further process of the exploration of the relationship between internal dialogical activity and other variables, one should differentiate between the types of dialogues, and use the IDAS on the level of subscales besides applying it on the general level of dialogicality. The study of the dialogical self as a multifaceted phenomenon deserves attention on the specific level of functioning.

REFERENCES

Brown, K. W. and Ryan, R. M. (2003) The benefits of being present: mindfulness and its role in psychological well-being, *Journal of Personality and Social Psychology*, **84**, 822–848

Bruner, J. S. (1990) *Acts of Meaning* (Cambridge, MA: Harvard University Press)

Campbell, J. D., Trapnell, P. D., Heine, S. J., Katz, I. M., Lavallee, L. F. and Lehman, D. R. (1996) Self-concept clarity: measurement, personality correlates, and cultural boundaries, *Journal of Personality and Social Psychology*, **70**, 141–156

Chmielnicka-Kuter, E. (2005) Role-playing game heroes as partners of internal dialogues, in P. K. Oleś and H. J. M. Hermans (eds.), *The Dialogical Self: Theory and Research* (Lublin: Wydawnictwo KUL), 231–243

Cooper, M. (2003) 'I–I' and 'I–Me': transposing Buber's interpersonal attitudes to the intrapersonal plane, *Journal of Constructivist Psychology*, **16**, 131–153

Costa, P. T. and McCrae, R. R. (1992) *Revised NEO Personality Inventory (NEO PI-R) and NEO Five-Factor Inventory (NEO-FFI)*. Professional manual (Odessa, FL: Psychological Assessment Resources)

Davis, M. H. (1980) A multidimensional approach to individual differences in empathy, *JSAS Catalogue of Selected Documents in Psychology*, **10**, 85–104

Fraley, R. C., Waller, N. G. and Brennan, K. A. (2000) An item-response theory analysis of self-report measures of adult attachment, *Journal of Personality and Social Psychology*, **78**, 350–365

Gough, H. G. and Heilbrun, A. B. (1983) *The Adjective Check List: Manual* (Palo Alto, CA: Consulting Psychologists Press)

Hermans, H. J. M. (1996) Voicing the self: from information processing to dialogical interchange, *Psychological Bulletin*, **119**, 31–50

(1999) Dialogical thinking and self-innovation, *Culture and Psychology*, **5**, 67–87

(2002) The dialogical self as a society of mind: introduction, *Theory & Psychology*, **12**, 147–160

(2003) The construction and reconstruction of a dialogical self, *Journal of Constructivist Psychology*, **16**, 89–130

Hermans, H. J. M. and Dimaggio, G. (2007) Self, identity, and globalization in times of uncertainty: a dialogical analysis, *Review of General Psychology*, **11**, 31–61

Hermans, H. J. M. and Hermans-Konopka, A. (2010) *The Dialogical Self: Positioning and Counter-Positioning in a Globalizing World* (Cambridge University Press)

Hermans, H. J. M. and Kempen, H. J. G. (1993) *The Dialogical Self: Meaning as Movement* (San Diego, CA: Academic Press)

Josephs, I. E. (1998) Constructing one's self in the city of the silent: dialogue, symbols, and the role of 'as-if' in self-development, *Human Development*, **41**, 180–195

Larsen, R. J. and Buss, D. M. (2005) *Personality Psychology: Domains of Knowledge about Human Nature*, 2nd edn (New York: McGraw-Hill)

Lewis, M. D. (2002) The dialogical brain: contributions of emotional neurobiology to understanding the dialogical self, *Theory & Psychology*, **12**, 175–190

Linell, P. (2007) Dialogicality in language minds and brains: is there a convergence between dialogism and neuro-biology?, *Language Sciences*, **29**, 605–620

Marková, I. (2005) *Dialogicality and Social Representations: The Dynamics of Mind* (Cambridge University Press)

McAdams, D. P. and Pals, J. A. (2006) A New Big Five: fundamental principles for an integrative science of personality, *American Psychologist*, **61**, 204–217

McAdams, D. P., Anyidoho, N. A., Brown, C., Huang, Y. T., Kaplan, B. and Machado, M. A. (2004) Traits and stories: links between dispositional and narrative features of personality, *Journal of Personality*, **72**, 761–784

McCrae, R. R. and Costa Jr, P. T. (1999) A five-factor theory of personality, in L. A. Pervin and O. P. John (eds.), *Handbook of Personality: Theory and Research* (New York: Guilford Press), 139–153

McGregor, I., McAdams, D. P. and Little, B. R. (2006) Personal projects, life stories, and happiness: on being true to traits, *Journal of Research in Personality*, **40**, 551–572

Oleś, P. K. (2009) Czy głosy umysłu da się mierzyć? Skala Wewnętrznej Aktywności Dialogowej (SWAD) [Is it possible to measure the voices of the mind? Internal Dialogical Activity Scale (IDAS)], *Przegląd Psychologiczny*, **52**, 37–50

Oleś, P. K., Batory, A., Buszek, M., Chorąży, K., Dras, J., Jankowski, T., *et al.* (2010) Wewnętrzna aktywność dialogowa i jej psychologiczne korelaty [Internal dialogical activity and its psychological correlates], *Czasopismo Psychologiczne*, **16**, 113–127

Pickering, A. D. and Gray, J. A. (1999) The neuroscience of personality, in L. A. Pervin and O. P. John (eds.), *Handbook of Personality*, 2nd edn (New York: Guilford Press), 102–108

Puchalska-Wasyl, M. (2005) Imaginary interlocutors – types and similarity to the self of the individual, in P. K. Oleś and H. J. M. Hermans (eds.), *The Dialogical Self: Theory and Research* (Lublin: Wydawnictwo KUL), 201–215

(2006) *Nasze wewnętrzne dialogi: O dialogowości jako sposobie funkcjonowania człowieka* [*Our Inner Dialogues: About Dialogicality as a Way of Human Functioning*] (Wrocław: Wydawnictwo Uniwersytetu Wrocławskiego)

(2007) Types and functions of inner dialogues, *Psychology of Language and Communication*, **11**, 43–62

Puchalska-Wasyl, M., Chmielnicka-Kuter, E. and Oleś, P. (2008) From internal interlocutors to psychological functions of dialogical activity, *Journal of Constructivist Psychology*, **21**, 239–269

Raggatt, P. (2000) Mapping the dialogical self: towards a rationale and method of assessment, *European Journal of Personality*, **14**, 65–90

Roberts, B. W., O'Donnell, M. and Robins, R. W. (2004) Goal and personality development, *Journal of Personality and Social Psychology*, **87**, 541–550

Rosenberg, M. (1965) *Society and Adolescent Self-Image* (Princeton University Press)

Shotter, J. (1999) Life inside dialogically structured mentalities: Bakhtin's and Voloshinov's account of our mental activities as out in the world between us, in J. Rowan and M. Cooper (eds.), *The Plural Self: Multiplicity in Everyday Life* (London: Sage), 71–92

Sternberg, R. J., Grigorenko, E. L. and Oh, S. (2001) The development of intelligence at midlife, in M. E. Lachman (ed.), *Handbook of Midlife Development* (New York: Wiley), 217–247

14 Spatial organization of the dialogical self in creative writers

Renata Żurawska-Żyła, Elżbieta Chmielnicka-Kuter and Piotr K. Oleś

Introduction

In this chapter we aim to show how dialogical self theory (DST) (Hermans 1996, 2002; Hermans and Kempen 1993; Hermans and Hermans-Konopka 2010) can inspire empirical research in creative writers. The process of writing a novel requires the creation of imaginary figures and the simulation of their relationships, which typically emerge in the form of dialogue. Dialogical relationships may also emerge between the author and the created figures. As Watkins (1986) and also Taylor *et al.* (2003) have indicated, many writers of novels take advantage of the relationships they develop with their characters, who may function as their imaginary companions. The invented character may become an important reference point or even a partner for the writer.

As we know from Bakhtin's (1929/1973) work, the author's position, as the creator of the figures introduced into the novel, is not always as dominant as one would expect. The characters, allowed some autonomy in their beliefs and attitudes, can present not only different points of view in comparison with the views of their creator, but sometimes – and even more interestingly – better ones. The dialogues in a novel have special dynamics and logic, as well as a creative power, which lead authors far beyond their own knowledge, basic beliefs, attitudes and preferences. An author who experienced his characters' autonomy in a way that not only exceeded his intentions but even terrified him, was Fyodor Dostoyevsky. In the chapter 'Pro and Contra' of his famous novel *The Brothers Karamazov*, Dostoyevsky allowed Ivan so much autonomy and authenticity that his atheistic arguments became more persuasive than even the religious arguments of Dostoevsky himself. Saintly Father Zossima, who was brought into the scene to weaken his attitude, was not convincing enough. Because of this, Dostoyevsky failed to accomplish his intent in the chapter, which was meant to be a strong argument against atheism (see Watkins 1986: 94).

DST proposes that dialogue in and of itself is a dynamic process achieved by the exchange of ideas between the *I*-positions which represent different parts of the self, or various points of view present in the environment and culture (Hermans 1996, 2001, 2002, 2003). According to the theory, the authors are conceptualized together with their literary figures as *I*-positions occupying an extended self-space. Each *I*-position is connected with different kinds of experiences and even with different world views (the real world of the author and the fictional world of a figure). Both the author's and the characters' *I*-positions can be endowed with a 'voice' to tell a unique story from their own stances and are also able to develop dialogical relationships with each other. Such relationships can potentially influence the artistic vision of the author (and perhaps also life alongside the artistic activity). The question is, to what extent do contemporary writers allow the figures in their novels to have a free and open expression of ideas in dialogical relationships, including those of the author? And – allowing such an opportunity – how do the authors portray the relationships with their figures?

This study introduces innovative concepts and is an interdisciplinary enterprise in which we connect psychology, psychobiography and the theory of literature, and it is original for at least two reasons. First, the participants are recognized Polish novelists who have agreed to reveal something important about their writing processes and about the relationships with their novelistic figures. Second – according to DST – we not only asked about the writers' gains and losses in their contact with the created figures, but we also were interested in the organization of their self-systems. We wanted to know how the *I*-position of an author is situated in the context of the *I*-positions representing novelistic characters.

Participants

Six Polish writers, aged 29 to 59, four men and two women, took part in this project. For all of them, literary creation was a subjectively important life activity. Four participants were popular novelists who are well known in Poland for their novels as well as interviews in journals and literary awards. The other two authors were less widely known; however, each has had at least three books published by well-recognized national publishers. The writers were asked to participate in our research via email or through personal contact. They agreed to take part in this investigation and accepted the proposed procedure. The research itself was based on personal contact and cooperation between the participants and the researcher.

The spatial self-representation procedure

As a research method for studying the organization of *I*-positions, the spatial self-representation procedure was developed. It provides a graphical description of the self in terms of the spatial organization of *I*-positions. The procedure refers directly to the basic metaphor of the dialogical self as a space stretched between voiced *I*-positions (Hermans 2001, 2002). The essential part of the method is an invitation to depict the self as a composition of different *I*-positions and corresponding voices and to depict them on a sheet of paper. In order to do this, the participants were each given a piece of white paper of A4 format with a circle in the central part of the sheet. It was explained that the whole sheet stands for one's psychological space and the circle for the self. In the first part of the procedure, the participants were asked to identify a number of *I*-positions representing relevant figures in their novels, to give them names, and to place them in the space inside or outside the circle. Next, they were asked to focus on their own *I-position as author* and to depict this special *I*-position on the sheet, inside or outside the circle, and then to mark the relationships – if there were any – between *I-as author* and each of the selected positions representing the figures. An unbroken line represented an important and positive relationship (e.g. agreement between author and character), a dashed line an ambivalent relationship (e.g. disagreement), and a crossed line opposition or a conflict relationship.

We have treated the number of *I*-positions, their names and particular locations, as well as other operations performed on these positions, as the raw material for the analysis of the writer's attitude to the characters and construction of the novels. However, in the study presented here, we focus mainly on the spatial relationships between an author's *I*-position and the figures created by this author. We used the circle as a metaphor of the self, referring to the circular representation of the self proposed by Hermans (2001, 2003), by Jung's (1951) theory of archetypes, and by Lewin's (1936) ideas concerning the field psychology.

Besides applying the spatial self-representation procedure, we also interviewed the writers. A semi-structured recorded interview was applied, which focused, among other topics, on the creation of literary characters, the relation between author and characters, and the nature of the imaginary dialogues with them.

Three kinds of relationships in the self of writers of novels

Analysing the results of the spatial self-representation procedure and the interviews, we found three kinds of relationships between the

Spatial Organization of the Dialogical Self 1

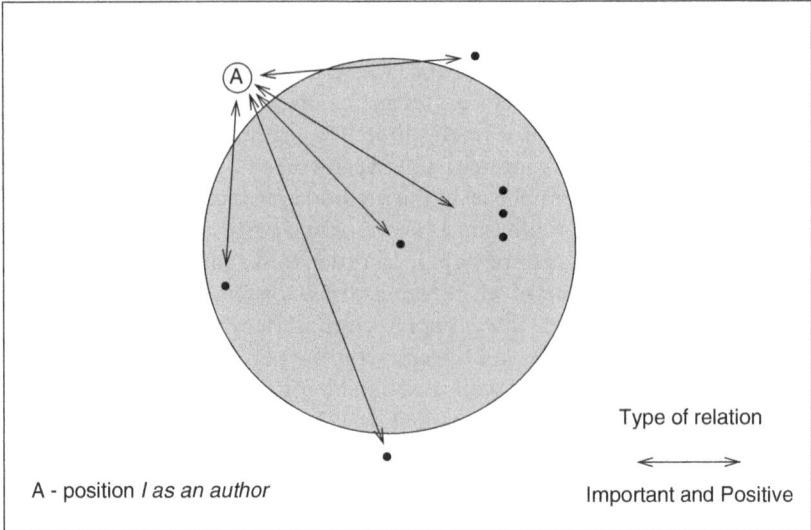

Figure 14.1 The author as an omniscient expert.

author's *I*-position and the characters' *I*-positions: (1) the author as an *omniscient expert*; (2) the author as a *spectator*; and (3) the author as a *partner* of the novelistic figure. In the case of the author as *omniscient expert*, the writer is distanced from his characters (see Figure 14.1). He holds the position of an 'expert', so he places, to take a stand, the characters in the role of 'laic' (the author knows more than the characters) and in the role of recipients of the creative activities of the author, with the characters as subordinated to the vision of the author. The characters are described by the author as reflecting his view rather than being allowed to speak independently. The author talks about the characters or speaks for them. The omniscient *I*-position of the author emphasizes distance and supreme reflection, and control and power over the characters. The interview revealed that the author prefers to use internal monologue in the creative process of writing. He also employs monologue as a dominant form of literary utterance and style of narrative. It is common for the authors in the position of an *omniscient expert* to avoid dialoguing with their novel characters. A statement from one of the writers illustrates this relationship: '*Such a direct talk with the characters in my mind – no, but thinking about them, thinking for them – yes.*'

Another author may assume a *spectator's* attitude in relation to his characters (see Figure 14.2). He neither enters into direct confrontation

Spatial Organization of the Dialogical Self 1

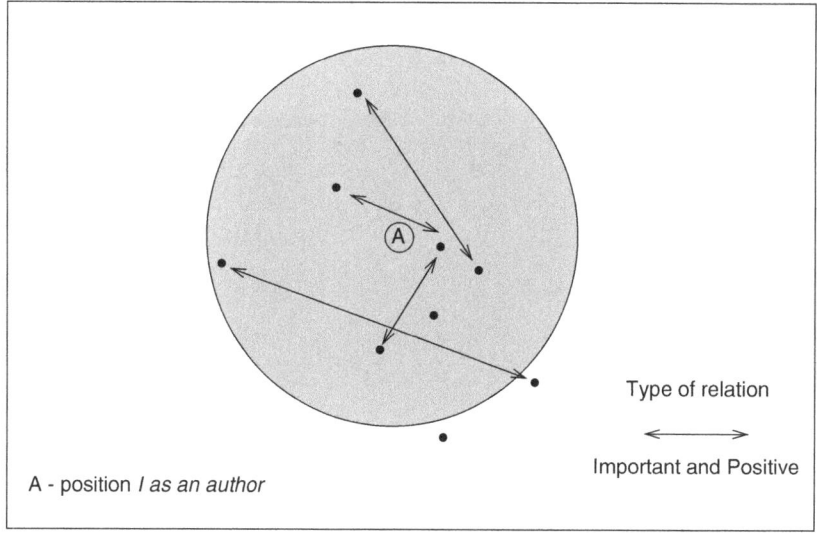

Type of relation

Important and Positive

A - position *I as an author*

Figure 14.2 The author as a spectator.

with the characters, nor tries to dominate them. The character is accepted as separate, autonomous and equal, but is not a partner. The dominant form for this type of writer is taking the perspective of others. In novels, it manifests as a third-person narration. A representative statement is as follows: '*It is very difficult for me to describe the meeting or the contact between two characters. I prefer to describe the conditions as they are perceived by someone else's eyes. I like the third person, I like to write it. Then, I have the feeling that it is the character's consciousness as if I stood behind him as a witness who follows his eyes.*' Such an author avoids getting in touch with the characters of his own creation and prefers to treat them as the objects of his observation.

We also found that some writers assume the position of a conversational *partner* with their characters (see Figure 14.3). In this case, the characters are placed in the same space as the author, who permits them to take the role of autonomous individuals. Moreover, the character becomes the co-author of the novel, being not only the recipient but also the originator of the author's creative activities. Dialogue with and taking the perspective of another person is the dominant form used in this process of novelistic creation. The authors of this type intensively confirmed internal conversations with the characters during their interviews. What is outstanding in their novels is the great number and

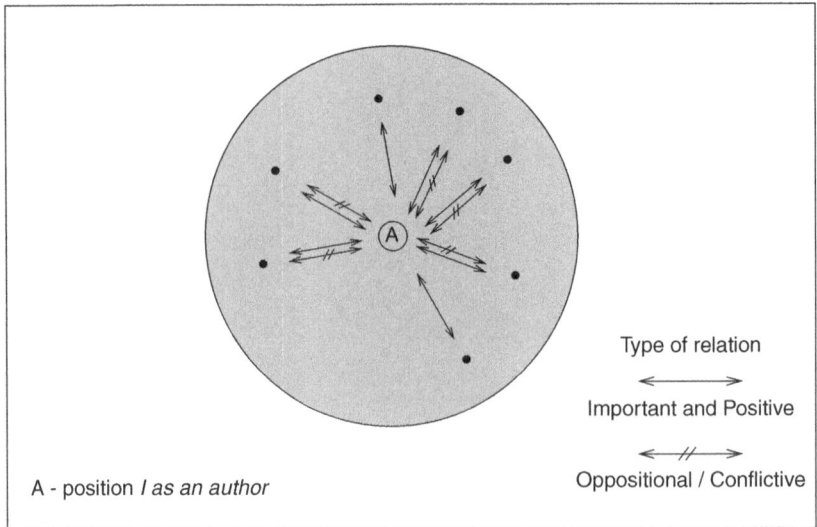

Figure 14.3 The author as a partner.

diversity of literary characters and the multitude of interactions among them. The characters actively discuss and confront their points of view. Consider the following example: '*I can think of a character as someone who is a little like me, but who is also against me, it's very stimulating to me, such an internal dispute.*' Or, to give another example: '*Yes, I almost always talk to my characters. All the time as I write. It is a monologue, no, it is a dialogue. They are in my head and I talk to them. Through the conversation with them I can build on these characters.*' As depicted in Figure 14.3, the author's *I*-position is located just in the middle of the circle, and she has direct relationships with all created figures. The author participates in this world of imaginal figures, exchanging ideas and receiving inspirations from them. Such relationships are reported by the author as both positive and important in some situations, and as oppositional and conflictive in other situations.

The results of the interviews with the writers show that each type of relationship with the characters (internal monologue, taking the perspective of the other, internal dialogue) is connected with different styles of positioning and with imaginative activity.

It was also found that oppositions and conflicts between the *I*-position of an author and the *I*-positions of the novelistic figures were present only for the writers who take the position of *partner* towards the characters. In the other types of writers' attitudes to the characters (*omniscient expert* and *spectator*), there were numerous positive relationships and no oppositional and conflictive relationships between the author and the characters. This means that the partnership relations between an author and his characters during the creation of these literary characters reveal not only an internal differentiation of the writer's self (multivoicedness), but also that this method of literary creation is used to reconcile conflicts by a constructive exchange of views. The *I*-positions which do not agree with the perspective of the author do not become a threat to the harmony of the self-system, but a challenge. The author in the position of *partner* does not seek to dominate his disagreeing or conflicting characters (as an *omniscient expert* would), or ignore or silence them (as a *spectator* would), but allows them to speak freely to him or her. We claim that this is a specific way of constructing the author's identity.

Discussion

The presented study is an illustration of the manner in which DST inspires research into the intersection of psychology, psychobiography and literary studies. The theory also encourages phenomenological analysis of the personal experiences of creative people. Furthermore, it enables meta-reflection on the creative process as well as on the relationships between the authors and the characters of their novels. Creative activity resulting in novelistic or story writing highly engages the self. The 'landscape of the mind' was introduced to the participants – in a metaphorical way – as a 'territory of voices' and presented as a circle. The analysis of relations between authors and their characters revealed three types of self-organization. Each type of author's attitude to the characters is connected with a characteristic spatial representation of *I*-positions engaged in artistic activity. In the first type (*omniscient expert*), the writers prefer the position of an expert towards their characters, while in the second type (*spectator*) they prefer the position of an empathic spectator. In the third type (*partner*), they become engaged as a dialogical partner who lets the characters speak with their own voices and negotiate their views with the author, which implies possible conflicts and even influences the writing process. Note that avoiding dialogical relationships with the figures, which is typical of an *omniscient expert*, enables a writer to protect his identity from change, while allowing such relationships, typical of a *partner*, inspires a writer's change of identity.

Our findings concerning the types of authors' attitudes to their characters can be related to Bakhtin's (1929/1973) distinction between the polyphonic and homophonic novel and to his idea that an author's attitude to the characters shapes the whole artistic work. The typology which emerged from our study is partly consistent with this distinction. The main characteristic of Bakhtin's polyphonic novel is a multitude of viewpoints represented by highly autonomous characters involved in dialogical relations both between themselves and with an author. The position of the author is far from privileged, as his or her vision of the story is only one of many and can be questioned, criticized and even ridiculed by the characters. The feature of the homophonic novel is the presence of the omniscient creator, whose complete and all-encompassing artistic vision leaves no space for the characters' viewpoints and claims.

There is an analogy between the polyphonic composition of a novel and the experience of our authors who describe themselves as the *partners* of their characters, ready to maintain dialogues with them and remaining open to their 'message'. Another analogy can be found between the homophonic composition of the novel and our authors who experience themselves as *experts* separated from their characters and free from potentially complicated relations with them. These authors strongly avoid dialogues with their characters and do not feel that such dialogues are necessary for the quality of their work.

However, there is at least one more type of self-organization possible: the authors who define their role as *spectators* of their imaginal figures. These authors take a kind of intermediate position, something between the authors in the role of partner and those in the role of expert. They let the characters interact and observe the drama taking place in the novel. At the same time they neither join the 'scene' in an active manner nor interrogate the characters after the 'play'. They experience it as witnesses and write about it, while taking the (imagined) perspective of the figures. The presence of this type of author encourages us to modify Bakhtin's typology of novels, extrapolating our findings to the types of novels. The results of our interviews with the writers necessitate this extrapolation in that each type of relationship between author and figure is connected with different styles of work: (1) using a different style of positioning towards the characters; and (2) using different types of imaginative activity (imaginary monologue, imaginary dialogue, the process of taking the perspective of the other).

Thus, we propose to distinguish two types of polyphonic novels depending on the (inter)activity between author and character: the multivoiced novel and the dialogical novel. The modified typology emerging from the presented study is introduced in Figure 14.4.

The dialogical novel in the modified version corresponds with Bakhtin's polyphonic novel, which results from an author and the

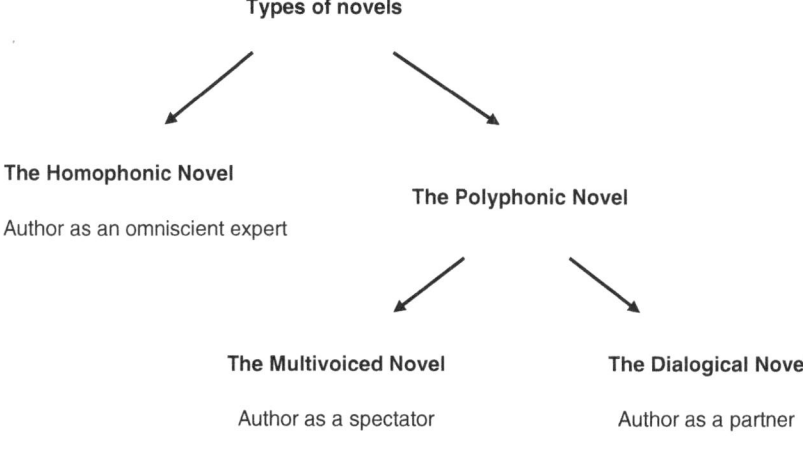

Figure 14.4 Typology of novels referring to the relation between author and characters.

characters overtly interacting with each other. The 'multivoiced novel' has been added as a variant of polyphony in which the multitude of viewpoints carries no necessity to establish voiced relationships between author and characters.

We note that the writers' activities connected with the creation of each type of novel probably serve different functions, relevant to their identity. Activities connected with creating a homophonic novel favour mono-logues as ways of expressing the writers' attitudes and personality, while those connected with creating a dialogical novel promote imaginal dia-logues as a way of overcoming one's own stereotypes and stagnation and as a way of striving for novelty. Assuming the perspective of the other, typical of the multivoiced novel and the dialogical novel, enables the writer to go into a deeper reflection about both his personal view of life and human experience, and to create his own stance.

The finding that opposite and conflicting relationships occur only between the *I*-positions of the novelistic figures and the *I*-position of an author as *partner* corresponds with the observation that the novels of those authors contain a great diversity of characters and interactions between them. The identity of the writer of the dialogical novel is shaped in the processes of dialogical exchange between various points of view that imply both relationships of agreement and disagreement. Opposite and conflicting relationships challenge the integration of the writer's self and at the same time make it more flexible and open to the innovation which is central to dialogue in DST (Hermans and Hermans-Konopka

2010), and it is also basic for creativity. Internal conflicts and oppositions bring about innovative results in one's identity and thinking, which can be expressed in the creative work.

The three types of relationships between author and characters which emerged from our study let us formulate arguments for the distinction between multivoicedness and dialogue as related but not synonymous phenomena described on the basis of DST (see also Chmielnicka-Kuter 2005). Multivoicedness is indispensable for the existence of dialogue. However, it does not automatically imply dialogue. For example, it may serve the type of author who takes the position of *spectator* in relation to his novelistic characters. This example shows that people can be multivoiced (moving from the one position and voice to the other) but not dialogical (not entertaining a dialogical relationship between the different positions and voices). People, like the authors assuming the role of *omniscient expert*, can even avoid an overt multivoicedness, preferring a single dominate voice that takes control of the multitude of other voices. However, there are also people – like the author who becomes a *partner* of his characters – for whom the existence of multiplicity of *I*-positions opens the possibility to entertain dialogical exchange of meanings and ideas. Even though such relationships imply conflicts and the necessity of negotiations, the juxtaposition of contrasting ideas can lead to an innovation of the self that manifests as flexible and creative functioning in a heterogeneous social environment.

We hope that this study has clearly shown that the concept of the dialogical self is especially inspiring with regard to explaining the process of literary creation. Too strict boundaries between the disciplines limit the potential of the study of creativity. We think that DST and literary theories still have a lot to offer to each other and provide a valuable source of mutual inspiration (see also Żurawska-Żyła 2011a, 2011b).

REFERENCES

Bakhtin, M. M. (1973) *Problems of Dostoevsky's Poetics* (Ann Arbor, MI: Ardis)
Chmielnicka-Kuter, E. (2005) Role-playing games heroes as partners
   of internal dialogues, in P. K. Oleś and H. J. M. Hermans (eds.), *The
   Dialogical Self: Theory and Research* (Lublin: Wydawnictwo KUL),
   231–243
Hermans, H. J. M. (1996) Voicing the self: from information processing to
   dialogical interchange, *Psychological Bulletin*, **119**, 31–50
   (2001) The dialogical self: toward the theory of personal and cultural
   positioning, *Culture & Psychology*, **7**, 243–281
   (2002) The dialogical self as a society of mind: introduction, *Theory &
   Psychology*, **12**, 147–160

(2003) The construction and reconstruction of a dialogical self, *Journal of Constructivist Psychology*, **16**, 89–130

Hermans, H. J. M. and Kempen, H. J. G. (1993) *The Dialogical Self: Meaning as Movement* (San Diego, CA: Academic Press)

Hermans, H. J. M. and Hermans-Konopka, A. (2001) *Dialogical Self Theory: Positioning and Counter-Positioning in a Globalizing Society* (Cambridge University Press)

James, W. (1954) *The Principles of Psychology* (New York: Dover Publications), vol. I

Jung, C. G. (1951) *Aion: Researches into the Phenomenology of the Self (Collected Works*, vol. 9, Part 2) (Princeton, NJ: Bollingen)

Lewin, K. (1936) *Principles of Topological Psychology* (New York: McGraw-Hill)

Taylor, M., Hodges, S. D. and Kohanyi, A. (2003) The illusion of independent agency: do adult fiction writers experience their characters as having minds of their own?, *Imagination, Cognition and Personality*, **22**, 361–380

Watkins, M. (1986) *Invisible Guests:* The Development of Imaginal Dialogues (Hillsdale, NJ: Lawrence Erlbaum)

Żurawska-Żyła, R. (2011a) The experience of illusion of literary characters' independence – an empirical and theoretical description attempt, in P. K. Oleś, M. Puchalska-Wasyl and E. Brygola (eds.), *Dialog with Oneself* (Warsaw: Wydawnictwo Naukowe PWN), 36–68.

(2011b) Patterns of internal self-organization and types of authors in literary work, in E. Dryll and A. Cierpka (eds.), *Narrative Psychology* (Warsaw: ENETEIA), 353–367.

15 Cognitive architecture of the dialogical self: an experimental approach

Katarzyna Stemplewska-Żakowicz, Bartosz Zalewski, Hubert Suszek and Dorota Kobylińska

> *The I has the possibility to move, as in a space, from one position to the other in accordance with changes in situation and time. The I fluctuates among different and even opposed positions. The I has the capacity to imaginatively endow each position with a voice so that dialogical relations between positions can be established.*
> (Hermans *et al.*1992: 28)

These words of Hubert Hermans are considered the classic definition of the dialogical self. Let us imagine what can happen when a social psychologist reads these words. It is likely that the first questions that arise in her or his mind would be: 'To what extent is it a metaphor? Does this refer to any actual processes? Or maybe it should be understood as a symbolic image that is to be translated yet into some more prosaic but precise language?' However, the question of crucial importance that our imagined social psychologist might ask would be, 'Is it possible to confront these ideas with empirical data?'

As far as we know, dialogical self theory (DST) as a scientific theory has not yet been experimentally verified. It is true that there are convincing reinterpretations of research (Hermans 1999; Hermans and Dimaggio 2007; Hermans and Kempen 1993) and illustrative case studies (Dimaggio 2006; Hermans and Hermans-Jansen 1995; Stiles 1999), as well as empirical studies where the concepts of *I*-position and positioning were used to analyse natural conversations and other material (e.g. Bamberg 1997; Ligorio and Spadaro 2006; Wortham and Gadsden 2006). However, showing that the proposed notions are useful in describing psychological reality may be regarded by many as an argument that is not strong enough to validate a new theory. Therefore, one of the first research

An elaboration of the theoretical concept presented here was enabled by a grant from the Ministry of Science and Higher Education (Poland), no. 1325/H03/2006/31. All questions and comments regarding this chapter should be directed to Katarzyna Stemplewska-Żakowicz. Email: katarzyna.stemplewska-zakowicz@chodkowska.eu problems in an attempt to verify DST should be to check whether the concepts of *I*-position and positioning do really have an empirical basis. Precisely that was the aim of our series of experiments (Stemplewska-Żakowicz *et al.* 2006; Stemplewska-Żakowicz, Walecka *et al.* 2005; for correlational studies, see also Oleś and Puchalska-Wasyl in the present volume).

DST has something very important to propose to mainstream psychology. The concept of multivoicedness, referring to the variety of inner perspectives which can be taken by a person, allows us to find and understand the manifestations of multiplicity of the subjective self in different contexts of our lives. However, if the mainstream theories really are to incorporate this idea, there is a need for a model of cognitive architecture of the dialogical self in which the concept of multivoicedness is given a form of precise structural and functional proposals. By such a proposal we mean a set of theses giving clear answers to questions of how the cognitive system is organized and what are the specific functions of its particular components.

In the present chapter we intend to outline such a proposal, which we call a model of the discursive mind. The reason for creation of the discursive mind model was to adapt DST to the requirements of experimental research. We came to the conclusion that in order to conduct the experimental research on DST, it is necessary to express its ideas in more cognitive terms. The discursive mind model, as described below, was formulated, and it can be understood as a tool which adapts the DST to experimental research.

The discursive mind model

Our model is based on the thesis of the cognitive system's discursive organization. This thesis states that a number of relatively autonomic, holistic modules of representation exist in our mind, of which every one is linked to a specific social context, present in one's socialization history. Different modules contain specific cognitive-affective resources, shaped by different ways of giving meaning to personal experience. These patterns of naming and weighting experience are developed within relationships with significant others, important groups or influential social backgrounds (Hermans 1999; Wertsch 1991).

There are three fundamental assumptions of the discursive mind model:

1. the modular character of one's knowledge structures
2. the social origin of one's knowledge structures
3. the specificity of the knowledge structures for the social context from which they stem.

The first two assumptions can be found in many contemporary psychological theories, whereas the third assumption does not play a key role in mainstream theories. However, it is crucial for the model of the discursive mind presented here.

According to the discursive mind model, *I*-positions are relatively autonomic modules of the cognitive system, which consist of script-like structures combining personal and socially shared knowledge. These structures are activated in certain conditions (automatically or intentionally) and henceforth – until the next *I*-position is activated – determine the range of processable information and the specific rules of this processing.

The process of taking up a certain *I*-position is called positioning (Harré and van Langenhove 1991; Hermans 1996, 2001), and it is essential in the discursive mind model, because it is crucial for the whole chain of events which happen afterwards. In the theoretical language of cognitive concepts, positioning means the activation of a particular representation module. Each of the modules has specific rules of discursive structuring and has access to specific cognitive contents. Different *I*-positions can even 'remember' the same things differently, because they are independent in their ontogenetic development, each developing in its own social context and at its own pace.

The model of the discursive mind assumes that the activation of different *I*-positions within the same person causes significant intra-individual variations in cognitive functioning. Metaphorically, it may happen that one of the *I*-positions of a given person is more neurotic or intelligent than another. It can be that only one of many *I*-positions within a given person shares stereotypes concerning a certain social group or is prejudiced, while others are not. This internal diversity and its complex, dynamic organization are well portrayed by the 'self as a society of mind' metaphor (Hermans 2002; Minsky 1985).

Experimental verification of the discursive mind model

We designed a series of experiments, in which we expected that manipulating particular characteristics of representation modules (the *I*-positions) will result in corresponding changes in their structural, functional and content properties. The experiments described below were based on an experimental positioning procedure that enabled us to observe the effects of activation of *I*-positions on several variables (e.g. self-narratives, personality traits, prejudice, intelligence and others). By activating different *I*-positions in different groups of participants or activating them within the same individual but at different times (repeated measure design), we could compare the specific functioning of particular *I*-positions (e.g. *I* in relation with my mother, with my partner, with a close person who is tolerant or intolerant, etc.).

Do I-*positions exist?*

Two studies were planned to check whether people really have different *I*-positions at their disposal as well as to see whether, in case they take up a position in a particular situation, they perceive the world and the self according to the specific perspective of this *I*-position as different from another one.

The aim of the first experiment (Stemplewska-Żakowicz *et al.* 2006; see also Stemplewska-Żakowicz, Walecka *et al.* 2005) was to check whether one can expect systematic differences in self-narratives that a particular person constructs in different relational contexts. The task for the participants (258 students of Warsaw universities) was to write a short narrative which would briefly present the story of their lives. The participants were invited to mention different significant others (mother, father, friend, partner and teacher), and to relate to them in three different ways: to imagine their faces, to address their story to them or just to describe their personality. This design made it possible to study different *I*-positions (*I* as mother's child, *I* as father's child, *I* as a friend, *I* as a partner, and *I* as a pupil) and the nature of their relation to corresponding significant others (mother, father, friend, partner and teacher, respectively). Given the theoretical assumption in DST that different *I*-positions are associated with different narratives, we focus here on the self-narratives as they were told from different *I*-positions. The results showed that self-narratives produced in different relational contexts differed both in content and formal characteristics. For example, the position of mother's child was the most talkative ($F = 4.251$; df $= 4$; $p < 0.01$), expressed most emotions ($\chi^2 = 11.31$; $p = 0.05$), had the most colourful stories ($\chi^2 = 11.44$; $p < 0.05$), most intensively expressed the needs of affiliation ($\chi^2 = 18.09$; $p = 0.001$) and intimacy ($\chi^2 = 22.98$; $p = 0.001$), and most often mentioned relations with other people ($\chi^2 = 12.75$; $p = 0.01$). We found also characteristic properties of narratives from other *I*-positions, as well as of each of the three methods of positioning (for details, see Stemplewska-Żakowicz *et al.* 2006). Generally, these findings are in agreement with the assumption of DST that people produce different self-narratives from the perspective of different *I*-positions.

The second study aimed to explore how people position themselves and their conversational partners as experts or laymen during dyadic conversations on the internet. The *I*-positions were experimentally evoked by informing two groups of subjects – 60 psychology students and 60 perspective students considering a degree in psychology – that they are 'experts' or 'laymen', respectively, in regard to the topic of the conversation ('Does psychology help in passing exams?'). In half of the dyads, both partners were informed about the nature of their position (expert or layman), but in the other half one party did not receive this information. The results generally showed that the experimental treatment was effective in that differences were found between three characteristics of the utterances: giving advice, asking for advice and information, and agreeing with the interlocutor. As expected, experts gave much more advice and asked for it less than laymen. Moreover, we found that these differences held even when the participants were *not* informed about the nature of their positions, but only their interlocutors were. This suggests that different positions produce different kinds of utterances even when participants are not aware of their own position (Stemplewska-Żakowicz, Walecka *et al.* 2005; more details can be found in Stemplewska-Żakowicz, Suszek *et al.* 2005).

The results of the two experimental studies show that positioning can be regarded as a real phenomenon. The experimental procedures of positioning did work (some of them stronger, others weaker) and led to a range of differences in self-narratives as well as in utterances in conversations, as produced by different *I*-positions.

Stability or variability of personality

In an attempt to explore the interface of personality theory and DST, Szymczyk (2010) decided to investigate whether different *I*-positions within the same person can appear as different personalities in standard tests. For this aim he used the Big Five Model and the NEO-FFI questionnaire (Costa and McCrae 1985). Two *I*-positions, '*I* in relation with my mother' and '*I* in relation with my father', were studied in repeated measurements separated by a delay of 1 week. In the experimental group every person was consecutively positioned in two different *I*-positions (with a rotation of sequence), whereas in the control groups participants were positioned two times in the same position (in relation with their mother or father).

On the basis of the theoretical model, we can expect that, when participants fill in the questionnaire from a given *I*-position, the results will be the same or very similar when they fill in the questionnaire a second time from the same *I*-position. However, when the questionnaire is filled in by two *different* *I*-positions successively, it is expected to reflect

Table 15.1 *Pearson correlation coefficients between the first and the second measurements of five dimensions of personality of NEO-FFI in the experimental and control group*

	Two different positions (experimental group) n = 38	The same position twice (control group) n = 36	p (significance of the difference between two correlation coefficients)
Neuroticism	0.83	0.92	0.14
Extroversion	0.88	0.89	0.94
Openness to experience	**0.84**	**0.96**	**0.01**
Agreeableness	0.83	0.85	0.82
Conscientiousness	0.94	0.90	0.29

Statistically significant results in boldface.

observable differences in the participants' 'personality'. This expectation was verified by comparing the Pearson correlation coefficient between the first and the second measurement in each of the two experimental conditions.

As shown in Table 15.1, all correlations are relatively high, confirming the well-known stability of NEO-FFI. As expected, for all variables, the raw values of correlation coefficients are lower in the experimental group than in the control group. However, only one of these differences – or Openness to experience – is statistically significant (for the relevance of Openness to experience to the dialogical self, see also the chapter of Oleś and Puchalska–Wasyl in this volume).

Comparable results were recently obtained by Niedopytalski (2010), who invited 24 members of the Polish Brotherhood of Knights to fill in the NEO-FFI questionnaire twice: one time in their homes (position of 'house mate') and during a tournament (position of warrior). The sequence of two repeated measurements was rotated in two halves of the groups. Again it appeared that some personality traits differ in different *I*-positions. In this research the differences were statistically significant for two dimensions of the Big Five: Neuroticism ($t(23) = -2.07$, $p < 0.05$) and Agreeableness ($t(23) = -2.85$, $p < 0.01$). The details are shown in Figure 15.1.

From the two experiments on stability, we learn that different pairs of *I*-positions are distinguished from one another on several (but not all) personality dimensions. The experiments described do not falsify the model of trait stability. However, the obtained results require further

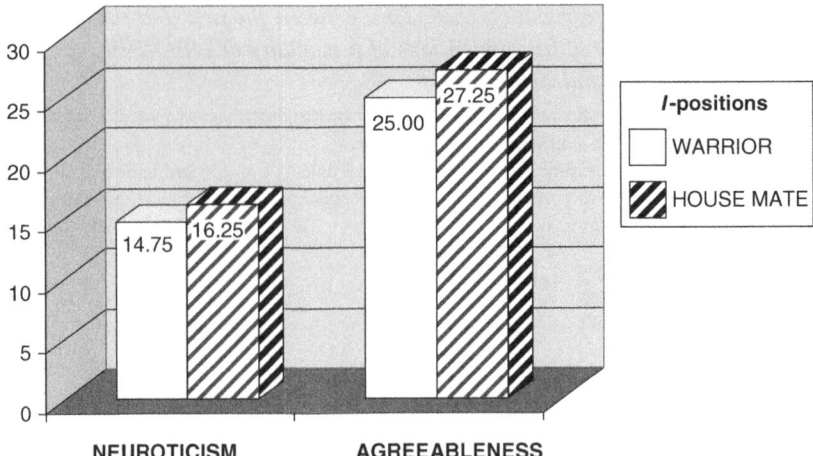

Figure 15.1 Activated positions of Warrior and House Mate and scores on scales of Neuroticism and Agreeability in NEO-FFI. *Source:* Niedopytalski 2010.

research on 'personalities' of *I*-positions and compel us to reconsider the problem of stability versus variability, which is central to the whole field of trait psychology. From the perspective of DST, it is expected that the more different the *I*-positions are, the stronger the differences in personalities. Future research could find an answer to the question of which personalities are sensitive to which *I*-positions. The results presented here suggest that, despite the assumed stability of traits, the answers on personality questionnaires are, to some degree, susceptible to differences in activated *I*-positions.

Unequal abilities of different I-*positions*

A few studies were undertaken to determine whether different *I*-positions within a person can vary in various abilities. In the field of intelligence and social context, the most interesting *I*-positions are the ones developed as a result of positive or negative feedback from tutors. These can be generally described as the positions of Good Student and Bad Student. Despite individual differences, probably both of them exist in every student. This is because both 'better' and 'weaker' students tend to have experiences of success and failure from time to time. Because students are sometimes under- or over-appreciated by their teachers, probably all of them are sometimes perceived as Good or Bad Students, and this helps to activate these positions in their minds.

The discursive model assumes that once the position of a Good Student is activated, students can use the cognitive-affective resources of this position in their current behaviour. It results in an increase of performance in different school competency tests, because it is in the Good Student position's resources where the majority of knowledge and skills taught in school is stored. The resources of the Bad Student are much poorer and so the performance in tests and exams is expected to be low when this position is activated. This assumption was subject of verification in experiments on intelligence and the school knowledge.

In the first study (Suszek *et al.* 2010), 48 adult high-school students were subjected to repeated (after 1 month) positioning in the Good Student and Bad Student positions. The sequence of activating these two positions was rotated in both classes which took part in the research. That is, one class was positioned in the Good Student position at time 1 and in the Bad Student position at time 2. For the other class the order was reversed. The experimental manipulation was performed with the help of tutors who gave feedback to classes of students in two different ways: emphasizing high (Good Students) or low (Bad Students) abilities of a given class and predicting their performance on the test tasks accordingly (after the research a profound debriefing was given to the students with the information about the aim of the experiment). After activating the positions, an intelligence test, the Standard version of Raven's Progressive Matrices, was given to the participants (in the repeated measurement another version of the test was used).

The results of the experiment showed a significant effect of interaction between the measurement and the sequence of activating the I-positions ($F(1, 46) = 7.40$; $p < 0.01$; $\eta^2 = 0.14$), as illustrated in Figure 15.2. This result means that regardless of whether the Good Student position was activated as first or second, it always caused an increase of the Raven's test results by 1 point on average. The scale of the effect is small; however, it occurred on a regular basis. No difference was found between first and second measurement, confirming the equality of the versions of Raven's tests used.

Verbal intelligence was examined in another experiment (Suszek *et al.* 2010), in which a Polish test, 'Leksykon' (Jurkowski 1997), was applied. Again the results revealed the expected differences (see Table 15.2). The 'Good Student' position activation led to considerable improvement in performance and this effect was particularly pronounced in the case of active verbal activities, which require a creative application of verbal resources.

Similar results were shown in three research projects based on a similar experimental schema, in which, instead of psychological tests of intellectual abilities, school tests of knowledge of mathematics, nature

Table 15.2 *Averages on two subscales – passive and active dictionary – and on the overall result of the Leksykon test in Good and Bad Student groups*

Variables	Means in groups		*t*	df	*p*
	Good Student ($n = 22$)	Bad Student ($n = 18$)			
Subscale: passive dictionary	19.13	17.16	−1.57	38	0.124
Subscale: active dictionary	**14.59**	**10.33**	**−2.48**	**38**	**0.018**
Overall result	**33.72**	**27.50**	**−2.31**	**38**	**0.027**

Statistically significant results in boldface.

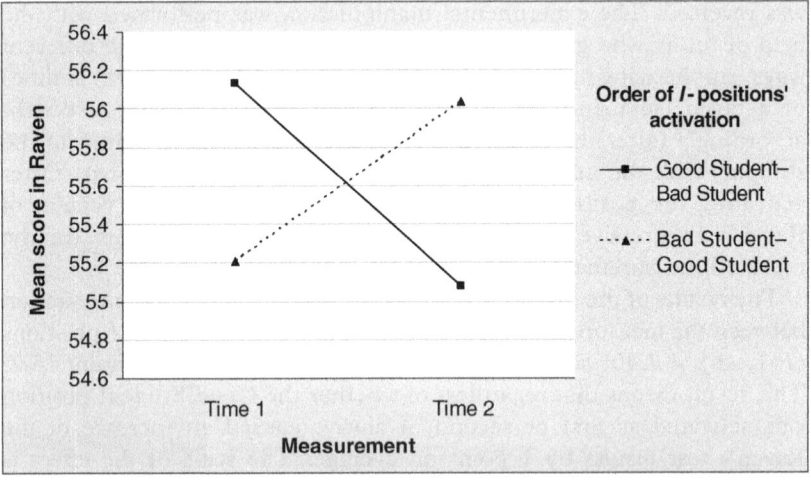

Figure 15.2 Activated *I*-position of Good Student and Bad Student and intelligence test performance level.

and English (as foreign language) were used (Suszek *et al.* 2010). Although the significance level of the results in this research ($p < 0.10$) was weaker than the one usually applied ($p < 0.05$), we mention the results because they followed the same pattern repeatedly. In the experimental tasks the Good Students performed better on average than the Bad Students, although there were no differences in the routine school tests given before by the teachers during lessons.

The effects shown in the described experiments seem similar to the well-known Pygmalion effect. From the rich empirical data on this effect (see Rosenthal 2002), the conclusion can be drawn that the expectations of teachers influence the intelligence and performance of the students at school as a self-fulfilling prophecy. At first, these research findings were received enthusiastically, but soon the methodology was criticized (Snow 1995; Spitz 1999). Later, it was shown that the influence of positive expectations on pupils' performance is quite constrained by the real abilities of children (Jussim and Eccles 1992). We neither offer to go back to the initial conceptualizations of the Pygmalion effect nor put forward a new theory on it. There is one important theoretical difference between the phenomena described in DST and the discursive mind model, on the one hand, and the Pygmalion effect on the other. The latter is – theoretically – based on a real, persistent and context-independent increase or decrease in the observed competency of a student due to a specific treatment by a positively or negatively biased teacher. However, because we take into account solely the positioning phenomenon (e.g. Good versus Bad Student), the increase in competence appears as temporary and limited to a particular relational context. It is an increase in the accessibility of the particular cognitive-affective resources, which refer to a particular latent *I*-position. This is no longer the Pygmalion effect but a context-dependent, positioning phenomenon. DST and the discursive mind model have conceptual tools to explain this phenomenon more precisely and to predict short- or long-term consequences. However, further research is needed to complete this task.

Positioning and social influence

Another experiment based on the assumption of the relative autonomy of the *I*-positions' resources was conducted by Zalewski (2010), who examined the social influence of a particular effect called 'foot-in-the-door'. From a dialogical perspective, social influence might be understood as the employment of an existing context for successful positioning of an interaction partner. A model of social influence, informed by DST, assumes the existence of hidden processes of positioning, which activate a specific identity and modify the relation among the persons involved. The classical effect of 'foot-in-the-door' technique shows that the likelihood of meeting a request is higher for a person who has already met a similar but smaller request from another person (Burger 1999; Freedman and Fraser 1966). According to the DST model of social influence, this effect should be stronger if the internal 'recipient' of both the first and the second request is the same *I*-position. In contrast, when two successive requests are addressed to different *I*-positions, the 'foot-in-the-door' effect should not take place or be weaker, because the processes responsible for this effect occur only one time in one position, which then faces the second request without this priming at a previous occasion.

In a natural experiment (see Zalewski 2010 for details), participants were positioned coherently (both requests addressed to the same *I*-position: Expert or Samaritan) or incoherently (the first request was addressed to Expert and a second one – to Samaritan, or reverse). The study was conducted at the parking lot adjacent to a mall. It was assumed that the Expert position would be triggered by appealing to the participants' knowledge (e.g. a question about one of the products sold in the mall), while the Samaritan position would be evoked by asking for help (e.g. a request to change money for coins that could be used to unlock a shopping cart). A total number of nine such requests was used.

It turned out that participants positioned coherently fulfilled the second request more often (85.6%) than did those positioned incoherently (73.3%; $\chi^2(1, n = 180) = 4.116, p < 0.05$; one-tailed). The effect was repeated in a second study (Zalewski, unpublished), which was based on the classic methodological scheme, traditionally used in research on the 'foot-in-the-door' technique. Again participants positioned coherently fulfilled the second request more often (65.0%) than participants positioned incoherently (41.7%; $\chi^2(1, n = 150) = 12.463, p < 0.05$; one-tailed).

The results show the explanatory power of the dynamic construct of positioning, which is at the heart of DST. These results cannot be reliably explained by a social-cognitive approach (Śpiewak 2005), which assumes limitations in information processing by the mind, understood as just one subject. The idea of a monolithic subject does not permit recognition of two requests as addressed to different internal subjects. Similarly, the classical explanation of the 'foot-in-the-door' effect – that is, self-perception theory (Bem 1967) – is limited to one subject position only. DST appears to explain better the results obtained because it allows a polyphonic vision of the self composed of different *I*-positions, each of which can be addressed by different appeals or requests.

Positioning and stereotypes

Some of our studies offer a new perspective in the field of stereotypes and prejudice. *I*-positions come from different sociocultural origins and contain knowledge collectively shared by different social circles (Hermans and Hermans-Konopka 2010). Therefore, they differ from each other as much as those circles do. It can be theorized then that some I-position within a person can be biased towards a certain minority group, while the other I-position of the same person is free of such prejudice. This hypothesis was investigated in two experiments (Suszek *et al.* 2010) devoted to prejudice against minority groups.

The first experiment investigated whether the intensity of dehumanization as a characteristic of racism (Goff *et al.* 2008) depends on the activated I-position. A group of 44 members of the All-Polish Youth organization (Młodzież Wszechpolska), famous for its extreme nationalistic and fascist political aspirations, took part in the experiment. The participants were randomly assigned to two groups in which two different I-positions were activated: 'I as a member of All-Polish Youth' (APY) or 'I in relation with John Paul II' (JP2). Special surveys were used in the experimental manipulation, in which the participants were asked to answer freely questions, an example of which is following:

JP2 group: the personality of John Paul II – $\Big\}$ **what does it mean to you personally?**
APY group: to be a true APY –

Then the participants completed a computer task (created by means of FLX Lab software), which was to categorize 45 pictures, sequentially exposed on the screen, into three categories: human, animal or object. Fifteen of the pictures presented a human face (five Caucasian, five African-American and five Asian), and the rest showed animals and objects. The level of dehumanization was indicated by the reaction times when the pictures of different colour faces where shown. We expected the time needed to categorize the pictures with Asian and African-American faces to be longer in the APY group than the JP2 group.

This expectation was fulfilled by the results of a two-factor MANOVA, which was used in a 2 (I-positions) × 3 (skin colour) design. All multi-dimensional effects were significant, but what is directly important for the hypothesis is the interaction effect of the activated position and the skin colour of the faces ($F(10, 33) = 4.27$; $p < 0.001$; $\eta^2 = 0.56$), which indicates that the time needed to assign a face of different colours to the 'human' category was shorter or longer depending on the I-position currently activated. Analysis revealed that participants in the JP2 position tended to dehumanize yellow coloured people less than participants from the APY group ($t(35, 15) = 1.96$; $p < 0.05$). For the pictures of black colour faces, no predicted differences were found. Thus, these results provide partial support for the hypothesis.

In critically reviewing the effect, it cannot be denied that it may have happened that other, simpler than discursive mechanisms worked in this experiment. Another explanation refers to the experimental manipulation, which can be also understood as activating a social identity (APY) or an individual identity (personal relation with the pope) of the participant. This former type of identity, as shown in classic research, is more prone to discrimination against minority groups than the latter one.

The second experiment offers more solutions to these problems, as the influence of the above mentioned factors (individual vs. collective identity) was controlled better. In an experiment on stereotypes of Romany people, a repeated-measures design was applied to make sure that the predicted effects were intra-individual differences. Another modification was the method of experimental positioning, which adopted two short descriptions, one of them an example of tolerant and one of intolerant behaviour (however, the word 'tolerant' or any similar word was not used). Then the participants ($n = 45$) were asked to recall a close friend or relative who could behave similarly to the person described (tolerant or intolerant), and then to spend some time imagining talking with this person. After activating one of these two *I*-positions, the level of negative stereotypes of the Romany was measured by means of two indicators: (1) the evaluation of stereotypical, not stereotypical, and neutral adjectives as relevant or not in describing Romany people; and (2) the reaction times for these adjectives. As predicted, the activated *I*-position influenced the level of the negative stereotypes of Romany people. A MANOVA in repeated-measures design revealed a significant interaction effect of the currently active *I*-position and the adjective category. This effect was discovered for both indicators – the assessment of relevant adjectives ($F(2, 88) = 6.84; p < 0.01; \eta^2 = 0.13$) and the reaction times ($F(2, 43) = 4.68; p < 0.05; \eta^2 = 0.18$). Details are shown in Figure 15.3.

In both cases the differences between the tolerant and intolerant positions were significant only for the stereotypical adjectives in agreement with the prediction. Note that in this case the results are not confounded with the distinction between individual and social identity.

Ego depletion: dynamics inside an I-*position*

Taking Baumeister's (2002) theory of ego depletion and ego power as a starting point, Monika Turowska (Kobylińska *et al.* 2009; see also Suszek *et al.* 2010) was trying to find an answer to the question of whether *I*-positions have separate resources of energy. In a research project with 143 students from two Warsaw colleges, participants were induced to use the energetic resources of two different *I*-positions to find out whether there were differences in resources of energy. Two

A

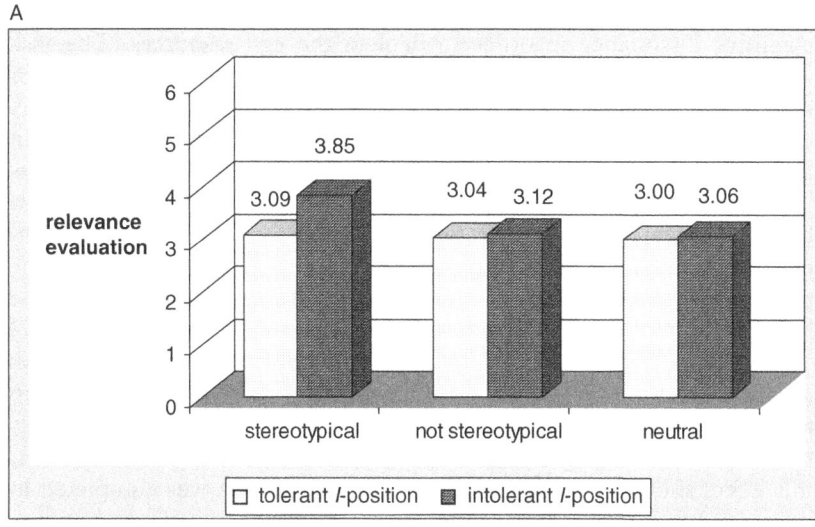

B

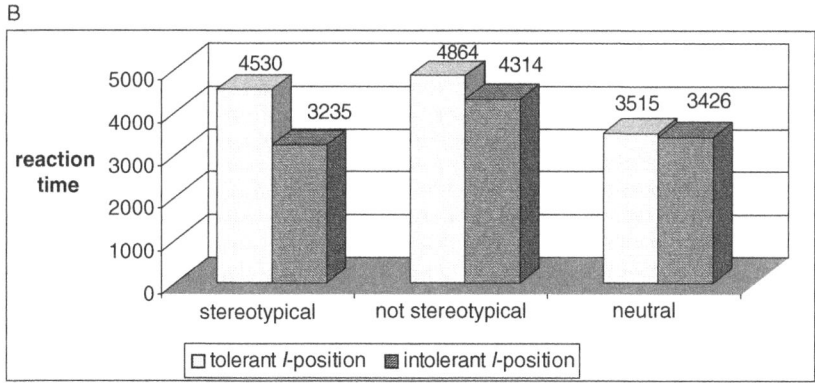

Figure 15.3 Relevance evaluation (A) and reaction times (B) for tolerant and intolerant positions from which minority groups are described in terms of stereotypical, not stereotypical and neutral adjectives. *Source:* Nowak (2008).

experimenters manipulated their own behaviour in order to activate two different *I*-positions among the participants: '*I* as a competent person' versus '*I* as an incompetent person'. In the experiment, methods of ego depletion and the depletion measurement were used (Baumeister 2002). An additional control group was planned in which the same procedure was used without the experimental positioning. The experiment started with positioning the participants in a particular *I*-position, after which they were asked to complete a first task aimed at causing a state of cognitive dissonance in order to deplete the ego resources. The task was to think of and note down as many arguments for paying fees for studies as the participants could find, arguments which were obviously contrary to their own interests as students of public universities (in Poland public schools are free). While the first experimenter was collecting the papers with the arguments, the second one appeared to replace him and activated the same or different *I*-position (competent or incompetent) depending on the experimental condition. Then he asked the participants to solve anagrams. The number of correct solutions was the indicator of the volume of resources available for the ego.

It was expected that activating a different *I*-position after the first task (experimental groups) would result in the restoration of the general ego resources, because the second *I*-position's resources became available, as they had not been depleted during the first task. In the control groups, this effect should not occur because the second task was completed in the same *I*-position as the first one. The regular ego-depletion effect was expected in these groups. The results are shown in Figure 15.4.

One-way ANOVA showed a significant main effect of the positioning variable ($F(2, 140) = 5.230; p < 0.01$). Additional analysis implied that in the experimental group, in which two different *I*-positions were activated, more correct anagrams were found than in the control group, in which the same position was activated twice. There were no significant differences between the experimental group and the neutral group, or between the control group and the neutral one.

This result is broadly in line with the expectations. However, before drawing the conclusion that the hypothesis was confirmed, further statistical analysis was conducted, revealing that only the result from one of the experimental half-groups (distinguished due to the order of position activation) was responsible for the observed differences ($F(4, 138) = 8.491; p < 0.001$). Most solutions were found by people in whom the '*I* as an incompetent person' position was activated prior to the 'competent person' position. In the second group, in which these positions were activated in a reversed sequence, the number of solutions matched the level of control group. Hence, not only was activating two different positions found to be important, but also the sequence of it.

Discussion and conclusion

A series of presented studies proved that specific and theoretically predicted effects of positioning can be observed in a variety of psychological phenomena, from personality traits, abilities and stereotypes to social

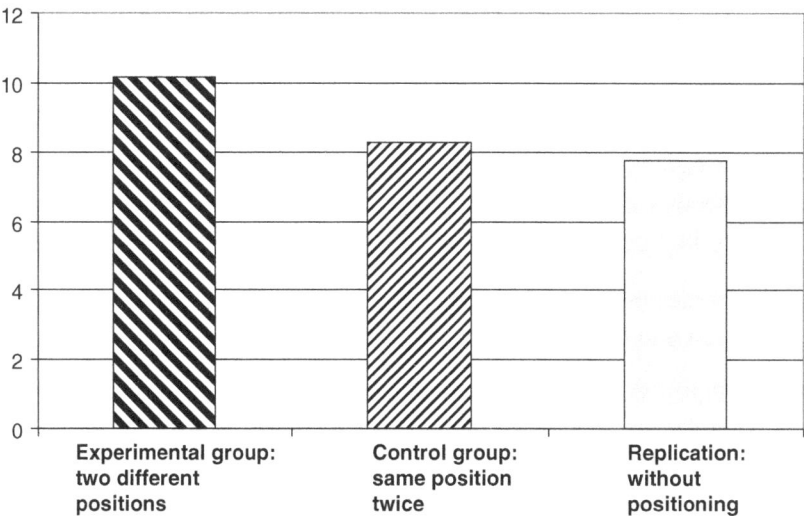

Figure 15.4 Mean number of correct anagrams in the experimental group and control group and in the group in which the original Baumeister's condition (without positioning) was replicated.

influence and ego depletion. It should be noted that in the above presentation we collected experiments that were mainly in line with the expectations drawn from the theoretical consideration of DST and the discursive mind model. However, among our studies, there were also ones which did not yield the predicted results. In particular, when we applied strong experimental control in a computer-designed lexical decision task to verify hypotheses about the accessibility of semantic categories in different *I*-positions, the results of more than 20 experiments following this procedure were inconclusive or even opposite to prediction. Following an idiographical procedure proposed by Daniel Cervone (Shadel *et al.* 2004), we conducted a reanalysis of these data, in which we tried to take into account – as far as it was possible *post factum* – individual differences in contents of particular *I*-positions. The results of this additional analysis are encouraging (see Suszek *et al.* 2010 for a detailed description). Here, too, further studies are needed.

Because of the limited frame of this chapter we did not describe here a series of experiments based on another procedure. The idea behind them was to start from different kinds of priming and then collect samples of internal dialogue. This procedure, inspired by the work of Elżbieta Dryll (2005), enables a researcher to measure a personal gallery of voices and to estimate their relative power. By changing the initial manipulation, we are able to compare dialogue samples in different contexts, which is another possible approach to verify the DST and the discursive mind model. Until now they have yielded a few theory-relevant theses or hypotheses, such as, for example, the insight that metacognition is most likely a product of internal dialogical activity (Stemplewska-Żakowicz *et al.* 2010) or the conclusion (Rumińska 2010) that a powerful voice of the mother in the self of young adults is associated with higher scores on some of the scales of the Personal Authority in the Family System Questionnaire (Bray and Harvey 1992). For the same reason we did not present here some more results that support DST and the discursive mind model. They show the usefulness of the adopted approach in some clinical applications (Siodmiak and Jędrasik-Styła 2009).

Generally, on the basis of our studies the discursive model, and particularly the assumption on the specificity of knowledge structures for the social context, can be acknowledged as worth a precise theoretical description and empirical verification. This seems particularly important in the context of new trends in mainstream psychology, which take greater account of phenomena of an intersubjective nature (Higgins 2000). The model of the discursive mind and DST offer an attractive explanation of this kind of social-cognitive phenomena.

The described model, like DST, with which it corresponds, is characterized by great complexity. Such a complexity makes an unequivocal verification harder to conduct. In an attempt to solve this problem, we used rigorous methodology and performed a series of different experiments, as described in this chapter (for more information, see Suszek *et al.* 2010). These empirical studies aimed to check the effects of the activation of different *I*-positions on cognitive processes and behaviour. We showed that cognitive-affective resources of *I*-positions, being activated in a particular context, are more easily accessible than resources of *I*-positions that are not activated, and this effect was visible in several experimental measures, such as reaction times and error rates.

Our results support the thesis that *I*-positions have their own specific cognitive-affective resources and that the main constructs of the DST – such as an *I*-position and positioning – are empirically real and can produce effects that are observable by means of empirical and experimental investigation. The model of the discursive mind and its empirical verification not only support DST, but also may be a vehicle of its contribution to theories stemming from other theoretical traditions. In particular, the idea of placing dialogue in sociocultural and relational contexts – as a basis for module formation in the mind – may be valuable in advancing general psychological understanding of cognition and personality.

A next step would be to describe how *I*-positions work together; that is, how different situations and circumstances prime the revelation of different voices in dialogue. We hope that future research in this direction can help us understand and capture the complexity and dynamics of the dialogical self and personality functioning in a better way.

REFERENCES

Bamberg, M. G. W. (1997) Positioning between structure and performance, *Journal of Narrative and Live History*, 7, 335–342

Baumeister, R. F. (2002) Ego depletion and self-control failure: a model of the self's executive function, *Self and Identity*, 1, 129–136

Bem, D. J. (1967) Self-perception: an alternative interpretation of cognitive dissonance phenomena, *Psychological Review*, 74, 183–200

Bray, J. H. and Harvey, D. M. (1992) Intimacy and individuation in young adults: development of the young adult version of the Personal Authority in the Family System Questionnaire, *Journal of Family Psychology*, 6, 152–163

Burger, J. M. (1999) The foot-in-the-door compliance procedure: a multiple-process analysis and review, *Personality and Social Psychology Review*, 3, 303–325

Costa Jr, P. T. and McCrae, R. R. (1985) *The NEO Personality Inventory: Manual* (Odessa, FL: Psychological Assessment Resources)

Dimaggio, G. (2006) Changing the dialogue between self voices during psychotherapy, *Journal of Psychotherapy Integration*, 16, 313–345

Dryll, E. (2005) Tatuś, koleżanka, Kmicic, policjant i pies: identyfikacja głosów w dialogu wewnętrznym podmiotu [My dad, my friend, Robin Hood, a policeman and a dog: identification of voices in an inner dialogue], *Przegląd Psychologiczny*, 48, 95–108

Freedman, J. L. and Fraser, S. C. (1966) Compliance without pressure: the foot-in-the-door technique, *Journal of Personality and Social Psychology*, 4, 195–202

Goff, P. A., Eberhardt, J. L., Williams, M. J. and Jackson, M. C. (2008) Not yet human: implicit knowledge, historical dehumanization, and contemporary consequences, *Journal of Personality and Social Psychology*, 94, 292–306

Harré, R. and van Langenhove, L. (1991) Varieties of positioning, *Journal of the Theory of Social Behavior*, 21, 393–407

Hermans, H. J. M. (1996) Voicing the self: from information processing to dialogical interchange, *Psychological Bulletin*, 19, 31–50

(1999) The polyphony of the mind: a multivoiced and dialogical self, in J. Rowan and M. Cooper (eds.), *The Plural Self: Multiplicity in Everyday Life* (London: Sage), 107–131

(2002) The dialogical self as a society of mind: introduction (Special Issue on the Dialogical Self), *Theory & Psychology*, 12, 147–160

Hermans, H. J. M. and Dimaggio, G. (2007) Self, identity and globalization in times of uncertainty: a dialogical analysis, *Review of General Psychology*, 11, 31–61

Hermans, H. J. M. and Hermans-Jansen, E. (1995) Self-Narratives: The Construction of Meaning in Psychotherapy (New York: Guilford)

Hermans, H. J. M. and Hermans-Konopka, A. (2010) Dialogical Self Theory: Positioning and Counter-Positioning in a Globalizing Society (Cambridge University Press)

Hermans, H. J. M. and Kempen, H. J. G. (1993) The Dialogical Self: Meaning as Movement (San Diego, CA: Academic Press)

Hermans, H. J. M., Kempen, H. J. G. and van Loon, R. J. P. (1992) The dialogical self: beyond individualism and rationalism, American Psychologist, 47, 23–33

Higgins, E. T. (2000) Social cognition: learning about what matters in the social world, European Journal of Social Psychology, 30, 3–39

Jurkowski, A. (1997) Test Językowy 'Leksykon': Podręcznik [The Language Test 'Leksykon': Handbook] (Warszawa: Pracownia Testów Psychologicznych PTP)

Jussim, L. and Eccles, J. S. (1992) Teacher expectations. II. Construction and reflection of student achievement, Journal of Personality and Social Psychology, 63, 947–961

Kobylińska, D., Stemplewska-Żakowicz, K., Zalewski, B., Suszek, H. and Turowska, M. (2009) Relacyjnie ustrukturalizowany umysł: Badania' [Relationally structured mind: Research], Przegląd Psychologiczny, 52, 87–110

Ligorio, M. B. and Spadaro, P. (2006) Digital positioning and on-line communities, in P. K. Oleś and H. J. M. Hermans (eds.), The Dialogical Self: Theory and Research (Lublin: John Paul Catholic University Press), 217–230

Minsky, M. (1985) The Society of Mind (New York: Simon & Schuster)

Niedopytalski, P. (2010) Wojownik czy domownik? Spostrzeganie siebie i cechy osobowości u członków ruchu rycerskiego w zależności od wzbudzonej pozycji Ja [A Warrior or a House Mate? Activated I-Position and Self-Perception and Personality Traits in Participants of a Historical Reconstruction Movement] (Warsaw: Warsaw School of Social Sciences and Humanities)

Nowak, K. (2008) Tolerancyjne i nietolerancyjne głosy umysłu. Aktualnie wzbudzona pozycja podmiotowa a występowanie stereotypów w spostrzeganiu społecznym [Tolerant and intolerant voices of the mind. Activated I-position and stereotyping in social perception]. Master's thesis, Warsaw School of Social Sciences and Humanities.

Rosenthal, R. (2002) Covert communication in classrooms, clinics, courtrooms, and cubicles, American Psychologist, 57, 839–849

Rumińska, M. (2010) Relacje rodzinne a struktura dialogowego Ja I siła wewnetrznych głosów [Family Relationships, the Structure of the Dialogical Self and the Strength of Internal Voices] (Warsaw: Warsaw School of Social Sciences and Humanities)

Shadel, W. G., Cervone, D., Niaura, R. and Abrams, D. B. (2004) Developing an integrative social-cognitive strategy for personality assessment at the level of the individual: an illustration with regular cigarette smokers, Journal of Research in Personality, 38, 394–419

Siodmiak, K. and Jędrasik-Styła, M. (2009) Wykorzystanie metodologii dialogowej w praktyce arteterapeutycznej i diagnozie klinicznej [Application of the dialogical methodology into artetherapeutic practice and clinical diagnosis], *Przegląd Psychologiczny*, **52**, 1, 111–122.

Snow, R. (1995) Pygmalion and intelligence?, *Current Directions in Psychological Science*, **4**, 169–171

Śpiewak, S. (2005) Seedcorn Grant Report: cognitive determinants of compliance techniques, *European Bulletin of Social Psychology*, **17**, 71–78

Spitz, H. H. (1999) Beleaguered Pygmalion: a history of the controversy over claims that teacher expectancy raises intelligence, *Intelligence*, **27**, 199–234

Stemplewska-Żakowicz, K. (2004) *O rzeczach widywanych na obrazkach i opowiadanych o nich historiach: TAT jako metoda badawcza i diagnostyczna* [*On Things Which Have Been Seen on Pictures and Stories Which Have Been Told About Them: Thematic Apperception Test as Research and Diagnostic Method*] (Warsaw: Academica)

Stemplewska-Żakowicz, K., Dimaggio, G. and Kozłowska, O. (2010) Dialogowa natura samoświadomości [Dialogical nature of self-awareness], *Czasopismo Psychologiczne*, **16**, 99–112

Stemplewska-Żakowicz, K., Suszek, H. and Zalewski, B. (2005) Pozycjonowanie a nieświadome procesy potwierdzania zachowaniem cudzych koncepcji [Positioning and nonconscious behavioural confirmation of other people's conceptions], *Przegląd Psychologiczny*, **48**, 33–52

Stemplewska-Żakowicz, K., Walecka, J. and Gabińska, A. (2006) As many selves as interpersonal relations (or maybe even more), *International Journal for Dialogical Science*, **1**, 71–94

Stemplewska-Żakowicz, K., Walecka, J., Gabińska, A., Zalewski, B. and Suszek, H. (2005) Experiments on positioning, positioning the experiments, in P. K. Oleś and H. J. M. Hermans (eds.), *The Dialogical Self: Theory and Research* (Lublin: John Paul II Catholic University of Lublin Press), 183–199

Stiles, W. B. (1999) Signs and voices in psychotherapy, *Psychotherapy Research*, **9**, 1–21

Suszek, H., Kobylińska, D., Stemplewska-Żakowicz, K. and Szymczyk, B. (2010) Explorations in the discursive mind, *International Journal for Dialogical Science*, **4**, 95–122

Szymczyk, B. (2010) Positioning and personality traits in five factor model, *International Journal for Dialogical Science*, **5**, 35–59

Wertsch, J. V. (1991) *Voices of the Mind: A Sociocultural Approach to Mediated Action* (Cambridge, MA: Harvard University Press)

Wortham, S. and Gadsden, V. (2006) Urban father position themselves through narrative: an approach to narrative self-construction, in A. de Fina, D. Schiffrin and M. Bamberg (eds.), *Discourse and Identity* (Cambridge University Press), 314–343

Zalewski, B. (2010) Positioning and the 'foot-in-the-door' social influence technique, *International Journal for Dialogical Science*, **5**, 61–73

16   Voicing inner conflict: from a dialogical to a negotiational self

Dina Nir

This chapter offers a new conceptualization of the dynamics of inner conflict within the framework of the dialogical self. Central to dialogical self theory (DST) is the notion that the self is organized as a dialogical interchange between mutually influencing *I*-positions in the society of the mind. Like different people in a group or social system, *I*-positions function in a relatively autonomous way. Each *I*-position is endowed with different views, memories, wishes, motives, interests and feelings, and therefore has a distinct story to tell from its own experience and its own stance. Moreover, just as in any social system, the internal society of *I*-positions is characterized by hierarchical order and political power. Indeed, some *I*-positions are dominant and overpowering, whereas others are more subdued. Some tend to cooperate and form coalitions, whereas others function in conflict, opposition and even in continuous battle (Hermans 1996, 2001, 2002; Hermans and Dimaggio 2007; Hermans and Hermans-Konopka 2010; Hermans *et al.* 1992; Hermans *et al.* 1993).

Drawing on the main tenets of DST, a negotiational view of the self in a state of inner conflict has been proposed (Nir 2009; Nir and Kluger 2008), termed negotiational self theory (NST). The theory suggests that whenever inner conflict erupts within the self and a decision is called for, the internal interchange takes the form of a negotiation process. In this internal negotiation, different and conflicting *I*-positions advocate their unique wants, concerns, fears and aspirations in a back-and-forth communication that is designed to bring the conflict to a conclusion and enable action to ensue. NST further proposes that just as in negotiation between people, the internal negotiation may lead to either a distributive (i.e. coercive win–lose) or an integrative (i.e. collaborative win–win) negotiation process and outcome (see Deutsch 1973; Fisher and Ury 1981; Follett 1942). When a distributive win–lose negotiation transpires within the self, dominating *I*-positions take over the negotiation space and direct the decision in their favour. As a result, the needs and concerns of the dominating *I*-positions are satisfied, whereas the interests and needs of the other *I*-positions remain lacking and unfulfilled. When a collaborative negotiation develops within the self, different and conflicting *I*-positions are equally acknowledged and heard, and an integrative solution is constructed that simultaneously incorporates and satisfies the needs of multiple *I*-positions.

Several scholars have previously acknowledged the concept of negotiations taking place within the self; however, the nature of these negotiations has been outlined in general terms only. For example, Freud (1923) maintained that to manage the internal conflict, the ego needs constantly to negotiate between the gratification-seeking id, the morally ideal superego and the demands of reality. In a different way, Minsky (1985) suggested that when internal conflict arises within the self, different agents or sub-parts of the self engage in a negotiation with one another in order effectively to allocate limited resources and direct behaviour. From a motivational perspective, Kenen (1986) suggested that making agreements with oneself is part of the ongoing process of self-direction, and maintained that different parts of the self act as arguers that bargain with each other in a way that is analogous to interpersonal negotiation. Hermans' (1996) account of the self has also inferred that the dialogical interchange between different conflicting *I*-positions may involve a process of negotiation. This is specifically reflected in Hermans *et al.*'s (1992) notion that some dialogical interchanges are aimed at reaching agreements and solving problems, while others focus on derogating, criticizing and battling one another.

To illustrate the internal negotiation process and to outline its characteristics and dynamics, a case study of an inner conflict will be presented and analysed. The example will demonstrate how different *I*-positions put forward their needs and claims in a back-and-forth communication until a decision is made. Then, using well-established criteria from the field of interpersonal negotiation, several hypothetical resolutions to the inner conflict will be presented and analysed to illustrate the differences between distributive and integrative internal negotiations. Finally, the notion of transforming win–lose internal decisions into integrative win–win resolutions will be discussed, and a four-stage NST intervention method, designed to direct systematically the inner conflict towards a collaborative and integrative resolution, will be delineated.

The internal negotiation process

Consider the case of Sara, a young woman, who after five years of working as a check-in attendant for a large airline, was deliberating whether to leave her current job at the airline, and take the position of an assistant producer in a small TV production company. When Sara was asked to report her internal dialogue in an open-ended questionnaire, she described her internal interchange in a series of consecutive sentences:

I want to develop myself in the area of production and television.

I want to fulfil my aspirations and dreams.

On the other hand, I want to take care of my future and receive financial benefits, and live in comfort and security.

As an airline employee, I'm entitled to free airline tickets, extended insurance, car expenses and in the future phone expenses, etc.

And as a producer I have to work without security. In a small private company like this one, people can be fired any day, depending on the situation in the country. There is no insurance and the pay changes according to the work done.

But on the other hand, I aspire for more for myself than merely sitting at a counter all day and receiving passengers. In this job, you don't need any imagination, courage, ambition or initiative. I am not interested in staying in this job for years to come.

My great ambition is to be a TV producer and this company is the first step on the way there.

A content analysis of the text revealed that four distinct *I*-positions took part in Sara's internal dialogue. These *I*-positions include: '*I*, the airline employee'; '*I*, the aspiring TV producer'; '*I*, the self-fulfilment seeker'; and '*I*, the security seeker'. While alternative classification of the four *I*-positions may be just as informative, this is of less importance to the purpose of demonstrating the internal negotiation process.

Sara's internal dialogue is initiated by '*I*, the aspiring TV producer', which clearly puts forward aspirations to develop in the area of production and television. In support of this stand, '*I*, the self-fulfilment seeker', joins in, and voices a desire to realize Sara's aspirations and dreams. In response to these two collaborating 'pro-change' *I*-positions, '*I*, the security seeker' emerges and voices concerns for Sara's long-term financial security and comfort. To strengthen this perspective, '*I*, the airline employee' enters the stage, and offers a detailed list of the different financial benefits that Sara is already entitled to in her current job.[1] Building on this information, '*I*, the security seeker' goes on to stress the serious risks Sara would be taking if she actually went ahead and took the new job. To counter this developing agenda, '*I*, the self-fulfilment seeker' puts forward several arguments against staying in the current job, detailing its unattractive qualities and clearly objecting to staying in such an unchallenging and dull job for years to come. Finally, '*I*, the aspiring TV producer', which was the first *I*-position to be voiced, abruptly concludes the internal interchange by declaring that becoming a TV producer is Sara's great ambition, and that the new company is a first step towards fulfilling this aspiration.

Many definitions can be used to portray an interpersonal negotiation process. Among these, the one most concurrent with our focus defines negotiation as 'a back and forth communication designed to reach an agreement when you and the other side have some interests that are shared and others that are opposed' (Fisher and Ury 1981: xiii). It is suggested that Sara's internal interchange reveals such a negotiation process. In this internal negotiation, a back-and-forth communication takes place between different and opposing *I*-positions until a decision is made. As the dialogue unfolds, *I*-positions react and counter-react to the previously voiced *I*-positions, backing their claims and arguments with concrete facts and conflict-relevant knowledge. Gradually, two opposing coalitions of *I*-positions are formed, each supporting a different pole of the conflict. On the one hand, '*I*, the aspiring TV producer' and '*I*, the self-fulfilment seeker', who are for taking the new job in hopes of fulfilling long sought after aspirations. On the other hand, '*I*, the security seeker' and '*I*, the airline employee', who are against taking the new job, as it risks uncertainty and a possible decrease in financial welfare. As all four *I*-positions are part of a single self, they share a common interest in Sara's well-being. Yet, as *I*-positions represent different and unique needs, concerns, fears and aspirations, each of the conflicting *I*-positions expresses different views regarding what is best for Sara.

The forming of coalitions within the self is another characteristic of the internal negotiation process. By joining forces with others, dominant *I*-positions are able to build up more power, and thus exert more influence on the opposing side. As demonstrated in Sara's case, the dynamics of the internal negotiation are such that statements are often supported by other closely associated statements, and counter-statements are equally supported by akin counter-statements. Indeed, the notion of coalitions of *I*-positions is a well-established concept in DST. Although relatively autonomous, *I*-positions do not necessarily work in isolation but rather collaborate with each other, much as people cooperate in society. As Hermans and Hermans-Konopka maintain, 'dominant positions usually have their companions, helpers, satellites, and auxiliary troops that together form stabilizing forces in the internal and external domains of the self' (2010: 152).

Another characteristic of the internal negotiation process is that it aims to culminate in a decision. In parallel to negotiating parties that aim to reach an agreement, the aim of the internal negotiation is to reach a resolution that alleviates the discrepancies among conflicting needs, and enables the self to move from deliberation to action. However, while parties in the interpersonal domain may choose to stop negotiating with one another and seek other alternatives, no such option exists within the self. Therefore, how the internal negotiation is concluded substantially affects both the current and future self. Next, the different modes of interpersonal negotiation will be delineated, followed by a discussion of the different possible outcomes to Sara's internal negotiation.

The different modes of negotiation

Negotiation scholars traditionally distinguish between two fundamental approaches to negotiation. A distributive (i.e. coercive win–lose) approach, on the one hand, and an integrative (i.e. collaborative win–win) approach on the other (Deutsch 1973; Fisher and Ury 1981; Follett 1942). Parties that adopt a distributive strategy tend to view the negotiation as a zero-sum game in which gains of one party come at the direct expense of the other. To maximize their benefit in this competitively perceived endeavour, negotiators often lock onto their initial positions and stands, and use coercive tactics such as threats, manipulation, intimidation and unilateral action to persuade the other party to yield. Consequently, distributive negotiations result either in one party winning and the other party losing, or at best in compromise agreements in which both parties gain some and lose some. Such distributive negotiations produce low joint benefit, and often strain the relationship between the negotiating parties, and this in turn reduces the chance for future collaboration. In contrast to coercive negotiations, an integrative approach leads to high joint benefit and to mutually satisfying agreements that create added value and 'expand the pie' (Pruitt 1981, 1983; Pruitt and Lewis 1975; Raiffa 1982; Schulz and Pruitt 1978). Through collaborative efforts, a creative solution is constructed that enables both parties to satisfy their different needs and interests (Weingart *et al.* 1990; Zubek *et al.* 1992). Moreover, it has been shown that reaching integrative agreements not only produces sustainable settlements but also strengthens the parties' relationship and promotes future cooperation (Deutsch 2000; Kremenyuk 1991; Pruitt and Carnevale 1993; Pruitt and Rubin 1986).

By applying these well-established definitions of interpersonal negotiation to the internal domain, a novel means of evaluating the resolutions of inner conflict emerges. Thus, the resolution of inner conflict may be evaluated by the extent to which the internal negotiation outcome is either coercive or integrative. To highlight the differences between coercive and integrative internal negotiations, Sara's case will be further expanded on, and different hypothetical outcomes, as well as her own reported decision will be presented and examined.

Coercive internal negotiation

One possible conclusion to Sara's inner conflict could be that she decides to stay in her secure job at the airline and forgo the opportunity to join the small production company. Although such a decision could be considered the 'rational' or 'responsible' thing to do, from an NST perspective it would nevertheless reflect a typical coercive win–lose decision. The reason is that the security-based I-positions would be fully satisfied, whereas the I-positions that seek self-actualization would remain lacking and unfulfilled. An alternative option could be that Sara decides to 'throw caution to the wind', and leave her secure job without any concerns or plans for her long-term financial comfort and security. Although in this alternative solution the winning and losing sides are reversed, it nevertheless represents a coercive win–lose decision as well.

Just as in negotiation between people, using coercion and forcing some I-positions into submission creates dissatisfaction, deepens the internal separation, and diminishes the chances that the internal agreement will endure. The reason is that I-positions that remain repressed and unsatisfied do not simply fade away or withdraw from the self. On the contrary, they continue to experience an energized discrepancy that will eventually resurface sometime in the future to seek recognition, alleviation and need satisfaction. Indeed, Freud observed that any repressed and unsatisfied drives and desires tend to reappear sometime in the future in consciousness, in behaviour or in both (Freud 1923, 1939; Westen 1998). Along the same lines, Minsky (1985) suggested that the longer a sub-part of the self remains unfulfilled, the more energized and activated it becomes, and, therefore, the more likely it will eventually take over the hierarchy of the self and direct the self's behaviour in the opposite direction. For instance, if Sara represses the I-positions that seek self-actualization, it is likely that these repressed I-positions would eventually re-emerge the first time she feels bored and frustrated at work, or learns about a friend who is pursuing her dreams. Alternatively, if Sara represses the I-positions that seek security, it is most probable that they would re-emerge with the first signs of instability in the small firm, or possibly when Sara receives her first pay cheque. Therefore, it is suggested that whatever the direction of a coercive win–lose decision, it does not produce a lasting and durable solution, and as such does not fully resolve or alleviate the inner conflict. Next, we will examine Sara's actual decision, which was reported in the following words:

I decided to take the job in the small company as a means of gaining experience and as a stepping-stone towards working in a large and well-established firm that will offer better terms and benefits, and that will provide me with long-term security.

At first glance, Sara's decision incorporates all the considerations that were elicited in her internal negotiation. She decides to take the job at the small production company, and at the same time acknowledges her need for financial comfort and security. Yet a close examination of her decision reveals that while '*I*, the aspiring TV producer' and '*I*, the self-fulfilment seeker', who campaigned for taking the new job, are clearly satisfied in the decision, the security-based *I*-positions are not concretely addressed and therefore may continue to experience some discrepancy regarding their needs. It seems that Sara is willing to put aside her current needs for financial security and welfare for the sake of gaining experience in the field of TV production. Yet, while she remains positive and hopeful regarding her chances to do better in the future, she does not specify exactly how she plans to meet these substantial needs. Therefore, from an NST perspective, although Sara's decision is not entirety a one-sided, win–lose decision, it is nevertheless far from an optimal win–win resolution.

Integrative internal negotiation

After we have outlined the different possible coercive decisions, the question is, does a solution exist that is able to satisfy all of Sara's conflicting *I*-positions at the same time? In other words, could the need for self-actualization and the need for security and financial comfort be met without subduing or compromising either? To answer this question, it is worthwhile examining how negotiation research has dealt with this issue on an interpersonal level. In general, negotiation researches agree that while most interpersonal negotiations appear as zero-sum situations, they nevertheless have the potential to produce integrative and mutually beneficial agreements (Blake and Mouton 1964; Deutsch 1973; Follett 1942; Raiffa 1982). To reach integrative agreements, negotiation research recommends building trust, asking questions, acknowledging each other's perspectives, clarifying misunderstandings, freely exchanging information and developing mutually beneficial settlements (Deutsch 1973; Pinkley *et al.* 1995; Thompson and Hastie 1990; Weingart *et al.* 1990).

As in the interpersonal domain, integrative solutions are also attainable within the self. To demonstrate this potential, several possible solutions to Sara's inner conflict are offered next. For example, Sara could decide to build on her current standing at the airline and apply for a transfer to a more challenging, creative and demanding position in another department, such as the marketing or public relations departments. Another possible integrative solution could be that Sara continues with her current job, yet enrols in a postgraduate programme that specializes in TV and cinema production. In a different vein, Sara could decide to continue her job at the airline for a few more months, while searching for a position as an assistant producer in a larger and more established production firm. Yet, in another, altogether different direction, Sara could ask for one year's leave of absence from her job at the airline, while she tries out the new job, thereby keeping all options open in case working in the small firm does not turn out well. In addition to each of these possible options, Sara could actively collect more information about the requirements needed for the position of assistant producer, and also find out whether the job in the small firm will indeed contribute to obtaining a future position in a large and established TV production company.

The alternatives suggested above put forward a number of possible directions Sara could pursue towards an integrative solution that would fully resolve her inner conflict. Yet, however different these alternatives may seem from one another, they nevertheless have one thing in common. They all simultaneously acknowledge and concretely address the different and opposing *I*-positions that took part in Sara's internal negotiation. The *I*-positions that are concerned with self-actualization are satisfied since action is taken towards fulfilling Sara's dreams and aspirations. At the same time, the *I*-positions that are concerned with financial security and future benefits are satisfied because the financial and employment issues are taken care of (e.g. either by staying in the airline, joining an established production firm, or creating a financial safety net). While a truly integrative solution may still lie elsewhere for Sara, these alternatives offer an indication of the rich array of possibilities that actually exist, and that can be pursued beyond a dichotomous, 'either-or' coercive approach.

In summary, Sara's case provides a porthole through which to view the internal negotiation process that takes place among *I*-positions in states of inner conflict. It also enables us to examine the two fundamentally different negotiation strategies that can be adopted within the self, and their consequent outcomes. While the mere act of making a decision enables putting an end to the often distressful and chaotic experience of inner conflict, the type of negotiation strategy applied and the consequent decision reached has a considerable effect both on our internal experience and on the results we achieve in the world.

The negotiational self method (NSM): facilitating the integrative resolution of inner conflict

Negotiation scholars have repeatedly demonstrated the effectiveness of training people to apply integrative strategies in negotiation. It seems that offering prescriptive directions as to how to overcome coercive tendencies and build mutually beneficial agreements, significantly helps people to become better, more efficient and more collaborative negotiators (Bazerman *et al.* 1985; Goldenberg *et al.* 2006; Neale and Northcraft 1986; Spector 1995; Thompson 1990, 1991; Thompson and De Harpport 1994; Thompson and Hastie 1990; Weingart *et al.* 1990). It is suggested that intrapersonal negotiation processes may similarly benefit from such guidelines and directions. To help people manage their inner conflicts and transform coercive negotiations and decisions into integrative win–win processes and outcomes, a four-stage intervention method, termed the negotiational self method (NSM), was developed and modified through numerous interviews (Nir 2009). The method draws both on negotiation literature and on the dialogical properties of the self to manage systematically the internal negotiation and direct the process towards a collaborative and democratic resolution. It is important to note that the method, which is presented next, could be applied independently – to help resolve an inner conflict on one's own, or as an intervention method for a counsellor or facilitator to guide another person in reaching an integrative resolution to his or her inner conflict.

Stage 1: identifying and framing the inner conflict

The first step in navigating the resolution of the inner conflict is to explicitly frame the conflict. To achieve this, NSM suggests first freely describing the conflict and its general background, and then focusing on what seems to be at the heart of the internal deliberation. That is, specifically identifying the 'for' and 'against' poles of the conflict. For example, in Sara's case, the two poles of the conflict could be described as 'for taking the job in the small firm' and 'against taking the job in the small firm'. Alternatively, it is also possible to frame the conflict in 'for' and 'for' or 'against' and 'against' terms. For example, the two 'for' poles could be 'for taking the job in the small firm' and 'for staying with the airline'. Framing the conflict in such a way is suggested to create a clear starting point from which to begin the process of managing the conflict space. Moreover, it sets the stage for a systematic elicitation of multiple conflict-relevant *I*-positions, as will be delineated next.

Stage 2: eliciting and mapping conflict relevant I-positions

The second stage suggests methodically eliciting a wide range of conflict-relevant *I*-positions under the two poles of the conflict as defined in stage 1. As each *I*-position conveys a unique perspective and a different segment of knowledge concerning the problem space, NSM encourages the elicitation of a broad as possible range of conflict-relevant *I*-positions. To achieve this, it is advised to start eliciting the different *I*-positions that are in support of one pole of the conflict (preferably the 'for' pole), and only when this process is exhausted, move on to elicit the *I*-positions that are in support of the opposing pole. The aim of this ordered methodology of *I*-position elicitation is to prevent the automatic process of internal coercion, and create a space for *I*-position divergence and for new knowledge to surface. A simple and effective means of encouraging *I*-position elicitation is repeatedly to ask: 'What else?' or 'What else is relevant in this situation?' It is important to stress that whatever the content of a voiced *I*-position, it should not be denied, repressed or ignored, but rather democratically acknowledged and empathetically accepted. Even those voices and *I*-positions that tend to be judged as negative (i.e. childish, petty, mean, lazy or weak) should be listened to, recognized and mapped, as they often represent underlying fears, frustrations and concerns that stem from deeply rooted human needs that seek expression and fulfilment (Maslow 1968). This systematic mapping process in which *I*-positions are encouraged to voice freely their unique views, concerns and aspirations promotes an internal state of active listening, one that is consistent with Rogers' (1951) humanistic notion of active listening and unconditional positive regard. Moreover, it is suggested that accepting all *I*-positions as valid, regardless of their place in the internal hierarchy, serves to reduce temporarily the power differences among the different parts of the self and allows for a more collaborative and democratic process to follow.

Stage 3: revealing underlying interests and needs

A fundamental principle in interpersonal negotiation is that in order to promote integrative win–win outcomes, negotiating parties should focus on revealing their underlying interests rather than on bargaining over their stands. Interests are considered the primary aspirations, concerns, desires and fears that stem from deeply rooted human needs that continually seek fulfilment (Burton 1984; Lewicki *et al.* 1999; Nierenberg 1968). In contrast, stands (i.e. otherwise known as positions in the negotiation literature) are the tangible demands that people declare, the concrete objectives they state, or the specific solutions they initially offer. For example, an employee may demand a 10 per cent increase in salary. This would be her stance. However, behind this standpoint, typically lie several different and unique interests and needs that have motivated her to ask for the increase. These interests may include a desire to receive recognition for her work, a need to be valued and rewarded for her contribution to the organization, a concern that she receive the same terms and salary as her male colleagues, or a combination of these diverse interests. Negotiation literature further proposes that by focusing on interests rather than on stands, seemingly resolution-resistant conflicts often become solvable. The reason is that since interests represent deep human motivations, they are also intangible and therefore can be addressed and satisfied in many different ways. However, a demand is specific in nature, and therefore can be met with either acceptance, rejection or compromise. Thus, focusing on interests enables the parties to expand their knowledge and understanding of what is important for each party, and consequentially use this knowledge to build resourceful solutions that might not have been evident when the issues were described in terms of stands and demands (Fisher and Ury 1981; Thompson 2001).

It is proposed that just like people in a negotiation, *I*-positions may voice either interests or stands in the internal negotiation interchange. Therefore, the third stage advocates revealing the interests behind different stands, by inquiring into the reasons and motives that underlie each voiced *I*-position. This is achieved by asking questions such as 'Why is this important for me?', 'Why do I want this?', 'How will achieving this benefit me?' and 'What else is important to me in this situation?' In some instances, these questions may lead to additional *I*-positions to be elicited. If so, the newly elicited *I*-positions may be added to the previously mapped perspectives, under the appropriate 'for' or 'against' poles. Indeed, the general aim of this stage is to allow unheard *I*-positions to be clearly voiced, to enable additional concerns, fears, aspirations and desires to become overt, and thus to achieve a deeper and more comprehensive understanding of the conflict space.

Overall, the three NSM stages described so far have focused on framing the two sides of the inner conflict, systematically and democratically eliciting diverse *I*-positions, and revealing the underlying needs and interests. These stages putatively lead to a more ordered and extensive mapping of the conflict space, to the elicitation of new self-knowledge and to a deeper understanding of the 'for' and 'against' forces that are at play within the self. Moreover, combined, they set the stage for the final step of the process – creating an integrative resolution that jointly satisfies the opposing *I*-positions.

Stage 4: building integrative win–win solutions

To progress towards building an integrative solution to the inner conflict, the fourth stage suggests formulating a creative solution that follows one single principle. The principle is that the constructed solution should simultaneously address, acknowledge and incorporate each and every *I*-position and interest that was elicited and mapped in the previous stages. This principle is neutral in nature since it does not rely on any subjective or normative standards, such as what is considered the 'right' 'good' or 'worthy' solution, nor does it rely on the hierarchical or political station of *I*-positions within the self. Rather, the principle is content-neutral, and suggests simply that all voices must be satisfied in the decision. Indeed, to reach a fully integrative solution, no voice should be left unacknowledged and unattended, not even those voices that are considered unworthy or undesired. In other words, each voice that has been mapped under the 'for' and 'against' poles in the second and third stages should be acknowledged, attended to and satisfied in the constructed decision. If, for instance, a solution has been formulated that satisfies all voices but one, the unsatisfied voice, which represents unsatisfied needs, should become the focus of attention and subsequently incorporated into the decision.

To aid people in the process of arriving at new and innovative solutions that can simultaneously satisfy diverse *I*-positions, different creativity strategies known in the field of negotiation may be applied. These strategies have been proven effective in solving complex negotiations and are traditionally advocated in negotiation literature. They include strategies such as expanding the range of conflict variables, introducing new issues and resources that are exogenous to the initial conflict space, unbundling issues into sub-issues, and changing and reformulating the relationship between different variables (Froman and Cohen 1970; Goldenberg *et al.* 2006; Lax and Sebenius 1986; Pruitt 1981). By applying these creativity strategies to the internal domain, new kinds of resolutions may be constructed that can concurrently address the multi-facetedness of the conflict.[2] When such integrative and composite solutions are formed, the different and opposing needs are satisfied, and a comprehensive and full resolution of the inner conflict is reached.

Discussion

Viewing the workings of the self in states of inner conflict as negotiational, and constructing the theoretical and applied framework of NST would not be possible if not for the advances put forward by DST. A negotiational view of the self draws on depicting the *I* as dialogical in its dynamics, and multifaceted and societal in its structure. In particular, NST is inspired by the notion of *I*-positions that advocate unique perspectives, cognitions and emotions within the self, and, like different people in a society, maintain a degree of autonomy alongside the proclivity to function as part of a larger collective. NST also draws on the idea that different *I*-positions are able to communicate and influence each other through dialogical interchanges, which resemble the way in which people interact and converse in any society.

Yet, it is suggested that NST puts forward several advances that may also serve to contribute to DST, from both a theoretical and an applied perspective. For instance, through demonstrating the back-and-forth negotiation dynamics that take place among *I*-positions, NST further supports the basic DST premise that the self is not only multifaceted but also dialogical in nature. Similarly, NST supports the DST notion that the self may function through the formation of coalitions and oppositions, and through the interchange that takes place among them. Furthermore, the emphasis NST places on the role of interests and needs as motivating forces within the self may offer an additional contribution. Specifically, NST proposes that, like people, *I*-positions are driven by an underlying set of interests (i.e. needs, concerns, fears and aspirations), and that these interests may be reflected either overtly or covertly in dialogical interchanges. In other words, *I*-positions may directly articulate their deep-seated interests and needs, or may imply them indirectly, through voicing stances, claims and declarations instead. Hence, it is suggested that differentiating between interest-based and stance-based interchanges may provide a novel criterion by which to evaluate internal dialogues at large, and analyse the communication style of any single *I*-position in particular.

It is further proposed that the NST method (NSM) presented here supports the developmental process of creating what is described by Hermans and Hermans-Konopka (2010) as a 'good dialogue'. Overall, the method promotes a democratic and equality-based process within the self, and as such aims to encourage an active and unconditional process of internal listening. More specifically, the first and second stages of framing and mapping the inner conflict create an organized 'space' in which new self-knowledge may be obtained. By encouraging a democratic elicitation of a wide array of *I*-positions, and accepting all *I*-positions as valid, regardless of their value or station in the internal hierarchy, the method is congruent with the DST notions of creating a broad bandwidth of *I*-positions, and accepting the other within the self. In addition, the third stage, which outlines the different genres of internal communication (interests-based vs. stance-based), also promotes the elicitation of deep motivations, fears and aspirations, thus further increasing self-knowledge, and reducing misconceptions and misunderstandings. Finally, the fourth stage, which directs the inner conflict towards a mutually beneficial win–win solution, creates constriction on the problem space, which is known to increase the potential for creative and innovative thinking to commence (see Boden 1994; Finke *et al.* 1996).

To conclude, evaluating the outcomes of inner conflicts by the same criterion we use to evaluate interpersonal negotiation sets a novel standard by which to measure and facilitate one's internal dialogues and decisions. If the dialogues and actions directed by the self lead to the mutual satisfaction of diverse *I*-positions, then well-being and personal thriving will be promoted. However, if internal control and coercion are in play, and the needs and interests of some *I*-positions are favoured over the others, then the discrepant *I*-positions will come out losing, and the self will consequently lose as a whole. Therefore, whether we apply coercion or collaboration in resolving our inner conflicts not only affects the decisions we make and the goals we attain, but may also subsequently influence and shape the fabric of our self.

NOTES

1 Note that '*I*, the airline employee', as referred to here, connotes an *I*-position that is content with the benefits provided by the job at the airline.
2 Applications of some of these creativity strategies appear in the hypothetical integrative solutions presented in Sara's example.

REFERENCES

Bazerman, M. H., Magliozzi, T. and Neale, M. A. (1985) The acquisition of an integrative response in a competitive market, *Organizational Behavior and Human Performance*, **34**, 294–313
Blake, R. R. and Mouton, J. S. (1964) *The Managerial Grid* (Houston, TX: Gulf)
Boden, M. A. (1994) What is creativity?, in M. A. Boden (ed.), *Dimensions of Creativity* (Cambridge, MA: MIT Press), 75–118
Burton, J. W. (1984) *Global Conflict: The Domestic Sources of International Crisis* (Brighton: Wheatsheaf Books)
Deutsch, M. (1973) *The Resolution of Conflict* (New Haven, CT: Yale University Press)

(2000) Justice and conflict, in M. Deutsch and P. Coleman (eds.), *The Handbook of Conflict Resolution: Theory and Practice* (San Francisco: Jossey-Bass), 41–64

Finke, R. A., Ward, T. B. and Smith, S. M. (1996) *Creative Cognition: Theory, Research, and Applications* (Cambridge, MA: MIT Press)

Fisher, R. and Ury, W. (1981) *Getting to Yes: Negotiating Agreement Without Giving In* (Boston: Houghton Mifflin)

Follett, M. P. (1942) Constructive conflict, in H. C. Metcalf and L. Urwick (eds.), *Dynamic Administration: The Collected Papers of Mary Parker Follett* (New York: Harper), 1–22

Freud, S. (1923) *The Ego and the Id – The Standard Edition of the Complete Psychological Works of Sigmund Freud* (London: Hogarth), vol. XIX (1939) *Moses and Monotheism* (New York: Vintage Books)

Froman, L. A. and Cohen, M. D. (1970) Compromise and logroll: comparing the efficiency of two bargaining processes, *Behavioral Science*, **30**, 180–183

Goldenberg, J., Nir, D. and Maoz, E. (2006) Creativity in negotiation, in L. Thompson and H. S. Choi (eds.), *Creativity and Innovation in Organizations* (New York: Lawrence Erlbaum), 43–65

Hermans, H. J. M. (1996) Voicing the self: from information processing to dialogical interchange, *Psychological Bulletin*, **119**, 31–50 (2001) The dialogical self: toward a theory of personal and cultural positioning, *Culture & Psychology*, 7, 243–281 (2002) The dialogical self as a society of mind: introduction, *Theory & Psychology*, **12**, 147–160

Hermans, H. J. M. and Dimaggio, G. (2007) Self, identity, and globalization in times of uncertainty: a dialogical analysis, *Review of General Psychology*, **11**, 31–61

Hermans, H. J. M. and Hermans-Konopka, A. (2010) *Dialogical Self Theory: Positioning and Counter-Positioning in a Globalizing Society* (New York: Cambridge University Press)

Hermans, H. J. M., Kempen, H. J. G. and van Loon, R. J. P. (1992) The dialogical self: beyond individualism and rationalism, *American Psychologist*, **47**, 23–33

Hermans, H. J. M., Rijks, T. I. and Kempen, H. J. G. (1993) Imaginal dialogues in the self: theory and method, *Journal of Personality*, **61**, 207–236

Kenen, R. H. (1986) Making agreements with oneself: prelude to social behavior, *Sociological Forum*, 1, 362–377

Kremenyuk, V. A. (ed.) (1991) *International Negotiation* (San Francisco, CA: Jossey-Bass)

Lax, D. A. and Sebenius, J. K. (1986) *The Manager as Negotiator: Bargaining for Cooperation and Competitive Gain* (New York: Free Press)

Lewicki, R. J., Saunders, D. M. and Minton, J. W. (1999) *Negotiation* (Boston: Irwin/McGraw-Hill)

Maslow, A. (1968) *Toward a Psychology of Being* (New York: Wiley)

Minsky, M. (1985) *The Society of Mind* (New York: Simon & Schuster)

Neale, M. A. and Northcraft, G. B. (1986) Experts, amateurs, and refrigerators: comparing expert and amateur negotiators in a novel task, *Organizational Behavior and Human Decision Processes*, **38**, 305–317

Nierenberg, G. I. (1968) *The Art of Negotiating: Psychological Strategies for Gaining Advantageous Bargains* (New York: Hawthorn Books)

Nir, D. (2009) The negotiational self: identifying and transforming negotiation outcomes within the self, unpublished Ph.D. thesis, Hebrew University of Jerusalem

Nir, D. and Kluger, A. N. (2008) The negotiational-self theory: from mayhem and inner conflict to harmony and integration within a dialogical self, paper presented at the 5th International Conference on the Dialogical Self, Cambridge, UK

Pinkley, R. L., Griffith, T. L. and Northcraft, G. B. (1995) 'Fixed pie' à la mode: information availability, information processing, and the negotiation of suboptimal agreements, *Organizational Behavior and Human Decision Processes*, **62**, 101–112

Pruitt, D. G. (1981) *Negotiation Behavior* (New York: Academic Press)

(1983) Strategic choice in negotiation, *American Behavioral Scientist*, **27**, 167–194

Pruitt, D. G. and Carnevale, P. J. (1993) *Negotiation in Social Conflict* (Buckingham: Open University Press)

Pruitt, D. G. and Lewis, S. A. (1975) Development of integrative solutions in bilateral negotiation, *Journal of Personality and Social Psychology*, **31**, 621–633

Pruitt, D. G. and Rubin, J. Z. (1986) *Social Conflict: Escalation, Stalemate, and Settlement* (New York: Random House)

Raiffa, H. (1982) *The Art and Science of Negotiations* (Cambridge, MA: Harvard University Press)

Rogers, C. (1951) *Client-Centered Therapy: Its Current Practice, Implications and Theory* (London: Constable)

Schulz, J. W. and Pruitt, D. G. (1978) The effects of mutual concern on joint welfare, *Journal of Experimental Social Psychology*, **14**, 480–492

Spector, B. I. (1995) Creativity heuristics for impasse resolution: reframing intractable negotiations, *Annals of the American Academy of Political and Social Science*, **542**, 81–99

Thompson, L. L. (1990) An examination of naive and experienced negotiators, *Journal of Personality and Social Psychology*, **59**, 82–90

(1991) Information exchange in negotiation, *Journal of Experimental Social Psychology*, **27**, 161–179

(2001) *The Mind and Heart of the Negotiator*, 2nd edn (Upper Saddle River, NJ: Prentice-Hall)

Thompson, L. L. and De Harpport, T. (1994) Social judgment, feedback, and inter-personal learning in negotiation, *Organizational Behavior and Human Decision Processes*, **58**, 327–345

Thompson, L. L. and Hastie, R. (1990) Judgment tasks and biases in negotiation, in B. H. Sheppard, M. H. Bazerman and R. J. Lewicki (eds.), *Research on Negotiation in Organizations* (Greenwich, CT: JAI Press), vol. II, 31–54

Weingart, L. R., Thompson, L. L., Bazerman, M. H. and Carroll, J. S. (1990) Tactical behavior and negotiation outcomes, *International Journal of Conflict Management*, **1**, 7–31

Westen, D. (1998) The scientific legacy of Sigmund Freud: toward a psychodynamically informed psychological science, *Psychology Bulletin*, **124**, 333–371

Zubek, J. M., Pruitt, D. G., Peirce, R. S., McGillicuddy, N. B. and Syna, H. (1992) Disputant and mediator behaviors affecting short-term success in mediation, *Journal of Conflict Resolution*, **36**, 546–572

Miguel M. Gonçalves and António P. Ribeiro

In dialogical self theory (DST), the way dialogical relations allow innovation and transformation of the previous dialogical patterns is of central importance (Hermans 2004). In this chapter we explore a dialogical process through which innovation is aborted in psychotherapy – a cyclical movement between two opposing voices, one dominant that organizes the client's problematic self-narrative, and one innovative, non-dominant voice. We also discuss two different paths of escaping this cyclical movement. In the first path the innovative voice gains power over the previously dominant one, while in the second path the two opposing voices engage in dialogue, transforming them. These processes will be illustrated with two different cases from psychotherapy. Finally, we analyse the implications of our findings by DST.

Self-narratives and the dialogical self

Self-development is regulated by processes of construction and reconstruction of meanings which occur in the context of narrating oneself to others. Each narrative account has external audiences or, as with stories told silently to oneself, internal audiences (Hermans 2003).

However, constructing a self-narrative, that is, a self-told life story by which the singular events narrated come to be articulated, is not simply a matter of organizing life events as they occur. In fact, it also entails a process of selection and synthesis of life experience (McAdams 1993) since only a small part of the multitude of the person's experiences is incorporated into the self-narrative (White and Epston 1990). This process of self-narrative construction is dialogical, in the sense that a self-narrative, as Hermans and Kempen (1993) have clearly shown, is not the result of an omniscient narrator, but the result of the dynamic interplay between the positions of the self, or *I*-positions, which organize the self at a given moment. These several *I*-positions may then animate inner and outer dialogues, in which several 'voices' can be heard and give meaning to the current experience.

In sum, self-narratives are the outcome of dialogical processes of negotiation, tension, disagreement, alliance and so on, between different voices of the self (Hermans and Hermans-Jansen 1995).

Problematic self-narratives

Self-narrative presents a meaningful framework of understanding life experiences, triggering repetition (Michel and Wortham 2002). This repetition becomes a problem if the self-told life story's content is 'unhelpful, unsatisfying, and dead-ended' and if 'these stories do not sufficiently encapsulate the person's lived experience' (White and Epston 1990: 14); that is, if the self-narrative is too rigid and systematically excludes experiences not congruent with it. Neimeyer *et al.* (2006) refer to this type of problematic self-narratives as dominant narratives, in the sense that there is a restriction in the meanings framed by the self-narrative. In such a case, they lead to applications of general rules (such as self-devaluation in depression) to the daily life context, becoming restrictive of clients' experiences, given that the same theme keeps repeating itself. Dominant self-narratives emerge in the client's dialogue, usually by the emphasis on a main theme, which can be a specific problem or a problematic situation, or even a set of recurrent themes.

As stated by Hermans and Hermans-Jansen, a problematic self-narrative is a 'narrative reduced to a single theme' (1995: 164). Obviously, we do not think that all forms of dominance are problematic. Most of the time, the self is stabilized around a type of dominant narrative, which is flexible enough to allow other narrative accounts subsequently to come to the foreground. By dominant narrative, Neimeyer *et al.* (2006) refer to a kind of dominance that precludes any flexibility to allow other narrative accounts to play a role in a person's life. This is akin to what White and Epston (1990) designate as problem-saturated narrative, in the sense that the problematic story totalizes the self, making other possible narrative accounts invisible. Thus, from now on, we use the term 'dominant narrative', implying this problematic facet, which results from the lack of flexibility and from excessive redundancy.

Dominant self-narratives are characterized by an asymmetrical relationship between the different *I*-positions involved. There is an *I*-position or a coalition of *I*-positions that tries to totalize the interchange (Cooper 2004), insisting on telling the same story over and over again. It is this redundancy that constitutes the problematic nature of the dominant self-narrative, given that other possible *I*-positions, some of them more viable for the current situation, are silenced or rejected.

The result of this type of *I*-position arrangement mirrors an attempt to deny the dialogical nature of existence and communication (Linell and Marková 1993).

The entry way for narrative reconstruction: innovative moments

As Bakhtin (1984/2000) suggested, the attempt to suppress the other (external or internalized) is never totally accomplished (Gonçalves and Guilfoyle 2006; Salgado and Gonçalves 2007; Valsiner 2004). Thus, internal (and external) voices are not inert and refuse to be treated as objects, devoid of agency. They could be silenced but they are still there, and power unbalances may occur that bring these silenced voices from the background to the foreground (Hermans 2004). According to this view, dominant self-narratives can be challenged by the emergence and amplification of 'novel ways of thinking, interacting, and behaving that the client narrates in the therapeutic conversation, which are different from the rule(s) he or she usually applies to his or her life' (Santos and Gonçalves 2009: 493). We consider these exceptions to the dominant self-narrative – which we call *innovative moments (IMs)*[1] – as new emergent meanings that have the latent power to promote change in psychotherapy (Gonçalves *et al.* 2009; Gonçalves *et al.* 2010). Dialogically, IMs are opportunities for new *I*-positions to emerge and tell their own stories, different from the dominant self-narrative, or even for non-dominant *I*-positions to move from the background to the foreground. If these alternative *I*-positions support each other and are amplified in the therapeutic conversation, they may result in the emergence of a network of interconnected *I*-positions which compete with the formerly dominant ones, attenuating their strength, and thereby promoting self-narrative transformation. In therapy, every time these dominated voices are heard, a novelty emerges in the self-system, which we call an IM. An IM is thus an exception to the rule which organizes the dominant self-narrative. As we shall see below, some exceptions are more powerful than others, some may emerge without significant change in the self-system equilibrium, and others disrupt more easily the dominant self-narrative, creating self-development.

Previous research has consistently shown that IMs can be reliably identified, using the *innovative moments coding system (IMCS)* (Gonçalves, Ribeiro, Matos *et al.* in press), and that they occur in psychotherapeutic change in different models of brief therapy (Gonçalves *et al.* 2010). Furthermore, research suggests that there are five different categories of IMs, which correspond to different narrative processes, namely:

1. *Action* IMs are specific behaviours which challenge the dominant self-narrative.
2. *Reflection* IMs are thoughts, feelings, intentions, projects or other cognitive products which challenge the dominant self-narrative.
3. *Protest* IMs entail new behaviours (like action IMs) and/or thoughts (like reflection IMs) which challenge the dominant self-narrative, representing a refusal of its assumptions. This active refusal is the key feature that allows the distinguishing of protest from action and reflection.
4. *Reconceptualization* IMs are the most complex type of innovations. The client not only describes some form of contrast between present and past (e.g. 'Now I've changed X or Y'), but he also understands the processes which allowed this transformation.
5. *Performing change* (previously named as new experiences) IMs are new aims, experiences, activities or projects, anticipated or in action, as a consequence of meaningful changes developed so far.

Thus far, findings from IMs in psychotherapy research have shown that poor and good outcome cases tend to be similar in the beginning of the therapeutic process, both characterized by IMs of action, reflection and protest. In the middle of the treatment, two significant differences start to differentiate good from poor outcome cases. First, action, reflection and protest IMs, which are dominant in the initial phase of therapy, usually increase their presence in good outcome cases and remain stable or even decrease in poor outcome cases. Second, and more important, as we shall see below, reconceptualization and performing change emerge and increase until the end of the treatment in good outcome cases, and are virtually absent in poor outcome ones (Matos *et al.* 2009).

From these studies our research team developed a heuristic model of change (Gonçalves *et al.* 2010) which posits reconceptualization as a central feature of successful psychotherapy. According to this model, action, reflection and protest IMs emerge in the beginning of the therapeutic process, starting the development of novelty emergence. However, the emergence of reconceptualization in the middle and late phases of the therapeutic process is central in developing and sustaining meaningful change. Two main features of reconceptualization are central in this process: it establishes a contrast between the formerly dominant position and the innovative position, and it allows access to how this transformation between the former and the new position occurred. Thus, reconceptualization posits the person as an *author* of the change, given the access to the process through which change is occurring, from a meta-position (Dimaggio *et al.* 2003; Hermans 2003; see also Dimaggio's chapter in this volume). By doing so, reconceptualization also allows us to give coherence to the other, more episodic IMs; namely action, reflection or protest and shaping a new narrative of the self. Performing change IMs, which appear usually after reconceptualization, represent the expansion of the change process into the future.

Our suggestions about the importance of the meta-position involved in reconceptualization IMs are congruent with other dialogical scholars' proposals. For example, Hermans (2003) has suggested that an observer position which manages the repertoire of positions is a necessary condition for successful psychotherapeutic change. This same process has been repeatedly researched by Dimaggio and colleagues (Dimaggio and Lysaker 2010), regarding metacognitive processes in therapy. Metacognition is a set of abilities, involving the capability to understand one's own (and others') emotional and cognitive processes and change them, which are stimulated in the psychotherapeutic process. This research makes it clear that these abilities are lacking or underdeveloped in the most disturbed patients (e.g. personality and psychotic disorders).

IMs, discontinuity and continuity restoration: the centrality of uncertainty

What processes block the path of successful psychotherapy in poor outcome cases? Why do the poor outcome cases fail to follow the pattern of increasing duration of IMs and the development from action, reflection and protest IMs into reconceptualization and performing change, in the middle and late phases of therapy?

Answering these questions involves taking into consideration IMs' potential to generate discontinuity and uncertainty, given that every innovation disrupts the usual, taken-for-granted, meaning-making processes. In fact, as Abbey and Valsiner (2005) suggest, 'all development is inherently based on overcoming uncertainty' (paragraph 14). When a system is disrupted by a significant modification, discontinuity is generated and the system must be rearranged or modified until relative stability is found again (Zittoun 2007). Accordingly, Hermans and Dimaggio have pointed out that although 'uncertainty challenges our potential for innovation and creativity to the utmost', it also 'entails the risks of a defensive and monological closure of the self and the unjustified dominance of some voices over others' (2007: 10).

Thus, sometimes, the emergence of IMs leads the self to strive to restore its sense of continuity, protecting itself from uncertainty, by aborting novelty exploration and returning to the dominant previous self-narrative. In the next section we further discuss this defensive movement facing innovation, which, if persistent during psychotherapeutic treatment, could lead to an unsuccessful outcome.

Mutual in-feeding and problematic self-stability

Each IM can be construed as a microgenetic *bifurcation point* (Valsiner and Sato 2006), in which the client has to resolve uncertainty; that is, the tension between two opposing voices – one expressed in the dominant self-narrative and the other expressed in the emerging IM. The client has to choose the *direction* of meaning construction, which, according to Valsiner (2008), can entail either *semiotic attenuation* or *semiotic amplification*.

Semiotic attenuation refers to the minimization, depreciation or trivialization of a particular innovative way of acting, feeling or thinking; that is, the maintenance of the old patterns. Inversely, semiotic amplification refers to the expansion of a given innovative way of acting, feeling or thinking, creating an opportunity to change and development to occur. This represents, after the emergence of the innovative voice, its permanence in the foreground, rejecting the control of the dominant voice. Looking at the therapeutic change as a developmental process, we argue that this microgenetic process, that is, choosing between IMs attenuation and amplification at each bifurcation point, may influence ontogeny by promoting change or protecting stability. This choice depends on the dialogical relations between the problematic voice(s) and innovative ones at a given moment and on the dialogical encounter with an *other* – the therapist.

Frequently, in poor outcome cases, particularly in the initial and middle phases of good outcome cases, clients tend to resolve the discontinuity created by the emergence of an IM, by attenuating its meaning, making a quick return to the dominant self-narrative. This may result in the disappearance of a particular innovative way of feeling, thinking or acting (Figure 17.1), reinforcing the power of the dominant self-narrative and, thus, promoting self-stability. By doing so, clients temporarily avoid discontinuity, but do not overcome it, as the non-dominant voice continues to be active and, thus, IMs emerge recurrently. Hence, each new IM is a new opportunity for a new attenuation through the return to the dominant self-narrative. In some cases this struggle between the dominant self-narrative and the IMs continues during the entire psychotherapeutic process. We have here two opposing wishes (expressed by two opposing voices): to keep the self stable, avoiding discontinuity and

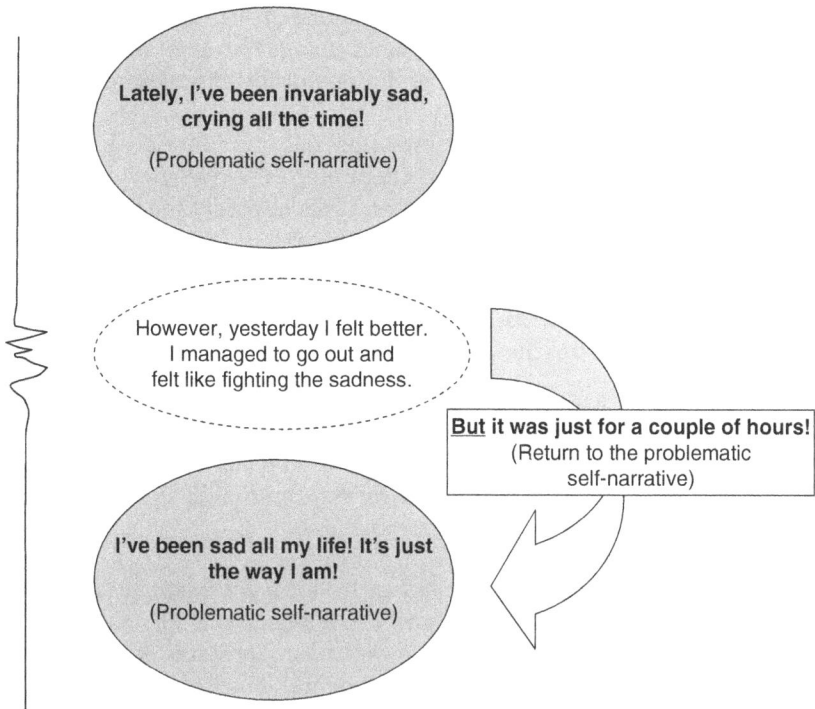

Figure 17.1 Restoring continuity through semiotic attenuation.
Source: Ribeiro and Gonçalves (2010). Adapted with permission.

the uncertainty generated by it, and to change the self, avoiding the suffering which the dominant self-narrative implies. When novelty emerges, the person 'resolves' the problem of discontinuity by returning to the dominant narrative. When the client feels too oppressed by the dominant self-narrative, he or she 'resolves' this problem by trying to produce novelty, but of course this poses the problem of discontinuity once again. Thus, the self is trapped in this cyclical relation, making ambivalence impossible to overcome within this form itself. This mirrors a form of stability within the self, in which two opposite *I*-positions keep feeding each other, dominating the self alternatively, a process which Valsiner (2002) has called 'mutual in-feeding' (see also Gonçalves *et al.* 2009; Gonçalves, Ribeiro, Conde *et al.* 2011).

Mutual in-feeding allows for the maintenance of the person's *status quo*, protecting one's self-identity and sense of integrity or coherence

(Ecker and Hulley 2000; Kelly 1955; Mahoney 1991). People who seek psychotherapeutic help look for personal change but often discover that change creates unpredictability and uncontrollability (Arkovitz and Engle 2007).

In what follows, it is not our intention fully to address why clients 'resist' change, but rather to draw attention to the dialogical processes involved in the maintenance of self-narratives in psychotherapy and the way we have been empirically observing them.

The empirical study of mutual in-feeding: the return-to-the-problem markers

We have proposed a measure of the mutual in-feeding process which grew from our observations of therapy passages in which an IM emerged and is immediately followed by a return to the problematic experience. We called such events a *return-to-the-problem marker (RPM)*. For example:

I don't want to be depressed anymore (reflection IM), *but I just can't* (RPM).

In this example, the client described an IM – *I don't want to be depressed anymore* – and then returned to the problematic voice by saying, *but I can't.* This clause introduced by the word *but* represents opposition or negation towards what is being said and hence constitutes the RPM.

The results obtained in a sample of narrative therapy with women victims of domestic violence showed that IMs were much more likely to be followed by a return to the dominant self-narrative in poor outcome cases than in good outcome cases (Gonçalves, Ribeiro, Conde *et al.* 2011). Even though the cases had similar levels of symptom severity at intake, poor outcome cases showed dramatically higher percentages of IMs containing RPMs. This observation is consistent with the theoretical suggestion that mutual in-feeding between the dominant self-narrative and IMs can interfere with therapeutic progress (Gonçalves *et al.* 2009). Furthermore, we found a lower incidence of RPMs in reconceptualization and performing change IMs than in reflection and protest IMs, and this is congruent with the theoretical assumptions (Gonçalves, Ribeiro, Conde *et al.* 2011), corroborating reconceptualization and performing change as markers of sustained therapeutic change.

Overcoming mutual in-feeding throughout the therapeutic process

Although RPMs as a marker of mutual in-feeding are more characteristic of unsuccessful psychotherapy, they may also offer opportunities for constructive therapeutic work. In fact, when mutual in-feeding is overcome, it could facilitate the change process, given that the struggle between the opposing voices is solved. Therefore, we have initiated a line of intensive qualitative research into how RPMs can turn into therapeutic movement; that is, how the relation between non-dominant voices and dominant voices evolves from mutual in-feeding to another form of dialogical relation. Hitherto, we have identified two possible processes: (1) *Escalation of the non-dominant voice(s) and thereby inhibiting the dominant voice*, and (2) *negotiating and engaging in joint action*. Below, these processes are illustrated in two cases.

Overcoming mutual in-feeding through escalation
of the non-dominant voice(s) and thereby inhibiting
the dominant voice: the case of Susan

Susan (a pseudonym) was a 38-year-old participant in a study of IMs in women victims of intimate violence followed in narrative therapy (Matos *et al.* 2009). In the initial phase of the therapy, Susan often oscillated between two contrasting positions: the dominant voice, which was described as justifying her husband's violent behaviours and even feeling responsible for them, leading her to keep forgiving him (e.g. 'things will change as time goes by') – a *forgiving* voice – and the non-dominant voice, which was described as thoughts and feelings that challenge the forgiving voice; that is, realizing that her husband was responsible for his actions and resisting internal and external pressures to forgive him (e.g. 'I've had enough!') – a *resisting* voice.

The following example illustrates the escalation of the resisting voice and the subsequent inhibition of the forgiving voice, resolving mutual in-feeding.

SUSAN: I see things from another perspective ... I no longer excuse or minimize his violent behaviour ... It's gone [referring to the forgiving voice].

THERAPIST: It's curious ... because there are a lot of people trying to convince you.

SUSAN: The more people try to convince me that I must forgive him, the more I convince myself that things cannot be fixed.

THERAPIST: What helps you resist others' pressures to excuse him?

SUSAN: I realized that things were worse than I ever imagined! ... I used to repress my feelings because I used to believe that if I thought too much about it I would become very depressed and wouldn't be able to take care of my son ... Now, I let things come [reconceptualization IM].

In this example, as a result of realizing that 'things were worse than I ever imagined!', the resisting voice escalates ('I no longer excuse or minimize his violent behaviour') and strives towards regulating the forgiving voice ('I convince myself that things cannot be fixed'), inhibiting its power ('It's gone [referring to the forgiving voice]').

This dialogical process can move towards a monological outcome (see Valsiner 2000 on process versus outcome distinction) since, although the opposing voices are in dialogue, the type of interaction is very asymmetrical. Hermans (1996a, 1996b) has characterized this process as a form of dominance reversal: the position that was once dominant is now dominated. However, in this example, the process does not stop with the reversal of the *I*-positions; there is an escalation of the power of the resisting *voice* and a strong inhibition of the dominated *I*-position, in this case the forgiving *voice*.

One can argue that this process of escalating one voice and inhibition of the other may risk creating another dominant self-narrative, given that once again a dominant *I*-position took over the others. However, we suspect that sometimes meaningful clinical changes occur by this process, as in Susan's case. First, the new dominant voice is more adjusted and congruent with Susan's preferences. Second, the dominance did not occur automatically, but resulted from the client's choice. We proposed that this was mediated by a meta-position over the reversal process, without which a reversal of positions may have been a mere substitution of one problematic pattern for another. Actually, this meta-position is present in the reconceptualization IMs as it was described before.

From our narrative view, and following Sarbin (1986), we suggest that the first form of dominance, which was present in the beginning of therapy in Susan's case, has positioned her as the actor of a narrative which she did not author. In the last form of dominance, Susan was the author of her own plot. We further suggest that the meta-position involved in the dominance reversal is essential to ensure this position of authorship. One important reason is that there is not only one position which dominates and silences others, but also a third one which manages the kind of dominance involved. Instead of two forces opposing each other, we have three positions: the dominant, the non-dominant and the meta-position which manages them. Thus, this new form of dominance is much more flexible than the previous one, and this flexibility is in part ensured by the meta-position (or authorship) involved.

In some cases, this asymmetrical regulation may be a transitory stage in the process of change, facilitating the client's adaptation to the immediate future in a given moment (e.g. a specific decision-making process: to leave or not to leave home, in the case of Susan). For instance, Susan worked towards the inhibition of the forgiving voice, which, according to her, was harmful. Congruently, these moments of monologization, in which a specific voice considered as helpful 'function[s] at a certain moment as an anchorage point around which the entire self-system organizes itself' (Rosa and Gonçalves 2008: 103), may be effective in the reduction of the ambivalence. Thus, this process of voices reversal may be a temporary stage which facilitates other subsequent, meaningful changes. While in the beginning Susan's life was constrained by the forgiving voice, and she was left without any choice about her future (besides continuing to forgive the abuse), now the dominance of the resisting voice allows new *I*-positions to come to the fore. For instance, Susan started to invest in a broader multiplicity of positions ('there are things that I recovered, things that I am doing again and that I will never again give up doing'). Thus, the potentiality for monologization of the self is precluded not only by the meta-position we referred to above, but also by the multiplicity of positions which were stimulated by the inhibition of the problematic voice (the forgiving voice).

Overcoming mutual in-feeding through negotiating and engaging in joint action: the case of Joan

Joan (a pseudonym)[2] was a 42-year-old female participant in a randomized clinical trial comparing process experiential/emotion-focused therapy with client-centred therapy (Greenberg and Watson 1998; see Honos-Webb *et al.* 1999 for the analysis of the assimilation process in this case).

In the beginning of therapy, Joan oscillated between two opposing voices: the dominant voice, which was described as seeking others' approval (e.g. 'I guess I'm scared I'll end up alone') – a *good-girl* voice – and the non-dominant voice, which was described as thoughts and feelings that challenge the good-girl voice (e.g. 'I think deep down I know I'm strong enough that I could survive on my own') – a *rebellious* voice.

The following example illustrates the negotiation between the good-girl and the rebellious voices, resolving mutual in-feeding (a two-chair[3] dialogue between the good-girl voice and the rebellious voice):

JOAN: It's always like I see myself as two split personalities [referring to her two voices] as two altogether different people and. . .

THERAPIST: So, who's sitting there right now? Which one is sitting there?

JOAN: I feel like the stronger part of me [referring to the rebellious voice] now is thinking, go over and come together, and it's overpowering and overpowering the weaker person [referring to the good-girl voice]...

JOAN: I wonder if it's a way to, to be supportive and to lend strength [reflection IM].
THERAPIST: So kind of like ... it just all of a sudden happened?
JOAN: Yes.
THERAPIST: So somehow it's almost like you didn't have to ask her – for what you wanted – and she didn't have to sort of tell you, it's sort of like, she, just kind of came over and you feel stronger.
JOAN: It's, it's just like when I was there [sitting in the good-girl voice's chair] and I was feeling so vulnerable and weak, and then it seemed like these [two voices] coming together as two things ... two people coming together is like, and one and all of a sudden I felt like a lot stronger [reconceptualization IM]...

JOAN: I guess we can confront the issues and talk to T. [husband] about it, it doesn't have to be so scary [reconceptualization IM].

In this example, the rebellious voice helped the good-girl feel stronger and therefore confront the issues that disturb her instead of giving in. The opposing voices appeared to be respectfully communicating with one another ('I wonder if it's a way to, to be supportive') and engaging in joint action ('I guess we can confront the issues and talk to T. [husband] about it').

This IM seemed to act as a *meaning bridge*, allowing both voices to serve as resources (Brinegar *et al.* 2006) – 'coming together as two things ... two people coming together' – thus becoming a source of flexibility in the self's meaning system, in so far as it appeared to enable a conditional dynamic movement between the opposites, rather than a fixation on one of them (J. Valsiner, personal communication, 16 May 2008). This is also akin to the concept of coalition of positions as proposed by Hermans and Hermans-Konopka (2010).

Thus, as reflected in these two cases, one pattern of overcoming mutual in-feeding promotes the escalating of previously silenced voices, and the inhibition of the dominant voice, whereas another pattern opens the space to negotiation between opposing voices, transforming the opposition through mutual regulation. Regardless of their differences in terms of dialogical outcome, both processes involve the development of a meta-position, present in the reconceptualization IM, which is capable of communicating openly and effectively with other positions, and having a function of management and coordination.

Reflecting about these two processes, we may hypothesize that the kind of resolution depends on the type of therapeutic strategies used and the problem the client is facing. Thus, specific strategies or exercises focused on fostering clients' reaction against the problem (e.g. cognitive restructuring in cognitive-behavioural therapy or externalization in narrative therapy) may support the dominance reversal, given the way therapists support a counter-position to the problem. Other strategies more centred on understanding and giving voice to different positions (e.g. two-chair dialogue) may facilitate cooperative dialogue between the positions involved.

Moreover, the case illustrations presented were very different from each other as far as the type of the problem clients were facing is concerned. Susan was coping with a very destructive situation as a victim of her partner's violence. Her situation in comparison with Joan's was much more severe and was clearly a situation of crisis (Roberts 2000). We wonder whether, in situations in which the suffering is very disturbing, as in Susan' case, the inhibition of the maladaptive dominant voice cannot be a necessary starting point to more complex changes. On the other hand, when the suffering is less intense, perhaps stimulating a cooperative dialogue between voices is an important resource to transform the dominant self-narrative.

Implications for DST

In this section we discuss two implications of our work for DST: the dialogical functions of reconceptualization, as a particular form of meta-position, and the way multiplicity in the self produces stability or change.

As the IMs change model suggests, reconceptualization is fundamental in transforming self-narratives. Reconceptualization IMs occurred in the clinical cases presented above, although, as we have also discussed, the paths of change were very different in these two cases. One important ingredient of reconceptualization IMs is the presence of a contrast between a past position and a current one, as well as access to the processes which allow the transformation from one to the other. As stated before, the articulation of the relationship between these two positions is only possible by a third one: a meta-position (see Hermans 2003). Recently, Hermans and Hermans-Konopka (2010) have argued that meta-positions have three main functions: unifying, executive and liberating. The unification refers to the way different *I*-positions are articulated or put in contact by the action of the meta-position. The executive function results from the decision-making processes, in which the meta-position has, at least temporarily, the power to organize the different positions involved. Finally, the liberating function has to do with the ability that the self has to stop habitual or automatic patterns associated with common positions and give priority to new ones, less automatic. In fact, these functions are very clear in reconceptualization: past and present have a temporal integration which gives meaning to the transition (unifying function), the present position is preferred and gets priority (executive function), and former habitual patterns, present in the dominant (problematic) self-narratives, are disrupted and stopped (liberating function).

One interesting phenomenon, from our perspective, is the repetition of reconceptualization in psychotherapy. As we stated before, reconceptualization emerges in successful psychotherapy in the middle of the treatment and increases until the end. In fact, quite often reconceptualization IMs represent the most common form of innovation in psychotherapy, occupying a significant amount of time. We believe that this repetition of different reconceptualization IMs is in fact therapeutic and no significant change would occur without it. Moreover, reconceptualization does not involve a meta-position between two current positions, but rather a meta-position that articulates a past position and an emerging new one. Thus, we propose that a fourth function of a meta-position is present here: a developmental one. That is, through the repetition of the meta-positioning involved in reconceptualization a *dis-identification* with the past *I*-position occurs, concomitantly with a progressive identification with the emerging new *I*-position, transforming the self in the process (Cunha *et al.* in press). This would explain the need of some redundancy of reconceptualization in psychotherapy (and perhaps also in every significant life transformation).

A second implication of our approach to the study of the dialogical self relates to the processes through which multiplicity of the self produces stability or change. This chapter shows that when uncertainty and ambivalence are not overcome throughout the therapeutic process, the dominant *I*-positions (present in the dominant narrative) and alternative ones (present in IMs) may establish a cyclical relation throughout the therapeutic process – a process of mutual in-feeding – blocking the development of the dialogical self. In such a case, 'the self-system is dynamic, but not developmental' (Valsiner 2002: 260).

This alternation between two opposite positions is more monological (at least as an outcome) than dialogical. This relates to a proposal from Hermans and Hermans-Konopka (2010) about the nature of 'good dialogue'. Moreover, from their point of view, the presence of two or more positions (internal and/or external) does not guarantee that dialogue will occur. One of the features of good dialogue is the production of some form of innovation, in which each participant takes the other into consideration and is open to change their own perspective in response to the other. This is exactly what is absent when mutual in-feeding is not resolved. The two positions keep alternating without any resonance to the other's perspective. They are each of them closed inside itself, not responding to the other, but just reacting to the other. That is, in the response, the other position is not integrated, and the original position stays unchanged. Thus, a mere automatic reaction (and not a responsive response) keeps going on, as illustrated above.

We have shown two types of resolutions for these situations: one, in which one position is temporarily blocked, and the other develops, and the other, in which the two positions enter into dialogue. The last resolution is congruent with the notion of 'good dialogue'. Of course, our chapter illustrates that this might not always be possible, and that change may start when the problematic position is blocked. One interesting question that remains for future studies is whether, for solid therapeutic change to occur, 'good dialogue' must be present at some point of the process.

ACKNOWLEDGEMENTS

This chapter was supported by the Portuguese Foundation for Science and Technology (FCT), by Grant PTDC/PSI/72846/2006 (Narrative Processes in Psychotherapy) and by the Ph.D. Grant SFRH/BD/46189/2008. We are very grateful to Leslie S. Greenberg and Lynne Angus for allowing us to analyse the transcripts of Joan's case.

NOTES

1 The concept of IM is a methodological application of the concept of unique outcome proposed by White and Epston (1990) (see Gonçalves et al. 2009 for an explanation about this topic).
2 The original pseudonym of this case was 'Jan'. We changed the pseudonym here to 'Joan' since in several languages Jan is a male name.
3 Two-chair work has its roots in gestalt therapy as described by Perls et al. (1951) and has been adapted and further developed by Greenberg and colleagues (e.g. Greenberg et al. 1993). This therapeutic task involves identifying two discrepant (often conflicting) parts of the self, and putting each one on a separate chair. The client is then coached to speak from each of the parts in turn, thus creating a dialogue between the two parts.

REFERENCES

Abbey, E. and Valsiner, J. (2005) Emergence of meaning through ambivalence [58 paragraphs], *Forum Qualitative Sozialforschung/Forum: Qualitative Social Research*, 6(1), Art. 23. Retrieved from http://nbn-resolving.de/urn:nbn: de:0114-fqs0501231

Arkovitz, H. and Engle, D. (2007) Understanding and working with resistant ambivalence in psychotherapy, in S. G. Hofmann and J. Weinberg (eds.), *The Art and Science of Psychotherapy* (New York: Routledge), 171–190

Bakhtin, M. (1984/2000) *Problems of Dostoevsky's Poetics* (Minneapolis, MN: University of Minnesota Press)

Brinegar, M. G., Salvi, L. M., Stiles, W. B. and Greenberg, L. S. (2006) Building a meaning bridge: therapeutic progress from problem formulation to understanding, *Journal of Counselling Psychology*, 53, 165–180

Cooper, M. (2004) Encountering self-otherness: 'I–I' and 'I–Me' modes of self relating, in H. J. M. Hermans and G. Dimaggio (eds.), *The Dialogical Self in Psychotherapy* (New York: Brunner-Routledge), 60–73

Cunha, C., Gonçalves, M., Ribeiro, A. P., Mendes, I. and Valsiner, J. (in press) Rehearsing renewal of identity: re-conceptualization on the move, in M. C. Bertau, M. Gonçalves and P. Raggatt (eds.), *Dialogic Formations: Investigations into the Origins and Development of the Dialogical Self*. (Charlotte, NC: Information Age Publishing)

Dimaggio, G. and Lysaker, P. (eds.) (2010) *Metacognition and Severe Adult Mental Disorders: From Basic Research to Treatment* (London: Routledge)

Dimaggio, G., Salvatore, G., Azzara, C. and Catania, D. (2003) Rewriting self-narratives: the therapeutic process, *Journal of Constructivist Psychology*, 16, 155–181

Ecker, B. and Hulley, L. (2000) The order in clinical disorders: symptom coherence in depth-oriented brief therapy, in R. A. Neimeyer and J. D. Raskin (eds.), *Construction of Disorder: Meaning-Making Frameworks for Psychotherapy* (Washington, DC: American Psychological Association), 63–89

Gonçalves, M. and Guilfoyle, M. (2006) Dialogism and psychotherapy: therapists' and clients' beliefs supporting monologism, *Journal of Constructivist Psychology*, 19, 251–271.

Gonçalves, M., Matos, M. and Santos, A. (2009) Narrative therapy and the nature of 'innovative moments' in the construction of change, *Journal of Constructivist Psychology*, 22, 1–23

Gonçalves, M., Ribeiro, A., Conde, T., Matos, M., Martins, C., Santos, A., *et al.* (2011) The role of mutual in-feeding in maintaining problematic self-narratives: exploring one path to therapeutic failure, *Psychotherapy Research*, 21, 27–40.

Gonçalves, M., Ribeiro, A., Matos, M., Santos, A. and Mendes, I. (in press) The innovative moments coding system: a coding procedure for tracking changes in psychotherapy, in S. Salvatore, J. Valsiner, S. Strout and J. Clegg (eds.), *YIS: Yearbook of Idiographic Science*, vol. 2 (Rome: Firera Publishing Group)

Gonçalves, M., Santos, A., Salgado, J., Matos, M., Mendes, I., Ribeiro, A., *et al.* (2010) Innovations in psychotherapy: tracking the narrative construction of change, in J. D. Raskin, S. K. Bridges and R. Neimeyer (eds.), *Studies in Meaning 4: Constructivist Perspectives on Theory, Practice, and Social Justice* (New York: Pace University Press), 29–64

Greenberg, L. S., Rice, L. N. and Elliott, R. (1993) *Facilitating Emotional Change: The Moment-by-Moment Process* (New York: Guilford)

Greenberg, L. S. and Watson, J. (1998) Experiential therapy of depression: differential effects of client-centred relationship conditions and process interventions, *Psychotherapy Research*, **8**, 210–224

Hermans, H. J. M. (1996a) Opposites in a dialogical self: constructs as characters, *Journal of Constructivist Psychology*, **9**, 1–26

(1996b) Voicing the self: from information processing to dialogical interchange, *Psychological Bulletin*, **119**, 31–50

(2003) The construction and reconstruction of a dialogical self, *Journal of Constructivist Psychology*, **16**, 89–130

(2004) The dialogical self: between exchange and power, in H. J. M. Hermans and G. Dimaggio (eds.), *The Dialogical Self in Psychotherapy* (New York: Brunner-Routledge), 13–28

Hermans, H. J. M. and Dimaggio, G. (2007) Self, identity, and globalization in times of uncertainty: a dialogical analysis, *Review of General Psychology*, **11**, 31–61

Hermans, H. J. M. and Hermans-Jansen, E. (1995) *Self-Narratives: The Construction of Meaning in Psychotherapy* (New York: Guilford)

Hermans, H. J. M. and Hermans-Konopka, A. (2010) *Dialogical Self Theory: Positioning and Counter-Positioning in a Globalizing Society* (Cambridge University Press)

Hermans, H. J. M. and Kempen, H. J. G. (1993) *The Dialogical Self: Meaning as Movement* (San Diego, CA: Academic Press)

Honos-Webb, L., Surko, M., Stiles, W. B. and Greenberg, L. S. (1999) Assimilation of voices in psychotherapy: the case of Jan, *Journal of Counselling Psychology*, **46**, 448–460

Kelly, G. A. (1995) *The Psychology of Personal Constructs* (New York: Norton)

Linell, P. and Marková, I. (1993) Acts in discourse: from monological speech acts to dialogical inter-acts, *Journal for the Theory of Social Behaviour*, **23**, 173–195

Mahoney, M. (1991) *Human Change Processes: The Scientific Foundations of Psychotherapy* (New York: Basic Books)

Matos, M., Santos, A., Gonçalves, M. and Martins, C. (2009) Innovative moments and change in narrative therapy, *Psychotherapy Research*, **19**, 68–80

McAdams, D. P. (1993) *The Stories We Live By: Personal Myths and the Making of the Self* (New York: William Morrow)

Michel, A. and Wortham, S. (2002) Clearing away the self, *Theory & Psychology*, **12**, 625–650

Neimeyer, R., Herrero, O. and Botella, L. (2006) Chaos to coherence: psychotherapeutic integration of traumatic loss, *Journal of Constructivist Psychology*, **19**, 127–145

Perls, F., Hefferline, R. and Goodman, P. (1951) *Gestalt Therapy* (New York: Julian Press)

Ribeiro, A. and Gonçalves, M. (2010) Innovation and stability within the dialogical self: the centrality of ambivalence, *Culture and Psychology*, **16**, 116–126

Roberts, A. (2000) *Crisis Intervention Handbook* (Oxford University Press)

Rosa, C. and Gonçalves, M. (2008) Dialogical self and close relationships: looking for ambivalences, *Studia Psychologica*, **8**, 89–108

Salgado, J. and Gonçalves, M. (2007) The dialogical self: social, personal, and (un)conscious, in J. Valsiner and A. Rosa (eds.), *The Cambridge Handbook of Sociocultural Psychology* (Cambridge University Press), 608–621

Santos, A. and Gonçalves, M. (2009) Innovative moments and change processes in psychotherapy: an exercise in new methodology, in J. Valsiner, P. C. M. Molenaar, M. C. D. P. Lyra and N. Chaudhary (eds.), *Dynamic Process Methodology in the Social and Developmental Sciences* (New York: Springer), 493–526

Sarbin, T. R. (1986) The narrative and the root metaphor for psychology, in T. R. Sarbin (ed.), *Narrative Psychology: The Storied Nature of Human Conduct* (New York: Praeger), 3–21

Valsiner, J. (2000) *Culture and Human Development: An Introduction* (London: Sage)

(2002) Forms of dialogical relations and semiotic autoregulation within the self, *Theory & Psychology*, **12**, 251–265

(2004) Temporal integration of structures within dialogical self, keynote lecture at the 3rd International Conference on the Dialogical Self, Warsaw

(2008) Constraining one's self within the fluid social worlds, paper presented at the 20th Biennial ISSBD meeting, Würzburg

Valsiner, J. and Sato, T. (2006) Historically structured sampling (HSS): how can psychology's methodology become tuned into the reality of the historical nature of cultural psychology?, in J. Straub, C. Kölbl, D. Weidemann and B. Zielke (eds.), *Pursuit of Meaning: Theoretical and Methodological Advances in Cultural and Cross-Cultural Psychology* (Bielefeld: Verlag für Kommunikation, Kultur und Soziale Praxis), 215–251

White, M. and Epston, D. (1990) *Narrative Means to Therapeutic Ends* (New York: Norton)

Zittoun, T. (2007) Dynamics of interiority: ruptures and transitions in self-development, in L. M. Simão and J. Valsiner (eds.), *Otherness in Question: Labyrinths of the Self* (Charlotte, NC: Information Age Publishing), 187–214

18 Methodological approaches to studying the self in its social context

Carol A. Jasper, Helen R. Moore, Lisa S. Whittaker and Alex Gillespie

'The literature in the dialogical self field,' Hermans (2008: 186) writes, 'shows more theoretical advances than methodological and empirical elaborations.' The idea, that the self is dialogical in its nature and origin, clearly fits with theoretical ideas not only within psychology, but also within literary studies, anthropology, sociology and clinical fields. But what methodologies are most suitable for guiding research? Research to date has been interdisciplinary, and, accordingly, a wide range of methodologies have been used. In the literature one can find experiments (Hermans 1999; Stemplewska-Żakowicz *et al.* 2006), self-report questionnaires (Rowiński 2008), the self-confrontation method (Hermans and Hermans-Jansen 1995), anthropological data (Gieser 2008), interview data (Aveling and Gillespie 2008) and close textual analysis of biographical material (Barresi 2008; Gillespie 2005). Our aim, in the present chapter, is to discuss some of the main methods for studying the dialogical self and, elaborating on that, to introduce an additional methodology that is of a more interpersonal nature than most of the existing methods. As we will argue, such an additional methodology is needed in the light of the mutual complementing nature of intra- and interpersonal dialogues in dialogical self theory (DST).

The first section of the present chapter will sketch some benefits of the existing methodologies and argue that, at present, the available methodologies are not designed to investigate the dialogical self as socially situated. Existing methodologies enable us to examine the voices within the dialogical self, but not the relation between intrapsychological voices within the self and the interpersonal and socially situated perspectives of significant others within social relations. The second section will introduce the interpersonal perception method (Laing *et al.* 1966) as a methodology that will enhance the ability of the researcher to examine systematically the socially situated self. In brief, this methodology enables us to examine not only the voices within the self but also the voices outside the self, and specifically the relation between these intrapersonal and interpersonal domains. We conclude with a discussion of how this methodology might be best adapted for studying the dialogical self.

Methods for studying the dialogical self

DST possesses high face validity and connects with personal experience of an internal dialogue and the tensions of indecision. It is, for many, an everyday experience that the perspectives of significant others are woven into private thought. Yet more than intuitive appeal is needed if we are to advance the theory and produce further insights (Hermans 2008). We argue that a methodology is needed which will enable an analysis of the relation between the social and the psychological, to examine how perspectives within the social world become perspectives within the dialogical self.

More methodological approaches have been suggested for studying the dialogical self than we can review (see Hermans 2008). We will focus our review on three distinctive approaches – namely, the self-confrontation method, the personal-position repertoire and the use of bi-plots to map internal and external *I*-positions – and a brief discussion of the experimental paradigm (Stemplewska-Żakowicz *et al.* 2006). The purpose of this review is to illustrate the benefits of these methodologies in enabling us to address particular questions but also to highlight that existing methodologies do not enable us to examine the relation between the voices within the dialogical self and the actual perspectives of significant others in the social environment.

Self-confrontation method

The self-confrontation method (Hermans and Hermans-Jansen 1995) addresses the process of personal meaning construction as individuals self-reflect and organize historical events and emotionally salient experiences into consistent and intelligible narrative structures (Lyddon *et al.* 2006). Clients are encouraged to orient to past and future selves through seven open stimulus questions. There are two questions about the past, two about the present and three concerning the future. The questions are unstructured and direct the client to consider unspecified focal events. For example, 'Was there something in your past that has been of major importance or significance for your life and which still plays an important part today?' (Hermans *et al.* 1990: 158). Clients evaluate their own responses to create valuations and consider the emotional component of these valuations. In practice, open-ended questions allow the participants to self-reflect upon their life in a temporal context and dialogically interact with significant others in addition to past and future selves. Self-confrontation with their valuations leads to understanding and personal meaning construction by providing clients with an overview of the boundaries of their self, taking the perspective of significant others, such as parents, siblings and employers, in dialogical exchange. Hermans describes this as a 'helicopter view' (Hermans and Hermans-Jansen 1995: 159).

An example of the self-confrontation method can be found in a study by Puchalska-Wasyl *et al.* (2008). Role-play was used to explore the impact of taking the perspective of a hero upon participants' self-narratives. A self-confrontation was established over three research sessions. In the first session both the participants and their heroes answered seven questions, with both the participant and the hero using imaginative positioning to construct life narratives. Subsequently, valuations were generated and rated with regard to emotional climate across 24 affective terms, such as joy, pride and worry. The second session focused upon the patterns of connections between the *I*-position of the participant and the alternative hero *I*-position. In the third research session, two to three months later, the participant was confronted with the valuations from the first session and could accept, reject, modify or create new valuations. Twenty out of thirty participants experienced a changed life narrative by using imaginative positioning to take the perspective of the hero in the second research phase. The researchers argue that the meaning making of participants was affected by taking the perspective of the hero. Specifically, the dialogical exchange between the two *I*-positions resulted in a self-confrontation which subsequently led to narrative innovation.

In a similar vein to Puchalska-Wasyl *et al.* (2008), Stemplewska-Żakowicz *et al.* (2006) also considered self-narrative construction. In an experimental paradigm, participants were asked to construct a self-narrative from implicit and explicit positions: imagining the face of the significant other, verbal description of the other and addressing an imagined other. The authors acknowledge that DST needs to move beyond internal and imagined positioning. In their introduction the authors state that explicit positioning involves 'addressing the subject's self-narrative directly to a significant other' (Stemplewska-Żakowicz *et al.* 2006: 75). While we value the inclusion of explicit positioning, addressing the actual other, we contend that this is not realized in their experimental procedure, as the method still relies upon the invocation of the imagined other.

A unifying strength of both the self-confrontation method and the experimental procedure used by Stemplewska-Żakowicz *et al.* (2006) is the creation of dialogical moments of transformation, thus enabling examination, of not just the voices within the self but also how they clash and the resultant dialogue which can produce change within the self. In the role-play example, the influence of heroes' positions had a far-reaching impact on the meaning-making systems of players. Confrontation with the hero is associated with positive experiences linked with autonomy and success (Puchalska-Wasyl *et al.* 2008). The self-enhancing outcome of such confrontation makes this a method with excellent applications in a therapeutic setting. The self-confrontation method is temporal; it focuses on change, and can be subtle enough to further psychological change within a therapeutic context.

A limitation of the self-confrontation method is that it does not relate voices, or *I*-positions, within the dialogical self to the perspectives of significant others within the social world. Of course, in the case of the method used by Puchalska-Wasyl *et al.* (2008), not all heroes exist in reality but real significant others are a key aspect of the dialogical self. As Hermans (2008) notes, social interaction is at the core of the dialogical conception of self. Yet, actual interactions with others are not explored, and therefore an extension of the method could move beyond the realm of imagined others and target the relations between interlocutors in their shared social experience.

Personal-position repertoire

The personal-position repertoire method (Hermans 2001) is a method for disentangling the myriad of *I*-positions within the self (and as such has a similar aim to the methodology proposed by Raggatt 2000). It introduces the innovation of distinguishing between internal and external *I*-positions. The self is composed of internal *I*-positions (e.g. *I*-as-mother, or *I*-as-academic-writing-a-chapter) and extends to positions which relate to others, external *I*-positions (e.g. the *I*-position of my children or the *I*-position of potential readers of this chapter). In the case study of Nancy, Hermans (2001) charts her repertoire of *I*-positions, both internal and external, for illustration. The relationships from internal *I*-positions to external *I*-positions extend beyond the realm of the individual, interact with the social environment and are reflected back into the self. The internal position '*I*-as-mother' can only exist in relation to the external position of child. *I*-positions can be inclusive of past, previous and future selves together with the organization of each perspective in terms of significance and priority. The young child going to school, for example, is suddenly confronted with a number of new *I*-positions. The introduction to a teacher creates a new and significant external *I*-position which relates to the new *I*-as-pupil internal position. The young child must rapidly reorganize and reposition herself to manage new *I*-positions and to relinquish the priority given to previous positions such as *I*-as-nursery child (Hermans 2001). The personal position repertoire allows exploration of the movement between *I*-positions, specifically with regard to problem solving, a concern originating in the observations of Mead (1913), who noted that problems could cause conflict and restructuring within the self, leading to perspective transcendence. Accordingly, it is expected that through tension and movement between internal and external *I*-positions, change within the self becomes possible (Hermans 2001, 2003).

The strength of the personal-position repertoire is the ability to chart the organization and flux of internal and external *I*-position changes within the self (Gonçalves and Salgado 2001; Hermans 2001, 2003). The grouping of *I*-positions, constructed around social positions, allows the researcher to develop matrices of the individual *I*-positions which are associated with particular social selves (Hermans 2001). The attribution of values and significance to specific positions, and the changes to these values during therapy, allow the therapist to chart progress and assist clients to reorganize their *I*-positions, attributing lower significance and value to those positions which generate tension (Hermans 2001, 2003). The methodology may be best applied therapeutically where dialogical manipulations involving significant others-in-the-self may be used to explore difficult personal circumstances.

The internal processes of any individual are private, and although the personal-position repertoire invites the introduction of imagined significant others and maps both internal and external *I*-positions thoroughly, the external *I*-position remains unconnected to the views of actual significant others. The method limits itself to studying intra-psychological dialogical thinking and not interpersonal dialogue, offering the potential to develop a methodology which relates the intra-psychological to the interpersonal.

Mapping the dialogical self: bi-plots

The bi-plot method provides a novel approach to the analysis of data resulting from the personal-position repertoire (Hermans 2001). Kluger *et al.* (2008) use a bi-cluster analysis to create a graphic map charting the range of internal and external *I*-positions evident in the case study of Nancy (Hermans 2001), mentioned in the previous section. Unrotated principal-components analysis was carried out for the data to create a scatter plot displaying visually the full spatial arrangement of internal and external *I*-positions, thus providing a 'global map of the internal theatre' (Kluger *et al.* 2008: 228). The bi-plot method reveals the patterns between *I*-positions. Each pair of points is plotted to incorporate the patterns of connectedness with all alternative points. For example, two points may be highly correlated with each other but will be located apart on the plot if they have differing patterns of connections with other positions (Kluger *et al.* 2008).

In her original personal-position repertoire matrix, Nancy selected 19 external positions and 33 internal positions of relevance (Hermans 2001) which were charted on the scatter plot. Kluger *et al.* (2008) propose that exploration of points close together on the plot can be illuminating, as these indicate important connections between positions. For example, in Nancy's plot, the external position of Nancy's 'employer' is closest to the internal position of Nancy as 'sacrificing' and closest to the external position of Nancy's 'father'. This suggests that the role of father and employer share commonalities for Nancy and evoke feelings of sacrifice. Kluger *et al.* (2008) also examine visually apparent clusters of related positions within Nancy's scatter plot. One cluster of related points contains the external position of Nancy's ex-partner and the internal positions of Nancy as 'aggressive', 'materialist' and 'demanding'. Engaging in dialogical activity with the ex-partner for Nancy will bring to the fore these internal positions, which may well have negative connotations. Exploration with the therapist of what these connections signify may provide insight and heightened self-knowledge.

The strength of bi-plots is that they go beyond the comparison within internal and within external *I*-positions in dyadic relations and instead enable the simultaneous examination of the whole range of positions. Thus, not only the relations within internal and external positions, but also, importantly, the relations *between* these positions can be seen on one plot. This allows for analysis of the global organization of dialogical relations elicited by the personal-position repertoire (Hermans 2001) and allows us to address the question of how all *I*-positions within the dialogical self fit together. The method also has significant benefits within therapeutic settings. The graphical representation of the plot is clear and easily intelligible and thus may assist in drawing the client into the process of joint sense-making alongside the therapist.

The bi-plot method successfully extends analysis of the personal position repertoire to incorporate concurrent analysis of both the internal and external *I*-positions elicited. However, as illustrated in the example, Nancy's external *I*-positions are related to the views of significant others as constructed by Nancy herself. The external positions in the plot do not relate to the actual viewpoint of significant others. As a result, the analysis still allows one to address intra-psychological dialogical relations only and does not extend to the exploration of inter-psychological relations and the impact of interactions with actual significant others in a socially pertinent context.

Summary: relating the self to society

'By placing internal psychological processes in the broader context of external social and societal process', Hermans and Hermans-Konopka (2008: 5) maintain that the concept of the dialogical self provides a link 'between self and society'. Indeed, the very term 'dialogical self' is meant to relate the external (dialogue) to the internal (self) (Hermans and Hermans-Konopka 2010: 1). While we agree that at a theoretical level the concept of the dialogical self does provide a link between the internal and the external, we suggest that available methodologies provide only limited means with which to study this link. In the three methodologies reviewed above, we can see an increasing concern with 'the-other-within-the-self' (Hermans 2008: 186), specifically, with the relation between internal and external *I*-positions within the self. However, each of these methodologies still takes the individual self as the unit of analysis. These methodologies study society within the self, but not the self within society or within social relations.

Focusing on the relation between the dialogical self and the social context opens up several important questions: What is the relation between external *I*-positions within the self and the actual perspectives of others? How do the voices in society become voices within the self? What are the processes of transformation? And how are the voices 'out there' woven into the construction of the self? These questions relate to one specific aspect of the concept of the dialogical self, namely the relation between the self and society. In the next section we introduce a methodology from the field of interpersonal perception which we suggest can be adapted to address these questions.

Interpersonal perception method (IPM)

Dialogical theory assumes that the voices within the self are internalizations of voices in society and dialogical responses to them. For example, when preparing for a job interview, we often rehearse the conversation we think we will have, taking the perspective of the interviewer. The extent to which an individual can take the perspective of the other is crucial for effective communication (Rommetveit 1974), and yet there is little access to this information contained, as it is, in silent, internal thoughts (Gillespie and Zittoun 2010). It is commonly assumed that our knowledge of others' perspectives is accurate. Indeed, research findings show that we have an accurate generalized view of what most people think of us (Kenny and DePaulo 1993; Norman 1969). However, other research reveals that the relation between what people think other people think and what those other people actually think is often quite weak (Cast *et al.* 1999; Shrauger and Schoeneman 1979). Moreover, therapeutic practice has shown that often it is the mismatch between perspectives within selves and between selves that is the basis of many problems. For example, mistaking their own vulnerability for hostility from others can cause difficulties in interpersonal relationships, resulting in psychological distress and ultimately in a 'destructive interpersonal cycle' (Cooper 2009: 89).

The interpersonal perception method (IPM) (Laing, Phillipson and Lee 1966) examines the relation between what people think other people think and what those other people actually think. The IPM is elaborate and enables the identification of many types of intersubjective relationships (Gillespie and Cornish 2010). However, it is used not only to assess the accuracy of perspective taking but also to identify relational patterns, misunderstandings and the origin of projected perspectives (e.g. Gillespie *et al.* 2010).

Describing the method

The IPM is a comparative, self-report, questionnaire methodology first developed by Laing, Phillipson and Lee (1966) as a useful measurement instrument in marriage and family counselling (White 1982). The original IPM questionnaire comprises 60 issues, grouped into six categories. Around each of these 60 issues, 12 questions require to be answered, giving a total of 720 questions.

The IPM assumes a theoretical framework in which the intersubjective relations between people are characterized by three levels, namely (1) direct perspectives, (2) meta-perspectives and (3) meta-meta-perspectives. The term 'meta-perspective' refers to what each member of the dyad thinks the other member thinks. Accordingly, the term 'meta-perspective' has a different meaning from the concept of meta-position used by Hermans and Hermans-Konopka (2010), who propose that the term should refer to the process of the *I* engaging in the act of self-reflection about a number of positions, and their patterning and origin. Laing *et al.* (1966) explain their concepts with reference to a married couple. Both members of the dyad are asked about their own view (direct perspective), their estimation of the view of the other (meta-perspective), and their estimation of how the other views them (meta-meta-perspective) (for a comparable view, see Verhofstadt-Denève's chapter in this book).

A unique feature of the IPM is that it takes dyadic relations as the unit of analysis. Most methods in psychological research, including research on the dialogical self, take the (multivoiced) individual as the unit of analysis. The IPM starts by looking at both sides of a relationship, thus enabling several comparisons to be made. Specifically, comparisons can be made *between* the perspectives of a dyad or group(s) and also *within* each member of the dyad or within each group, thus revealing the actual and perceived convergences and divergences of perspective.

Comparisons between individuals or groups reveal several key insights including the existence of agreements/disagreements and understandings/misunderstandings and, crucially, whether there is any realization of misunderstandings between each individual or group. Agreement occurs when two individuals or groups have similar direct perspectives. By contrast, disagreements arise when their direct perspectives differ, but they are each aware of this. Misunderstandings arise when direct perspectives differ, but there is no awareness of this. The underlying argument is that disagreements and divergences in perspectives occur, but it is misunderstanding and the feeling of being misunderstood that can cause problems within relationships (Sillars *et al.* 2005).

Comparisons within each member of the dyadic relation reveal perceived intersubjective relations. Perceived agreement occurs when there is alignment between what one person thinks and what they think the other person thinks. Feeling understood entails an alignment between what one person thinks and what they think the other person thinks they think. Comparisons within each individual or group reveal perceived agreement/disagreement, feeling understood/misunderstood and perceived understanding/misunderstanding (for comparable sequences, see Ho's chapter in the present book).

The IPM is a systematic self-report methodology for analysing interpersonal perception within dyadic relations. It is suited to studying dialogicality because it is based on the assumption that people have multiple perspectives, and are able to think about themselves or some issue from both their own perspective and the perspective of others. It shares this assumption with the self-confrontation method. However, it is distinctive as a methodology for studying the dialogical self because not only does it analyse the perspectives within an individual or group but it compares these to the actual perspectives of significant others.

Many authors have discussed interpersonal perception (for example, see Cook 1971; Hinton 1993; Jones 1990), but the focus has tended to be on questions of accuracy (for example, Funder 1980; Kenny and DePaulo 1993) rather than the role of interpersonal perception in constructing the self. Towards the end of his book, Jones (1990: 201) turns his attention to getting to know ourselves and states that 'self-knowledge can be a direct consequence of perceptions of others in our presence ... it is obvious we can learn about ourselves by learning how others respond to us in the interaction sequence'. This 'obvious' fact had been highlighted previously by Laing *et al.*, who stated, 'self-identity is a synthesis of my looking at me with my view of others' view of me' (1966: 5). The IPM enables us to analyse how this synthesis of views occurs.

Finally the IPM is also a flexible methodology. It is possible to take the original IPM questionnaire and adapt it to address the relevant issues within any given interaction, such as those between an individual, dyad or family (White 1982). The IPM is amenable to a variety of research questions. Because it is questionnaire-based, it can yield a large quantity of data with relatively little effort compared to other methods such as qualitative interviews.

Example: young people and employers

Whittaker (2010) adapted the IPM in order to compare the perspectives of employers and unemployed adolescents seeking work. Young job seekers often become frustrated and disheartened after several failed attempts to gain employment. Each failed attempt adds a negative voice into their dialogical selves. In order to understand the dialogical selves of young people in their social context, Whittaker used IPM to analyse not only their views but also the views of potential employers. On the basis of interviews and discussions, Whittaker developed a questionnaire with nineteen statements focusing upon employment. Both employers and young people answered the questionnaire from their own perspective, the perspective of the other, and what they thought the other would think they thought.

Several interesting misunderstandings emerged. For example, employers thought that qualifications are not important, but young people thought that employers place a great importance on qualifications. Employers place most emphasis on what a prospective employee can do, but the education system continues to emphasize academic achievements above other skills. This misunderstanding is unfortunate because within the dialogical selves of underachieving young people, the lack of good grades can be a source of feelings of stigmatization and failure.

Using the IPM to connect the *I*-positions within these young people (*I*-as-seen-by-employers) with what potential employers actually think makes both theoretical and practical contributions. At a theoretical level it shows us that the view of employers which these young people have 'internalized' does not originate in the perspective of the employers. Instead it might originate in the academic institutions in which these young people have lived most of their lives and which tend to over-emphasize grades. At a practical level, the IPM provides an avenue for intervention, namely bolstering the identity of these young people by correcting their misunderstanding of the perspective of employers.

The use of the IPM, in this context, reveals the intra-psychological dynamics, namely the feeling of failure associated with having low grades and thinking that other people value grades. But the IPM goes beyond intra-psychological dynamics, to reveal interpersonal and intergroup dynamics. It shows us that this general view of young people does not originate in the views of employers and is not as supportive of their identity as the real views of employees. Thus the IPM augments the intra-psychological analysis by situating the self socially and also, in this case, suggesting interventions which might benefit these young people.

Beyond self-report

Research on the dialogical self has focused upon intra-psychological relationships between *I*-positions. The IPM was not developed to examine the dialogical self; rather, it was developed to examine interpersonal relationships. We have suggested that the IPM can be adapted to contribute to the aim of 'placing internal psychological processes in the broader context of external social and societal process' (Hermans and Hermans-Konopka 2008: 5).

The IPM, however, is also a limited methodology. It is based upon self-report (people's responses to questionnaires are limited by their own self-insight). But this limitation is not unique to the IPM. The questions asked in the self-confrontation method and personal-position repertoire and analysed in the bi-plot method also depend upon self-report. But, to what extent can people self-report *I*-positions? Gillespie and Cornish (2010) argue that *I*-positions are not transparent to speakers, and they often need interpretation. To base our analyses on the self-reports of participants would be to limit severely our window on the self, and possibly risk reproducing common-sense notions of selfhood. Researchers need to be independent observers of the dialogical self and accordingly should not limit themselves to self-report methodologies.

The limitation of respondent's self-report is most evident when answering questions about meta-meta-perspectives. In Whittaker's (2010) study, the majority of participants struggled to comprehend questions about what they thought the other thought they thought. But, such difficulty does not mean that meta-meta-perspectives are not important in the data. On the contrary, they are often observable in everyday interactions. For example, one employer in Whittaker's study who struggled to answer the meta-meta-perspective questions was able to say fluently, when talking about a young person who had not been committed to work, 'I thought, they actually think that they're doing me a favour coming here.' Within this utterance there is a meta-meta-perspective: the speaker thinks that the young person thinks that they are doing her a favour by coming to work. Yet, while such an utterance can often be found in everyday conversation, it does not follow that the employer discussed previously would be able to identify or elucidate upon the meta-meta-perspective which she articulates fluently.

Moreover, it is not just at the levels of meta-perspective and meta-meta-perspective that self-report methods are problematic. Gieser (2008: 50) has pointed out that the embodied aspects of the dialogical self have been neglected. The tendency has been to study, usually by interview or self-report methods, the *I*-positions within the individual at a cognitive, or self-reflective, level. But what about *I*-positions which are implicit and manifest only in embodied action? For Mead and James, the *I* is an embodied precondition of self-reflection not necessarily aware of itself: it is the knower, not the known. Too much reliance upon self-report is likely to overlook the importance of the pre-reflective and reactive nature of many *I*-positions (see Lewis 2002, for the relevance of pre-linguistic forms of positioning in the dialogical self).

One potential way to avoid the limitations of self-report in research on the dialogical self is to adapt the IPM into a framework for analysing naturalistic discourse and action. Gillespie and Cornish (2010) have argued that Laing *et al.* (1966) developed a powerful framework but that the operationalization in self-report was limited. Taking a Bakhtinian approach to the study of language (Aveling and Gillespie 2008; Wertsch 1991), they show how the framework of direct, meta- and meta-meta-perspectives can be used as a coding frame to systematize dialogical analyses of discursive or observational data. Actions and utterances are coded in terms of what they reveal about the speaker or actors' direct perspective and what they implicitly assume and explicitly state about the perspectives of others. As with the standard IPM, such a coding frame should be used on data relating to both sides of a dyadic inter-action in order to enable the aforementioned comparisons.

There are two advantages to using Laing, Phillipson and Lee's (1966) framework as a coding frame for naturalistic data. First, because the data do not rely on self-report, it is possible to identify implicit *I*-positions (which speakers themselves might not be able to articulate or be aware of, in response to a questionnaire). Second, using the IPM as a coding frame still yields the main benefit of the IPM questionnaire; namely, it allows researchers to understand the dialogical self in its social context, provided, of course, that two or more people/groups in relation are studied. The main limitation with using the IPM framework as a coding frame, in contrast to a self-report questionnaire, is that it is much more time-consuming as it requires interpretation and coding of individual utterances.

Conclusion

Understanding the self as fundamentally dialogical entails research, not only on dialogues within the self but also on the social dialogues in which the self is embedded. It is an ambitious aim to develop a concept that is so explicitly positioned as a bridge between the self and society. The project requires a broad range of methodological tools. In the present chapter we have sought to review some of the most prominent methods for studying the dialogical self, and we have argued that existing methodologies do not explicitly study the self as viewed by other people, nor, consequently, how these views relate to the self's own views. Research has focused on the other within the self, but has not sought to relate this to the other outside the self.

We have introduced the IPM into the discussion of the dialogical self in order to make available a tool for self-report survey research which aims to situate the self within social relations. This methodology does not replace existing methodologies, but rather provides a complement. It enables researchers to address a specific question concerning the relation between the dialogical self and the social context. However, we have not advocated the IPM without reservation. We have argued that the methodology needs to be recognized as limited, as all questionnaire methods are, by the nature of self-report. *I*-positions are often implicit, and thus, by definition, closed to self-report analysis. Building on the work of Gillespie and Cornish (2010), we concluded by suggesting that at times it is necessary to engage in more qualitative analyses in order to reveal the more subtle dynamics of implicit meanings and positionings.

Clearly, the methodological trajectory outlined in the present chapter is not finalized, and more empirical explorations are needed in order to understand how best to study the self in its social context. In this regard, perhaps the most important contribution of the IPM for researchers of the dialogical self is that it opens the door to studying the dialogical self from both the inside and the outside. Whether one uses the IPM as a questionnaire or a coding frame, the key insight is thus that one should examine not only how people view themselves or feel themselves to be viewed, but also how they are actually viewed by significant others, and thus how they are actually situated within the field of social interaction.

REFERENCES

Aveling, E.-L. and Gillespie, A. (2008) Negotiating multiplicity: adaptive asymmetries within second generation Turks' 'society of mind', *Journal of Constructivist Psychology*, **21**, 200–222

Barresi, J. (2008) Black and white like me, *Studia Psychologica*, **8**, 11–22

Cast, A. D., Stets, J. E. and Burke, P. J. (1999) Does the self conform to the views of others?, *Social Psychology Quarterly*, **62**, 68–82

Cook, M. (1971) *Interpersonal Perception* (Harmondsworth: Penguin Education)

Cooper, M. (2009) Interpersonal perceptions and metaperceptions: psychotherapeutic practice in the interexperiential realm, *Journal of Humanistic Psychology*, **49**, 85–99

Funder, D. C. (1980) On seeing ourselves as others see us: self–other agreement and discrepancy in personality ratings, *Journal of Personality*, **48**, 473–493

Gieser, T. (2008) Me, my prey, and I: embodiment and empathy in the dialogical self of a Siberian hunter, *Studia Psychologica*, **8**, 41–54

Gillespie, A. (2005) Malcolm X and his autobiography: identity development and self-narration, *Culture and Psychology*, **11**, 77–88

Gillespie, A. and Cornish, F. (2010) Intersubjectivity: towards a dialogical analysis, *Journal for the Theory of Social Behaviour*, **40**, 19–46

Gillespie, A., Place, M. and Murphy, J. J. (2010) Divergences of perspective between people with aphasia and their family caregivers, *Aphasiology*, **24**, 1559–1575

Gillespie, A. and Zittoun, T. (2010) Studying the movement of thought, in A. Toomela and J. Valsiner (eds.), *Methodological Thinking in Psychology: 60 Years Gone Astray?* (Charlotte, NC: Information Age Publishing), 69–86

Gonçalves, M. and Salgado, J. (2001) Mapping the multiplicity of the self, *Culture and Psychology*, **7**, 367–377

Hermans, H. J. M. (1999) Dialogical thinking and self-innovation, *Culture and Psychology*, **5**, 67–87

  (2001) The construction of a personal position repertoire: method and practice, *Culture & Psychology*, **7**, 323–365

  (2003) Clinical diagnosis as a multiplicity of self-positions: challenging social representations theory, *Culture & Psychology*, **9**, 407–414

  (2008) How to perform research on the basis of dialogical self theory? Introduction to the special issue, *Journal of Constructivist Psychology*, **21**, 185–199

Hermans, H. J. M., Fiddelaers, R., de Groot, R. and Nauta, J. F. (1990) Self-confrontation as a method for assessment and intervention in counselling, *Journal of Counselling and Development*, **69**, 156–162

Hermans, H. J. M. and Hermans-Jansen, E. (1995) *Self-Narratives: The Construction of Meaning in Psychotherapy* (New York: Guilford Press)

Hermans, H. J. M. and Hermans-Konopka, A. (2008) Dialogical self theory: introduction to the special issue, *Studia Psychologica*, **8**, 5–10

(2010) *Dialogical Self Theory: Positioning and Counter-Positioning in a Globalizing Society* (Cambridge University Press)

Hinton, P. R. (1993) *The Psychology of Interpersonal Perception* (London: Routledge)

Jones, E. E. (1990) *Interpersonal Perception* (New York: W. H. Freeman)

Kenny, D. A. and DePaulo, B. M. (1993) Do people know how others view them? An empirical and theoretical account, *Psychological Bulletin*, **114**, 145–161

Kluger, A., Nir, D. and Kluger, Y. (2008) Personal position repertoire (PPR) from a bird's eye view, *Journal of Constructivist Psychology*, **21**, 223–238

Laing, R. D., Phillipson, H. and Lee, A. R. (1966) *Interpersonal Perception: A Theory and a Method of Research* (London: Tavistock)

Lewis, M. D. (2002) The dialogical brain: contributions of emotional neurobiology to understanding the dialogical self, *Theory & Psychology*, **12**, 175–190

Lyddon, W. J., Yowell, D. R. and Hermans, H. J. M. (2006) The self-confrontation method: theory, research and practical utility, *Counselling Psychology Quarterly*, **19**, 27–43

Mead, G. H. (1913) The social self, *Journal of Philosophy, Psychology, and Scientific Methods*, **10**, 374–380

Norman, W. T. (1969) 'To see ourselves as others see us!' Relations among self-perceptions, peer-perceptions, and expected peer-perceptions of personality attributes, *Multivariate Behavioral Research*, **4**, 417–443

Puchalska-Wasyl, M., Chmielnicka-Kuter, E. and Oleś, P. (2008) From internal interlocutors to psychological functions of dialogical activity, *Journal of Constructivist Psychology*, **21**, 239–269

Raggatt, P. (2000) Mapping the dialogical self: towards a rationale and method of assessment, *European Journal of Personality*, **14**, 65–90

Rommetveit, R. (1974) *On Message Structure: A Framework for the Study of Language and Communication* (London: Wiley)

Rowiński, T. (2008) Virtual self in dysfunctional internet use, *Studia Psychologica*, **8**, 107–130

Shrauger, J. S. and Schoeneman, T. J. (1979) Symbolic interactionist view of self-concept: through the looking glass darkly, *Psychological Bulletin*, **86**, 549–573

Sillars, A., Koerner, A. and Fitzpatrick, M. A. (2005) Communication and understanding in parent–adolescent relationships, *Human Communication*, **31**, 102–128

Stemplewska-Żakowicz, K., Walecka, J. and Gabińska, A. (2006) As many selves as interpersonal relations (or maybe even more), *International Journal for Dialogical Science*, **1**, 71–94

Wertsch, J. V. (1991) *Voices of the Mind: A Sociocultural Approach to Mediated Action* (Cambridge, MA: Harvard University Press)

White, J. (1982) The application of Laing's interpersonal perception method (IPM) to the counselling context, *Family Therapy*, **9**, 167–173

Whittaker, L. (2010) A dialogical analysis of the identities of adolescents not in education, employment or training (NEET), unpublished Ph.D. thesis, University of Stirling, Scotland

Part III

Domains of application

Introduction

Hubert J. M. Hermans and Thorsten Gieser

In the course of time, dialogical self theory (DST) has led to applications in a variety of fields. In this part, contributions are presented in the following areas: psychotherapy, education, transcendental awareness in emotion work, and consumer behaviour. Each of the chapters has a theoretical background in DST but links it to other perspectives and approaches. All chapters have immediate practical applications.

In his contribution Rowan argues that in the concepts of positioning, repositioning and counter-positioning, counsellors and psychotherapists have a vocabulary available that is highly dynamic and avoids the problem of reification. It is compatible with existing approaches, such as gestalt therapy, transactional analysis, psychosynthesis, transformational chair work, voice dialogue and others. However, while existing concepts, such as subpersonalities, subselves or images, are often treated as static entities in the self, the dynamic nature of *I*-positions allows them to become modified and even developed depending on the person–situation interaction. Moreover, by developing dialogical relations between them, they can be entered (as a space), explored and even changed. Another advantage of the concept of *I*-position, Rowan reasons, is that it enables us to make a transition from the personal to the transpersonal. It makes a space for such concepts as soul, spirit or god/goddess, which are not sub anything. The author provides extensive case material of working with *I*-positions in his psychotherapeutic practice.

In his chapter Dimaggio sees psychopathology as a dysfunction in the inner- and interpersonal dialogues people conduct with both internalized and real-world others, and psychotherapy as a dialogical co-construction of meaning. In his discussion of personality disorders, he makes a distinction between *metacognition*, *meta-position* and *self-reflection*, which have some degree of overlap with each other but with different emphases. He uses these concepts to analyse three dysfunctional forms of organization of the self in case of personality disorders: barren, monological and cacophonous. Dimaggio applies these notions, which were already introduced in Lysaker and Lysaker's chapter about schizophrenia, to clients with personality disorders. He gives extensive examples of his own clients in order to show how these forms of organization can be recognized and treated.

Central in Neimeyer's chapter is the experience of loss of significant others and the meaning of death and dying in the self of their relatives. On the basis of his own experiences with clients, he has found that familiar conceptualizations that view the death of loved ones merely as a 'stressful life event' producing temporary disequilibrium or descriptions of grief in terms of universal 'stages' of adaptation, are too obsolete to understand the hard and subtle emotional work in the wake of a difficult death. Instead, he employs three threads of inspiration, concerned with *meaning making, narrative* and the *dialogical self*, and braids them together into a strand of coherence, flexible enough to permit a variety of novel interventions. He sketches the contribution of each of these strands and exemplifies them with specific therapeutic procedures in the context of contemporary scientific literature on death and dying.

From an eastern perspective, Morioka investigates how therapeutic meaning is generated in a counselling process that gives central significance to the notion of space. In this context, he finds the process term 'positioning', in combination with the notion of 'meta-positioning', as particularly relevant. On the basis of his experiences with clients, he shows how the dynamic movement of positioning and meta-positioning creates a dialogical space that is shared with the client. Elaborating on this view, he introduces the Japanese cultural concept of *ma* in order to explain the dynamics of shared space. One of the central characteristics of this concept is that it refers to a spatial experience that emerges *between* existing *I*-positions. Moreover, the concept of *ma* makes creative use of the dialogical potentials of this in-between area. Finally, Morioka explains how clients can reflect on and transform their unresolved emotions in the active space of *ma*.

Also relevant to the East–West dialogue is Ho's contribution. He argues that DST resonates with constructions of relational selfhood informed by Eastern intellectual traditions. These constructions meet two requirements: inclusion of both self-in-other and other-in-self, and giving full recognition not only to personal responsibility (for one's own well-being) but also social responsibility (for the other's well-being). He presents *dialogical action therapy* (DAT), which integrates two cardinal ideas, dialogue and action, into a coherent framework for effective problem solving under the slogan: action speaks louder than words. DAT is founded on the thesis that selfhood is dialogical in nature. He emphasizes that the dialogical self may divide itself into different positions that become engaged in internal dialogues with one another, a process in which the self participates in its own transformation. Ho develops a detailed formal notation system in order to provide systematic symbolization of complex interpersonal perceptions and meta-perceptions.

In her chapter Hermans-Konopka notes that in virtually all DST studies the focus is on the content and organization of positions, on the assumption that the *I* as a reflexive and dialogical agency is always and even necessarily bound to the flow and change of positions. In contrast to this assumption, she argues that the *I* is not necessarily defined by a position but has the capacity to *deposition* itself; that is, it has the ability to leave any position and enter a form of consciousness that is portrayed in the literature in terms of a witnessing, thought-free, transcendental awareness. In the second part of her chapter, she presents a stage model for emotional training and coaching, giving examples of her own clients who are caught up by intense emotions, but move, often suddenly and unexpectedly, beyond the spur of the moment, and experience their emotions in a more detached and nonjudgemental way. At such moments they 'dis-identify' themselves from the ongoing experience, being at the same time very present, alert and open to it.

The topic of Ligorio's chapter is the reciprocal enrichment of DST and recent trends in educational research. She reasons that an encounter between these developments is justified by the need of educational researchers to overcome the limitations of traditional cognitive learning theories. In order to overcome these limitations, she discusses three recent trends: (1) distributed cognition, which holds that cognition is dependent on context; (2) the so-called CHAT (cultural-historical activity theory), which emphasizes the cultural-historical basis of learning; and (3) social-constructivism, which favours the idea that knowledge building takes advantage of technological tools. Building on these developments, she reviews research and applications of DST in student identity, in teachers' professional identity and in student–teacher interactions. Finally, she emphasizes the importance of a stimulating learning environment in which the processes of positioning, repositioning and counter-positioning in students' and teachers' dialogical selves are facilitated.

In their contribution, Winters and her colleagues are interested in the interface between education and career development in contemporary society. They propose that students on this interface are in need of career competencies such as 'career reflection' (reflection on behaviour and choices), 'career shaping' (proactive behaviour that influences one's career) and networking (interactive behaviour to build contacts in the job market). Then they argue that the enhancement of these competencies needs the development of 'career dialogue', which is based on the idea that real-life problems are the basis for reflective conversation between students, teachers and workplace mentors. They present a model that is based on the assumption that effective and practice-based learning starts from broadening the range of relevant (possibly contradictory) *I*-positions and then runs via consecutive dialogical shifts from these *I*-positions to the level of meta-position, and from there to the level of promoter position. In this way, they claim, students are invited to enter a dialogue in a multivoiced and reflexive way that enables them to learn from their experiences in their preparation of a career.

In her chapter on consumer preferences, Bahl notes that researchers of consumption behaviour, although they are interested in the notion of identity, often do not take into account what goods and services mean to the consumers from the lens of their *different* identities. To use one of the author's examples, when I say that I love chocolate, do all my identities, or *I*-positions – the mother, the romantic partner, exhausted worker, and health-conscious consumer – love chocolate and do they all love it in the same way? And, if my different *I*-positions have inconsistent feelings and meanings for dark chocolate, how do I decide if I like chocolate and if I should eat it? In order to address such questions, Bahl studies consumption preference on different levels. She explores consumption on the level of specific *I*-positions, in which she is interested in the similarities and contradictions between the preferences of these positions. Moreover, she studies the preferences on the 'higher' level of the consumers' meta-positions so that she can investigate to what extent the preferences on this level deviate from those on the level of specific *I*-positions. She gives extensive examples of her informants' narratives and argues that insight into the contradictions between positions facilitates dialogue that may be helpful for changing one's consumption behaviour.

19   The use of *I*-positions in psychotherapy

John Rowan

In this chapter, I argue that one of the main advantages of the dialogical self approach in psychotherapy is that it offers, in the concept of *I*-positions, a more effective way of approaching the multiplicity within the person than any previous method. As is well known from a great deal of previous work (Rowan 1990), many different schools of psychotherapy have embraced such multiplicity and found ways of working with it. The most common of these ways is to use chair work – that is to say, by personifying a character which has emerged during the course of therapy, and talking directly to it, and then talking back as the character itself. In the concept of *I*-positions we have a way of approaching chair work which is less loaded with unnecessary assumptions than any previous approach. It is compatible with all the existing approaches, such as gestalt therapy, transactional analysis, persona therapy, psychosynthesis, psychodrama, schema therapy, experiential process therapy, transformational chair work, voice dialogue, narrative therapy and so forth, and offers them, for the first time, a really adequate vocabulary. The dangers of reification, such a temptation in many of these other schools, are virtually eliminated. The possibility is also opened up of working in a productive way with the transpersonal, as we shall see in due course.

One of the most important aspects of dialogical self theory (DST), as developed in a number of books and papers since the early 1990s by Hubert Hermans and his colleagues, is its idea of *I*-positions. The notion of the 'dialogical self' considers the self as 'a dynamic multiplicity of relatively *autonomous I*-positions in the landscape of the mind' (Hermans 2010: 174). These *I*-positions offer a way of talking which neatly sidesteps the problem of reification inherent in such older concepts as subpersonalities, and ego states and parts. *I*-positions come and go with the situation, and are not regarded as solid, continuous entities. It also gets over the problem of making a space for such concepts as soul, spirit or god/goddess, which are clearly not sub-anything, nor are they ego states or parts of the person. Some clients, and some therapists, make use of such ideas, and in most theories they are hard to handle. But they can be *I*-positions.

Hence, of all the possible names for the multiple locations within the person, *I*-positions is the most flexible, and the least liable to lead to problems in practice. This means that in therapy we can escape from the tyranny of just one unconscious mind, which can be so complex and difficult to consult that we can seldom be sure of what it says or what it wants. It may seem unnecessary to contest the concept of the unconscious, but many different voices nowadays are urging us to do just this (Chiari and Nuzzo 2010; van Deurzen 2010; Wilber 1997). Perhaps the concept of the unconscious, like so many of the older ideas in psychotherapy, is not needed now that we have more adequate and interesting theories.

Instead of saying – 'Consciously you say it is OK for me to go on holiday for six weeks, but at an unconscious level you may resent or fear it' – it is more natural (in the sense of being closer to everyday speech) and more accurate to say – 'From your immediate *I*-position you may say that it is OK for me to go on holiday for six weeks, but you may have another *I*-position (perhaps an adolescent) who resents it, or another *I*-position (perhaps a child) who feels abandoned, or another *I*-position (perhaps an infant) who is screaming and going crazy. Let's explore that a bit.' It may be worth saying here that therapists who use everyday speech in this way often find it easier to relate to the client in the room. One of the advantages of doing it this second way is that we can actually talk directly from one *I*-position to another, and get a reply back again. The one who resents the long holiday may be a teenager who can be interrogated; the one who feels abandoned may be a child who can be talked with; and the one who is screaming and going crazy may be an infant, who 'by some miracle' can also talk back. By encouraging the client to take up these *I*-positions, we can find out more about what is going on within the client. And this puts us as therapists in a position to do something to change the situation. We can reason with the teenager; we can empathize with the child; we can attend to the needs of the infant and get to the bottom of the screaming and apparent craziness.

Out of the theory of the dialogical self has come the notion of *I*-positions, as we have just pointed out. Yet it seems curious to me that so little of the research involving *I*-positions has featured the practice of letting the *I*-positions talk to each other. Of course, there have been some examples, such as can be found in Verhofstadt-Denève's psychodramatic application of DST (Verhofstadt-Denève 2003); Neimeyer's chapter with Buchanan-Arvay, using Westwood's idea of therapeutic enactment (Westwood *et al.* 2002), in the Hermans and Dimaggio book (2004); and the recent Hermans and Hermans-Konopka book (2010). What I want to do in this chapter is to show how useful it can be to use *I*-positions in this way. In other words, I want to add to what has been done in the existing literature, and relate it to other work in the field.

The notion of an *I*-position is the latest and I think the most defensible version of a long-standing idea – the idea of multiplicity within the person. We are all familiar with the idea, so well used in literature and the arts generally, of different parts of the person with possibly conflicting needs and interests. In psychology we have had the Freud (1923) who wrote of the ego, the id and the superego; the Jung (1928) who talked about the complexes or the archetypes; the Federn (1952) or Berne (1961) or John Watkins (1978) who spoke of ego states; the Lewin (1936) who wrote about subregions of the personality; the Perls (1951) who referred to the topdog and the underdog, or retroflection; the Klein (1948) or Fairbairn (1952) or Guntrip (1971) who talked about internal objects; the Balint (1968) who delineated the child in the patient; the Mary Watkins (1986) who described imaginal objects, such as the imaginary friend; the McAdams (1985) who deployed the concept of imagos as a key to life histories; the Hilgard (1986) who discovered the 'hidden observer' in hypnotic states; the Tart (1986) who spoke of identity states; the Denzin (1987) who talked about the emotionally divided self; the Winnicott (1965) or Lake (1966) or Janov (1970) or Laing (1976) who referred to the false or unreal self; the Gurdjieff (1950) who introduced the concept of little *I*'s; the Goffman (1974) who referred to multiple selfing; the Stone and Winkelman (1985) who used the concept of energy patterns; the Mahrer (1978) who theorized deeper potentials coming to the surface; the Wake (2008) who talks about parts of the person; the Watkins and Barabasz (2008) or Hunter (2007) who refer to alters; the Mair (1977) who opened up the possibility of a community of self; the Ornstein (1986) who spoke of small minds; the Gazzaniga (1985) or Minsky (1988) who discovered agents and agencies within the brain; the Gergen (1972) or Martindale (1980) or O'Connor (1971) or Shapiro (1976) who refer to subselves; the Strauss or Rossan who talk about subidentities; the Markus and Nurius (1987) who speak of possible selves; the Kihlstrom and Cantor (1984) who introduce the concept of self-schemas; the Bogart (2007) who speaks of personas; the Mearns and Thorne (2000) who speak of the configurations of self; the T. B. Rogers (1981) who writes about prototypes; the Beahrs (1982) who refers to alter-personalities; or the Assagioli (1975) or Redfearn (1985) or Rowan (1990) or Sliker (1992) who talk about subpersonalities – all the time we are talking about the same thing – multiplicity within the person. One of the distressing features of all the psychotherapeutic literature is the way in which each school ignores parallel work, and just the few favoured writers and researchers are featured all the time. There is a kind of professional narcissism involved here.

There are two main reasons why the nomenclature of *I*-positions is superior to any of those just mentioned. One is that it is less liable to reification. When we succumb to the temptation of reification, we make the inner selves too strong, too solid, too long-lasting – we tend to think of them as permanent or at least semi-permanent, living for weeks, months or years within the person. Reification is of course rampant in the psychological sciences, with various authorities bandying about personages like the oral type, the masochistic position, the macho man, the inner child and so forth. With *I*-positions there is none of this. It is quite clear and explicit that they can come and go with great frequency at times, and are 'of the moment' rather than 'of the essence'. This is a great advantage, because reification is rife throughout the psychotherapeutic literature, as we have pointed out, and any method or approach which avoids this is to be welcomed.

The other great advantage of *I*-positions is that there is no suggestion with them of subordination, of their being lesser in some way than the whole person. This makes it possible to think of the soul, of the spirit – even of God – becoming an *I*-position. All we mean by this is that we can, in therapy, put the soul (for example) on the empty chair, visualize it, talk to it, and then take up that position on the chair and talk back as the soul. If we do not like the word 'soul', there are plenty of synonyms, such as the higher self, the inner teacher, the *daimon* and so forth. If we accept the idea of the transpersonal – and there is now a vast research literature on this, usefully summarized in Shorrock (2008) – this is particularly valuable in transpersonal therapy. This is important because of the way in which the transpersonal is ignored in much of the psychological literature and in psychotherapy, and counselling and coaching. But if we want to do justice to the whole person (and most psychotherapeutic approaches give at least lip service to such an ideal), it is not valid to omit all mention of the soul and the spirit. These may well be concepts or *I*-positions that are important to our clients and hence considered real from within their experienced life world. We certainly do not want to omit or ignore anything that is meaningful to the client.

How to use *I*-positions in theory

I call the process of using *I*-positions 'personification' – in other words we are effectively turning the entity, whatever it may be, into a person for the purposes of dialogue. There are basically three forms of personification in the world of therapy, counselling and coaching.

Empty-chair work

This is the basic idea, pioneered by Jacob Moreno (Moreno *et al.* 2000), and popularized by Fritz Perls (1969), of asking the client to imagine that the object of his or her affections or enmity or questioning is sitting on an empty chair. The client then first of all describes and talks to the character involved, and then moves over into the other chair and enters into and speaks for that character. In recent years this has been formalized by the Integral Institute as the 3–2–1 method: first we describe the character in the third person (he or she is like this or that), then in the second person (addressing the person as 'you'), and finally in the first person (turning the person into an *I*). Fritz Perls was the great master of this method, and showed that we could put into the empty chair such things as 'the number plate in your dream', 'your smirk', 'the dream you did not have', and so forth. This is the classic way of bringing people who are hard to reach into the room, such as your mother, your dead father or your aborted foetus. The more recent work has been well written up by Goldman (2002).

Two-chair work

In this version we identify two (often incompatible) parts of the client, and put each one on a separate chair. The client is then encouraged to speak for each of the parts in turn, and may then be encouraged to engage in a dialogue between the two parts: perhaps they may want to convince the other part that they are more necessary or more valid than that other part. Robert Elliott and others in the group led by Les Greenberg has done much research on this technique in recent years (Greenberg *et al.* 1998). This is important because it is only in recent years that there has been the present emphasis on research and evidence, and of course the dialogical self tendency has been responsible for some of this big surge. More examples are to be found in the work of Victor Bogart (2007).

Multiple-chair work

This is particularly often used by the voice dialogue school, who may use up to ten or more chairs to personify different parts of the person (Stone and Winkelman 1985). Again they may speak individually or engage in dialogues with other 'persons' on the other chairs. The idea has been taken up by Professor Kellogg (2004) in recent years, and more research is now on the way. It has been used very creatively in the last few years by Genpo Roshi in his Big Mind workshops, a transpersonal approach. He introduces characters such the Controller, the Skeptic, the Vulnerable Child, the Damaged Self, the Seeking Mind – and then the Non-Seeking Mind, Big Mind, Big Heart and so forth, and invites people to enter such states for short periods, and speak from that position. In this way ordinary people can be introduced to some extraordinary ways of seeing the world.

This is therefore a very flexible idea, which can take a number of forms. In recent years I have been urging that it is now possible, using the idea of *I*-positions, to have dialogues with one's soul or even one's spirit (Rowan 2010). This idea was pioneered by Moreno again, who sometimes asked a protagonist to stand on a chair and be God. But it was refined and developed further by the psychosynthesis practitioners, particularly Molly Young Brown (1993).

It is obvious that the notion of an *I*-position makes all these moves more transparent and less worrying conceptually. It is important not to regard this as merely a technique (or set of techniques) which are useful in therapy, but to realize that it is a very free and flexible way of construing or understanding what people are really like. John Beahrs put it very well: 'When is it useful or not useful to look upon an individual as a single unit, as a "Cohesive Self"? When is it useful or not useful to look upon anyone as being constituted of many parts, each with an identity of its own? When is it useful to see ourselves as part of a greater whole? I use the term "useful" rather than "true" since all are true – simultaneously and at all times' (Beahrs 1982: 4–5).

This last statement is helpful, I think, to all those who want to work with the dialogical self. They will continually be faced by critics who question the whole idea that the person can be multiple. To realize that this can be true, yet not the whole truth, is an important step forward. Since I have criticized some of the dialogical self researchers for not using these techniques in their work very much, it behoves me to give an example myself. This has to do with the difficulty of working with extreme emotions. Let us look at the case of 'Sarah' (not her real name).

Black Witch and giant spider

For good reasons, which there is no space to go into here, Sarah was preoccupied with her mother. In the early days of the therapy, we spent most of the time on Sarah's mother, just following her feelings back into her childhood again and again. We found that her mother kept on turning up in the most extraordinary disguises, in dreams and in fantasies: for example, we spent some time wrestling with a 'death skeleton' which was extremely frightening and threatening, and this turned out in the end to be her mother again. One of the most fearful versions for Sarah was the Black Witch, who came up in dreams and fantasies, and actually laid a spell on the child Sarah to strike her dumb. This was a very accurate statement of what happened when Sarah's mother came on the scene: Sarah was dumbstruck.

For a long time it seemed that we were stuck, because Sarah could find no way of facing her mother without being overcome immediately. There seemed to be no strength, no resource, within her that was strong enough to resist. She lost her voice; she couldn't think of anything to say or do; it was as if she were paralyzed.

After one or two failed attempts to deal with the Black Witch, we were working on a dream about a giant spider. As I often do, I suggested, after going through the dream and finding that the spider represented her mother, that we put the spider on to a cushion and talk to it. Sarah agreed to this, and we set it up, but I could see that she was experiencing some fear. I remembered a previous session where I had taken her side, and it suddenly occurred to me how we might make it work better.

This time I said, 'Now there is a magic glass screen just here [I indicated a line] between you and the spider. You can talk to the spider, but the spider can't get through the screen. The spider can still hear and see and talk through the screen, but is completely blocked by the screen. You can get at the spider if you want to, but the spider can't get at you. And the screen will stay there until I take it down again.'

Now I lined up with Sarah as before, and supported her against the spider, shouting back to the spider that she had no right to attack Sarah, that Sarah had seen through her game, that she wasn't going to stand for it any more and so on. This time, as we went back and forth between Sarah and the giant spider, the spider diminished in size and paled in colour. It became smaller and smaller and weaker and weaker, until Sarah felt capable of facing it and dealing with it by herself.

For the first time, we had the feeling of victory against her mother. For the first time, her mother respected Sarah. We had broken through, and the positive feeling was tremendous. Sarah afterwards said that the magic screen was like a protection that made her feel safe. It made her feel that she was allowed to communicate. Before this, she had felt no right to communicate, particularly where her mother was concerned.

But of course there were other things going on too. It may be felt that I was perhaps functioning on one level as a bigger magician than the

Black Witch, and beating her on a magical level. At an unconscious level, perhaps I was her father come back to rescue her this time. Perhaps the glass screen was simply a schizoid defence, a temporary neurosis. Sarah's own view, expressed later, was that I was showing her how to talk back to her mother: she had no model or script for it, so did not know how to do it until she saw me do it. Once she had picked up the model, she was able to use it, and this seemed to break the dumbness spell put on the child by the Black Witch.

Here we have a good example of the case put forward by the dialogical self school: 'As we argued earlier, the self is characterised by oppositions, ambivalences, and ambiguities, in which a broad variety of positions play their part, not only those that are foregrounded as presentations to the outside world but also those that are backgrounded as "shadow positions" (Hermans 2001), "exiles" (Schwartz 1995) or "disowned selves" (Stone and Winkelman 1989) in the darker spaces of the self' (Hermans and Hermans-Konopka 2010: 178).

I give this example to illustrate the point that dialogical work can lead us into some very deep areas, and may suggest ways of working which are theoretically quite unusual. It can also be used in group work, as has been well described by Sewell *et al.* (1998).

The transpersonal

The transpersonal is a vast realm for psychotherapy, counselling and coaching, and it has been emerging as a really important aspect of the therapeutic engagement over the past 30-odd years. I focus on it because it is all too common in our psychological work to leave out the element of spirituality, which has been well written about recently by David Mattison (2008), for example. If we want to do justice to the whole person it is not valid to leave out such important components as the soul or the spirit. The term 'transpersonal' is superior to the term 'spirituality' for the reasons succinctly stated by Roberto Assagioli: he described the transpersonal as 'a term introduced above all by Maslow and by those of his school to refer to what is commonly called spiritual. Scientifically speaking, it is a better word; it is more precise and, in a certain sense, neutral in that it points to that which is beyond or above ordinary personality. Furthermore it avoids confusion with many things which are now called spiritual but which are actually pseudo-spiritual or parapsychological' (Assagioli 1991: 16).

The clearest and most useful map of the transpersonal, in my opinion, has been given to us by Ken Wilber (2000). What he says is that we are all on a path of psychospiritual development, whether we know it or not and whether we like it or not. And this process has three main phases. Firstly, there is the 'prepersonal' – the whole realm of childhood development when we see ourselves as part of a family rather than as a separate and distinct personality. Secondly, there is the personal – the vast realm of role-playing in society, where we grow up believing that we have to defend and enhance our self-image. This process ends up with a mature ego, as psychology generally describes it, capable of self-defence and self-enhancement in very effective ways. Thirdly, there is the transpersonal – the later realm where we first of all shake off the shackles of the self-image and discover authenticity; and then later perhaps admit that we are spiritual beings capable of enjoying symbols, images and archetypes, exploring altered states of consciousness, and opening ourselves up to inspiration and joy; and then later perhaps again shake off all that and open up to the total freedom of the One, the All or the None, where we no longer need concrete representations of the divine. This is all very well described in the relevant literature (Cortright 1997; Ferrer 2002; Washburn 2000; Wilber 2000).

There is no suggestion in Wilber that we should all go to the transpersonal, and indeed it seems that to go very far along this path is rare and difficult. The path to the mature ego is easy, because society is right behind us, encouraging us to be a better and better role-player. In fact, it very often takes a crisis, perhaps quite painful, to get us to leave the familiarity of the personal – what has sometimes been called the 'consensus trance'. When we do, it is very often along the lines of – 'I have spent thirty years building up my social self, and learnt very well how to play my roles for the benefit of other people, but what about me? Who am I really, behind all the roles?' And at that point we may get into counselling or psychotherapy, or even take a course to become a therapist, as many people have done in recent years. In fact, therapy is of great help to put us on the road to the transpersonal, because it enables us to deal with our shadow material. The shadow is a concept introduced by Jung (1951) originally, but it is vitally necessary for us to understand it if we are to move on into the transpersonal realm without self-deception. The shadow comprises all those aspects of us which we either reject or do not understand or do not even know about, although its effects are very often obvious to others. To go on into the transpersonal without dealing with the shadow is asking for trouble, and Wilber is very clear about this (Wilber 2006: 126). This leads us to the idea of resistance in psychotherapy, because it is resistance that can make it hard for us to explore and deal with our shadow material. This is a very common and very useful idea, as has been pointed out by Michael Guilfoyle (2006). How do we deal with it in the dialogical self model? The first thing is to identify the resistance. This can be done very gradually and tactfully if necessary: 'Do you ever feel that there is a voice within you which is saying just the opposite to your conscious intentions?'; or 'Do you ever get the sense that some part of you wants nothing to do with your plan or your programme?' In doing this work, of course, we must always respect the client's belief system and way of seeing things.

Having identified the resistance – for example, as a saboteur, or a perfectionist or a procrastinator – the next step is to put it in a chair, or on a cushion, or in some other convenient location. For example, if it just takes the form of a wall, we could just visualize the wall in the middle of the floor.

The next step is to visualize the resistance. Encourage the client to bring some picture, image or vision to mind that puts the resistance into some concrete form. This may need some shaping to make it easier to handle: for example, if the client says it is a fog, encourage him or her to visualize it as a particularly deep and dark fog, almost solid in its thickness. Once the client is visualizing the resistance, ask him or her to speak to it. There is no need to put words into the client's mouth – just wait until the client produces something. What the client says to the resistance does not matter very much. It is the dialogue itself that is the important factor. Don't let the client talk about the resistance – he or she must talk directly to it, as if it were some kind of person. Keep on encouraging the client to talk until it seems clear that some reply is needed. Then ask the client to change places, positioned in such a way that it is easy to talk back to the space where the client was sitting.

Now the client is the resistance. Help the client to take a moment or two to really get into role. Often the voice changes at this point. Answer the requests or accusations or whatever the client has been saying. This is the crucial point, and the interaction can be quite intense. Encourage the resistance to talk more. At an appropriate moment, it is often a good idea for the therapist to talk to the resistance direct, finding out what role it is taking in relation to the client – what it thinks it is doing. Much can emerge from this kind of dialogue.

It is worth pointing out that if we have the concept of the dialogical self we do not need to preserve or use the concepts of transference or counter-transference. Twenty years ago David Smith (1991) was demonstrating that there was actually no theoretical justification for the concept of transference, using a very careful examination of the classic documents in psychoanalysis, and we can now see that if we have *I*-positions we do not need transference. Instead of saying, 'Perhaps your strong reaction to me is really directed at your father', we might say instead, 'Perhaps you could express these strong feelings to this empty chair, and see who appears there.' If this worked, a dialogue could then ensue, which would reveal the material needing to be dealt with here. Similar considerations apply to counter-transference – the therapist may need to work on this in her or his own therapy.

Discussion

As suggested earlier in this chapter, the implications here run very deep. Historically, the concept of the unconscious emerged from the discovery of persons within the person (Chertok and de Saussure (1979) and Ellenberger (1970)). It grew and developed from the middle of the eighteenth century until today, as these authorities have shown in great detail. But if it was invented to account for the evident multiplicity within the person, it is not needed now that we have the improved theory of the dialogical self, which states that this multiplicity is not something odd or strange that needs special explanation to handle, but rather something natural and basic to what human beings are. All this highly complicated and unusual apparatus (Freud's system Ucs and so forth) can go into the fire. The many arguments and reported research in books like that of Hermans and Dimaggio (2004) bring alive the theory in extremely convincing ways, and we do not need to shrink from applying the lessons in a radical way.

Working with the dialogical self in this way is, I believe, the wave of the future. It arises very naturally out of the work with clients and coachees. It was exciting, for example, to pick up the recent book by Robert Neimeyer (2009) on constructivist psychotherapy and find in the very first chapter a case vignette in which a woman was encouraged to put her dead father in a chair and dialogue with him, with good results. It was enthralling to discover the work of Scott Kellogg (2004), who actually calls his approach 'transformational chair work' and uses the idea as to the manor born. It has been very encouraging to see how Les Greenberg and his colleagues (1998) have been conducting serious research on empty-chair work and two-chair work, as, for example, in the chapter by Barry Wolfe and Patti Sigl on experiential psychotherapy of the anxiety disorders, or by Robert Elliott, Kenneth Davis and Emil Slatick on process-experiential therapy for post-traumatic stress, in the same volume.

But it is important to go back to the basic breakthrough being canvassed here. It is that when we work with human beings, what we are actually doing in all cases is to facilitate the processes of positioning, repositioning and counter-positioning which enable us as therapists to address the self in highly dynamic and non-reifying ways. By working in this way, we enable new configurations of the self to open up. And it is interesting to note that in the person-centred school, which many of us have regarded as very simple and basic, the concept of 'configurations of self' is now part of the basic theory being taught (Mearns and Thorne 2000). The dialogical self is not a sport, an exception, a peripheral thing, but part of a broad movement towards a new vision of the person, which is more and more popular in the therapeutic world of today.

Much of the important work has been put together in my own (2010) book, which goes very thoroughly into the historical use of these ideas by virtually all the great names in the field of psychotherapy. It also goes into the question of how we can believe at one and the same time in the unity of the self and the multiplicity of the self: both of these are vitally necessary. It does seem to me that this is the way to go if we are to do justice to what human beings are, and how to conduct therapy with them.

REFERENCES

Allison, R. and Schwartz, T. (1980) *Minds in Many Pieces* (New York: Rawson-Wade)
Angyal, A. (1941) *Foundations for a Science of Personality* (New York: Commonwealth Fund)
Assagioli, R. (1975) *Psychosynthesis* (London: Turnstone)
    (1991) *Transpersonal Development: The Dimension Beyond Psychosynthesis* (London: Crucible)
Balint, M. (1968) *The Basic Fault* (London: Tavistock)
Beahrs, J. O. (1982) *Unity and Multiplicity* (New York: Brunner/Mazel)
Berne, E. (1961) *Transactional Analysis in Psychotherapy* (London: Evergreen Books)
Bogart, V. (2007) *Explore the Undiscovered You: Three Paths to Self-Discovery and Empowerment* (Walnut Creek, CA: Baskin Publishing)
Brown, M. Y. (1993) *Growing Whole: Self-Realization on an Endangered Planet* (Center City, MN: Hazelden)
Chertok, L. and de Saussure, R. (1979) *The Therapeutic Revolution: From De Saussure to Freud* (New York: Brunner/Mazel)
Chiari, G. and Nuzzo, M. L. (2010) *Constructivist Psychotherapy* (Hove: Routledge)
Cortright, B. (1997) *Psychotherapy and Spirit: Theory and Practice in Transpersonal Psychotherapy* (Albany, NY: SUNY Press)
Denzin, N. K. (1987) A phenomenology of the emotionally divided self, in K. Yardley and T. Honess (eds.), *Self and Identity* (Chichester: John Wiley), 287–296
Dunkel, C. and Kerpelman, J. (eds.) (2006) *Possible Selves: Theory, Research and Applications* (New York: Nova Science)
Dyak, M. (1999) *The Voice Dialogue Facilitator's Handbook* (Seattle, WA: Life Energy Press)
Ellenberger, H. (1970) *The Discovery of the Unconscious* (New York: Basic Books)

Fairbairn, W. R. D. (1952) *Psychoanalytic Studies of the Personality* (London: Tavistock)

Federn, P. (1952) *Ego Psychology and the Psychoses* (New York: Basic Books)

Ferrer, J. N. (2002) *Revisioning Transpersonal Theory: A Participatory Vision of Human Spirituality* (Albany, NY: SUNY Press)

Freud, S. (1923) *The Ego and the Id and Other Works, Collected Works*, vol. IXX (London: Hogarth Press)

Gazzaniga, M. (1985) *The Social Brain* (New York: Basic Books)

Gergen, K. J. (1972) Multiple identity, *Psychology Today*, 5, 31–35

Goffman, E. (1974) *Frame Analysis* (New York: Harper and Row)

Goldman, R. N. (2002) The empty-chair dialogue for unfinished business, in J. C. Watson, R. N. Goldman and M. S. Warner (eds.), *Client-Centered and Experiential Psychotherapy in the 21st Century: Advances in Theory, Research and Practice* (Llangarron: PCCS Books), 427–447

Greenberg, L. S., Watson, J. C. and Lietaer, G. (eds.) (1998) *Handbook of Experiential Psychotherapy* (New York: Guilford)

Guilfoyle, M. (2006) Using power to question the dialogical self and the therapeutic application, *Counselling Psychology Quarterly*, 19, 89–104

Guntrip, H. (1971) *Psychoanalytic Theory: Therapy and the Self* (New York: Basic Books)

Gurdjieff, G. (1950) *Meetings with Remarkable Men* (London: Routledge)

Hermans, H. J. M. (2001) The dialogical self: towards a theory of personal and cultural positioning, *Culture and Psychology*, 7, 243–282
    (2004) The dialogical self: between exchange and power, in H. J. M. Hermans and G. Dimaggio (eds.), *The Dialogical Self in Psychotherapy* (Hove: Brunner-Routledge), 13–28

Hermans, H. J. M. and Dimaggio, G. (eds.) (2004) *The Dialogical Self in Psychotherapy* (Hove: Brunner-Routledge)

Hermans, H. J. M. and Hermans-Konopka, A. (2010) *Dialogical Self Theory: Positioning and Counter-Positioning in a Globalizing Society* (Cambridge University Press)

Hilgard, E. R. (1986) *Divided Consciousness* (New York: Wiley)

Hunter, C. R. (2007) *The Art of Hypnotherapy*, 3rd edn (Dubuque, OH: Kendall-Hunt)

Janov, S. (1970) *The Primal Scream* (New York: Putnam)

Jung, C. G. (1928) *The Structure and Dynamics of the Psyche*, in *Collected Works*, vol. IIX (London: Routledge)
    (1951) *Aion: Researches into the Phenomenology of the Self*, in *Collected Works*, vol. IX, part 2 (London: Routledge)

Kapleau, P. (1967) *The Three Pillars of Zen* (Boston: Beacon)

Kellogg, S. H. (2004) Dialogical encounters: contemporary perspectives on 'chairwork' in psychotherapy, *Psychotherapy: Research, Theory, Practice, Training*, 41, 310–320

Kihlstrom, J. F. and Cantor, N. (1984) Mental representations of the self, in L. Berkowitz (ed.), *Advances in Experimental Social Psychology* (New York: Academic Press), vol. 17

Klein, M. (1948) *Contributions to Psychoanalysis* (London: Hogarth Press)

Laing, R. D. (1976) *The Facts of Life* (Harmondsworth: Penguin)

Lake, F. (1966) *Clinical Theology* (London: Darton, Longman and Todd)

Lewin, K. (1936) *Topological Psychology* (New York: McGraw-Hill)

Mahrer, A. R. (1978) *Experiencing* (New York: Brunner/Mazel)

Mair, M. (1977) The community of self, in D. Bannister (ed.), *New Perspectives in Personal Construct Theory* (London: Academic Press)

Markus, H. and Nurius, P. (1987) Possible selves: the interface between motivation and the self-concept, in K. Yardley and T. Honess (eds.), *Self and Identity: Psychosocial Perspectives* (Chichester: John Wiley), 157–172

Martindale, C. (1980) Subselves: the internal representation of situational and personal dispositions, in L. Wheeler (ed.), *Review of Personality and Social Psychology* (Beverly Hills, CA: Sage), vol. I, 193–218

McAdams, D. P. (1985) The 'Imago': a key narrative component of identity, in P. Shaver (ed.), *Self, Situations and Social Behavior* (Beverly Hills, CA: Sage), 116–141

Mearns, D. and Thorne, B. (2000) *Person-Centred Therapy Today: New Frontiers in Theory and Practice* (London: Sage)

Minsky, M. (1988) *The Society of Mind* (London: Picador)

Moreno, Z., Blomkvist, L. D. and Rützel, T. (2000) *Psychodrama, Surplus Reality and the Art of Healing* (London: Routledge)

Neimeyer, R. A. (2009) *Constructivist Psychotherapy* (Hove: Routledge)

Neimeyer, R. A. and Buchanan-Arvay, M. (2004) Performing the self, in H. J. M. Hermans and G. Dimaggio (eds.), *The Dialogical Self in Psychotherapy* (Hove: Brunner-Routledge)

O'Connor, E. (1971) *Our Many Selves* (New York: Harper and Row)

Ornstein, R. (1986) *Multimind: A New Way of Looking at Human Behavior* (Boston: Houghton Mifflin)

Perls, F. S. (1951) *Gestalt Therapy* (New York: Dell)

(1969) *Gestalt Therapy Verbatim* (Moab, UT: Real People Press)

Redfearn, J. W. T. (1985) *My Self, My Many Selves* (London: Academic Press)

Rogers, T. B. (1981) A model of the self as an aspect of the human information processing system, in N. Cantor and J. F. Kihlstrom (eds.), *Personality, Cognition and Social Interaction* (Hillsdale, NJ: Lawrence Erlbaum), 193–214

Rowan, J. (1990) *Subpersonalities: The People Inside Us* (London: Routledge)

(2010) *Personification: Using the Dialogical Self in Psychotherapy and Counselling* (Hove: Routledge)

Schwartz, R. (1995) *Internal Family Systems Therapy* (New York: Guilford)

Sewell, K. W., Baldwin, C. L. and Moes, A. J. (1998) The multiple self-awareness group, *Journal of Constructivist Psychology*, **11**, 59–78

Shapiro, S. B. (1976) *The Selves Inside You* (Berkeley, CA: Explorations Institute)

Shorrock, A. (2008) *The Transpersonal in Psychology, Psychotherapy and Counselling* (Basingstoke: Palgrave Macmillan)

Sliker, G. (1992) *Multiple Mind* (Boston: Shambhala)

Smith, D. L. (1991) *Hidden Conversations* (London: Routledge)

Stone, H. and Winkelman, S. (1985) *Embracing Our Selves* (Marina del Rey, CA: DeVorss)

(1989) *Embracing Our Selves: The Voice Dialogue Manual* (San Rafael, CA: New World Library)

Tart, C. (1986) *Waking up: Overcoming the Obstacles to Human Potential* (Boston: New Science Library)

Van Deurzen, E. (2010) *Everyday Mysteries: A Handbook of Existential Psychotherapy*, 2nd edn (Hove: Routledge)

Verhofstadt-Denève, L. (2003) The psychodramatical 'social atom method': dialogical self in dialogical action, *Journal of Constructivist Psychology*, **16**, 183–212

Wake, L. (2008) *Neurolinguistic Therapy: A Postmodern Perspective* (Hove: Routledge)

Washburn, M. (2000) Transpersonal cognition in developmental perspective, in T. Hart, P. L. Nelson and K. Puhakka (eds.), *Transpersonal Knowing: Exploring the Horizon of Consciousness* (Albany, NY: SUNY Press), 185–212

Watkins, J. G. (1978) *The Therapeutic Self* (New York: Human Sciences Press)

Watkins, J. G. and Barabasz, A. (2008) *Advanced Hypnotherapy: Hypnodynamic Techniques* (Abingdon: Routledge)

Watkins, M. (1986) *Invisible Guests* (Hillsdale, NJ: Analytic Press)

Westwood, M. J., Keats, P. A. and McLean, H. B. (2002) A re-entry program for peacekeeping soldiers, *Canadian Journal of Counselling*, **36**, 221–232

Westwood, M. J., Keats, P. A. and Wilensky, P. (2003) Therapeutic enactment: integrating the individual and group counselling models for change, *Journal for Specialists in Group Work*, **28**, 122–138

Wilber, K. (1997) *The Eye of Spirit: An Integral Vision for a World Gone Slightly Mad* (Boston: Shambhala)

(2000) *Integral Psychology: Consciousness, Spirit, Psychology, Therapy* (Boston: Shambhala)

(2006) *Integral Spirituality* (Boston: Integral Books)

Winnicott, D. W. (1965) *The Maturational Processes and the Facilitating Environment* (London: Hogarth Press)

20 Dialogically oriented therapies and the role of poor metacognition in personality disorders

Giancarlo Dimaggio

Dialogue is the heart of psychotherapy conversation. Patients enter a session with a story to tell, a head full of phantasms and fears, and expectations about how the therapist will react to their complaints, anguishes and requests for care. Going to an appointment, patients anticipate in their imaginal space how the conversation will unfold. And then the talk begins and a meeting of minds takes place, one where I as a therapist must tactfully, to the extent that I can, become a member of their inner society, while letting them in turn speak within my mind and stimulate an appropriate responding voice, which might bring them relief.

Psychopathology can be seen as a dysfunction in the inner and inter-personal dialogues people conduct with both internalized and real-world others, and psychotherapy as a dialogical co-construction of meaning (Dimaggio *et al.* 2003; Hermans and Dimaggio 2004; Lysaker and Lysaker 2002). In this chapter, I briefly summarize some tenets common to dialogically oriented psychotherapies and then try to introduce an element of psychopathology; that is, the difficulty in thinking about thinking, both by oneself and others, henceforth termed *metacognition* (Dimaggio *et al.* 2007a; Dimaggio and Lysaker 2010; Semerari *et al.* 2003). The aim is to tailor such psychotherapies to the needs of adults suffering from severe pathologies and often so unable to describe the features of both the voices inhabiting their imaginal space and of the others with whom they interact that a dialogue can scarcely commence. Throughout the whole chapter, I will use the terms *metacognition* (Dimaggio and Lysaker 2010; Semerari *et al.* 2007), *meta-position* and *self-reflection*, which have some degree of overlap with each other. By metacognition, I refer to a broad range of skills concentrated on decoding and thinking about mental states, both of oneself and others. In Carcione and colleagues' (2010) definition, metacognition is the set of skills necessary for: (1) identifying mental states and ascribing them to oneself and others on the basis of facial expressions, somatic states, behaviour and actions; (2) reflecting on and reasoning about mental states; (3) using information about mental states to decide, solve problems or psychological and interpersonal conflicts, and master subjective suffering.

Metacognition involves both semi-automatic processes, such as deducing an emotion from another's face or recognizing variations in one's own arousal as specific emotions, and conscious ones, such as taking a critical distance from a formerly firmly held belief. By self-reflection, I simply refer here to metacognitive operations applied to the self-domain – as opposed to focusing on others, which is often termed 'theory of mind' or 'mind-reading'.

Meta-position (Hermans and Hermans-Konopka 2010) instead is a part of the dialogical self-system capable of assuming an overarching view of other *I*-positions. Meta-position necessarily involves a content and is affective-laden. For example, I might achieve a meta-position from which I see two different *I*-positions: *I*-as-a-hardworking scientist and *I*-as-a-playful-father. From this meta-position, I would perceive that they are very different aspects of my personality but be happy about my ability to adapt to circumstances, thus defining this meta-position as *I*-as-often-committed-to-tasks-but-flexible. Meta-positions are a special kind of *I*-position, with the unique quality of a bird's-eye view of other self-aspects; one person can thus, according to the perspective endorsed at a specific moment and the *I*-positions being viewed, embody different meta-positions.

Meta-position, according to the above definition, is a specific part of the metacognitive system: *integration* (Dimaggio *et al.* 2010a; Semerari *et al.* 2007), that is, the ability to form a consistent perspective of oneself across a lifespan or in different situations. The main difference between the two concepts is that metacognition is a function, such as a memory, and neutral in meaning-making attributions; in other words, it involves abilities like describing emotions or recognizing that thoughts are self-generated. Meta-position instead intrinsically implies affective-laden meaning attributions.

For the sake of space and clarity, I will focus here on persons with personality disorders (PD) with limited ability to perceive and describe their inner world and poor understanding of what is passing through others' minds. In a dialogical therapy context, I will principally try to develop the idea that in persons with PD a barrier to healing is their inability to describe aspects of themselves and others in mentalistic terms, thus preventing the formation of a full-fledged, flexible, adaptive and open-to-innovation dialogical self. I start by briefly summarizing the common aspects of dialogically oriented therapies. I next provide an overview of what metacognitive dysfunctions are, and why they hamper healing. Finally I describe technique elements that may help in treating more severe sufferers by taking into account their metacognitive disorders.

Dialogically oriented psychotherapies: common concepts

Dialogical self theory (DST) has developed principles for dealing with persons whose inner and interpersonal dialogues are problematic (Hermans and Dimaggio 2004). Key features are that: (1) the self is multiple and is a narrative construction where its different facets dialogue with each other both in patients' imaginal conversations and in the therapy relationship; (2) the dialogue of people with psychological suffering is dysfunctional – that is, it is impoverished, barren, repetitive and closed to innovation, or disorganized; (3) therapy should aim at helping patients get in touch with previously overshadowed voices, or build new self-aspects which will enrich their construction of the world and lead to better health and adaptation. Therapy should also aim at constructing positions capable of an overarching view of the many sides of who an individual is. In other words, psychotherapy is about forming meta-positions able to reflect upon the more crystallized aspects of the self and provide new solutions to problems. Meta-positions also help in forming a more integrated self-view, compared to a previously only fragmented understanding of the connections among the inner cast of voices. Finally, through dialogue therapy should aim at opening new gateways to previously blocked narratives (Gonçalves *et al.* 2009; Santos *et al.* 2009; see also Gonçalves and Ribeiro's chapter). I will deal with each of these three points in the following section.

A dialogical, multiple and narrative self in therapy: theory and clinical examples

One core aspect of DST is that the self is made of multiple facets or voices, each possessing their own characteristics, expressing different emotions and taking distinct perspectives on events and social interactions. These voices, in both the imaginal space and social arena, dialogue with each other; they agree, disagree, negotiate meanings and influence each other, while forming a series of self-narratives (Hermans, Kempen and van Loon 1992). A dialogical self therefore implies a multiple and narrative self.

As the various parts surface, persons act, feel and process information differently and anticipate different reactions from others. The different voices, each with their own set of wishes, needs and action tendencies, surface in line with the demands of interpersonal situations and the problems to be confronted (Dimaggio and Stiles 2007; Hermans 1996; Neimeyer 2000). The different voices noted in a person's verbalizations have distinct bodily features – for example, prosody and intonation – express different emotions and have unique perspectives and informa-tion-processing modes (Stiles 2007). The dialogical interaction between them weaves a web of personal and psychological knowledge in the form of a set of autobiographical narratives.

Narrative is a way of making sense of the world and providing consist-ency to perceptions and communications (Angus and McLeod 2004; Bruner 1990; Gonçalves et al. 2009; Salvatore et al. 2004). The stories we tell ourselves and others give meaning to and anticipate events, provide for action planning, consolidate our self-understanding, estab-lish our characteristic range of emotions and life goals, and guide our performance on the social world stage (Neimeyer 2000). Stories can be rewritten and evolve, thanks to the gradual working of inter- and intrapersonal dialogue. Psychotherapy is a specialized field where con-versation with an expert stimulates the rewriting of stories that were previously blocked or barren. A therapist can propose him/herself as a new element capable of changing barren and constricted narratives by, for example, embodying a voice validating meanings and emotions that have never found an interlocutor willing to accept them.

DST-based psychopathology

A series of problems affecting the dialogical, multiple and narrative self has been detected in clinical populations (Dimaggio et al. 2010a): (1) dialogical impoverishment or barren discourse; (2) monological narratives, and dominant voices or meta-positions; (3) disorganization, dialogical cacophony and dissociation (see also Lysaker and Lysaker's chapter in this volume).

Dialogical impoverishment or barren discourse

Many patients possess a limited position-repertoire, a set of representa-tions of who they and significant others are, so that they lack the cognitive resources necessary to meet different societal demands and have an inadequate and restricted set of strategies for coping with the many difficulties of social life. Moreover, the dialogue among the differ-ent I-positions is repetitive and stereotyped. Such patients' imaginal world does have a dialogical form, but the reciprocal positioning of utterer and recipient always leads to the same end, with a very limited potential for openness and innovation (Dimaggio *et al.* 2003).

Psychopathology arises when the self is impoverished to the extent that there are no voices, or, when there are, patients are unaware of or actively repress or dissociate them. In their imaginal dialogues they tend to let others almost always speak with the same voice. Their daily interactions also repeat the same pattern, and they are unable to perceive that others are offering them the option of new solutions to their problems.

Monological narratives and dominant voices

Many people suffer because their meaning attribution system is colonized and dominated by a few voices which dictate the story plot and outcome, hampering the potential for new solutions when they face different life challenges. This is typical, for example, of people with schizophrenia (see Lysaker and Lysaker's chapter in this volume) suffering from paranoid delusions, who are only able, whatever happens around them, to ascribe evil intentions to others, thus blocking any potential for a fruitful exchange. The lives of many sufferers from abuse – or other trauma (Neimeyer 2000) – are afflicted by the presence of dominant positions in their imaginal space that block the possibility of finding alternative solutions to problems. For example, a battered woman might feel that her wish for a life free from violence will always remain unfulfilled, because her abusing partner's voice denies her any possibility of leaving the relationship. There is scarcely ever a potential caretaker in such abused persons' dialogues (Santos *et al.* 2009).

One possible reason for discourse being barren is that meta-positions (Hermans 2001), that is, voices with a superordinate stance vis-à-vis the cast of characters in a person's imaginal space, either silence any other perspective or share the negative self-image other voices have. For example, Silvia, a patient of mine, had a life narrative dominated by a tyrannical meta-position. She featured a dominant ugly and despised – both physically and morally – self, faced with a harsh and spiteful other. She suffered from dysmorphophobia and featured obsessive-compulsive PD with prominent dependent and passive-aggressive traits. When she looked at herself in the mirror, she felt she was fat and horrible and imagined others mocking her for this. She recalled memories of her late brother, who died in a car accident while under the effect of drugs, and his friends joking about her physical appearance; she remembered trying to rebel but being unable to utter any word. She then usually burst into tears, ran home, shut the door and did her school homework in order to reach an idealized *perfect-student* position. Her life had little room for pleasure. One likely reason for this inability to experience happiness was the commanding tone of her father's internalized voice. She recalls that when she was eight years old and asked him if she could play with some friends, he inflexibly forced her to serve as a waitress in the family restaurant instead. During psychotherapy I asked Silvia to give a name to the spiteful character and she called it *the giant octopus* because it was dark, tentacular and controlled everything. I applied the two-chair technique to get her into a dialogue with the octopus. To my surprise, when she was back in her normal *I*-position, her face still looked worried. I asked her to reply to the octopus, and she said: 'I agree with you. I'm ugly and stupid.' As this example suggests, Silvia's self was dominated by a tyrannizing voice that tended to subordinate all other voices in her self.

Disorganization, dialogical cacophony and dissociation

Having an integrated identity means that the different voices forming our personality can engage in a dialogue allowing mutual recognition and reciprocal awareness of different perspectives and negotiation of conflicts when different urges scream to be satisfied first. With patients unable to form an integrated self-narrative, symptoms or social dysfunctions are likely to appear.

Many with schizophrenia (Lysaker and Lysaker 2008), trauma-related or dissociative disorders (Liotti and Prunetti 2010) or PD (Dimaggio *et al.* 2007a) are inhabited by a mob of voices, all talking at once and with no relevance hierarchy. This makes it impossible for a listener, and for the person him/herself, to discern the main theme of the story or real problem to be solved, or to find a stance providing a consistent action guide. In other cases there is no mutual recognition of the voices, as in the case of many with borderline PD, who describe themselves or others as a *loved/respectful* dyad at one moment and a *betrayed/cheater* one just a few minutes later in the same session.

Finally, many with PD tend to lack a superordinate stance, a meta-position capable of providing a necessary bird's-eye view and telling them the wisest course of action to take. Patients' different and often contrasting wishes tear them into opposite directions as if they head east and west at the same time. A lack of meta-positions often leaves a person in a world of chaos and confusion (Salvatore *et al.* 2006). (For descriptions of patients featuring disorganized narratives, see Lysaker and Lysaker's chapter in this volume and Salvatore *et al.* 2006.)

Dysfunctions in the metacognitive system

Understanding what we and others think and feel is something some people unsuccessfully struggle for all their lives. It requires us to comprehend internal signals telling us whether we feel tired or energetic, infer the motivations driving others' actions, and effectively pursue profitable goals based on this information. We have to decode facial expressions and consider background information to understand whether others are sincere or lying or what has motivated them to behave in a particular way. We also need to distinguish our perspective from others' and, the more we can do this, the more likely we are to find ways of meeting our needs and regulating our emotions.

Metacognitive dysfunctions need to be taken into account when adapting DST-oriented therapies to more severe sufferers' needs. Many forms of DST-oriented therapy take for granted that patients in psychotherapy are able, with appropriate therapist prompts, to describe the voices inhabiting their imaginal landscape. Moreover, these therapies assume that patients are able to form nuanced descriptions of others with whom they interact, in both their fantasy and real worlds. Also it is taken for granted that patients have the capacity to engage in dialogical question and answer and agreement and disagreement processes and to negotiate the meaning of what happens in their inner society. In severe disorders, such as the avoidant, narcissistic, obsessive-compulsive and borderline PDs which I focus on here, and in schizophrenia, this is often not the case. Many with avoidant PD can barely perceive their changes in emotional arousal and are even less able to understand that a specific event, such as the impending risk of being abandoned, triggers an affect. As a result, instead of telling detailed autobiographic episodes, they rely on over-generalized statements (Dimaggio *et al.* 2007a), thus depriving their therapist of an understanding of what they feel and think at specific moments in their lives. Two metacognitive system deficit forms prevent the formation of dialogical processes: poor self-reflection (Dimaggio *et al.* 2009a) and impaired mind-reading (Dimaggio *et al.* 2009b).

Poor self-reflection

A dysfunction in understanding one's own mind has been found in people with PD and schizophrenia, and research supports the notion that increased self-awareness is linked to positive therapy outcomes (Dimaggio *et al.* 2007b; Lysaker *et al.* 2010). With severe damage to the self-reflexive ability to tell what one feels and why, and what makes one react to what stimuli coming from relevant others, scarcely any dialogue can arise.

Therapists need instruments to tackle problems similar to the one presented by Rick, a 30-year-old biologist suffering from a severe avoidant PD, with prominent passive-aggressive and schizoid traits, and covert narcissism features. In his self-justifying, generalized narratives, he endorsed an abstract meta-position, which did not in fact reflect anything in his everyday life: he portrayed himself as a benevolent and detached entity, untouched by anything and motivated by the desire to bring calm and relief to everyone around him. It is worth noting that his father, described more and more during therapy as intrusive and domineering, suffered from a bipolar disorder, with prominent symptoms of mania leading to hospitalizations when Rick was a child. Rick did not report any suffering on account of his father's condition or anger at the plans his father made for his life. Rick led an isolated life, had not had a girlfriend in years and had no plans for the future. He felt capable of doing everything but never made a choice.

Rick attempted suicide by cutting his wrists in a park the year before seeking therapy. In his words, this attempt was merely a form of aesthetic experience and he decided not to let himself bleed to death because 'it was less beautiful than I expected, with blood staining everything'. No sign of awareness of specific factors leading to the suicidal gesture appeared in his discourse, no painful emotion was present in his words, and I could see no signs of pain in his face, except for a hint of disgust. After some months of therapy he started a relationship with a girl of his age, but he constantly denied any involvement, and I could detect no emotion in his face. Furthermore, Rick told that the girl became pregnant and then left him, while deciding to keep the baby. Rick then displayed distress at the separation and declared he was involved. Again this came in the form of an abstract statement, uttered from an idealistic meta-position: he felt he was losing the chance to fulfil his wish for a family, which would represent a perfect love circle, a desire he never mentioned while dating the girl. But even this new account, with the appearance of love for the girlfriend he had lost, was inconsistent with the real nuances in his inner experience, due to his deficient self-reflective skills. I discovered the tragic inconsistency a few months later. The baby was born and Rick attempted suicide again, this time with pills. He did not mention any suicidal wish before this act, although I repeatedly asked him about this possibility. He was not lying, as we thought after the act, but was obviously unaware of what was happening inside his mind. Only two months after this act, we were able to reconstruct that he felt overwhelmed by the responsibility of rearing a child and by the distance the mother put between him and the baby.

In short, how could I promote new forms of dialogue, if the very aspects of Rick's self-system were inaccessible to both of us? Stories like Rick's call for a therapy primarily aimed at fostering self-awareness, starting from understanding and naming affects, then discovering their triggers and consequences, and finally becoming aware of the nature of emotionally laden meaning-making attributions.

Problems in mind-reading

Many with adult mental disorders experience difficulty in inferring others' feelings and thoughts (Dimaggio and Lysaker 2010). In the PD area, there is an emerging consensus that many patients are barely able to form a nuanced picture of others' intentions or recognize that others have different wishes, opinions and agendas from theirs (Dimaggio *et al.* 2009b; Fonagy *et al.* 2002).

A significant part of the mind-reading dysfunction depends on relationship quality (Fonagy *et al.* 2002). People with PD often stick to their expectations of negative reactions from others, pay only selective attention to signals such as criticism or rejection, and trigger negative cycles in which others' reactions confirm their expectations (Safran and Muran 2000). At such moments their ability to reflect on mental states is likely to diminish.

There are reasons for mind-reading being impaired in a context-specific manner. For example, patients with histories of abuse or violence learn to be scared about what passes through a caregiver's mind, so that under the activation of the attachment motive they automatically shut off the mind-reading system as a dissociative protection against psychological pain (Fonagy *et al.* 2002). Alternatively, they bias their attributions of the intentions of others towards evil ones, a process hampering the development of a dialogical self in which others are recognized as distinct and unique human beings.

These preconceived attributions are rigid, inflexible and easily activated. Moreover, once they are ignited in real-world relationships, they tend to elicit schema-congruent reactions in others (Safran and Muran 2000), thus providing further material to prevent an alternative positioning of others. For example, people with paranoid personalities see themselves as weak and with poor self-efficacy vis-à-vis hostile others (Dimaggio *et al.* 2007a). In reaction, they attack first, thus evoking the expected hostile reaction and narrowing their mind-reading further.

A difficulty in forming a nuanced, mature and realistic theory of the other's mind was evident in Marcel, a 32-year-old clerk, who suffered from avoidant PD with paranoid traits. He felt constantly ashamed and reluctant to self-disclose in social interactions because he constantly feared criticisms and humiliation. During group psychotherapy, it became clear that, no matter how other group members reacted, he was only able to note signals of criticism or refusal, thus leaving the sessions with a sense of being an outcast with nothing to share with the others. A first step towards his recovery occurred after a few sessions, when he reacted to a girl even more prone to shame than he by giving her advice and support, thus embodying a *caretaker* position.

In sum, poor mind-reading leaves little room for dialogue. The other is positioned according to pre-existing scripts, because patients find it hard to read emotions in faces or listen to points of view not foreseen by their schemas (Dimaggio *et al.* 2009b). Such patients take a long time to form a mature theory of the other's mind and to be able to say, for example, 'I thought he was cross at me, but his gloomy expression probably signified he was annoyed at his boss not giving him a raise.'

Dialogical therapy with PD taking account of metacognitive dysfunctions

A dialogically based treatment can be tailored to treating metacognitive disorders. It is impossible to enrich a personal position repertoire if clinicians and patients have only vague ideas of what the latter feel and think. Many therapeutic operations need to be performed before verbal dialogues arise in therapy and are detailed enough to be worked through. I notice here that in such cases dialogues do appear, but mostly in the non-verbal bond between patient and therapist. In this interpersonal space, action and reaction patterns and silent requests for wishes to be met encounter unintended reactions from the other. Therapists need to pay attention to these non-verbal dialogues, tactfully transforming them into the content of conversations which are accessible to the observing selves and then amenable to enrichment and change.

The therapy agenda can be set to prepare PD patients for a flexible, dialogical form of meaning-making, of the sort that would then be amenable to more classical, DST-oriented interventions. I limit myself here to proposing three therapy steps to follow in a hierarchical order; that is, if the earlier steps are not successfully achieved, I discourage therapists from proceeding further and trying to engage patients in mentalistically complex processes they would be unable to perform. The three steps are as follows: (1) *evoking detailed autobiographical narratives*; (2) *promoting self-reflection in order to let voices enter consciousness*; (3) *promoting mind-reading through the therapy relationship*. The goal of these steps is to construct a narrative landscape where new, previously inchoate and unnoticed, voices are allowed to speak and become precursors of the constructions of others as unique human beings, and not according to the patient's pre-existing patterns. These new voices can progressively activate a flexible dialogical functioning of the mind.

Evoking detailed autobiographical narratives

Clinicians need to collect details of self-narratives before working through psychological contents, in order to avoid pointless discussions on abstract, theory-like, value-laden statements, which would make the therapy a clash of values. With a shared narrative landscape rich in emotions and contents, it is possible to cooperate and work on shared goals. What I look for are specific examples, located in well-defined moments (*when*) and specific places (*where*), clearly portraying the actors on stage (*who*) and the dialogue among them, and with a defined plot, which should include a theme encompassing the protagonist's wishes and vicissitudes during interpersonal relationships (*what*), and, lastly, the reason (*why*) the story gets told; that is, the problem the patient wants to be solved or the message that the story conveys to the therapist (Hermans and Dimaggio 2004; Neimeyer 2000).

This is a hard-to-accomplish task in people with PD, as in my therapy with Carmen, a young woman suffering from narcissistic PD, dysthymia and worries about important decisions in her life (see Dimaggio *et al.* 2007c). I struggled for months to access narrative scenarios. My questions were focused on eliciting examples, but she completely denied having recent or remote memories, and, in accordance with her narcissistic character, she was annoyed by my questions. Session after session, she described herself as 'depressed'. I asked, 'Could you tell me about a moment when you were depressed?' She answered, 'I'm always depressed. I'm the black sheep of the family.' I could not obtain anything more so there was no way of changing her mood. Then I asked her to focus slowly on her daily life between sessions. Although she was sceptical about the procedure, she provided more and more memories, which I focused on by asking for as many details as possible, until a key episode finally arrived: she woke up feeling it was a black day. She and her partner had spent the night before with two couples of friends, one about to get married, the other likely to separate. Her partner was open to both possibilities: a couple can get married or it can separate if things are going badly. This scene provided a path to a shared understanding of her emotional world: she was depressed because she felt both constricted at the idea of getting married and sad about the prospect of being abandoned. These – the *constricted position* and the *abandoned position* – were the first elements to surface in her consciousness, and I could now promote mutual contact between them in a dialogical context. I now describe the steps for improving metacognitive awareness of emotions once a narrative scene has been set up.

Promoting self-reflection in order to let voices enter consciousness

Therapists should foster a shared understanding of the emotions nesting in patients' discourses. In PD patients with limited emotional language, trying to promote awareness of emotions and of why and under what relational conditions an emotion is experienced is a basic operation. Such patients do not convey the appropriate affects – in particular positive ones – to stimulate clinicians' empathy. Therapists therefore need devices for promoting emotional awareness and working on the therapy relationship, in order to prevent and repair alliance ruptures (Dimaggio *et al.* in press).

As emotions are the basic form of meaning-making, I first always ask patients about the emotional correlates of an episode. A typical question I posed to Rick was, 'What did you feel while your father started preparing the game for your son in your place?' Starting from a detailed analysis of the episode and from my reading of his face and posture, I pointed out to Rick that there was a striking contrast between his description of the episode ('My father was playing very well with him') and his non-verbal reaction ('You look pretty annoyed'). I then proposed an alternative reading of these signals: 'Can it be you felt encroached on and wanted instead to be yourself deciding what to play with your kid?' I also showed him that I myself was feeling tense while listening to him. I told him that I felt annoyed when other parents tried to decide what my children should do. Rick felt understood and supported, and started to perceive a protesting voice entering his consciousness. Before reaching this assertive position, Rick had had two positions towards his father: I-*as-taking-care of a suffering father* and I-*as-trying-to-comply with father's wishes and expectations.* Understanding that he had a complex and con-flictual reciprocal positioning with his father paved the way for the emergence of an *assertive position*, capable of disagreeing with others and taking an agentive stance. In spite of this first success, the improvement in Rick's awareness of emotions occurred only falteringly, and years after this moment I still have to struggle to make contact with his disagreements with relevant figures – e.g. spouse, ex-girlfriend – and get the agentic self to take the lead.

Promoting mind-reading through the therapy relationship

Most PD patients have difficulty in adopting others' points of view and consider them to have intentions reflecting their own anticipatory schemas, with such attributions being negative – *she is criticizing, abusing* or *rejecting me* – or tainted by self-serving biases – *he adores me.* It is almost mandatory *not* to prematurely push patients to adopt others' perspectives or ingenuously get them to *empathize* with relatives, spouses or colleagues. This is counterproductive in many instances, as *real* others scarcely exist in these patients' expectations. If forced to explore others' minds and assume their perspective, they feel forced to take sides with the 'enemy', 'tyrant' or 'rejecting caregiver'. Promoting mind-reading or, in DST terms, recognizing others as separate and unique human beings, is a later therapy step (Dimaggio *et al.* 2010b, 2011). One needs first to gain a fine-grained access to formerly suppressed parts of the self. For example, persons with narcissism are likely to feel others are hampering their goals through envy, incompetence or neglect, and therefore react angrily. Most of all, they are unable to pursue their uttermost life goals unless admired by others. It is therefore pointless to try to convince a man with narcissistic features that his wife is not neglecting him because she does not love him, but simply because she is exhausted from taking care of their newborn child. He would react simply by constructing the therapist as allied to the neglecting internalized other. Instead I spend time on helping patents to focus on their wishes and slowly discover they depend on others' approval and support, while lacking an *inner supporter*, which therapy will try to develop later.

A second step, to be achieved before promoting mind-reading and a full-fledged dialogical self, is making patients understand that they do not suffer because of what happens around them, but because of their *constructions* of reality. I therefore focus on helping them see the similarities in their reciprocal positioning of the self and others as time, characters and situations change. Only when they are aware of tending to construct relationships in a fixed and rigid way and recognize that problems lie in their minds, do I encourage them to see others as separate and unique human beings.

An action within the therapy relationship that can promote mind-reading is therapists' self-disclosing what they are actually feeling about the patient, especially when the alliance is strained. Self-disclosure needs to be carefully delivered, after anticipating patients' potential reactions, and therapists need to be aware that patients may interpret it differently from their intentions. Therapists should expect describing their own mental states to be misunderstood. More precisely, therapists can disclose their thoughts and feelings but only after covertly disembedding themselves of any problematic pattern on the part of the patient.

I resorted to the self-disclosing strategy during group sessions with Marcel. He was describing his relationship with women – their roommates, friends or potential romantic partners – with a mixture of fear, distrust and contempt. This elicited negative reactions in the female group members, which in turn made him more and more disdainful and defensive. My co-group leader (a woman) and I attempted to make Marcel understand that what was happening in the group was just a problem that could be solved, but nothing helped soothe his tension. I then asked him what he thought I was thinking about him. He answered that he felt criticized, blamed and misunderstood. I asked Marcel how he had come to perceive this: from my words or hints of contempt or rejection in my face? He answered that it was just a vague sensation. Then I told him that I was worried because I could see his distress and wanted to find a way, especially in the here-and-now of the group situation, to relieve his suffering, make contact with him and make him feel understood, but was not finding any viable option, so that I felt rather powerless. After describing my mental state, I asked him to tell me straightforwardly if he felt I was sincere or not. He answered he thought I was honest. At that moment Marcel looked more relaxed. I noticed that, under the burden of the criticisms which he expected and sensed from others, he was motivated to protect his self-image from humiliation. I also told him that at such moments he was focused only on self-defence, so that he could not explore others' minds. I finally stated that my real goal was just to show him that there was no real danger and I deeply wanted him to not feel threatened, at least not by me. Marcel accepted my observations and started to build a meta-position in which he recognized that this feeling of impending humiliation might be not only a reflection of reality but also part of his own pattern of expectations.

In this excerpt one can see the beginning of a transformation from a fixed positioning of self and others to one in which the other, the therapist in this case, can be positioned by patients in a manner inconsistent with their monological narrative. This transformation paves the way for full-fledged dialogical exchanges in which exploration of different perspectives in self and other is possible. Therapist self-disclosure is a fruitful way to open new dialogues, because therapists, positioning themselves in relationships with other human beings, face similar life challenges and complex mental states regarding stressful relationships.

Conclusions

DST-oriented therapies have provided clinicians with many useful concepts. These help persons build a more nuanced construction of the self-with-others and enrich their narrative landscape by the introduction of new self-voices, which bring innovation through dialogue (Hermans and Hermans-Konopka 2010). The new voices can flexibly dialogue with pre-existing voices in persons' imaginal space and social environment, helping them to break formerly crystallized patterns. DST-oriented therapies also aim at promoting the construction of overarching vantage points, that is, meta-positions, from which a person can observe self-aspects from different angles and learn new ways to overcome barriers to health and adaptation. I have proposed in this chapter that considering impairments in the human ability to make sense of mental states, here termed 'metacognition', is required to broaden the application of DST-oriented therapies to the needs of more severe sufferers, such as PD patients. With them therapists should first promote access to their mental states, an operation in which patients often fail, and form a picture of their mind that both patient and therapist can then use as a basis for treatment planning. Until mental state understanding is adequate, open-ended and flexible, dialogical processes among different self-positions cannot start, because patients are unable either to describe facets of their self-experience or to portray what is passing through others' minds. I contend that clinicians first need to work at length to collect details of narrative episodes, in order to base exploration of mental states on autobiographical knowledge and not on abstract theories. A next step is to promote awareness of the inner experience depicted in these narratives, in particular emotions and their triggers, until a clear-enough picture of the voices within the self appears. Only when a nuanced knowledge about the multiplicity of self-positions is reached, can therapists try to promote new perspectives on others' minds, when previously others were constructed only according to sketchy descriptions or crystallized attributions. Once mental state knowledge has been collected, it is possible, even with the more severe sufferers, to start therapeutic question/answer and agreement/disagreement processes, negotiation of conflicts, and a search for new solutions to pre-existing problems, which are the features of a full-fledged dialogical self in action.

REFERENCES

Angus, L. E. and McLeod J. (eds.), (2004) *The Handbook of Narrative and Psychotherapy: Practice, Theory and Research* (Thousand Oaks, CA: Sage)

Bakhtin, M. (1973) *Problems of Dostoevsky's Poetics*, 2nd edn (Ann Arbor, MI: Ardis)

Bruner, J. (1990) *Acts of Meaning* (Cambridge, MA: Harvard University Press)

Carcione, A., Dimaggio, G., Conti, M. L., Fiore, D., Nicolò, G. and Semerari, A. (2010) *Metacognition Asssessment Scale* V. 4.0, unpublished manuscript, Rome

Dimaggio, G., Carcione, A., Conti, M. L., Nicolò, G., Fiore, D., Pedone, R., *et al.* (2009) Impaired decentration in personality disorder: an analysis with the Metacognition Assessment Scale, *Clinical Psychology and Psychotherapy*, **16**, 450–462

Dimaggio, G., Carcione, A., Salvatore, G., Nicolò, G., Sisto, A. and Semerari, A. (2011) Progressively increasing metacognition through a step-by-step procedure in a case of obsessive-compulsive personality disorder treated with meta-cognitive interpersonal therapy, *Psychology and Psychotherapy: Theory, Research and Practice*, **84**, 70–83

Dimaggio, G., Carcione, A., Salvatore, G., Semerari, A. and Nicolò, G. (2010c) A rational model for maximizing the effect of regulating therapy relationship in personality disorders, *Psychology and Psychotherapy: Theory, Research and Practice*, **83**, 363–384

Dimaggio, G., Fiore, D., Salvatore, G. and Carcione, A. (2007c) Dialogical relationship patterns in narcissistic personalities: session analysis and treatment implications, *Journal of Constructivist Psychology*, **20**, 23–51

Dimaggio, G., Hermans, H. J. M. and Lysaker, P. (2010a) Health and adaptation in a multiple self: the role of absence of dialogue and poor metacognition in clinical populations, *Theory & Psychology*, **20**, 379–399

Dimaggio, G. and Lysaker, P. H. (eds.) (2010) *Metacognition and Severe Adult Mental Disorders: From Basic Research to Treatment* (London: Routledge)

Dimaggio, G., Procacci, M., Nicolò, G., Popolo, R., Semerari, A., Carcione, A., *et al.* (2007b), Poor metacognition in narcissistic and avoidant personality disorders: analysis of four psychotherapy patients, *Clinical Psychology and Psychotherapy*, **14**, 386–401

Dimaggio, G., Salvatore, G., Azzara, C., Catania, D., Semerari, A. and Hermans, H. J. M. (2003) Dialogical relationships in impoverished narratives: From theory to clinical practice, *Psychology and Psychotherapy: Theory, Research and Practice*, **76**, 385–410

Dimaggio, G., Salvatore, G., Fiore, D., Carcione, A., Nicolò, G. and Semerari, A. (in press) General principles for treating the overconstricted personality disorder: toward operationalizing technique, *Journal of Personality Disorders*

Dimaggio, G., Salvatore, G., Nicolò, G., Fiore, D. and Procacci, M. (2010b) Enhancing mental state understanding in the over-constricted personality disorder with metacognitive interpersonal therapy, in G. Dimaggio and P. Lysaker (eds.), *Metacognition and Severe Adult Mental Disorders: From Basic Research to Treatment* (London: Routledge), 247–268

Dimaggio, G., Semerari, A., Carcione, A., Nicolò, G. and Procacci, M. (2007a) *Psychotherapy of Personality Disorders: Metacognition, States of Mind and Interpersonal Cycles* (London: Routledge)

Dimaggio, G. and Stiles, W. B. (2007) Psychotherapy in light of internal multiplicity, *Journal of Clinical Psychology: In-Session*, **63**, 119–127

Dimaggio, G., Vanheule, S., Lysaker, P., Carcione, A. and Nicolò, G. (2009a) Impaired self-reflection in psychiatric disorders among adults: a proposal for the existence of a network of semi-independent functions, *Consciousness and Cognition*, **18**, 653–664

Fonagy, P., Gergely, G., Jurist E. L. and Target, M. (2002) *Affect Regulation, Mentalization, and the Development of the Self* (New York: Other Press)

Gonçalves, M., Matos, M. and Santos, A. (2009) Narrative therapy and the nature of 'innovative moments' in the construction of change, *Journal of Constructivist Psychology*, **22**, 1–23

Hermans, H. J. M. (1996) Voicing the self: from information processing to dialogical interchange, *Psychological Bulletin*, **119**, 31–50

(2001a) The dialogical self: toward a theory of personal and cultural positioning, *Culture & Psychology*, **7**, 243–281

Hermans, H. J. M. and Dimaggio, G. (eds.) (2004) *The Dialogical Self in Psychotherapy* (London: Brunner-Routledge)

Hermans, H. J. M. and Hermans-Konopka, A. (2010) *Dialogical Self Theory: Positioning and Counter-Positioning in a Globalizing Society* (Cambridge University Press)

Hermans, H. J. M., Kempen, H. J. G. and van Loon, R. J. P. (1992) The dialogical self: beyond individualism and rationalism, *American Psychologist*, **47**, 23–33

Liotti, G. and Gilbert, P. (in press) Mentalizing, motivation and social mentalities: theoretical considerations and implications for psychotherapy, *Psychology and Psychotherapy: Theory, Research and Practice*

Liotti, G. and Prunetti, E. (2010) Meta-cognitive deficits in trauma-related disorders: contingent on interpersonal motivational contexts?, in G. Dimaggio and P. Lysaker (eds.), *Metacognition and Severe Adult Mental Disorders: From Basic Research to Treatment* (London: Routledge), 196–213

Lysaker, P., Dimaggio, G., Buck, K. D., Carcione, A., Procacci, M., Davis, L. W., *et al.* (2010) Metacognition and schizophrenia: the capacity for self-reflectivity and prospective assessments of work performance over six months, *Schizophrenia Research*, **96**, 124–130

Lysaker, P. and Lysaker, J. (2002) Narrative structure in psychosis: schizophrenia and disruptions in the dialogical self, *Theory & Psychology*, **12**, 207–220

(2008) *Schizophrenia and the Fate of the Self* (Oxford University Press)

Neimeyer, R. A. (2000) Narrative disruptions in the construction of the self, in R. A. Neimeyer and J. D. Raskin (eds.), *Constructions of Disorder* (Washington, DC: APA Press), 207–241

Safran, J. D. and Muran, J. C. (2000) *Negotiating the Therapeutic Alliance: A Relational Treatment Guide* (New York: Guilford Press)

Salvatore, G., Conti, C., Fiore, D., Carcione, A., Dimaggio, G. and Semerari, A. (2006) Disorganized narratives: problems in treatment and therapist intervention hierarchy, *Journal of Constructivist Psychology*, **19**, 191–207

Salvatore, G., Dimaggio, G. and Semerari, A. (2004) A model of narrative development: psychopathology and implication for clinical practice, *Psychology and Psychotherapy: Theory, Research and Practice*, **77**, 231–254

Santos, A., Gonçalves, M., Matos, M. and Salvatore, G. (2009) Innovative moments and change pathways: a good outcome case of narrative therapy, *Psychology and Psychotherapy: Theory, Research and Practice*, **82**, 449–466

Semerari, A., Carcione, G., Dimaggio, M., Falcone, G., Nicolò, M., Procacci, M., *et al.* (2003) How to evaluate metacognitive functioning in psychotherapy? The Metacognition Assessment Scale and its applications, *Clinical Psychology and Psychotherapy*, **10**, 238–261

Semerari, A., Dimaggio, G., Nicolò, G., Procacci, M. and Carcione, A. (2007) Understanding minds: different functions and different disorders? The contribution of psychotherapeutic research, *Psychotherapy Research*, **17**, 106–119

Stiles, W. B. (2007) Signs and voices in psychotherapy, *Psychotherapy Research*, **9**, 1–21

White, M. and Epston, D. (1990) *Narrative Means to Therapeutic Ends* (New York: Norton)

21 Reconstructing the self in the wake of loss: a dialogical contribution

Robert A. Neimeyer

Like other contributors to this volume, I have found a multiplistic, dialogical conception of self to be an indispensable conceptual and practical aid, especially in my work as a psychotherapy theorist and clinician. Confronted with the considerable complexity of loss of key attachment figures, I have found that well-worn formulations that view the death of loved ones merely as a 'stressful life event' producing temporary disequilibrium, or that conceptualize grief in terms of universal 'stages' of adaptation, are simply too threadbare to support the hard and subtle work of therapy in the wake of a difficult death. Instead, I have drawn on three strands of inspiration, concerned with *meaning making*, *narrative* and the *dialogical self*, braiding these together into a flexible and durable strand of coherence that runs through my therapy, and supports a great variety of novel interventions. I will therefore sketch here the contribution of each of these strands, reserving space to illustrate specific therapeutic procedures animated by an understanding of aspects of the self as intrinsically in dialogue with other aspects, which can include internalized *I*-positions that originate in relationships with other persons. In so doing, I hope to encourage the further development of dialogical self theory (DST) (Hermans and Dimaggio 2004; Hermans and Kempen 1993), to which my own extrapolations are a footnote. First, however, I will briefly sketch the landscape of loss as viewed through the contemporary scientific literature, in order to frame the field to which a dialogical, meaning-oriented model makes a distinctive contribution.

Grief and the quest for meaning

> To live is to suffer; to survive is to find some meaning in the suffering.
> –*Friedrich Nietzsche*

Until recently, popular and professional accounts of bereavement were beguiling in their simplicity: the death of a loved one represented a normative, if stressful life event, one which set in train a series of emotional adaptations that proceeded with stage-like regularity from initial shock and protest through phases of depression and disorganization towards eventual acceptance and recovery (Bowlby 1980; Kübler-Ross 1969). When this process of 'grief work' encountered obstacles in moving forward and 'moving on', such impasses were understood chiefly in terms of the bereaved person's inability to detach or withdraw emotional energy from the one who had died in order to invest it in other people (Freud 1917/1957).

In recent years, nearly every aspect of this modernist model of mourning has been called into question by quantitative and qualitative research (Neimeyer *et al.* 2011; Stroebe *et al.* 2007). For example, studies of large cohorts of both older (Maciejewski *et al.* 2007) and younger adults (Holland and Neimeyer 2010) provide limited support for stage-like models of adaptation, as those emotional markers that are in fact most prominent at various points following loss depart greatly from traditional models. Likewise, evidence that maintaining, rather than relinquishing, a 'continuing bond' with the deceased may be the normative pattern of bereavement adaptation, challenges the assumption that the goal of grieving is 'letting go' of the deceased to reinvest in other relationships (Klass *et al.* 1996). With this conceptual ferment has come a critical assessment of the status of contemporary grief therapy, which the latest review of controlled trials demonstrates is far less universally efficacious than had once been supposed (Currier *et al.* 2008). As a consequence of these and other developments, it is becoming clearer when grief is and is not a problem that will benefit from intervention, and the range of potentially efficacious strategies for grief therapy is expanding (Currier *et al.* 2008; Neimeyer and Currier 2009). Simultaneously, there is greater emerging support for the resilience of the bereaved even in the face of enormous loss (Bonanno 2004), and accruing evidence that traumatic loss can occasion significant personal growth as well as stress (Calhoun and Tedeschi 2006).

As both researchers and practitioners cast about for frameworks with which to orient to this new landscape of loss, one approach to receive attention draws on constructivist psychology, with its central emphasis on how people individually, relationally and socially impose meaning on life events, seeking recurrent themes that permit them to interpret, anticipate and negotiate life challenges and transitions (Kelly 1955; Neimeyer 2009b). From a constructivist standpoint, grieving for the death of a loved one entails reaffirming or reconstructing a world of meaning that has been challenged by loss (Neimeyer 2002).

Consider the experience of Cara, an African-American mother in her mid-thirties mourning the stillbirth of her daughter, whom she named 'Spirit', because 'that was how she came to us – as a spiritual being, rather than a living baby'. For her, the birth and death of her child, fused unimaginably in the same unforgettable moment of delivery, posed a serious crisis of meaning, one accentuated by every encounter in a restaurant with a mother holding a newborn infant, one replayed every night when she would dream of her daughter playing with her siblings, only to find, upon approaching her, a lifeless little body in her place. Spirit's birth and death for Cara invalidated key elements of her 'assumptive world' (Janoff-Bulman 1989), which held that the world was just, that life was predictable, and that she was a 'good mother' who could ensure the safety of her child. Perhaps still more perturbing, Cara found herself looking back to the ultrasound image of her living daughter at 4 months' gestation, seeing in retrospect the ominous portent of her death in the ghost-like image of a 'woman' who appeared to be moving towards her child's fœtal outline. As her physician had been at a loss to explain the shadowy form, merely reassuring her it was not an anatomical picture of the umbilical cord, Cara began to see in it a malevolent spirit, a kind of death angel, sent to 'take her baby'. The reconsideration of the image in light of her loss therefore launched a quest to make sense of the death in spiritual terms, as well as to find some sustainable meaning in the life she herself now led in its wake.

Research on bereaved parents makes clear that Cara's experience is by no means unique. Indeed, the majority of those who lose young children are thrown into an anguishing struggle to 'make sense' of the seemingly senseless loss, with 45 per cent confessing an inability to find sustainable answers even an average of six years later (Lichtenthal *et al.* 2010). Moreover, those who fail in their effort after meaning are at substantially higher risk of poor bereavement outcomes, as sense-making accounts for as much as fifteen times more of the variability in parents' report of complicated grief symptomatology than such factors as the passage time or whether the child died a violent or natural death (Keesee *et al.* 2008). In contrast, when meaning is found, either in spiritual terms (e.g. concluding that the death was God's will) or secular ones (e.g. reordering life priorities), parents report bearing the loss with less disabling grief symptomatology.

Data on other populations reinforce these observations about the centrality of meaning-making processes in adapting to loss. For example, sense-making is such a potent mediator of the impact of bereavement by suicide, homicide or fatal accident that it accounts for nearly all the difference in complicated grief symptomatology between such violent forms of loss and those arising from the natural deaths of loved ones (Currier *et al.* 2006). Even in the context of the normative death of a spouse in later life, making sense of the loss early on predicts positive mood, well-being and resilience even four full years in the future (Coleman and Neimeyer 2010). Thus, the development of strategies that support meaning reconstruction in the context of loss would seem to have high priority (Neimeyer 2001).

Loss and the narration of transition

> There is not one big cosmic meaning for all, there is only the meaning
> we each give to our life, an individual meaning, an individual
> plot, like an individual novel, a book for each person.   *–Anais Nin*

As useful as the concept of meaning-making is in the context of loss and transition, it under-specifies both the processes by which a world of meaning is disrupted and those by which it is restored. How can we understand the challenge posed to our prior ways of making sense of life by a cardinal loss? How do people characteristically, naturally, attempt to cope with such a challenge, when not guided by psychologists? And when psychological intervention is warranted, what form or forms might this usefully take? The variety of concrete answers that might be given to these questions suggests the need to identify a more abstract process that could encompass them, a kind of higher-order principle adequate to describe some of the many ways that loss intrudes in life, and that people attempt to re-establish or reassert meaning in its aftermath. One candidate for such a process is that of *narration*, the organization of life experiences in storied form.

As Hermans has argued, people can be understood as 'motivated storytellers'; that is, as beings drawn naturally to the narrative organization of events in time and space, telling them to both real and imaginal audiences, and motivated to thread the plot structure of their lives through with themes that suggest a sense of purpose and direction (Hermans 2002). This narrative impulse is nowhere clearer than when people are faced by unwelcome transitions in the form of losses of persons, places, projects and possessions that are identity defining, leading them to seek receptive others who can help them make sense in story form of a world that does not.

When losses are profound, however, significant disruptions of narrative processing can result, leading to narrative *disorganization, dominance* or *dissociation* (Neimeyer 2000, 2006b). That is, the story of one's life-altering injury, trauma or bereavement may give rise to a chaotic story that resists clear 'emplotment' in a coherent account, to an oppressive fixation in a hopeless story that 'colonizes' the life of its protagonist, or to a 'silent story' that cannot be acknowledged in its essential details – perhaps not even to oneself. Under such circumstances professional intervention may be indicated to help the client-as-narrator rediscover a significant 'through line' in his or her *self-narrative* (Neimeyer 2004b), defined as 'an overarching cognitive-affective-behavioural structure that organizes the "micro-narratives" of everyday life into a "macro-narrative" that consolidates our self-understanding, establishes our characteristic range of emotions and goals, and guides our performance on the stage of the social world' (2004b: 53–54). A growing number of narrative interventions in the field of bereavement can serve this aim (Neimeyer *et al.* 2009). These include evidence-based practices of encouraging the client to revisit the story of the loss in vivid, slow-motion detail (Shear *et al.* 2005), retell the story as if to a friend (Wagner *et al.* 2006), or write for oneself as the only relevant audience about the possible 'silver lining' or unsought benefit in the experience (Lichtenthal and Cruess 2010). The specific narrative processes facilitated by these methods have in common the goal of helping the storyteller master the experience of loss in a way that entails less emotional reactivity and complication.

An example of narrative disruption and reconstruction in the wake of loss is provided by Daniel, a medical intern whose life script was shattered along with his leg in a major automobile accident. A runner and track star since his youth, Daniel had been on the 'fast track' in more ways than one, winning a series of academic as well as athletic awards as he moved quickly towards a career bright with promise, the rising star in an immigrant family, and seemingly destined to marry his college sweetheart and achieve great things in his career in medicine. All that changed in an instant when a pickup truck ran through a red light, slamming into the side of the car he was driving, and splintering the bones in his leg in a dozen places. Extensive surgeries over the course of a long hospitalization narrowly averted an amputation.

At the point of his consultation with me, Daniel was despondent and disillusioned, ruminating endlessly on the accident and all that it had taken from him. Gone were his speed, his agility, a year of his education – in a word, his entire progressive self-narrative that had long seemed ensured. No less substantial were the intangible losses of his sense of invulnerability, direction and 'specialness', as he now found himself distancing from his partner, gaining substantial weight and questioning the spiritual discourse that he once shared with his parents. Although he was completing his medical training, he seemed to be going through the motions mechanically, without purpose or passion, to an extent that was beginning to be noticed by his supervisors. Given this cluster of symptoms, Daniel could be fairly described as grieving for not the death of another, but the death of a core aspect of himself.

As we neared the end of our first session of therapy, I thought spontaneously of a narrative technique I find helpful in assisting people struggling to find meaning in their loss, through encouraging them to frame such unwelcome transitions in terms of the broader structure of their life story. I therefore introduced the idea to Daniel of considering his life as a book, and asked if he would be willing to spend some time between sessions writing the 'table of contents' of that life to capture its plot developments, including the accident and his subsequent adaptation (Neimeyer 2006a). Intrigued, Daniel readily agreed, and returned the next week with a substantial series of chapter titles, which read:

Chapter 1. *Ten years of Timelessness: The Cheerful and Captivated Child*
Chapter 2. *Nowhere to Fit: The Insignificant Adolescent*
Chapter 3. *From Outcast to King: The Teen Athlete*
Chapter 4. *Loss of Self in a Foreign Land: Life as a College Freshman*
Chapter 5. *Seeking That Which Was Lost: Competing on a Smaller Field*
Chapter 6. *No Way Back: Injury, Insult and the Return to Obscurity*
Chapter 7. *The Dark Time: Dominance of the Noon-Day Demon*
Chapter 8. *Painful Paralysis: A Firm Lesson in Infirmity*
Chapter 9. *Reclamation: Preparing Body and Mind for an Unknown Future*
Chapter 10. *A Juggernaut of Purpose: Preparing for a Great Destiny*
Chapter 11. *King Once More: Readying for a Brilliant Launch*
Chapter 12. *Cut Down by Fate: The Destruction of Destiny*
Chapter 13. *Pit of the Unknown: Hospitalized, Bedridden and Shattered*
Chapter 14. *Holding Firm: Living in Limbo*
Chapter 15. *Frozen in Time: Surviving as Life and Love Move On*

As Daniel responded with animation to my curious queries about the gist of each of the chapters, I learned of the secure and loving home environment in which he had been raised, captivated by wonder at the natural world that surrounded his small town. But soon enough, there was trouble in paradise, as Daniel, a slightly chubby, bookish and unfashionably dressed immigrant boy, entered an adolescence in which looks and conformity were paramount, only to find social acceptance and eventual acclaim on the high-school athletic field. Unfortunately, this 'field of dreams' was lost once more upon entry into a gigantic state university with its cloak of anonymity, shed only when he transferred to a smaller college where he again found visibility through athletics until a spinal injury 'cut him down', and introduced him to the 'noon-day demon' of depression. Daniel's way back was gradual as he slowly transferred his physical exertions into intellectual ones, preparing for a brilliant career in medicine and gaining admission to an elite school. It was at this propitious moment, borne up by the pride of his family, the devotion of his girlfriend and the admiration of his small town that Daniel drove through the wrong intersection at the wrong time. Once again he was 'cut down by fate', and accompanied once more by his dark demon, he limped despondently through the remainder of medical school, ultimately finding his way to my office.

In addition to outlining his chapters, Daniel had accepted my suggestion to address a subset of further 'deconstructive questions' that prompted him to reflect in novel ways on the organization, pattern, thematic structure and alternative readings of the chapters of his life (Neimeyer 2006a). For instance, in response to a question that asked him to consider where his self-narrative ended, and how it might develop if projected into the future, Daniel responded, 'My narrative ended at my present state, a state of stagnation in which I can't seem to find my way forward... I believe I could marry, have children, work for 35 years or so, and then die. As time marches on, any remnant of my life would be forgotten.' He then projected his future chapters, sparely titled, 'Marriage and Children', 'Work', 'Retirement', 'Death' and 'Eternal Obscurity'. Prompted by another question to consider how he determined when one chapter ended and another began, Daniel quickly discerned how 'across the whole of my life the chapters seem to stop and begin by the acquisition and loss of a positive identity that is admired by others... This seemed attainable once, but it now seems like childish thinking.' Still another question encouraged Daniel to reflect on the basic themes threaded through his chapters, leading him to recognize the *leitmotif* of 'ever rising to find my place in the world only to lose it once more... From my perspective, I am not growing toward or into anything, just more slowly deteriorating now.' Asked what literary genre his life story would fall into, Daniel acknowledged that although some aspects of it 'could readily be seen as a tragedy, a comedy, or even a cliché romance ... what seems missing is the *adventure* story... I would like to again see myself as, and more importantly *feel* like an adventurer.' In subsequent sessions we then turned to precisely this task, exploring the core motifs that informed his early memories, role models, favourite books, movies, mottos and interests (Savickas 2005). What emerged as a through line was a heroic sense of life as a noble quest, undertaken with courage and compassion, and open to the wisdom that can be cultivated in adversity. Looking back and forward from his current impasse, we then began experimenting creatively with first discerning these themes in his most central life projects and then extending them more boldly in hoped-for directions. Daniel quickly gained traction, began exercising and dieting, losing weight, deepening contact with others, and excelling in his internship, while also cultivating greater philosophic depth and empathy for the suffering of others. Using narrative as a method as well as a metaphor, Daniel was able to restore forward movement to a life story seriously disrupted by loss.

Enactment and the dialogical self

> A new kind of mind thus begins to come into being which is based on the development of a common meaning that is constantly transforming in the process of the dialogue.   *–David Bohm*

Viewed in its simplest terms, a narrative framing of human experience merely implies storytelling, our species-specific penchant for formulating our experiences in accounts that can be related to others of our kind. Helpful though this may be, however, it has come to feel too constraining to me to encompass, guide or inspire the healing stories that are articulated, reconstructed and transformed in the crucible of therapeutic conversation. What seems missing from a straightforward conceptualization of storytelling is the deep recognition of the *multivocality* of all accounts, even when the narrator, the protagonist and the audience of the account are all the same person. It is precisely for this reason that I find a model of the dialogical self, a subjectivity shot through with sociality and capable of encountering and addressing aspects of the self as if they were 'other', to be an indispensable aid to my efforts to help people contending with disconcerting loss and transition. Thus, a dialogical self model might appropriately be viewed as an elaboration of a meaning-focused narrative approach, rather than a competing formulation.

Among the several advantages this entails is a clearer conception of narration as performance, of language as a way of 'doing something' in the social world (Gergen 2000), such as positioning the speakers in a morally sympathetic, admirable or heroic fashion, or perhaps victimized by antagonists or fate. Sensitivity to this dynamic contributes to my 'deconstructive listening' to my clients' stories. This implies engaging them with one ear attuned to the function of the narration in conjuring a world that (1) reifies the motives of relevant actors, (2) defines the implicit theme and (3) sets invisible constraints on the development of the plot in ways that the client may experience as disempowering or confining.

A second advantage of a dialogical conception of meaning is more concrete. A central principle of practice that guides my approach to therapy is that *all significant moments of therapeutic change are experientially intense*; everything else that happens in a session is merely commentary (Neimeyer 2009a). That is not to say that reflective commentary, either in the literal dialogue of therapy or in the subsequent private dialogue of a client in her or his personal journal, has no place – indeed, it is typically essential in helping both participants hold and harvest the lessons learned in the more vivid and emotional aspects of their encounter. But it in no way substitutes for the affectively charged encounter with self (and others) that pivots clients into deeper awareness and agency in producing significant shifts in their evolving self-narrative. To foster the latter, therefore, I frequently draw on evocative visualization to meet, confront and dialogue with internalized others, as well as unattended parts of the clients themselves (Neimeyer 2004a, 2008, 2009a; Neimeyer and Arvay 2004). It is a sampling of such methods that I will attempt to illustrate in the remainder of this chapter.

Reopening a dialogue foreclosed by death

More than two years following the death of her mother from complications associated with diabetes, Deborah remained inconsolable. Tearful and dishevelled in our first session of therapy, she spoke of how her own life had somehow slipped out of focus with the loss of her mother's. Although she was 43, she continued to live in the home she had shared with her mother, and still shared with some of her adult siblings. Her desperate yearning for her mother's presence was palpable each morning, as she padded from a sleepless night in her own bedroom to peer into the room that was once her mother's, as if she expected the nightmare to end by seeing the older woman sleeping peacefully where she belonged. But, reminded each day of her mother's absence, she found herself unable to perform simple chores, unable to work in the field of elder care she had once found satisfying, and vacillating between periods of dissociative 'blankness' and unpredictable bouts of painful emotion, both public and private. Deborah confessed that she was stuck in an agonizing grief that 'seemed to get worse instead of better' as the months of her bereavement grew into years.

As we moved towards the end of our first session, a spark of hope leaped up with Deborah's spontaneous comment, 'I try to open whatever doors I can, and accept that she's gone. I *can* make decisions.' Giving more tinder to the spark, I observed that there were indeed two parts to the story, and two parts of her, one of which wanted to close the door on life and withdraw, while another wanted to get some footing back in life, and make it more as she wanted it to be. Getting her nonverbal assent, I therefore wondered aloud 'whether there was some small and specific step that we could take in the direction of that hope', and sketched the idea of a narrative intervention: her writing a letter to Mum, to resume an intimate conversation with her mother that had been interrupted by death. Deb showed a muted sign of interest, but noted, 'We'd have to write that down, because it was already lost' to her impaired concentration and memory. I therefore picked up a pen and paper, and prompted her by asking what she called her mother, gradually eliciting the first few lines of a heartfelt letter that came haltingly through a torrent of tears. Converting Deborah's third-person statements (e.g. 'I miss her', 'she always listened') into first-person affirmations (e.g. 'I miss you', 'you always listened'), I handed her the letter we had begun, and inquired how it would be to continue it as therapeutic homework, an idea to which she assented. We closed with her noting hopefully that the letter might be a way to 'reconnect' with Mum and with 'her positive thoughts', something she realized tearfully that she greatly needed.

Deborah's appearance for the next session immediately caught my attention: dressed in bright 'business casual' attire with a smart pair of glasses and hair that clearly benefited from her attention, she seemed to step more lightly, meeting my gaze and taking a seat eagerly for our conversation to begin. In response to my inquiry about her reaction to our first meeting in the ensuing week, Deborah permitted the flicker of a smile, and noted that 'I feel that I have gotten through some of the "yuck" I was feeling. I liked the idea of writing a letter, and wrote it three or four times', although she confessed that doing so was accompanied by 'a lot of anxiety'. The writing, she informed me, had helped her realize that her mother 'was in a better place', as well as to recognize that 'her presence was within', especially within herself, in a way that was difficult to articulate. What was certain, however, was that some welcome form of reconnection had begun. At my invitation, Deborah slowly read aloud the letter she had drafted:

Dear Mum,

I miss you. It's hard without your guidance and encouragement, but I'm doing what you told me to do almost 26 years ago. I'm completing my associate's degree. It's very hard for me to function. . . I pray to God I'm doing what I'm meant to do in this lifetime. How I miss your words of wisdom, and how you always told me to 'keep up the good work'. I know you're in a better place and I will see you again. I send you the biggest hug, and I'm trying to be the person you raised me to be. I pray that the blankness of thought goes, and I am able to concentrate on the gift God gave me of having a mother like you for 43 years. I know you're keeping track of us, as your love lives in us all.

Until we meet again, hugs and kisses,
Deborah

Smiling broadly, I shared my appreciation of her 'loving letter, filled with such gratitude in relation to Mum'. It seemed to us both that some important kind of dialogue had begun – in this case between two *I*-positions (Hermans and Dimaggio 2004), one associated with her contemporary sense of self, and one representing an 'external' position reflected in a version of her mother, now clearly accessible within her.

Exploring a bit more the family system's response to the loss, I soon learned that Deborah had identified with her mother's role in the family, monitoring and 'worrying over' her adult siblings as Mum has once done. At the same time, she recognized 'that's not a good place for me to be, and it's something my family doesn't have acceptance of anyway. So I need to let that go, and let them be them.' 'Let them be them,' I echoed, adding, 'and let *you* be *you*, and not just Mum's placeholder in the family… Do you think that Mom would approve of that, your relinquishing her role a little bit?' Deborah responded, 'I don't know how my mother would feel about that,' adding, 'It sounds hard… That's one of my greatest fears – if I stop being her portion [of the family], if everything's going to be okay, if *I'm* going to be okay.' Deborah's response suggested the gist of some further dialogue with Mum, under the title, 'Returning my Mother's Legacy to Her'. Deborah readily accepted my suggestion that she write on that theme as therapeutic homework, seeking Mum's permission to relinquish some of the over-identification with her advice-giving presence that had been resisted by her adult siblings. We closed the session with her noting, 'This sounds neat. I think I'm going to enjoy it. It's going to be a big milestone in my life.'

Our third session of therapy opened with Deborah noting that she began 'feeling down' on the intervening 'monthly anniversary' of her mother's death, but that when she started writing, 'it was a kind of release'. 'What was released with that writing?' I asked. 'Just the identification,' she responded, 'that I was trying to be my mother, and wasn't identifying with myself. It was this obsession.' The writing, it seemed, had led to an insight, 'that I was becoming this worry-wart of a person… It's almost like I was playing hide-and-seek with myself,' she added thoughtfully, to which I inquired, 'What an extraordinary image, playing hide-and-seek with yourself! What were you hiding, and what were you seeking?' Responding, she noted that she was creating an identity that wasn't her own, one that wasn't being asked for by others. She then accepted my invitation to read the remarkable letter in which so much had become clear:

Dear Mum,

You were always the key-holder for our family's problems. You had an instinct about what to do in every situation, always made sure we felt loved and special. Since you've been gone from this world I've tried to be you within our family. I am returning your legacy to you. You had one bad characteristic, and that was that you worried about us a lot. I picked up that characteristic, and this is something I've gone overboard with... Mum, I am asking your permission to be me. I'm going to allow myself to be okay with who I am. I need to practise on my own individuality, and have faith that I'll be okay with myself. I have all the wonderful wisdom you taught me, and one of those things is the power of prayer.

Love, your daughter and friend,
Deborah

To explore any further relational impediment that could block Deborah's reconstruction of her bond with her mother, I then suggested a novel intervention, one that entailed accessing her mother's voice as an external *I*-position within Deborah's dialogical self: 'As we were talking about this notion of getting Mum's permission for the changes you want to make ... I wondered if we could have a conversation in here, in which I interviewed your mother, briefly, about the person her daughter, Deborah, is becoming. Would that be interesting to you?' Deborah chuckled a little nervously, but agreed, and so I immediately suggested that we switch chairs 'to allow us to be someone else', and began to interview her as her mother by her name, Pat: 'I've been having some conversations, Pat, with your daughter Deborah... And one of the things she's been talking about is that she's looking for a way to let your legacy be yours, and for her to step back into being Deborah. And she's been a little bit worried as to how you feel about that... What do you think of this move your daughter is trying to make ... to make room for who she is as a person?' Deborah, as Pat, affirmed that her daughter should be who she is, and especially should 'erase' any negative traits she might have given her. Alerted to this incipient metaphor, I introduced the image of a 'magic pencil with lead on one end, and an eraser on the other', and asked 'Pat' alternately about 'what traits you would write out for Deborah to carry forward in her life', and what she would give her daughter permission to erase or relinquish. I picked up my notepad and took dictation as she pensively formulated the list of the qualities she hoped Deborah would cultivate (e.g. a loving understanding of herself, a great love of people), those she regarded as 'precious' in her daughter (e.g. that she thinks before she speaks, is confident in what she knows) and those she would encourage her to let go (e.g. being the family caregiver, needless worry). Invited to share some 'final words for this part of the conversation', 'Pat' concluded that she hoped her daughter 'would find total joy'. After we ended the conversation with 'Pat's' permission and took our former chairs, I reread her 'mother's' words slowly and evocatively, as Deborah brushed away a tear. 'I'm crying,' she said, 'but it feels good. It's encouraging. I get caught up in the fact that she's not here, and I don't think she would want that.' She paused and smiled. 'Of course not,' I replied, 'she wouldn't want to be banished, because she *is* here with you. When you invite her, she steps right back in.' Accepting the paper with my interview notes, Deborah remarked, 'This is something I may type up, because they are words of wisdom. These are like words she could have said, and when I need her words, I can have them.' She continued, unprompted: 'Typing them will keep me in the positive swing that has been transforming in my life the last couple of weeks... It's funny when things start to roll in the right direction.' Having reanimated her mother's voice within herself, Deborah seemed to have reconstructed a meaningful ongoing bond that both reaffirmed her attachment to Mum and gave Deborah freedom to live her own life.

Coda

As a constructivist theorist, researcher and therapist, I have found it helpful to view life-altering loss as a challenge to people's worlds of meaning, calling for a deep understanding of the role that such transition can play in disorganizing, dominating or dissociating a self-narrative that now calls for significant revision. Far from being a cerebral, intellectual process, the quest for meaning in both the loss and in their changed lives is typically a profoundly emotional one for survivors, and one that calls for professionals to step with them into the darkness and disruption, while also looking for potential pathways to integrate a difficult passage into a life story that ultimately finds new coherence. In this, I have found meaning-oriented, narrative and dialogical procedures to be invaluable aids in reconstructing a sense of self and world that respects the loss, without being restricted by it.

What might the field of dialogical self studies learn in turn from a meaning reconstruction approach to grief and grief therapy? Among other things, I would hope that psychologists drawn to a conception of a multivocal self might explore the rich voicing of the complexity of the *I*-positions that characterize such healing encounters, perhaps using rigorous qualitative procedures to analyse transformative dialogues and emerging coalitions of voices, including prominently (but not exclusively) those involving the still-accessible voice of the deceased, as illustrated above. Doing so should enrich a conception of narrative practices in therapy, extending them to the performance of written or spoken dialogues within the self or between the self and enacted others in a way that opens to new patterns of (self-) relating and (self-) understanding. Such a cross-fertilization of theory and practice, informed by relevant research, could thereby make a contribution to our common humanity, as we strive for a thread of consistency in a life story punctuated by unwelcome change.

REFERENCES

Bonanno, G. A. (2004) Loss, trauma and human resilience, *American Psychologist*, **59**, 20–28

Bowlby, J. (1980) *Attachment and Loss: Loss, Sadness and Depression* (New York: Basic Books)

Calhoun, L. and Tedeschi, R. G. (eds.) (2006) *Handbook of Posttraumatic Growth* (Mahwah, NJ: Lawrence Erlbaum)

Coleman, R. A. and Neimeyer, R. A. (2010) Measuring meaning: searching for and making sense of spousal loss in later life, *Death Studies*, **34**, 804–834

Currier, J. M., Holland, J. and Neimeyer, R. A. (2006) Sense making, grief and the experience of violent loss: toward a mediational model, *Death Studies*, **30**, 403–428

Currier, J. M., Neimeyer, R. A. and Berman, J. S. (2008) The effectiveness of psychotherapeutic interventions for the bereaved: a comprehensive quantitative review, *Psychological Bulletin*, **134**, 648–661

Freud, S. (1917/1957) Mourning and melancholia, in J. Strachey (ed.), *The Complete Psychological Works of Sigmund Freud* (London: Hogarth Press), vol. XIV, 239–260

Gergen, K. (2000) From identity to relational politics, in L. Holzman and J. Morss (eds.), *Postmodern Psychologies* (New York: Routledge), 130–150

Hermans, H. (2002) The person as a motivated storyteller, in R. A. Neimeyer and G. J. Neimeyer (eds.), *Advances in Personal Construct Psychology* (Westport, CT: Praeger), 3–38

Hermans, H. and Dimaggio, G. (eds.) (2004) *The Dialogical Self in Psychotherapy* (New York: Routledge)

Hermans, H. and Kempen, H. (1993) *The Dialogical Self* (New York: Guilford)

Holland, J. and Neimeyer, R. A. (2010) An examination of stage theory of grief among individuals bereaved by natural and violent causes: a meaning-oriented contribution, *Omega*, **61**, 105–122

Janoff-Bulman, R. (1989) Assumptive worlds and the stress of traumatic events, *Social Cognition*, **7**, 113–116

Keesee, N. J., Currier, J. M. and Neimeyer, R. A. (2008) Predictors of grief following the death of one's child: the contribution of finding meaning, *Journal of Clinical Psychology*, **64**, 1145–1163

Kelly, G. A. (1955) *The Psychology of Personal Constructs* (New York: Norton)

Klass, D., Silverman, P. R. and Nickman, S. (1996) *Continuing Bonds: New Understandings of Grief* (Washington, DC: Taylor & Francis)

Kübler-Ross, E. (1969) *On Death and Dying* (New York: Macmillan)

Lichtenthal, W. G. and Cruess, D. G. (2010) Effects of directed written disclosure on grief and distress symptoms among bereaved individuals, *Death Studies*, **34**, 475–499

Lichtenthal, W. G., Currier, J. M., Neimeyer, R. A. and Keesee, N. J. (2010) Sense and significance: a mixed-methods examination of meaning-making following the loss of one's child, *Journal of Clinical Psychology*, **66**, 791–812

Maciejewski, P. K., Zhang, B., Block, S. D. and Prigerson, H. G. (2007) An empirical examination of the stage theory of grief, *Journal of the American Medical Association*, **297**, 716–723

Neimeyer, R. A. (2000) Narrative disruptions in the construction of self, in R. A. Neimeyer and J. D. Raskin (eds.), *Constructions of Disorder: Meaning Making Frameworks for Psychotherapy* (Washington, DC: American Psychological Association), 207–242

(ed.) (2001) *Meaning Reconstruction and the Experience of Loss* (Washington, DC: American Psychological Association)

(2002) *Lessons of Loss: A Guide to Coping* (Memphis, TN: Center for the Study of Loss and Transition)

(2004a) *Constructivist Psychotherapy* (video) (Washington, DC: American Psychological Association)

(2004b) Fostering posttraumatic growth: a narrative contribution, *Psychological Inquiry*, **15**, 53–59

(2006a) Narrating the dialogical self: toward an expanded toolbox for the counselling psychologist, *Counselling Psychology Quarterly*, **19**, 105–120

(2006b) Widowhood, grief and the quest for meaning: a narrative perspective on resilience, in D. Carr, R. M. Nesse and C. B. Wortman (eds.), *Spousal Bereavement in Late Life* (New York: Springer), 227–252

(2008) *Constructivist Psychotherapy Over Time* (video) (Washington, DC: American Psychological Association)

(2009a) *Constructivist Psychotherapy* (London and New York: Routledge)

(2009b) *Constructivist Psychotherapy: Distinctive Features* (London and New York: Routledge)

Neimeyer, R. A. and Arvay, M. J. (2004) Performing the self: therapeutic enactment and the narrative integration of loss, in H. J. M. Hermans and G. Dimaggio (eds.), *The Dialogical Self in Psychotherapy* (New York: Brunner-Routledge), 173–189

Neimeyer, R. A. and Currier, J. M. (2009) Grief therapy: evidence of efficacy and emerging directions, *Current Directions in Psychological Science*, **18**, 252–256

Neimeyer, R. A., Van Dyke, J. G. and Pennebaker, J. W. (2009) Narrative medicine: writing through bereavement, in H. Chochinov and W. Breitbart (eds.), *Handbook of Psychiatry in Palliative Medicine* (New York: Oxford University Press), 454–469

Neimeyer, R. A., Winokuer, H., Harris, D. and Thornton, G. (eds.) (2011) *Grief and Bereavement in Contemporary Society: Bridging Research and Practice* (New York: Routledge)

Savickas, M. L. (2005) The theory and practice of career construction, in R. W. Lent and S. D. Brown (eds.), *Career Development and Counseling: Putting Theory and Research to Work* (Hoboken, NJ: Wiley), 42–70

Shear, K., Frank, E., Houch, P. R. and Reynolds, C. F. (2005) Treatment of complicated grief: a randomized controlled trial, *Journal of the American Medical Association*, **293**, 2601–2608

Stroebe, M., Hansson, R., Schut, H. and Stroebe, W. (eds.) (2007) *Handbook of Bereavement Research and Practice* (Washington, DC: American Psychological Association)

Wagner, B., Knaevelsrud, C. and Maercker, A. (2006) Internet-based cognitive-behavioral therapy for complicated grief: a randomized controlled trial, *Death Studies*, **30**, 429–453

22 Creating dialogical space in psychotherapy: meaning-generating chronotope of *ma*

Masayoshi Morioka

In today's world, the voices of many people get lost among those of dominant others. Consequently, it has become difficult to enter into a dialogue between oneself and another person. This entails the risk that each person tends to speak his or her own language and retreats to monologue. It is then difficult to form a linkage between two persons engaged in a dialogue. At times, it is also difficult to hear our own voices in the dialogical double space of both internal and external dialogues, but it is necessary to create this double space through conversation with others.

The question, then, is how we can develop a Bakhtinian chronotope, which refers to the compound of space and time, in order to have access to our own voices and those of others. In fact, the psychotherapist, serving as an active listener, could benefit from this process. Here, I discuss dialogicality in the course of the practice of psychotherapy, with a focus on the meaning-generating process which is central in dialogical self theory (DST).

When a client talks about different parts of the self, each part has a unique voice. The therapist listens as openly as possible to all the different parts, meanings and conflicts that are gradually unveiled by the client. Some of those parts may be very familiar to the client and might even have been given names. Others may be hidden or unknown. How can these different parts become integrated? What were the parts at earlier times in one's life? What did they say then? The therapist and client collaboratively investigate such questions. From the viewpoint of DST, the self is conceived as a dynamism or process arising in a conversation between people. The practice of the dialogical self involves talking about oneself to others and also of talking to oneself silently. This double conversation, that is, self-to-self and self-to-other, creates a dialogical space that articulates and differentiates one's self-narrative on the basis of inner and outer dialogues. Various selves in this space are involved in communication with each other. They are articulated and further developed by a process of dialogical movements in an imaginary space (Hermans 1996).

This concept of experiencing many *I*-positions in an imaginary or metaphorical space is one of the peculiarities of the psychotherapeutic process, as informed by DST. Thus, in this space where the self is constructed in close connection with the other, meanings are generated as part of a therapeutic listening process. Therapeutic conversations facilitate continuous internal dialogues within the client's self. When one creates such self-narratives, a significant distance will appear between the different voices of the self. The act of narrating to the self creates a division between the self and the not-self. This new sphere entails 'the others' and as a consequence, may evoke tension and conflict within the self.

The talking and conversation with an 'other' divides the self repetitively, and may sometimes create a severe problem within the self. It is thus necessary to organize and connect the different positions in the self. The self is structured on the basis of hierarchically organized voices (dominance–subdominance relation) together with the need or necessity for dialogical interactions between those voices. The self needs to create a multivoiced structure in interaction with an organizing or disorganizing living world. But how can this take place? What kinds of conditions are required to accomplish this?

Talking does not necessarily construct the self. Rather, the individual undertakes this project through re-experiencing, at a new reflective level, the narratives about the self as a central topic of the conversation. In the therapeutic situation, the therapist remains receptive when the different positions of the self begin to talk and enter into a dialogue with one another. The therapist makes an effort to receive the expression of the client's authentic sense of self at any moment.

In this chapter, I investigate how therapeutic meaning is generated in the counselling process. The idea of 'positioning' in DST is useful in this context, especially the notion of 'meta-positioning'. I will show that the dynamic movement of positioning and meta-positioning develops a dialogical space. Then, I introduce the Japanese cultural concept of *ma* in order to explain the characteristics of therapeutic shared space. I argue that therapeutic meaning may be generated through semiotic activity in this space. The concept of *ma* explains the dialogical features of this in-between area. Finally, I shall indicate how clients can reflect on and transform their unresolved emotions in the active space of *ma*. In the practice of counselling and psychotherapy, clients usually express contradicting emotions in their dysfunctional narrative. In the dialogical self, this contradiction may be a significant condition for change.

The other and double dialogical space

Which characteristics of the dialogical space contribute to making the therapeutic conversation creative and meaningful? In answering this question, it should be emphasized that the attitude of the listening other is crucial. The therapist plays a double role in the relationship with the client. Therapists must be able to attend simultaneously to both the inner and outer conversations (Anderson and Goolishan 1992). Consciousness can hold two opposite voices in an internal dialogue. There is some tension in the dialogue between the self and the inside other, or alter ego. For the sake of dissolving this tension, we have to develop an invisible internal listener in the mind space and maintain the internal dialogue with the self. Our utterance is constructed according to the viewpoint of this invisible listener, who determines the intonation, selection and arrangement of words. If one were to lose this internal listener, one's personality would be in crisis.

However, the internal conversation with the imagined other only is not genuinely polyphonic (Hermans 1999). The therapist has to simultaneously attend to and facilitate both the inner and outer conversations. A double dialogical space emerges from the heterodialogue (with others, including imaginary others) and the autodialogue (within oneself) (Valsiner 2002).

The third realm in-between

In the psychotherapeutic situation, many referred others appear in the client's narrative as if they were characters in a drama, and the client himself is presented as one of the characters of the narrative. The present other, the therapist, is important for the change of the self of the client. He is the orchestrating participant of the therapeutic conversation. His response is important for the co-construction of the client's story.

It is equally important to accept the other's perspective for self-construction. We can create a sense of reality through an exchange of the perspectives of self and others. A new space is formed in which two perspectives of two persons cross over towards each other. It is a potential space with another reality that is constructed within and between persons. The boundary zone between self and others in the therapeutic conversation allows the construction and reconstruction of meanings. In the dialogical space, people spontaneously construct their joint actions, which are experienced (sensed) as a 'third realm of activity' (Katz and Shotter 1996; Shotter and Katz 1999).

Dialogical space is generated gradually in-between two persons where this 'third realm' can be activated. This process of co-constructing the dialogical space as a third area is itself a basic form of psychotherapy. In the space of the dialogical self, a self of one moment talks to the self of the next or previous moment. Continuous conversation takes place from self to self and from self to other. If one talks with one's actual voice to the other, a new meaning sometimes emerges. This new outcome will be an experience of recovery for one's own voice. In a therapeutic conversation, joint construction takes place in an effort to express one's own experiences with one's unique words.

In dialogical relationships, the dialogical model is based on not two but three steps. Step 1 is A to B, step 2 is B to A, and step 3 is A to B again. In step 3, position A is no longer the same as A in step 1 but has changed somewhat in the course of the dialogical process itself (Hermans 1999; Marková 1987). In this three-step dialogical process, one can increase therapeutic novelty via self-positioning.

According to the dialogical self perspective, the clients' narratives are concerned with the dialogues between the characters in the narrative. Psychological problems are considered to be the result of fragmentation between the *I*-positions and/or suppressive dominance of one *I*-position over the others. Psychotherapy is conducted to facilitate a reconstruction of the client's repertoire in such a way that the client can move flexibly between positions.

Thinking via the position of external others, without returning to the initial position, does not create novelty. Dialogical thinking that takes place via another person only (step 2) is not sufficient for an increase in novelty. Returning to the initial position and further developing it as a result of the dialogical interchange has a greater chance of introducing novelty in the position repertoire. It is thus one of the main goals of psychotherapy to initiate a dialogue between positions.

Meta-positioning and coalition of positions

Given the need of creating novelty, it is useful to focus on the dynamic movement of positioning in dialogical space. Hermans and Hermans-Konopka (2010) indicate that meta-positioning enables people to distance themselves from the stream of experiences. As a result of self-reflection from a meta-position in the context of a therapeutic dialogue, people are able to see relevant linkages between various positions. The meta-position thus contributes to the integration and continuity of the self-positioning.

Hermans and Hermans-Konopka (2010) explain that a meta-position has the following specific qualities:

(1) It provides an overarching view on several positions.
(2) It enables participants to link the positions as part of their personal history.
(3) It helps people find a direction of change.

Yet, unity and integration can be realized not only by meta-positions but also by the construction of a *third position*. Hermans and Hermans-Konopka (2010) indicate that a conflict between two positions in the self can be reconciled by the creation of a third position. The third position has the potential of unifying the two original ones without denying or removing their differences. This dynamic movement between positions creates a dialogical space where a third position can be activated. Therapeutic conversation can be initiated by creating a third sphere of dialogical in-between space as a basis of meta-positioning. I will argue that, for the emergence of a dialogical space, the intonation of the voices and a positive tension built up during the therapeutic conversation are crucial.

Recovery of one's voice: intonation and tension in dialogue

In the space of the dialogical self, a self of one moment talks to the self of another moment and, at the same time, it is involved in a conversation with the other. If we talk with our actual voice to another one, a new meaning can emerge that is experienced as a recovery of our own voice. In a therapeutic conversation, a joint construction takes place that leaves space for one's own experience expressed in unique words.

In the following, I present two vignettes that show how a dialogical space can emerge in the therapeutic situation and how intonation of the voice plays a crucial role in this space. From a Japanese perspective I will elaborate on this discussion by referring to the concept of *ma*.

Clinical vignette 1

Mr A was a 27-year-old office worker. He visited our counselling service because of strong anxiety. He felt overly tense in public, especially when using the phone. This problem became acute when he noticed that he spoke to an answer machine during a phone call. After that, he became afraid of making any call in the office. His anxiety was related to the feeling that he was always being checked on and listened to.

Mr A was constrained by only one voice. Surely, he had other voices but they were suppressed. So, each voice had to be taken care of in the therapeutic dialogue. Various other voices were latent in the client's silence. It is fundamental to the therapeutic progress to voice suppressed parts of the self, but we do not need to 'en-voice' them directly.

From a Bakhtinian perspective, we can say that a word has many voices in a dialogical situation (Bakhtin 1981). We can hear different voices in a word. One's speech occurs when being in contact with the other. Conceptualizing the self as a dynamic interplay among voiced positions opens a range of possibilities for recognizing individual differences and differences between situations (Hermans 1996).

One's voice can get overtones mingled with another's voice. When a voice contacts another's voice, a dialogical process is facilitated. This polyphonization is realized by constructing a system of positions that is filled with opposites, contrasts and narrative fragments (Hermans 2001b). Linking these contradicting aspects into an inclusive experience is central in dialogical therapeutic work, as we can see in the case of Mr A.

Mr A reflected upon his social relationships and discerned a new point of view (he began to conduct a dialogue with his past self):

THERAPIST 1:   You have made no big mistake yet, am I right?
A1:   No, I have not. I was the leader of my group [he was talking
               about a situation when he was about 10 years old], but
               I was afraid of making a mistake. Despite having a number
               of members in the group, I would still feel isolated.
THERAPIST 2:   You didn't have any intimate friend in your childhood, did you?
A2:   Frankly speaking, I didn't have any friendly acquaintance.
               I was usually suspicious and my relationships could not
               continue for a long time.
THERAPIST 3:   It seems to me that you are extremely attentive toward your
               co-workers, much more than toward others. But the
               others may not notice this . . . they may mistakenly think
               that you lack compassion and warmth.
A3:   I remember something that happened when I was a child.
               A companion said to me, 'I don't enjoy being with you!' We
               were playing, and most often, when we were confronted with
               a dangerous situation, for example, when we had to climb
               over a fence or jump over a ditch, I usually took a
               roundabout route.
THERAPIST 4:   If one person is not enjoying himself, the others are not
               enjoying themselves either.
A4:   Well, I am surely in the same situation in my office. . .
A5:   But to whom does anyone talk about such private things?

In this fragment, the intonation of the voices changed during the conversation. At the end it became more intimate. The intonation is the clearest index of the social value of the speech. Our speech always reflects an evaluative accent. This is clearly seen in expressive intonation. One can say that the exchange in intonation is the main communication means in our ordinary conversation, coloured as it is by the exchange of emotion. Even if one's speech is diffused on a syntactic level, we can communicate sufficiently via intonation.

Even if speech is used repetitively, the intonation of evaluation changes when the same sentence is expressed by a different person in a different context. A dialogue, at least two speeches in interaction, is the basic unit of language (Bakhtin 1981). From the viewpoint of this stance, we may say that one can never speak the same word twice. When one's speech comes in contact with that of others, differences or even conflicts become manifest, and have the possibility of generating new meaning.

In the case of Mr A, his strained relationships with others culminated when he was not able to communicate well with the answering machine. The machine can never 'answer' with an embodied voice. The tension resulting from this lack of natural communication was not dissolved. Moreover, the tension was amplified by the lack of response from his co-workers, the silent others. When he cannot get a clear answer from the other, he tries to initiate a pseudo-dialogue in his psychic space where internalized others speak with him in a negatively evaluating intonation. Mr A seems to become anxious on the basis of his experience of not being accepted positively by others.

Mr A recalled the situation where an acquaintance told him that he did not enjoy being with him and he tried to talk with the therapist about this. Once he did this, he was able to determine an encounter with the acquaintance's words, which had been difficult to accept (A3–A5). Our task was to co-construct an open space so that the tension between positions in the dialogical self could be worked through and resolved. The intonation of the word changes in a different context and receives another meaning. The word that was earlier part of the client's repetitive rumination receives a different meaning when it is expressed and shared with an actively listening psychotherapist.

Sense of tones in the therapeutic relationship

As already explained, Mr A remembered a small traumatic event that had occurred when he was about 10 years old. The therapist tried to deal with the episode – wherein his companion had told him that he did not enjoy being with the client – and looked, together with the client, for new meanings included in this word. We repeated this word and tried to find its new meaning.

The therapist responded, 'If one person is not enjoying himself, the others are not enjoying themselves either' (Therapist 4). In response, Mr A disclosed his self, saying that he could not be frank or open about his own weakness. At that instance, the tension of the field changed largely and the intonation of his words changed as well. He made a shift in the evaluation of the traumatic episode. At the same time, his sense of time expanded. His sealed memory was opened and vividly connected to the present.

The therapist functions as a supporter who tries to transform the space of the dialogical self towards the future and in this sense he acts as a promoter position in the self of the client (Hermans and Hermans-Konopka 2010). He facilitates an active conversation to expand the dialogical space, where *I*-positions become reconstructed. The dialogical self is structured through the transformation of time into space. When we integrate the multivoiced selves, the structure of the dialogical self promotes future possibilities.

We can grasp a change in the quality of the time experience through the change in the tension felt in the therapeutic relationship. Mr A vividly remembered his experience at age 10. We can say that his past space of playing with companions appears here and now. The past event, which was separated from the present, was accepted in 'its meaning now' in the contact with the psychotherapist. From the moment that this spatial juxtaposition occurred, he could talk more frankly and freely.

The sense of tone that the therapist tentatively receives in the here-and-now situation is a sensor for catching the internal state of the client and the quality of the therapeutic relationship. When I heard Mr A's negative episode, I felt that he cannot move in a small group. Being alone with him, I noticed that the atmosphere of the room changed slightly. This sense of tone guided the subsequent orientation of the interview.

Meaning making in a potential chronotope of *ma*

Apart from the above example, I have examined conversational exchanges in several clinical cases in more detail (Morioka 2008a). In order to understand what happened during the psychotherapeutic process, I have introduced a Japanese cultural concept *ma* (間) in order to explain the space where therapeutically meaningful outcomes are generated. In order to understand the nature of this concept, the following considerations have to be taken into account:

(1) The unique Japanese word *ma* has multiple meanings. It can imply a space between two things, or it can indicate a space between one moment and another moment. *Ma* is a concept that includes both time and space (Kimura 2005). The Japanese perceive space according to the dynamism inherent in the non-separation of space and time. This fusion of time and space is expressed by the concept of *ma*.

(2) The word *ma* is also used to describe the quality of interpersonal relationships. The process of talking and listening creates unique *ma* between persons. Japanese can pronounce the Chinese character (間) as both *ma* and *aida*. The character *ma* (間) also indicates the space between two or more things, when it is pronounced as *aida*. The word *aida* is used in a limited way to refer to relationships between persons and between things, while *ma* indicates the creative lively tension between me and you. If this tension diminishes, *ma* is lost. The word 'human being' is written as (人間) in Japanese, which includes the same character *ma* or *aida*. A human is always depicted as a 'human-*I* between' and is said to have a 'relational existence'.

(3) The 'in-between' not only refers to a person's relationship with another human being but is also concerned with the distance from voice to voice in an internal dialogue. When one remains in an internal dialogue, a distance is created between the narrating self and the narrated self in one's internal world. This distance can also be called *ma*.

(4) *Ma* is generated, both in internal and external relationships, in taking a pause, maintaining silence and experiencing the deepened chronotope (time-space). As Hermans and Hermans-Konopka put it, 'Silence, too, giving space for inner recapitulation, rehearsal, and imagination, is a facilitating factor in dialogical relationships' (2010: 294). The silence which gives this space can be called *ma*. The Japanese Noh theatre is sometimes called the art of *ma*. The action of the Noh actor pays attention to the creation of a space of *ma*. The potential dreamlike effect of *ma* must be understood in the context of the aesthetics of the play. *Ma* is to be understood as the shared reality of an intersubjective sphere (Botz-Bornstein 2004). There remains a vital tone in this sphere.

(5) The concept of *ma* may be concerned with the boundary zone, A vs. non-A field, where meaning is constructed and reconstructed (Valsiner 2004). The therapist and client co-investigate the emotional experiences of ambivalence to realize a new form of feeling (see also Valsiner and Cabell's chapter in this book).

These five characteristics are closely interrelated in the compound concept of *ma* that reveals a latent context in Japanese culture. I will examine this concept of *ma* as the distance in self-to-self reflection and as the boundary zone of meaning construction in another clinical vignette.

Clinical and psychotherapeutic implications: emotions and self

From a psychotherapeutic viewpoint, DST provides various basic ideas. One such idea is the theme of the dynamic relationship between emotions and self. The dialogical view on emotions as exposed by Hermans and Hermans-Konopka (2010) suggests that self and emotions are intensely interconnected; emotions change the self, and the self can change emotions. Dynamic and complex relationships exist between self and emotions. Self-reflectivity influences affective processes. 'The concept of a self as a self-reflective agency . . . has profound implications for understanding the relationship between self and affect' (Hermans and Hermans-Jansen 2001: 121).

Self-reflective emotions are differentiated in the dynamism of 'first-order phenomenology' and 'second-order awareness' (Lambie and Marcel 2002; see also Hermans and Hermans-Konopka 2010). The first-order phenomenology is an emotional experience that has phenomenological truth. The emotional experience refers to 'how I am' or 'how he is'. In the second-order awareness, a person is reflexively aware of his own emotional experience. There is a recognition and awareness of the self experiencing something in this or that (subjective) way.

Ma is depicted as the distance of self to self, which refers to reflective second-order awareness. Emotional awareness is not about thinking but about feeling; it involves experiencing the feeling of lively awareness in *ma*.

Emotions have not only bodily and spatial implications but also narrative and dialogical connotations; that is, they have something to tell. Emotions, conceived as *I*-positions, can assume a voice and can convey a message. 'We are not only positioning ourselves in an emotion . . . but also are positioned by emotions' (Hermans and Hermans-Konopka 2010: 260). We can listen to and receive the message of emotions.

In DST, emotions are understood as temporary *I*-positions and as participating in a process of 'com-positioning'. The psychotherapist makes an effort to focus on and facilitate the dialogicality of emotions. In order to develop dialogical relations between emotions, the therapist tries to focus on a counter-emotion. An emotion can be changed by another emotion (e.g. anxiety can be countered and reduced by receiving a consoling message from a significant other). According to Hermans and Hermans-Konopka (2010), an emotional counter-position, in combination with a meta-position, is an especially powerful tool in changing dominant emotions.

A dialogical relationship between emotions implies that the different emotions have something to tell and are able to send out different messages to the self and to each other. I examine this work of developing dialogical relations between emotions in psychotherapeutic work on dysfunctions.

Clinical syndromes such as eating disorders and self-injury are common in Japan. I noticed that many people seem to lose their capacity of expanding their reflective consciousness. When they feel uncomfortable, with negative affect and tension, they try to dissolve these feelings by indulging in inadequate conduct such as wrist cutting (Morioka 2008b). Paradoxically, the aim of self-injury is to decrease psychological pain. The act itself seems to be an effort to regulate affect. Then, they experience a serious dilemma with regard to their conduct through which they try to self-regulate their emotions. Being unable to cope with serious conflicts, clients cannot refrain from repeated self-injury. Apparently, they have an incomplete dialogical access to healthy counter-emotions as these may emerge from the other-in-the-self (e.g. the encouraging voice of an interiorized parent). I illustrate this problem with the next case.

Clinical vignette 2

Ms B was a 22-year-old office worker. She had continued to injure herself by cutting her wrist until she went to high school. She had many scars on her left arm, from wrist to elbow. She had also cut her side and thigh. She sometimes also used to bang her head against a wall. She had adapted quite well to her place of work. Every co-worker had a good impression of her. She found it hard to express her own conflicts. In the assessment interview she also found it hard to express her feelings freely.

Self-injury is not simply a form of impulsive conduct but typically has an intention. There are some purposes behind the act of self-injury. How can we capture the intention of the action? One could argue that the action is maladaptive as well as self-destructive and that it seems to function as a defensive skill. It involves ambiguous meanings that need to be uncovered by psychotherapy.

I encouraged Ms B to accept and to clarify her vague, uncertain emotions. She began to talk about her emotional experiences. She said, 'There are two me's, the first one is nervous and restless, and the other is calm and stands still. The first one tries to "cut" the other.' In another session, she said, 'I am always slow in making decisions. Sometimes I am on one pole and at other times I am at the extreme opposite. There isn't a middle way for me.'

As a therapist, I tried to elicit the report of events that occurred from the beginning to the end of the self-inflicted injury. Was there anything particular happening before the action? Ms B usually said that she could not clearly remember what happened in the middle of the act of self-injury. Therefore, it was important to listen carefully to her steps towards self-care after the injured action.

Gradually, Ms B took a reflecting view on herself in the course of the therapeutic sessions. She began to reflect and take care of herself. She could remember and talk about her own episodes associated with the self-injuring act.

A significant dialogical moment was introduced when I asked her, 'Is there anyone who knows about your cutting conduct?' Ms B said, 'Nobody noticed my conduct of cutting except one of my friends from high school. I remember that my friend noticed that I had injured myself repeatedly. She asked me to stop but I could not.' Then I asked her, 'What do you think now?' She answered, 'I guess no one will pay such strong attention to me as my friend' (counter-emotion).

The act of self-injury itself may express her epitomized life story. The action has meaning in her life story, particularly in her attachment history. I invited her to take a meta-position from which she could view from some distance the several emotions and their connections and then co-create a composition of emotions through dialogical movements between the emotion and counter-emotion.

Ms B had a negative father image. She said she could not have a close relationship with her father. Her mother usually made negative comments about her conduct. Sometimes, she ran away from home but she felt she had no choice but to come back.

Ms B said, 'But I hope the constraints set by my father will help reduce my instability. I need strong constraint.' She gradually expressed natural but ambivalent emotions such as anger, complaints and ambivalent emotions of dependence. She said, 'My father commented rudely on my ordinary conduct but was rather indifferent about my career change. I was controlled by him. But I wanted to speak with him "naturally".'

If one has received repeated negative feedback from one's family, the sense of self may become ambiguous. The capacity to accept one's own feelings will be uncertain. This sense of uncertainty about oneself is a latent theme in the act of self-injury.

When she could take a meta-position to her different emotions, she had access to the configuration of her emotional experience, as resulting from her personal life story. In the next few sessions, there came moments when Ms B said that she gradually made the effort to be independent of her father. She said, 'I talked with my father frankly after having repeatedly attempted to talk with him directly about the difficulties in my life. I told him what I was thinking.'

Such an actual conversation has the potential to activate and develop the patient's distorted internal positions (e.g. '*I* as inferior' or '*I* as hating myself') intimately related as they are to the image of her father as an external position in the self (e.g. 'My father as rejecting me, yet being important to me'). Her ambivalent compound emotion can be shared with the therapist through telling her self-narrative. In the case of Ms B, her father image gradually changed in the course of the therapeutic conversation.

For the stimulation of second-order awareness (Lambie and Marcel 2002), it is necessary to recover self-reflective emotions. Self-reflective emotions are clear indications of the interpersonal regulation of our affectivity (Salgado and Ferreira 2007). These emotions are given adequate symbolic expression that differs from non-reflective 'raw' emotions. In the case of self-injury, the emotion experienced before and during the action seems to be non-reflective.

Self-reflective emotions and emotions related to the other person are undivided. Reflective consciousness will emerge through a particular form of conversation, which has non-linear simultaneous modes and not causal linear modes. The conscious mode of one's self emerges from a specific mode of relationship and in a particular context. Access to this mode helps clients to recover their sense of agency, enabling them to appropriate their own experiences.

Emotional coaching is useful for coping with psychological difficulties. As therapists, we invest effort to stimulate an internal dialogue in our clients through the internalization of their experiences of talking with us. Emotions represent movements in space and time as central in the theoretical basis of 'dialogical emotional coaching', as proposed by Hermans and Hermans-Konopka (2010). Such movements create a space for dialogue and exploration of the self-space, that is, *ma*, which emerges not only between self and other, but also between the different positions in a multivoiced self.

Conclusion

The therapist constructs and develops a shared reality with the client through therapeutic conversation. This reality offers a fertile ground for revising existing meanings and creating new ones as part of the client's self-narrative.

Therapeutic conversation can be made by creating a third sphere, a dialogical in-between space, *ma*, in which meta-positions, counter-positions and new coalitions of positions may emerge. In this space, which is stretched into the self of client and therapist, each *I*-position offers a particular view of the world and a particular horizon that limits this view. When a dominating emotion has a particular perspective, the counter-emotion offers a different one. When there is a conflict between two positions in the self, this can be reconciled by the creation of a third area, *ma*.

In the space of the dialogical self, the self of one moment talks to the self of the next moment. There is continuous conversation from self to self. This dynamic movement of *I*-positions contributes to the construction of a dialogical space where a third sphere is activated. *Ma* is the dynamic and playful space of potentiality where therapeutic meaning is generated.

REFERENCES

Anderson, H. and Goolishan, H. (1992) The client is the expert: not-knowing approach to therapy, in S. McNamee and K. Gergen (eds.), *Therapy as Social Construction* (London: Sage), 25–39

Bakhtin, M. M. (1981) *The Dialogic Imagination: Four Essays*. Ed. Michael Holquist. Trans. Caryl Emerson and Michael Holquist (Austin, TX and London: University of Texas Press)

Botz-Bornstein, T. (2004) *Place and Dream: Japan and the Virtual* (Amsterdam: Editions Rodopi)

Hermans, H. J. M. (1996) Voicing the self: from information processing to dialogical interchange, *Psychological Bulletin*, **119**, 31–50

(1999) Dialogical thinking and self-innovation, *Culture & Psychology*, **5**, 67–87

(2001a) The dialogical self: toward a theory of personal and cultural positioning, *Culture & Psychology*, **7**, 243–281

(2001b) The construction of a personal position repertoire: method and practice, *Culture & Psychology*, **7**, 323–365

Hermans, H. J. M. and Hermans-Jansen, E. (2001) Affective processes in a multivoiced self, in H. A. Bosma and E. S. Kunnen (eds.), *Identity and Emotion: Development Through Self-Organization*. Studies in Emotion and Social Interaction (New York: Cambridge University Press), 120–140

Hermans, H. J. M. and Hermans-Konopka, A. (2010) *Dialogical Self Theory: Positioning and Counter-Positioning in a Globalizing Society* (Cambridge University Press)

Hermans, H. J. M. and Kempen, H. J. G. (1993) *The Dialogical Self: Meaning as Movement* (San Diego, CA: Academic Press)

Katz, A. M. and Shotter, J. (1996) Hearing the patient's 'voice': toward a social poetics in diagnostic interviews, *Social Science and Medicine*, **43**, 919–931

Kimura, B. (2005) *Kankei tositeno Jiko* [*The Self as Relationships*] (Tokyo: Misuzushobo)

Lambie, J. A. and Marcel, A. J. (2002) Consciousness and the varieties of emotion experience: a theoretical framework, *Psychological Review*, **109**, 219–259

Marková, I. (1987) On the interaction of opposites in psychological processes, *Journal for the Theory of Social Behaviour*, **17**, 279–299

Morioka, M. (2005) *Utushi: Rinsyou no Shigaku* [*Utushi: Clinical Poetics*] (Tokyo: Misuzusyobo)

(2008a) Voices of the self in the therapeutic chronotope: utushi and ma, *International Journal of Dialogical Science*, **3**, 93–108

(2008b) On the recovery of self-reflective emotions in the therapeutic relationships, paper presented at the Fifth International Conference on the Dialogical Self, Cambridge, UK

Salgado, J. and Ferreira, T. (2007) Dialogical relationships as triads: implications for the dialogical self theory, in P. K. Oleś and H. J. M. Hermans (eds.), *The Dialogical Self: Theory and Research* (Lublin, Poland: Wydawnictwo KUL), 141–152

Shotter, J. and Katz, A. M. (1999) 'Living moments' in dialogical exchanges, *Human Systems*, **9**, 81–93

Valsiner, J. (2002) Forms of dialogical relations and semiotic autoregulation within the self, *Theory & Psychology*, **12**, 251–265

(2004) Temporal integration of structures within the dialogical self, paper presented at the Third International Conference on the Dialogical Self, Warsaw, Poland

23   Therapeutic applications of dialogues in dialogical action therapy

David Y. F. Ho

The East and the West appear to resonate in current conceptions of understanding and relating with others. In the East, conceptions grounded in a world view that stresses the relational character of human existence have always been dominant. In the West, there is growing awareness of the tension between two conceptions of selfhood in terms of self–other relationships. The first, rooted in individualism, is primacy of the autonomous self, through which the world is perceived and understanding is achieved; the second is the dialogical self, to which engagement in self–other dialogues is fundamental. Long eclipsed by the individualistic, the relational conception is now demanding to be heard.

Dialogical self theory (DST), developed by Hermans and his colleagues, represents a contemporary construction of relational selfhood in the West. A decentralized conception of the self as multivoiced and dialogical is articulated (Hermans 2001). The dialogical self is defined in terms of a dynamic multiplicity of *I*-positions or voices in the mind, intertwined as this mind is with the minds of other people. Positions are not only 'internal' (e.g. *I* as a husband, psychologist) but also 'external', belonging to the extended domain of the self (e.g. my wife). Dialogues may take place among internal positions (e.g. a conflict between my position as a husband and my position as a hard-working scientist), between internal and external positions (e.g. I had an argument with my colleague), and between external positions (e.g. disagreement between my colleagues).

Hermans' work resonates with constructions of relational selfhood informed by Eastern intellectual traditions. One such construction is the *self-in-relations* by Ho, Peng *et al.* (2001); another is the dialogical self by Ho, Chan *et al.* (2001). These constructions meet two requirements: (1) inclusion of both self-in-other and other-in-self, and (2) giving full recognition to the whole range of capabilities and potentialities unique to humans. The first follows from the dialectic between selfhood and otherness: self and other are inextricably intertwined; each derives its meaning from the coexistence of the other. It is a restatement of the

Eastern world view concerning the relational character of human existence. The second recognizes the importance of higher cognitive capabilities, such as self-consciousness, other-consciousness and metacognition, for the emergence of selfhood.

In Hermans' (2002) conception, the dialogical self is not only part of the society at large but also functions as a 'society of mind', with tensions, conflicts and contradictions as intrinsic features of a healthy functioning self. As in society, the different *I*-positions are involved in not only processes of interchange but also struggles in which some positions are more dominant than other positions.

Similarly, Ho, Chan *et al.* (2001) accord a positive role to tensions and contradictions in the generation of the dialogical self. In the parlance of dialectical psychology, internal dialogue, being a process internal to the individual, belongs to inner dialectics; external dialogue, being an interaction between the individual and its external world, belongs to outer dialectics. Dialectical psychology demands attention to the interdependence, as well as tensions and contradictions, between inner and outer dialectics. Inner dialectics is not just a reflection of outer dialectics; it has a self-generative capability, leading to new possibilities for thought and action. At the same time, outer dialectics is essential for consensual validation and is a source of nourishment for new ideas. Without consensual validation, inner dialectics would be autistic; devoid of new ideas, inner dialectics withers. Thus, interaction between inner and outer dialectics creates the dialogical self. Facilitated by both internal and external dialogues, the dialogical self creates, and is created by, its social environment. It acts on and changes the external world, transforming itself in the process. The theoretical import is that the dialogical conception ascribes a prominent role to inner–outer interactions in the construction of selfhood, and indeed of mind.

To advance DST, this chapter gives an account of the dialogical self in psychotherapy, specifically therapeutic applications of dialogues in dialogical action therapy (DAT) as explicated by Ho and Wang (2009) (for the notion of dialogical action, see also Verhofstadt-Denève's chapter). Informed by Eastern intellectual traditions, DAT is relation centred: the participation of others in extended conceptions of selfhood comes naturally to the dialogical self. It gives recognition to the paramount role metacognition plays in the therapeutic process (see also Dimaggio's chapter). The chapter will also touch on the inadequacies of some therapies, specifically rational-emotive and person-centred, as they are currently practised. Therapeutic strategies of DAT are illustrated. Finally, suggestions for research in DST are made, using the notation and analytic tools developed in DAT.

Dialogical action therapy

DAT integrates two cardinal ideas, dialogics and action, into a coherent framework for effective problem solving and meaningful living. Both ideas are quintessential to defining what it means to be human. Dialogics may be defined simply as the study of all forms, aspects and processes of dialogues. Virtually all therapeutic systems entail not only dialogues between persons, therapist and client(s), but also internal dialogues within each person. In DAT, the therapist exploits these dialogues to achieve therapeutic gain. DAT stresses that action is essential to successful therapy. The defining characteristics of action are intentionality, voluntariness, self-knowledge and self-consciousness (Ho and Wang 2009: 85). Grounded in dialectics, DAT promotes the unity of action and thought. It demands taking corrective, effective actions as an outcome indicator. It accords with the time-honoured adage, 'Action speaks louder than words.'

Dialogues, internal and external

Before proceeding further, a clarification of terminology is needed. The word *dialogical* is usually meant to refer to conversations between two or more people, or external dialogues. In the context of self psychology, *dialogical* refers no less to internal dialogues – 'talking with oneself'. The idea of talking with oneself is likely to invite an association with egocentric speech (or even madness). However, in adults there is no necessary association, or lack of it, between egocentricity and internality-externality. One may be egocentric while engaged in a dialogue with others, or empathic while engaged in a dialogue with oneself. This is not to deny that there may be qualitative differences between internal and external dialogues.

In DAT, the term *internal dialogue* (or *self-directed dialogue*) is used, without prior theoretical commitment, to refer simply to intrapersonal dialogue; that is, dialogue involving only one person, acting as both 'speaker' and 'listener'. Internal dialogue may be overt (spoken aloud) or covert (silent). It takes varied forms: imaginary dialogues between one's different selves (e.g. the actual and rejected, the present and the future), between oneself and others, between oneself and one's deceased significant other, and so forth. *External dialogue* (or *other-directed dialogue*) is interpersonal, referring to dialogue that the self engages in with other(s) – with the self still being the point of reference. To avoid confusion, it is best to make explicit, when necessary, the distinction between actual external dialogue and imaginary 'external' dialogue, which is really internal, involving others participating in the extended domain of the self.

The interaction between internal and external dialogues acts as an engine for the generation of new ideas and, indeed, for the continual renewal of the dialogical self. In daily life, we shift back and forth between outer speech and inner self-talk (covert, to be discreet) when we converse with others. Internal dialogue plays a key role in bidirectional social calculus, and serves as a social compass for interaction.

But we must go further and grant internal dialogue to others, no less than to ourselves. That is, we assume our thoughts and actions are considered by others and, furthermore, others also assume that their thoughts and actions are considered by us. This line of reasoning leads to an inevitable conclusion: an account of dialogicality demands attention to interaction between dialogical selves; the dialogical self can never be considered in isolation. This conceptualization resonates with Hermans' idea of the dialogical self as a society of mind. It points to a paradigmatic shift from methodological individualism to methodological relationalism (Ho, Peng *et al.* 2001).

Fundamental features of DAT

The two cardinal ideas, dialogics and action, underscore differences between DAT and other therapies. First, DAT stresses the need for assuming social responsibility, personal and social, through taking action. Currently, many therapies emphasize the word at the expense of the deed, and personal responsibility (for one's own well-being) at the expense of social responsibility (for others' well-being). Second, DAT places great emphasis on the participation of others in the construction of selfhood. It does not rest on individualism, the foundation on which most Western therapies rest. Third, DAT gives due recognition to the full range of human capabilities and potentialities, enabling it to reach the higher domains of life, the metacognitive, creative or transformational. Thus, self-reflective thought plays a vital role in the therapeutic process. These differences imply radical change in therapeutic approaches.

DAT accords a central role to the joint creation of a therapeutic relationship by therapist and client. Ho and Wang define therapy as '*the process of jointly creating a therapeutic relationship, in the context of which the client (and the therapist) may grow psychologically and deal more effectively with problems of living*' (2009: 85; emphasis added). This definition embodies several implications: (1) a therapeutic relationship has to be created – it is not present at the beginning; (2) creating this relationship is a joint endeavour; and (3) the act of creation may transform its creator. In an important sense, therefore, therapeutic change is self-transformation. DAT repudiates treating the individual therapist or client as a fundamental unit of analysis. Instead, it employs two units: persons-in-relation (e.g. therapist and client interacting within a particular therapeutic context) and person-in-relations (e.g. a therapist or client functioning in different therapist–client contexts, or a client functioning in different interpersonal relationships).

DAT is founded on the thesis that selfhood is dialogical in nature. The dialogical self may split itself into different selves, engaged in internal dialogues with one another, in the process of which it may participate in its own transformation. Thus, the dialogical self has immense potentiality for creative self-transformation, even self-creation (Ho, Chan *et al.* 2001). In the course of engaging in dialogues, the reciprocity of perceptions between persons plays a paramount role. DAT attends to the social 'presence' of others, real, imagined or implied. Moreover, this presence is bidirectional, in the self-to-other as well as the other-to-self direction: one assumes that others consider one's own presence; in the same way, one also assumes that others assume that their presence is considered by oneself. Thus, bidirectionality is a fundamental feature of the therapeutic process. Ho and Wang (2009) have formulated a systematic directional analysis of perceptions in the therapist-to-client and client-to-therapist directions.

In DAT, the conception of selfhood is extended by employing social self (aspects of one's self presented or revealed to others) and social image (aspects of one's self publicly and collectively perceived by others) as reciprocal constructs. A methodological implication is that two approaches to assessment are complementary: one focusing on the social self, with the person serving as informant or respondent; the other on social image, with others serving as informants. These two approaches may well reveal discrepant perceptions, reflecting tensions between the social self as perceived by oneself and the social image as perceived by others. Such discrepant perceptions are a source of strain and conflict in self–other relationships, the resolution of which is integral to therapeutic movement. Bidirectionality is thus a fundamental feature of the therapeutic process. Empirical research on therapeutic communication informed by this conception has been conducted by Ho (2010).

DAT is conceived at a high level of generality. It is receptive to diverse intellectual traditions, techniques and theoretical orientations (e.g. systemic, psychodynamic, person-centred, cognitive-behavioural). Under this diversity, however, are unifying principles that emphasize (1) putting prevention first; (2) creative synthesis of East–West learning; (3) integration of theory and practice (action again); (4) unity of thought and action; and (5) a holistic-systemic framework for therapeutic intervention at the individual, interpersonal, family, group, community, societal and cultural levels. Receptive to diverse ideas, it nonetheless demands theoretical coherence. DAT is integrative, not eclectic. Its assumptions about selfhood and therapy are made explicit.

DAT may be regarded as a general approach to effective and meaningful living, or as therapy for helping people in distress. Although articulated as therapy, DAT may be generalized to become a methodology that has universal applicability for problem solving, learning from experiences and taking corrective actions in daily living. It is 'therapy for all seasons'.

Metacognition and extended conceptions of selfhood

The brief exposition above makes clear that metacognition and extended conceptions of selfhood are central to DAT. In the therapeutic process, therapist and client engage in dialogues that entail metacognition and metaperception. One result would be extended conceptions of selfhood, which refer to increases in the participation of others in one's self-concept. By metacognition, I mean self-reflective, higher thought processes. It may be defined simply as thinking about a thought or thinking itself; similarly, metaperception may be defined as the perception of another perception. Metacognition and metaperception are intertwined: metacognition is involved in metaperception, and vice versa.

Examples of metacognition abound in Chinese literary and philosophical, particularly Daoist, traditions. A tale relates that Zhuangzi once dreamt he was a butterfly and was happy as a butterfly, not knowing that he was Zhuangzi. When he awoke, he did not know whether it was Zhuangzi dreaming that he was a butterfly or a butterfly dreaming that it was Zhuangzi. This tale reveals the workings of metacognition, and suggests an avenue *par excellence* for exploring the dialogical self.

Notation

A formal notation has been introduced by Ho and Wang (2009) to clarify constructs and to provide systematic symbolization of complex interpersonal perceptions and metaperceptions. As applied to therapy, for instance, the capitalized letters S, T and C may be used to denote supervisor, therapist and client, respectively; they are regarded as both perceivers and percipient objects. Other capitalized letters may be added, for instance, O may be added to denote other people. Lowercase letters are not used to denote perceivers, but may be used in the symbolization of objects. They are particularly useful for indicating direction, for instance, tc trust and ct trust denote therapist-to-client trust and client-to-therapist trust, respectively. (Note that direction is indicated by the order of the letters *t* and *c*.) Objects are placed within parentheses; perceivers are placed outside, to the left, of the parentheses. For instance, S(T) and T(tc trust) read as supervisor's perception of the therapist and as therapist's perception of therapist-to-client trust, respectively. Any perception may be treated as an object of perception, placed within an outer pair of parentheses. For instance, C(T(tc trust)) reads as client's perception of the therapist's perception of therapist-to-client trust. In informal notation, parentheses may be dropped. Thus, CTtc trust is deemed to be equivalent to C(T(tc trust)).

Degrees of complexity

Perceptions or construals differ in degrees of complexity (DC), which may be indexed (Ho, Peng *et al.* 2001; Ho and Wang 2009). We first distinguish between the perceiver and the object of perception (including the perceiver himself). By convention, we may designate perceived objects, without the perceiver being specified, as zero-degree perceptions. Common examples of perceived objects are the attributes of persons or relationships. Self-perceptions and other-perceptions (i.e. perceptions of other people) are first-degree perceptions; metaperceptions are second-degree perceptions; perceptions of metaperceptions are third-degree perceptions; and so forth. In short, any perception may be itself the object of a higher-degree perception. In the case of first-person perceptions, the phrase, 'I perceive/think/see/feel that' is presumed; thus, 'I trust him/he trusts me' is deemed equivalent to 'I perceive/think/see/feel that (I trust him/he trusts me)' (first degree). Note that, however, whereas '(he loves me)' is a first-degree perception, '(he thinks that (he loves me))' is a second-degree perception, and '(he thinks that (I perceive (he loves me)))' is a third-degree perception. Using formal notation facilitates the determination of degrees: the number of parentheses used corresponds to the degree. Thus, tc trust is a zero-degree perception; T(tc trust) is a first-degree perception; C(T(tc trust)) is a second-degree perception; and so forth. Note that the order in which perceptions are formed corresponds to that in which successive parentheses are added.

Perceivers and perceiver alterations

The number of distinct perceivers (P) and the number of perceiver alterations (PA) provide two more indices of complexity. Both P and

PA in any degree of perception may be counted. Obviously, P cannot exceed the degree of perception. PA, distinct from P, refers to the number of alterations from one perceiver to another, and is always smaller than the degree of perception. For example, the therapist's verbalization '(the client knows what (other people think of (him)))' (third degree) involves three perceivers (therapist, client, other people) as well as two alterations (from therapist to client and from client to other people). Note that, if there is only one perceiver (by the first-person *I*), there is no alteration; accordingly, PA is zero. In particular, PA is always zero for first-degree perceptions. Note, however, that PA may exceed P. For instance, '(She knows that (I feel (she thinks (she trusts me))))' (fourth degree) has three alterations, but only two perceivers. The formal notation, if used, would help in coding: simply count the number of *distinct* capitalized letters that denote perceivers for P, and the number of alterations for PA.

Metacognition

In DAT, metacognition plays a crucial role in assimilating incongruent perceptions towards cognitive reintegration. An increase in complexity signifies cognitive reintegration at work, extended selfhood and hence therapeutic movement.

Cognitive reintegration, or repositioning, cannot be reduced to a frontal attack on the client's irrational beliefs in rational-emotive therapy, as practised by Albert Ellis (Yankura and Dryden 1990). By what standard are judgements of rationality made? By the therapist's standard? One might even question rationality itself as the ultimate value. Even if the question of standards were set aside, another would arise, concerning the cognitive demands put on the therapist. From a dialectical vantage, therapist and client have separate cognitive systems; understanding one from the standpoint of the other requires meta-systematic capability (Ho, Chan et al. 2001: 402). Moreover, logicians distinguish rationality of beliefs from logicality of reasoning: proceeding from irrational premises, one may logically draw irrational conclusions. This consideration suggests a more efficacious strategy: attack the premises, rather than the conclusions, if one must attack. Still, merely replacing irrational beliefs with rational ideas leaves untouched the cognitive system that generates the irrational beliefs in the first place. To use a metaphor, it is cognitive surgery and implant. It is preferable to achieve cognitive reintegration through inviting clients to self-examine their thinking, whence they may better judge the rationality of their beliefs.

This orients the therapist to work with and *through* the client's cognitive system, rather than attacking directly the irrational beliefs it generates.

Additionally, standards of judgements may vary across cultures as well as within cultures through time. Thus, what appears irrational to the therapist may be quite 'rational' to clients from a different cultural background. This is an instance of a more general problem: failure to consider the client's cultural background may erect barriers to therapist–client communication.

Extended conceptions of selfhood

The apparent simplicity of identifying different degrees of perception is deceptive. Consider the complex nature of self-perceptions. The self-concept is typically treated as a first-degree self-perception. However, self-perception may include what one reveals to others (perception of one's own social self – first degree), and what others think of oneself (perception of one's public image as perceived by others – second degree). One may reflect on one's self-concept: 'I revel at the thought that I am so smart' (second degree). Going further, one may reflect upon about how another person perceives oneself: 'I laugh, upon reflecting on my wife thinking that I am so smart' (third degree). Clearly, the self-concept is a complex composite of various components at different degrees of perception, each of which may be measured (Ho, Peng *et al.* 2001) (Table 23.1). Thus conceived, selfhood is a dynamic construct fraught with contradictions and tensions between perceptions. These contradictions provide opportunities for their resolution, which signifies therapeutic movement.

Such an extended conception of selfhood exposes fundamental inadequacies in the self psychology on which person-centred therapy is based. First, selfhood is far more encompassing than what can be fathomed with traditional assessments of the self-concept limited mostly to first-degree perceptions. Second, the notion of the individual, autonomous self is incomplete; it cannot account for the richness of the dialogical self, let alone a community of dialogical selves. Third, Rogers (1951), the progenitor of person-centred therapy, champions empathy as fundamental to understanding. DAT regards empathy as necessary, but not sufficient; full understanding requires metacognition. Fourth, Rogers' notion of self-consistency, which has dominated self psychology, leads to a sterile conception of human functioning in which contradictions have no place. Contradictions are, however, a part of life – a source of change, adaptation and creativity.

Table 23.1 *Directional trust*

Directional trust	Notation	DC/P/PA	Invitation to exploration
Client's trust (direction not specified)	C(trust)	1/1/0	Creating a trusting relationship is the first order of everything we do. It's a joint effort. Do you feel there is trust between us?
Client's perception in the client-to-therapist direction	C(ct trust)	1/1/0	Do you feel you trust me?
Client's metaperception in the client-to-therapist direction	C(T(ct trust))	2/2/1	Do you see that I feel you trust me?
Client's perception in the therapist-to-client direction	C(tc trust)	1/1/0	Do you believe I trust you?
Client's metaperception in the therapist-to-client direction	C(T(tc trust))	2/2/1	Do you see that I myself feel I trust you?

Therapeutic strategies

The therapist exploits dialogues, internal and external, for therapeutic gain. This may be done through inviting the client to explore his (1) relationship with the therapist, (2) own self, (3) perception of others, (4) internal dialogues with others and (5) internal dialogues with or between his different selves (or self-positions). Illustrative examples are provided in Tables 23.1–23.6. A word of caution: as illustrations, they should not be construed as formulaic prescriptions on how to conduct DAT.

Invite the client to co-create a trusting relationship with the therapist

The first order of DAT is to co-create a trusting therapeutic relationship. The idea of directional trust is illustrated in Table 23.1.

Invite the client to explore his own self

DAT is not easy. Cognitive demands on the therapist are formidable. In order to induce higher-degree perceptions in the client, the therapist must invoke construals at least one degree higher than those

Table 23.2 *Components of the self-concept*

Components of the self-concept	Notation	DC/P/PA	Invitation to exploration
Self-perception and social self			
Client's self-perception (what the client thinks of himself)	C(C)	1/1/0	Tell me something about yourself. What are you like as a person?
Reflection on one's self-perception	C(C(C))	2/1/0	You don't like the way you see yourself. Nobody feels good about that.
Social self (what the client reveals to others)	C(social self)	1/1/0	How do you present yourself in front of others?
Private self (what the client wants to hide from others)	C(private self)	1/1/0	Everyone needs to hide something about themselves from others. There are parts of you that you don't want others to know. But, here, you are encouraged to talk about them.
Social image			
Social image (what others think of the client)	O(C)	1/1/0	Let's explore how other people see you.
Client's perception of his social image	C(O(C))	2/2/1	You think other people see you as a nice guy.
Reflection on one's perception of one's social image	C(C(O(C)))	3/2/1	You find it hard to believe other people see you as a nice guy.
Reflection on friends' perception of one's self-perception	C(O(C(C)))	3/2/2	You think you are an awful person. Are your friends aware of what you think of yourself? ... What are their reactions to your thinking that you are awful?

of the client. Regarding the client's perception of his social image in Table 23.2, for instance, the therapist must first perceive accurately that (1) The client perceives that other people see him as a nice guy T(C(O(C))), a third-degree perception; and (2) the client finds it hard to believe in his own perception that other people see him as a nice guy T(C(C(O(C)))), a fourth-degree perception. The invitation, which should be verbalized in simple, ordinary language, brings to the client's awareness the incongruence within his self-concept, a necessary step towards cognitive reintegration.

Table 23.3 *Other-perception*

Other perception	Notation	DC/P/PA	Invitation to exploration
Client's other-perception (what the client thinks of others)	C(O)	1/1/0	Tell me something about your friend. What's she like as a person? ... So you think poorly of her.
Refection on one's other-perception	C(C(O))	2/1/0	You feel you've been rather harsh in judging others, such as your friend.
Client's perception of his friend's self-perception	C(O(O))	2/2/1	What does your friend think about herself?
Client's perception of his friend's reflection on her self-perception	C(O(O(O)))	3/2/1	What does your friend think about what she thinks of herself? ... Has she reflected on how she sees herself?
Client's perception of his friend's perception of what he thinks of his friend	C(O(C(O)))	3/2/2	What does your friend think about what you think of her?
Client's perception of how his friend perceives him	C(O(C))	2/2/1	What does your friend think about you? ... So she doesn't think well of you.
Client's perception of his friend's reflection on how she perceives him	C(O(O(C)))	3/2/1	What does your friend think about what she thinks of you? ... Has she reflected on how she sees you?
Client's perception of how his friend perceives his self-perception	C(O(C(C)))	3/2/2	What does your friend think about what you think of yourself? ... Does she feel you judge yourself even more harshly than you judge others?

Similarly, the therapist's supervisor must invoke still the next higher degree to understand what goes on between the client and therapist. Theoretical formulations of therapy in general entail yet higher degrees of cognitive construal. Such is the nature of human cognition.

Invite the client to explore his perception of others

Table 23.3 gives illustrations of how the client may be invited to self-examine his perceptions at different degrees of complexity. For instance, the client thinks poorly of his friend C(O), and perceives that his friend reciprocates in what she thinks about him C(O(C)). After reflection, the

Table 23.4 *Other people*

Other people	Invitation to exploration
Spouse	There's something you have wanted to tell your wife for a long time. Now start telling her. . . If you find this difficult, write her a letter. You can decide later whether you'll let her see it.
Parents	Say to your parents: 'I wish you would . . .'
Deceased parents	Your mother has been dead for a long time. You still feel guilty. What would she say to you (from wherever she is)? . . . How do you react to what she has said? . . . What would you want to say to her?
Your significant others	Take a look at the important people around you. What are they doing or thinking? What do they have to say about you? What would you want to say to them?
Your nemesis	You say this person has caused you great pain. You can't beat him. Now what would you like to say to him? . . . How are you going to deal with him?
Self and others in a dream	In your dream, you saw yourself and others. What happened? . . . So you saw yourself talking with those people, and sometimes even with yourself. . . Sometimes you became another person, talking with someone else, and sometimes with yourself. . . What do these tell you about your life? Your fears, your aspirations?

client becomes aware that he may have been too harsh in judging his friend C(C(O)). This may alter his subsequent perceptions: possibly, his friend does not think of him as harshly as what he has thought of her. Ho and Wang (2009) have formulated a systematic analysis of interpersonal perceptions, using constructs borrowed from social psychology: agreement, reciprocity, accuracy and congruence.

Internal dialogues with others

The idea of the self engaged in internal dialogues with others is illustrated in Table 23.4. Nowhere else is internal dialogue as rich and intriguing as in dreams (see Ho, Chan *et al.* 2001 for a description).

Internal dialogues between the client's different selves

The idea of different selves, engaged in internal dialogues with one another, is illustrated in Table 23.5. In particular, the idea of an imaginary self that has assumed the identity of another person may be very useful for strengthening interpersonal sensitivity and confronting

Table 23.5 *Different selves*

Different selves	Invitation to exploration
Actual self	Talk with yourself, the way you actually are.
Ideal self	Think of yourself as you would like yourself to be. Now close your eyes, and visualize your ideal self. Talk with him.
Rejected self	Look at the dark side of yourself. Find out what he is really like... What makes you dislike him so much?
Good (ideal) and bad (rejected) selves	Let your good self and your bad self talk with each other... Your good self is kind, right? Can he treat his rejected partner like a brother?
Past self	Let's move back in time, to a point when you *are* a little boy... What *are* you doing and thinking? ... *Are* you a good boy or a bad boy?
Future self	Fast forward to 5 years from now. Describe yourself. What *are* you like as a person?
Imaginary self	Imagine that you are a different person, different from the way you are now... Suppose you are going to do something you have never before done. What would that be?
Self-in-crisis	You're facing a crisis, and you don't know what to do... Now you may summon the strength deep inside you. This gives you an opportunity to confront your crisis.
Extinguishing self	You have limited time left. How are you going to use it wisely? ... You have had a quick review of your past. Now, the important thing is to list the things you feel must be completed before you die.
Extinguished self	Suppose you are dead already. Watch your funeral. What are the people attending your funeral doing? What do they say about you? Openly and in their hearts? What about the people closest to you?
Reborn self	You believe in rebirth. Whom would you choose to be your parents-to-be? What kind of a life would you choose to lead?
Selfless self	You have been dwelling on your miseries. Enough is enough. Now, ask yourself, 'What can I do to make other people around me less miserable?' 'Blessed is the person who finds the greatest joy in making others happy.'
Transformed self	You have been tormented by your past deeds, but your actions haven't changed. 'Lay down your butcher's knife, and be transformed into a Buddha on the spot.' That's action. So when will you act differently, like a transformed person?
Empty self	We don't know what the empty self is. So stop thinking about it. Just close your eyes. Attend to only the here and now. Empty your mind, until you are completely empty. Rid yourself of all thoughts. Experience emptiness, total emptiness... All gone... 'The empty, mindless mind minds nothing and everything all at once.' (The idea of the empty self is Buddhist. Great discipline is required to reach it.)

prejudices. The client may be invited to assume the identity of a member of the opposite sex, a minority group, a low-status group (e.g. domestic helpers) or caste (e.g. untouchables in India), or a mentally or physically handicapped group (e.g. deaf, blind).

Call to action in seven steps

DAT recasts therapy as *helping clients to learn to take dialogical action for solving problems of living and be masters of their own lives.* The methodology is scientific in orientation. It incorporates induction, deduction, even hypothesis testing. Developed to its full potential, dialogical action flows from the workings of a mature mind that goes beyond the hypothetical-deductive. Operationalized, dialogical action is a cycle of action and thought taken in seven steps (Ho, Chan *et al.* 2001).

(1) Learn from accumulation and summation of experience.
(2) Formulate a plan for action.
(3) Act according to plan.
(4) Evaluate and reflect on the action taken (consequences, effectiveness, etc.).
(5) Reformulate plan for action.
(6) Act according to reformulated plan.
(7) Learn from newly gained experience.

These steps constitute only a segmental description of the dialectic between action and thought. In actuality, the cycle of thought–action–thought never ends, as long as there is life. Although most people think of thought as preceding action, it is not necessarily the case. Thus, we could have chosen action–thought–action as the basic cycle instead.

Implications for theory advancement: from conceptualization to operationalization

Dialogue as a three-step procedure

In applying DST to counselling, Hermans (2006), drawing on Marková (1987), treats dialogue as a three-step procedure between two persons, A and B, in a dialogical relationship: (1) A directs an utterance to B; (2) B responds to this utterance; and (3) A revises his initial utterance in the light of B's response. As an illustratration, I construct Table 23.6 to capture the complexities that may be involved, using the notation and analytic tools developed in DAT.

Table 23.6 *Steps 1, 2 and 3*

Step	Utterance	Example	Process
Step 1: A to B	Uab1	'You think poorly of me, don't you?' symbolized as A(B(A poor)).	Uab1 becomes an object of perception by B, symbolized as B(Uab1). B thinks that Uab1 reflects A's poor self-perception, prompting him to respond with Uba1.
Step 2: B to A	Uba1	'You are the one who thinks poorly of yourself,' B(A(A poor)).	Uba1 as perceived by A = A (Uba1). A becomes more aware of his poor self-perception, prompting him to revise Uab1, and respond with Uab2.
Step 3: A to B	Uab2	'I may have been too harsh in judging not only you, but also myself,' A(A(B poor)) and A(A(A poor)).	Uab2 as perceived by B = B(Uab2). This entails two perceptions, symbolized as B(A (A(B poor))) and B(A(A(A poor))). Having become aware of A's revision, B may then, in turn, revise his perception of A.

Of course, the three-step procedure is only a segment, or basic unit, of an extended dialogue. However, DAT has the flexibility to capture extended dialogues for analysis in research. Both external and internal dialogues may be captured. For instance, A and B may represent (1) two different persons and (2) a person engaged in an internal dialogue between two self-positions, or with an imaginal person or even an inanimate object.

In a dialogical relationship, both partners engage in self-perceptions, other perceptions (i.e. perceptions of the partner) and, more importantly, reflections on these perceptions. Moreover, each partner assumes that his perceptions and reflections are considered by his partner; each partner also assumes that his partner makes a similar assumption. In short, a truly dialogical relationship is characterized by reciprocity and bidirectionality. Each partner adopts this attitude: 'I try to understand what you are thinking, and what you are thinking about what I am thinking; I also expect you to do the same thing.'

Methodological principles

The preceding analysis suggests several guiding principles for studying dialogical movements.

(1) Dialogical movement consists of cycles of Hermans' (2001) positioning–counter-positioning–repositioning. Polyvocality may entail multiple dissenting voices (counter-positioning) coming from one's own different selves or from others, real or imaginary. Unity with diversity may be achieved through a process of cognitive integration–disintegration–reintegration.

(2) A full account of dialogical movements includes interactions between inner and outer dialectics: between internal and external dialogues, and between thought and action.

(3) Individual differences in cognitive organization, metacognition in particular, should be considered. Hermans (2006: 15), for instance, reported that remarkable individual differences were found in the way clients went through the three-step procedure. Higher degrees of cognitive complexity are indicative of greater dialectical, and hence dialogical, capability. Thus, charting changes in terms of cognitive complexity provides an operational scheme to index dialogical movements.

Opportunities for research also abound for charting movements in therapy. We would expect, as therapy progresses, more higher degree perceptions and perceiver alterations, specifically more perceptions from another's perspective and reflections on one's own perceptions. Ho, Chan *et al.* (2001) illustrate therapeutic movement in terms of positioning–counter-positioning–repositioning, in which corresponding degrees of perception are charted. Ho, Fu *et al.* (2004) illustrate how emotional responses (guilt and shame) at different degrees of perception may be involved in various components of the self-concept.

Conclusion

Therapy based on the dialogical self promises to transform therapeutic practice, just as the thesis that selfhood is dialogical in nature promises to revolutionize self psychology. Future developments of DST require elaborations on self–other interactions in extended conceptions of selfhood. To advance to the next stage of development, elaborations are required on interactions between dialogical selves; after that, interactions within a community of dialogical selves. Metacognition plays an essential role in these developments. In particular, indices of cognitive complexity (degrees, numbers of perceivers and perceiver alterations) can serve as valuable analytic or research tools.

Resonations between the East and the West may be heard in such exciting developments. Although the present chapter owes much to

Eastern intellectual traditions, virtually everything it says about dialogical therapeutic practice is applicable in the West as well. In this respect, kindred minds countenance no barriers to intercultural communication. They are, however, challenged to engage in more East–West dialogues.

REFERENCES

Hermans, H. J. M. (2001) The dialogical self: toward a theory of personal and cultural positioning, *Culture and Psychology*, **7**, 243–281

(2002) The dialogical self as a society of mind, *Theory & Psychology*, **12**, 147–160

(2006) Moving through three paradigms, yet remaining the same thinker, *Counselling Psychology Quarterly*, **19**, 5–25

Ho, D. F. Y. (2010) Pooled ratings, self-ratings, and estimated ratings of therapeutic communication and popularity: a relational analysis, *The Humanistic Psychologist*, **38**, 317–335

Ho, D. F. Y., Chan, S. F., Peng, S. Q. and Ng, A. K. (2001) The dialogical self: converging East–West constructions, *Culture & Psychology*, **7**, 393–408

Ho, D. F. Y., Fu, W. and Ng, S. M. (2004) Guilt, shame, and embarrassment: revelations of face and self, *Culture & Psychology*, **10**, 159–178

Ho, D. F. Y., Peng, S. Q., Lai, A. C. and Chan, S. F. (2001) Indigenization and beyond: methodological relationalism in the study of personality across cultures, *Journal of Personality*, **69**, 925–953

Ho, D. F. Y. and Wang, H. L. (2009) Interpersonal perceptions and metaperceptions in dialogic action therapy: a relational methodological approach to theory construction, *The Humanistic Psychologist*, **37**, 79–100

Marková, I. (1987) On the interaction of opposites in psychological processes, *Journal for the Theory of Social Behaviour*, **17**, 279–299.

Rogers, C. (1951) *Client-Centered Therapy: Its Current Practice, Implications, and Theory* (Boston: Houghton Mifflin)

Yankura, J. and Dryden, W. (1990) *Doing RET: Albert Ellis in Action* (New York: Springer)

24 The depositioning of the *I*: emotional coaching in the context of transcendental awareness

Agnieszka Hermans-Konopka

From its inception, the dialogical self has been described in terms of a dynamic multiplicity of *I*-positions in the landscape of the mind, in the context of dialogical relationships between positions in the self and between those of different individuals (Hermans 2001; Hermans, Kempen and van Loon 1992). This description, which allows us to study the self as a 'society of mind' and part of society at large, has provided a fertile soil for the production of a variety of theoretical, empirical and professional studies over the years. In these studies, much attention has been paid to the content and organization of positions, guided by the implicit or explicit assumption that the *I* as a reflexive and dialogical agency is always and even necessarily bound to the flow and change of positions. In its most simple form, this assumption implies that the *I* is *always* a positioned *I*. In contrast to this assumption, I will argue that the *I* is not necessarily defined by a position but has its own specific nature and qualities.

I propose that the *I* can become engaged in a process of *depositioning*; that is, it can dis-identify from any position and enter a form of consciousness that is described in the literature in terms of a witnessing, thought-free, transcendental awareness (Cahn and Polich 2006).

In the second part of this chapter, I will show how moments of depositioning emerge when people are involved in processing their emotions. In my work with emotional coaching (Hermans and Hermans-Konopka 2010), I have observed that, when clients are caught up by intense emotions, they can sometimes move to a space beyond them from which they experience themselves in a more detached and non-judgemental way. It is as if they 'dis-identify' themselves from the ongoing experience, being at the same time very alert, present and open to it. It is my purpose to give specific examples of such moments and to show in which phases of the process of emotional coaching they occur.

Depositioned *I* as awareness

Attention to transcendental awareness can be found in a variety of psychological, cultural and religious contexts. For example, Hermans and Hermans-Konopka maintain that the notion of the depositioned *I* opens new ways of exploring experiential domains that are lying beyond the content of the position repertoire of the self. In a study titled '"I" = awareness', Deikman argued that awareness should be distinguished from any content. It is 'that which witnesses – not that which is observed' (1999: 421). The author maintains that awareness is prior to any content, that it is rather 'the ground in which the mind's contents manifest themselves; they appear in it and disappear once again' (1999: 421). Seeing awareness as devoid of content is very close to the conception of awareness as 'formless', as described by Tolle (2006). His main point is that people are often preoccupied by form (e.g. material, thoughts, emotions, plans), losing contact with the formless ground. Likewise, in Buddhist texts this ground has been described as a 'mother ground', 'sky-like essence' or 'Buddha nature' (Rinpoche 1992). A similar view can be found in the texts of Meister Eckhart, who talks about the 'ground of the soul', or the 'most inner space', which is unchangeable and silent, like a desert or ocean (McGinn 2001).

The process of transcendental awareness is not only known to spiritual traditions or mystical experiences, but it has also attracted the attention of scientists. Their focus is typically on the psychological and physiological effects and correlates of meditation, as focused in states of mind that can be described in terms of transcendental awareness. Recently, Cahn and Polich (2006) have presented an extensive review of empirical studies on the effect on meditation over the past decades. They note that 'the development of a transcending observer's perspective on their mental contents is an implicit or explicit goal of most meditative traditions' (2006: 180). The authors observe that meditation practices have an influence on psychological functioning not only during meditation (state changes) but also after it (trait changes). As a result of long-term meditation, many of the studies reported 'a deepened sense of calmness, increased sense of comfort, heightened awareness of the sensory field, and a shift in the relationship to thoughts, feelings, and experience of self. States of awareness sometimes referred to as "the witness" or "transcendental experience" are also claimed to ensue over time' (2006: 181). This experience is described as a 'contentless awareness that is independent of mental activities', producing 'a perception of an altered self-identity' wherein the separation perceived between the observer and the observed is reduced. For our purposes, the following observation is particularly relevant: 'As the perceived lack of separation develops, the sense of self seems to shift from mental thought centered in the body to an impersonal *beingness*. This awareness is related to the essential emptiness of a separate and isolated self-identity' (2006: 181). As this quotation suggests, the dynamic nature of the process of positioning and repositioning is changed into a form of 'beingness' (for an extensive review of electroencephalographic (EEG) and neuroimaging and imaging studies of meditative states, see Cahn and Polich 2006).

Awareness and emotions

In this chapter, I am bringing together work on transcendental awareness and work on emotions which we have described as 'temporary *I*-positions' (Hermans and Hermans-Konopka 2010). In this way, I explore the relationship between emotions as influential ways of positioning and awareness as a factor of depositioning. My purpose is to show how awareness can play a central and productive role in dealing with emotions. The space of the self, temporarily devoid of content, can become a vital experience in the coaching of emotions. An important reason for combining work on emotions and awareness is that the globalizing self with its increasing multiplicity and heterogeneity of *I*-positions and emotions (Hermans and Dimaggio 2007) is at risk of becoming overcrowded and needs the space of awareness in order not to be lost in a cacophony of voices. The space of awareness will allow contradictive tendencies in the self to exist and helps to deal with strong decentralizing movements, permitting one to step back from any experience of storm and turbulence.

Emotions and positions come and go; their natural multiplicity and changeability cannot offer much continuity in one's life. On the other hand, if an emotion becomes fixed and over-stabilized, losing its fluidity, it becomes an *I*-prison, limiting the horizon of the self. Awareness can be seen as a counter-force against the natural discontinuity of emotions and also has the power to liberate the person from *I*-prisons.

My purpose in this exposition is to find a balance between positioned content and formless space. Work on emotions needs space of awareness and, the other way around, a meaningful place of awareness in everyday life needs recognition of emotions and *I*-positions. I want to argue that along these lines we can profit from two traditions: Western psychology, which emphasizes the potential of working with emotions as a basis for authenticity, uniqueness and richness of the individual self; and the Eastern traditions, or even broader, the spiritual traditions, which open the gate to the transforming character of awareness.

In the following I start with an exposition of a stage model as a procedure of working on emotions in coaching, counselling and training, and I will show how awareness can be included in this model, in such a way as to offer not only going into emotions and positions but also going beyond them.

Stage model of emotions

Taking into account the transforming potential of emotions (Averill 1992; Greenberg 2002; Morgan and Averill 1992), we designed a stage model of work with emotions (Hermans and Hermans-Konopka 2010) which can be introduced in coaching, psychological training or counselling.

The model consists of seven stages which can be applied in a flexible way according to the needs and possibilities of the client:

Stage	Name
1	Identifying and entering an emotion
2	Leaving the emotion
3	Identifying and entering a counter-emotion
4	Leaving the counter-emotion
5	Developing dialogical relations between emotion and counter-emotion
6	Creating a composition of emotions
7	Developing a promoter position

The processes of entering and leaving emotions (stages 1–4)

In the first stage a client is asked to enter into an emotion, experienced as important and problematic (entering stage). It can be a rigid emotion that limits one's actions, like anxiety that prevents building authentic relations with others. In the next phase (leaving stage) a person is invited to let the emotion go and to move on freely. During the two next stages the same process is repeated with the counter-emotion: a person enters a counter-emotion (e.g. happiness), explores its quality (by entering the counter-emotion) and then lets it go (leaving the counter-emotion). In these four stages the movement of the *I* between different emotional landscapes is stimulated by the coach in order to increase the flexibility of experience and the accessibility of varied emotions, preventing their rigidity.

What can transcendental awareness mean for the process of entering and leaving emotions? I argue that it adds an experiential space beyond the emotion which creates a chance to feel this emotion without over-identifying with it. This space helps to deal with difficult emotional experiences, which could otherwise be too overwhelming or imprisoning. Where there is no space beyond the dominating experience, the person becomes totally immersed in the emotion, with the consequence that alternative perspectives fall beyond the constricted horizon of the self. Participating in the space of awareness offers a 'safety buffer' that encourages a person to go into difficult experiences, at the same time reducing the risk of becoming lost in them. Awareness, opening a space to step back, does not exclude an intimate contact with the emotional experience. It helps to *be with* whatever is arising and leads to allowing a broader range of feelings. Avoidance or suppression of the emotion does not take place, because awareness creates a 'continuity in discontinuity', which allows one to stand still while moving and to be with whatever appears in the successive stream of experience.

As an example, I present here an experience of my client, a 50-year-old manager, Robert, who did not feel able to deal with his overwhelming emotions. Trying to present himself as a rational and self-controlled man, according to the expectations prevailing in his organization, he had a strong tendency to control the expression of his emotions by suppressing them. He used to sit in a tense posture, never taking enough space for himself, and not being able to relax. He explained that, in his work situation, he sometimes lost his emotional control and could explode with anger, accusing other people in destructive ways and making rude, insulting statements. During the process of dialogical emotional coaching, he arrived at a point where he experienced a space *between* and *around* his emotions. This was a space not filled by any emotion or thought but by space *per se*. He felt this space and he could be *in* it, while being at the same time in contact with his emotions, but not totally immersed in them. From that moment on, he could experience his emotions more and more without attempting to avoid or suppress them. He gradually learned to 'feel all these energies from the space in myself'. In one of the sessions, he described this process in the following way: 'Space, a sky-like experience, I never experienced this space before, just space, I am bigger now and I can use all these characters, all these emotions. I can move easily from one to another.'

Experiencing the space of awareness in himself, he could be better in touch with the variety of his emotions, while not being lost in them. He said: 'The experience of the space is developing. There is more and more inner space. I can be angry, I can be sad, there is place for more, and when I feel this space I am not so afraid of being lost in my emotions.' The growing awareness prevented him from being overwhelmed by the flux of emotions and from falling back to his protective avoidance. He pointed out: 'I have a space to look at whatever comes, I know it is possible not to be taken by it.' His emotions stopped being threatening as he realized that he had a space to step back, even in the middle of his emotional storm. The development of awareness changed the relation with his emotions: 'I feel less need to struggle with all these emotions, there is enough space for all of them.'

The relation between self (and awareness in the self) and emotion is a central focus in a dialogical perspective on emotions (Hermans and Hermans-Konopka 2010). Including awareness in the practice of dialogical self theory (DST) is concerned more with improving the relation between self and emotion than with changing the emotion. In the majority of cases, people are attempting to change their negative emotions (Parkinson *et al.* 1996) rather than allow them to exist. Robert was struggling with his emotions, investing a great deal of energy in it. Not being able to allow and accept his emotions, he could not feel relaxed or relate to people in an authentic way. The development of awareness showed him a very different attitude towards his feelings and he realized that he could let them be and diminish his inner war. From an attitude of fighting against his emotions, he moved towards freedom to allow the whole range of emotions: 'This space gives me freedom to feel them all, to become them all.' Awareness implies the emergence of a space from which a person can relate to his emotions in a non-oppositional way, allowing them to be and to be heard, but not being dominated by them.

The process of dis-identification seems to be essential to awareness as an experience of widening one's horizon and space, as indicated by Robert's statement: 'I can look at all of them from my space.' The relevance of dis-identification is also pictured by an exercise proposed by Wilber (2009), in which a person is invited to think in the following way: 'I have a thought, I am not my thought.' A similar practice has been developed by Assagioli, as discussed by Rowan (2010; see also his chapter in this volume), in which a person, invited to identify different parts of himself, came up with characters like Clown, Gorilla, Caveman and Child. In the next step, the person had to dis-identify from these parts, saying: 'I have a Clown, but I am not a Clown; I have a Gorilla, but I am not a Gorilla' (Rowan 2010: 58). Probably many of us have a part in ourselves which can be symbolized as a gorilla, crocodile, monster or any other animal. Some people *have* these gorillas or crocodiles in themselves; other experientially *become* like gorillas or crocodiles. Awareness allows us to keep the advantages of having or even loving a gorilla or a crocodile but prevents us from becoming one (for the process of identifying with an animal, see the phenomenon of shape-shifting, Gieser 2006).

Development of awareness seems to stimulate flexibility to move from one emotion to another, facilitating movements in the 'leaving phases' of the model. When a person identifies with an emotion, there is a risk of clinging to it. When my anger becomes my identity ('I am angry') or when my depression coincides with my identity ('I'm depressed'), it has some fixing quality. As a consequence of such identification, losing my anger or my depression would be losing part of who I am, or, in extreme cases, losing a central part of my identity. Participating in the background awareness rather than entirely identifying with the experience helps to become engaged in emotions and to leave them before they become *I*-prisons. Awareness creates a space for emotional freedom, so that the movement from one emotion to another becomes more flowing. Leaving an emotion in this way is not entering a void emptiness but an emptiness full of presence and witnessing. This space has much to offer to the developing self as moving through the 'landscape of the mind'. Of special significance for the self moving in space is the next phase of the stage model.

Dialogue between emotions (stage 5)

In this phase the dialogue between two emotions is stimulated. Emotions as 'voiced positions' define the way of perceiving the world, the self and others. From a dialogical perspective, emotions have something to tell to the person. Anxiety may have the message that the world is threatening, while joy tells him that the world is inviting and enjoyable. When these emotions with their message meet in a dialogue, they may influence and even renew each other (Hermans and Hermans-Konopka 2010). In this dialogue the two emotions, as different 'emotional schemas', influence each other with the possibility of merging into a new synthesis (Greenberg 2002). Such a synthesis is in agreement with the centring (organizing) movements in the dialogical self. In contrast, moving back and forth from the one to the other (opposite) emotion can have a decentring (disorganizing) effect. Research on emotions and the self (Hermans-Konopka and Hermans 2010) showed that the self under the influence of one emotion (e.g. anger) reacts in a very different way than when under the influence of another emotion (e.g. feeling down). When the person goes from one emotion to a very different emotion, a sudden increase of discontinuity works as a decentring movement in the self. As a reaction, centring movements are required in order to restore the organization in the self. It is this sequence of decentring and centring movements that is activated when the person moves between different emotions and establishes a dialogue between them.

One of my clients, Jane, 45 years old, complained about intense anxiety. During one of our sessions, we stimulated the dialogue between two of her emotions: '*I* as anxious' and '*I* as happy'. Giving a voice to her anxiety, she said, 'There is always a hidden danger. Do not say anything, just be quiet, otherwise you will again spoil these relations; people will not like you; they will leave you.' When she let the anxiety go and entered happiness as a counter-emotion, she said, 'Let yourself be who you are, it is enough as it is.' These two statements were for her contradicting messages emerging from her own emotions. Looking at the world from the perspective of happiness meant that she could not recognize herself in the message coming previously from her anxiety.

A dialogue between two contradicting or opposing emotional voices results in strong decentring movements in the self. I have learned that in such situations silence can act as an important centring counter-force in the self. Particularly, when there is an increasing density and heterogeneity of positions which are involved in dialogue, silence, as an essential feature of awareness, functions as an antidote to an over-crowded mind.

I want to argue that inner dialogue between emotional voices, particularly when they are involved in conflict or opposition, needs space for silence so that the dialogue between the voices comes to an end. A constant interaction and exchange between the voices would be unproductive and, therefore, needs to be balanced by silence and stillness.

Awareness serves as a factor of stability in dealing with the reality of emotions and positions. Awareness offers a background from which centring forces introduce stillness in the midst of a whirlpool of emotions. As an experience of being and witnessing, it creates continuity in the self, in the midst of emotions. Only the content of awareness changes but not the witnessing presence itself. According to Hayward, 'Gradual identification with the background, rather than with the illusion of a permanent self, brings a sense of harmony, clarity, wisdom and energy to one's life' (1999: 393).

It appears not only that emotions, positions or thoughts are parts of our identity, but also that awareness, as a result of practice, can become increasingly part of the sense of who we are. The capacity of dis-identification from emotions leads to more openness for change provoked by dialogue, because letting go of an emotion is no longer felt as a threat to one's identity.

Composition of emotions (stage 6)

The sixth stage of the stage model is focused on making a composition of emotions: 'The notion of composition reflects the conceptualization of the self as an organized position repertoire and, at the same time, allows us to consider this organization from an artistic perspective. The essential quality of a composition is its *pattern*, and, as parts of this pattern, positions and emotions can be viewed as receiving their place in a larger whole' (Hermans and Hermans-Konopka 2010: 309–310). In the practice of emotional coaching, a client is asked to create an artistic composition in which emotions receive a place in a context of the broader position repertoire. The composition can consist of varied positions, including emotions as temporary positions (e.g. '*I* as anxious', '*I* as happy'), other internal positions (e.g. '*I* as rational', '*I* as professional') or external positions (e.g. 'my friend', 'my mother', etc.). In this phase a client takes the perspective of an artist who expresses himself and his emotions in an imaginative way. This process itself can lead to a development of awareness, because, as Epstein argued, 'Art is another portal into the space of bare attention' (Epstein 2007: 188). Looking at the composition of one's self through the eyes of an artist allows a non-judgemental attitude which leads to seeing things as they are in their full expression, colours, shapes and richness, and this attitude becomes more important than striving for perfection. Finding perfection not in changing emotions but rather, in the terms of Huxley (1957), in their 'itsness' and 'suchness' (perceiving things as they are in non-evaluating ways) brings together composition and awareness.

Art is, according to Hermans and Hermans-Konopka (2010), an antidote for splitting identities. Art has the potential to transcend the pervasively used good–bad dichotomy by bringing them together as parts of a composition. When the good–bad dichotomy loses its predominance, emotions and positions that would be otherwise rejected as shadow positions (unacceptable parts of the self) are allowed to become part of an integrative composition. Art helps us to transcend any mutually exclusive opposition between 'good' and 'bad' and between 'positive' and 'negative' and in this way favours a synthesis of otherwise unrelated or fragmented parts of the self.

Awareness supports this artistic process by going beyond one's natural tendency to become attached to the pleasant and to reject the unpleasant. Just trying to keep one, positive, side of emotional experiences and rejecting the other, unpleasant, side, as a natural human tendency, leads to a never-ending struggle against one side of life. This struggle can be reduced by art and awareness of being *with* all experiences as they manifest themselves. Including emotions in art and awareness becomes more important than clinging to their positive sides. My client Robert described it in the following words: 'This is a space of looking at different feelings. Including them all makes me feel a more complete human being, not only positive, not only this or that, but all, richer. It means to be human.' When we are able to make art which includes our deepest sorrow and pain and feel it while *standing still towards* the experience in the middle of the experience, art becomes a transforming experience. Strength is built up when we stop running away from our demons and we dare to look straight into their faces. This is a strength different from just feeling strong and good; it is rather a form of strength that grows in the midst of pain and weakness. It seems that working with artistic compositions and developing awareness can cooperate in the process of developing a non-dualistic form of strength.

Learning to look and just to see, to be with whatever arises, is the opposite of trying to change anything. Emotional change in the context of awareness is often a paradoxical one, as it starts when a person stops striving for change. Epstein presents the example of a client who was depressed and tried to get rid of his difficult feelings. Paradoxically, 'His feelings began to change only when he stopped wishing them to' (Epstein 2007: 157). Striving for change is often an escape from what is and cannot lead to a real encounter with one's emotions. Allowing emotions as they are and discovering their artistic quality allows one to make art from any experience. As Greenberg (2002) holds, even if an emotion needs to be changed, first of all it must be accepted and allowed to exist. By its nature, awareness intensifies the process of allowing, and learning to be with whatever arises, without rejecting and clinging, including the dark sides of experiences and painful emotions. However, awareness goes a step further than acceptance, as mentioned by Green-berg, and it should not be confused with an accepting attitude. It is neither rejecting nor accepting; it is rather being *with* and allowing experience as it is without any evaluation. Both art and awareness are characterized by non-judgemental attitudes because uniqueness becomes more important than the way a person would like to see the experience or to feel the emotion in an idealistic way.

Irene (44 years old) experienced anxiety as an obstacle to her spon-taneous relations with others and as detrimental to the development of her company. In the trajectory of emotional coaching, we worked on a composition using a variety of stones as material. Each stone was repre-senting an *I*-position or an emotion. She included in her composition the following positions: '*I* as anxious', '*I* as lonely', '*I* as feminine', '*I* as artistic', '*I* as spiritual', '*I* as relaxed', '*I* as resting in my body',

'*I* as depressed' and '*I* as a girl'. After exploring these positions and allowing their voices to speak, we focused on the composition as a whole and on the experience of anxiety as part of this context. I invited Irene to go into the experience of anxiety, represented by a heavy, grey stone. At some moment she noticed an experience in the background which she described in terms of 'pain' and she took another black stone to represent it. Silently she looked at this stone and placed it in the middle of her composition. I asked her where she was, and she answered, 'Somewhere here, I would say, here, in awareness.' After a session with much silence, we discussed what had happened and she said, 'I just want to let it be as it is, for now; it is OK to feel this pain, it brings me a relief.' She discovered that deeper, under her anxiety, was a hidden emotional pain that she had wanted to escape for many years. It was the pain that she was so afraid of and had never dared to face. It seems that this moment of awareness, as she called it herself, helped her to face her own pain, not trying to escape or change it. The stone representing the pain was placed 'out there', at some distance from her. It represented a content of experience which was even in physical space differentiated from the experiencer. She did not coincide with the experience, but she was there, *with* it, in awareness.

In artistic composition not only positions or emotions are objects of attention. The spaces between are also essential. Morioka (2008), a Japanese psychologist, introduced the concept of *ma* and defined it in this way: 'We use the word *ma* for a space between a thing and another thing, and also between one moment and another moment' (2008: 105). It is a place of receptive listening to what is said and what is not said. The space between two emotions or two thoughts is also an object of meditation in Dzogchen Buddhism, a Tibetan school of Buddhism which focuses attention directly on the experience of 'rigpa', described as ground of awareness. According to Trungpa (2008), rigpa can be experienced in the 'gap of mind', in a space between one emotion and another, between one thought and another. The essence of the Dzogchen meditation can be described in this way: 'When one past thought has ceased and a future thought has not yet risen, in that gap, in between, isn't there a consciousness of the present moment; fresh, virgin, unaltered by even a hair's breadth of concept, a luminous, naked awareness? Well, that is what Rigpa is!' (Rinpoche 1992: 160). According to Hayward (1999), rigpa is accessible within the gap between two moments of dualistic experience, as spacious and vast, with a quality of peacefulness and brilliance. The space 'in-between' is an entrance to the field of awareness and has intrinsic value to the spiritual path.

Usually, in work with composition in the dialogical self, the space 'in-between' refers to the relation between positions with an emphasis on how the two positions or emotions are placed in the space. The focus is then not so much on the space itself but on the positions and their connections. In this way, the space 'in-between' is defined by the relationship between *I*-positions as located in that space. However, if we consider a composition from the perspective of awareness, the space between is treated as prior to any relation which takes place in it. It is not only in the service of understanding the relationship between entities (like the relation between positions), but also has a meaning in itself. When we follow this line, the space 'in-between' can be experienced in itself. Being in this space allows one to experience opposites and contradictions in their presence and suchness without being lost or overwhelmed by them.

Promoter function (stage 7)

In the last stage of the model (promoter stage), the voice of a promoter position is included in the work with emotions. This position has a special meaning for the development of a person. It stimulates the development of a variety of positions and integrates older and new positions in the self. It reorganizes the self towards a higher level of development and creates some continuity, at the same time giving space for discontinuity in the self (Hermans and Hermans-Konopka 2010). A promoter position can refer to a significant other (e.g. inspiring teacher, parent of spiritual figure) or to an internal *I*-position (e.g. *I* as compassionate or *I* as a fighter). An emotion treated as a temporary *I*-position can also become a promoter position and as such is included in the stage model.

Central to our chapter is the argument that awareness can have a promoter function as well, but it is different from positions. As I argued at the beginning of this chapter, awareness has no content, no form; it is rather a witnessing presence of any content or form. Awareness, as a promoter, should not be treated as just another *I*-position. Following this line, awareness in work with emotions could become a basis for allowing different, even contradictive emotions and for giving space for a variety of new *I*-positions, at the same time integrating them. As my client Robert said: 'From my sky position I can allow *all* these energies.'

In particular, I see the promoter function of awareness in the potential of developing the *receptive* side of the self by going from 'the art of doing' towards the 'art of being'. As such it becomes a counter-force to active positions in the self and opens the door to an appreciation of existence itself. Being is not dependent on doing and achieving but is able to encompass it. In this way the sense of the self and self-worth receives a broader basis than one's actions and achievements. Discovering the sense of the self and self-worth in one's existence as a being liberates the person from conditional self-esteem. In this way, awareness can invite an unconditional love for self and other, directed towards one's being and not merely dependent on actions, achievements or qualities.

Conclusions and consequences

In this chapter, I wanted to show that emotions are experienced on two levels: content and awareness. On the level of content, the person identifies, in a more or less transient way, with a particular emotion. On the level of awareness, the emotion is 'there', but it is distinguished from the 'experiencer'. I have argued that this two-level approach has important implications for working with emotions in the stage model (Hermans and Hermans-Konopka 2010). It allows us to bring together personal (emotions) and transpersonal (awareness) processes in coaching, counselling and training methodology based on DST.

In order to understand the specific nature of awareness as a process of depositioning, it makes sense to distinguish between awareness and meta-position. According to Hermans (2003), a meta-position enables the person to start a process of self-reflection about one or more specific positions. A meta-position has several qualities: it creates a certain distance from other positions, allows one to order them, creates an overview, helps one to link positions with one's personal history, and stimulates a comparison and evaluation of the organization of positions. It can also help to sketch a direction of change in the further development of a person. In this way a meta-position can have an important function in coaching, training or counselling as stimulating insight and change.

While a meta-position permits a process of active ordering, comparing and evaluating, awareness, on the contrary, is a depositioning presence that generates a receptive attitude to everything that arises. Awareness is oriented towards the here and now, and it is not concerned with any form of comparison or evaluation. While meta-positioning implies a movement between past, present and future with a focus on resemblances, contrasts and evaluations, awareness is non-judgemental and non-evaluative. While meta-positioning is immersed in categorizations and concepts, awareness goes beyond conceptual thinking to the realm of presence and being.

A common feature of meta-position and awareness is the dis-identification from an emotion or position. Taking a meta-position enables one to move above positions or emotions and to create some overview. Awareness also allows dis-identification from emotions by going into a space beyond them.

Both awareness and meta-positioning have important but different functions in coaching and counselling. Meta-position and self-reflection provide a basis for understanding the organization of the self, seeing interconnections between positions, and moving in a particular develop-mental direction. Awareness in coaching and training helps participants to allow all experiences while not being overwhelmed by these experi-ences. It allows the opening of people to the experience of the here and now, liberating them from the limitations of concepts and categoriza-tions, and helping them to go beyond rigid and imprisoning emotions and positions.

The majority of methods based on or connected with DST, such as the personal-position repertoire (PPR) method (Hermans 2003), or the self-confrontation method (Hermans and Hermans-Jansen 1995), empha-size self-reflection or meta-positioning. The application of these methods could be significantly enriched by including coaching and training procedures that stimulate awareness, especially when it becomes important to relate to one's positions and emotions in an open, allowing and non-judgemental way.

REFERENCES

Averill, J. R. (1992) William James's other theory of emotion, in M. E. Donnelly (ed.), *Reinterpreting the Legacy of William James* (Washington, DC: American Psychological Association), 221–229

Cahn, B. L. and Polich, J. (2006) Meditation states and traits: EEG, ERP, and neuroimaging studies, *Psychological Bulletin*, **132**, 180–211

Deikman, A. J. (1999) 'I' = awareness, in S. Gallagher and J. Shear (eds.), *Models of the Self* (Thorverton, UK: Imprint Academic), 421–427

Engler, J. H. (1984) Therapeutic aims in psychotherapy and meditation: developmental stages in the representation of self, *Journal of Transpersonal Psychology*, **16**, 25–62

Epstein, M. (2007) *Psychotherapy Without the Self: A Buddhist Perspective* (New Haven, CT, and London: Yale University Press)

Gieser, T. (2006) How to transform into goddesses and elephants: exploring the potentiality of the dialogical self, *Culture & Psychology*, **12**, 443–459

Greenberg, L. S. (2002) *Emotion-Focused Therapy: Coaching Clients to Work Through Their Feelings* (New York: American Psychological Association)

Hayward, J. (1999) A r-Dzogs-chen Buddhist interpretation of the sense of self, in S. Gallagher and J. Shear (eds.), *Models of the Self* (Thorverton, UK: Imprint Academic), 379–394

Hermans, H. J. M. (1996) Voicing the self: from information processing to dialogical interchange, *Psychological Bulletin*, **119**, 31–50

(2001) The dialogical self: toward a theory of personal and cultural positioning, *Culture & Psychology*, **7**, 243–281

(2002) The dialogical self as a society of mind: introduction, *Theory & Psychology*, **12**, 147–160

(2003) The construction and reconstruction of a dialogical self, *Journal of Constructivist Psychology*, **16**, 89–130

(2004) The dialogical construction of coalitions in a personal position repertoire, in H. J. M. Hermans and G. Dimaggio (eds.), *The Dialogical Self in Psychotherapy* (New York: Brunner-Routledge), 124–137

Hermans, H. J. M. and Dimaggio, G. (2007) Self, identity, and globalization in times of uncertainty: a dialogical analysis, *Review of General Psychology*, **11**, 31–61

Hermans, H. J. M. and Hermans-Jansen, E. (1995) *Self-Narratives: The Construction of Meaning in Psychotherapy* (New York: Guilford Press)

Hermans, H. J. M. and Hermans-Konopka, A. (2010) *Dialogical Self Theory: Positioning and Counter-Positioning in a Globalizing Society* (Cambridge University Press)

Hermans, H. J. M. and Kempen, H. J. G. (1993) *The Dialogical Self: Meaning as Movement* (San Diego, CA: Academic Press)

Hermans, H. J. M., Kempen, H. J. G. and Van Loon, R. J. P. (1992) The dialogical self: beyond individualism and rationalism, *American Psychologist*, **47**, 23–33

Hermans-Konopka, A. and Hermans, H. J. M. (2010) The dynamic features of love: changes in self and motivation, in J. D. Raskin, S. K. Bridges and R. Neimeyer (eds.), *Studies in Meaning 4: Constructivist Perspectives on Theory, Practice, and Social Justice* (New York: Pace University Press)

Huxley, A. (1957) *The Doors of Perception* (London: Chatto and Windus)

Kluger, A., Nir, D. and Kluger, Y. (2008) Personal position repertoire (PPR) from a bird's eye view, *Journal of Constructivist Psychology*, **21**, 223–238

McGinn, B. (2001) *The Mystical Thought of Meister Eckhart: The Man from Whom God Hid Nothing* (New York: Crossroad Publishing)

Morgan, C. and Averill, J. R. (1992) True feelings, the self, and authenticity: a psychosocial perspective, in D. D. Franks and V. Gecas (eds.), *Social Perspectives on Emotion* (Greenwich, CT: JAI Press), vol. I, 95–124

Morioka, M. (2008) Voices of self in the therapeutic chronotope: 'Utushi' and 'Ma', *International Journal for Dialogical Science*, **3**, 93–108

Parkinson, B., Totterdel, P., Briner, R. B. and Reynolds, S. (1996) *Changing Moods: The Psychology of Mood and Mood Regulation* (London and New York: Longman)

Raggatt, P. (2007) Forms of positioning in the dialogical self: a system of classification and the strange case of Dame Edna Everage, *Theory & Psychology*, **17**, 355–382.

Rinpoche, S. (1992) *The Tibetan Book of Living and Dying* (London: Random House)

Rowan, J. (2010) *Personification: Using the Dialogical Self in Psychotherapy and Counselling* (Hove: Routledge)

Shikpo, R. (2005) The highest Maha Ati teachings: Chogyam Trungpa Rinpoche in Great Britain, in F. Midal (ed.), *Recalling Chogyam Trungpa* (Boston and London: Shambhala), 221–241

Tolle, E. (2006) *A New Earth: Awakening to Your Life's Purpose* (New York: Penguin Group)

Trungpa, C. (2008) *True Perception: The Path of Dharma Art* (Boston and London: Shambhala)

Wilber, K. (1997) *The Eye of Spirit: An Integral Vision for a World Gone Slightly Mad* (Boston and London: Shambhala)

(2009). Subject becomes object. Retrieved from www.youtube.com/watch?v=NQ_HsQkBkJA

25   The dialogical self and educational research: a fruitful relationship

M. Beatrice Ligorio

This purpose of this chapter is to discuss the reciprocal enrichment of the encounter between dialogical self theory (DST) and recent trends in educational research. Such an encounter is justified, on the one hand, by the need of educational research to overcome the traditional cognitive approach and to encompass a larger view of the educational mission, particularly in formal contexts such as schools. On the other hand, the encounter is instigated by the many suggestions coming from the idea of positioning, repositioning and counter-positioning of DST and the need to incorporate this idea in a contemporary school context.

This encounter is not merely a juxtaposition of two streams of thought but is based on many common points between the two fields – learning theories and DST – such as the attention to the social dimension of human development, the relevance of the material tools, and the significance of the physical and cultural spaces where individuals meet and act. These dimensions are the starting point for a reciprocal enrichment and will lead towards the mutual advancement sought by both fields. In fact, educational research attempts to define a more comprehensive research area, a learning science where the learning processes are the basis of human development. Conversely, DST seeks to expand and generalize methods and outcomes to many applied contexts – beside psychotherapy and clinical situations – in order to define a psychological theory of individual and cultural changes in modern society.

This chapter is an attempt to demonstrate that this encounter is not only possible but also needed and will lead to a general advance in the understanding of the functioning of individuals in educational contexts.

The limits of a traditional educational approach

Experts in education strongly contend that traditional approaches to learning – such as the cognitive approach – show insufficient explicative power (Brown and Campione 1990; Kruger and Tomasello 1996; Scardamalia and Bereiter 2005; Simons *et al.* 2000). Many of the phenomena occurring nowadays within educational contexts cannot be sufficiently understood through the cognitive approach. Events such as student failure, teacher burnout, classroom management difficulties, or failure to create a positive relationship between school and family are difficult to understand through approaches based exclusively on the cognitive lens. In fact, all these situations are, directly or indirectly, related to cultural and situational issues, and the impact of these issues on students' and teachers' self-representation, and on their professional and personal identities, should be adequately taken into consideration. A new theoretical and methodological apparatus is therefore needed. A more comprehensive understanding of educational situations should be pursued by amplifying the focus of research so that the cognitive dimension also includes emotional, social, cultural and personal perspectives. Three important approaches have contributed to explaining why the traditional cognitive approach can no longer be considered adequate to understand education and to carry out research in the field of learning and instruction: (1) the distributed cognition approach; (2) cultural-historical activity theory (CHAT); and (3) social-constructivism. I will first discuss each of these approaches separately and then argue for the reciprocal enrichment of learning theories and DST in the service of advanced educational research.

The first approach, distributed cognition (Hollan *et al.* 2000; Salmon 1993), argues that cognitive processes do not belong exclusively to individuals. External sources and individual cognition should be considered as a unit, and not as two separate dimensions. Cognition remains an important focus, but this approach contends that cognitive processes can only be understood when looking at how cognition works when interacting with tools and other people, within specific contexts. Individual cognitive processes depend strictly on context; therefore, the network of people with whom each individual works, the tools used and all the resources – symbolic or material – available within the context are part of the individual processes.

When applied to education, this means that the individual learner is no longer the exclusive centre of attention and that, in order to understand how people learn, their network of tools and social interaction needs to be addressed.

CHAT (Cole and Engeström 1993) is the second tradition challenging the cognitive approach. CHAT argues that individuals are strongly rooted in the history and development of their species. In this sense, humans are cultural and historical beings. This approach is strongly rooted in Vygotsky's work (1978; Vygotsky and Luria 1994) and represents a fervent attempt to develop a new psychology based on Marxist

dialectical materialism (Levitin 1982; Yaroshevsky 1989). In opposition
to the Freudian vision of psychology, Vygotsky rejected the idea of a
'psyche' formed at a very early stage in life and strongly objected to the
idea of unconscious forces. Instead, the activities humans undertake at
any stage of life, the goals and the aims they pursue, the tools they use
and develop, all have a deep impact on the psychological structure of
human beings. Since these elements vary depending on the cultural and
historical contexts people live in, human psychology is historically and
culturally shaped. In other words, who we are depends on what we do,
on the type of activity we are involved in, on the people we interact with,
and on the types of tools we use. The 'psyche' and the external world are
interdependent and are not separable. For education, this implies that
the external world should be rich and complex so as to promote higher
levels of thinking.

The third approach is social-constructivism (Gergen and Davis 1985).
To illustrate the basic assumption of this approach, the concept of
'mediation' should be considered. Human beings are not capable of
direct access to an objective reality because of their inescapable inclination to interpret what they see (Bruner 1990; Cole 1996). Furthermore, interpretation is not possible without the mediation of tools
provided by nature, or artefacts made by humans. Therefore, the relationship with the world is never direct; instead, it is always mediated by
tools and artefacts, which have a crucial role in shaping and directing the
sense-making process of the world, of events and even of who we are.
Humans interpret what they see under the influence of the resources that
a specific context makes available to them. Just to give a trivial example,
if we use a magnifying lens, we will see different things than just with
the naked eye. The tool we use shapes what we see and influences
the representation of our world and of our place in it. When social-
constructivism is applied to education, learning cannot be considered
simply a transfer of knowledge, but rather an active and complex
knowledge-building process, occurring within a community of learners
sharing aims and practices (Brown and Campione 1990; Lave and
Wenger 1991; Scardamalia 2002; Wenger 1998). The aim is no longer
to improve individual knowledge, but rather to improve collective knowledge and have each individual contribute to this goal. Therefore, suitable, rich and varied mediation tools should be provided to ensure
students have a wide perception of knowledge and many possibilities
for the development of the self.

All these three approaches promote a vision of education as a
means of providing rich contexts and of fostering active 'knowledge
builders', committed not only to personal improvement but also to the

advancement of communal knowledge. Consequently, learning theories have widened their focus, from the centrality of cognitive processes to the relevance of social interaction and of the cultural dimension. This vision implies a change in the perception of ourselves as learners and as students. Because identity formation and innovation have been acquiring a new significance for learning in these frameworks, DST can play an important role.

Dialogical self theory and learning theories: a reciprocal enrichment

According to DST, the self is composed of a set of *I*-positions constantly in movement and in change (Hermans 1999; Hermans and Dimaggio 2007; Hermans and Kempen 1993). Changes depend upon contextual situations, where many elements play a role: personal and cultural history, future perspective, and people and tools one may come into contact with. According to this view, the self is involved in a constant process of change and innovation, constantly striving for a balance between many tensions within the *I*-positions featuring the self. The vision of the self proposed by DST is perfectly in tune with the criticism regarding the limitations of the cognitive vision on education, and it may offer a better understanding of how the perception of the self may be affected by learning experiences. On the other hand, DST can take advantage of educational research, especially in understanding the forces driving the processes of positioning, repositioning and counter-positioning (Hermans and Hermans-Konopka 2010). Many aspects can influence these processes, and some of them can be explicitly organized so as to acquire a positive direction and an improvement of the current *I*-positions. After all, the general aim of applying DST is to obtain a resourceful and healthy organization of the *I*-positions composing the self in any type of setting. This could be a shared goal of both DST and educational research.

Learning is a fundamental device producing changes not only in terms of the acquisition of information or the development of competences, but also regarding the improvement and enrichment of the organization of *I*-positions within the identity landscape. This vision gives a new 'power' to the educational context, which becomes a place where students and teachers can experiment with new ways of thinking about themselves, and where learning becomes a resource for personal and cultural changes. Therefore, the reciprocal enrichment between DST and learning theories can be conceived as follows: DST offers to learning theories a framework that both broadens and deepens the understanding of changes of the self within educational contexts, while learning theories may enrich DST with ideas on how to improve the movements, changes and dialogue between *I*-positions. I will discuss this reciprocal enrichment by looking at educational research conducted by the dialogical approach, and by embracing one or more of the three approaches I outlined in the first paragraph. In order to facilitate this discussion, I have grouped the research into three trends, namely: (1) student identity; (2) teachers' professional identity; and (3) student–teacher interaction. Each of these trends will be discussed in the following paragraphs.

Student identity

The first trend of research I will analyse concerns student identity. The introduction of DST to the study of an educational context has amplified the social-constructivism approach by underlining that not only is knowledge built during the learning process, but also the person involved in the building process undergoes some changes in the organization of the self and its dialogical functioning. The learner's self inevitably changes while he or she is involved in knowledge building. Educationalists have often observed that the most significant results of a successful learning process occur when learners become 'different', in the sense that they become critical thinkers and better arguers (Muller *et al.* 2009), creative problem solvers (Whitebread 2004), and competent in participating in dialogical interactions (Brown and Renshaw 2006; Fisher 2007; Wegerif 2007). At the same time, research based on learning theories has helped DST to understand how the educational context may support the evolution and development of *I*-positioning. For instance, Yamakawa *et al.* (2009) introduced positioning as a conceptual and analytic tool to examine identity work that goes on in a Third Grade (8–9-year-olds) mathematics classroom community. This study empirically illustrates how, over time, positioning provides a powerful tool for educational researchers and practitioners to understand the social construction of identities for students as learners of mathematics in evolving classroom interactions. It also underlines the relevance that key elements of school life, such as teachers' feedback, participation in the social life of the classroom, and the type of discourse emerging during different activities, have in shaping student identity. Even within a specific domain of learning, like mathematics, which may seem strongly content-based, offering little space for discussion and reflection on student identity, there appears to be a continuous rethinking of *I*-positions and the construction of new ones.

The constant moving and flowing of students' *I*-positions at school can be directed by teachers in many ways. Some of the research I have conducted has had exactly this focus; that is, how to organize the educational context so as to offer new and stimulating opportunities for students to appropriate and elaborate new *I*-positions (Ligorio 2009, 2010). In one study in particular (Lagrasta and Ligorio 2009), we adapted the self-confrontation method, constructed by Hermans (1998; Hermans and Hermans-Jansen 1995), to the school environment. The confrontation was carried out in written form – instead of discursively – with the intention of helping students develop a positive vision of their future by: (1) first, asking them to write an essay, anonymously, about how they see themselves in the present; (2) secondly, inviting them to share in a discussion group the topics that emerged from the essays (as assessed through a qualitative content analysis); and (3) finally, asking them to write a second essay about how they see themselves in the future. The students involved in this study were teenagers (aged 16–17) showing signs of depression, since one of their classmates had committed suicide the year before. After the students had written essays about themselves, these texts were read by the teacher together with the researcher, to obtain a list of sensitive topics to be used with the purpose of organizing a focus group in the classroom. During the focus group, students developed an awareness of their negative *I*-positions as collective and common positions rather than individual positions, and, at the same time, the teacher helped them to realize that the class could be a resource to overcome their present difficulties. Consequently, the second essay, written again anonymously but this time after the classroom discussion, contained in general more positive *I*-positions, a higher sense of agency concerning their lives, and a lower sense of isolation. By openly addressing and disclosing specific *I*-positions emerging in the classroom context, the entire learning experience was conceived as a symbolic resource for the development of the self in the future as well as in the present.

In fact, schools are places characterized by a high level of interaction (between teachers, peers, other adults, parents and so on) and by the extensive presence of symbolic and material tools (books, writing, media, etc.) (Zittoun 2006). Therefore, the number of 'voices' – in a Bakhtinian sense (Bakhtin 1981, 1984, 1986) – to which students are exposed is potentially enormous, and the classroom can be considered as a powerful dialogical context (Hermans 2004; Koschmann 1999; Linell 2009; Marková 2003). Understanding conflicts or struggles within identity landscapes, and introducing new 'voices' especially addressing problematic issues, could be a relevant task for teachers and schools.

Teachers' professional identity

The effects of education on identity building concern not only students but also teachers, as they are crucial agents in such contexts. Looking at how teachers develop their professional identity illustrates the essential point of the second trend I select as representative of the meeting between DST and research on education.

Teaching is a complex activity, always striving to find a balance between coping with social change and maintaining a professional standard in the disciplinary content of teaching. Recently, the professional identity of teachers has been conceived as depending on their personal attitude and motivation, on how they perceive themselves as professionals, and on their awareness of the impact of their educational actions (Beijaard *et al.* 2004). Following this line of research, the dialogical approach contributed enormously to reconsidering the dimensions implied in the teachers' professional activities. A good example of research conducted along this line comes from Vloet and her colleagues (Vloet 2007, 2009; Vloet and van Swet 2010). Through a narrative-biographical method, Vloet shows how the identity and teaching practices of teachers are in fact composed of many 'voices' coming from the present context, from past experiences and from the future – for instance, thinking of situations after the students have left the school and how they might use what they are learning now. The cultural-historical dimension clearly emerges through the many temporal links retrieved from the teachers' narratives. From each temporal stage explored in biographies (past, present and future), several sub-identities emerge, in harmony or in conflict with one another, so that their ensemble composes a complex perception of their own professional experience. The sub-identities have both a personal and professional nature and emotional, cognitive and social issues are continuously mixed and combined. They are not unilaterally acquired during the training programme, but are elaborated at the crossroads of the individual motivation and the cultural perception of what it means to be a teacher. As CHAT suggests, the dialogues teachers engage in (during the narrative of their biographies) involve real and internalized others – people and institutions – as well as material and immaterial aspects. Therefore, materialistic aspects enter the dialogue, and *I*-positions connected to significant others (colleagues, students, teachers) interact with *I*-positions based on the use, for instance, of a book read and a relevant person met in their career and, as reported also in similar research conducted by Ligorio and Tateo (2008), the level of salary and the school's and classroom's resources and facilities.

Furthermore, Geijsel and Meijers (2005) underline the relevance of learning for teachers. Teaching is not a static practice; indeed, the ever-changing nature of the profession keeps teachers in constant challenge with themselves. These changes are emotionally charged to a large extent, and are strictly connected to identity changes. In this sense, teachers find themselves taking on the role of learners. Becoming a learner, from a teacher's position, means stepping down from the position of teacher to the position of student, in this way realizing a multi-voiced self (Hermans and Hermans-Konopka 2010). From a pedagogical point of view, this is considered a very positive and effective strategy. The community of learners model (Brown and Campione 1990) looks upon swapping roles between teachers and students as a way to support and consolidate collaborative and active learning. Never-theless, for teachers, this challenge has two facets. First, it implies working through a psychological process of adjusting to dual identities, implying very different meanings for the same person. Second, what is learnt cannot remain at a theoretical level, but should be put into practice. Both challenges involve a struggle between the need to learn new knowledge and skills, and the tendency to stick to beliefs and strategies used in their everyday practice. For the teacher, taking up the role of active learner is not only a pedagogical choice, but also a psychological decision requiring a new understanding of teaching and learning. This shifting, from teacher to learner and back, involves both giving a meaning to, and making sense of, the educational context and the dialogical relationship between teachers and students. In fact, the *I*-position-as-learner can act as a promoter position (Hermans and Hermans-Konopka 2010) and can trigger a more positive relationship between teacher and learners, as well as among teachers.

Student–teacher: a dialogical relationship

The third trend in the meeting between the DST and educational research concerns the relationship between students and teachers. This trend is based on the assumption that an understanding of the self always involves some sort of integration of the first and third person (Barresi and Moore 1996), and it recognizes the role of dialogue with the inner 'alter' (Marková 2006). Just as infants first come to understand their own or another's activity through a process of imitation or spontaneous mimicry of the activity of another person, so students engage in a process of imitation or mimicry with their teachers. First the imitation, and later the internalization, of significant others is at the base of the evolution toward new zones of proximal development (ZPD) (Vygotsky 1978).

Students and teachers reciprocally internalize each other's 'voice' and, consequently, they jointly build a representation of how the educational content should be learnt, why it is important to learn, and what are the 'normal' ways of behaving in the classroom.

The quality of the teacher–student relationship seems to be one of the most relevant factors influencing learning outcomes. For instance, de Abreu *et al.* (1997) demonstrated that students are seriously affected by what teachers consider to be the skills for being a good mathematician. Therefore they may consider themselves as good mathematics learners in accordance with the perception of mastering those skills. Again in the field of mathematics, Apple (1995) and César (2009) analysed how power relations work in formal educational scenarios. One would expect mathematics to be a neutral ground where cultural differences are not accentuated and where various types of students (such as immigrants or students with hearing disabilities) could find a refuge. Instead, it was found that, even when teaching mathematical concepts, issues about students' culture and their future perspective emerge. While explaining and talking about mathematics, teachers foreground general beliefs and cultural stereotypes (Alrø *et al.* 2009). So, in order to understand student–teacher dialogues, we should be aware that *I*-positions influence and affect, in implicit or explicit ways, the interaction between the participants in the educational process.

The reciprocal influence of teachers and students can be illustrated by a research project (Ligorio and Mirizzi 2010), in which we interviewed a teacher who taught most hours in a classroom (Eighth Grade; 13–14-year-olds) and four of her students. The interview was conceived to collect their personal biographies, their perception of educational practices and the way they saw the school. Through content analysis of the interviews, the individual sets of *I*-positions of each respondent were retrieved. A peculiar mechanism was found in the way the teacher's *I*-positions were organized. She manifested herself as a good, well-prepared, expert teacher, representing a well-defined professional *I*-position, crucial for the learning context. This *I*-position was at the centre of a net where many other *I*-positions were connected to each other. One of them was the young teacher's ambition to become an actress – left behind for family reasons that led her to choose a more stable profession. Strikingly, this position was revitalized by the central *I*-position (good, well-prepared, expert teacher) because many activities she conducted in her classrooms were related to theatre and poetry. The central *I*-position works as a pivot through which many other *I*-positions emerging during the interview, even hidden ones from the past, acquire sense. These *I*-positions dialogically converged around the most prevalent *I*-position the teacher displayed, together forming a coalition of *I*-positions around the central one (Hermans and Hermans-Konopka 2010). Past, present and future *I*-positions remain in the background, blurred and mixed, and they acquire realization through the central one. When we looked at the *I*-positions of the students, one finding seemed highly relevant from a dialogical point of view. All the interviewed students displayed the same type of mechanism which we found in their teacher: an evident, central, firmly defined *I*-position that is adequate for the school context, sustained by other *I*-positions that are re-elaborated and reinterpreted in light of the central one, again mixing past, present and future. It seems that these students learnt from this teacher not only concepts related to the curricula, but also how to organize their *I*-positions in the form of meaningful coalitions in the school context.

The results of our research as reported above emphasize the reciprocal influence and the mutual interdependency between teacher and students. They allow us to conclude that the 'didactic contract' (Schubauer-Leoni 1996) goes far beyond intellectual and instructive scopes. They involve ways of reconstructing the self at school as the result of productive dialogical relationships.

Conclusions

In this chapter, I have discussed the following three developments: (1) the distributed cognition which underlines that cognitive processes are not individual but are strongly dependent upon others and upon the tools available in the context; (2) the so-called CHAT, which entails the reconceptualizing of learning as a process of knowledge building rooted in the cultural-historical dimension; and (3) social-constructivism, focused on the idea that students are actively building knowledge. I discussed the ways in which DST and these three developments can profit from each other in giving shape to the learning process in educational settings. I applied these approaches in three areas of educational research: student identity, teachers' professional identity and student–teacher relationship.

After having discussed recent theoretical trends in educational research in close connection with DST, I want to draw three conclusions which refer to the cross-fertilization of DST and educational research. First, the process of positioning can be defined as 'distributed' across many participants and many tools. In fact, students' and teachers' positioning is built through interaction, and it is interdependent and strongly shaped by the perception others have of us (Falmagne 2004). Therefore the positioning, repositioning and counter-positioning and the dialogue involved should be considered as distributed across the network of people and tools. The landscape of the self necessarily exceeds the individual and covers a distributed dialogue, with many forms and patterns depending on the counterparts and the means involved. Furthermore, *I*-positions should be observed and analysed in relation to *we*-positions, in order to stress the social nature of the self.

Second, to understand the forces acting on the shaping and reshaping of *I*-positions, the educational context should be taken into consideration. Each context is potentially a source for generating specific positions. The educational context spotlights certain actors, certain expectations about the future, and certain values partially negotiated in the present and partially coming from the cultural background within which the classroom is located. Understanding how new positions are learnt in this context requires an examination of the educational activities performed within the community. For theories such as the community of practice (Wenger 1998) and the community of learners (Brown and Campione 1990), this is a solid principle. Applied to DST, this principle can offer interesting insights in analysing the positioning, counter-positioning and repositioning of the self. Understanding how positions are learnt through participation in a community could be an interesting advance for DST and, at the same time, learning could be redefined as the ability to cover new *I*-positions or modify old ones by participating in practices and by performing activities that are culturally grounded in a community.

Third, to paraphrase a suggestion of Stetsenko and Arievitch (2004), the development of the self may be considered as a fundamental 'dialogical' activity. This is an activity locally aimed at obtaining practical results and, at the same time, globally aimed at developing and improving people's identity system and the dialogical relationships, both among the positions and between the positions and the context and significant others. This means, on the one hand, that DST should consider *I*-positions in relation to the activity performed and should consider that each activity may trigger a specific set of *I*-positions and a particular type of dialogue, learnt within a particular community. On the other hand, DST can enrich the analysis of the learning activity by inquiring into its dialogical nature, considering it not only as being aimed at a pragmatic goal, but also as potentially able to change and reshape identity.

Finally, the cross-enrichment between learning theories and DST suggests that the set of *I*-positions should always be contextualized by articulating the specific context to which it refers. Furthermore, whenever possible, the *I*-positions at the start should be explored in connection with the *I*-positions obtained as a consequence of the exposure to an educational experience. In this way, it will be possible to understand who and what can be regarded as a source of change and development, and under what conditions.

REFERENCES

de Abreu, G., Bishop, A. and Pompeu, G. (1997) What children and teachers count as mathematics, in T. Nunes and P. Bryant (eds.), *Learning and Teaching Mathematics: An International Perspective* (Hove: Psychology Press), 233–264

Alrø, H., Skovsmose, O. and Valero, P. (2009) Inter-viewing foregrounds: students' motives for learning in a multicultural setting, in M. César and K. Kumpalainen (eds.), *Social Interaction in Multicultural Settings* (Rotterdam: Sense Publishers), 13–38

Apple, M. (1995) Taking power seriously: new directions in equity in mathematics education and beyond, in W. Secada, E. Fennema and L. Adajian (eds.), *New Directions for Equity in Mathematics Education* (Cambridge University Press), 329–348

Bakhtin, M. M. (1981) *The Dialogic Imagination: Four Essays.* Ed. Michael Holquist. Trans. Caryl Emerson and Michael Holquist (Austin, TX, and London: University of Texas Press)

   (1984) *Problems of Dostoevsky's Poetics.* Ed. and trans. Caryl Emerson (Minneapolis, MN: University of Minnesota Press)

   (1986) *Speech Genres and Other Late Essays.* Trans. Vern W. McGee (Austin, TX: University of Texas Press)

Barresi, J. and Moore, C. (1996) Intentional relations and social understanding, *Behavioral and Brain Sciences*, **19**, 107–122

Beijaard, D., Meijer, P. and Verloop, N. (2004) Reconsidering research on teachers' professional identity, *Teacher and Teacher Education*, **20**, 107–128

Brown, A. L. and Campione, J. C. (1990) Communities of learning or a context by any other name, in D. Kuhn (ed.), *Contributions to Human Development* (Basel: Karger, 1990), 108–126

Brown, R. and Renshaw, P. D. (2006) Positioning students as actors and authors: a chronotopic analysis of collaborative learning activities, *Mind, Culture and Activity*, **13**, 247–259

Bruner, J. (1990) *Acts of Meaning* (Cambridge, MA: Harvard University Press)

César, M. (2009) Listening to different voices: collaborative work in multicultural maths classes, in M. César and K. Kumpulainen (eds.), *Social Interactions in Multicultural Settings* (Rotterdam: Sense Publishers), 203–233

Cole, M. (1996) *Cultural Psychology: A Once and Future Discipline* (Cambridge, MA, and London: The Belknap Press of Harvard University Press)

Cole, M. and Engeström, Y. (1993) A cultural-historical approach to distributed cognition, in G. Salomon (ed.), *Distributed Cognitions: Psychological and Educational Considerations* (Cambridge University Press), 1–46

Falmagne, R. J. (2004) On the constitution of 'self' and 'mind': the dialectic of the system and the person, *Theory & Psychology*, **14**, 822–845

Fisher, R. (2007) Dialogic teaching: developing thinking and metacognition through philosophical discussion, *Early Child Development and Care*, **177**, 615–631

Geijsel, F. and Meijers, F. (2005) Identity learning: the core process of educational change, *Educational Studies*, **31**, 419–430

Gergen, K. and Davis, K. E. (1985) *The Social Construction of the Person* (New York: Springer-Verlag)

Hermans, H. J. M. (1998) Meaning as an organized process of valuation: a self-confrontational approach, in P. Wong (ed.), *Handbook of Personal Meaning: Theory, Research and Application* (New York: Erlbaum), 317–334

(1999) Dialogical thinking and self-innovation, *Culture and Psychology*, **5**, 67–87

(2004) Introduction: the dialogical self in a global and digital age, *Identity: An International Journal of Theory and Research*, **4**, 297–320

Hermans, H. J. M. and Dimaggio, G. (eds.) (2004) *The Dialogical Self in Psychotherapy* (New York: Brunner and Routledge)

(2007) Self, identity and globalization in times of uncertainty: a dialogical analysis, *Review of General Psychology*, **11**, 31–61

Hermans, H. J. M. and Hermans-Jansen, E. (1995) *Self-Narratives: The Construction of Meaning in Psychotherapy* (New York: Guilford Press)

Hermans, H. J. M. and Hermans-Konopka, A. (2010) *Dialogical Self Theory: Positioning and Counter-Positioning in a Globalizing Society* (Cambridge University Press)

Hermans, H. J. M. and Kempen, H. J. G. (1993) *The Dialogical Self: Meaning as Movement* (San Diego, CA: Academic Press)

Hollan, J., Hutchins, E. and Kirsh, D. (2000) Distributed cognition: toward a new foundation for human-computer interaction research, *ACM Transactions on Computer–Human Interaction*, 7, 174–196

Koschmann, T. (1999) Toward a dialogic theory of learning: Bakhtin's contribution to understanding learning in settings of collaboration, in C. Hoadley and J. Roschelle (eds.), *Proceedings of the Computer Support for Collaborative Learning 1999 Conference* (Stanford, CA: Laurence Erlbaum), 308–313

Kruger, A. C. and Tomasello, M. (1996) Cultural learning and learning culture, in D. R. Olson and N. Torrance (eds.), *The Handbook of Education and Human Development: New Models of Learning, Teaching and Schooling* (Malden, MA: Blackwell), 369–387

Lagrasta, A. and Ligorio, M. B. (2009) Il Sé dialogico nel contesto classe. Esperienza di narrazione di sé e condivisione [The dialogical self in the classroom context. Experience of self narration and sharing], *Orientamenti Pedagogici*, **56**, 661–668

Lave, J. and Wenger, E. (1991) *Situated Learning: Legitimate Peripheral Participation* (Cambridge University Press)

Levitin, K. (1982) *One Is Not Born a Personality: Profiles of Soviet Education Psychologists* (Moscow: Progress)

Ligorio, M. B. (2009) Identity as a product of knowledge building: the role of mediated dialogue, *Qwerty*, **4**, 33–46

(2010) Dialogical relationship between identity and learning, *Culture & Psychology*, **16**, 93–107

Ligorio, M. B. and Mirizzi, P. C. (2010) Posizionamenti identitari a scuola: una pluralità di voci [*I*-positions at school: a plurality of voices], *Rassegna di Psicologia*, **27**, 89–116

Ligorio, M. B. and Tateo, L. (2008) 'Just for passion': dialogical and narrative construction of teachers' professional identity and educational practices, *European Journal of School Psychology*, **5**, 115–142

Linell, P. (2009) *Rethinking Language, Mind, and World Dialogically* (Charlotte, NC: Information Age Publishing)

Marková, I. (2003) *Dialogicality and Social Representations* (Cambridge University Press)

    (2006) On 'the inner alter' in dialogue, *International Journal for Dialogical Science*, **1**, 125–147

Muller Mirza, N. and Perret-Clermont, A. N. (eds.) (2009) *Argumentation and Education: Theoretical Foundations and Practices* (New York: Springer)

Salmon, G. (ed.) (1993) *Distributed Cognitions: Psychological and Educational Considerations* (Cambridge University Press)

Scardamalia, M. (2002) Collective Cognitive responsibility for the advancement of knowledge, in B. Smith (ed.), *Liberal Education in a Knowledge Society* (Chicago: Open Court), 67–98

Scardamalia, M. and Bereiter, C. (2005) Does education for the knowledge age need a new science?, *European Journal of School Psychology*, **3**, 21–40

Schubauer-Leoni, M.-L. (1996) Étude du contrat didactique pour des élèves en difficulté en mathématiques. Problématique didactique et/ou psychosocial, in C. Raisky and M. Caillot (eds.), *Audelà des didactiques, le didactique: Débats autour de quelques concepts fédérateurs* (Paris: De Boek Université), 159–189

Simons, P. R. J., van der Linden, J. and Duffy, T. (eds.) (2000) *New Learning* (Dordrecht: Kluwer Academic Publishers)

Stetsenko, A. and Arievitch, I. (2004) The self in cultural-historical activity theory: reclaiming the unity of social and individual dimensions of human development, *Theory & Psychology*, **14**, 475–503

Vygotsky, L. S. (1978) *Mind in Society: The Development of Higher Psychological Processes* (Cambridge, MA: Harvard University Press)

Vygotsky, L. S. and Luria, A. (1994) Tool and symbol in child development, in R. van der Veer and J. Valsiner (eds.), *The Vygotsky Reader* (Cambridge, MA: Blackwell), 99–174

Vloet, C. (2007) Building professional identities on the platform: stories in dialogue, in J. Swet, P. Ponte and B. Smit (eds.), *Postgraduate Programmes as Platform: A Research-Led Approach* (Rotterdam: Sense Publishers), 69–82

    (2009) Career learning and teachers' professional identity: narratives in dialogue, in M. Kuijpers and F. Meijers (eds.), *Career Learning: Research and Practice in Education* ('s-Hertogenbosch, The Netherlands: Euro-guidance), 69–84

Vloet, K. and van Swet, J. (2010) 'I can only learn in dialogue!' Exploring professional identities in teacher education, *Professional Development in Education*, **36**, 149–168

Wegerif, R. (2007) *Dialogic, Educational and Technology: Expanding the Space of Learning* (New York: Springer-Verlag)

Wenger, E. (1998) *Communities of Practice: Learning, Meaning, and Identity* (Cambridge University Press)

Whitebread, D. (2004) Teaching children to think, reason, solve problems and be creative, in D. Whitebread (ed.), *The Psychology of Teaching and Learning in the Primary School* (London: Routledge Farmer), 140–164

Yamakawa, Y., Forman, E. and Ansell, E. (2009) Role of positioning: the role of positioning in constructing an identity in a Third Grade mathematics classroom, in K. Kumpulainen, C. E. Hmelo-Silver and M. César (eds.), *Investigating Classroom Interaction Methodologies in Action* (Rotterdam: Sense Publishers), 179–202

Yaroshevsky, M. Y. (1989) *Lev Vygotsky* (Moscow: Progress)

Zittoun, T. (2006) *Transitions: Development Through Symbolic Resources* (Greenwich, MA: Information Age Publishing)

26 The self in career learning: an evolving dialogue

Annemie Winters, Frans Meijers, Reinekke Lengelle and Herman Baert

Although it is broadly accepted that modern society poses a significant challenge to an individual's career development, there are as yet few theoretical frameworks that provide a holistic perspective on how to understand and meet this challenge successfully. Such a framework should incorporate an acknowledgement of both the complexities of the modern labour market and the requirement of individuals to navigate it consciously and creatively. We propose that dialogical self theory (DST) offers a helpful view as it accepts the multidimensionality and multivoiced nature of individuals, who, in order to achieve a successful career, must be able to construct a flexible and workable narrative and do so as a result of an engaged dialogue where '*I-*', 'meta-' and 'promoter' positions feature prominently.

From monologue to dialogue in career construction

In modern society, career paths have become more and more unpredictable (Arthur *et al.* 2005), and therefore it is increasingly difficult to make rational and information-based career choices. The idea that careers can be chosen by matching an individual's skills and aptitudes to particular work is outmoded. Moreover, modern careers are no longer chosen in one finite moment, but continue to develop over a lifetime. Within career development theory, attention has shifted from the narrow focus on cognition, to understanding career development as the result of learning processes in which emotions and intuition also play an important role (Krieshok *et al.* 2009). In an effort to conceptualize this, 'career competencies' were introduced (Kuijpers and Scheerens 2006; Kuijpers *et al.* 2006): research has shown that youths must develop competencies in order to recognize and make use of the opportunities they encounter while developing their aspirations (Guindon and Hanna 2002; Mitchell *et al.* 1999).

In a nationwide, questionnaire-based study of Dutch vocational education, Meijers *et al.* (2006) identified three career competencies: *career reflection* (i.e. reflective behaviour based on experiences and choices that reveal personal qualities and an awareness of motives that are important for future career development), *career shaping* (i.e. proactive behaviour that influences the course of a career; researching jobs, making deliberate decisions, and taking action to ensure work and study choices match one's personal qualities and motives), and *networking* (i.e. interactive behaviour to build and maintain contacts in the internal and external job market, aimed at career development).

Kuijpers *et al.* (2011) showed that the existence of these competencies among students in vocational education correlates with a learning environment that is characterized by a practice-based and inquiry-based curriculum, and that offers students the opportunity to engage in a career dialogue. A career dialogue is a dialogue where real-life problems are the starting point for professional development and where the relevant and experiential learning that takes place is at the heart of a reflective conversation between students, teachers and workplace mentors. It is the existence of a *career dialogue* that proved to be crucial for the development of career competencies: indeed, without a dialogue, the learning potential of a practice- and inquiry-based curriculum has proven to be limited. In the words of the educator Rosenstock, 'rigor is being in the company of a thoughtful, passionate, reflective adult who invites you into an adult conversation which is composed of the rigorous pursuit of inquiry' (Wagner 2010).

However, it is still unclear *why* and *how* a career dialogue can impact the process of career learning. A first answer is offered by constructivist learning theory, which states that meaning is constructed when we engage in a dialogue with oneself and others (Bruner 1990; Lengelle and Meijers 2009). The theory of career construction (Savickas 2002, 2005) is the most developed constructivist approach with respect to career learning. In it, three areas are emphasized: vocational personality, career adaptability and life themes. Savickas advanced the idea of life themes at the level of personal narrative and subjective career; he positions life stories in a way that shows they are the crucial threads of continuity that make meaningful the elements of vocational personality and career adaptability. Career-related stories express the uniqueness of an individual and explain why he or she makes choices and explicates the meanings that guide those choices. Career stories 'tell how the self of yesterday became the self of today and will become the self of tomorrow' (Savickas 2005: 58). Savickas also suggests that individuals generate their own career life themes. However, in its current form, his theory does not, according to McIlveen and Patton (2007), offer a psychological explanation for *how* individuals enact a process of self-construction via 'storying'. Savickas states that career construction, at any given stage, can be fostered by conversations, but an explanation of this statement is required to explore further the life-themes component of the theory and its dialogical implications.

Career construction and dialogical self theory

DST (Hermans and Hermans-Konopka 2010) may offer a promising framework for understanding and analysing how conversations foster career construction. The starting point of the DST is that the formation of an identity is dialogical in nature (Hermans and DiMaggio 2007; Hermans and Kempen 1993). This is because – according to Hermans *et al.* (1992) – the self is actually a kind of 'polyphonic novel' or combination of various voices embodied in one person. Although written by one person, the polyphonic novel is spoken by many 'sub-selves' or *I*-positions: 'as different voices these characters exchange information about their respective Me's and their world, resulting in a complex, narratively structured self' (Hermans *et al.* 1992: 28–29).

The dialogical self is not static and is inherently transformed by the exchanges among *I*-positions (the internal dialogue with ourselves) and with other people (the external dialogue). This means that there is room in this model to explore the self's decentralizing tendencies, as opposed to the interpretation of the self as logically consistent and as a rational whole, which was a dominant idea in earlier, career-learning theories. Compared with more cognitive approaches, the DST stresses that an individual is much more capable of acting adequately towards his or her career, once he or she recognizes and acknowledges the existing complexities without resorting to rationalizing or finding simplistic explanations (e.g. deciding prematurely on an actual career choice). At the same time such an approach offers more room for exploring one's life history, acknowledging emotions and fostering an ability to make intuitive decisions – the usefulness of which is demonstrated by modern neuropsychology (Dijksterhuis 2008) and has been described recently in the trilateral model of career decision-making by Krieshok, Black and McKay (2009).

From the perspective of the DST, the trajectory from real-life experiences to an appropriate (career) choice ideally starts with the formulation of an *I*-position and the subsequent broadening of this *I*-position by means of a dialogue to other relevant *I*-positions, and runs, via consecutive dialogical shifts, from these *I*-positions to a meta-position and from this meta-position to the formulation of a promoter-position (Hermans and Hermans-Konopka 2010). By inviting *I*-positions, we mean that a student is asked to enter a dialogue in a multivoiced way – experiences from practice may even be discussed in ambiguous and contradictory ways (e.g. I like working with seniors; I don't like working with them when they don't interact; I like working with them when we are both quiet). The myriad of positions honours the complexity of both the work situation and the individual doing the practice-based learning. However, in order to turn dialogues into competences and actions, an ability to witness the presence and influence of the various '*I*'-positions is needed. This is where a meta-position is valuable, as it allows the individual to view one's *I*-positions from a distance. This allows for a usefully detached look at a given situation and provides an opportunity to discover that 'I am this multivoiced self, but I am also the part that is aware of the various parts.' In career learning this means that we are able to develop and express various perspectives and explore options without becoming 'married' to any one of them from the outset. The integrative understanding gained through a meta-position is intended to lead us to action or at least the intention to act, while remaining aware of the complexity and changeability of ourselves and our work environment. The 'position' that is capable of taking action, with the intention to give a developmental impetus to future *I*-positions, is called a promoter position. We assume that the development of the three kinds of positions (*I*-, meta- and promoter positions) is central to the development of a multivoiced career dialogue.

We propose to combine the perspective of career construction through dialogue with the DST into a comprehensive model for the developing self in career learning. This will be illustrated in the context of competence-based education.

Career learning in competence-based education

Competence-based education is about 'creating opportunities for students and workers, close to their world of experience in a meaningful learning environment (preferably professional practice) where the learner can develop integrated, performance-oriented capabilities for handling the core problems in practice' (Biemans *et al.* 2004: 530). This context seems full of potential to study career learning. The development of career stories is fostered by realistic experiences (Bailey *et al.* 2004). In Dutch secondary vocational education (students aged 16–20), such experiences are offered by means of internships in labour organizations. During these internships, students receive guidance from a mentor from school (usually a teacher) as well as from a mentor in practice (e.g. an experienced employee of the labour organization in which the student works). Teacher, mentor and the student have at least two meetings to discuss the work experiences of the student: one at the beginning of the internship and one at the end. Based on the findings of Kuijpers *et al.* (2011) about the learning environment for career competencies, we hypothesized that these 'training' conversations offer the best possible opportunity for studying a career dialogue.

A previous study of training conversations in Dutch secondary vocational education (Winters *et al.* 2009) showed that it is not the student who is at the heart of the conversation, but the curriculum, and furthermore that mentors in school and from work placement talk mostly *to* (65 per cent) and *about* (21 per cent) students, but hardly ever *with* (9 per cent) them. In this trialogue, the students sit with their teacher and their mentor from practice, but this does not mean that they can take part in the conversation and direct it to their personal learning goals. Little opportunity is given to students to express what they think of their experiences in the workplace, let alone that they can say what they have learned or want to learn from them. Training conversations are almost completely aimed at evaluation and on transferring expert opinions from teacher and mentor to the students (see also Mittendorff *et al.* 2008). Following this analysis of the training conversations, we embarked on a longitudinal study in which the training conversations of 32 students – both at the start and at the end of their internships – were analysed. In a quasi-experimental condition, teachers were offered career-oriented training between the first and last training conversation, intended to develop both their understanding of and skills in co-creating a true career dialogue *with* the students. This training was not provided to subjects in the control group.

In the first study, reported in Winters *et al.* (2009), the training conversations were analysed by means of a framework with four general themes: formal characteristics (e.g. who is talking, who poses the questions?), content (is the conversation about the school, the occupation, the student or the career?), form (e.g. aimed to give information to the student, to stimulate action or reflection, and to motivate) and relational components (talking to, with or about the student). This model only partially registered the extent to which training conversations enable students to develop a career story. Therefore, we started to use an adjusted framework, based on the assumption that career stories can be developed when – in training conversations – the development of *I*-, meta- and promoter positions is fostered. In this, we explore which *I*-positions are formulated in training conversations with special attention to the bandwidth that is allowed to *I*-positions and which of the *I*-positions have the quality of meta- and promoter positions. We are also interested to see which aspects of the learning environment are responsible for these forms of positioning.

Case study of career dialogues: analyses of training conversations

Sample, background and selection

For the present contribution, we have selected three cases to illustrate the potential to study the developing self in career learning based on training conversations. In order to explain our choice of the three cases, we need to provide some background information on the evolution of training conversations. During the analysis of the original training conversations in 2007/8, the school was just starting to introduce the concept of competency-based education. By 2009/10, this had led to the introduction of new policies and procedures for student guidance conversations. Based on our experience with these conversations, we can define at least three types of conversations in school practice.

First, there are the traditional conversations in which the school presents its demands and learning aims to students and where the contact with a mentor from practice serves to check whether the specific context of work allows the student to realize these aims. In this type of conversation, the student is (merely) required to listen to what especially the teacher and the mentor advise (*teacher-dominant*). Second, there are conversations in which students can and must determine what is talked about. Much like the first type, these conversations are guided by strong directives, but in these conversations teacher and mentor understand their role as one of non-interference: self-directiveness means that students must do it themselves (*student-directed*). We consider these two types of conversations to be at opposite ends of a continuum; between them is a third conversation type, which combines the school's demands with the student's personal learning goals. We consider this conversation to be '*dialogical*': both parties are active participants in the exchange and a myriad of *I*-positions can be expressed. Additionally, it is a conversation in which reflective (i.e. meta-positions) abilities can be developed and career-shaping (i.e. promoter) competencies can be learned.

To draw the most elaborate picture possible of what actually happens in training conversations from a career-learning perspective, we have chosen three illustrative cases from within the Department of Health Care – given the emphasis on students' personality in this sector. The following conversation fragments were chosen to illustrate how the different types of conversations affect a student's positioning towards a desired career.

Conversation 1: teacher-dominant

The following dialogue comes from a first vocational training conversation (first contact between the teacher and the mentor from practice) for a student during this apprenticeship. She is a second-year student from the Department of Health Care and her workplace is a nursing home. (T = teacher, M = mentor in internship, S = student.)

T1:   Let's take a look at the personal learning goals that you have sent me. I summarized them a little. Your first learning goal is 'understanding of disease presentation' (*T starts writing*).

S1:   Yes.

T2:   How is that going?

S2:   I haven't really worked on that yet.

T3:   Hmm. Haven't worked on that yet?

S3:   No.

T4:   So this learning goal remains...? (*T looks up again*).

S4:   Yes.

T5:   Then, as your second learning goal, I summarized it as (*reads notes*) 'dealing with the severely ill, mortality and with family'.

S5:   Yes, yes.

T6:   (*silence*).

S6:   When I had just arrived here, two people had passed away. It was my first week here and ... well, I hadn't connected yet (*T is writing again, occasionally saying hm 'hmm'*). And as for deaths, we haven't really ...

T7:   You haven't had any since?

S7:   No.

T8:   How about your contact with severely ill patients?

S8:   Um, yes, actually every day, right? (*looks at M, who smiles*).

T9:   (*looks up*) Yes. And how does that go? How do you feel about that?

S9:   Um, it's hard sometimes. There are times when I don't know what to say to them and how, well, what would be a good way to put things.

T10:   (*starts writing*) Hmm. Do you mean the part about how to interact in those situations?

S10:   Yes, I just don't know how to be supportive then. That to me is really difficult.

S11:   And that sort of goes back to the learning goal of making conversation with someone. I feel, well, I find that difficult to do.

T11:   Yes. Making conversation.

T12:   Can you talk about that with M?

S12:   I can (*starts laughing; T looks up*), but I haven't yet. But I could.

T13:   Or can you go to any of your supervisors or colleagues in your ward?

S13:   Yes, sometimes I tell them, 'I find this quite hard' or something, and then we talk about it. But the next time I find it just as hard. So ... But I can talk about it.

s14: I think I really have to do that for myself.
t14: It has to find a place, for you?
s15: Yes. I have to learn to do that.
t16: (*writes first; then without looking*) And it is hard.
t17: Especially if I consider, just briefly, your previous apprenticeship with 'care at home'. Seeing this work next, it really is quite a change.
s17: Absolutely, totally different.
t18: But anyway, you described it as a learning goal, so you can still work on it (*formulates the next learning goal*).

This conversation overall was organized in a relatively instrumental fashion, with the teacher playing a dominant role: the goal of the communication was to check the student's progress in learning goals (personal, but *reformulated* by the teacher) with no link to careers. In this fragment, we recognize a significant experience (S6, clients dying in the student's first week) and subsequently the formulation of an *I*-position (S10, the student finds it difficult to be supportive of clients who are ill) following the teacher's inquiry about the student's feelings. The teacher goes on to *talk to* the student and does not elaborate on the other apprenticeship (T17) to contrast experiences (in order to take a meta-position) or networking as a possible action (resulting from a promoter position). The responsibility for repositioning (actually to *do* something with what was said) is passed from the mentor(s) to the student, but in an implicit manner: there is no verbal agreement and it remains unclear whether the student is actually conscious of (or up to) the task.

Conversation 2: student-directed

The following fragment is from a first training conversation (first contact between the teacher and the mentor from practice) during an apprenticeship. The student is a first-year student of the Department of Health Care, and his workplace is an activity centre for people with a mental disability.

t1: You wanted to work with people with a mental disability. How do you like that, now that you're doing it?
s1: Um, well, I like it, but then again I have quite frequent contact with people with a mental disability (*T: 'Yes'*). So for me, it wasn't really new.
t2: But the actual working with them – you like it?
s2: Um, yes. I just think the variety in also working with the elderly, that's actually something that appeals to me. Working with the elderly (*T: 'OK'*). Because I find it very interesting to hear their stories.

M3:   That's a good one, to me that's a really good one. The thing with most youngsters is that when it comes to the elderly (*makes a waving gesture*), they aren't really interested. They want to work with little kids (*T: 'Yes'*) and teenagers and (*T: 'Yes, yes'*). But to turn that around and appreciate the stories, that's really important in guidance. What I mean to say, these people get older and when they talk about their father and mother you might think, 'How long has he or she been dead, for 50 years now?' But these stories are still their stories (*T: 'Yes'*), and these stories remain important (*T: 'Yes'*), whether it was just now or many, many years ago. And clients may tell them time and time again. And the fact that you are someone who wants to listen … Well, to me, that makes you an invaluable colleague.

T3:   And you seem to like it.

S3:   I do, I think it's interesting to hear these things.

S4:   It's just that here … well, for example, I work with John and he doesn't articulate very well (*T and M: 'Yes'*). So it is sometimes hard to understand him, and especially for me because he uses these words … (*T: 'That make you think: what do you mean?'*; *tells anecdote*). And even when it's stuff I usually dislike, when I do it with him, I really enjoy it.

M5:   And so does John.

S5:   Yes, exactly. And meanwhile, he feels like 'let me show him' (*T: 'Nice'*). So that's when I like it too.

T6:   So if I summarize: you say that it's the diversity of this client group that makes it fun for you, as well as the experience you get here working with the elderly?

S6:   Yes. But still, for example, in people with a mental disability… (*tells anecdotes to illustrate that he wants to learn how to communicate with this client group*).

There were no explicit assignments or learning goals directing this conversation, just the teacher's invitation to talk about what was important to the student. In this fragment, this resulted in the teacher trying to find a balance between what the student was actually saying (route to action without reflection: how to get better at communicating with clients with a mental disability) and what both he (from the perspective of reformulating experiences into learning goals; e.g. T6) and the mentor from the practice (from the perspective of his own *I*-position; e.g. M3) thought was important. The student articulates two different *I*-positions (S2/3 and S5), but is not prepared to stand still and actually look at them (a first step to construct a meta-position). The conversation progresses as a search for a mutual focus, and does not result in repositioning.

Conversation 3: dialogical

The following anecdote comes from a first training conversation (first contact between the teacher and the mentor from practice) during the student's apprenticeship. The student is a second-year student of the Department of Health Care, and her workplace is a nursing home for clients with dementia. The teacher had been involved in a two-year development trajectory in which she made recommendations for and was trained in how to make training conversations more career-oriented.

T 1:   From what I hear, you are someone who pays attention to who is in front of you and how you can best respond to that specific client, and you're conscious of the fact that every client is different in that respect.

S 1:   Yes, I noticed that (*the student relates an anecdote that illustrates this*). I noticed that, yes.

T 2:   I feel that's a positive thing, because it means that – in what you do – you're always thinking about the other. It's not your situation that's the starting point, but the client's and what he or she needs at that moment.

S 2:   I actually experienced this myself (*tells anecdote that illustrates this*).

T 3:   (*laughing*) So that experience made you think, 'I'll never do that again' (*S: 'No'*). Well, that's learning too. And actually, you just named a really positive trait.

T 4:   If you compare it with your previous apprenticeship, do you notice that you have grown here?

S 4:   Yes, in that other place it was more about learning basic care. Communication with the people there was not really necessary, because they had each other (*T: 'Yes'*) and family, and people that lived there communicated more with each other (*T: 'Yes'*). And now here, clients here do communicate of course, but not in the same way (*T: 'Yes'*). You really learn to deal with people here (*T: 'Yes'*).

T 5:   It seems to me that you need to rely much more on all your senses here (*S: 'Yes'*), it's not just making conversations the way we do now...

S 5:   No, like there was this lady ... (*tells anecdote that illustrates this*).

T 6:   If you look at your development, do you think there's anything you can take with you to your next apprenticeship?

S 6:   For the next, if I can go to a hospital next year, for example, and there's a client with dementia, and in the hospital they don't know what to do with her, then I know what to do (*T: 'Yes'*). Because I learned that in this apprenticeship (*T: 'Yes, yes'*) (*S tells another anecdote about a skill she learned in a previous apprenticeship and that she could use in the present work context*).

T 7:   What I find especially positive about the way you talk about your learning, is that it's a very conscious process. You have shown here and there, and in the way you tell this now, that you can disassociate from yourself and look at yourself and think, 'I should do that this way', or 'I did it like that last year, so now I will try it this way.' Do you recognize that?

M7:   Yes, absolutely (*T: 'Yes'*). I have to say it's typical of the student. Yes.

T8:   You have a very natural talent for reflection (*M: 'Yes'*). That's a real quality, I think. I've told you this before (*S: 'Yes'*). I've also noticed that this enables you to take new steps in your learning process and – as a matter of fact – you can now reflect on how you can use what you learned here for your next apprenticeship.

S8:   Yes, I haven't really given it much thought, it just goes like this.

In this conversation a lot of effort was made to make sure the school's agenda could support the progress of the student. In this fragment, the teacher quite literally takes time for the student to understand and become conscious of each step in her reflection (with the student admitting that this is new to her). The student talks about her experiences (e.g. S4 and anecdotes in S1, S2 and S5) and compares different experiences from a meta-point of view, and it is the teacher who structures this fragment and puts words to what's relevant (e.g. formulates an *I*-position in T1). We chose this fragment because it is a unique example of a teacher articulating the repositioning steps *without being aware of the framework* (the model was not part of the training as described earlier): in T7/8, the teacher formulates this student's ability to go from *I*-positions to meta-positions (verbalized in T4 and T6) and then (in T8) to a promoter position that serves to integrate the previous *I*-positions and to stimulate their future development. This promoter position is endorsed by the student while the teacher is phrasing it (T8) and later when the student expresses the need for more attention to this position (S8).

Discussion

Successful career development increasingly depends on an individual's ability for self-determination in and of his or her career. This ability, according to Savickas (2005), is based on the presence of career stories that must be developed in a dialogue. In a first study of training conversations in Dutch vocational education, we used a framework based on formal characteristics, content, form and relational components. This enabled us to conclude that these conversations are *not actual dialogues*, because teacher and mentor were mostly talking to and about the student. But because the framework did not include a qualitative construct for dialogue development, it remained unclear whether in the training conversations there were chances to realize the potential of developing career stories and – if so – how these chances could be better utilized. Including elements of the DST in our framework seemed like an appropriate solution to this problem: we hypothesized that the mechanism through which a dialogue contributes to the construction of career stories is via the development of *I*-, meta- and promoter positions, so we included this as a theme in the framework.

The biggest challenge is that the ideal sequence of a student going from *I*-position to *I*-positions (i.e. broadening of the bandwidth) to a meta-position to a promoter position, is a theoretical notion that requires a dialogical learning environment. In reality, the culture of schools and thus of training conversations is still very monological – this is largely due to the fact that the transmission of so-called undisputed knowledge is the pivot around which everything turns in education as we know it (Gatto 2009). Research shows that in vocational education nowadays teachers, mentors and students are reluctant to engage in (career) reflection (Kuijpers *et al.* 2011; Meijers 2008), and the examples in this paper illustrate that a career dialogue, in which an *I*-position is broadened and eventually evolves into a meta- and promoter position, is actually possible but difficult to realize in the current educational climate.

An analysis based on DST does show where there may be opportunities for teachers and mentors from practice to make use of a broader range of possibilities in the career dialogue. It also shows what kinds of issues those entering the conversation encounter when they are working in an environment with a 'monological' tradition. In general, when confronted with a problem or uncertainty, students and mentors are motivated to find a quick solution (Gladwell 2006). Reflection, by definition, slows them down (Willingham 2009). The primary goal of students and mentors in training conversations is not the development of the student's self, but rather seeing his or her efforts rewarded with a diploma; and the most effective way to do this is by making guidance conversations impersonal and instrumental. Students do not seem to participate in a career dialogue willingly; they are barely motivated to participate in reflective activities about their careers when these are prescribed as part of the curriculum (Law *et al.* 2002; Mittendorff 2010). Guidance in general still aims to be rational (i.e. non-emotional) and logically consistent. Transformation of the self asks for a different process, one that allows for uncertainty (e.g. realizing that different *I*-positions are not in agreement) and working with emotions (both positive and negative) in order to create or arrive at a dialogical shift (Hermans and DiMaggio 2007). These kinds of conversations are by no means easy and require both specific competences by those involved in the training conversations (especially teachers and mentors from practice) and an institutional environment that values the processing of emotions and respect for the time and attention this requires.

Conversations in which students are invited to develop *I*-, meta- and promoter positions ask more of the teacher than conversational 'techniques' do. In the first place, teachers and mentors need an appropriate vision of learning and education, embedded in specific competencies to engage students in reflective career dialogues (Willingham 2009: 147 ff.). It is likely that teachers and mentors lack these skills because they have little experience in having conversations with students, and with career conversations in particular. Besides knowledge about how the minds of their students work, the teacher and the mentor from the workplace must be genuinely interested in the student's development and keep in mind that each student is a trans- forming polyphonic self with both thoughts and emotions. A teacher can invite the student to bring this out only in an atmosphere that offers the student both structure and space – each in the right proportion. Asking specific and open-ended questions, as well as summarizing and tentatively interpreting a student's reply, makes it possible for students to act. Students appreciate this so-called 'helping behaviour' (Zijlstra and Meijers 2006), although teachers must be careful not to provide hasty interpretations or to draw premature conclusions. The teacher must not only allow a student to tell his or her 'first story' in response to a challenge or boundary experience, but also invite the student to widen and deepen this story and turn it into an energizing second story (Lengelle and Meijers 2009).

Teachers find this deepening conversation and further development of the student's career story difficult (Wijers and Meijers 2009). Even after being trained in this area and focusing on getting *I*-positions above board, they are not, as yet, able to help students to develop meta- and promoter positions. In order for this to happen, a more thorough mentor training is essential, which would focus on how to become effective and efficient in coaching students in the development of their careers and career identities. However, training individual teachers will probably be insufficient to formulate and develop students' career stories. As schools do not have the space – institutionally or culturally – to organize career conversations, teachers would need to learn collectively. Their starting point would be to look at actual practical problems and to engage in a group dialogue about those (Fenwick 2008; Garavan and McCarthy 2008; Rowe 2008). Such a dialogue does not, by definition or in the first place, seek consensus, but assumes pluralism and even conflict (Chiva *et al.* 2007). In other words, a dialogue is needed where teachers also have the opportunity to formulate *I*-positions, broaden the bandwidth of those positions, and ultimately transform them into meta-positions and promoter positions.

REFERENCES

Arthur, M. B., Khapova, S. N. and Wilderom, C. P. M. (2005) Career success in a boundaryless career world, *Journal of Organizational Behaviour*, **26**, 177–202

Bailey, T. R., Hughes, K. L. and Moore D. T. (2004) *Working Knowledge: Work-Based Learning and Education Reform* (New York: Routledge Farmer)

Biemans, H., Nieuwenhuis, L., Poell, R., Mulder, M. and Wesselink, R. (2004) Competence-based VET in The Netherlands: background and pitfalls, *Journal of Vocational Education and Training*, **56**, 523–538

Bruner, J. (1990) *Acts of Meaning* (Cambridge, MA: Harvard University Press)

Chiva, R., Alegre, J. and Lapiedra, R. (2007) Measuring organisational learning capability among the workforce, *International Journal of Manpower*, **28**, 224–242

Dijksterhuis, A. (2008) *Het slimme onbewuste: denken met gevoel* [*The Smart Unconscious: Thinking with Feeling*] (Amsterdam: Bert Bakker)

Fenwick, T. (2008) Understanding relations of individual-collective learning in work: a review of research, *Management Learning*, **39**, 227–243

Garavan, T. N. and McCarthy, A. (2008) Collective learning processes and human resource development, *Advances in Developing Human Resources*, **10**, 451–471

Gatto, J. T. (2009) *Weapons of Mass Instruction* (Gabriola Island, Canada: New Society Publishers)

Gladwell, M. (2006) *Blink: The Power of Thinking Without Thinking* (New York: Little, Brown)

Guindon, M. H. and Hanna, F. J. (2002) Coincidence, happenstance, serendipity, fate, or the hand of God: case studies in synchronicity, *Career Development Quarterly*, **50**, 195–208

Hensel, R. (2010) The sixth sense in professional development: a study of the role of personality, attitudes and feedback concerning professional development, unpublished Ph.D. thesis. Enschede, The Netherlands: Twente University

Hermans, H. J. M. and DiMaggio, G. (2007) Self, Identity and globalization in times of uncertainty: a dialogical analysis, *Review of General Psychology*, **11**, 31–61

Hermans, H. J. M. and Hermans-Konopka, A. (2010) *Dialogical Self Theory: Positioning and Counter-Positioning in a Globalizing Society* (Cambridge University Press)

Hermans, H. J. M. and Kempen, H. J. G. (1993) *The Dialogical Self – Meaning as Movement* (San Diego, CA: Academic Press)

Hermans, H. J. M., Kempen, H. J. G. and van Loon, R. J. P. (1992) The dialogical self: beyond individualism and rationalism, *American Psychologist*, **47**, 23–33

Krieshok, T. S., Black, M. D. and McKay, R. A. (2009) Career decision making: the limits of rationality and the abundance of non-conscious processes, *Journal of Vocational Behavior*, **76**, 275–290

Kuijpers, M., Meijers, F. and Gundy, C. (2011) The relationship between learning environment and career competencies of students in vocational education, *Journal of Vocational Behavior*, **78**, 21–30

Kuijpers, M. and Scheerens, J. (2006) Career competencies for the modern career, *Journal of Career Development*, **32**, 303–319

Kuijpers, M., Schyns, B. and Scheerens, J. (2006) Career competencies for career success, *Career Development Quarterly*, **55**, 168–179

Law, B., Meijers, F. and Wijers, G. (2002) New perspectives on career and identity in the contemporary world, *British Journal of Guidance and Counselling*, **30**, 431–449

Lengelle, R. and Meijers, F. (2009) Mystery to mastery: an exploration of what happens in the black box of writing and healing, *Journal of Poetry Therapy*, **22**, 59–77

Luken, T. (2009) *Het dwaalspoor van de goede keuze: Naar een effectiever model van (studie)loopbaanontwikkeling [The Wrong Track of the Good Choice: Towards a More Effective Model of Career Development]* (Tilburg: Fontys Hogeschool HRM en Psychologie)

McIlveen, P. and Patton, W. (2007) Dialogical self: author and narrator of career life themes, *International Journal of Educational and Vocational Guidance*, **7**, 67–80

Meijers, F. (2008) Mentoring in Dutch vocational education: an unfulfilled promise, *British Journal of Guidance and Counselling*, **36**, 235–252

Meijers, F., Kuijpers, M. and Bakker, J. (2006) *Over leerloopbanen en loopbaanleren: Loopbaancompetenties in het (v)mbo [About Learning Careers and Career Learning: Career Competencies in Vocational Education]* (Driebergen: Het Platform BeroepsOnderwijs)

Meijers, F. and Wardekker, W. (2002) Career learning in a changing world: the role of emotions, *International Journal for the Advancement of Counselling*, **24**, 149–167

Mitchell, K. E., Levin, A. S. and Krumboltz, J. D. (1999) Planned happenstance: constructing unexpected career opportunities, *Journal of Counselling and Development*, **77**, 115–124

Mittendorff, K. (2010) Career conversations in senior secondary vocational education, unpublished Ph.D. thesis. Eindhoven, The Netherlands: School of Education, University of Technology of Eindhoven

Mittendorff, K., Jochems, W., Meijers, F. and den Brok, P. (2008) Differences and similarities in the use of the portfolio and personal development plan for career guidance in various vocational schools in The Netherlands, *Journal of Vocational Education and Training*, **60**, 75–91

Rowe, A. (2008) Unfolding the dance of team learning: a metaphorical investigation of collective learning, *Management Learning*, **39**, 41–56

Savickas, M. (2002) Career construction: a developmental theory of vocational behaviour, in D. A. Brown (ed.), *Career Choice and Development*, 4th edn (San Francisco, CA: Jossey-Bass), 149–205

(2005) The theory and practice of career construction, in S. D. Brown and R. Lent (eds.), *Career Development and Counselling: Putting Theory and Research to Work* (Hoboken, NJ: Wiley), 42–70

Wagner, T. (2010) *The Global Achievement Map* (New York: Basic Books)

Wijers, G. and Meijers, F. (1996) Career guidance in the knowledge society, *British Journal of Guidance and Counselling*, **24**, 185–198

(2009) *Resultaten van het onderzoek 'Reflectievragen, suggesties en succesfactoren BPV-gesprekken in het kader van het project Loopbaanleren'* [*Results of the Research Project 'Reflective Questions, Suggestions and Success Factors in Training Conversations'*] (Oss/Veghel: ROC De Leijgraaf)

Willingham, D. T. (2009) *Why Don't Students Like School?* (San Francisco, CA: Jossey-Bass)

Winters, A., Meijers, F., Kuijpers, M. and Baert, H. (2009) What are vocational training conversations about? Analysis of vocational training conversations in Dutch vocational education from a career learning perspective, *Journal of Vocational Education and Training*, **61**, 247–266

Zijlstra, W. and Meijers, F. (2006) Hoe spannend is het hoger beroepsonderwijs? [How exciting is higher vocational education?], *THMA – Tijdschrift voor Hoger Onderwijs and Management*, **13**, 53–60

27 Navigating inconsistent consumption
preferences at multiple levels
of the dialogical self

Shalini Bahl

Introduction

Many consumer studies have examined the role of consumption in
defining identity (e.g. Ahuvia 2005; Fournier 1998; Schouten 1991;
Thompson 1997; Tian and Belk 2005). This stream of research recognizes identity conflicts and consumers' use of marketplace goods and
experiences to achieve a coherent sense of self (Ahuvia 2005). However,
past consumer research has not explored what marketplace goods and
services mean to the consumers from the lens of their different identities.
For example, when I say that I love dark chocolate, do all my different
identities – the mother, the romantic partner, exhausted worker and
health-conscious consumer – love chocolate and do they all love it in
the same way?

Further, past research in consumer behaviour has found that mixed
emotions in consumers generate avoidance behaviour and negative attitude towards the object creating ambivalence (Luce 1998; Nowlis *et al.*
2002; Williams and Aaker 2002). However, it is not uncommon for
people to feel ambivalence and continue consumption of the object
causing ambivalence. Continuing with the above example, if my different identities have inconsistent feelings and meanings for dark chocolate,
how do I decide whether I like chocolate and whether I should eat it?

Dialogical self theory (DST) provides a useful framework to explore
multiplicity in consumers' self-concepts by recognizing the self at three
levels – the meta-position, *I*-positions and *me*'s. The dialogical self
comprises a multiplicity of *I*-positions, thereby allowing multiple subject
positions to exist in the individual, among which dialogical relations can
emerge. Researchers can get a better understanding of identity conflicts
and inconsistent consumption narratives by attending to the consumers
at different levels of their dialogical selves and their inner dialogue
between *I*-positions. More specifically, in this chapter, I use DST to

address two research questions: (1) How do consumers experience consumption at different levels of their dialogical selves, and (2) How do consumers make decisions when faced with seemingly inconsistent consumption preferences within themselves?

The chapter is organized in the following manner. First, I describe how DST provides a unique lens to study consumer behaviour. Next, I briefly describe a mix of methods used to address the research questions. Following this, I draw from different cases to illustrate the major findings of our research (Bahl and Milne 2010) with respect to consumption meanings at multiple self levels and how internal inconsistencies are managed. I conclude with a discussion on how these findings extend our understanding of consumer behaviour in the context of identity conflicts and inconsistent consumption preferences, with some suggestions for future research.

Dialogical self theory in consumer research

Narratives are becoming increasingly popular in consumer research to study issues that cannot be easily understood by more conventional approaches of data collection and analysis (e.g. Ahuvia 2005; Escalas and Bettman 2000). Narrative approaches used to study consumer identities embrace the Jamesian distinction between *I* and *me*, where *I* refers to the self as knower and *me* is the self as known and comprises everything and everyone that people experience as belonging to themselves. DST extends the narrative view by acknowledging multiple *I*-positions in the consumer. The *I* can move from one spatial position to another and imaginatively endow each self-position with a voice so that dialogical relations between positions can emerge. Each voice has its own perspective based on its experiences and may agree or disagree with other voices. DST thus, requires researchers to understand consumer behaviour from the perspective of the different *I*-positions and as an outcome of the relationship between these positions.

Consumer research studying identity conflicts has focused on the role of possessions and specific brands in creating a coherent sense of self (e.g. Ahuvia 2005; Fournier 1998; Schouten 1991; Thompson 1997; Tian and Belk 2005). Resolution between conflicting identities is seen as an ongoing process of choosing some consumption objects and experiences that define the person's dominant behaviour and identity. However, the task of creating a coherent identity narrative lies with a single authorial *I*. DST, on the other hand, can be used to attend to multiple *I*-positions and the dialogical relations between positions to understand how internal inconsistencies are resolved. While marketplace interactions are important in defining identity and conflict resolution, understanding the dialogical relationships in the context of marketplace acquisitions can provide new insights into consumers' conflict resolution and decision making.

Postmodern research in consumer behaviour has moved away from unified meanings and meta-narratives to the fragmented subject with multiple narratives reflecting multiple realities (Askegaard *et al.* 2005; Firat and Venkatesh 1995; Üstüner and Holt 2007). The postmodern studies in consumer research have looked at the fluidity between conflicting cultural identities and the different ways that consumers' identities deal with acculturation issues. However, this research stream does not address the question that if people have multiple voices, some of which are in opposition, how do they resolve the conflict to make consumption decisions? DST provides a useful framework to address this question. The dialogical self is defined by inter- and intrasubjective exchange and social domination. The notion of dominance is not seen as necessarily negative because an intrinsic aspect of dialogue is turn taking, which requires temporary dominance of one voice in order to make exchange possible (Hermans and Kempen 1993). Like a society, the dialogical self involves oppositions, conflicts, negotiations, cooperation and coalition between positions (Hermans 1996). The internal tensions and conflicts provide a 'fertile basis for the innovation of the self in particular and for creativity in general' (Hermans and Hermans-Konopka 2010: 151). There is much to be learned about consumer behaviour by understanding how the different voices interact to arrive at new identities and consumption choices. In this dynamic conception of the self, dialogical relationships between the different *I*-positions may lead to the emergence of meanings that are not given at one single position (Hermans and Kempen 1993).

Given the multiplicity of positions and dominance in relationships, Hermans and Kempen (1993) describe the organization among these positions by introducing a meta-position. The meta-position reflects the ability of the self to observe the different positions from a distance and see how they relate with each other. It provides an overview and evaluation of the different positions, their linkages and their accessibility, allowing the individual to have a broader perspective in decision-making (Hermans and Hermans-Konopka 2010). The meta-position is different from notions of core self or an agency that guarantees a coherent sense of self. Rather, 'the meta-position is typically influenced by one or more internal or external positions that are actualized at the moment of self-examination' (Hermans and Hermans-Konopka 2010: 148). Moreover, different meta-positions emerge depending on different social

Table 27.1 *Participant information and* I-*positions*

	Informant	Age	Profession	I-positions
1	Ari	40	Musician and teacher	Sensitive, artist and teacher, striver, survivor, helpless
2	Beth	54	Activist	Quilt-maker, teacher, activist, spiritual, mother and grandmother, lover of nature
3	Brad	26	Realtor (estate agent)	Athletic, closed, open, spiritual, experience with women, critical
4	Dee	37	Project manager	Strong, competitive, giving, low self-esteem, insecure
5	Jessica	21	Student	Irish, social, concerned with appearance, realistic, goal-oriented, politically aware
6	Sam	57	Artist	Connected with world, spiritual, enjoying life, healing, expressive

situations. Given its special nature, how do consumption meanings at a meta-position differ from those at the specific positions? What role does a meta-position play in dealing with identity conflicts? Consumer researchers have yet to explore the role of meta-position in consumer decision-making and meaning-making of consumption activities.

Methodology

Our study used a fully integrated, mixed-methods approach (Bahl and Milne 2006) that included narratives, multidimensional scaling (MDS), cluster analysis and metaphors. Guided by the research purpose, and consistent with other interpretative research (Belk *et al.* 1989; Miles and Huberman 1994), we pre-specified a purposive sample to include three men and three women across different age groups. See Table 27.1 for informants' descriptions. The small sample size allowed an in-depth study of each informant's important I-positions at the time of study and their relationships with respect to six different consumption experiences, which resulted in 90 possible relationships between I-positions (Bahl and Milne 2010).

The study involved four stages. The first two stages adapted Raggatt's (2000, 2002) personality web protocol in order to discern important I-positions in the informants. The self was studied as a repertoire of narrative voices, wherein each voice has a unique web of affective attachments to people, events, beliefs and consumptions (Raggatt 2002). Informants' narratives provided important attachments that were used as input for MDS and cluster analysis. The resulting MDS and cluster solutions were analysed in combination with the informants' narratives in order to discern and understand I-positions in the informants.

The third stage provided a deeper understanding of the *I*-positions and their relationship through metaphor analysis (e.g. Zaltman 1997). Informants brought in 3–5 images (clipped from magazines) that represented their feelings and thoughts about their *I*-positions discerned in the previous stages. After describing the metaphorical meanings for each *I*-position, the informants were asked to create a montage that would provide the overview from the meta-position of how the different *I*-positions relate to each other. In addition, the informants were asked to describe dialogues that are typical between the different *I*-positions.

In the fourth stage, metaphors were used to understand the meaning of consumption at different levels of the self and dialogical relations between them in the context of consumption choices. Informants were asked to bring three to five metaphorical pictures for each of their three most positive and three most negative consumption experiences with respect to products, brands and/or services. After describing each consumption experience from the meta-position, informants were invited to describe the experience from the perspective of each *I*-position, providing examples from real situations involving the different *I*-positions and possible dialogue between different positions with respect to the consumption experience.

Consumption meanings at multiple self levels

In this section, I report how consumption narratives vary across the meta-positions and *I*-positions in the informants mentioned in Table 27.1. I will discuss some examples depicting informants' consumption narratives at a meta-position and their *I*-positions discerned at the time of this study.

Our general finding was that, when consumers describe their consumption experiences at a meta-position level, their descriptions are not consistent across all *I*-positions. In fact, consumption objects and activities differ in their importance and meaning across the informants' *I*-positions. The narratives from the different *I*-positions have some overlap in feelings and meanings but also some unique perspectives, which point to the specific needs and concerns at the different *I*-positions with respect to the consumption object. I will explain this in more detail with examples from the informants' narratives with respect to their consumption experiences, which involved mixed, positive and negative feelings at the meta-position.

Mixed feelings

A meta-position exists as a distant observer that juxtaposes different *I*-positions relevant in that situation. As such, the consumption narratives at a meta-position comprise a dispassionate reflection of different voices associated with the consumption activity. If some voices in the consumer view the product as positive and others as negative, the meta-position is likely to convey the positive and negative meanings associated with that product. For example, Ari's description of Doritos, a brand of chips (crisps), from a meta-position includes positive and negative feelings. His metaphors at the meta-position about eating Doritos convey feelings of 'wearing food', needing 'damage control', 'love them (Doritos) but can kill me', 'unhealthy but appealing', and 'seductive'.

The source of the mixed feelings can be understood better by attending to the specific I-positions in consumers. Continuing with our example with Ari, this means that the source of mixed feelings expressed by Ari at a meta-position can be traced to his I-positions. Ari's negative feelings related to Doritos are mostly associated with his *helpless* I-position, which becomes dominant when he is in pain due to auto-immune disorder. When he is in pain, he uses Doritos as a 'distraction' and finds that he gives into the seduction more easily. From his *helpless* I-position, Ari can eat 'a whole bag of Doritos' because he is feeling 'weak and helpless'. He describes Doritos as being 'a crutch, a drug' to help him get through the pain. From his *survivor* I-position, Ari feels he is in more 'control' and has the 'awareness', so he will either 'not eat the Doritos' or 'control' what he does eat. Ari's *survivor* I-position speaks about exercising when he is not in pain, which allows him to 'enjoy the appeal and not worry about how it's not good for him'. From this I-position, Doritos can be described as a 'reward'. His *spiritual* I-position sees the 'humour' in the 'seductive' aspects of Doritos. From this I-position, Ari can focus on the 'flavour' and see what a 'great product' it is. The *spiritual* voice can 'take out the guilt' and make it a 'joyous experience' that involves satisfaction after eating only a few chips. From this position Ari describes Doritos as a 'tasty treat'.

Ari experiences Doritos differently depending upon which voice is describing the experience. His *helpless* voice has the most negative feelings associated with Doritos, while his *survivor* voice has more control over his consumption of Doritos, and his *spiritual* voice removes all guilt and experiences only joy. Studying consumers' feelings at the level of I-positions is more informative, as it is closer to the I-position from which it is being experienced rather than being a distant view of different perspectives.

Positive feelings

When the primary feelings across the consumer's important I-positions are positive, the meta-position also reflects positive feelings. Brad discusses playing soccer as one of his favourite activities. And playing soccer is positive at the meta-position and all his *I*-positions other than his two negative *I*-positions, the *critical* and *closed* voices. His *closed* voice describes soccer as a 'release', but it can be 'painful when the release isn't achieved' because when he is trying too hard it does not happen. He experiences 'frustration', which makes him 'more closed' and he does not play as well. Even if he scores goals, 'they're not satisfying'. His *critical* voice speaks to feeling 'not good enough and undeserving' with reference to soccer.

It is important to note that even consumption objects described by consumers as positive experiences can involve negative feelings when experienced from the lens of a particular *I*-position. Interestingly, the negative tone for positive consumption experiences was found to belong to undesirable *I*-positions in our informants.

Negative feelings

When the primary feelings across *I*-positions are negative, the meta-position echoes that. For example, Sam described his struggles associated with not wearing his partials (dentures), which he selected as a negative consumption activity from his meta-position. Partials are a part of his grooming ritual that he finds time-consuming and painful but feels pressured to wear them primarily because of cultural pressures. His overall metaphors from a meta-position talked about 'suffering for long-term benefit', 'reminder of old age', being 'a poor slob', 'decrepitude', 'a time-consuming process', 'a symbol of insecurity', 'discomfort' and lacking 'sex appeal' without them. His *I*-positions further endorsed the negative feelings by speaking to some themes overlapping with the meta-position, while adding other perspectives unique to that *I*-position. For example, his *connected-with-world I*-position described the role of the media in adding to his insecurity associated with not wearing dentures; his *healing* voice described his 'pattern of not putting in partials and then feeling stupid about it'; and his *expressive* voice raised concerns about not being able 'fully to express without partials' and being 'caught in a negative drama that takes away from positive expression'. Sam's *spiritual I*-position was more compassionate towards old patterns and his *enjoying-life I*-position 'felt wonderful even without wearing it (the partials)'; but overall the meta-position reflected the negative dramas that each of the *I*-positions associated with not wearing dentures.

Meta-position dominated by I-position

A meta-self juxtaposes the major *I*-positions related to consumption but can be dominated by a single position, in which case the consumption narrative reflects the voice of the dominant *I*-position. We see this in Jessica's overall narratives about junk food, which were all negative. Her initial metaphors depict junk food in terms of 'obstacle', 'guilt', 'jumbo heavy feeling' and 'consumed with thoughts' about feeling 'gross' about what she ate and feeling that she had to do something about it. Yet, when we listen to Jessica's different voices speak about junk food, the tone and feelings are very positive and all the negative feelings reflected in the initial metaphors map only on her *concerned-with-appearance* voice:

When I eat junk food it makes me concerned with my appearance. When I'm concerned with my appearance, I therefore don't eat lots of junk food. That would be a little bit of all of these then (the initial negative metaphors). It is the enemy.

While her *political* and *Irish I*-positions don't have anything to do with junk food, other *I*-positions speak of junk food in favourable ways:

Social: Basically when my friends and I get together we are eating, that's just how it is. We wouldn't be friends if any of us liked to go on diets. We're all concerned with weight to a certain point, but we all have that side of us that's like shut up and eat the burger. We all find it really annoying when people won't let themselves have fun because they're concerned with calories... It's definitely like a bonding thing that we do, something that we all share in common.

Realistic: I guess the realistic part of me knows how to balance the two. I know that if I'm gonna go out and like, you know, have a huge dinner tonight, then tomorrow I'll just you know eat healthy food or I'll go to the gym or something, so I just have a good balance between indulging and keeping myself on track and that's why I can do that without feeling guilty.

Goal-oriented: It can be like a comfort. Sometimes when I'm really stressed out, I'm a stress eater definitely so, I just don't care as much when I'm like focused on something else. If I have a huge test the next day and I'm eating the calzone I'm not like, ooh I have so many calories.

Other voices in Jessica recognize the negative effects of junk food but continue to enjoy junk food and describe it in positive terms such as a 'bonding activity' and 'like a comfort'. Yet, when asked to reflect on junk food at an overall level, she described it with extremely negative metaphors, suggesting that her concerned-with-appearance voice dominated other voices including the meta-position when asked to speak about junk food. Even when prompted to speak at a meta-position, Jessica was not able to do so as her concerned-with-appearance voice dominated all other voices.

Navigating inconsistent consumption preferences

If consumption narratives at different *I*-positions involve contradictory feelings, how do consumers make decisions? In this section, I discuss specific characteristics of the dialogical self that help to explain how consumers navigate inconsistent consumption preferences across their *I*-positions. These are discussed under three broad headings of dialogical relationships, the meta-position and domination.

The role of the dialogical self in dealing with inconsistent preferences

An important aspect of the dialogical self is dialogical relationships between different *I*-positions. I discuss the different attributes of dialogue that explain how consumers deal with inconsistent preferences across their *I*-positions.

Dominance

Dominance is a normal aspect of dialogue between *I*-positions. Dialogue between any two positions requires the speaking voice to gain dominance while other voices recede. The theory also speaks of dominance reversal, suggesting that different *I*-positions take turns in being dominant. As such, consumption decisions are driven by the *I*-position that is dominant in that situation. We observed in many situations described above that the consumption object involves mixed emotions, and consumption is a decision made by the position that is dominant at the time. For example, Jessica's preference for junk food and Ari's experience with Doritos both involve inconsistencies in preferences and feelings across their *I*-positions. The decision to engage in the activity and to what extent depends upon the *I*-position that is dominant.

Fluidity

What renders the possibility for consumers to choose among different identities and consumption choices is the notion of fluidity. The celebratory nature of the fragmented self (Firat and Venkatesh 1995) and the protean self (Lifton 1993) speak to the freedom postmodern consumers have in moving between different *I*-positions without any conflict. The ease with which informants move between their *I*-positions is noted by Brad: 'Sometimes I indulge one or the other [I-position]; in fact, I guess I always do.' A good example is Jessica's decision to smoke although this is a negative consumption for her. Jessica continues to enjoy smoking in company even though all her other voices are against smoking, because she can compartmentalize her smoking to her social *I*-positions (Bahl and Milne 2010):

When I'm here [at school], [I] don't view [myself] as like a smoker, it's just when I go out, people see me smoking, but I associate that more with like a different part of my lifestyle. When I'm here it's like I'm not a smoker and I'm goal-oriented, ambitious Jessica, not the smoker Jessica.

Compartmentalization is one way for people to continue to engage in negative or seemingly contradictory consumption behaviours. Other informants' stories also illustrate the relative ease with which they move between different positions. Consumer researchers have studied the liberatory aspect of moving between *I*-positions in the context of cultural identities (Askegaard *et al.* 2005; Üstüner and Holt 2007). However, Hermans and Hermans-Konopka (2010) warn against trends in consumerism promoted by the choices available that can lead to levelling enjoyment and lacking depth of experience. This is certainly an important area of investigation that needs further exploration in consumer research.

Innovative solutions

Dialogue between positions leads to innovative outcomes that wouldn't have been possible in the absence of dialogue (see also Gonçalves and Ribeiro's chapter). Two distinct types of dialogical relationships that offer innovative possibilities are coalition and conciliation (Bahl and Milne 2010; Hermans and Hermans-Konopka 2010). Coalition involves two or more *I*-positions working together to come up with a win–win solution that caters to the needs of both *I*-positions. For example, the *quilt-maker* and the *activist* in Beth have been in conflict over how her time should be spent. But this dialogue allows her to see a new way of meeting the needs of both her *I*-positions (Bahl and Milne 2010):

I can't really be a *quilt maker* when I'm spending time as an *activist*. I don't have enough time really to do both. Well, I'm making a choice. I'm looking at my life and finding choices that reflect who I am now, and I might give up a certain amount of the activism so I can have this other life. Otherwise I'm gonna miss out on having a life that I would really like.

I guess there's another way to look at it in that my making quilts and giving them away to children in orphanages is also being an activist. It's a different kind of activism. My activism is gonna take a different turn now. It has to somehow incorporate the quilting thing, so that I can be an activist in a way of giving something lovely to someone. I might not be an activist standing on a street corner trying to change what's happening. I'll be an activist by offering my love to children.

The above dialogue in Beth brings a new resolution for how her time will be spent that satisfies both positions. A variation of *I*-positions working together is conciliation, which actually results in the creation of a new position that resolves the conflict between the earlier positions (Hermans and Hermans-Konopka 2010). For example, Beth's *spiritual* and *activist* positions have conflicted because she does not see spirituality and activism as compatible. She creates a new position defined by the Native American approach to spirituality that allows her to pursue activism in a spiritual way:

> There's a lot of people who are spiritual who meditate a lot and they aren't activists. I can't do that. It's like if I care about something, I have to be out there, if it's a tree being killed, find out why and do something about it. You can't let corporations do things like just damage anything or poison the water. To me spirituality, especially eco-spirituality, ecological spirituality is caring about the planet, caring about the land. I guess it's more of a Native American approach to spirituality – I have to be out there and saying, doing something.

The positive role of meta-position: balance and compassion

The meta-position has the important quality of seeing multiple *I*-positions and the ability to juxtapose apparently different perspectives so that they can be compared. Thus, the meta-position can play a positive role in dealing with inconsistent consumption preferences in consumers. This special position can bring balance and compassion in situations involving conflict. This quality is reflected in Jessica's *realistic* *I*-position. In the above example of junk food, Jessica says, 'I guess the realistic part of me knows how to balance the two [indulging with friends and concerned about weight].' In another example, Sam's different voices realize the harm of sugar but give in when depressed and then are angry for giving in. Sam's *spiritual* voice speaks from a meta-position when it is able to see the pattern in other voices related to overconsumption of sugar products.

> OK, you [his *healing I*-position] aren't doing something very smart here but I'm not gonna get down on you for doing it. Because you have a lot of patterns of doing something stupid, which get reinforced because there's a part of you that is dying to feel stupid and this is the way to feel stupid and so you keep on doing the stupid thing. If you're gonna do any bad habits whatsoever, the less you can feel about it the better. Because it's feeling bad will make you do it more in association with a behaviour that reinforces it.

By being compassionate towards other voices, the *spiritual* position helps Sam to deal with sugar addiction. These findings are consistent with the work on self-compassion, which is emerging as an important coping mechanism to deal with negative or unpleasant situations in psychology (e.g. Adams and Leary 2007; Crocker and Canevello 2008; Neff 2003). The positive impact that the meta-position can have on consumer decision-making makes it a viable topic for further research in consumer behaviour.

The negative role of dominating voices: overconsumption

One way that consumers deal with contradictions is by allowing an *I*-position to dominate the opposing voices such that they cannot be heard and consumption choices are made by the dominating position. The conflict in such situations is more discreet and may not even appear to exist, as only one voice is dominating the decisions. In such situations, there is no scope for innovations in consumption decisions that the dialogical self promises. Instead, the consumption basket is narrowly confined to the preferences of the dominant position. The consequences of many of these consumption activities are less than optimal because the dominant self may overdo certain activities to retain dominance, and this can involve negative outcomes such as stress and pain. These findings corroborate Cooper's (2004) finding that a dominant self can cause discomfort because of its need for constant vigilance that the subjugated positions do not take over.

I found incidents of overconsumption in my informants related to dominant voices in the informants. Typically, overconsumption is studied in the context of negative behaviours like overeating and addiction. But our study suggests that too much of even a good thing can be bad. For example, the *goal-oriented* position in Jessica is a desirable voice, which drives her need to excel in school. But in order to remain goal-oriented and focused Jessica takes more classes and participates in more school activities than required. Her *goal-oriented* voice drives her to overcommit to activities that will enhance this position, but it has other negative consequences like feeling 'burnt out'.

This [metaphorical picture for *goal-oriented I*-position] is obviously like busy blurry and sometimes you feel like you're just going at such fast pace that you are burnt out. I've definitely driven myself to that point where I was just like I need to stop doing all this stuff but sometimes I feel like if I don't live like this [fast pace] then I'm just gonna be like this [picture of woman lying down] and not doing anything, you know what I mean – just kind of like lying there. I feel like the more I do, the better I do it, which is kind of weird, but I feel like if I don't do stuff then I get lazy or I just lose that momentum.

Dee also noted that her *strong I*-position, which is a desirable position, engages her in running ultra-marathons and intense training despite being hurt and in pain, because if she does not, her *insecure I*-position, which is an undesirable position, will show up. Both Jessica and Dee describe overdoing activities that consume their time and energy in enhancing their desirable *I*-positions but which have negative outcomes like feeling 'burnt out' and physical 'pain'. Even though the activities described are not tangible products, they do involve monetary transactions and expenditure of energy in pursuit of constructing their desirable *I*-positions and are thus important consumption activities from their perspective.

Discussion

DST introduces many new concepts that this study used to explain how consumers give meaning to consumption and navigate inconsistent consumption preferences. From the perspective of consumer research, findings related to the multiple levels of the dialogical self, meta-position, innovative nature of dialogue, and domination holds lay the foundation for future research. In this section, I summarize the major findings of this study with suggestions for future consumer research using DST.

Multiple I-*positions and post-purchase evaluations*

Consumer research suggests that products that evoke primarily positive emotions during the consumption experience are positively evaluated (Oliver 1992; Stokemans 1998; Westbrook and Oliver 1991), and this was also found in our study (Bahl and Milne 2010). However, when understood from the perspective of certain *I*-positions, even products that are positively evaluated at the overall level can involve primarily negative emotions, at the level of specific positions, as in the case of Brad's *closed* and *critical* selves playing soccer.

More interestingly, it was observed that some experiences that the informants had picked as their most negative consumption experiences and that evoked overall negative feelings in the initial metaphors were very positive experiences from certain *I*-positions. For example, Jessica's overall metaphors for junk food were negative, but a deeper investigation revealed that the negative thoughts were primarily related to her *concern for appearance* voice. Other voices, especially her *social* voice, had very positive feelings. These findings emphasize that the methods employed by consumer researchers need to incorporate an understanding of the consumption phenomenon at multiple levels of the self relevant to the phenomenon. The lens of the dialogical self and methodologies that speak to the different voices in consumers would be very useful in understanding complex consumer processes such as post-purchase emotions and evaluations. More specifically, there is a future research question: if some *I*-positions have favourable feelings and others do not, how do consumers arrive at their post-purchase evaluation?

Meta-position and mindful consumption

The meta-position provides a distant view of several positions. Even though it may be drawn to some positions more than others, the meta-position offers an overarching view of different *I*-positions and their relationships with each other (Hermans and Hermans-Konopka 2010). This position has the potential to offer several advantages to consumers in making more mindful decisions. The initial findings in this study suggest that the ability to see different positions with compassion and non-judgemental acceptance assists in overcoming overconsumption and addiction problems (e.g. Ari and Sam eat less unhealthy foods when they are compassionate towards other *I*-positions addicted to such foods). The ability to see different positions also creates the possibility of bringing balance by alternating unhealthy consumption with healthier choices. For example, Jessica's realistic position allows her social *I*-position to enjoy eating with her friends, knowing that she can go to the gym the next day to make up for any overeating. The initial findings about the positive role of decision-making at a meta-position are very promising and lay the foundation for future research that could evaluate the differences in outcomes of decisions made at individual *I*-positions and a meta-position.

Innovative potential of dialogue and consumer well-being

Much evidence in consumer studies points to consumers' need to avoid conflicts and create a coherent and unified sense of self (e.g. Ahuvia 2005). DST provides an alternative perspective in which conflicts and contradictions are not necessarily negative, as they offer the potential for innovations in the self. Dialogue between *I*-positions can bring creative outcomes like coalition and conciliation that offer win–win solutions for the concerned *I*-positions or the creation of new *I*-positions that embrace the goals of conflicting *I*-positions in innovative ways. (For win–win relationships, see Nir's chapter.)

This study also finds that consumers are not always looking to resolve internal inconsistencies among *I*-positions because of their ability to compartmentalize. As seen in Jessica's case, even though smoking is not a preferred consumption, she allows herself to smoke when in company because smoking is part of her social identity. People's ability to move between *I*-positions allows them to embrace seemingly inconsistent consumption preferences. However, it is important to explore further under what conditions consumers seek to resolve internal inconsistencies and when they find it useful to compartmentalize. It would also be interesting to compare outcomes such as customer satisfaction and consumer well-being as a result of different relationships between positions, including compassion, coalition, conciliation, compartmentalization and domination.

Domination as the antithesis of innovations in self

Domination is the antithesis of innovations made possible by dialogue between *I*-positions. Domination by an *I*-position means that the sub-servient voices are not heard. As such, consumer decisions driven by a single dominating *I*-position can lead to overconsumption of experiences preferred at that position without any counter-arguments provided by other *I*-positions. What makes this situation more damaging is when the dominating *I*-position is a desirable position because then the situation can go unchecked and lead to overconsumption with negative consequences. For example, in this study, Jessica's *goal-oriented* and Dee's *strong I*-positions were desirable *I*-positions based on their narratives. However, even these *I*-positions can overindulge in activities (such as extra classes and running even when hurt) to retain their power, which can have negative outcomes (like mental and physical stress).

Consumer studies have examined the role of consumption in enhancing desirable selves (e.g. Ahuvia 2005; Belk 1988; Firat and Venkatesh 1995; Thompson and Hirschman 1995). In our study, I point out that even desirable *I*-positions in situations of domination can have negative outcomes for the consumers' overall well-being. This makes domination an important area of study for consumer researchers. Future research needs to explore more how marketplace activities, dominant cultural discourses and social contexts shape dominant *I*-positions in consumers. Domination would also be an interesting construct to study in other marketing contexts such as brand loyalty and customer satisfaction. Do *I*-positions from a place of domination exhibit brand loyalty more than the fluid *I*-positions? Moreover, is the level of customer satisfaction at the dominating *I*-position more or less favourable, given that such positions can lead to overconsumption with negative effects?

DST is a very useful framework to understand different aspects of consumer behaviour, as it facilitates studying consumers at different levels of the dialogical self. Especially, as interest in transformative consumer research grows (Mick 2006), researchers are going to need innovative theoretical frameworks to explore identity formations and negotiations in a fragmented, postmodern world. DST provides such a framework to consumer researchers by introducing important concepts including dialogical relationships, meta-position and domination. Such concepts were lacking in previous investigations of how consumers make decisions given the plethora of choices in identities and consumption activities available to them. DST opens new doors for transformative consumer researchers to engage in cross-disciplinary work that has a real impact on consumer well-being. It provides a conceptual framework to study the effects of dialogue in decision-making related to mindful consumption choices and lifestyles.

REFERENCES

Adams, C. E. and Leary, M. R. (2007) Promoting self-compassionate attitudes toward eating among restrictive and guilty eaters, *Journal of Social and Clinical Psychology*, **26**, 1120–1144

Ahuvia, A. C. (2005) Beyond the extended self: loved objects and consumers' identity narratives, *Journal of Consumer Research*, **32**, 171–184

Akkerman, S., Admiraal, W., Simons, R. J. and Niessen, T. (2006) Considering diversity: multivoicedness in international academic collaboration, *Culture & Psychology*, **12**, 461–485

Askegaard, S., Arnould, E. J. and Kjeldgaard, D. (2005) Postassimilationist ethnic consumer research: qualifications and extensions, *Journal of Consumer Research*, **32**, 160–170

Bahl, S. and Milne, G. R. (2006) Mixed methods in interpretive research: an application to the study of self-concept, in R. W. Belk (ed.), *Handbook of Qualitative Marketing Research* (London: Edward Elgar), 198–218

(2010) Talking to ourselves: a dialogical exploration of consumption, *Journal of Consumer Research*, **37**, 176–195

Barresi, J. (2002) From 'the thought is the thinker' to 'the voice is the speaker': William James and the dialogical self, *Theory & Psychology*, **12**, 237–250

Belk, R. W. (1988) Possessions and the extended self, *Journal of Consumer Research*, **15**, 139–167

Belk, R. W., Wallendorf, M. and Sherry, J. F., Jr (1989) The sacred and the profane in consumer behaviour: theodicy on the Odyssey, *Journal of Consumer Research*, **16**, 1–38

Bhatia, S. and Ram, A. (2001) Locating the dialogical self in the age of transnational migrations, border crossings and diasporas, *Culture & Psychology*, **7**, 297–309

Brown, K. W. and Ryan, R. M. (2003) The benefits of being present: mindfulness and its role in psychological well-being, *Journal of Personality and Psychology*, **84**, 822–848

Cooper, M. (2004) Encountering self-otherness 'I–I' and 'I–me' modes of self-relating, in H. J. M. Hermans and G. Dimaggio (eds.), *The Dialogical Self in Psychotherapy* (New York: Routledge), 60–74

Crocker, J. and Canevello, A. (2008) Creating and undermining social support in communal relationships: the role of compassionate and self-image goals, *Journal of Personality and Social Psychology*, **95**, 555–575

Escalas, J. E. and Bettman, J. (2000) Using narratives to discern self-identity related goals and motivations, in S. Ratneshwar, D. G. Mick and C. Huffman (eds.), *The Why of Consumption: Contemporary Perspectives on Consumer Motives, Goals, and Desires* (London: Routledge), 237–258

Firat, F. A. and Venkatesh, A. (1995) Liberatory postmodernism and the reenchantment of consumption, *Journal of Consumer Research*, 22, 239–267

Fournier, S. (1998) Consumers and their brands: developing relationship theory in consumer research, *Journal of Consumer Research*, 24, 343–373

Gieser, T. (2006) How to transform into goddesses and elephants: exploring the potentiality of the dialogical self, *Culture & Psychology*, 12, 443–459

Hermans, H. J. M. (1996) Voicing the self: from information processing to dialogical interchange, *Psychological Bulletin*, 119, 31–50

(2001) The construction of a personal position repertoire: method and practice, *Culture & Psychology*, 7, 323–265

Hermans, H. J. M. and Dimaggio, G. (eds.) (2004) *The Dialogical Self in Psychotherapy* (New York: Brunner and Routledge)

Hermans, H. J. M. and Hermans-Konopka, A. (2010) *Dialogical Self Theory: Positioning and Counter-Positioning in a Globalizing Society* (Cambridge University Press)

Hermans, H. J. M. and Kempen, H. J. G. (1993) *The Dialogical Self: Meaning as Movement* (New York: Academic Press)

Josephs, I. E. (2002) 'The Hopi in me': the construction of a voice in the dialogical self from a cultural psychological perspective, *Theory & Psychology*, 12, 161–173

Lewis, M. D. (2002) The dialogical brain: contributions of emotional neurobiology to understanding the dialogical self, *Theory & Psychology*, 12, 175–190

Lifton, R. J. (1993) *The Protean Self: Human Resilience in an Age of Fragmentation* (New York: Basic)

Luce, M. F. (1998) Choosing to avoid: coping with negatively emotion-laden consumer decisions, *Journal of Consumer Research*, 24, 409–433

Mick, D. G. (2006) Presidential address: meaning and mattering through transformative consumer research, in C. Pechmann and L. Price (eds.), *Advances in Consumer Research*, 33, 1–4

Miles, M. B. and Huberman, A. M. (1994) *Qualitative Data Analysis* (Thousand Oaks, CA: Sage)

Neff, K. D. (2003) Self-compassion: an alternative conceptualization of a healthy attitude toward oneself, *Self and Identity*, 2, 85–102

Nowlis, S. M., Kahn, B. E. and Dhar, R. (2002) Coping with ambivalence, *Journal of Consumer Research*, 29, 319–334

Oliver, R. L. (1992) An investigation of the attribute basis of emotion and related affects in consumption: suggestions for a stage-specific satisfaction framework, in J. F. Sherry, Jr and B. Sternhal (eds.), *Advances in Consumer Research* (Provo, UT: Association for Consumer Research), vol. XIX, 237–244

Raggatt, P. T. F. (2002) Mapping the dialogical self: towards a rationale and method of assessment, *European Journal of Personality*, 14, 65–90

(2002) The landscape of narrative and the plural self: exploring identity using the Personality Web Protocol, *Narrative Inquiry*, 12, 290–318

Schouten, J. W. (1991) Selves in transition: symbolic consumption in personal rites of passage and identity reconstruction, *Journal of Consumer Research*, 17, 412–425

Stokemans, M. (1998) The relation between post purchase evaluations and consumption experiences of hedonic products: a case of reading fiction, *European Advances in Consumer Research*, 3, 139–145

Thompson, C. J. (1997) Interpreting consumers: a hermeneutical framework for deriving marketing insights from the texts of consumers' consumption stories, *Journal of Marketing Research*, 34, 438–455

Thompson, C. J. and Hirschman, E. C. (1995) Understanding the socialized body: a poststructuralist analysis of consumers' self-conceptions, body images, and self-care practices, *Journal of Consumer Research*, 22, 139–153

Tian, K. and Belk, R. W. (2005) Extended self and possessions in the workplace, *Journal of Consumer Research*, 32, 297–310

Üstüner, T. and Holt, D. B. (2007) Dominated consumer acculturation: the social construction of poor migrant women's consumer identity projects in a Turkish squatter, *Journal of Consumer Research*, 34, 41–56

van Meijl, T. (2006) Multiple identifications and the dialogical self: Maori youngsters and the cultural renaissance, *Journal of the Royal Anthropological Institute*, 12, 917–933

Westbrook, R. A. and Oliver, R. P. (1991) The dimensionality of consumption emotion patterns and consumer satisfaction, *Journal of Consumer Research*, 18, 84–91

Williams, P. and Aaker, J. L. (2002) Can mixed emotions peacefully coexist?, *Journal of Consumer Research*, 28, 636–649

Zaltman, G. (1997) Rethinking market research: putting people back in, *Journal of Marketing Research*, 34, 424–437

Epilogue
A philosophical epilogue on the question of autonomy

Shaun Gallagher

One of the great strengths of dialogical self theory (DST) is that it is not just a theory of the self, since even in being a theory of the self, it is also a theory of the social other. The chapters gathered together in this volume demonstrate in great detail, across a number of issues, how DST is able to explain the self only in relation to the other, whether that other be a different person, a different social set of persons, or a different position that stands, in some degree, as other to self, and yet, as Chaudhary (Chapter 9) suggests, an 'otherness in the self'. I want to stay with this thought, while at the same time acknowledging that these chapters bring to bear a comprehensive set of resources to address a wide range of issues, from developmental questions to the effects of changing cross- and multicultural factors; from psychodrama and narrative to action in lived space as well as cyberspace; from specific methodologies to various maladaptations and psychopathologies; from theories to therapies and applications in the areas of education, counselling and consumer preferences. The ability to see DST as applicable to all of these various aspects of knowing and living is part of why I think it holds promise to address a particular philosophical problem that is essentially related to the question of how the self *is* only in relation to the other. The problem is that of autonomy.

As Ho (Chapter 23) suggests, there is an ambiguity involved with the possible transpositions of self-in-other and other-in-self, and at the same time a call for personal and social responsibilities. The starting point for thinking about autonomy is not a consideration about the coercive or collaborative nature of social relations, to use Nir's terms (Chapter 16), but something more primary that precedes any claim about coercion or collaboration. It lies closer to the developmental origins of the dialogical self, discussed by Bertau (Chapter 3). The issue concerns the fact that we are immersed in interactive relations with others before we know it.

488

I have argued, in other places (Gallagher 2005, 2008), for the interaction theory of social cognition as an alternative to the standard theories found in philosophy of mind, psychology, and neuroscience – theories that frame the problem of intersubjectivity in terms of mind-reading the other's mental states from an observational standpoint. The standard theories assume, as part of the problem, a clear separation of minds, and accordingly a lack of access to the other person's mental states. Moreover, they look for a solution that reinforces this assumption with another one: the assumption of methodological individualism; that is, the working assumption that access to knowledge about the minds of others depends on cognitive capabilities or mechanisms of an isolated individual, or on processes that take place inside an individual brain.

The standard solution, therefore, is cast in terms of a 'theory of mind module' (Leslie 1992) or a set of neurons the activation of which constitutes a simulation of the other person's mind (Gallese 2001; Goldman 2006).

In contrast, interaction theory appeals to developmental studies to show that we are not third-person observers of others, but rather are involved, from the earliest point in infancy, in second-person interactions and dialogical relations with others, and that we start to 'understand' others through a variety of embodied practices.

I will not rehearse the evidence here (but see Gallagher 2005; Hobson 2002; Reddy 2008). I will, however, emphasize the importance of timing and emotional attunement as essential to the kind of interaction involved. Infants and caregivers are affectively and temporally attuned to each other in their dialogical vocalizations and gestures (e.g. Gopnik and Meltzoff 1997, and experiments by Tronick *et al.* 1978, and Murray and Trevarthen 1985). The upshot of interaction theory is that meaning and emotional significance are co-constituted *in the interaction* – not in the private confines of one or the other person's head, and that such embodied interactive practices continue to characterize our mature adult behaviour – supplemented and transformed via communicative and narrative practices (Gallagher and Hutto 2008). In communication, for example, we coordinate our perception–action sequences; our movements are coupled with changes in velocity, direction and intonation of the movements and utterances of the speaker (Issartel *et al.* 2007; Kendon 1990; Lindblom and Ziemke 2007). Our movements are imperfectly synchronized in resonance with others, following either in-phase or phase-delayed behaviour, and in rhythmic co-variation of gestures, facial or vocal expressions (Fuchs and De Jaegher 2009; Gergely 2001). In this interactive process, attunement, loss of attunement and re-established attunement maintain both differentiation and connection.

There is significant evidence that a pre-social, pre-personal interaction develops prenatally and primes the kind of post-natal intersubjective interaction we find in infants. A variety of behavioural and neuroscientific studies show that the proprioceptive and kinaesthetic registration of bodily movement develops prenatally, and that this development is facilitated by foetal movement. Cortical connections and body-schematic proprioceptive processes are in place by 26 weeks of gestational age, but proprioceptors in the muscles (muscle spindles) first appear even earlier, at 9 weeks of gestational age (Humphrey 1964). Parts of the vestibular system develop as early as the fourth month of gestation (Jouen and Gapenne 1995). In addition, a differential perception (which may be conscious or non-conscious) of stimuli occurs in the late-term foetus. For example, in response to auditory stimuli, starting around 24 weeks of gestational age, foetal heart rate changes; and after 25 weeks the foetus responds by blinking its eyes or moving its limbs. Cortical response to such stimuli has been demonstrated in premature infants of 24–29 weeks of gestational age (Fifer and Moon 1988). The foetus shows preference for some sounds (such as the mother's voice) rather than others (DeCasper and Spence 1986). Bright light directed on the lower abdomen of the mother in the third trimester can elicit foetal eye blinks (Emory and Toomey 1988). Foetal facial movements prompted by music or voice may be indicative of a similar differential awareness (Birnholz 1988).

There is also evidence that a dialogical sensitivity to the difference between touching and being touched, moving and being moved, develops prenatally since a certain kind of embodied interaction predates all of these late-term developments, and can be found in the initial and very early movements of the foetus. For example, at 10 weeks of gestational age, foetuses display structured bodily movements, which they develop through habituation (Krasnegor *et al.* 1998), such as regular mouth opening and closing, and swallowing, as well as movement in response to stimuli such as the mother's laugh or cough. From 12 weeks of gestatational age, spontaneous and repetitious movements, such as movement of the hand to mouth, occur several times an hour (De Vries *et al.* 1982; Prechtl 2001; Tajani and Ianniruberto 1990). Moreover, in a study of twins *in utero*, kinematic analysis shows that between 14 and 18 weeks of gestational age movements of one twin towards the other are different in duration and deceleration compared to movements directed towards the uterine wall or self-directed movements (Castiello *et al.* 2010).

The neuroscientific principle is that movement influences morphology: brain development *results* from the system as a whole adapting to new levels of organization at more peripheral levels, rather than the neurological developments unfolding to 'allow' increasing proprioceptive capacities (Edelman 1992; Sheets-Johnstone 1998; van der Meer *et al.* 1995). If asked about this originating movement that sets the train of development in motion, we should say that it is a kind of intercorporeal interaction. Some early foetal movement is spontaneous and repetitive and starts out as a reflex that unfolds genetically (De Vries *et al.* 1982). Other early foetal movement, however, appears regulated and practised – non-reflex (Krasnegor *et al.* 1998) – and it starts out as a response to stimuli. That is, even at this early stage, the foetus is not simply bouncing around in a container. It is responding to something. To what is this movement a response? Quite likely, to the mother's movement:

It is likely that these earliest regulated movements, which are prior to proprioceptive capacity, are a response within and to, the maternal body in *her* regulated and habituated, body schematic movement... Add to physical movement the regular maternal heart beat, digestion, and breathing and we can see that the intrauterine world is not only a moving but quite rhythmic or regulated animate world. (Lymer 2010: 230)

Of course, this is not strictly *interpersonal* interaction (the mother does not even know she is pregnant this early; and the foetus is not an experiencing subject), but it is what we might call *intercorporeal* interaction – a non-conscious motor coupling between mother and foetus driven towards and then driven by proprioception and touch. This kind of movement and intercorporeal interaction is, accordingly, sub- or pre-personal. To such pre-personal aspects of interaction, which remain immanent in what later becomes interpersonal interaction, we need to add super-personal aspects.

As suggested above, the intersubjective interaction that is found in infancy and that continues through adulthood is not reducible to mechanisms that belong to the individuals involved in the interaction – it is not reducible to a sum of individual capacities (De Jaegher *et al.* 2010). Rather, interaction produces a surplus where 1 + 1 is greater than 2. That is, the interaction goes beyond each participant; it results in something (the creation of meaning) that goes beyond what each individual *qua* individual can bring to the process. Just as when two people dance the tango, something dynamic is created, which neither one could create on their own. Moreover, as we just saw in regard to the pre-personal aspects of interaction, we are in the tango before we even know it.

If we consider both the pre-personal and the super-personal aspects of interaction, then, not just in its origins, but as an ongoing process, interaction seems to transcend the control of the participants (De Jaegher and Di Paolo 2007). Merleau-Ponty (1964: 40) talks about the infant getting caught up in the 'whirlwind of language' – but prior to that the infant is caught up in the whirlwind of interaction – and even as adults we remain in that whirlwind.

This, then, motivates the following question: if I, always, already even before birth, am caught up in a whirlwind of interaction, and that interaction always goes beyond me and my ultimate control, is there really any room for individual autonomy or self-agency?

There are current lively debates about self-agency and the related concept of autonomy, with a variety of positions being staked out. From materialist and reductionist perspectives, and based on neuroscientific studies, or the results of psychological experiments, numerous theorists argue that self-agency is an illusion (e.g. Banks *et al.* 2006; Wegner 2002). Those who defend the notion of self-agency often appeal to processes that are *in the head*, or to mind–body connections – mental causation, intention formation, reflective decision-making or the phenomenological sense of agency. These approaches follow a traditional view that conceives of self-agency (or the lack of it) as a matter of individual subjectivity. Agency and autonomy are either in the individual system or they do not exist. Even those theories that take social phenomena into account often use the individual as a measure: thus, for social determinists, individual free will does not exist precisely because we are fully determined by our social interactions or our culture.

In general, discussions of autonomy and self-agency are framed in terms of methodological individualism – they focus on the individual – the question is framed in just this way if we ask about individual autonomy. Just here I want to argue that we can conceive of autonomy and self-agency in different terms if we conceive of the agent as something other than an individual who either has or does not have free will. If we view the self as something that emerges from intercorporeal and intersubjective interactions, and develops in social interactions with others, then we are forced to face the question of autonomy in a different way. Can we still speak, and do we have a good model for speaking, about self-agency in a system that is not reducible to a simple individual?

An important step for this way of thinking involves the concept of the dialogical self. If we view the dialogical self as something that is won in social interactions with others, then this could offer a good model for self-agency that is not based on the assumption of methodological individualism. Beyond the idea that the concept of the dialogical self allows us to think about the self-in-the-other and the other-in-the-self, it also allows for a certain volitional space to open up – the possibility of taking a critical perspective on ourselves.

We can think of this in a number of different ways. For example, we can think of it as the possibility of having what Harry Frankfurt (1971) calls *second-order volitions* – that is, volitions about volitions – volitions in which we consider our own first-order action volitions. In Frankfurt's view, this, or what Charles Taylor (1989) calls the possibility of a strong evaluation of our own desires, is what is essential for attaining the status of moral personhood. We might think, however, that this way of putting it is still too closely tied to methodological individualism.

From an interactionist/dialogical perspective, we should say that this kind of strong evaluation is possible only as a result of a social process. For Taylor especially, this is a hermeneutical and dialogical enterprise. Not only do we gain self-understanding as we understand others, but there is a dialogical dimension built into self-understanding and self-evaluation. In strong evaluation, I take a position on myself – and I am able to occupy such a position because I have always occupied such a position vis-à-vis others.

Hubert Hermans (2011: 660) puts it this way: the dialogical self is a

dynamic multiplicity of relatively autonomous '*I*-positions' ... involved in processes of mutual dialogical relationships that are intensely interwoven with external dialogical relationships with actual others... When positions emerging from social interactions are interiorized, the self is able to *respond* to these positions in the form of counter-positions. In the interplay between positions and counter-positions the agency of the self comes to its full expression.

The autonomy of the self, then, is not constituted in just an internal intra-individual negotiation made by one self-position with respect to another, but is 'intensely interwoven with external dialogical relationships with actual others'.

Self-agency – and a proper sense of autonomy (which comes along with a proper sense of responsibility) – can be found only in the context of social interaction, which is dialogical, and which is where our intentions are formed in or out of our interactions with others. After all, we learn to act, and we learn our own action possibilities, from watching and interacting with others acting in the world. Through our interactions with others, we generate shared intentions and we form our own intentions out of the same fabric. In this regard, self-agency becomes a matter of degree rather than an all-or-nothing issue.

In case this notion sounds a little too abstract, let me add a few clarifications about how this kind of autonomy can emerge. Interaction theory holds that, starting early in development, communicative and narrative practices play a major role in intersubjective relations (Gallagher and Hutto 2008). Just such communicative and narrative practices allow for the possibility of strong evaluation – the possibility of taking a critical perspective on ourselves. I do not mean to rule out other possible attitudes, such as the non-evaluative attitude that Hermans-Konopka (Chapter 24) calls *depositioning* oneself; that is, the possibility of leaving a particular dialogical position and entering a form of consciousness that witnesses, in a transcendental and non-judgemental way. What evaluative and non-evaluative positions have in common, however, is a narrative distance established between the narrating self (evaluating or witnessing self) and the narrated (evaluated or witnessed) self.[1] From an interactionist perspective, importantly, this is possible only as a result of a social process, in a social world, where we act, and where we gain communicative and narrative competence. The autonomy that comes with this set of socially constituted possibilities (i.e. possibilities of communicative and narrative practices, and of whatever strong evaluation or depositioning such practices afford) is the possibility of what I would happily call, following Gonçalves and Ribeiro (Chapter 17), 'innovative moments' – moments of insight into my own possibilities of actions that are not divorced from others, but that are either fostered or discouraged by others, where others may be other persons, or other dialogical self-positions.

NOTE

1 Narrative distance is a concept that goes back to Aristotle's *Poetics*, and holds for autobiographical (or self-) narrative as well as other kinds of narrative. Specifically, one can ask about the distance between the self who narrates and the self who is narrated. For an empirical study of narrative distance in cases of deception, see Bedwell *et al.* (2010); and for a discussion of this concept in relation to psychopathology, see Gallagher and Cole (2010).

REFERENCES

Banks, W., Pockett, S. and Gallagher S. (eds.) (2006) *Does Consciousness Cause Behavior? An Investigation of the Nature of Volition* (Cambridge, MA: MIT Press)

Bedwell, J., Gallagher, S., Whitten, S. and Fiore, S. (2010) Linguistic correlates of self in deceptive oral autobiographical narratives, *Consciousness and Cognition* (published online October 2010). doi:10.1016/j.concog.2010.10.001

Birnholz, J. C. (1988) On observing the human fetus, in W. P. Smotherman and S. R. Robinson (eds.), *Behavior of the Fetus* (Caldwell, NJ: Telford Press), 47–60

Castiello, U., Becchi, C., Zoia, S., Nelini, C., Sartori, L., Blason, L., et al. (2010) Wired to be social: the ontogeny of human interaction, *PLoS ONE*, **5**. doi:10.1371/journal.pone.0013199

DeCasper, A. J. and Spence, M. J. (1986) Prenatal maternal speech influences newborns' perception of speech sounds, *Infant Behavior and Development*, **9**, 137–150

De Jaegher, H. and Di Paolo, E. (2007) Participatory sense-making: an enactive approach to social cognition, *Phenomenology and the Cognitive Sciences*, **6**, 485–507

De Jaegher, H., Di Paolo, E. and Gallagher, S. (2010) Can social interaction constitute social cognition?, *Trends in Cognitive Sciences*, **14**, 441–447

De Vries, J. I. P., Visser, G. H. A. and Prechtl, H. F. R. (1982) The emergence of fetal behaviour. I. Qualitative aspects, *Early Human Development*, **7**, 301–322

Edelman, G. (1992) *Bright Air, Brilliant Fire* (New York: Basic Books)

Emory, E. K., and Toomey, K. A. (1988) Environmental stimulation and human fetal responsivity in late pregnancy, in W. P. Smotherman and S. R. Robinson (eds.), *Behavior of the Fetus* (Caldwell, NJ: Telford Press), 141–161

Fifer, W. P. and Moon, C. (1988) Auditory experience in the fetus, in W. P. Smotherman and S. R. Robinson (eds.), *Behavior of the Fetus* (Caldwell, NJ: Telford Press), 175–188

Frankfurt, H. (1971) Freedom of the will and the concept of a person, *Journal of Philosophy*, **68**, 5–20

Fuchs, T. and De Jaegher, H. (2009) Enactive intersubjectivity: participatory sense-making and mutual incorporation, *Phenomenology and the Cognitive Sciences*, **8**, 465–486

Gallagher, S. (2005) *How the Body Shapes the Mind* (Oxford University Press) (2008) Inference or interaction: social cognition without precursors, *Philosophical Explorations*, **11**, 163–173

Gallagher, S. and Cole, J. (2010). Dissociation in self-narrative, *Consciousness and Cognition* (published online October 2010). doi:10.1016/j.concog.2010.10.003

Gallagher, S. and Hutto, D. (2008) Understanding others through primary interaction and narrative practice, in J. Zlatev, T. Racine, C. Sinha and E. Itkonen (eds.), *The Shared Mind: Perspectives on Intersubjectivity* (Amsterdam: John Benjamins), 17–38

Gallese, V. (2001) The 'shared manifold' hypothesis: from mirror neurons to empathy, *Journal of Consciousness Studies*, **8**, 33–50

Gergely, G. (2001) The obscure object of desire: 'nearly, but clearly not, like me': contingency preference in normal children versus children with autism, *Bulletin of the Menninger Clinic*, **65**, 411–426

Goldman, A. I. (2006) *Simulating Minds: The Philosophy, Psychology, and Neuroscience of Mindreading* (New York: Oxford University Press)

Gopnik, A. and Meltzoff, A. N. (1997) *Words, Thoughts, and Theories* (Cambridge, MA: MIT Press)

Hermans, H. J. M. (2011) The dialogical self: a process of positioning in space and time, in S. Gallagher (ed.), *The Oxford Handbook of the Self* (Oxford University Press), 654–680

Hobson, P. (2002) *The Cradle of Thought* (London: Macmillan)

Humphrey, T. (1964) Some correlations between the appearance of human fetal reflexes and the development of the nervous system, *Progress in Brain Research*, **4**, 93–135

Issartel, J., Marin, L. and Cadopi, M. (2007) Unintended interpersonal coordination: 'Can we march to the beat of our own drum'?, *Neuroscience Letters*, **411**, 174–179

Jouen, F. and Gapenne, O. (1995) Interactions between the vestibular and visual systems in the neonate, in P. Rochat (ed.), *The Self in Infancy: Theory and Research* (Elsevier Science), 277–301

Kendon, A. (1990) *Conducting Interaction: Patterns of Behavior in Focused Encounters* (Cambridge University Press)

Krasnegor, N. A., Fifer, W., Maulik, D., McNellis, D., Romero, R. and Smotherman, W. (1998) Fetal behavioral development: measurement of habituation, state transitions, and movement to assess fetal well being and to predict outcome, *Journal of Maternal-Fetal Investigation*, **8**, 51–57

Leslie, A. M. (1992) Pretense, autism, and the 'theory of mind' module, *Current Directions in Psychological Science*, **1**, 18–21

Lindblom, J. and Ziemke, T. (2007) Embodiment and social interaction: implications for cognitive science, in T. Ziemke, J. Zlatev and R. Frank (eds.), *Body, Language, and Mind: Embodiment* (Berlin: Mouton de Gruyter), 129–162

Lymer, J. (2010) The phenomenology of the maternal-foetal bond, unpublished Ph.D. dissertation, Wollongong University, Australia

Merleau-Ponty, M. (1964) *Signs*. Trans. R. C. McCleary (Evanston, IL: Northwestern University Press)

Murray, L. and Trevarthen, C. (1985) Emotional regulation of interactions between 2-month-olds and their mothers, in T. M. Field and N. A. Fox (eds.), *Social Perception in Infants* (New York: Ablex Publishers), 177–197

Prechtl, H. (2001) Prenatal and early postnatal development of human motor behavior, in A. F. Kalverboer and A. A. Gramsbergen (eds.), *Handbook of Brain and Behaviour in Human Development* (Dordrecht: Kluwer Academic Publishers), 415–418

Reddy, V. (2008) *How Infants Know Minds* (Cambridge, MA: Harvard University Press)

Sheets-Johnston, M. (1998) Consciousness: a natural history, *Journal of Consciousness Studies*, **5**, 260–94

Tajani, E. and Ianniruberto, A. (1990) The uncovering of fetal competence, in M. Papini, A. Pasquinelli and E. A. Gidoni (eds.), *Development Handicap and Rehabilitation: Practice and Theory* (Amsterdam: Elsevier Science), 3–8.

Taylor, C. (1989) *Sources of the Self* (Cambridge, MA: Harvard University Press)

Tronick, E., Als, H., Adamson, L., Wise, S. and Brazelton, T. B. (1978) The infant's response to entrapment between contradictory messages in face-to-face interactions, *Journal of the American Academy of Child Psychiatry*, **17**, 1–13

van der Meer, A. L., van der Weel, F. R. and Lee, D. N. (1995) The functional significance of arm movements in neonates, *Science*, **267**, 693–695

Wegner, D. (2002) *The Illusion of Conscious Will* (Cambridge, MA: MIT Press)

Index

9 781107 681064